I0424209

THE

ANCIENT WORLD-WIDE SYSTEM:

STAR MYTHS OF THE WORLD

VOLUME ONE

SECOND EDITION

The
Ancient
World-Wide
System:

Star Myths of the World,
Volume One

Second Edition

David Warner Mathisen

Published by Beowulf Books, Paso Robles, California

Mathisen, David Warner.

The Ancient World-Wide System: Star Myths of the World, Volume One / David Warner Mathisen. – 2nd ed.

1. Mythology.   2. Astronomy.   3. Spirituality.

ISBN 978-0-9960590-7-7

Cover Images: Wikimedia commons

https://commons.wikimedia.org/wiki/File:Lagoon_nebula_(Messier_8).jpg

https://commons.wikimedia.org/wiki/File:Toutankamon-expo_36_cercueil-ext.JPG

https://commons.wikimedia.org/wiki/File:Madurai_si0727.jpg

Dedicated to

the Divine Spirit in each and every
Man and Woman

to

Blessing instead of Cursing

to

My Teachers,
for encouraging and inspiring me

to

My Family
for loving and sustaining me

and to

Social uplift
and
an end to
oppression, colonialism, imperialism,
racism and the privatization of
the gifts given by nature
and the gods to all
Men and Women

Contents

Introduction to the Second Edition

This updated edition of *Star Myths of the World, Volume One*, the original edition of which was first published in 2015, revisits some of the myths explored in the first edition with the expanded perspective of having now explored hundreds more Star Myths in great detail, including the wealth of myth left to us from the culture broadly referred to as "ancient Greece" (examined in *Star Myths of the World, Volume Two*), the sacred stories collected in what we commonly call the Old and New Testaments of the Bible (examined in *Star Myths of the World, Volume Three*), and the Norse myths (examined in *Star Myths of the World, Volume Four*), as well as the collection of myths examined more thematically (or by "oicotype") in *Astrotheology for Life*.

With the benefit of this added perspective, some of the analysis contained in the first edition of *Volume One*, dealing with a broad range of myths from the cultures of Australia, Africa, the Americas, the Pacific, ancient Egypt, ancient Mesopotamia, ancient India, China and Japan, can be expanded upon and (in some cases) corrected or emended, with the goal of providing the best possible introduction to a series purporting to help readers explore the incredible treasure bequeathed to the various cultures of humanity in the ancient myths, and to begin to understand the worldwide celestial language with which these ancient myths are speaking and through which they convey their profound message to us.

Some additional myths will be examined, in addition to most of those contained in the original edition of *Volume One*.

For better clarity, as well as to help keep the price of this volume as affordable as possible, illustrations and star-charts will be grayscale instead of full-color, and star-charts will use a newer

1

"inverted" color-scheme, in which the dark background of the night sky will appear light, and the stars and Milky Way will be dark. Constellations will be outlined with dark gray lines, rather than in the various colors used in the first edition.

The physical dimensions of the book will also be changed, to a smaller form, in order to reduce cost (the same dimensions are also used in *Star Myths of the World, Volume Four: Norse Mythology*, as well as in my two previous books, *Astrotheology for Life* and *Ancient Myths, Ancient Wisdom*).

Perhaps the biggest change from the first edition will be the elimination of the "two-part" format used in the first edition, which will enable a deeper look at more myths more deeply, because the two-part format necessarily expands the book's length.

The two-part format was designed to enable to the reader to be presented with the myth in the first half of the book and then turn to the second half of the book to read the celestial interpretation of the same story, thus allowing the reader to try to determine the celestial interpretation himself or herself. The drawback of that format is that it thus requires each chapter to be "doubled," so to speak, with one part in the first half of the book and the other in the second half, thus increasing the amount of text devoted to each story (since some aspects of each myth are necessarily described twice), as well as disrupting the "flow" of the reader's journey through the myths to some degree. Therefore, in this volume, the two "halves" will be combined, and each aspect of the myths will be explored with discussion of its celestial foundations and possible spiritual meaning in the same chapter.

The purpose of the "doubled" format was to teach the reader to learn to spot the clues in the stories that point to the distinctive characteristics of the various constellations in the night sky. Those wishing to see these myths in the "two-part" format instead can still consult the first edition of *Star Myths of the World, Volume One*, as well as *Star Myths of the World, Volume Two* and *Volume Three*, which also use that "doubled" format.

Despite these changes, however, the core message of this second edition does not change from that of the first. The world's myths are based on the stars and heavenly cycles, and they are speaking an esoteric and allegorical language. This fact, which by now should be indisputable based on the overwhelming volume of evidence, argues that the ancient stories are not based on terrestrial history, characters, or events. They are not about external persons living thousands of years ago, or events external to our lives which happened to someone else in lands now buried under the sands of time. The ancient myths are based on the stars because the myths are describing an infinite realm -- the realm of spirit, the realm of the gods -- and the things they are describing apply directly to our own lives. The sacred stories, as Alvin Boyd Kuhn once explained, are about us -- and they are not grasped in their "full force and applicability" unless and until each man and woman encountering those myths discerns *himself* or *herself* to be, as Kuhn puts it, the *central figure* in them!'

Thus, contrary to the message repeated by the literalizers of ancient myth for the past seventeen centuries, the message of the world's ancient wisdom is *not* that we must seek for answers and for completion, redemption, rescue and salvation from a source outside of ourselves.

To assert this truth, as Alvin Boyd Kuhn argues in a different text (his encyclopedic and definitive work, *Lost Light*, published in 1940), is not to deny the existence of an Absolute and Ultimate

Eternal -- far from it. Indeed, the ancients did not deny the reality of the Eternal, but they "had the discretion to leave it alone!"[2] The ancient wisdom points us towards the accessibility of divinity "with a god dwelling immediately within the human breast"[3] and the myths demonstrate time after time (in stories such as the episodes in the Odyssey, for example) that the gods work out their will through our own actions and efforts.

Because of this fact, the gods are always available to us, at any moment -- a fact which is demonstrated in the myths of ancient India, where the gods and goddesses appear in an instant when they are called upon . . . and the same is true in the Norse myths (for example), where the god Thor also appears the moment that his name is called.

We see a similar dynamic at work in the fifth "book" (or chapter) of the Odyssey, when an exhausted Odysseus is trying to make landfall on a rocky and forbidding shoreline, after spending three days cast adrift in the open sea, during his escape from Ogygia. The poem describes the man's thoughts, as he almost begins to panic, despairing of safely landing where the great waves are crashing against jagged rock-faces of the cliffs, while also fearing that if he does not make it to shore he will be swept back out to the fish-infested deep, perhaps to encounter one of the monsters with which, he imagines, the waters are undoubtedly teeming.[4]

In the midst of this despair, the goddess Athena inspires the hapless castaway, and he redoubles his efforts, making his way to a point where a wide river empties out into the ocean, creating a spot free of rocks where he can make it to shore -- but only after, perceiving the river's god, he prays for and receives a favorable current, and is able to swim to safety with the last reserves of strength left in him.[5]

In this significant episode, we see that the gods stand ready to help, and that their help is very real and decisive -- but that it is, in effect, synergistic with the actions and resolve of the one who calls upon them. We have within us what we already need -- including the access to the divine realm of the gods, through our own inner connection to the Infinite, if we learn how to avail ourselves of it.

Odysseus, as we see in the above episode and as we learn throughout his other adventures in the Odyssey, exemplifies the man or woman attuned to the voice and presence of the gods at all times, who are always present and available if we cultivate such awareness. The deleterious impact of centuries of insistence on the literalization of ancient scriptures (particularly of the Bible), and the literalist tendency towards externalizing their message (because, almost by definition, if the ancient stories are describing literal, terrestrial history, then they are describing things *external* to ourselves) has been the loss of contact with divinity where it *could* be accessed (within), by instead turning our gaze outward.

As Alvin Boyd Kuhn puts it, the understanding that we have access to the gods right where we are at any given moment implies no disrespect to the Eternal: on the contrary, "the real heresy and apostasy is to miss deity where it is to be had in the blind effort to seek it where it is not available."[6] In the path laid out for us in the ancient wisdom bequeathed to humanity in the myths of the world, "No reaching after the moon of the Absolute diverted conscious purpose from actual touch with the god who stood at one's elbow."[7]

This approach to the ancient wisdom resembles the ancient Buddhist teaching of the "Lion's Gaze," related in writings attributed to the 11th century Tibetan yogi Milarepa.[8] He observes that while a dog will chase a stick one throws, over and over, always focusing on the stick, you can only throw a stick at a lion one time, because the lion will not focus on the stick: he will turn and face the thrower of the stick, and chase him instead![9]

The meaning, as elucidated by researcher of ancient wisdom Richard Cassaro in a 2015 article on "The Lion's Gaze," is that like the lion we should not waste our effort chasing after that which is external (exemplified by the dog chasing after a stick) but rather that we should turn our attention to the heart of the issue, which is to be found *within ourselves* and not in any external distraction.[10]

In doing so, we ourselves can begin to manifest the characteristics associated with the lion: majesty and dignity and focus -- all attributes which cannot be obtained by chasing after "sticks" of external achievement or external "religion," even if we dutifully retrieve thousands of such sticks which are thrown for us.

This is a very powerful teaching indeed, and one which encapsulates the message of the world's ancient wisdom. The answers we seek, and the resources to deal with the issues we face, are already present within us -- and we do not need to chase after external sticks, like a dog would do. The gods are real, and available to us in time of need -- and our connection to them is internal. We are already equipped with what we need to avail ourselves of their assistance -- but, like Odysseus upon the waves, we often forget this truth, and indeed begin to panic and despair and even sink down beneath the billows (Peter exemplifies the same lesson, in the "walking on water" episode described in Matthew 14: 24 - 32).

The ancient myths stand ready to remind us, and to correct our perspective, and to turn our "Lion's Gaze" towards the divine where it is available, to our great blessing as we make our way through this incarnate life.

It is my hope that by learning to hear the myths in the language that they are actually speaking, you will be able to hear their profound message in an entirely new way, and that you will be able to converse with them and hear their incredible wisdom, which is as fresh today as it was so many thousands of years ago.

Paso Robles, California
August 5th, 2018

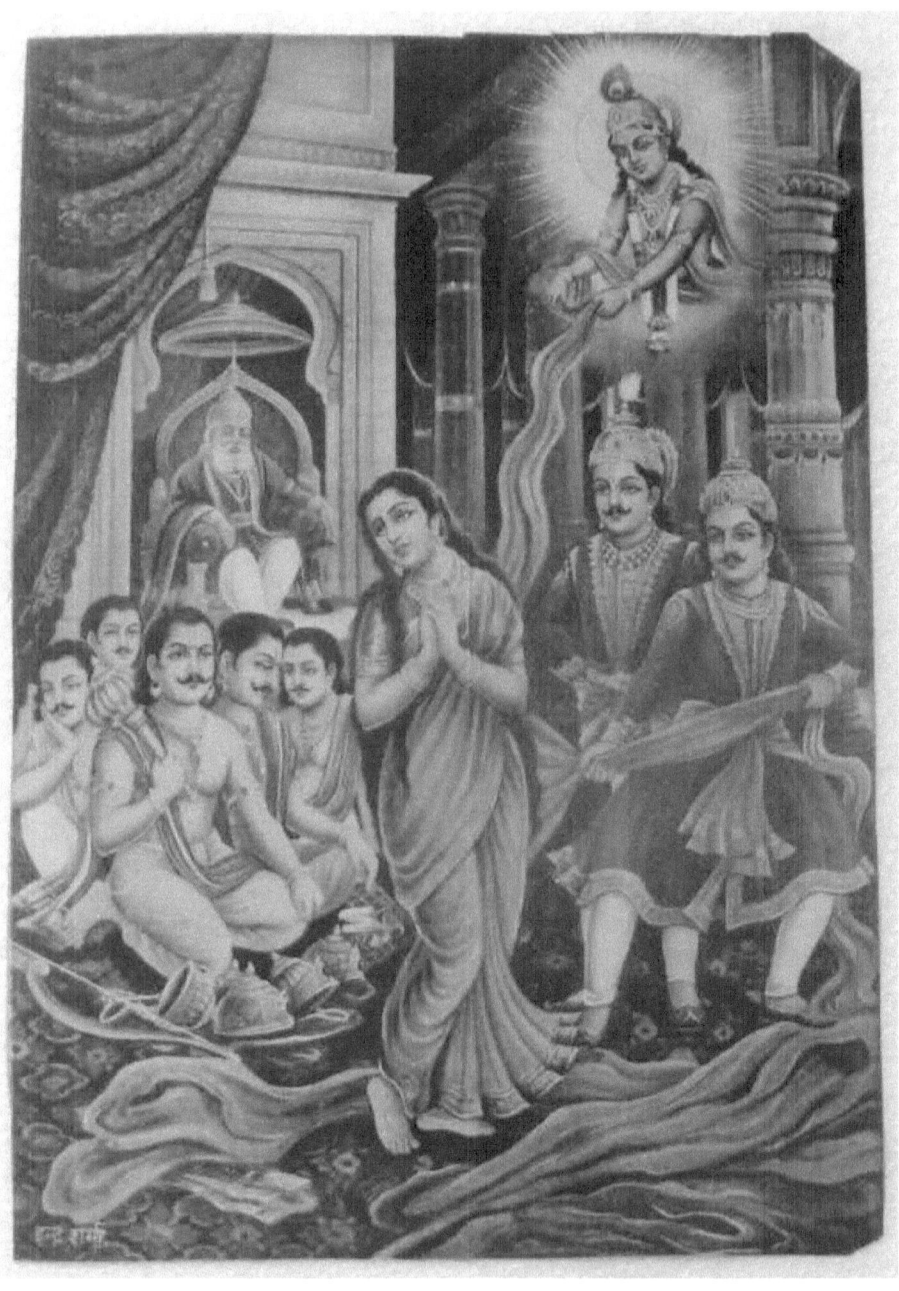

8

Introduction to the First Edition

The world's sacred traditions share a common system of celestial metaphor, with unmistakable patterns that can be traced across oceans and across centuries – even across millennia.

The outlines of this system have been tantalizingly described by Hertha von Dechend and Giorgio de Santillana in *Hamlet's Mill*, published in 1969.

Details of it have been systematically analyzed most thoroughly perhaps by the Reverend Robert Taylor of England (1784 – 1844), working with the stories found in the scriptures we call the Old and New Testaments of the Bible.

But although the insights of these and many others who have sought to clear away the "dust of centuries" (as de Santillana and von Dechend describe it) from this vast ancient edifice have been invaluable to my own work, it is also true that even after many readings of the writings of these authors, the comprehensive structure and underlying rules, as well as the deeper purpose of the great system remained elusively out of reach.[11]

Over the course of much examination of the myths – and especially of the stars themselves – and through the process of analyzing them, publicly writing about them, and even dreaming about them for the past seven or so years, a clearer and clearer picture of the outline of a central pillar of this ancient system has presented itself to me, with different parts of it resolving into view at different times, often with the feeling that new images and connections came without any effort, the realizations being handed across, as it were, from the realm of the stars themselves.

Interested readers can trace the course of the development of my understanding of this system over the course of three books:

> ➤ my first effort, published in 2011, which began to connect celestial aspects of the myths from ancient Sumer, Babylon, and Egypt with some similarly celestial features found in the sacred traditions and rituals found in the Americas and elsewhere, but in which I was still taking the scriptures of the Old and New Testament in a literalistic manner;

> ➤ my next book, *The Undying Stars*, published in 2014, by which time I had accepted the fact that the system of celestial metaphor I had been exploring forms the foundation of virtually *all* of the world's myths, sacred traditions, and ancient scriptures – including those in the Old and New Testaments of the Bible, which I had spent a large part of my life taking literally – and in which I tried to explain the system in a more comprehensive manner, while also examining the possible implications of this evidence and presenting some possible explanations as to *why* the world's ancient wisdom would use such a system of celestial metaphor, and what it intended to convey; and . . .

> ➤ This present work, in which the details of the system have come into even clearer view, and in which I attempt to share with the reader the keys to interpreting nearly any celestial myth, along with additional thoughts on their meaning.

The method I have used here was inspired by a request from a reader who mentioned a wish that I would create some kind of a course or methodology for readers to begin to analyze and interpret and unlock the ancient myths for themselves, rather than simply reading my descriptions of the celestial metaphors at work in particular myths (as I do in my second book and especially in certain posts published to the web in the ongoing blog that I have maintained on a fairly regular basis since the month of the publication of my first book in 2011). "Teaching to fish instead of giving a fish."

Thank you, Jed / Jody, for that inspired recommendation!

Therefore, in this present work, I have come up with a method by which you (dear reader, fellow sojourner in this material-spiritual incarnate realm of earth and water, and fellow child of the stars) will be presented with the myths, as well as with some "hints" or points of possible significance to consider for yourself, and then you learn how to unlock their celestial metaphors . . . and ultimately, it is hoped, you grow more and more able to perceive and to *receive* - directly, from those ancient sources - the profound spiritual knowledge that these incredible metaphors were intended to convey to us.

Each myth will be described in the first part of the book, along with a series of questions intended to "point you in the right direction" towards possible celestial connections, and then there will be a page number listed at the end of the myth, corresponding to a page found in the second part of the book which contains an explanation of the myth based on my own interpretation of the ancient system [this system has been changed in this edition] .

Of course, it's not an "answer key," because my interpretation could be incorrect. I present my reasoning for the interpretation that is offered, but the simple fact is that the ancient myths and scriptures do not generally come with accompanying celestial diagrams -- although some of the ancient art, including that of ancient Egypt, Sumer, and Babylon as well as some found in other parts of the world, could be argued to be performing that exact function, in addition to being incredible art from an aesthetic standpoint.

The ancient texts *do* contain clues and details which clearly seem intended to point us in the right direction – but sometimes there may be more than one possible explanation.

What does seem to be undeniable, however, is that this ancient system of celestial metaphor can be seen to be at work in virtually *every* set of sacred traditions, myths, and ancient scriptures of the human race.

The scope of this book is to demonstrate the system – not to analyze the entirety of any given myth-cycle or specific system from any given culture or part of the world. Therefore, only a few samples from a large number of different cultures were selected.

Necessarily, some myths which could have been used to demonstrate this system have been left out – in the future, it is very certain that entire books or even entire multi-volume studies could easily be devoted to the celestial aspects of any *one* of the many different myth-cycles and traditions which are touched upon in this volume.

Necessarily as well, some of the many incredibly varied cultures and myth-systems of humanity have not been included – but I hope that I have included enough to conclusively demonstrate that the system of Star Myths is virtually universal across every continent and across a wide sampling of different representative cultures of our human race. *The goal is to prove that this celestial allegory is in fact universally present,* and to teach you how to see it for yourself: not to cover every single possible example.

Descriptions of the myths, and discussions in their corresponding analysis sections, are deliberately kept shorter at first, in order to introduce the elements a few at a time, and become more elaborate as the "tour" proceeds.

The question of "What it all means" (or might mean – what it might have been intended to convey to us) has been touched upon here and there as we go through the different myths and their possible explanations. We will take it up again at the very end, by way of conclusion – but ultimately I believe that the myths themselves are the best teachers of what they are trying to convey.

I will give what I believe are some of the broad outlines of the system and the spiritual world and spiritual truths towards which I believe these celestial metaphors were intended to lead us – but once the basic outlines are grasped, I believe that the depths to which we can dive within the incredible sacred stories of humanity are literally without end, and that they will continue to reward deeper and deeper exploration and consideration, without ever exhausting their riches, for an entire lifetime (perhaps for many, many lifetimes).

Thus, it may be best to simply sketch some of the spiritual connections which I believe are supported by the evidence, and which I believe to be operating *across* the different myths and traditions (for example, the assertion that the realm of the stars was used *throughout* the myths, in whatever culture or part of the world we examine, to represent the realm of spirit, the realm of the infinite), and then leave it to the reader to plumb the depths of the myths themselves for the insights and awakenings which await each of us therein.

The study of the celestial foundations of the world's sacred myths is often called "astro-theology," probably taking its name from the title of a book of the lectures of the aforementioned Robert Taylor of England, an ordained minister who appears to have wrestled with the texts of the Bible at the very points that create the most difficulty for a literalistic interpretation, until he realized that the stories – all of them – are actually celestial in nature, and that their intended message was not as literal history.

In an attempt to explain this celestial interpretation, the Reverend Taylor regularly gave sermon-style lectures in which he eloquently, wittily, and at times condescendingly and with vicious sarcasm and ridicule expounded the evidence that the stories of the Bible, from the opening of the Old Testament to the closing of the New, are based upon the motions of the sun, moon and stars.

For his pains, he was kicked out of the Church of England, and locked up on different occasions, spending a total of three years behind bars. Two collections of his lectures were published in 1857, more than twelve years after his death: one was entitled *The Devil's Pulpit: or Astronomico-Theological Sermons by the Rev. Robert Taylor, B. A.* and the other was called *The Astronomico-Theological Lectures of the Rev. Robert Taylor, B. A.*

Since then, the term *astrotheology* has become somewhat well known (the shorter version "astro-theology" being much more common today than "astronomico-theology"), and while it is useful, it does not transform easily into a handy label for the astronomical *stories themselves* (calling them "astro-theologisms" doesn't really work). Astrotheology *is* a useful term, and one which is becoming more widely understood and familiar as it gains greater usage through the efforts of those researchers who labor to demonstrate the celestial origins of the world's myths. However, I would like to explain my preference for adding the term "Star Myths" as well. I believe that the term "Star Myths" has some advantages which recommend that term to us, and not least of these is the fact that the meaning of this phrase ("Star Myths") is immediately apparent, unlike the meaning intended by "astrotheology" – a term which can actually be somewhat confusing.

This is especially true because the term "theology" really means the study of the aspects of God or the divine, and refers to an entire discipline with a huge corpus of literature, most of which corpus comes from a perspective of "literalism," meaning from the perspective of taking scriptures as if they were intended to describe literal events rather than the allegorized motions of celestial actors such as the sun, moon, and stars. The term "Star Myths" avoids that problem altogether, because "myths" are generally understood to be allegorical and not literal right from the start, and the term itself conveys a very different set of thoughts and connotations than does the term "theology."

The term "Star Myth" is also much more direct and less intimidating, which may not seem important but certainly must be counted as an advantage, if our aim is to spread knowledge and help others to understand, rather than to try to keep this incredibly beneficial knowledge to ourselves, as if we were its owners or its appointed guardians.

The term "Star Myth" is simply more approachable than "astrotheology," largely for the simple reason that it is not a Latinate term. Its benefit on this score should not be overlooked. When someone hears the word "astrotheology" for the first time, they will probably ask "what's that?" because it isn't easily self-explanatory, whereas "Star Myths" is fairly self-explanatory.

Additionally, in recent years some researchers have begun using the term "astrotheology" to refer to the entire host of theological questions surrounding the possibility of the existence of advanced extraterrestrial lifeforms, which may be an interesting and important topic of exploration, but which is very different from the field of study originally intended by the term "astrotheology," which primarily focused on the evidence that the world's scriptures are based upon the stars and the heavenly cycles

For all these reasons, I believe the phrase "Star Myths" is valuable, although I also believe that the word "astrotheology" has continuing value as a word used to describe the field of study which looks at the Star Myths themselves and which explores the evidence for their allegorical connection to the motions of the heavenly players.

And so this present work was born – its intention being to examine the Star Myths of the world, in order to observe this ancient universal esoteric system in action.

Through the process of analyzing them for yourself, you will begin to match the celestial clues included in the stories with the distinctive features of the various constellations, as well as at times with the distinctive features of the various aspects of the *celestial cycles* (the relative motions of the earth, moon, sun, visible planets, and constellations).

The first volume of this study will begin in Australia, and then go on to examine myths from Africa, from the Americas, from the Pacific, and then from some of the most ancient texts known to be extant to this day – the hieroglyphics of ancient Egypt, and the cuneiform tablets of ancient Sumer and Babylon. Also examined in this volume will be the myths of the Sanskrit texts of ancient India, focusing in particular on some of the stories and characters found in the Mahabharata, which contains the Bhagavad Gita. We'll conclude with an examination of some of the ancient texts and traditions of China and Japan.

It is my belief that these ancient myths are not just powerful literary works (although they *are* certainly powerful literary works, conveying a tremendous range and depth of exploration and depiction of the human condition), and they are not just ingenious metaphors (although on that level their mastery is absolutely superlative, and almost seems to indicate a superhuman origin of some sort), but that they are in fact *sacred*: that they treat subject matter that is "set apart" from the mundane and the material world – subject matter that has to do with the realm of the immortal, the infinite, and the divine.

The myths do not have to be literal or historical in order to be sacred. In fact, it is when they are seen to be metaphor or esoteric allegory that these ancient stories truly begin to convey their sacred truths to our understanding. They do not lose their sacred character when they are perceived for what they truly are: quite the contrary. It is through this understanding that they begin to command an even greater sense of reverence and awe than ever.

It is my sincere hope that you will be blessed by your interaction with and investigation of the ancient Star Myths that form a precious part of the combined inheritance of all humanity.

Envisioning the Constellations

The constellations of the night sky can be an endless source of pleasure for those who have the opportunity to go out and see them in person. Additionally, becoming familiar with the constellations, and being able to envision their outlines, is in fact essential to perceiving the connection between the myths and the stars.

The best way to get to know the constellations is to devote a little time each night, observing how the actors on the great stage of the heavens change throughout the year due to the motion of the earth along its annual cycle around the sun.

It is also ideal if you can find a way to take a walk along a round-trip pattern that will enable you to have views of all the different parts of the sky, and all the different horizons in the four different directions of north, east, south and west, as you go along. If you can take that same round-trip walk each night (or early morning), at roughly the same time, for an entire year, you can gain a tremendous level of familiarity with the constellations of our night sky.

However, most of the constellations themselves do not simply "jump out" at the unpracticed viewer – and without a guide to the constellations it will be next to impossible to "pick them out" just based on a vague awareness that you are supposed to be looking for a Lion or a Crab or a set of Twins somewhere.

Therefore, a good understanding of the shape and major characteristics of each constellation is an absolute must – and it is here that we run into some complications, because the methodologies for outlining the constellations that have been published in print and even on the internet or in planetariums over the years (and indeed over the centuries) are often terribly lacking.

In fact, they are often so poor that it makes one wonder whether someone designed them to deliberately mask the important characteristics of the constellations, rather than to reveal those characteristics and to help people to see the constellations for themselves.

There is an exception to this lack of good literature on constellation identification, however: the star books of H. A. Rey (1898 - 1997), who is perhaps best known as the author and illustrator, along with his wife Margret Rey (1906 - 1996), of the *Curious George* series of storybooks.

H. A. Rey himself also lamented the prevailing systems used to depict the constellations, and in their place he presented his own system: one which would, in his words, "remedy the situation" with a method that would seek to illustrate the constellations, as he says:

> in a new, graphic way, as shapes which suggest what the names imply: it shows the group of stars known as the Great Bear, in the shape of a bear; the Whale in the shape of a whale; the Eagle as an eagle, and so on. These shapes are easy to remember, and once you remember them you can retrace them in the sky.[12]

For anyone who wishes to have the glories of our night sky and the celestial realm come to life, Rey's book *The Stars: A New Way to See Them* is an absolute must.

Not only does H. A. Rey's system enable us to remember the shapes of the constellations and find those constellations in the heavens, but it also has another tremendous advantage, and one which to my knowledge neither Rey himself nor anyone else has ever attributed to it: his system of outlining the constellations enables us to perceive the significant characteristics of each heavenly character, characteristics which appear to have been known to whoever imparted to the human race the collective treasure of ancient knowledge which we know of as *the myths, scriptures, and sacred traditions* whose origins are lost in the mists of earliest human history.

The characteristics which belong to each particular constellation will surface again and again in myths and sacred stories, whether those myths belong to the cultures who lived in the islands of Japan or in the fjords and mountains and forests of Scandinavia, whether those myths were recorded on fired clay tablets from the cultures of ancient Mesopotamia or inscribed upon the walls of some of the earliest Egyptian pyramids or whether they are still preserved and passed down in oral tradition among cultures who have retained their heritage right up to the present day (or until recent decades or centuries), in the Pacific islands or among the Native American nations and tribes.

In other words, across the entire vast surface of our planet, and across all the millennia of known human history from the most ancient to the most recent, the myths embody and bring to life these constellations, and they do so with specific references to details and characteristics intrinsic to those constellations – *details and characteristics that are evident when using the outlining system as published by H. A. Rey.*

If this assertion seems strange or unbelievable to you now, I think that by the end of this volume, you will have seen enough evidence to convince you many times over that this nearly unbelievable situation is indeed the case [indeed, if during the first several chapters you are skeptical, please push on, because by the time we reach Egypt and Mesopotamia, the evidence becomes simply undeniable].

Below we see an example of one section of the night sky, with selected constellations outlined according to one common outlining system which is still in use to this very day. In fact, this is the default outlining system which pops up when you use the excellent open-source planetarium app, Stellarium, which was used for creating all the star-charts in this series. The outlines are similar to you will find on popular websites such as Wikipedia when looking up a constellation, as well as in many mobile apps offered as tools for helping you to find the constellations in the night sky:

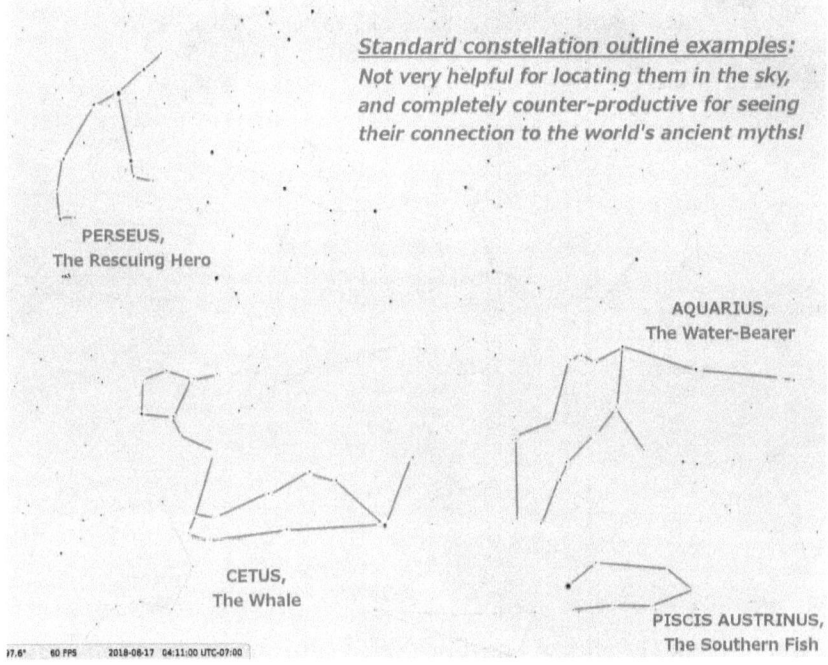

Standard constellation outline examples:
Not very helpful for locating them in the sky, and completely counter-productive for seeing their connection to the world's ancient myths!

PERSEUS,
The Rescuing Hero

AQUARIUS,
The Water-Bearer

CETUS,
The Whale

PISCIS AUSTRINUS,
The Southern Fish

Note that none of these rather abstract outlines are easy to remember, and none of them give even the slightest suggestion of what the actual constellation is supposed to envision. Looking at these outlines, one would wonder what exactly the ancients were thinking when they designated such star-groupings as a Whale, or a Fish, or a Hero, or a Water-Bearer!

Below, in contrast, is a star-chart showing the exact same stars depicted on the previous page. This time, the same selected constellations are outlined using the system published in 1952 by H. A. Rey in his book *The Stars: A New Way to See Them.* Now the underlying character envisioned by the constellation is completely clear! Not only that, but specific features and aspects of the outline and of the figure in the sky can be matched to specific descriptions in the ancient stories and texts containing the world's Star Myths:

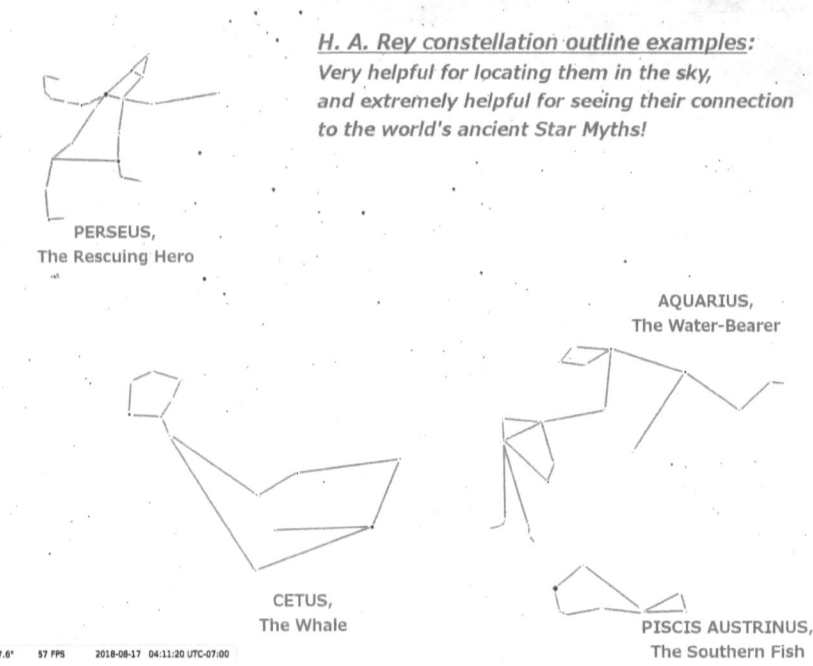

H. A. Rey constellation outline examples:
Very helpful for locating them in the sky,
and extremely helpful for seeing their connection
to the world's ancient Star Myths!

PERSEUS,
The Rescuing Hero

AQUARIUS,
The Water-Bearer

CETUS,
The Whale

PISCIS AUSTRINUS,
The Southern Fish

17.6°   57 FPS   2018-08-17 04:11:20 UTC-07:00

Note that the benighted outlines offered up on the previous page would give you no hint of the fact that the constellation Perseus, for example, wears a pointed hat and carries a hook-shaped sword, both of which are important features which appear in ancient myth and ancient artwork surrounding characters based on this constellation (including, but by no means limited to, the mythical character named Perseus in the Greek myth of that name).

They would give you no hint of the fact that Aquarius plays the role of a "headlong runner" in many ancient myths, most explicitly in both of the famous ancient pre-classical epics of Greece, the Iliad and the Odyssey, due to the "piteched forward" outline of the constellation which resembles a person running at full tilt.

And the uninspired "modern" outlines would give you no way of envisioning the constellation of Cetus as a mighty whale, whose mouth was also sometimes envisioned as having a "tusk" reaching up to the star that serves as the "eye" of the whale, thus giving rise to myths which also envision Cetus as a great boar, a role the constellation can be shown to play in myths from ancient Greece but also from the ancient Norse (as will be examined in later volumes in this series).

Amazingly, the myths of cultures literally around the world can be shown to be using *this same system* of envisioning the constellations as the foundation for an inspired language of esoteric metaphor. The evidence which points to this conclusion is voluminous and compelling -- and, I would argue, decisive. Each of the books in this series contains hundreds of pages and together they examine hundreds of characters and episodes from cultures as far removed as the northern regions of Scandinavia and the tropical islands of the Pacific – and yet the examples presented in this series only barely scratch the surface of the myths that could be explored which point towards this worldwide celestial connection.

Of course, such a discovery, if true, would seem to have tremendous ramifications for our understanding of the nature and purpose of these sacred myths of humanity – and indeed for our understanding of human history itself. We will briefly address some of those ramifications in a final concluding chapter at the end, as well as at various points throughout the analysis of the myths which follows in the pages of this and the other volumes.

First and foremost, it is important to state at the outset that I believe that these myths and stories are sacred: that they treat matters which are "set apart" from that which is mundane, material, or related to the common physical exigencies of existence. They treat matters related to spirit, to the invisible realm, to the infinite realm, and to all that lifts us beyond the merely material aspects of our existence.

There are some who would seize upon the explanation of the allegorical and celestial nature of these sacred texts and traditions in order to try to denigrate their sacred nature – to exclaim, "See! Nothing more than nature-worship, or encoded descriptions of the natural world and seasonal cycles! So there really *is* nothing but the material universe after all! I knew it all along!"

Those who would seize upon the celestial nature of the sacred texts in order to deny our essentially spiritual nature, and to deny the existence of a spiritual realm which interpenetrates and permeates every single aspect of our seemingly material universe, and which is in fact the source and origin for everything we see that is finite and manifest in the material realm, have completely missed the point of the Star Myths, and reached the completely opposite conclusion from what the myths were actually intending to convey through their system of celestial metaphor.

The Star Myths, as will be discussed during some of the analyses which follow, and again in depth in the subsequent volumes, were in fact using the celestial realm and the heavenly cycles as metaphors to help explain and convey knowledge of the existence and importance of the spiritual and invisible realm. We cannot see the invisible realm (using our ordinary senses, at least), and so they used the most majestic possible aspects of the material realm as their chosen visual aids to help convey to us what it is all about. They selected the most awe-inspiring canvas available to us in the physical universe in order to paint their stories conveying to us the reality of the infinite realm – and of our inherent connection to it.

I believe that these Star Myths were exquisitely crafted to convey profound truths which are absolutely essential to human life and to the human experience. This is not to say that one cannot learn those truths if one does not learn them through the myths: there are many other disciplines and paths which have been given to humanity or which have been discovered or developed through the millennia to put us in touch with the same vital knowledge – but I believe that these myths were in fact given in order to convey sacred and essential knowledge.

Thus I do not believe that perceiving their celestial and allegorical nature takes away from their sacred purpose: on the contrary, I believe that this perception of their celestial and allegorical nature is the best way for us to learn what they were intended to teach us.

Conversely, failing to understand them as powerful metaphors or allegories which point towards spiritual matters can cause us to miss their true meaning. By this I mean failing to understand their metaphorical nature by reading them as describing literal-historical figures, and beginning our interpretation from that understanding.

A helpful analogy (and one I often use) would be the "teaching aids" that Mr. Miyagi employs in order to teach Daniel-san the "ungraspable" or "invisible" truths of his karate system in the popular 1984 movie, *Karate Kid.* If we were to mistakenly conclude that Mr. Miyagi was actually teaching Daniel-san how to wax cars or paint fences, we would miss the point entirely, because those motions were about something else altogether.

In just the same way, these stories are not about literal or historical figures, and to focus on them as though they are is analogous to focusing on the motions "wax the car" or "paint the fence" as if their primary purpose were waxing more cars and painting more fences.

Nor, however, are these stories really about the constellations and stars, the sun and moon and planets. Those too are actually metaphors for the real layer of meaning that lies behind even those glorious celestial bodies, and towards which the ancient myths and sacred stories are trying to point our understanding.

Second, I believe that whenever possible it is best to use the original texts or very direct, literal translations of the texts, if the myth being examined was committed to writing. Often, details and clues were deliberately included in the myths, but later translators have "paraphrased them away" because they did not know the celestial meaning of the detail that they decided to re-word in their translation.

The scriptures which found their way into the collections that we today call the Old and New Testaments of the Bible will be examined in *Star Myths of the World, Volume Three* (*Star Myths of the Bible*), but there are many examples where older translations (such as the so-called King James version) preserve the celestial details (as confusing as those details may be for someone who tries to read the text as if it were describing a literal-historical person or event) but where newer translations (such as the New International Version) have tried to "helpfully" provide a better translation – and in doing so the "modern" version obscures the celestial detail altogether.

One fairly obvious example is the use of the term "unicorn," which is found in the King James translations (for instance in Psalms 22, 29 and 92, and in Numbers 23: 22) but which modern translators found completely unacceptable and thus decided on their own that the original text must have been referring to some terrestrial species of animal, which they then substitute in their "translation," subverting the intention of the original text.

The original term would alert a Star Myth investigator that he or she should be looking for a constellation that has an outline that might feature a protruding feature or features that could be allegorized as the horn or horns of a unicorn – but if the "translators" substitute some other animal in their zeal to re-write the texts into "literal-historical records," the celestial allegory will become impossible to decipher.

In this particular case of the unicorn, for instance, the NIV translators have substituted "wild ox," which relieves them of having to deal with any "mythical creatures," but which might then send the Star Myth investigator off in the wrong direction – looking at the constellation Taurus, for example, when in fact the original text was hinting at a different constellation found in a different part of the sky altogether (most likely Sagittarius).

Third, it is important to note that my diagrams are attempts to place on a flat page of paper a planetarium-style representation of the great "dome of the heavens" (it's not really a "dome," of course, but it resembles one to an observer on earth), and thus the shape of the constellations will occasionally have some distortion and differences in size and shape from one image to another, depending on where that constellation is in the sky. If closer to the horizon, for instance, the planetarium app that I have used for the star images will make the constellation look larger, because it is trying to give the impression to the viewer that the constellation is following an arcing path across the sky in the same way that constellations actually travel to an observer outside.

The result is some variation in some of the images in this book, but once you become familiar with the constellations themselves and their outlines and relative locations, and once you begin to spend some time looking at them outside (if possible), these differences will not throw you off at all and you will begin to understand why the planetarium makes them look that way.

Also, I occasionally will *outline* the shape of the constellation slightly differently (and in some cases, very differently) from one section of the book to another. These differences are usually relatively minor, but when they are significant, it is because the constellation has another very different role that it can sometimes play in Star Myths around the world, and because it will be important to know two ways of looking at it (the most important example of this phenomenon is probably the constellation Hercules). Again, once you become more familiar with the constellations (and especially with finding them outside, if you are able to go out to see them for yourself) then these differences will no longer pose any difficulty for you – but it does take some time to get familiar with the constellations.

Finally, it should be noted that almost all of the descriptions of the constellations, and almost all of the Star Myth analysis discussions, take what can be termed a "northern-hemisphere-centric" approach; that is, they describe the constellations and star motions as they appear to an observer in the northern hemisphere.

Strangely enough, this approach appears to be fairly universal in its scope, even for sacred myths and traditions coming from cultures found in the southern hemisphere, such as Australia, much of Africa, South America, and many of the islands of the Pacific. There are a few myths from southern latitudes in which the southern-hemisphere orientation of the sky may play a role, and when this is the case it is noted in the discussion of the myth during the Star Myth analysis portion, but for the most part the same system appears to operate around the globe with very little variation.

There could be many reasons for this somewhat surprising feature of the system, but in reality the fact is that the constellations and the heavenly cycles operate pretty much the same way no matter where on planet earth you are located: it is only their relative orientation in terms of "up" and "down," and the horizon along which the ecliptic path and zodiac band appears to travel more closely (the southern horizon for observers in the northern latitudes, and the northern horizon for observers in the southern latitudes) that changes dramatically from one hemisphere to the other.

Otherwise, the observation of the night sky is the same all over, and the descriptions of the constellations given in the discussions of the Star Myths which follow should make sense no matter where on the planet you happen to reside, with some minor mental adjustments necessary for those in southern latitudes when translating a description into something they can go out and locate in their own night sky.

Star Myths of Australia

The many tribes and cultures of Aboriginal Australians are thought by anthropologists to be one of the oldest living populations on our planet with perhaps the longest stream of unbroken and continuous preservation of culture and tradition of any group. Although certainty is impossible and various academic researchers disagree, it is generally accepted based on a variety of evidence that the Aboriginal peoples of Australia may have been isolated from other cultures for thousands of years or even for tens of thousands of years (with some exceptions).

Thus, the evidence we find that these myths, recorded by researchers in previous decades or even previous centuries, who presumably had no knowledge of the "Star Myth" theories and correspondences outlined in this series of books, belonging to the various Aboriginal peoples of Australia, appear to be built upon the very same system of celestial metaphor which forms the basis for the myths of ancient India and ancient Greece, and which forms the basis for the stories in the Old and New Testaments of the Bible, is significant indeed, and argues that whatever the original source is of this worldwide system, it predates anything known or admitted by conventional historians.

The example myths related here contain clear connections to celestial figures -- and, what's more, to myths from other cultures around the world as far removed from Australia as northern Europe and even the Americas! Once again, if during the first few chapters of the book the connections to the constellations seem to be "a stretch," please press on, because by the time we reach the myths of ancient Egypt, Mesopotamia, and India, the cumulative examples and connections will pile up to a point where their foundation in celestial metaphor becomes impossible to deny.

The Warramungu fire myth of the Bandicoot Woman

In his collection of myths from around the world entitled *Myths of the Origin of Fire*, first published in 1930, James Frazer recounts the fire-myth of the Warramunga tribe of north-central Australia, now usually spelled Warramungu.

We learn that fire was first made by two "hawk ancestors" named Kirkalanji and Warra-pulla-pulla, who had fire-sticks which they carried about with them at all times.[13] One day, however, "Kirkalanji lit a fire that was bigger than he intended to make," and was himself caught in the conflagration, and burnt up.[14] Warra-pulla-pulla was so distraught at this terrible episode that he flew away in the direction of Queensland, never to return.

Onto this scene then came the moon, who in those ancient and far-off days walked upon the earth in the form of a man. We learn that:

> He met a bandicoot woman near the spot where Kirkalanji had kindled the fire, and he strolled about with her. Then they sat on a bank with their backs to the fire and were so long talking to one another that they did not notice it till it was close upon them. The bandicoot woman was badly singed and swooned away or died outright; however, the moon man, being no ordinary mortal, brought her to life or to consciousness, and together they went up into the sky.[15]

The celestial clues in this story are actually quite abundant. At the end of the account, of course, we are told quite plainly that the moon man and the bandicoot woman "went up into the sky," and the implication is that we can still see them there to this day.

Chapter One

This myth of the Warramungu people of Australia contains numerous correspondences to myths from other cultures, myths which we will encounter later in this volume as well as in future volumes of this series, from cultures seemingly unconnected to the ancient and long-isolated cultures of Australia. The connection, in my opinion, may perhaps be traced back to some extremely ancient predecessor culture -- perhaps one which was almost-entirely wiped out by some terrible catastrophe, long before the time of ancient Egypt and ancient Babylon, whose primordial wisdom survives in barely-audible echoes within the world's sacred myths.

Can you guess the identity of the two hawk ancestors, one of whom was burnt to death in the blaze of the fire he had kindled? Can you find a place in the sky where there are the constellations of a man and a woman with their backs to this blaze, and can you see why they are described as sitting with their backs to the fire, and why the woman is described as either dying or swooning away? Perhaps you can even venture to speculate as to why they are identified as a moon man and a bandicoot woman, based on their outlines!

Let's begin with the figures of the "two hawk ancestors," Kirkalanji and Warra-pulla-pulla. There are two mighty celestial birds who can be seen flying towards each other along the shining silvery band of the Milky Way: the constellations Aquila the Eagle and Cygnus the Swan. These two great birds feature in many sacred stories from around the world, sometimes being described as various different birds, sometimes two falcons, sometimes two eagles (in this story as recorded by James Frazer, of course, they are two hawks).

Note that the hazy band of the Milky Way itself can be imagined to be the rising smoke from some great fire, and the widest and brightest part of the Milky Way (which astronomers believe to be the Galactic Core or the Galactic Center) could in fact be the blazing fire itself, which produces the "smoke" that makes up the rest of the column of the Milky Way.

And that is just how the shining band of the Galaxy features in this story, in which Kirkalanji kindles a blaze that is too great for him to escape, and he is trapped in it and perishes. Based on the relative locations of these two constellations within the smoky path of the Milky Way, it is likely that Aquila plays the role of Kirkalanji, who is caught in the conflagration, and Cygnus is Warra-pulla-pulla, who eventually migrates to the region now called Queensland. Below is a star-chart showing the scene:

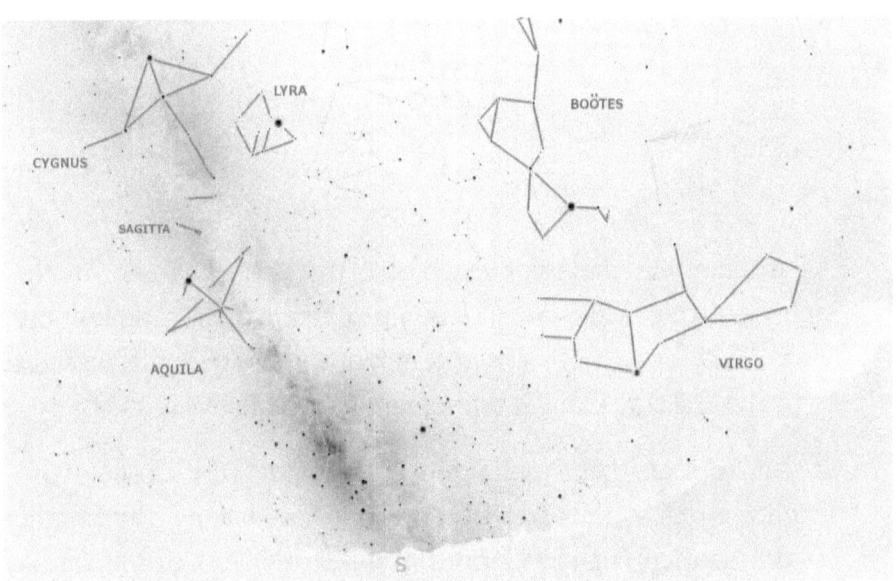

The viewer can see the forms of the two great birds of the Milky Way, Aquila the Eagle and Cygnus the Swan, which are both located in the vicinity of the brightest and thickest portion of the

Galaxy (the darker any part of the Milky Way appears in these inverted star-charts, the brighter that portion of the Galaxy appears in the night sky).

For readers who are not (yet) personally familiar with the Milky Way and who may have difficulty tracing its outlines following the cloudy band in the preceding chart, below is the exact same chart, but this time the path of the Galaxy has been outlined:

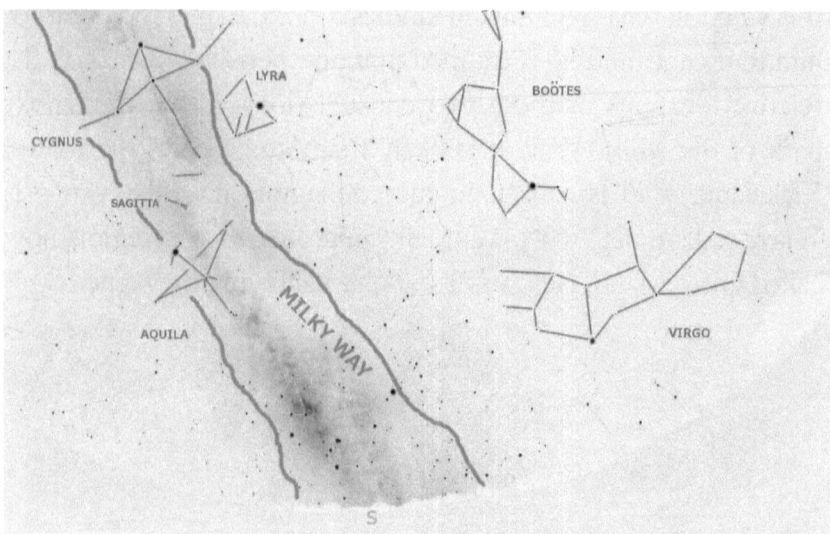

As we can see, the brightest part of the Milky Way is in the vicinity of the "Milky Way" label in the above chart (below the word "Way" in fact): this brightest and thickest region is thought to be the Galactic Core at the center of the Milky Way itself.

It can be seen that Aquila and Cygnus are very close to this brightest region and can be envisioned as having started the "blaze" at the Galactic Core from which the rest of the smoky band arises.

The myth tells us that the two hawk-ancestors carried fire-sticks with them wherever they went. Most likely these sticks correspond to figures we can see near Cygnus and Aquila or even between Cygnus and Aquila -- possibly one of them being the stick-like shape of Sagitta the Arrow, which is labeled in the star-chart. Nearby and almost parallel to it is another "line" between two stars just above Sagitta in the star-chart above. This line has been designated as Vulpecula, or the Little Fox, but this is a modern constellation and does not play a role as a fox in any ancient myths. It is possible, however, that this line-shaped constellation plays a fire-stick in this myth of Australia, along with Sagitta the Arrow.

Another possibility for the "fire-sticks" in this story might be the two parallel lines in the body of the constellation Lyra the Lyre, which is located adjacent to the constellation Cygnus the Swan. These two parallel lines within Lyra play the role of strings of the Lyre when it is envisioned as a musical instrument (as it is in many other important Star Myths from around the world), but in this case might be the fire-sticks described in the story.

It is even possible that the "fire-sticks" mentioned in this myth and some of the others we will examine are associated with the constellation Ophiuchus. We will see that Ophiuchus-figures in various myths often carry *two spears*. We will also see (in this volume's examination of myths from ancient India) that Ophiuchus plays the role of the "great churn" which churns the heavens -- which in other myths might be envisioned as a spinning fire-stick generating friction to start a fire.

In any event, we can see that the pair who strolled along and then sat down with their backs to the fire are played by Boötes the Herdsman, in the role of the moon man, and Virgo the Virgin, in the role of the bandicoot woman. The seated posture of Boötes is evident from the image, as is his fairly round and bulbous head, which may account for his being called a "moon" man. Note that his "back is towards the fire" of the smoky column of the Milky Way.

Virgo, who is playing the role of the bandicoot woman, has either fainted away or perished from the flames, as she is lying down in her familiar recumbent posture. This aspect of Virgo will turn up some in other myths around the world as a female character who is described as lazy, or who doesn't want to get up and do something she is supposed to do, and who then has to be coaxed or encouraged or begged to come out and show herself.

Additionally, the description in this myth -- from a culture in one of the furthest south pieces of land on earth -- of the man as being a "moon man" due to the shape of the head of the constellation Boötes will be seen again in a myth from a culture in one of the furthest north regions on the planet, the Norse myths (discussed in *Star Myths of the World, Volume Four*).

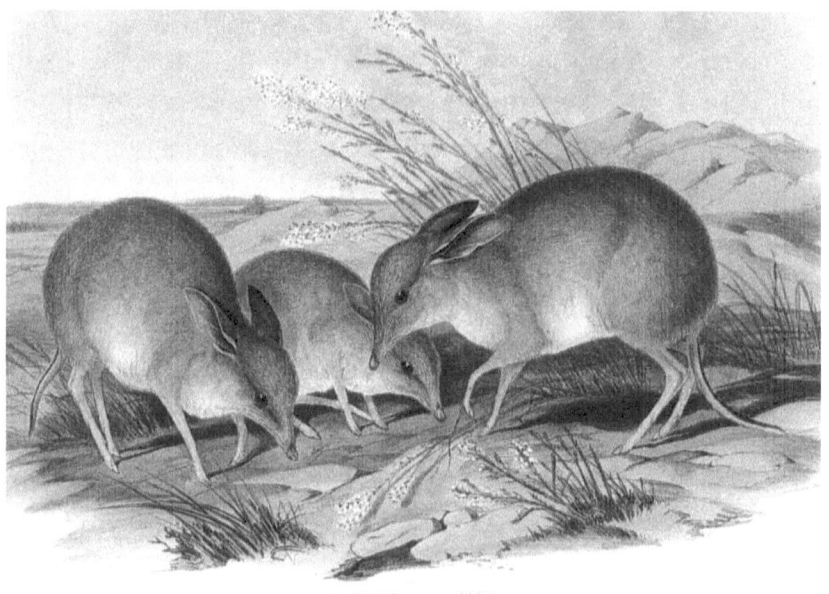

Equally important is the description of the woman as a "bandicoot woman." This description is undoubtedly inspired by the rather long head in the outline of the constellation Virgo, which can be seen in the preceding star-charts. That a figure in this myth who almost certainly corresponds to Virgo is described as having the characteristics of a bandicoot, which is a small marsupial indigenous to Australia and Papua New Guinea, with a somewhat rodent-like head featuring mouse-like ears and a pointed snout, will be important in the analysis of other myths around the world in which Virgo plays the role of a mouse-like figure in some way.

In fact, in a later section of this volume when we examine the story of the god Ganesha or Ganapati, the mouse-like or rodent-like aspects of the constellation Virgo will play an important role in the analysis. This myth was not included in the first edition of this first volume of the Star Myth series -- and is an example of details encountered in a myth examined later helping to confirm connections found in a previously-examined sacred story. Such confirmations have happened many times over the years as I have explored the Star Myths of the world.

The clues in this Warramungu legend are abundant enough to strongly suggest that this story encodes the motions of the actors in the heavenly sphere, and the details provided in the myth itself (and recorded by James Frazer in 1930, apparently without knowledge of the connections to the heavens) make the above interpretation seem very likely to be the correct one.

The River Yarra Fire-Myth of Karakarook & Waung

Another myth from Australia cited in Frazer's *Myths of the Origin of Fire* comes from the Aboriginal people of the Yarra River valley, near present-day Melbourne.[16] Here is their story to explain the origin of fire:

Long ago, there was a woman named Karakarook, who alone knew the secret of making fire, and who refused to share it with anyone else. Karakarook kept the secret fire with her, in the end of a yam-stick which she used as a simple digging tool to hunt for edible roots, such as yams, as well as for the insects and lizards that she and her people liked to eat.

Because Karakarook refused to share the secret of the fire, Waung (whose name itself means "Crow") devised a ruse to get some of the fire from her. Knowing that Karakarook greatly enjoyed making a delightful meal of ant eggs, which she would dig out of ant mounds with her yam-stick, Waung either created or found a great number of serpents, and hid them underneath a likely ant-hill.

Then, Waung went to find Karakarook, and told her about the ant-hill he knew of, which appeared to be a very likely source of the woman's favorite dinner. Karakarook came along with Waung and, seeing the mound and deciding there would certainly be ant eggs galore inside, she took out her yam-stick and began to dig into it.

It didn't take long for the woman's digging to uncover the snakes, which immediately began issuing from the ant mound and slithering towards her. At Waung's urging, she began to strike at the snakes with her yam-stick, and when she did, the hidden fire began to fall out of the tip of the stick as she struck the serpents slithering on the ground.

Waung immediately picked up some of the fire, and made off with it. Unfortunately, he was just as secretive with the fire as Karakarook had been, and the story goes on to explain that Pundjel, the Creator, ended up punishing Waung and placing Karakarook in the sky among the stars, and the rest of humanity obtained fire from Waung, but not before he had tried to burn the people, and in some versions of the story he burned two humans to death in the process.

Again, this story gives clear indications that we should look for the origin of this story in the heavens, most notably in the placing of Karakarook among the stars forever. There are other clues which can help you determine who is playing what role: Look for a part of the sky which might contain a constellation of a woman, a crow, and a serpent. Moreover, the "yam-stick" carried by the woman is a strong clue.

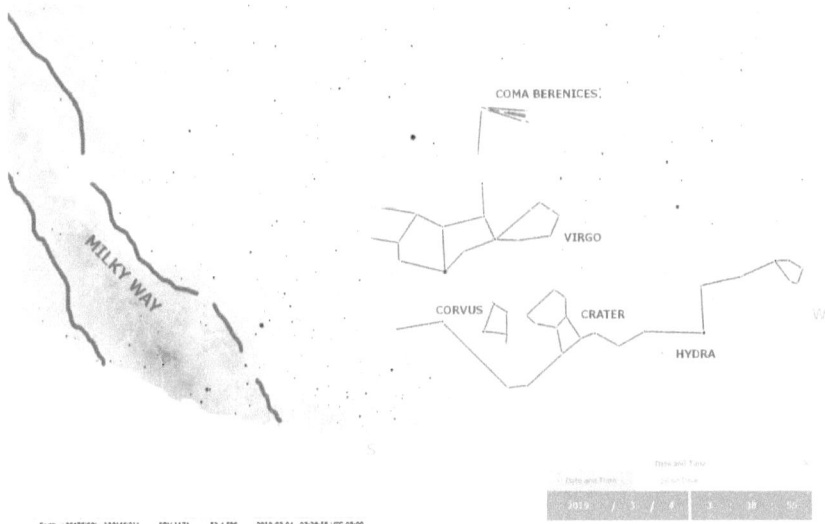

A woman carrying a stick is a clear indicator that we are almost certainly here dealing with a manifestation of the zodiac constellation Virgo the Virgin. The outline of Virgo is marked by the distinctive feature of her outstretched arm, which figures in many Star Myths around the world. The outstretched arm of Virgo is marked by the star Vindemiatrix. In this myth the outstretched arm becomes the yam-stick which Karakarook uses to hunt for edible roots.

Note that in this story from the Aboriginal people of the Yarra River area, the yam-stick has fire hidden "in the tip" of the stick. In the above star-chart, we see that the extended arm of Virgo reaches towards the constellation Coma Berenices, and can in fact be imagined to "connect" to that constellation, creating a longer "yam-stick" in the heavens – and one which does indeed seem to have fire hidden at the end of the stick, just as related in this story.

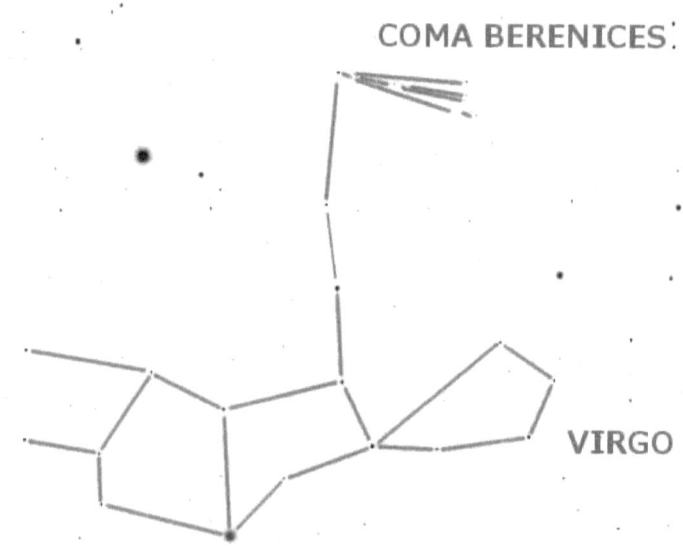

Coma Berenices, a constellation whose name means "Hair of Berenice" in Latin (or, more commonly, "Berenice's Hair") is a faint but important constellation which features in many Star Myths from cultures around the world. H. A. Rey outlines it as a kind of "pom-pom" consisting of faint streamers emanating from a sort of stick-like handle. Above, the imaginary "line" between the end of Virgo's outstretched arm and the base of Coma Berenices has been added.

Because the shimmering "streamers" of Berenice's Hair are difficult to see (requiring a dark night and low light pollution) the description of the fire as being *concealed* at the end of Karakarook's yam-stick is most apt for this story's combination of Virgo and Coma Berenices.

If we accept that Karakarook in the story corresponds to Virgo in the heavens, Waung the Crow would then be played by the nearby constellation of Corvus, who is always staring at Virgo's brightest star, Spica. The Crow in the heavens is perched on the back of the sinuous form of Hydra, the Serpent, and we note of course that serpents play an important role in this story as well:

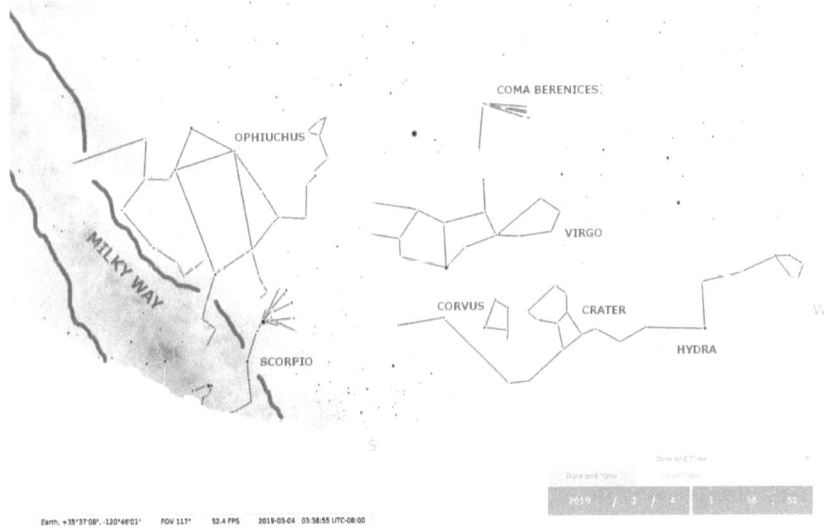

However, in the above star-chart we see that there is another candidate for the serpents which Waung either made or placed underneath the ant-mount in the story, in addition to Hydra: the constellation Scorpio, which is found immediately underneath the looming form of the constellation Ophiuchus (see above).

As we will see throughout our examination of the myths and the stars, including in later volumes in this series such as *Star Myths, Volume Two* (*Myths of Ancient Greece*), *Star Myths, Volume Three* (*Star Myths of the Bible*), and *Star Myths, Volume Four* (*Norse Mythology*), the constellation Ophiuchus does in fact play the role of a hill or mound or mountain in many, many myths around the world.

Opposite is an image of a huge termite mound in Australia, showing how well the oblong shape of the constellation Ophiuchus could play the role of a great ant-mound or termite mound in this story. The mound pictured, located in the Litchfield National Park in Northern Territory, Australia, is approximately five meters high, and is home to a colony of cathedral termites, *Nasutitermes triodiae*, so named because of the very high mounds they construct.

When Karakarook digs up the mound in which Waung has hidden the serpents, thinking that there must be ant-eggs inside, the serpents slither out and she is obliged to strike at them with her stick, allowing Waung to make off with the coveted fire.

If we consider the star-chart on the previous page, we can see that the constellation Scorpio, which is depicted in a "multi-headed" outline because this constellation often plays the role of a multi-headed serpent in various myths from around the world, could be envisioned as the many serpents beneath the mound of Ophiuchus. The constellation Hydra would then represent one serpent which is out ahead of the others, quite close to the woman in the story (Virgo) and her fire-tipped yam-stick (outstretched arm, continuing on to Coma Berenices).

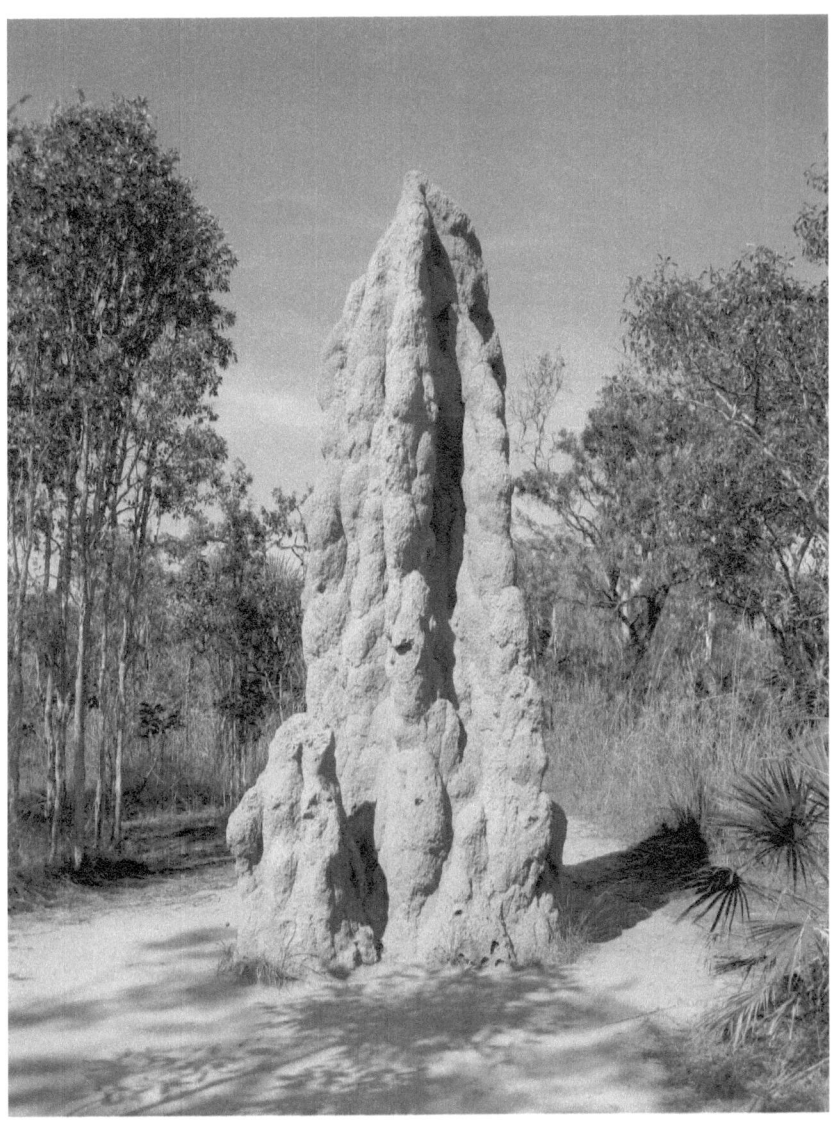

While Karakarook is striking at the snakes, some of the fire hidden within the yam-stick falls out, allowing Waung the Crow to steal it. He then continues the tradition of hoarding the fire, and in one version of the story burns two humans to death with it - possibly the Twins of Gemini, who are located on the other side of the sky.[17] The Twins are positioned such that the smoky-looking path of the Milky Way billows past their feet, and so they may be the humans burned by Waung in some versions of the story.

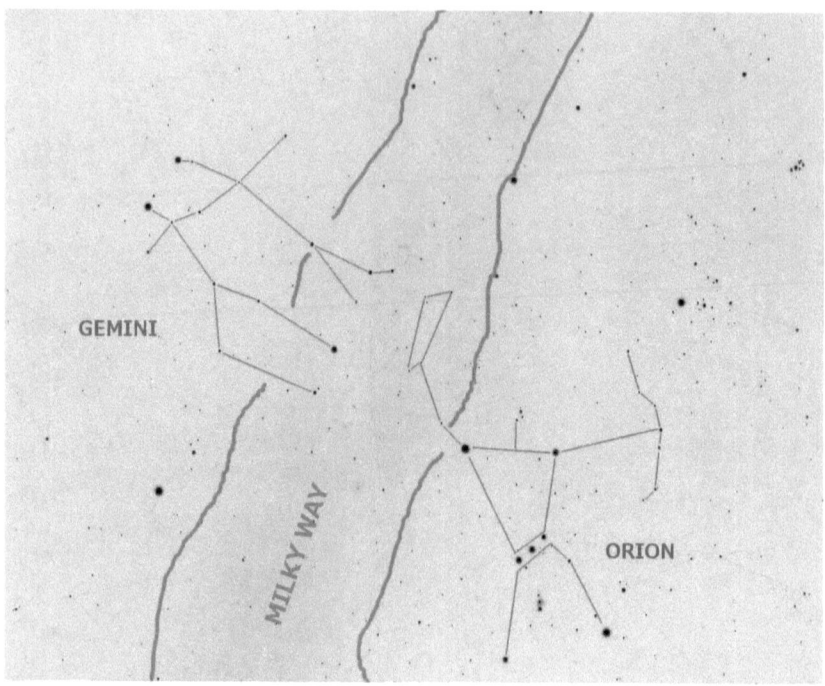

In any event, the identities of Karakarook (Virgo), Waung (Corvus), and the serpents (Hydra) are hard to deny, given the proximity of these three constellations, and given the sure clue of the "yam-stick" carried by Karakarook.

The inclusion in the myth of the direct admission that Waung and Karakarook were later placed in the sky among the stars is a compelling piece of evidence which pretty much clinches the case for a celestial interpretation.

Frazer's account of this myth of Australia declares that Karakarook is placed in the heavens as the Pleiades, which is on the opposite side of the heavens from Virgo, such that when

Virgo is rising the Pleiades are setting, and when the Pleiades are rising Virgo is setting.

Why the myth should specify that Karakarook becomes the Pleiades is not easy to determine based on the recorded accounts, which give no further detail on that aspect of the story. However, it should be quite evident that during the action of the story involving the fire-stick and the serpents beneath the termite mound, Karakarook is seen in the heavens in the figure of Virgo with her extended arm, and Coma Berenices just beyond.

It should also be mentioned at this point that the constellation Virgo appears in many world myths involving the origin of fire -- we have already seen Virgo playing a role in each of the two myths we have examined thus far. It is very likely that the reason has to do with the fact that these myths are not necessarily attempts to explain the "origin of fire" among human cultures so much as they are pointing towards a specific station in the great cycles of the heavenly machinery: the point of fall equinox, when the "fire" of the sun (and the sun's path) "plunges down" to the lower half of the year.

In their ground-breaking 1969 examination of the connection between the myths and the cosmology of the great heavenly cycles, *Hamlet's Mill*, Professors Hertha von Dechend and Giorgio de Santillana argue that when "fire" appears in myth, it figures the entire equinoctial "colure" which was imagined to run through each equinox and through the celestial poles.[18] Without going into depth here regarding the full explanation of the concept of a "colure," I agree with their interpretation up to a point: I believe that the "fire" represents the path of the sun through the heavens, and that myths mentioning fire almost certainly point to the two places where the sun's path crosses the celestial equator, which are the two equinoxes (one in the fall and one in the spring).

These two points mark the days each year when the sun "crosses down" into the lower half of the year (when hours of darkness are longer than hours of daylight) and again when it "crosses back up" into the upper half of the year (when hours of daylight are longer than hours of darkness).

The descent of the sun into the "lower half" of the year can be seen as analogizing the plunge of the divine spark into the lower realm of this incarnate life -- describing in esoteric language what happens at the birth of each and every child into this world. It is *this downward plunge* of divine fire into the lower realm which these myths on the "origin of fire" are commemorating and describing, in my opinion, and not the acquisition of fire by "early humans."

This argument is supported by the abundant evidence found in the Star Myths from cultures around the globe in which Virgo plays a prominent role. Virgo is situated at the "crossing down" point on the zodiac wheel and associated with the fall equinox and the "plunge downward" into mortal existence in many world myths.

Intriguingly, this point of fall equinox is only autumnal in the northern hemisphere: because of the tilt of our planet on its axis, the summer months in the northern hemisphere (when the north pole is pointing more directly towards the sun) are actually the winter months in the southern hemisphere (because the south pole is pointing away from the sun when the north pole is pointing towards the sun). Thus, Virgo is stationed at the fall equinox for the *northern* hemisphere.

This seems to argue at least the *possibility* that the ancient original of these Star Myths may have come from the northern hemsiphere, and then spread out around the globe later -- perhaps during the long recovery from some great catastrophe or cataclysm, for which there appears to be abundant evidence from many sources.

In any case, we will have occasion to see other myths from around the world in which Virgo and the constellations around Virgo play important roles and which have to do with the descent of the divine spark into the "lower realm" of this incarnate existence -- including other myths involving the "origin of fire."

Mirragan and Gurangatch

Aboriginal sacred tradition tells the story of Mirragan, the Fisherman, and his pursuit of the marvelous fish Gurangatch, which took place ages ago, in the Dreamtime. Gurangatch dwelt deep in a waterhole in what is today New South Wales, Australia, at the junction of the Wollondilly and Wingeecaribee Rivers:

> Gurangatch was half fish and half reptile, with shimmering scales of green, purple and gold. His eyes shone like two bright stars through the clear green water of his camping ground. At mid-day, when the sun was high, he basked in the shallow water of the lagoon, and at nightfall retired to the dark depths of the pool.[19]

Mirragan was a famous fisherman, who was too proud to pursue small fish, but only pursued the largest and most dangerous of them all. When Mirragan happened past the waterhole of Gurangatch and saw his blazing eyes beaming up from the depths, he immediately tried to spear the monster, but Gurangatch retreated deep into the waterhole, out of reach.

Then commenced a battle of wits and strength between Mirragan and Gurangatch. Mirragan first began to poison the waterhole with bark in hopes that Gurangatch would have to rise to the surface, but the fish was too strong and was only sickened, and remained in the depths.

When Mirragan went to search for more bark, Gurangatch took the opportunity to burrow underground from one lagoon to another, deep beneath mountain ranges, forming the extensive subterranean caves known as the Jenolan limestone caves and the Whambeyan limestone caves. When he plowed along the surface of the earth, his passage created the great river valleys where today flow the Wollondilly, the Guineacor, and the Cox Rivers.

All through the country Mirragan pursued Gurangatch, and whenever he caught up to the great fish, Mirragan attacked with his spear and Gurangatch fought back with blows from his powerful tail. Finally, both of them were worn out. Gurangatch was taken by his relations down into a deep waterhole where he could recover from the many blows he had received from Mirragan.

Mirragan met up with his friends, whom he found engaged in the process of roasting eels over a fire. They offered him some of the food, but he replied:

> I do not want such little things. I have been hunting a great fish for many days and nights. His eyes shine like stars when the night is cold, and his body shimmers like the noonday sun. His friends have taken him over the mountains to the Joolundoo waterhole. Will you send the best divers in the camp with me so that we may kill him?[20]

And so, his friends thought about it for a long time, and finally settled on Billagoola the Shag, Goolagwangwan the Diver, Gundhareen the Black Duck, and Goonarring the Wood Duck.

They went back with Mirragan to the waterhole where Gurangatch was hiding, and each dove as deep as he could, but could not descend far enough to reach Gurangatch. At last, Billagoola descended all the way to the mud, where Gurangatch was wedged fast into a crevice for protection, while a school of smaller fish were busy covering the great fish with mud to hide him.

Billagoola seized the back of the great fish with his bill, and strove with all his might to bring Gurangatch up, but he was wedged too tightly. All he could do was tear a chunk of flesh from the back of the mighty creature. This Billagoola brought back up to the surface.

Far from being disappointed, Mirragan was overjoyed and exclaimed, "This is a piece of the fish I have hunted many days and nights." They roasted the meat over a campfire and had a feast. Then they returned to their homes . . . but you can still see the pathways that the great Gurangatch made, over the ground and under it, as he was pursued by Mirragan the Relentless.

To find the celestial basis for this story, look for a part of the sky which contains a fish whose eye is a star of dazzling brightness. Near him, you will find the fisherman, who is always ready to deploy his spear. The duo are actually near the rising column of smoke where Mirragan's friends were roasting a mess of eels. You can see the place where the chunk of flesh was torn from the back of Gurangatch, and on *that* side of the fish there is a group of birds who probably play the role of the divers in this Aborigine Star Myth from the days of the Dreamtime.

In myths dealing with a Fisherman and a Fish, we are very often dealing with the constellations Aquarius (who takes the shape of a man) and Piscis Austrinus, the Southern Fish. We will see, for example, that the apostle Peter in the New Testament is almost certainly associated with Aquarius, particularly in the story in which Jesus tells Peter he will find a coin in the mouth of the first fish he catches (in Matthew chapter 17).[21]

As the name implies, Piscis Austrinus is located in the southern portion of the celestial sphere, and viewers in northern latitudes may have difficulty spotting anything but its brightest star,

Fomalhaut. The other stars may be lost in the haze and glow usually seen along the horizon, since the Southern Fish will not rise far above the southern horizon for viewers in the northern hemisphere above about 33° north latitude.

But even if its fainter stars are difficult for many northern hemisphere viewers to see, its brightest star is a real show-stopper: Fomalhaut is one of the brightest in the sky. It is located on the "head" portion of the Southern Fish constellation, and can be thought of as its eye – or perhaps as a brilliant jewel or (as in the New Testament account) a coin in the mouth of the fish.

In the story of Mirragan and Gurangatch, we are almost certainly dealing with these two constellations, Aquarius and Piscis Austrinus. The storytellers have left us a strong clue in the mention of the spear of Mirragan, with which he tries to plumb the depths to reach the mighty Gurangatch, but cannot quite reach the great fish-monster. This spear is mentioned more than once in the story.

Aquarius has a very distinctive outstretched "leg," which can best be envisioned through the use of the outlines suggested in 1952 by H. A. Rey, whose outlines of the constellations are frequently essential for unlocking the ancient meaning hidden in the myths. Other "modern" methods for connecting the stars of the most well-known constellations or depicting their outlines seem almost perversely designed to thwart the star-gazer's ability to either find the constellation or (more importantly, for this study) to connect the features of the constellations to descriptions preserved in the world's celestial myths (see the contrasting outline examples on pages 16 and 17 of this volume, which include Aquarius and Piscis Austrinus).

Aquarius is a prime example: the modern methodologies of outlining this constellation are horrendous. The outline suggested by H. A. Rey, however, is brilliant – and reveals the reason why this constellation appears in so many myths around the world. In his outline, Aquarius is pitched-forward, in a running posture, almost as if he has been running with his water-jar and has tripped, flying forward but still stretching out his forward leg in order to try to recover before he loses his balance (and the water) completely.

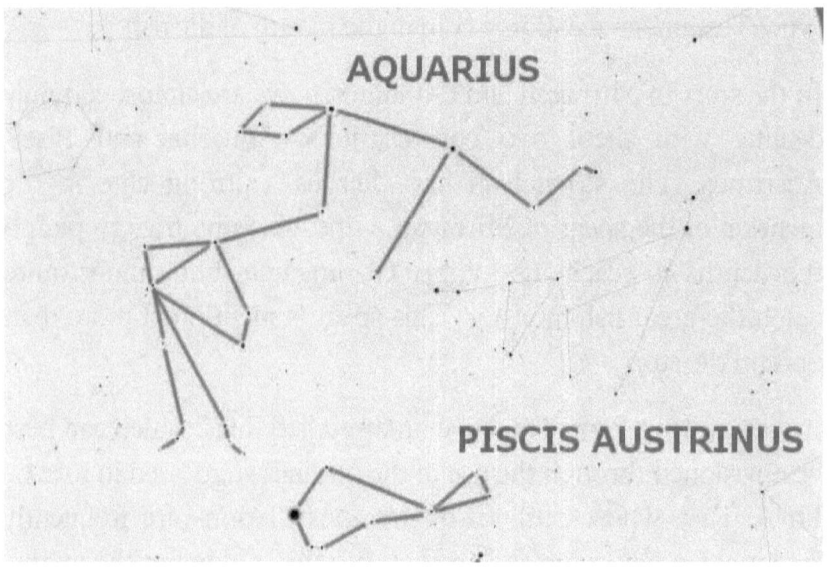

This outstretched leg will appear in different myths around the world in different ways, and here it takes the form of a spear, extended towards the Southern Fish.

Below it, and just out of reach, crouches Gurangatch, whose eyes the myth itself tells us blaze up from the depths of the pool like the glorious stars of the sky.

Below him are four bird-shaped constellations, not very well-known and not participants in many other myths with which most of us would be familiar. These are the Crane (or Grus), the Phoenix, the Toucan (or Tucana), and the Peacock (Pavo), and they are definitely southern constellations: arrayed south of the Southern Fish in the night sky, they will not be visible at all to most northern hemisphere viewers.

However, if we realize that in the southern hemisphere the stars and constellations appear to an observer as being "upside down" relative to their position in the northern hemisphere's sky, we can see that the "back" or dorsal region of the Southern Fish constellation (the side facing the four bird-companions) does indeed look as though a great chunk of flesh has been ripped out of it – perhaps by the deep-diving Crane, who is the closest of the four bird-constellations to the Fish.

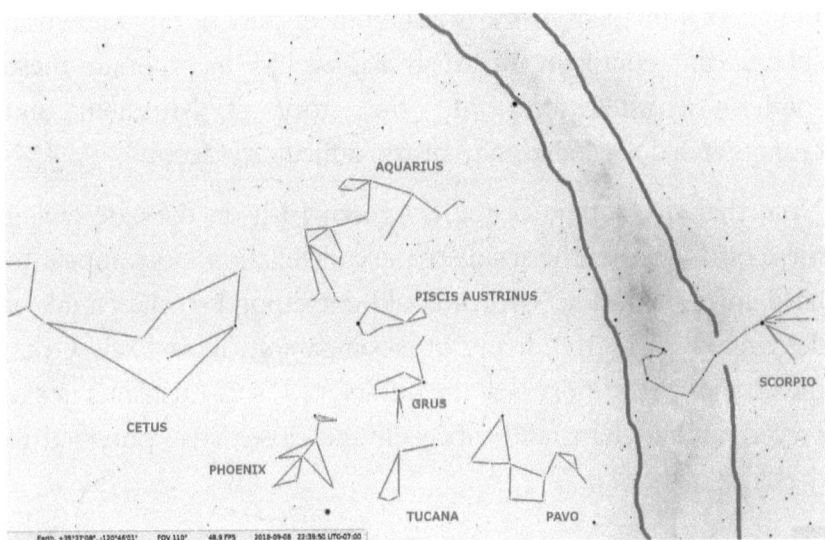

Note that there are in fact four "Southern Birds" in the region of the sky beneath (to the south of) the Southern Fish: the Crane, the Phoenix, the Toucan, and the Peacock (Pavo).

The four "Southern Birds" shown in the star-chart are all in fact "modern" constellations: not attested in any ancient source and only found in texts dating to the sixteenth century. However, as we will see in *Star Myths of the World, Volume Two* (*Myths of Ancient Greece*), there is some artistic evidence that the ancients imagined mythical figures corresponding to the constellation Pavo (with Pavo often playing the role of a defeated Titan or other figure on the battlefield, being crushed beneath the boulder of Ara the Altar, which is found just above Pavo in the Milky Way band, between Pavo and the tail of Scorpio).[22]

I have not encountered any other Star Myths thus far which incorporate Phoenix, the Toucan, or the Crane into the action of the myth itself, and so the association of these Southern Birds with the companions of Mirragan is somewhat tenuous -- and yet the outlines do strongly resemble birds, and the fact that an Indigenous myth from the southernmost part of our terrestrial sphere, the continent of Australia, would incorporate these southern constellations into the story of Mirragan and Gurangatch does not seem to be too difficult to accept.

Note that the outline of the Southern Fish on the side facing these birds (the southern side of the constellation) does appear to have an "indentation," which could correspond to the chunk of flesh removed by the diving bird-companion (most likely Grus, the Crane) in the story: see the outline of Piscis Austrinus in the preceding star-chart, and especially the closer view provided in the chart on page 52.

Finally, some additional supporting evidence is provided by the detail in the story which says that Mirragan's friends were busy roasting eels when the Fisherman came upon them. This reference in the story likely points to the constellation Scorpio, which is partly positioned within the rising column of the Milky

Way at its brightest and widest section – suggesting that it is being roasted in a fire.

Scorpio is often envisioned as having multiple heads, in various Star Myths from around the world (including the story of the battle of the Greek hero Heracles, or Hercules, with the Lernaean Hydra). Thus Scorpio almost certainly accounts for the detail in the story regarding Mirragan's friends and the roasted eels. In the New Testament account of the baptism of Christ, we are told that John the Baptist (also an "Aquarius figure") refers to the Pharisees and Sadducees as a "generation of vipers" (such as in Matthew 3: 7), and I would argue that this accusation is also referring to the nearby constellation of Scorpio with its multiple, serpentine heads.[23]

Thus, the evidence which supports the conclusion that this Aboriginal Australian myth from the Blue Mountains of New South Wales is celestial in nature and describes figures associated with the constellations in the region of the sky surrounding Aquarius and Piscis Austrinus is quite compelling.

In concluding this examination of this particular myth, it is worth noting that there is another, even larger "fish" constellation in the vicinity of Aquarius, and that is the form of Cetus the Whale (see preceding Star Myth chart). The monstrous size and power of Gurangatch in the story makes it possible that this mythical fish is played by Cetus in the heavens, rather than by Piscis Austrinus.

However, I favor the identification of Piscis Austrinus with Gurangatch, due to the fact that the myth itself clearly says that the bright and glowing eyes of Gurangatch are one of the distinctive features of this adversary -- and Piscis Austrinus has one of the brightest stars in the heavens at its mouth (the star Fomalhaut, whose very name means "mouth of the fish").

Additionally, the "spear" of Mirragan receives prominent mention in the Aboriginal myth, and is the implement of choice with which Mirragan pursues Gurangatch. From the preceding star-charts, it is clear that the "forward leg" of Aquarius (which almost certainly plays the spear of Mirragan in this story, and which will be shown to play the role of a spear in many other Star Myths from around the globe, such as in the battle-scenes described in the Iliad of ancient Greece, which are described in *Volume Two*) points almost directly towards Piscis Austrinus, and not towards Cetus.

From the evidence in this myth and the others we have examined, it becomes difficult to deny that the myths of the Aboriginal cultures of Australia are speaking a celestial language – and, what's more, that they are using the same system of celestial metaphor which underlies the world's other ancient myths, from cultures far removed and clearly not in contact with the southern island-continent.

This evidence and this conclusion have far-reaching implications.

We will now turn our attention to Star Myths found on another continent -- Star Myths which will also be shown to be built upon the same ancient system.

Star Myths of Africa: the Retreat of the Sky

In his 1967 text *African Mythology*, Geoffrey Parrinder (1910 - 2005) notes that:

> One of the best known of all African myths, found in many parts of the continent, tells of God leaving the world. It is generally agreed that in the earliest times God lived on earth but, generally due to some human fault, God got angry and went up to heaven. There is some idea of a Golden Age in the past, when God and man's ancestors were closer together, and some resemblance to the Biblical story of the Garden of Eden, though there it is men who are expelled from the paradisal state.[24]

Parrinder explains that the features of this particular myth-pattern are very similar wherever found, from the western side of the continent along the Atlantic, in Ghana and Nigeria and the Ivory Coast and other regions, straight across to the eastern side of Africa, along the Indian Ocean, among (for example) the Nuba and the Dinka of the Sudan.

In all of these sacred stories, the High God once dwelt close to and in fact among humanity, and the sky itself was much lower in those days and was physically accessible to the people (in some instances, people would break off a piece of the sky when they needed something extra for the cooking pot). However, the people became too familiar with the heavens and treated it without much respect, with children wiping their hands on it after their meals, and human beings everywhere generally taking the sky for granted.

But the final affront in every one of the stories involves women banging into the sky with their pestles when beating out grain in their pounding-bowls or mortars. Usually, in these stories, there is one particular woman who is especially enthusiastic and energetic in her pounding, and it is her carelessness in striking the sky that eventually causes the heavens – and the High God – to retreat to their current distance:

> Especially women would knock against the sky when pounding their meal. This is one of the great female occupations of Africa, where mechanical flour mills have not been introduced. The grain is pounded in a wooden mortar, a scooped out piece of log, and a long wooden pestle is thumped down on the grains of corn. It is said that there was a woman once who had a very long pestle, and whenever she pounded her corn the wooden pole hit against God who lived just above the sky.[25]

Elsewhere in Africa it is a long wooden spoon with which the women would stir their millet porridge while cooking it, and due to the close proximity of the heavens, they had difficulty stirring the pot and would often burn their hands on their pots, so low was the sky. When one of them got annoyed at constantly bumping the handle of her spoon against the heavens, and of burning her fingers on her cooking, she gave an especially vigorous thrust with the spoon, so vigorous in fact that it stabbed right through the sky. This so angered the sky that it retreated to its present distance above the earth.

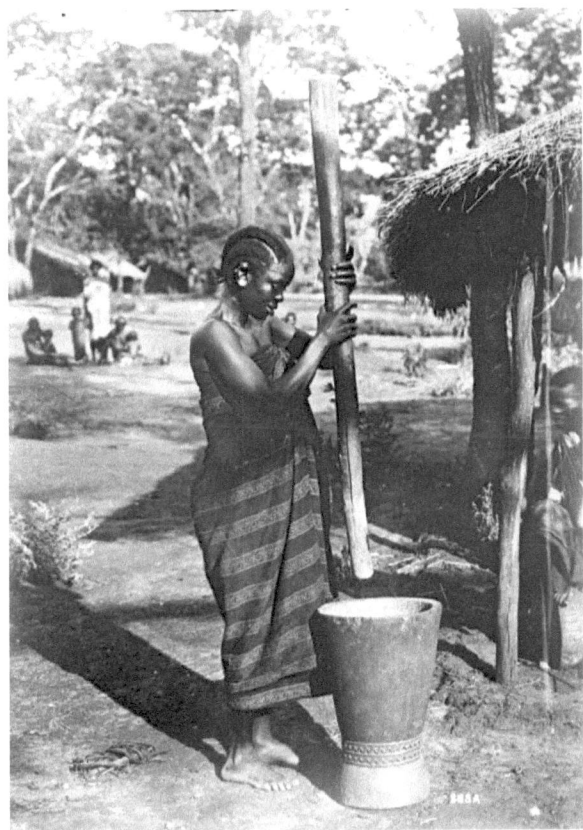

Woman with Mortar & Pestle, Tanzania , c. 1906 – 1918.

Parrinder speculates that in the various versions of this story, it always seems to be the woman who is blamed for the disaster of the retreat of the sky and the loss of intimate contact with the High God, "perhaps because the stories were told by men."[26]

But, just as with the Genesis story, it may be that there is a celestial explanation for this commonality. At this point, it should not be difficult to guess who plays the role of the woman with the long pestle or spoon (and, for that matter, who is the High One whom she strikes with her pounding stick, in some versions of the story). Can you guess which portion of which constellation is most likely the inspiration for these stories, found across the continent of Africa?

Further, there is a celestial "bowl" in close proximity to the woman: can you identify the constellation that probably represents the mortar in which the woman was pounding her grain, or in which she was cooking her millet porridge?

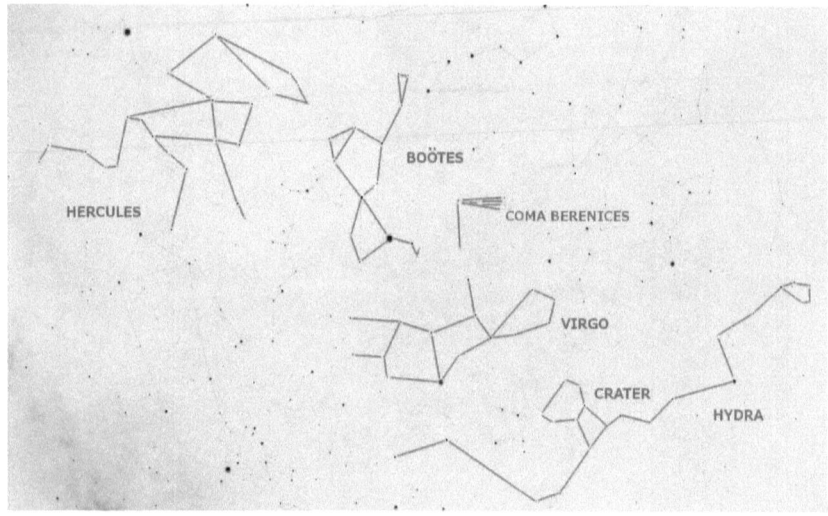

I would argue that in this myth, found across Africa, we are clearly dealing with the constellation Virgo. Her distinctive "extended arm" will be seen to play an important role in many of the world's Star Myths.

The extended arm of the constellation Virgo is marked by the bright star Vindemiatrix, pronounced "Vin-duh-MEE-uh-trix," a Latin word which roughly means "the female grape-pluckster" or "the female who plucks grapes" (the ending "-trix" is a Latin ending indicating a female role, and translates into the English ending "-tress" which is found in words such as "mistress" or "actress" and which in its Latin form survives in English in words such as "matrix" or "Bellatrix").

We have also seen, in the previous examinations of myths from the continent of Australia, that the "line" of the arm of Virgo can at times be extended to connect to the constellation of Coma Berenices (Berenice's Hair) when envisioning a longer stick or similar instrument. As can be seen in the photographs of actual pestles used in various cultures on the continent of Africa, these implements could be extremely long.

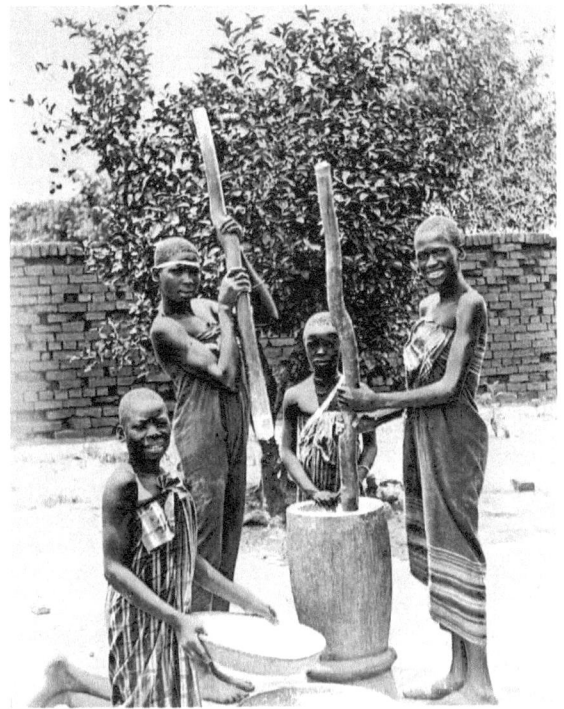

Young Ngoni girls, Malawi, c. 1910.

In this story, the extended arm of Virgo (possibly connecting to Coma Berenices) is viewed as either the pestle with which the women beat the grain into flour, or as a spoon with which they stir the millet porridge. The fact that it is generally pointing "upwards" as Virgo is arranged in the sky, appearing to recline on her back (for observers in the northern hemisphere) with her extended arm and Vindemiatrix pointing upwards in the direction of the constellation Boötes and the region of the north celestial pole, no doubt gives rise to the fact that in all the stories it is the *woman*, associated with Virgo, who pokes the sky with her implement (either her pestle or her spoon).

That it is the woman who pokes the sky and causes it and the High God to retreat to their current distance thus has less to do with any prejudice against women or greater culpability on the part of women than it has to do with the constellations as they are arranged in the night sky – and we will see that the same holds true for the story of Adam and Eve in Genesis, although that story has obviously been used by literalists for centuries as evidence to support the theory that women are somehow to blame for the entry of sin into the world (based upon a misinterpretation of stories that actually point to the stars).

In this story we also see an additional element not present in previous Star Myths, and that is the "mortar" in which the woman is pounding the grain, or the cooking-pot in which she is stirring her millet porridge. This feature *may* be played by the constellation Crater the Cup, located very close to the constellation Virgo – just beneath her, in fact – along the back of Hydra the Serpent, and between the Serpent and the Virgin. However, we will see mortars associated with another nearby constellation: Ophiuchus, a constellation of great importance in the ancient worldwide system.

In one version of the African myth, the woman is sorry for hitting the sky and causing God and the heavens to retreat to the distance at which they are no longer so accessible to humanity. As Parrinder tells the story:

> This meant that people could no longer approach God so easily as before. The woman tried to get over this difficulty

by telling her children to collect all the wooden mortars that they could find. These were all piled one on top of another and nearly reached up to heaven. Just one more mortar was needed, but they could not find one. So the old women told her children to take the lowest mortar out from the bottom and put it on the top. When they did this all the other mortars fell down and many people were killed. The Ila story will be recalled, of the old woman who tried to pile up trees to reach heaven, like a Tower of Babel.[27]

The similarity of this story to other Star Myths from around the world – including those in the Old and New Testaments of the Bible – is significant, and unmistakable, and Parrinder here points out one such parallel. In this case, we have a loss of access to divinity, and a loss that is precipitated by some fault or mistaken action on the part of humanity, no matter how seemingly innocuous (the overzealousness of pounding meal – although in some aspects of the myth, the woman also wanted more of the meal than everyone else). There is also the common theme of a lost "Golden Age" during which the deity walked among humanity before leaving.

In this case, we see the aftermath, in which humanity tries to regain access by climbing to the heavens, but the plan – as always – is frustrated and fails.

The identity of the High God who retreats from along with the sky itself and becomes more removed and less familiar to humanity can also be seen in the heavens. Based on the locations of the constellations seen in the star-chart on page 60, we might initially suspect that the constellation of Boötes in the sky corresponds to the highest deity who retreats from the poking of the woman. However, there are also reasons to believe that the

High God actually corresponds to the constellation Hercules, rather than to Boötes.

We shall see, in the subsequent volumes in this series, that the constellation Hercules plays the role of the highest deity in many other cultures around the world -- including in the stories of the Bible, in both the Old and New Testaments, but also in the myths of ancient Greece, where the constellation corresponds to the thunder-god Zeus, who is also known as Jove and as Jupiter among the Latins.

Of course, just because the constellation Hercules plays the highest deity in other cultures does not *necessarily* argue that Hercules plays the role of the High God in this story of the retreat of the sky found across the continent of Africa. However, as we will also see over the course of this series on the Star Myths of the world (as well as in a subsequent volume entitled *Astrotheology for Life*, published in 2017), the level of correspondence between the celestial metaphors used in the ancient myths and sacred stories around the world strongly suggests that they are all somehow connected, employing the same system of envisioning the constellations and the same blueprint of mapping the myths to the stars in cultures which are separated by vast distances of geography.

Additionally, there are reasons to suspect that in the story of the retreat of the sky which is found across so many cultures on the African continent, the figure of the High God can be confidently understood to correspond to the constellation Hercules in the night sky. The detail of the stacking of the mortars, to try to regain the familiarity with the deity which had been lost, in a story which has strong echoes to the incident of the Tower of Babel described in Genesis, points strongly to the identity of the High God with the constellation Hercules.

In the version of the story from Africa, related by Parrinder in his collection of African mythology, the people stack mortars in order to try to regain their connection with the High God. The overturned mortars, stacked up to reach almost to heaven, almost certainly correspond to the figure of Ophiuchus in the sky – which reaches nearly to the figure of Hercules, found immediately above Ophiuchus in the heavens:

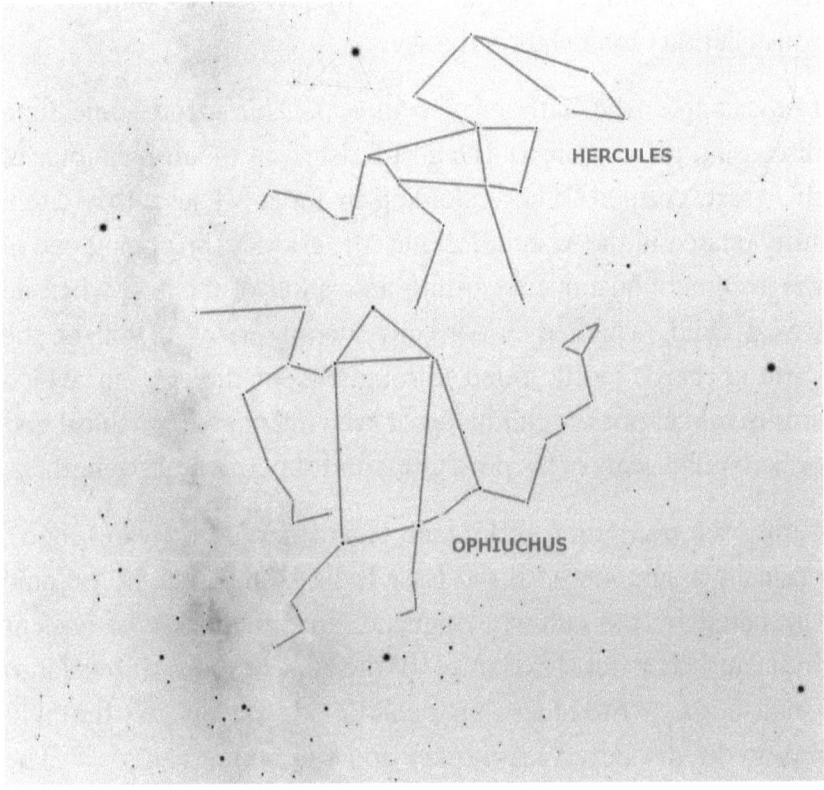

The outline of the central body of Ophiuchus can be seen to resemble a tower (and thus likely plays the role of the Tower of Babel in Genesis), but it can also be seen to resemble an overturned mortar, as in the version of the Tower of Babel story recounted above. Notice that it reaches *almost* to the place occupied by Hercules -- a constellation which plays the role of the highest deity in many myths and sacred stories the world over.

Indeed, the possibility that the tower of overturned mortars in the African story of the retreat of the heavens corresponds to the constellation Ophiuchus receives some confirmation from the fact that an overturned mortar features in myths from other cultures around the globe -- and receives additional support from the fact that in those myths, further details are present which help confirm that the overturned mortar does in fact correspond to the constellation Ophiuchus in the sky.

For example, the authors of *Hamlet's Mill* spend some time discussing the exploits of the god Krishna in the fifth chapter of their text, entitled "The Unfolding in India." There, they cite a story related in the Vishnu Purana (the god Krishna being one of the avatars of Vishnu) regarding an exploit of the god when he was a child, which they correctly identify as a version of the "Strong Boy" motif found throughout mythology, in which stories told about the childhood or even infancy of a mythical god or hero relate feats of his prodigious and supernatural strength.

Citing the translation of Horace Hayman Wilson (1786 - 1860), orginally a surgeon with the East India Company who became fascinated by the culture, language, and mythology of ancient India and later translated many of the ancient Sanskrit texts into English, they write of Krishna's childhood that "one day the child repeatedly disobeyed his mother and she became angry."[28] The Vishnu Purana then says (Wilson translation):

> Fastening a cord round his waist, she tied him to the wooden mortar Ulukhala, and being in a great passion, she said to him, "Now, you naughty boy, get away from hence if

you can." She then went to her domestic affairs. As soon as she had departed, the lotus-eyed Krishna, endeavouring to extricate himself, pulled the mortar after him to the space between the two ariuna trees that grew near together. Having dragged the mortar between these trees, it became wedged awry there, and as Krishna pulled it through, it pulled down the trunks of the trees. Hearing the crackling noise, the people of Vraja came to see what was the matter, and there they beheld the two large trees, with shattered stems and broken branches, prostrate on the ground, with the child fixed between them, with a rope round his belly, laughing, and showing his little white teeth, just budded . . .[29]

We will have occasion to examine the celestial identity of Lord Krishna in a later section of this volume, but for the present it is sufficient to note that the mortar which the infant Krishna pulled after him until it was wedged between "two ariuna trees that grew near together" can almost certainly be identified with the figure of Ophiuchus in the night sky, which has a central body (shaped like an overturned mortar) flanked by two twisted shapes which are usually envisioned as serpents, but which are also envisioned as vines, olive trees, and various other plants or animals in different myths from different cultures.

We can be quite certain that the Vishnu Purana is referring to the constellation Ophiuchus at this point when talking about Krishna being tied to a mortar, because just prior to this the text tells us that he was implicated in the destruction of a wagon – and as we will see later in this volume when we explore the celestial foundations of ancient Sanskrit texts such as the Mahabharata, the constellation Ophiuchus can also be envisioned as a wagon, or as a war-cart such as the one in which Krishna will later drive Arjuna during the cataclysmic battle of Kurukshetra

Note that the authors of *Hamlet's Mill* relate this example of the myth-pattern of the "Strong Boy" in the life of Krishna to an episode in the poems of Finland describing the life of Kullervo, in which the infant Kullervo destroys his cradle when he was only three days old, in an exhibition of preternatural strength.[30]

Such motifs or patterns found in myths across multiple cultures were dubbed "oicotypes" by the pioneering Swedish folklorist Carl Wilhelm von Sydow (1878 - 1952).[31] Another well-known example of this "Strong Boy" oicotype is of course the story of baby Heracles strangling the two enormous serpents sent by the goddess Hera, while he himself was yet in his cradle.

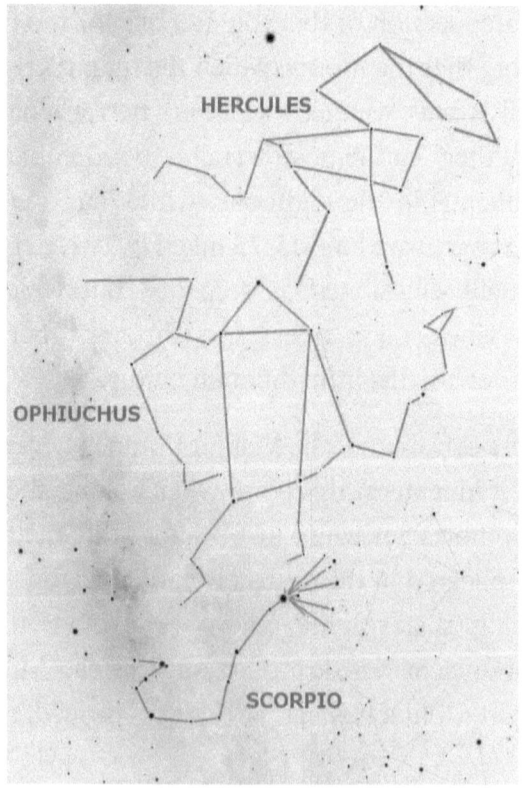

Here again we have an episode which is almost certainly based upon the constellation Ophiuchus in the sky. In this case, I see Ophiuchus playing the role of baby Heracles, who is holding (and strangling) a serpent in each hand (the two "serpent-halves" on either side of the central body of Ophiuchus). It is possible that the constellation Scorpio, just below Ophiuchus, plays the role of the "cradle" in which baby Heracles is sitting, when he strangles the two great snakes. Just above Ophiuchus, of course, we see full-grown Heracles, in the outline of the constellation which we call by the Latin name of that same hero: the constellation Hercules.

From this analysis of a myth recorded in the texts of ancient India, that of Krishna's mortar wedged between the ariuna trees, we can be quite confident that the stack of mortars in the African myth discussed above also corresponds to the constellation Ophiuchus (and, incidentally, from the same analysis we can be fairly confident that Ophiuchus plays the Tower of Babel in the text of Genesis as well).

The story found across Africa describing the loss of connection with the High God and indeed with the entire heavenly realm, and the futile efforts to regain that lost intimate connection, can be seen to belong to a pattern which manifests again and again in myths around the world. It is a pattern which speaks to our condition in this incarnate life, in which we find ourselves plunged into a physical body, while yet knowing that we are more than our merely physical and material nature. The infinite realm has retreated beyond our ordinary grasp, and yet we realize that we are also spirit not merely matter, and in some sense properly belong to that infinite realm, with which we long to reconnect and become integrated.

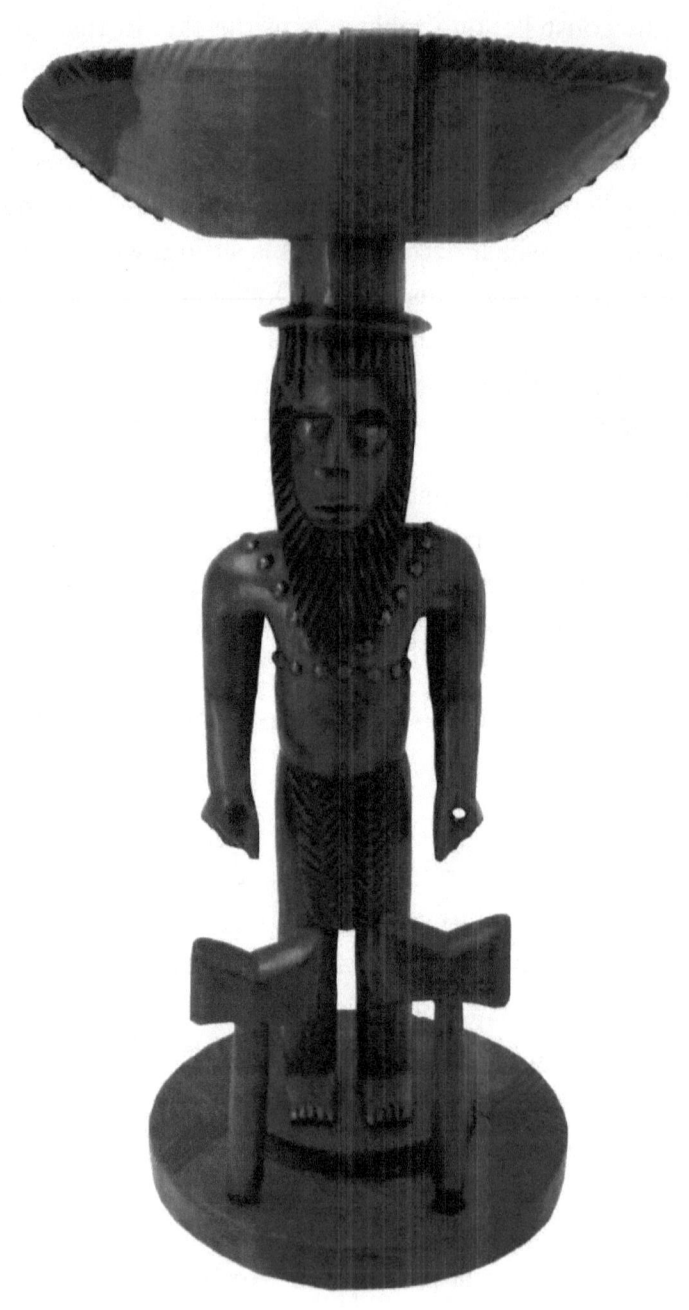

Shango and Oya of the Yoruba

One of the myth-cycles whose celestial foundations could be explored in its own full-length book would be the myths and traditions surrounding two important Yoruba deities or Orisha: Shango and Oya.

Shango is a powerful Orisha of fire and of thunder and lightning.

The Yoruba are a large ethnic and cultural group of the Niger and Congo region of western Africa, in the area covered by the modern-day nations of Nigeria, Benin and Togo, centered around the Gulf of Guinea.

In his 1980 study of Yoruba oral tradition and divination entitled *Sixteen Cowries*, William Bascom (1912 - 1981) writes of Shango (sometimes also spelled *Xango*):

> Shango is a God of Thunder. Living in the sky he hurls thunderstones to earth, killing those who offend him or setting their houses afire. His thunderbolts are prehistoric stone celts which farmers sometimes find while hoeing their fields; they are taken to Shango's priests, who keep them at his shrine in a plate supported by an inverted mortar, which also serves as a stool when the heads of initiates are shaved (cf. Bascom 1972: 6). The stones in Shango's sacrifices may be an allusion to his thunderbolts, and in one verse Shango kills a leopard by putting an inverted mortar over it. [. . .]

He was noted for his magical powers and was feared because when he spoke, fire came out of his mouth. One verse has Shango lighting a fire in his mouth with itufu, oil-soaked fibers from the pericarp of the oil palm, which is used in making torches and starting fires. In a state of possession it is said that a Shango worshiper may eat fire, possibly using itufu, carry a pot of live coals on his head, or put his hand into live coals without apparent harm.[32]

Shango is a formidable deity or Orisha -- but so also is his favorite consort, the goddess Oya. William Bascom describes her thusly:

> Oya is the favorite wife of Shango, the only wife who remained true to him until the end, leaving Oyo with him and becoming a deity when he did. She is Goddess of the Niger River, which is called the River Oya (odo Oya), but she manifests herself as the strong wind that precedes a thunderstorm. When Shango wishes to fight with lightning, he sends his wife ahead of him to fight with wind. She blows roofs off houses, knocks down large trees, and fans the fires set by Shango's thunderbolts into a high blaze. When Oya comes, people know that Shango is not far behind, and it is said that without her, Shango cannot fight. The verses tell that Oya is the wife of Shango, "The wife who is fiercer than the husband." Her town is Ira, which is said to be near Ofa.[33]

Bascom also notes that Oya is associated with buffalo's horns, and that a set of buffalo horns will be rubbed with cam wood to make them red and placed on Oya's shrine. In another book discussing the mythology of the Yoruba, *Yoruba Myths* by Ulli and Georgina Beier (1980), we learn that one time, when Shango and Oya were having a fight,

> she charged him with mighty horns. But Shango appeased her by placing a big dish of akara (bean cakes) in front of her. Pleased by the offering of her favourite food, Oya made peace with Shango and gave him her two horns. When he was in need, he only had to beat these horns one against the other and she would come to his aid.[34]

Based on these details from the different sacred traditions involving Shango and Oya, I believe we can very confidently identify Shango and Oya with the constellations Hercules and Virgo, respectively.

In nearly every ancient myth-system, the powerful figure who wields a thunderbolt weapon will be associated with the figure of Hercules in the sky, whether that thunderbolt weapons is wielded by a god in the Maya account contained in the Popol Vuh, by a god in the myths of ancient Greece and Rome, by a god in the myths of the Norse, or by a god in the myths of the Yoruba.

Images of Shango and symbolic scepters sacred to Shango usually feature a double-axe motif, a potent symbol which is also found around the world. The carved wooden image of Shango shown at the beginning of this chapter features a wide double-axe above the figure's head, as well as two additional smaller double-axes placed in front of the image in the carving.

It is possible that the great weapon held menacingly aloft by the constellation Hercules in the sky, which in some myths becomes a club or a sword, can also be seen as a double-axe shape, just as in the myths of far northern Europe and the Norse, the same weapon held by the constellation Hercules is envisioned as a double-headed hammer (the mighty hammer of the god Thor).

On the following page is an image showing the stars of the constellation Hercules, using the outlining system suggested by H. A. Rey in *The Stars: A New Way to See Them*. Below it is another image of the same stars, this time showing how the mighty weapon held aloft over the head of the constellation (and usually envisioned as a club, or as a giant sword, as well as playing the role of various thunderbolt-weapons in myth-systems around the world) could also be envisioned as a double-headed hammer, or a double-headed axe. In fact, very similar diagrams appear in Volume Four of this series during the discussion of the identity of the thunder-god Thor of northern Europe.

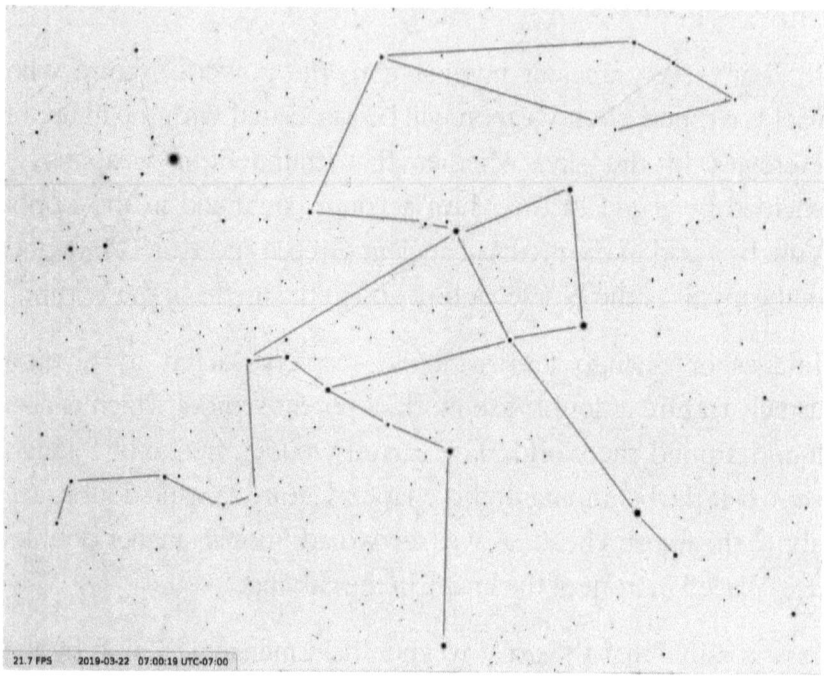

If you look closely at the stars which make up the outline of the tremendous weapon held aloft over the head of the constellation, you can see four stars which make up the "double-axe" outline:

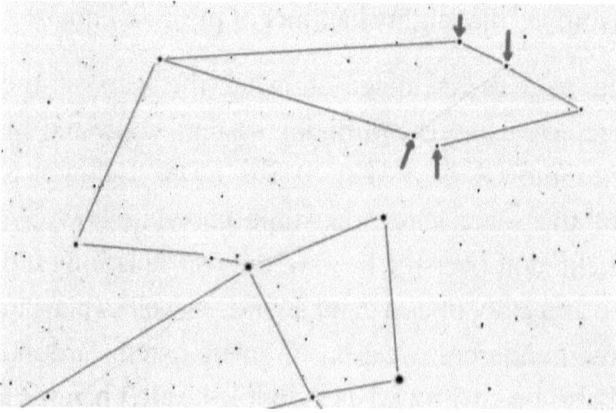

If we envision lines connecting those four points we will create a quadrilateral (something of a trapezoid, due to the positioning of the indicated stars). This quadrilateral, I believe, explains the fact that in some cultures, deities associated with the constellation Hercules (including both Thor and Shango) wield a weapon that is described as an axe, or a hammer:

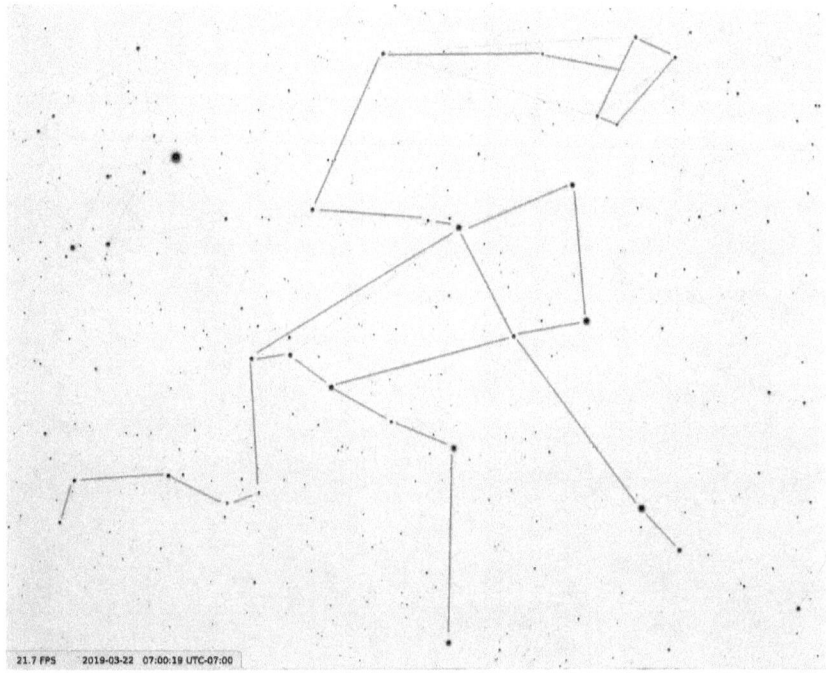

21.7 FPS   2019-03-22   07:00:19 UTC-07:00

As with so many other mythological figures associated with Hercules, Shango is a god of thunder. He is also depicted as having a full beard, as seen in the carved statue at the beginning of this chapter. Many male figures in myth who are associated with the constellation Hercules have a full beard, which can be easily understood by looking at the distinctive square-shaped head of the constellation. Besides the thunder-god Shango, other mythical figures associated with Hercules who are depicted with such a beard include Zeus (and also Jove or Jupiter), Thor, and of course the hero Heracles himself (also known as Hercules).

There are other details in the myths which give added certainty to the identification of Shango with the constellation Hercules, which we will examine in a moment. First, however, let's look at the identity of the goddess Oya, who is so powerful that Shango cannot fight without her, and who is described as *going ahead of Shango* in everything.

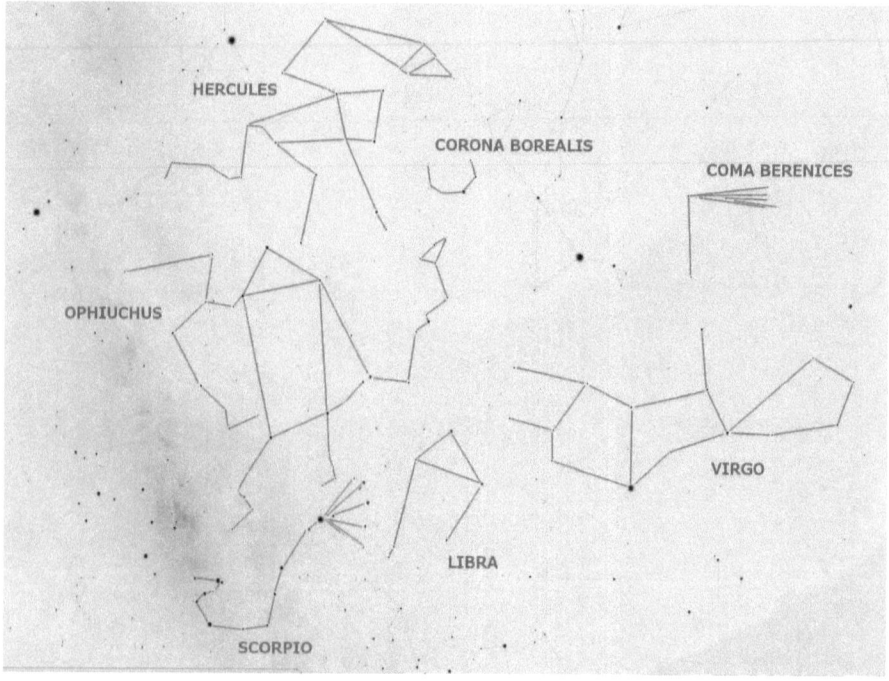

I am convinced that Oya is associated with the constellation Virgo: can you see how this arrangement gives rise to the tradition that Oya always precedes Shango? The motion of the stars each night is from east to west (just like the motion of the sun each day -- both are caused by the rotation of the earth towards the east on its daily rotation). In the star chart above, which looks towards the south, east is on the left and west is on the right, and the constellations move from left to right as we face the page.

The definitive clue that Oya is associated with Virgo is the fact that she is sometimes called the "Mother of Nine" (*Iyansan,* or *'Yansan*) in Yoruba tradition.[35] The constellation Virgo, as we will see in many other myths from around the world, is often envisioned as a mother about to give birth, due to her posture in the sky, lying on her back with feet elevated.

Virgo is sometimes envisioned as giving birth to the multi-headed figure of Scorpio, which follows Virgo in the sky. Scorpio, as we will also see in our later examinations of many of the world's myths and sacred stories, is often envisioned as having *multiple heads*. Sometimes the heads are three in number, but more often they number seven, eight, or (most commonly) nine -- as with the dreaded nine-headed hydra which Heracles must fight during his twelve labors, in the myths of ancient Greece. The fact that Oya is called "Mother of Nine" pretty much seals her association with the constellation Virgo in the heavens.[36]

You can also see the "buffalo horns" which Oya gave to Shango, almost certainly identified with the beautiful arc of stars known as the Northern Crown (or Corona Borealis), very close to Shango-Hercules in the sky and included in the diagram above.

It is also possible that the two-pronged outline of the zodiac constellation Libra (the Scales or Balances) might play the role of the buffalo-horn weapon of Oya, since Libra is very close to Virgo in the night sky. However, the fact that Oya is described as giving her horns to Hercules probably implicates the Northern Crown.

What about the details of the story in which Shango breathes fire out of his mouth? The star chart below shows that the "lower arm" of the constellation Hercules (the arm not holding a club or weapon) can be envisioned as proceeding out of the mouth of the constellation. It is possible (but not certain) that this downward-reaching "arm" could be the source of the association of "breathing fire" with this particular Orisha.

There is also a "torch" in the sky not far from Hercules and Virgo, in the form of the constellation Coma Berenices, which actually plays the role of a torch in many other Star Myths. This may be the itufa torch that appears in the myths of Shango.

The aspect of the myth in which Shango is described as killing a leopard by crushing it beneath "an inverted mortar" no doubt has to do with the constellation Ophiuchus, directly beneath the constellation Hercules. We have already discussed the fascinating evidence that Ophiuchus is specifically described as playing the role of a "mortar" in another sacred story from the mythology of the many cultures of Africa, including one with parallels to the story of the Tower of Babel in Genesis. We have also seen evidence that Ophiuchus plays a similar role as a mortar in a myth preserved in the Sanskrit texts of ancient India.

The body of Ophiuchus has a distinctive oblong shape with triangle at top. This almost certainly represents the inverted mortar: Ophiuchus could be envisioned as a tall mortar, turned upside down so that its conical base is at the top).

Note that the head and tail of the unfortunate leopard can be seen protruding from one or the other side of the upturned mortar of Ophiuchus! Alternately, it is possible that the form of Scorpio, splayed out below Ophiuchus, was envisioned as the crushed body of the leopard in this particular myth. We will have occasion to see Scorpio play a variety of different objects and animals in the different Star Myths from around the world. One common animal that Scorpio plays is a dog – often described as a "fawning dog" (in other words, a dog which is crouching or bowing-down in a subservient manner). Thus it is very possible that Scorpio plays the role of a "crushed leopard" in this Star Myth from Africa.

Note also that Shango is sometimes described as defeating his enemies with a cudgel, which is another weapon very closely associated with the outline of the constellation Hercules (and Hercules-figures throughout the world will often carry a club or cudgel as their favorite weapon). William Bascom cites Yoruba verses in which Shango uses a cudgel (in the verse labeled "L1" in *Sixteen Cowries*), and he mentions this fact on page 44 as well. This cudgel is yet another clue that Shango corresponds to the constellation Hercules. With such an abundance of clues, I believe we can be quite confident in associating Shango with Hercules, and Oya with Virgo.

In another set of verses cited by William Bascom, we learn of Shango that: "He drove away the hartebeest that had been eating the children of the people of Ijagba, and became the deity that all the people of Ijagba worshipped."[37]

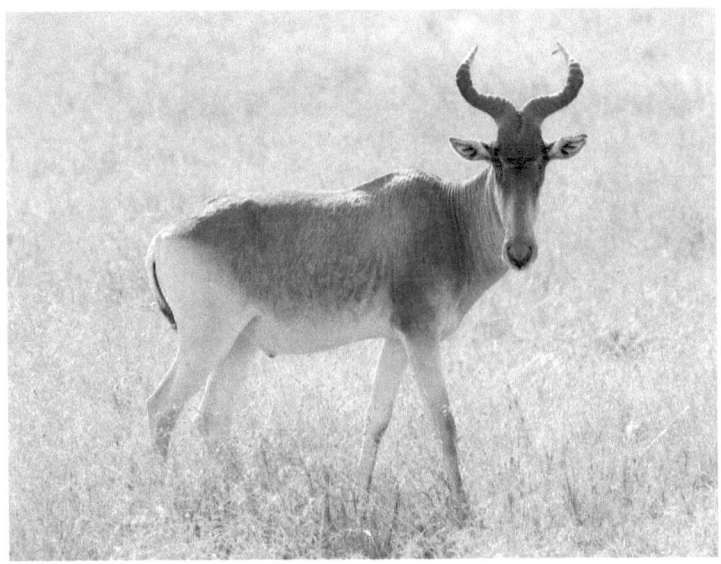

Chapter Five

A hartebeeste is a large African ungulate, with majestic curving horns. As you can see in the image above (on the preceding page), it is very possible that this hartebeest which Shango drives away might be associated with the outline of the horned figure of Taurus the Bull, which can also be said to resemble a hartebeest.

As the constellations Virgo and Hercules rise over the horizon in the east, the constellation Taurus can be seen to be sinking down into the west. This perfectly describes the situation in which Shango (Hercules) "drives away" the hartebeest (Taurus). There are other Star Myths from around the world in which the arrival of a god or goddess associated with Hercules or Virgo signifies the demise of a figure associated with Taurus (for instance, the traditions associated with the goddess Durga, discussed later in this volume).

Below is a star-chart showing Hercules rising in the east, as Taurus sinks down in the west:

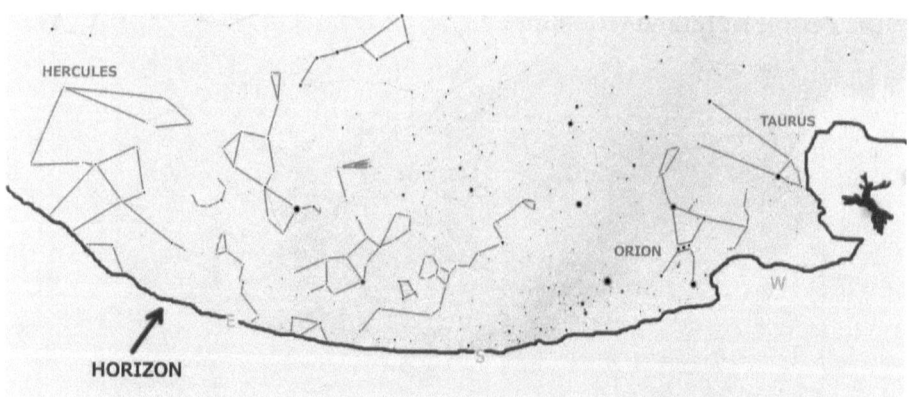

Note that in this diagram, we are facing towards the south. This means that east is towards our left as we face the page, and west is towards the right. The stars (and thus the constellations) will move across the sky from the east towards the west as our earth turns on its axis (just as the sun will move across the sky from the east to the west during the day). Thus, the constellation Taurus (on the far right-hand side of the chart as we face the page) is about to sink beneath the horizon and disappear into the west. However, at the same time we can see the looming figure of the constellation Hercules, rising up from the eastern horizon, on the left side of the chart as we face the page.

The line of the horizon has been drawn-in for ease of reference in the preceding diagram. Note that the open-source planetarium app Stellarium, which was used for this star-chart, has a large clump of trees jutting up from the horizon on the far-west side of the chart (on the rightmost edge of the star-chart). Taurus is about to sink behind those.

Note as well that in the diagram, the planetarium app distorts the size of constellations along the east and west, in order to simulate the "wraparound" effect you would see outside (the left and right of the image represent turning towards the eastern and western horizons, respectively. The app makes constellations look smaller when they are in the middle of the diagram, and larger when they are near the east or the west (to your left and right).

In *Yoruba Myths*, we read that the goddess Oya was originally an antelope who periodically took off her antelope skin to reveal a beautiful woman:

> Oya was an antelope who transformed herself into a woman. Every five days, when she came to the market in town, she took off her skin in the forest and hid it under a shrub.
>
> One day Shango met her in the market, was struck by her beauty, and followed her into the forest. Then he watched, as she donned the skin and turned back into an antelope.
>
> The following day Shango hid himself in the forest, and

when Oya had changed into a woman and gone to market he picked up the skin, took it home and hid it in the rafters.[38]

We learn that Shango's other two wives become jealous of Oya, who bears Shango twin babies, and they tell Oya where to find her skin, hanging in the rafters. She dons the antelope form again and disappears into the forest.

Previously, I have written that I thought that this story is also based upon the same celestial mechanics shown in the star-chart above. When Virgo takes off her antelope skin and hides it beneath a bush, Taurus is sinking down into the horizon (into the bushes of the horizon, you might say). Thus, I argued that Oya might be represented by Virgo when in the form of a woman, and by Taurus when in the form of an antelope.

However, I have since concluded that an even better explanation for this aspect of the myth is found in a constellation much closer to Virgo in the night sky, and one which can be shown to be associated with Virgo in many other Star Myths from around the globe, including in some of the stories in the scriptures of the Bible, as well as in the myths of ancient Greece -- the constellation Centaurus.

Centaurus is located immediately below (south of) and slightly west of the constellation Virgo. As discussed in my 2014 book *The Undying Stars*, and again in *Star Myths of the World, Volume Two* (*Myths of Ancient Greece*), published in 2016, the constellation Centuarus is commonly envisioned as a centaur: a man from the waist up, with the torso and arms and head of a human, and a horse from the waist down. However, the outline of the constellation Centaurus can also be envisioned as a stag, in which the narrow set of stars which form the "torso" of the human part of the centaur can instead be envisioned as the triangular head of a stag -- and the outstretched "arms" of the human part of the centaur can instead be envisioned as the sweeping antlers of the stag. Below are two star-charts showing the outline of Centaurus, one as a centaur and then as a stag:

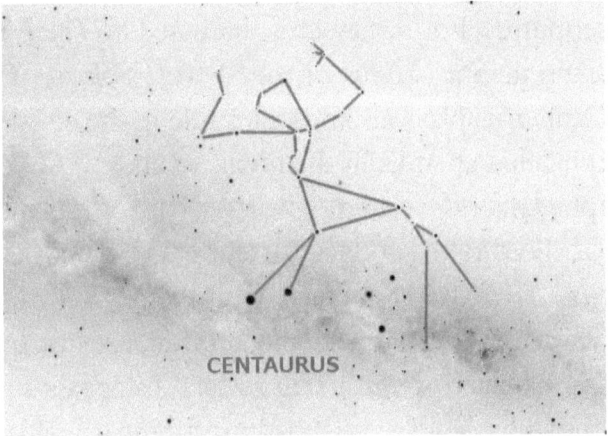

In the above chart, the stars of the constellation are outlined as suggested by H. A. Rey, and we can see a *centaur* consisting of a human torso, arms and head arising from a four-legged body. However, below are the same stars, less just one connecting line:

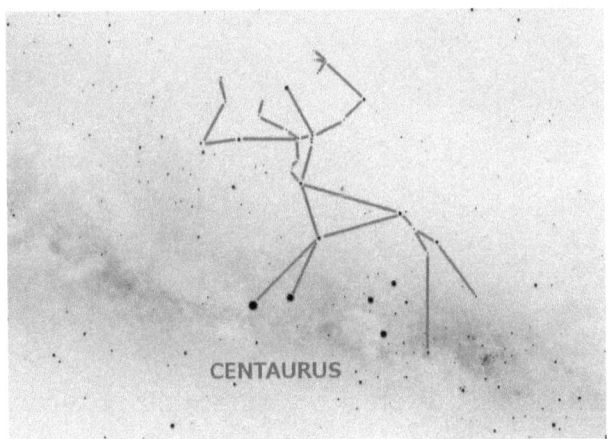

Now the outline resembles a *stag* instead: the stars that were the human "head" of the centaur have become prongs on the antlers, as do the stars that formed the human "arms" when the constellation was a centaur. And thee stars that formed the torso of the centaur are now the head of the stag instead.

Thus we can see why the constellation Centaurus so often plays the role of a stag in so many of the world's ancient myths and scriputres. For instance, as discussed in *The Undying Stars*, and again in *Star Myths of the World, Volume Two*, the figure of Centaurus plays an important role in the story of the sacrifice of Iphigenia at Aulis in the myths of ancient Greece. In that story, Iphigenia (associated, I believe, with Virgo the Virgin) is to be sacrificed to the goddess Artemis (associated, as I demonstrate in *Star Myths Volume Two*, with the constellation of Sagittarius), but at the last moment the goddess rescues Iphigenia from the sacrifice, and sends a stag to take Iphigenia's place on the altar (the stag becomes the substitute for the maiden).

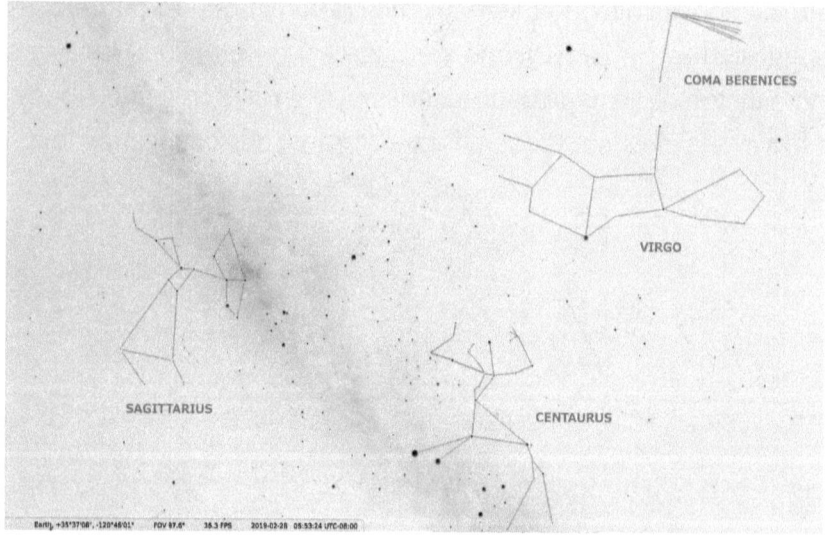

In the above diagram, we can see the proximity of Centaurus to the constellation Virgo in the sky. It is almost a certainty that Iphigenia in the Greek myth corresponds to Virgo, because in some versions of the story, the maiden later becomes (or is in some way associated with) the goddess Hecate, who is often depicted holding a torch or two torches (and note again the torch-shaped constellation Coma Berenices which, with the addition of a signle connecting line, can be seen as if held by Virgo in her outstretched arm).

In the myth of the sacrifice of Iphigenia, the young woman is "exchanged with" a stag. In the myth of Shango and Oya, the goddess Oya exchanges form between an antelope and a divine woman (both from an antelope to a woman, and later back to an antelope again).

The part about hanging the skin up in the rafters resonates with a very common oicotype in Star Myths around the world -- for instance, in the Maui myths of the Pacific, Maui's grandfather hangs Maui up in the rafters when he is a baby! In that case, the grandfather is undoubtedly Hercules, and Maui the infant is almost certainly Corona Borealis (the Northern Crown). This identification is discussed in greater detail later in this volume. The Northern Crown, oddly enough, plays a baby in many other Star Myths.

In the story of Shango and Oya and the hanging of Oya's skin in the rafters, Shango (who corresponds to the constellation Hercules) performs an act of "hanging something in the rafters" which is very similar to that performed by Tama-nui-ki-te-Rangi in the myths of the Pacific involving Maui.

When the other wives tell Oya where her skin is hanging (they do this using a chant, in which they sing about its location), she resumes her antelope form and bounds away into the forest so that Shango cannot find her.

For those who wonder whether the constellation Centaurus (or, alternately, the constellation Taurus) -- both of which are clearly horned – could play the role of the *female* antelope which is one of the shapes of the goddess Oya (female antelopes not always being horned, in many species of antelope), note that in Africa the female of the many species of antelope often has horns, in addition to the horns of the male antelope.

Below is an illustration of the female Hirola, an antelope found in the areas where the Yoruba cultures traditionally have lived for thousands of years:

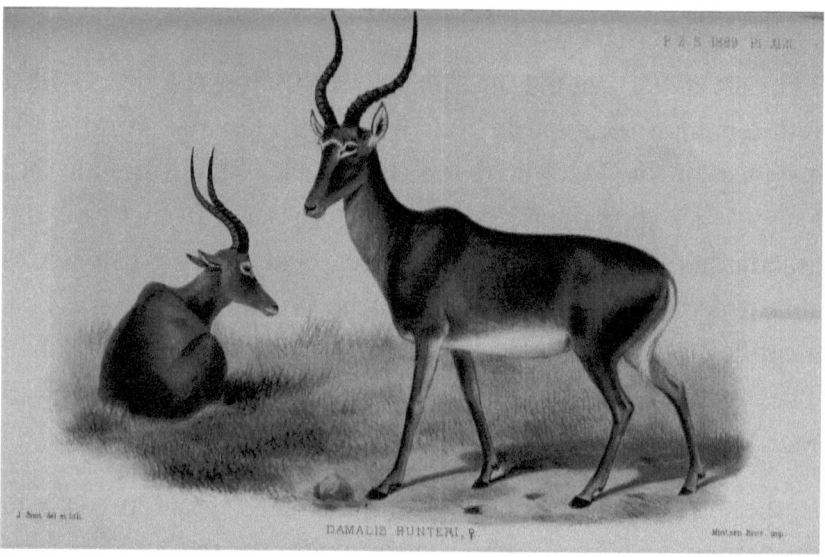

DAMALIS HUNTERI, ♀

There are still more stories of Oya and Shango which point to a celestial foundation associated with the constellations Virgo and Hercules. One of the stories involves the mother of Shango, the goddess of the River Yemoja (*odo Yemoja*), which flows through Yoruba lands. In one version of the story, Yemoja was pursued by her husband Okere (who is not the father of Shango) and he knocks her down, causing her to turn into a river which flows out of pots of water she was also carrying.[39]

This story may also involve the constellation Virgo, which is located in the sky adjacent to the constellations Crater the Cup and Hydra the Snake (see star-charts on pages 60 and 80, above). When Shango's mother Yemoja falls down (and note that Virgo is recumbent), she may become a river associated with the flowing form of Hydra, directly beneath Virgo and beneath the water-cup-like outline of the constellation Crater.

Shango and Oya are very important deities in the Yoruba mythology, with many devotees around the world to this day. Their clear celestial parallels provide still more evidence which argues that the system of celestial metaphor, which we can see operating in the stories of the Bible and in the other myths of the world, is in fact a common system which somehow provides the underlying bedrock upon which all the world's ancient traditions have their foundation.

Shango is a god of fire. I believe that the world's Star Myths convey powerful truths regarding the Invisible World -- the realm of spirit, the realm of the gods, the infinite realm, which we cannot see with our eyes but which we can learn about through the figures fixed in the "higher elements" of air and fire (as opposed to the "lower elements" of earth and water, through which we are traveling in this incarnate life, when we take on a body of "clay," symbolic of the lower elements of earth and water). The stars are firey orbs, in the higher realm of the heavens, representative of that realm of spirit (the realm of the gods) which we cannot see, but which is nonetheless very real.

One of the lessons that they teach is that, just as the stars themselves can be seen to rotate down to sink into the western horizon, so also we ourselves came down to this incarnate realm from a spirit realm -- and that we all contain a divine spark, an internal divine fire, through which we have immediate access to that Invisible Realm at all times, if we learn how to become reacquainted with that aspect of our nature.

I am convinced that the ancient myths, scriptures and sacred stories which were entrusted to humanity the world over are here to help show us how to do that.

Kintu and Nambi and the King of Heaven

Geoffrey Parrinder's *African Mythology* relates that:

> Many stories are told in Buganda, Uganda, of Kintu the
> first man and ancestor. When he came to the country
> from the gods he lived by himself with only one cow and
> lived on her milk. Then a woman named Nambi came and
> fell in love with him, but she had to go back to her father,
> Gulu, who was king of heaven. Nambi's relatives despised
> Kintu because he knew of no food but milk and they
> objected to the marriage. To test him Gulu robbed Kintu
> of his cow and the man had to live on herbs and leaves.
> But Nambi saw the cow, and went and told Kintu that it
> was in heaven and invited him to fetch it.[40]

Here begins a classic series of tests, in which Nambi's brothers
and their father Gulu, along with the other denizens of the
heavenly realm, set up a series of challenges for Kintu, which they
think no one can possibly accomplish.

First, they arrange an enormous feast for Kintu, enough to feed a
hundred, and lock him in a house with the instructions that if he
does not eat it all, he will be killed. Kintu eats as much as he
possibly can, but there is still great quantities remaining, and he
does not know what to do with the rest. However, as he casts
about for a solution, he notices a hole in the floor, into which he
begins dropping all the remaining food and beer, and when he is
finished with that he calls for the people to come take away all the
empty baskets.

Gulu is quite surprised that Kintu has passed this test, so he
sends Kintu his copper axe and tells Kintu that here in heaven he
is accustomed to chopping firewood from a rock, rather than

from wood the way ordinary people do. Kintu searches around for a rock with cracks in it, and breaks it apart and brings the pieces to Gulu.

Next Gulu demands that Kintu draw a pot full of water, but specifies that the water must be only dew. Kintu takes the pot and, unsure what to do, sets it down in the field while he thinks of an idea. Perhaps he even falls asleep while wrestling with the problem. In any event, when Kintu goes to pick up the pot again, he finds it is full of dew.

Gulu at this point is duly impressed, and has decided that Kintu really is a powerful being after all. He summons Kintu and announces that he has changed his mind and will allow Kintu to marry his daughter. He tells Kintu that he can also have his cow back, which Gulu had taken to heaven to start this whole series of tests in the first place. But, Gulu must select only his own cow, and this again will be a test, because the herds of heaven contain many cows nearly identical to his own. Gulu will have his sons bring groups of cows to Kintu for him to examine.

As Kintu is surveying the vast herds, he is suddenly visited by a bee, who flies up and tells him that he should choose the cow upon whose horns the bee alights.

When the first herd of cattle is brought to Kintu, the bee remains in a tree and does not go to any of them. So Kintu announces that his cow is not among this group, and asks Gulu's people to take it away. Again, another herd is brought and again Kintu announces that his cow is not among this group either.

Finally, when the third herd of cows is brought before Kintu, the bee sails into the air and lands right between the horns of a large cow. It then moves on and lights on three calves as well. Kintu announces that this is his cow, and also announces that he will take the three calves, which must have been born during the cow's stay up in heaven.

Gulu is so happy to have found a son-in-law whom no one can deceive that he gives his blessing to his marriage to his daughter, and Kintu and Nambi are married in great happiness.

This story is already explicitly telling us that it has to do with events in the heavenly realm. Gulu is the king of heaven, and he takes Kintu's cow up to heaven, where the rest of the story takes place. It thus seems to be inviting us to consider the heavenly figures which might be associated with the characters and events in the myth.

Let's first explore the possible celestial identity of Kintu, the man who, at least while on earth, lives entirely on milk and who has one cow (which is taken up to heaven).

Note that it is very possible that a character such as Kintu may "move through" different constellations at different stages in a story -- and that such movement is not at all uncommon in other Star Myths from around the world, as we will have occasion to see time and again later in this series.

While on earth, however, we are told that Kintu subsists entirely on the milk from his cow. Based on this description alone, we might suspect that Kintu may be located near the band of the Milky Way galaxy -- and that he might be associated with a constellation nearby to the figure of a cow of some sort. Is there a constellation located near the band of the Milky Way, and what is more a constellation next to a bovine?

In fact there is, and one of the most famous constellations in the celestial sphere: Orion the great hunter, the constellation with the highest ratio of very bright stars to total stars, and a constellation with tremendous importance in the myths of the world. Orion is located directly adjacent to the stream of the Milky Way galaxy, which parallels his upright form and runs through the region between Orion and the nearby constellation of Gemini the Twins.

Just above Orion and to the other side of Gemini is the distinctive "V" of the Hyades, part of the zodiac constellation of Taurus the Bull. Taurus has two long horns stretching from the front of the two tips of the "V" of the Hyades – and these could be the horns of a milk-cow as well, especially in Africa where the cow in many of the species of cattle sports beautiful horns just as does the bull. It is very probable that Kintu, who lives alone with just his cow and exists by consuming only milk, is Orion himself, and that Taurus represents his bovine companion.

On the opposite page we see a star chart containing the stars of Orion and Taurus. Note the length of the horns of the Bull of Taurus, which extend out from the "V"-shaped Hyades, and compare them to the majestic horns of the Ankole or Watusi bulls and cows found in the same part of Africa where we find this myth of Kintu and Nambi.

The Milky Way band runs through this region of the sky, between Orion and the feet of the Twins of Gemini. It would thus cut through the region just above the upper-left corner of the star-chart image shown here, as we face the page. Thus, the story's assertion that in his original condition Kintu subsisted entirely on the milk of his cow is understandable from Orion's location in the heavens. In addition, there is a constellation called the River Eridanus which originates near the foot of the constellation Orion at the lower-right as we face the page, which could also be envisioned as the flow of milk on which Kintu

As we have seen previously, Star Myths containing a lovely woman often refer to Virgo, who is located in the sky next to Boötes, who sometimes appears in the story as her husband, sometimes as her father or even her grandfather, and in this story it is very likely that Nambi is the constellation Virgo and that Gulu may be associated with either Boötes (close to Virgo) or with the constellation Hercules (who plays the ruler of heaven in numerous Star Myths from cultures around the world).

When Orion and Taurus rise in the east, Virgo and Boötes are sinking down out of sight into the west, and the same is true of Orion (sinking into the west) as Virgo rises in the east, because these constellations are located in nearly opposite directions as we look out into the heavens from our vantage point on the rotating globe of the earth. This feature of these specific constellations plays a role in other Star Myths from other cultures which we will examine during the ecourse of our investigation, including the slaying of Mahishasura by the goddess Durga in the myths of ancient India, and the story of the angel with the flaming sword positioned at the east of Eden when Adam and Eve are driven from the Garden in the book of Genesis, and the story of Perseus slaying Medusa and then chased by the other Gorgons in the myths of ancient Greece. The same "dual-horizon action" may feature in this story of Kintu and Nambi, when Nambi is taken from Kintu by her father Gulu.

When Kintu ventures into the realm of heaven to try to find his beloved Nambi, he is given a series of seemingly-impossible tasks. This specific myth-pattern or oicotype is very common in the myths and folklore of the world. In nearly every example (perhaps in every example), the impossible tasks can only be accomplished with supernatural help, or at least with what we could call "unusual" help from members of the natural world (such as birds or bees). We see this pattern, for example, in the fairy tale from Russia of the young and beautiful Maria Marina, which was one of my favorites as a child (and which I can now see to be filled with celestial allegory).

I would interpret this particular myth-pattern, of the mortal who is assigned a series of seemingly-impossible tasks by the gods themselves, or by a representative of the spirit world (such as a mysterious old woman who turns out to have supernatural powers, as we find in the story of Maria Marina and in many other folktales from various cultures), as teaching an esoteric truth about our own condition in this incarnate life. In this world, we ourselves face overwhelming demands and seemingly-insurmountable obstacles on a regular and recurring basis. The only way to successfully navigate these challenges, the ancient myths seem to be telling us, is to become attuned to the available help from a higher realm -- from our Higher Self, from the natural world to whose lessons we are usually blind, and from the Invisible Realm of the gods themselves.

We can become more attuned to the voice of our Higher Self and the resources of the infinite realm through ancient disciplines including meditation, Yoga, martial arts such as Tai Chi, forms of shamanic drumming, and many other practices that have survived in certain societies for millennia. As well, it seems that some men and women, either by upbringing or temperament, are innately more attuned to the voice of intuition and their Higher Self, and less prone to "doubt themselves" or engage in the forms of "self-sabotage" with which most of us are all too familiar.

I am convinced that one of the recurring themes of the myths, found across cultures, is our need for overcoming our own self-doubts and tendencies towards self-sabotage, by becoming more attuned to the assistance that is available to us at all times, if we only learn how to listen for it or to see it.

It is difficult to say if every one of the tests given to Kintu by Gulu refer to specific celestial details, but some of them have very clear ties to celestial patterns found in other myths, indicating that at least some of the tasks Kintu must accomplish have a celestial foundation, and I suspect that all of them have such a foundation, even if the celestial interpretation is more tenuous for some tasks than for others.

The first task involves locking Kintu inside a house with enormous amounts of food -- enough to feed a hundred -- and the demand that if he cannot eat all of it, he will be killed. In the first edition of this volume, I suggested that Kintu's solution of eating as much as he could before dropping the remainder down a hole in the middle of the floor of the house might refer to the central point in the celestial sphere around which all the stars appear to turn, which was anciently described in many myths as the center of a great whirlpool as well as being seen as a hole which led to another world (sometimes the hole leading to the world of giants, as the authors of *Hamlet's Mill* discuss in reference to a myth from Finland – note that both Orion and Boötes are gigantic figures in the sky and appear in other Star Myths as giants themselves). I suggested that the fact that Boötes is located near the Big Dipper and that this constellation turns around the central north point of the sky (where the helpful North Star, Polaris, marks the hub around which the northern celestial hemisphere appears to turn) makes it very likely that this central point is the "hole in the floor" of the "house" in which Kintu is imprisoned when he is given his first test (the house being the northern celestial hemisphere itself, and the hole in the center being the point around which it turns).

Kintu and Nambi and the King of Heaven

However, having now written three additional volumes in the series and examining the celestial foundations of literally several hundred more myths than I had examined when I wrote the original first volume of the series, I can now see some parallels of which I was not at first aware.

The house in which the king and his sons imprison Kintu is almost certainly seen in the heavens in the form of the constellation Ophiuchus, which is shaped like a hut, a tower, or a rectangular building with a triangular roof -- and which plays the role of all of these kinds of structures in various Star Myths from other cultures. Indeed, the figure of Ophiuchus can be shown to be associated with food and drink as well, such as in the story of the figure of Melchizedek in the book of Genesis, a figure who offers Abraham bread and water (discussed in *Star Myths of the World, Volume Three*).

The hole into which Kintu throws the excess food is almost certainly the nearby constellation of Hercules, when envisioned in its "whirling" outline. This constellation is much closer to the "hut" of Ophiuchus than is the north celestial pole (even though Hercules is a fairly northern constellation and is not too far from the north celestial pole). Additionally, as discussed in *Star Myths of the World, Volume Two* (and again in *Star Myths of the World, Volume Four*), the "whirling" outline of the constellation Hercules plays the gaping maw of various whirlpools in ancient myth, including the dreaded whirlpool of the monster Charybdis in the Odyssey. I strongly suspect that this same celestial feature plays the hole into which Kintu is able to dispose of the great quantities of food he has been ordered to consume.

In the first edition of this volume, I also offered an interpretation of the "copper axe" which Gulu sends to Kintu. In that edition, I suggested that this implement may refer to the sun itself, which was anciently described as an "axe" by virtue of the fact that it "cleaves" through the sky on its daily journey, and to support this I noted that there are indeed many ancient texts in which the axe is a solar symbol. However, in that first edition, I wrote that it is more likely that the copper axe in the story of Kintu is not the sun but rather the "V-shaped" Hyades, a grouping of stars located very close to Orion and which feature in many myths from around the world as an implement which Orion grasps in order to accomplish incredible feats. Since we have already seen that Kintu (at least when he was on earth and had his cow) is probably associated with Orion, this interpretation of the episode of the axe seems to make sense. Additionally, I noted, the Hyades contain the orange-red star Aldebaran, one of a small number of important reddish stars in the night sky (along with Antares and Arcturus), and this can perhaps explain the description of this heavenly axe as being made of copper.

However, once again I believe that there may be a better interpretation than the one that I settled upon in the first edition of this volume. As we have just seen in the previous examination of the figure of the god Shango of the Yoruba, the powerful weapon wielded by the constellation Hercules can be envisioned as an axe (just as it can also be envisioned as the hammer of the god Thor in the far north of Europe). The story itself tells us that Gulu gives the axe to Kintu – and we have just seen that Gulu may be identified with Boötes, because he and Nambi are on the other side of the celestial sphere from Orion and thus when Nambi returns to her father and leaves Kintu behind on earth, she can be seen to be disappearing into the opposite horizon with the constellation Boötes.

If Gulu gives the axe to Kintu for this particular challenge, and if the axe in question is the weapon brandished by the constellation Hercules (as I now believe), then it is very likely that Kintu is associated wih the constellation Orion when he is still on earth, with his cow, but that when he goes up to the heavenly realms to win the approval of Gulu and to be reunited with Nambi, then he takes on the form of the constellation Hercules. Note that Hercules plays a vital role in Kintu's solution to the first challenge (consuming enough food to feed a hundred) as well as being the one who wields the axe in this, Kintu's second challenge.

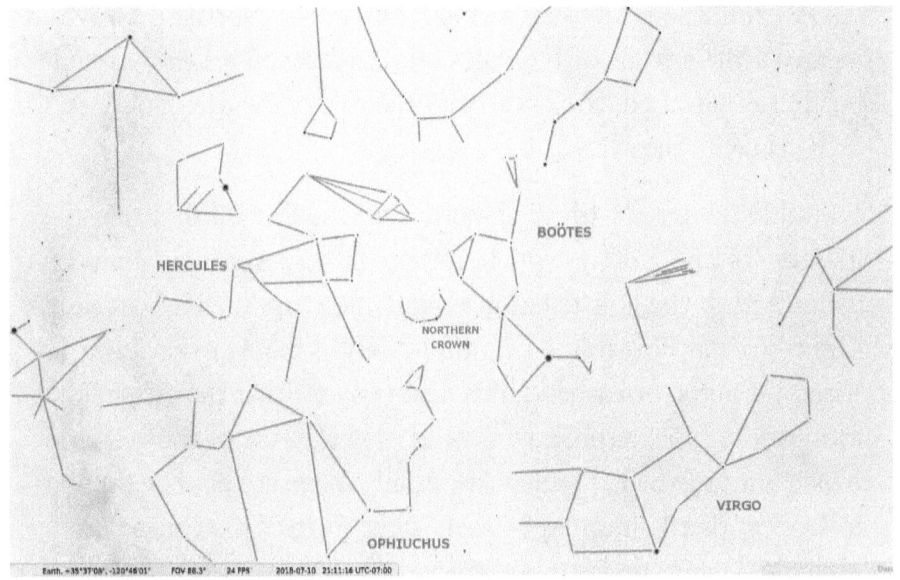

In the above star chart, we can see the proximity of Hercules to Boötes, as well as to Ophiuchus. The alternate "axe" or "hammer" feature of the weapon brandished by Hercules is indicated, within the traditional outline of the same celestial feature, which often becomes a sword or a club in other mythical figures associated with the constellation Hercules, but which can also appear as a mace or even as a thunderbolt.

If this is indeed the correct identification for the constellations involved in this second test of Kintu (as I am now convinced that it is), then the identity of the rock, which Kintu must crack open with the copper axe, becomes much more clear. We can see in the preceding star chart that the figure of Hercules appears to be reaching down towards Ophiuchus with the "lower arm" of Hercules, even as the "upper arm" brandishes the weapon. The part of Ophiuchus towards which Hercules appears to be reaching is the "serpent-head" on the west side of the constellation -- which could play the role of the rock which Kintu cuts with the axe. Alternately, the figure of the Northern Crown, located just in front of Hercules and directly above the serpent-head just described, could also play the role of the rock, split open by Kintu with the axe.

I would still agree with the assertion in the first edition that the identity of the pot in which Kintu gathers the dew may be connected to the constellation Crater the Cup, which is located in the heavens next to the beautiful Nambi (that is to say, next to Virgo). On the other hand, it is also possible that the arc-shaped form of the Northern Crown could play the role of the vessel in which Kintu gathers the dew, especially as we are now beginning to suspect that Kintu may be seen in the form of the constellation Hercules, when he journeys to the celestial realm to try to find Nambi.

In the first edition of this volume I argued that the helpful bee is almost certainly the Beehive Cluster in the zodiac constellation Cancer the Crab. I have found abundant evidence in other myths involving bees that the Beehive Cluster usually plays a role in these stories. The Beehive is a beautiful grouping of stars, visible with the naked eye, which figures in many ancient myths around the world.

The constellation Cancer itself has two "horns" (the outstretched "arms" of the Crab), and so the imagery of the helpful bee landing in the center of the horns points us to the conclusion that this bee, as in so many others in the world's sacred stories, is associated with the Beehive Cluster.

However, I now believe it is also very possible that the bee settling on the original cow belonging to Kintu may refer to the Pleiades, a beautiful and well-known cluster of stars located just above Taurus (the original cow belonging to Kintu, as we argued earlier). It is possible that *both* these explanations are envisioned by the myth, since the bee lands not only on Kintu's original cow but on three calves as well.

Additionally, there is a feature within the outline of the head of Hercules which upon close examination resembles the outline of a fly or a bee, and which plays a role in other myths involving figures associated with Hercules (including the Greek myth in which Zeus swallows Themis, the mother of the goddess Athena, and the Norse myth in which Loki takes the form of a fly to try to harass the dwarf Brokk who is forging the Mjolnir of Thor).

This specific feature of the constellation Hercules will be shown in a close-up star-chart on the following page, which presents two views of the same set of stars. In the bottom chart, the stars which make up this "fly" or "bee" in the head of Hercules have been indicated with lines which connect the small grouping of stars, to indicate the outline of the flying insect which comes to give Kintu advice, in the African myth (and which flies in the face of the Hercules figure to distract him, in the Norse myth, and which is envisioned as being swallowed by the Hercules figure, in the Greek myth).

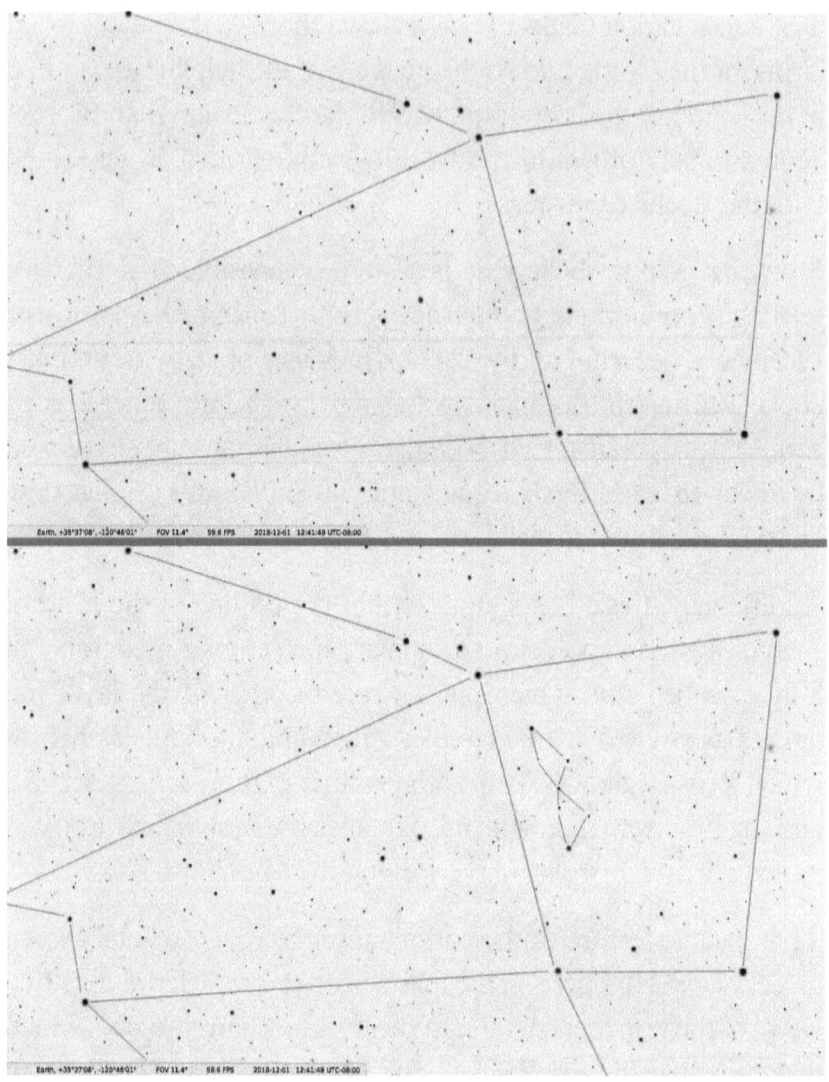

This outline of an insect may seem to be fairly far-fetched to some readers -- and indeed it would be a bit of a stretch to assert with confidence that this set of stars forms the helpful bee that flies up to Kintu to tell him where to find his missing cow, if it weren't for the fact that we can find other myths from other cultures in which figures who are very certainly associated with the constellation Hercules also have an encounter with a similar insect, as noted above. As it is, I would argue that this aspect of the story, in which Kintu is visited by a helpful bee, forms another important confirmatory clue that when Kintu goes to the heavenly realms, he takes on an identity that is associated with the constellation Hercules.

The "ascension" of Kintu from Orion to Hercules is significant, and points to a possible esoteric interpretation of this Buganda myth, while at the same time connecting it to other important myths from around the globe. Figures associated with Orion are often associated with separation and with descent into the lower realm -- such as the god Osiris of ancient Egypt (discussed later), as well as the god Kronos or Saturn of ancient Greece (who is banished to the undersea cave of Ogygia -- as too is Odysseus, when he languishes on the isle of Ogygia at the start of the Odyssey, separated from his family and from his proper home).

But, when Kintu goes up to the realm of Gulu to try to regain his stolen cow, and to undergo a series of impossible tests, he actually "moves through" the heavens and takes on the identity of the constellation Hercules. As discussed in *Star Myths of the World, Volume Two*, particularly in the analysis of the celestial foundations of the Odyssey, an identification with Hercules is significant, because my analysis of the Odyssey finds evidence that the "ascension" of our consciousness and our spirit and our re-integration with our Higher Self is frequently depicted in this world-wide myth system as moving up along the Milky Way band, often towards the constellation Hercules (we see this again in the story of Jacob's Ladder in the book of Genesis, discussed in *Star Myths of the World, Volume Three*).

Indeed, the figure of Cancer the Crab -- located at the very top of the zodiac cycle at the "high point" of summer solstice -- is also indicative in the ancient myth-system of the ascension of the spirit towards integration with the Higher Self and the divine realm, after being "cast down" into the lower realm of incarnate life. The Beehive Cluster, located in the very "forehead" of Cancer the Crab, may well have been seen as indicative of the pineal gland and the crown chakra and thus with the elevation of the consciousness to a higher vibration, as we will see time and again in our examination of the ancient myths.

But we would not be able to see any of these incredible esoteric aspects of the story of Kintu and Nambi if we were not able to decipher the celestial elements underlying the action in this Buganda myth (even though the story itself clearly indicates that it is dealing with celestial personages). Clearly, it is a myth dealing with truths of great value to us in this modern day -- and just as clearly, it is employing a system of celestial metaphor which underlies other ancient myths and scriptures from many other cultures.

These ancient myths constitute a precious inheritance, handed down in remote antiquity to all the different cultures of humanity -- an inheritance which can still benefit us today, if we can learn to understand the language they are speaking, which is the language of the stars.

Star Myths of the Americas:
the Old Man and his Daughter

An important myth in Frazer's *Myths of the Origin of Fire* which is discussed in *Hamlet's Mill* by Hertha von Dechend and Giorgio de Santillana is the myth given to one of the First Nations of British Columbia from the region of Vancouver Island, identified in Frazer's text as the Catloltq people, who lived "to the north of the Nootka."[41]

Citing an account recorded from the Catloltq by Franz Boas in the 1800s, Frazer tells us that according to the Catloltq, there was a time in the distant past when humanity had no fire. At that time, there lived an Old Man, who had a Daughter who was possessed of a miraculous bow and arrows, with which she could hit anything she aimed at.

However, much to the Old Man's distress, his Daughter "was very lazy, and slept constantly."[42] This made her father very angry.

One day, fed up with her constant lying around and wishing that he had the secret of fire, the Old Man said to the maiden:

> "Sleep not always, but take your bow and shoot into the navel of the ocean, that we may get fire."[43]

For according to the legend, the navel of the ocean was a great whirlpool, in which there were sticks caught in the churn, circling the center of the whirlpool, and in particular there were sticks which were capable of making fire by friction: fire-sticks.

So the Daughter took her bow and fired an arrow at the navel of the ocean, and because of her wonderful ability and her possession of a magic bow, she immediately hit the firesticks and caused them to fly out of the whirlpool and onto the shore.

Delighted, the Old Man built a great fire, but he wanted to keep it all for himself and his Daughter. So he built a house with but a single door, "which opened and shut with a snap like a mouth and killed every body who tried to enter."++ The rest of the people knew that the Old Man and his Daughter were inside, enjoying the warmth of the fire and all its benefits, but they could not get through the magic door to obtain fire for themselves.

At last, it was Deer who determined to bring the gift of fire to all of them, and to steal it from the Old Man who was keeping it all to himself. He lashed together two ocean canoes and decked them over, so that he might have a place to stand, and then he found some resinous wood and split it into kindling-sized splinters which he hid in his own coat of hair. Then he set off on the boats towards the place where the old man had built his house.

As he approached, Deer began dancing and singing on the deck he had made, repeating this song: "Oh, I am going to fetch the fire!"

The maiden heard Deer approaching, and implored her father to let him in, for he sang and danced so beautifully, she said. Closer and closer Deer came, and then he disembarked and came bounding towards the door, as if about to enter – but he knew better than that, and only pretended as though he were about to bound inside.

Snap! The door slammed shut with enough force that it would have crushed Deer, had he not already planned for this and stopped short. But now, as the door opened back up, he was ready for that moment and leapt through while it was unable to reverse direction in time, and so he gained access to the house.

He sat down as if he needed to warm himself by the fire, and continued his singing. As he did so, he bent over the fire until the kindling splinters he had concealed in his hair ignited from the heat. At that point, Deer sprang up and shot out of the house, bearing the fire in the splinters along with him – and gave these to the people so that from then on all could share in this wonderful gift.

Here again we see an important role of a woman in the obtaining of fire, and this time not with a yam-stick or digging implement but rather with a miraculous bow and arrows. But here we are also introduced to another character who is found in many other myths and accounts of the origin of fire among humanity: the figure of Deer. Can you guess the identity of this character? A hint is that he is actually very close by to a woman among the stars, but may not be identified as a Deer constellation but rather as something else.

This Native American story illustrates several important concepts that resonate with other Star Myths around the globe. First, as has already been suggested, stories which deal with the subject of the *first fire* among men and women are not simply dealing with the technology of making fire, as important as fire is to our comfort, quality of life, and even our very survival in a harsh world.

The centrality of myths centered on the gift of fire (or, very often, the *theft* of fire) in so many myth-systems from various cultures around the globe may be seen by some (condescendingly) as "guesses invented by men in the infancy of thought to solve a problem which would naturally obtrude itself on their attention as soon as they began to reflect on the origin of human life and society," in the words of J. G. Frazer, writing in 1929.[45] Yet as Frazer himself notes in his collection of myths on the origin of fire, there has never been any group of people encountered anywhere in the world which did not have the technology of fire, and thus "it is very unlikely that these narratives embody any real recollection of the events which they profess to record."[46]

Frazer judging by his writings was apparently ignorant himself of the evidence that the world's mythologies are linked by a common system of celestial metaphor, a fact which would suggest that all the myths are remembered "fragments of a lost whole" (in the words of de Santillana and von Dechend in *Hamlet's Mill*)[47] evidence which suggests that they may be about something much different than Frazer's patronizing description of them as "guesses invented by men in the infancy of thought."

The system can clearly be seen to be esoteric in nature -- using stories and metaphors which illuminate a deeper meaning, allowing the mind to grasp truths or concepts which are difficult to perceive through logical progression but which can be intuitively grasped in an instant of recognition once the parallel is understood (remember the example of the famous scene in the first *Karate Kid*, in which Mr. Miyagi finally shows Daniel-san the connection of the motions he has been learning while waxing the car or painting the fence to the deeper meaning that Mr. Miyagi has wanted to impart to Daniel all along, discussed previously beginning on page 25).

These stories about the theft of fire are part of a world-wide esoteric system which overwhelmingly appears to have to do with truths about the *Invisible* Realm, while using metaphors drawn from the mundane and material world (one in which making fire, for example, is a necessity to keep alive). However, to conclude that the stories are thus about the technology of making fire would be as mistaken as it would be to conclude that because Mr. Miyagi employed the teaching method of waxing the car, he was really trying to impart lessons about car-waxing, rather than about something completely different and much more intangible.

These world-wide myths describing the origin of fire can be seen when viewed in their entirety as being part of a once-intact system (or as fragmented descendants of that system) dealing with the descent of the divine spark into the incarnate realm -- an event which happens in the birth of each and every man and woman who has ever lived, each one of us constituting a curious mixture of a spiritual nature and a physical nature, conjoined in one person.

One giveaway that this interpretation is intended by these myths is the fact that the fire itself is seen as *coming from the realm of the supernatural*, or the realm of the gods. In the Prometheus story, of course, it is the fire from the hearth of Olympus itself, which Prometheus must steal and hide within a thyrsus (a kind of thistle-stalk, discussed in *Star Myths of the World, Volume Two*) in order to bring to mankind.

We can see similar symbology employed in the manifestation of this same metaphor in the New Testament texts, such as the story of the descent of the Holy Spirit in the form of a dove at the scene of the baptism of Christ, or the story of the descent of the tongues of fire upon the gathered faithful at the Pentecost described in the book of Acts (and indeed, these Bible stories are based on the same constellations which appear in many of the "origin of fire" myths from Australia and Africa and the Americas).

Those myths can all be shown to employ celestial metaphor -- and so can these stories from other cultures involving the origin of fire, such as this story of the Old Man and his Daughter and the intrepid Deer.

As with so many other myths relating the origin of fire among humanity, this one features a woman as a central figure in the story (think back to similar "origin of fire" myths we've examined from Australia and Africa which also center on a woman), and as with those myths we can probably identify her with the zodiac constellation of Virgo. The fact that she is described as "lazy" and "always sleeping" no doubt relates to the horizontal orientation of that important zodiac constellation in the sky.

The fact that this Daughter also possesses a magical bow and arrows may be a clue that we are dealing with the constellation Virgo, whose "outstretched arm" indicated by the star Vindemiatrix is variously depicted in Star Myths as being an implement such as a stick, a sword, or in many cases including this one, a bow and arrow, held out from the body in the act of shooting. We shall have occasion to examine some of the myths of ancient India surrounding the goddess Durga which confirm without much room for doubt that Virgo-figures can be envisioned as holding out a bow while riding on the back of a Lion (the proximity of Leo to Virgo being a strong indication that such female figures on lions are associated with Virgo).

However, as we will also see from countless other Star Myths from around the globe, many of them discussed in future volumes of this series, the figure of the constellation Sagittarius (which features a prominent bow) can take on the role of both male and female personalities in the myths -- as indeed can just about every other constellation -- and there are many myths in which a mortal or divine *female archer* is seen in the heavens in the outline of Sagittarius. Additionally, as we will see in many other myths from around the world, the figures of Virgo and Sagittarius have esoteric significance as the "two mothers" who give us the "first birth" (into our physical body) and the "second birth" (the birth of awareness of our inner connection to the Infinite -- our innate divine spark which dwells within the "body of death" which is our physical nature). It is certainly possible that the figure of the Daughter in this myth from North America is associated with *both* Virgo and Sagittarius in some way -- especially because the constellation who plays the role of Deer can be seen to be positioned in between both of them (between Virgo and Sagittarius).

Given the centrality of Deer in this story as well as the importance of deer- or stag-figures in other myths from other cultures, let us examine the evidence for the celestial identity of this figure in myth. As we've just discussed in the previous chapter examining the figures of Shango and Oya of the Yoruba, the constellation Centaurus when envisioned as a deer or stag often makes a good fit with the celestial interpretation of the rest of the action of the story and the other characters featured. I first realized that Centaurus could play this role when analyzing the story of the sacrifice of Iphigenia in the myths of ancient Greece (discussed in *The Undying Stars* as well as *in Star Myths of the World, Volume Two*), and later saw the same constellation playing an important role as a deer in the story of Artemis and Actaeon, and in many other myths.

Likewise, in this story from the Indigenous nations of the northwest Pacific region of North America, the constellation of the Centaur can be seen to play the character of Deer, who steals the fire and brings it to humanity.

Below for ease of reference we show again the two charts depicting the exact same stars of the constellation Centaurus, but with one slight difference in the imagined "connecting lines" which form the outline of the figure. On the top we see the constellation, outlined as suggested in 1952 by H. A. Rey in *The Stars: A New Way to See Them*. Below that is the same constellation, but a single connecting line has been removed:

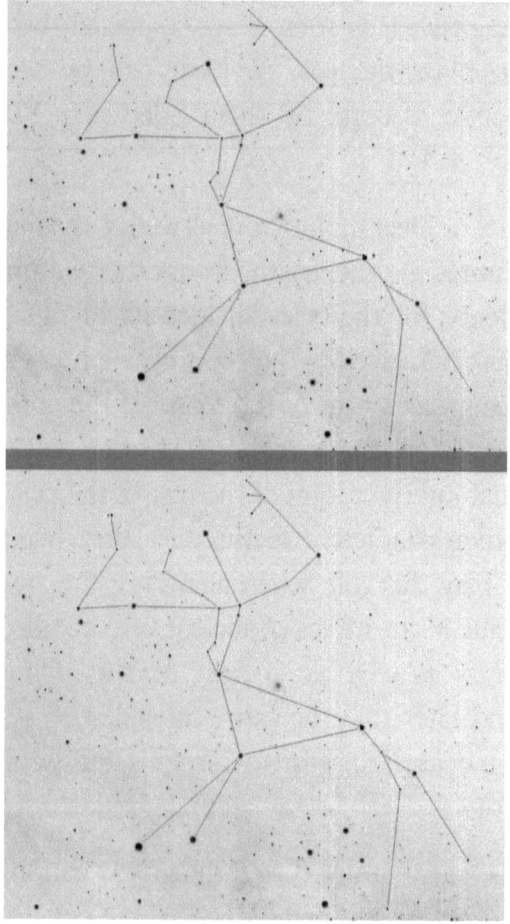

The removal of that single imagined connecting line in the constellation changes the interpretation entirely. In the top image, the figure resembles a centaur: we see the triangular body with its four legs (two forward and two rearward -- the lead foreleg marked by the famous star known as Alpha Centauri), and above the triangular body we see the torso, head, and arms of a human figure (the head is rather large).

However, when we remove just one imagined line at the top of the head of the Centaur, then we can imagine the figure in a completely different way. Now, the outline becomes a great Deer or Stag, with the outstretched arms of the erstwhile Centaur becoming the spreading rack of antlers of the majestic buck. What used to be the torso of the human part of the Centaur is now the somewhat triangular head of the Deer, and what used to be the sides of the human head of the Centaur figure are now two inner prongs of the outstretched antlers of the Stag.

This identification of Centaurus with the figure of Deer in this Native American myth may, along with the other details in the story, help us to perceive a possible esoteric message, which the myth may be intended to convey.

On the following pages we see a star chart showing many of the celestial figures likely to be playing roles in this important Indigenous fire-myth. Some of the identifications are not certain: based on the details in the story, we can make some educated guesses, but there may be two or more possible candidates for the celestial identification underlying the story detail.

Below we see the section of the sky containing Virgo, Centaurus and Sagittarius, along with the band of the Milky Way (which, because the colors are inverted for ease of reference, appears as a darker cloudy pillar running from the bottom of the star chart through the feet of Centaurus, up through the tail of Scorpio, and then on towards the top of the page, passing between Aquila and Ophiuchus):

113

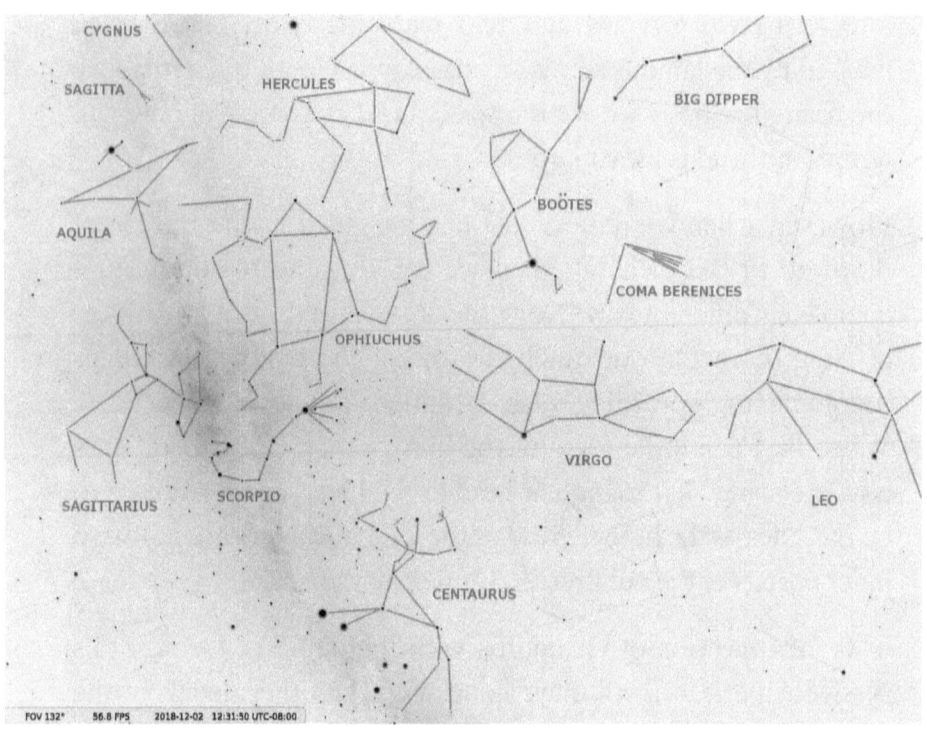

Note that the brightest and thickest part of the entire Milky Way band is found between Scorpio and Sagittarius, in the region towards which Sagittarius can be seen to be pointing a great bow: this region is today identified with the Galactic Core or the Galactic Center, the very nucleus of our Milky Way Galaxy and believed to be the region where stars in our galaxy are born.

Since publishing the first edition of *Star Myths of the World, Volume One* in 2015, I have modified some of my suggested celestial interpretations for this myth. I continue to believe that the Old Man in the story is likely Boötes, who appears alongside Virgo in many myths as either her husband, lover, or father and who in this case is criticizing her for lying around, as Virgo appears to be lying on her back compared to Boötes, who is "sitting upright" in comparison. The outline of the constellation Boötes can be envisioned as being somewhat "hump-backed" if a fairly bright star along the back of the figure is used in the outline, as I do in my drawings here – although H. A. Rey leaves this star out and draws the body of Boötes as a triangle without the "humped back." The hump-back outline does make the figure of Boötes appear to be more aged, which is appropriate to this story's description of the Old Man and his Daughter.

In the first edition, I argued that Virgo's outstretched arm is envisioned as her bow-arm in this story -- and there is precedent, for instance in the myths surrounding Durga (as mentioned before and as examined later in this volume), for this interpretation -- and if so then it is possible that the identity of the "navel of the ocean" into which the Old Man instructs his Daughter to shoot her arrow in order to retrieve the fire-sticks is indeed the north celestial pole itself, as argued in that first edition.

When Virgo is lying on her back with her outstretched arm – or her outstretched bow – pointing upwards, she is pointing towards the northern portion of the celestial dome, and indeed towards the central point around which the entire night sky appears to rotate (due to the rotation of the earth). This central point may be the "navel of the ocean" containing the great whirlpool, around which all the stars of heaven appear to swirl in their nightly motion. As can be seen in the opposite star chart, Virgo's arm does point towards the north celestial pole, which is located above the Big Dipper and pointed towards by the Dipper's bowl's front two stars.

Hertha von Dechend and Giorgio de Santillana present extensive evidence from other ancient myths that the starry sky was referred to as a silent, celestial "Ocean," encircling the land on which any of us live, on all sides (go out at night and see).[48] Thus the central point around which this Ocean appears to turn can be envisioned as a whirlpool at the center.

However, I believe that it is also possible to interpret the Daughter in this myth as being identified with Virgo when she is lying around to the frustration of the Old Man, but later as Sagittarius when (at the instigation of the Old Man) she gets up and uses her magic bow to retrieve the primordial fire.

As mentioned above, we can find abundant evidence from the Star Myths of the world's various cultures to support the conclusion that Virgo and Sagittarius play the roles, respectively, of the mythical "two mothers" involved in the "two births" of every man and woman -- the first birth being physical (into the body) and the second being spiritual (when we begin to realize our connection to the world of spirit, and to our own inner divine spark). One of the clearest metaphors of the "two mothers" is found in the story of the Judgment of Solomon in the text of the book of 1 Kings, which is discussed in some detail in *Star Myths of the World, Volume Three* (*Star Myths of the Bible*).

In this myth from the Indigenous people of the Pacific Northwest, there are not two distinct mothers as there are in the story of the Judgment of Solomon -- but we are told that the Daughter is sluggish and lazy at first (characteristics of our material nature, and our "body of death"), but that later she uses her bow to obtain the blessing of fire that no one else could retrieve.

Note in the zodiac wheel diagram shown below that Virgo is located immediately prior to the horizontal line between equinoxes (the fall equinox being at the "3 o'clock" point on this diagram) -- at which point on our annual cycle we "plunge down" into the "lower half" of the year, when hours of darkness are longer than hours of daylight during each of our daily rotations on

116

the axis. Three signs later, Sagittarius stands immediately prior to the lowest point of December or winter solstice (the solstices being connected on this diagram by a vertical line, between the winter solstice at the bottom and the summer solstice at the top), the point on the annual cycle at which the "plunge downward" makes a great turn, and begins back upwards again (on its way towards spring equinox). I've indicated the position of Sagittarius with a large arrow just before that lowest point (just before the "6 o'clock" point on the wheel as depicted in this diagram).

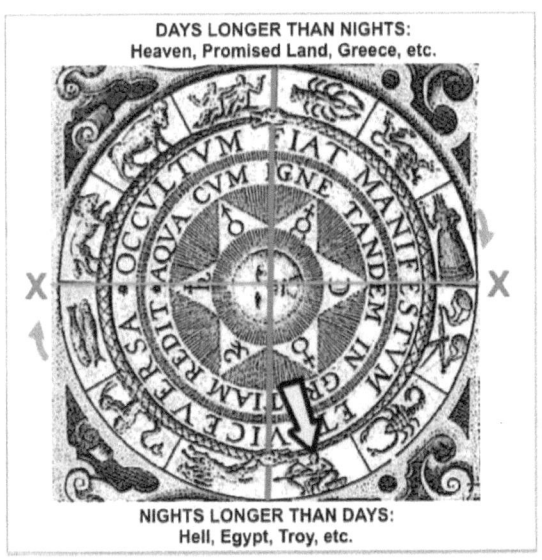

DAYS LONGER THAN NIGHTS:
Heaven, Promised Land, Greece, etc.

NIGHTS LONGER THAN DAYS:
Hell, Egypt, Troy, etc.

It is not difficult to understand why the ancient esoteric system would designate the winter solstice point as the "turning point" where our "second birth" takes place, when we begin to elevate our spiritual awareness and reverse our "downward course" into sluggish matter.

If this interpretation is correct and the Daughter is associated with Sagittarius when she takes her bow and obtains the fire (and, it should be noted, the outline of Sagittarius undeniably includes the outline of a great bow), then the "navel of the ocean" towards which the Daughter points her bow would more likely be identified with the very Galactic Center itself, towards which Sagittarius points the bow. This would make the point from which *humanity obtains the fire* be the same point from which the very stars of our galaxy are thought to originate -- and around which they all whirl, like a whirlpool! Such an interpretation would be compatible with the esoteric interpretation of this fire-retrieval myth pattern, which (as I have argued above) is most likely to dramatize the recovery of their innate connection to the divine fire of the spirit nature by individual men and women, at the point described in some myth allegories as the "second birth."

Further, this central point in the visible band of the Milky Way (the brightest and widest point of the entire river of the galaxy) could be accurately described as the "navel" of the Ocean, if the Ocean in this sense is understood as a great circular river (as we know the Ocean was sometimes envisioned in antiquity).

The identity of the "fire-sticks" which the daughter retrieves when she shoots her arrow into the navel of the Ocean is difficult to determine conclusively. In the first edition of this Star Myth volume, I argued that the fire sticks are most likely seen in the sky in the form of the two parallel lines of the Twins of Gemini. There are some aspects of Gemini which support this interpretation, including the fact that the individual heads of the two Twins are indicated in the sky by two bright stars: Castor and Pollux, as if tipped with fire. Additionally, the starry band of the Milky Way galaxy "washes" right across the "feet" of the Twins, passing between them and the constellation Orion. Thus, if we see them as two fire-sticks instead of as two human figures, then the Twins appear to be igniting a fire that generates a rising column of smoke in the heavens.

However, at this point in my examination of the world's myths, I am more hesitant to declare with any certainty which exact celestial feature plays the "fire sticks" which appear in more than one culture's mythological system (the presence of fire sticks and their possible celestial identity is discussed at some length in *Hamlet's Mill*).[49] As noted in the discussion of another set of "fire-sticks" described in a myth from the Aboriginal Australian people, on page 35, there are good reasons for seeing the two "serpent-halves" which are held by the constellation Ophiuchus as candidates for the fire-sticks described in so many myths around the globe. Remember that the constellation Hercules, just above Ophiuchus, can be envisioned in "whirling form" -- and thus as playing the "whirlpool" around which the fire-sticks are found. We will also see abundant evidence that Ophiuchus plays the role of the "churning stick" in the myth of the Churning of the Ocean of Milk, in ancient India, which suggests a parallel to the fire-sticks and churning motion in this and similar fire myths.

However, it could also perhaps be argued that the "fire sticks" are seen in the heavens in the constellation Coma Berenices, which is located immediately above the outstretched arm of Virgo. Perhaps, after the Old Man tells the Daughter to shoot her bow and retrieve the fire, she obtains the fire in the form of the constellation Coma Berenices (which does indeed resemble a flaming bundle of sticks) and brings these to the Old Man (note that Virgo can be imagined to be extending the flaming bundle of Coma Berenices towards the constellation Boötes). This interpretation seems to have some merit, and would work just fine even if we imagine that the Daughter shooting her bow is seen in the form of Sagittarius: she is Virgo when she is first criticized for simply lying about, and then Sagittarius when she goes and shoots the bow to retrieve the fire, and then she is Virgo again when she brings the fire sticks to the Old Man.

It is also possible that the mysterious fire sticks were somehow associated with the two "great birds" of the Milky Way, who after all play a very central role in many other myths regarding the origin of fire. In the chart below, we can only see the long neck of Cygnus, but note that Cygnus has a long neck and Aquila can be envisioned as having a long tail -- and thus these two birds might in some way have been envisioned as possessing the fire sticks. Note that in between Cygnus and Aquila there is a small constellation resembling an arrow and known as Sagitta (which means *arrow*) -- and this could have something to do with the shooting of the arrow and retrieval of the fire sticks, if these fire sticks are identified in some way with Cygnus and Aquila:

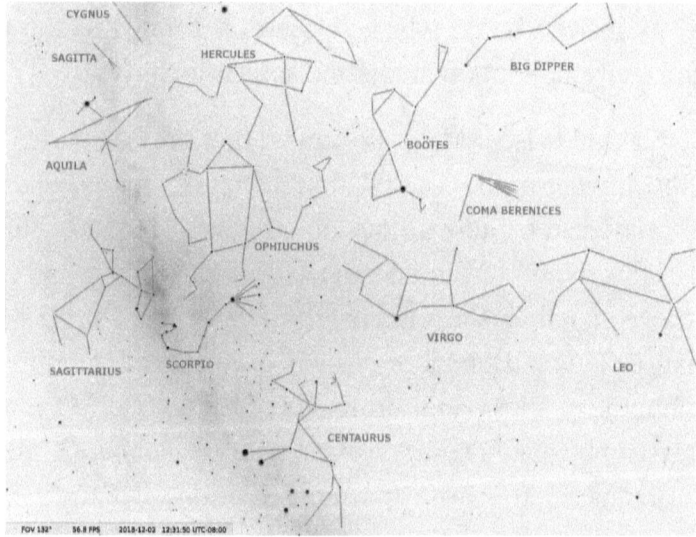

Once the Old Man has the fire, he builds a house on the shore of the celestial sea, a house which has the noteworthy feature of doors snapping open and shut, like a mouth. This aspect of the hut recalls the story of Jason and the Argonauts from ancient

Greek myth, who were confronted with the dreaded Symplegades, or "Crashing Rocks," which they were able to successfully sail through, creating a "new passageway" (the rocks stopped clashing together once the Argo had successfully shot between their dreaded gateway).

This similarity is noted by von Dechend and de Santillana in *Hamlet's Mill*, who argue convincingly that this heavenly "doorway" or "crossing point" represents none other than the equinox point, which functions as a "crossing point" in many ways.[50]

Most technically, the equinox points of the year are literal *crossing points* in that they represent the point at which the ecliptic path of the sun crosses the celestial equator in the sky, twice each year at the March and September equinoxes. You can see this "crossing" between the "angled up" ecliptic ring, containing the zodiac constellations, and the celestial equator which like the earth's equator is located ninety degrees "down" from the north pole (and ninety degrees "up" from the south pole), depicted on any armillary sphere (and as the armillary sphere spins, the ecliptic ring can be seen to yawn open and then snap shut, opening widest at the two solstices and snapping shut at the equinoxes).

The equinoxes also mark the two points dividing the year itself into two "halves," the upper and lower halves. In the upper half the days are longer than the nights, and in the lower half the nights are longer than the days. The equinoxes mark the "crossing over" from one half to the other, with the fall equinox being the crossing-over from the upper to the lower half of the year – where the sun's "fire" literally "goes down" to the lower world: hence, the place where fire is brought from the divine to the mortal realm.

This interpretation of the ecliptic at the equinoxes as the doors that gape open and then snap shut is certainly a likely solution, and in the first edition of this volume that is as far as I went with my own interpretation, agreeing with the authors of *Hamlet's Mill* that the snapping door, like the crashing rocks of the Symplegades, points us to the equinoxes.

However, having now examined hundreds of additional myths for their celestial interpretations, I would add that the house of the Old Man and his Daughter described in this story is almost certainly associated with the celestial figure of the constellation Ophiuchus. The outline of Ophiuchus resembles a hut, a booth, a canopy tent, or a house with a peaked roof, and plays these roles in many myths from around the globe.

In this story of the origin of fire from the Catloltq, the house is described as being on bordered in some way by water, for Deer is explicitly described as approaching the house on a raft that he makes. Note that the constellation Ophiuchus in the night sky is positioned adjacent to the stream of the Milky Way band, strengthening the argument that Ophiuchus is the house of Old Man and his Daughter, in which the Old Man is hoarding the fire and keeping it from other men and women who would like to share it.

Intriguingly, the constellation Ophiuchus can be envisioned as being surrounded by a pair of "jaws," just as it is described in this story. This association was not clear to me until writing *Star Myths of the World, Volume Four: Norse Mythology*, when I discovered unmistakable connections between the description of the slaying of Fenris Wolf by Odin's son Vidar in the Ragnarok account (in which Vidar splits the Wolf apart by the jaws), and the imagery on the huge sarcophagus lid discovered inside the

Temple of Inscriptions at Palenque (in the Chiapas region of the southern part of the modern-day nation of Mexico) thought to be the tomb of the Maya ruler Pakal (AD 603 - 683), in which scholars see the human figure as being enclosed by the jaws of the White-Bone Snake. In both cases, I argued, there are clear connections to the constellation Ophiuchus.[51]

This story from the Catloltq nation of the Pacific Northwest thus appears to be another example of an Ophiuchus figure with "snapping jaws" -- in this case, the house of Old Man and his Daughter, with its door that snaps open and shut.

In the star charts on the preceding pages, we can see Deer (in the form of the constellation Centaurus) pausing as he faces the constellation Ophiuchus (and his feet are in the band of the Milky Way, which is why his approach to the hut is described as being by water, on a raft). When he dodges through the snapping door to retrieve the fire for humanity, it is as though he is snatching spiritual life from between the jaws of death.

Thus, spiritual life comes to us from an agency that is beyond the merely natural -- originating in this story in the navel of the celestial Ocean (identified perhaps with the north celestial pole, but more likely I think with the center of the Milky Way itself, around which all the stars of our galaxy are orbiting and from which all are thought to have originated, according to current models), from the heart of the infinite realm, seen in the infinite heavens above, through the mechanism of the miraculous bow possessed by the Daughter, and finally brought to the rest of humanity by the brave actions of the singing and dancing figure of Deer (who is obviously no ordinary deer).

This important sacred story from the Indigenous people of North America thus illustrates a number of extremely profound truths, regarding issues that we ourselves face in our own lives, to this very day. We ourselves and everyone we meet are in need of the same spiritual "fire" that is being discussed in this myth -- and which can only be found in the realm of spirit. In fact, we already have access to it -- it is already available to us -- but only if, like the Daughter in the story, we stop simply lazing about and wallowing in our physical nature.

The story has many fascinating connections to myths in other cultures from other parts of the world, including Greek myths and Norse myths. The fact that this same system appears to be operating in so many cultures around the globe argues strongly that all of these different Star Myths may be remnants of some earlier common ancient knowledge, which later took on various forms in different cultures, and all pointing back to some now-forgotten ancient source.

The Story of Rabbit Boy

In the excellent collection *American Indian Myths and Legends*, edited by Richard Erdoes (1912 - 2008) and Alfonso Ortiz (1939 - 1997) and generally related in the same "voice" as the Native American story-teller who remembered the sacred story, the very first myth recounted in the book is very noteworthy for a variety of reasons, including the strong parallels it contains to an important theme found around the world (including to one of the central myths of ancient Egypt, the Osiris story, which itself can also be shown to have strong parallels to the New Testament gospels).

As related by Jenny Leading Cloud on the White River Rosebud Indian Reservation in 1967, the White River Sioux tell the story of the first boy, who was initially just a small blister of blood, in the days when "the earth was not quite finished."[52] Here is how the story goes. One day, as he was out walking, just enjoying himself, a playful, good-hearted rabbit came across a little blood clot, of unknown origin.

The rabbit began kicking the little clot around, as if it were a ball to play with, and the mysterious power of Takuskanskan, the power of motion, whose "spirit is in anything that moves," which "animates things and makes them come alive" got in harmony with the rabbit's kicking, and the little blister of blood began to change through this mysterious power.[53] It slowly grew and grew and began to take on the form of a human person, in the shape of a little boy.

The rabbit named the boy We-Ota-Wichasha, which means "Much-Blood Boy," but Jenny Leading Cloud explains that he is better known among her people as Rabbit Boy.[54]

The rabbit took the boy home, where he and his wife loved the boy and treated him as if he were their only son. They gave him a beautiful buckskin shirt, dyed in the sacred color red and decorated with porcupine quills – a shirt so beautiful it would later elicit jealousy among other people, much as Joseph's beautiful coat caused jealousy in the Genesis story.

As the boy grew up among the rabbits, the old rabbit eventually had to tell him that he was in fact a human being, and not a rabbit like him. Although it pained him to say it, the old rabbit said that it was time for Rabbit Boy to leave and find his own people.

Rabbit Boy began to walk, and eventually arrived at a village filled with people like himself. They were all amazed at his good looks and his beautiful fine clothes, and wondered where he was from. He told them he was from another village, but this was actually not true, for there were no other villages yet.[55]

In the village, there lived a beautiful girl, who fell in love with Rabbit Boy, "not only for his fine clothes, but also for his good looks and kind heart."[56] The people of the village thought as well that the two would be a fine match and be happy together, and they would be happy to have Rabbit Boy settle down among them, for he was also possessed of a great vision, in which he played with the sun, and wrestled with the sun, and raced with the sun, and engaged in hand-games with the sun – and always won.

But, Rabbit Boy's power, wisdom, generosity, and success angered Iktome, the evil Spider Man, who was also a prankster and a trickster and a powerful medicine man, and who began to stir up trouble. He began saying things about Rabbit Boy, saying "Look at him - showing off his buckskin outfit to us who are too poor to have such fine things!"[57] He also taunted the men for thinking of letting this stranger marry a girl from their village, as if their own sons weren't good enough. Iktome said that he had a magic hoop which he could throw over the newcomer, and make him helpless.

After enough of this kind of talk, the men of the village came around to Iktome's line of thinking, and agreed to let the medicine man fight Rabbit Boy. Iktome threw his magic hoop over Rabbit Boy, and although Rabbit Boy realized that the hoop actually had no power over him, he played along and pretended to be helpless as the men and boys of the village tied him to a tree with rawhide thongs.

Then Iktome the Spider Man said, "Let's take out our butchering knives and cut him up!"[58]

Rabbit Boy said to them, "Friends, *kola-pila*. If you are going to kill me, let me sing my death song first."[59] Then Rabbit Boy sang:

> *Friends, friends,*
> *I have fought the sun.*
> *He tried to burn me up,*
> *But he could not do it.*
> *Even battling the sun,*
> *I held my own.*[60]

When he was finished, the villagers killed Rabbit Boy and cut him up, putting the pieces into a soup pot.

But, Rabbit Boy had power beyond anything they had previously experienced. A storm began to brew, and a great cloud hid the sun, and everything on earth seemed to turn into night. When the storm passed and the cloud had again uncovered the sun, Rabbit Boy's pieces were no longer in the pot – they had disappeared without a trace. Some in the village, who had watched very closely, had seen the chunks of meat into which they had cut the miraculous stranger coming together and forming again into a body, which then rose up into heaven on a beam of sunlight.

One wise old medicine man of the village said, "This Rabbit Boy really has powerful medicine: he has gone up to see the sun. Soon he will come back stronger than before, because up there he will be given the sun's power. Let's marry him to that girl of ours."[61]

The jealous spider was beside himself. He screamed at the people to forget Rabbit Boy, and told them he himself was much more powerful than the stranger. He demanded that they tie him up too, and cut him into pieces. But, when Iktome tried to sing Rabbit Boy's song, thinking its power was the secret to protect him, he did not remember the words right, and sang:

> *Friends, friends,*
> *I have fought the moon,*
> *She tried to fight,*
> *But I won.*
> *Even battling the moon,*
> *I came out on top.*[62]

Then they cut up Iktome, but he never came back to life: he had outsmarted himself. "Evil tricksters always do," Jenny Leading Cloud concluded.[63]

This story has important parallels to myths of the "slain god" found in many cultures around the world. In particular, the analysis that has been done on the Osiris legend by some researchers including de Santillana and von Dechend in *Hamlet's Mill*, and Jane B. Sellers in her book *Death of Gods in Ancient Egypt*, help us to see that this story of the cutting up of Rabbit Boy may well have parallels to the killing and cutting up of Osiris as well, a myth which also finds parallels in the story of the death of Baldr in Norse mythology (discussed in *Star Myths of the World, Volume Four*) and of course the death of Jesus in the Bible (discussed in *Star Myths of the World, Volume Three*).

Can you guess who this miraculous boy, who grew from a blood clot and is located near a rabbit in the heavens, might be? What constellation might the represent a figure bound to a tree before being sacrificed? The identity of Iktome the Spider Man may be open to debate, but there is a figure in the heavens who does have somewhat "spidery" splayed limbs, and who in addition is seen raising a great knife or sword or club over his head in a different version of the constellation's outline and who thus may perhaps play the role of the evil magician in this myth.

There are strong parallels between this Native American sacred story in which an evil trickster "kills" and cuts up Rabbit Boy and the story of the god Osiris of ancient Egypt, who was also "tricked" by an evil malevolent figure (his brother Set) and cut up into pieces. In the Norse myths, the death of Baldr is likewise due to a malevolent jealous trickster: Loki. Baldr in particular allows himself to be shot at with all kinds of weapons, much as Rabbit Boy allows himself to be tied to the tree and then attacked.

There is historical evidence that the ancient Egyptians themselves associated the constellation Orion with the Osiris, and there is some evidence to suggest that in this story about the wise and wonderful Rabbit Boy, the constellation Orion plays an important role as well.

First, Orion is located in the night sky immediately above the constellation Lepus, the Hare – who actually looks like a rabbit (as well as bearing a certain resemblance to the god Set of ancient Egypt).

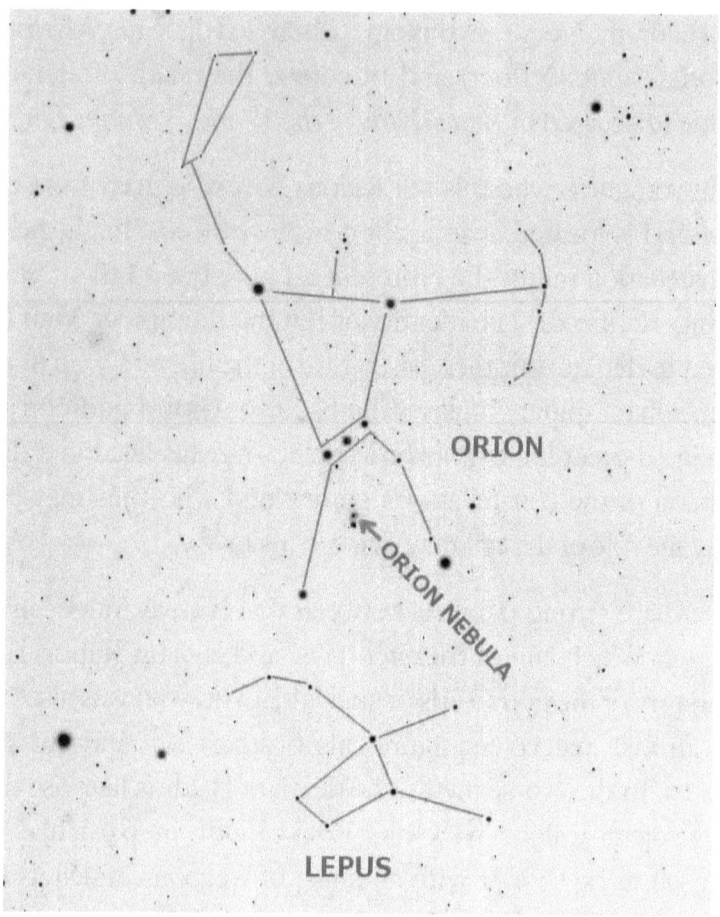

The constellation Orion also contains a fuzzy glowing hazy object (in the "sword" which dangles from Orion's storied three-star belt, towards the lower tip of the sword). This glowing hazy object is the Great Orion Nebula, and it is very possible to speculate that perhaps this is the original "blood clot" from which the entire boy We-Ota-Wichasha eventually emerged as Rabbit played with it and kicked it around. Orion is so large that it is easy to imagine that this miraculous boy has now grown much larger than his father, Lepus the Hare, even though for a time Rabbit Boy did not realize that he was different from his adoptive rabbit family.

In the examination of this myth found in the first edition of this volume, I did not realize that although the identification of Rabbit Boy with Orion is almost certainly correct (especially given the connection of the slain god Osiris with the same constellation), the identity of Rabbit Boy probably "moves through" more than one constellation during the course of this story (a pattern we will see again and again with other important mythical figures, such as Moses in the Bible for example).

I now believe that when Rabbit Boy travels to the distant village, he probably takes on the identity of the constellation Ophiuchus. There are a number of clues in the story which seem to support this interpretation -- one of them being the part in which Rabbit Boy is tied to a tree. This feature of the story is reminiscent of the part of the Osiris myth of ancient Egypt (examined later) in which the coffin containing the body of Osiris is swallowed up by a tree. It is also reminiscent of the famous episode in the Odyssey of ancient Greece (examined in *Star Myths of the World, Volume Two*) in which Odysseus allows himself to be tied to the mast of his vessel by his crew, so that he can listen to the bewitching song of the Sirens as he and his men sail by.

In both of these cases, I believe the action of the mythical episode centers around the constellation Ophiuchus -- and the same holds true for the episode in which Rabbit Boy allows himself to be tied up to a tree and eventually butchered by Iktome, and thrown into a stew-pot, before rising again.

Tellingly, as we will see in *Star Myths of the World, Volume Three* (*Star Myths of the Bible*), there is abundant evidence to identify Christ on the Cross with Ophiuchus as well. And, as we will see in *Star Myths of the World, Volume Four: Norse*

Mythology, there is every reason to believe that Baldr the dying god is associated with the constellation Ophiuchus when he allows himself to be attacked in sport by all the other gods of Asgard.

Thus, in this story of Rabbit Boy we see an important pattern emerge, which also surfaces in many other myths from many other cultures around the globe. Now let's examine the evidence which supports this analysis.

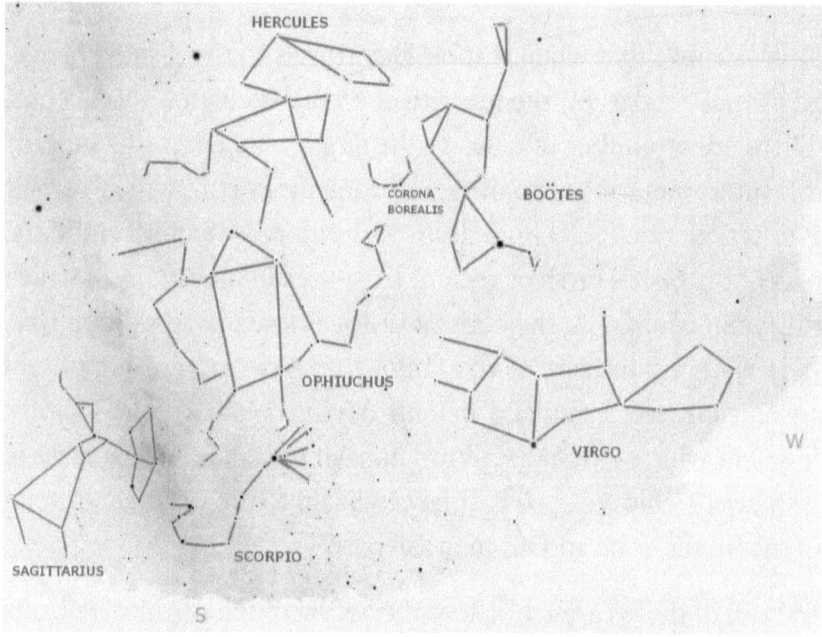

In the star chart above, it should be fairly evident that Ophiuchus can be envisioned as being bound or tied -- the two "serpent-halves" on either side of the central body can be envisioned as ropes or thongs or cords binding him (and indeed, in many myths this aspect of Ophiuchus bound is evident, including in the binding of Loki in the Norse myths).

Additionally, looming above the "bound" figure of Ophiuchus we see the menacing figure of the constellation Hercules, brandishing a weapon which could be envisioned as the butcher knife with which Iktome chops up Rabbit Boy in the story. Note that Iktome is also described as a Spider Man -- and as we will have occasion to observe in the Star Myths time and time again, the constellation Hercules sometimes shows up in myth in the form of a powerful figure brandishing a weapon, but at other times as a central square "head" or "disc" from which a number of arms (usually four) radiate outwards, very much resembling a spider.

Below is a comparison of the two main ways the stars of the constellation Hercules will be envisioned in Star Myths.

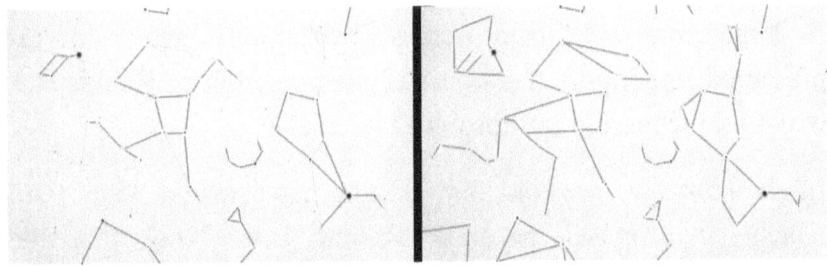

In each case, the stars shown are identical -- only the outlines are different. On the left, the outlines shown are those usually presented in modern conventional outlining systems. Note that the constellation Hercules appears as a square central body from which four arms radiate outwards. On the right, the same stars are shown, this time with outlines as suggested by H. A. Rey in *The Stars: A New Way to See Them*. The square portion of the constellation Hercules that forms the "central body" or "central disc" in the "whirling form" shown on the left is now seen as the head of the powerful figure brandishing a sword or club or mace or axe or hammer overhead.

In this myth from the White River Sioux, Iktome apparently displays both aspects of the constellation Hercules – as a Spider

Man figure and as a figure wielding a butcher knife with which he cuts up Rabbit Boy (associated now with the constellation Ophiuchus, directly below Hercules).

Note that there is precedent in other myths for seeing this "whirling" outline of the constellation Hercules as a spider: in *Star Myths of the World, Volume Two*, I provide evidence which argues that when Arachne is turned into a spider after the famous contest of weaving (in which Arachne challenges, and then insults, the goddess Athena, and insults all the other Olympian gods and goddesses at the same time), the constellation Hercules plays the role of Arachne when condemned to spider form.

And there are still further details in the Sioux sacred story as presented to support this celestial interpretation of Rabbit Boy with Ophiuchus and Iktome with Hercules.

In the story, we are told that Iktome has a magic hoop, with which he proposes to bind Rabbit Boy. Note that the constellation can be envisioned as reaching towards the arc of the Northern Crown with its "lower arm" -- and the Northern Crown itself could play the role of the "hoop." There are a great number of important myths in which a Hercules figure is envisioned as grasping the Northern Crown (Corona Borealis) as part of the action of the story.

Additionally, we are told that in this story, Rabbit Boy is cut up and put into a soup pot. Ophiuchus can be envisioned as a central figure (the rectangular body) thrown into a great cooking vessel (framed by the "jaws" of Ophiuchus on either side). In the previous chapter, we saw that the serpent-halves of Ophiuchus could be envisioned as "jaws" surrounding the central body of the constellation: the same jaws could be envisioned as the walls of a cauldron in which the central body is being cooked or boiled.

There is another "dying god" who is found in Greek myth, who is also torn to pieces -- the god Dionysus (or Dionysos). In *Star Myths of the World, Volume Two*, I also concluded that when Dionysus is torn asunder by the Titans, he is almost certainly associated with the constellation Ophiuchus. Note, of course, that like Rabbit Boy in North America and like Osiris in ancient Egypt, Dionysus also rises again after being dismembered, in the myths of ancient Greece.

And there is yet further astonishing evidence which suggests that this pattern of Iktome (associated with Hercules) slaying Rabbit Boy (associated in this part of the story with Ophiuchus) may be part of an ancient pattern with echoes around the globe. Giorgio de Santillana and Hertha von Dechend named their seminal book *Hamlet's Mill* in part because they discovered that the myths and ancient stories which Shakespeare used as the seeds for the famous play *Hamlet* have very ancient roots -- and these "Amlethus myths" reflect a pattern stretching back to the story of the slaying of Osiris by his treacherous brother Set. Set's murder of Osiris parallels the backstory of the play *Hamlet* in which the elder King Hamlet is slain by his treacherous brother Claudius (in the case of Osiris in the myths of ancient Egypt, the slain god is avenged by his son Horus, while in the Shakespeare play the same task will fall to the king's conflicted son, young Hamlet).

It is most remarkable, therefore, to note that the method in which Claudius is said to have slain the elder King Hamlet helps reveal the celestial identities of Claudius and the king -- and that these celestial identies parallel those of Iktome and Rabbit Boy! Claudius is said to murder King Hamlet by pouring poison into the king's ear as he is sleeping. Note that Hercules in the sky can be seen to be reaching down towards the "serpent-head" of the

western half of the serpent held by the constellation Ophiuchus --
and note also that this "serpent -head" is often envisioned in other
myths as a goblet or a drinking horn or a glass of wine. In the
story of the murder of King Hamlet by his treacherous brother
Claudius, it is quite possible that the pouring of poison into the
ear of the king can be seen in the heavens -- with King Hamlet
(like Osiris and Rabbit Boy, associated with Ophiuchus) being
slain by his treacherous brother Claudius (like Iktome, associated
with Hercules). We can see Claudius bending forward and
reaching down towards a kind of "cone" that leads to the "ear" of
Ophiuchus, if the poison is envisioned as running down from the
"goblet-shaped" serpent-head of the western serpent-half of
Ophiuchus and then back up to the "ear" of Ophiuchus:

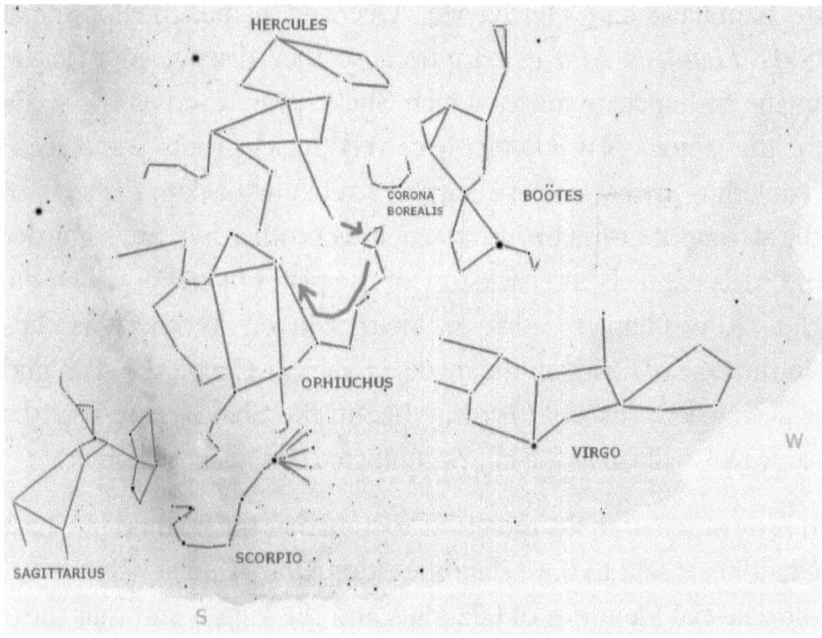

In the star-chart above, I have added arrows to illustrate the path
of the poison, from Claudius dropping it into the long
"cone" or "drinking horn" that runs down and then up to the "ear"
of the king.

We have seen that Iktome is almost certainly associated with the constellation Hercules, and that Rabbit Boy is almost certainly associated with Ophiuchus. How remarkable, then, to discover that another story with strong parallels to the Osiris myth -- the story of the murder of King Hamlet by his brother Claudius, and a story which the authors of *Hamlet's Mill* show to be rooted in various much older myths and folktales from northern Europe – appears to be based on the very same constellations, with a Hercules-figure (Claudius) murdering an Ophiuchus-figure (old King Hamlet).

As for the other features in the story, I believe that the beautiful maiden from the village who falls in love with Rabbit Boy when he first arrives is likely associated with the constellation Sagittarius, although it is also possible that she could be associated with Virgo instead. Sagittarius-figures often appear in myth as beautiful women, and what's more, Ophiuchus and Sagittarius are paired in many, many Star Myths from around the world.

The aspect of the story in which Rabbit Boy sings a song about playing with the sun and always emerging victorious is also very important. I spent some pages of text in the first edition of this volume arguing that this song (and some of the other aspects of the myth) indicate a precessional theme in the Rabbit Boy myth – and it is certainly true that "slain god" myths (including the Osiris myth) often do have precessional elements in the story. It is very possible that the Rabbit Boy myth has precessional elements – and the theme of "playing with the sun" could be interpreted as hinting at precessional themes.

The myths of ancient Egypt in which Orion is "cast down" by his brother and killed can be seen to be related to the ages-long motion of precession which slowly "holds Orion down" below the horizon – "drowns him" so to speak (just as Set casts the casket containing the body of Osiris into the sea, after usurping his throne). This interpretation has been presented in detail by Jane B. Sellers in her book, *Death of Gods in Ancient Egypt.*

In the first edition, I argued that the likelihood that this myth is related to the precessional cycle is strengthened by the details of Rabbit Boy's dream or vision, in which he plays with the sun and wrestles with the sun, and always wins. The precessional cycle itself is associated with the rising of the sun in the different constellations, and can be seen as a sort of "gaming with" or "contending with" or "wrestling with" the sun.

Further, Rabbit Boy sings his "death song" before the villagers try to kill him, and like his vision, this song has a theme of fighting with the sun. In his song, Rabbit Boy says that the sun "tried to burn me up" but could not, which is very suggestive of the possibility that Rabbit Boy is a constellation in which the sun rises. Does the sun ever rise in Ophiuchus?

In fact, the sun does rise in Ophiuchus, even though Ophiuchus is not traditionally counted among the twelve constellations that make up the zodiac band. The ecliptic path does cross Ophiuchus, which means that the path of the sun and of the visible planets will cross through Ophiuchus. We will have more to say about Ophiuchus as the mysterious "thirteenth zodiac constellation" as we proceed through this volume.

Ophiuchus-figures (including Rabbit Boy, Dionysus, Baldr, Osiris, Jesus on the Cross, and others) appear to have a mysterious connection to the inexorable motion of precession, and also with the "second birth." The ancient myths may employ Ophiuchus-figures in their transcendent role due to the proximity of Ophiuchus to the great turning-point of winter solstice (Ophiuchus being located in the sky above Scorpio and Sagittarius, and thus near the same annual turning-point which we discussed in the previous examination of the story of the Old Man and his Daughter).

Both the great turning at the winter solstice and the grinding-out of precession over the course of millennia deal with related themes. The Ages-long motion of precession causes the "dislocation" of the background of stars, and can be seen as representative of our own "dislocation" during this incarnate life, in which we find ourselves "dismembered" -- divided from our own identity, our conscious mind separated from our subconscious mind, alienated from our spiritual nature, out of touch with our Higher Self (and dubious even of the existence and reality of the Higher Self). No wonder precessional figures such as Osiris, Dionysus, and Rabbit Boy are cut or torn to pieces in the ancient myths!

But at the same time, these figures all transcend their own dismemberment, ultimately rising again in triumph. Associated with the constellation Ophiuchus, they are positioned near the point of the year's great upward turn, after reaching the lowest point of winter solstice. This turning point, sometimes described as a "second birth," is necessitated by the first condition -- our dislocation and "dismemberment."

The story of Rabbit Boy, then, is about us: it describes our own condition in this incarnate life. As Alvin Boyd Kuhn wrote in 1936, ancient myth depicts "the drama of our history here and now; and it is not apprehended in its full force and applicability until every reader discerns himself [or herself] to be the central figure in it!"[64]

Deer Hunter and White Corn Maiden

Another story found in *American Indian Myths and Legends*, collected and edited by Richard Erdoes and Alfonso Ortiz and published in 1984, is the haunting tale of Deer Hunter and White Corn Maiden, told by the Tewa-speaking Pueblo people of the southwest desert region of what is today the united states, with this myth specifically identified in that book as being from the Tewa people near San Juan, northwest of Santa Fe and southeast of Taos, on the western side of the Rio Grande. The story is from the people who lived in the area of San Juan, and who have been called the San Juan Pueblo, but their own name for their people is the O'ke Oweenge or Ohkay Owingeh Tewa.

In Alfonso Ortiz's translation, we learn that long ago in the sacred land of the O'ke Oweenge, there arose two young people - a boy and a girl - who were gifted by the gods with superlative grace and talent and divine favor. We learn that while they were still children, the boy was given the name Deer Hunter, "because even as a boy, he was the only one who never returned empty-handed from the hunt." Meanwhile, the girl, who was named White Corn Maiden, "made the finest pottery, and embroidered clothing with the most beautiful designs of any woman in the village."[65]

The two sets of parents and the entire village watched the two grow up into young adulthood and assumed that the pair would eventually marry, since even as children they had naturally gravitated towards one another's company. And sure enough, one happy day the two were married, Deer Hunter and White Corn Maiden, and all the people felt in their hearts that each of them would be destined to become respected members of the nation

140

whom everyone would respect and whose talents would be a great blessing to all the people, young and old.

However, once they were married, the couple became so entranced with one another that they began to spend more and more time together, to the extent that they began to ignore everything else. Soon, we are told:

> White Corn Maiden began to ignore her pottery making and embroidery, while Deer Hunter gave up hunting, at a time when he could have saved many of his people from hunger. They even began to forget their religious obligations. At the request of the pair's worried parents, the tribal elders called a council. This young couple was ignoring all the traditions by which the tribe had lived and prospered, and the people feared that angry gods might bring famine, flood, sickness, or some other disaster upon the village.[66]

The council presented their concerns and their guidance to the couple, but Deer Hunter and White Corn Maiden ignored the voices of everyone else, and only became even more engrossed with one another, withdrawing even further from society, and swearing vows to one another of deepest devotion, that they would never part.

Seeing them withdrawing further and further to themselves and ignoring the council of the people, the whole village was filled with a sense of foreboding, even though it was late spring when the entire world was filled with the unfolding of new life.

Then, without warning, White Corn Maiden fell grievously ill and, in just three days, she died.

Deer Hunter was overwhelmed with grief. He sat up beside his wife's body, refusing to move from the spot or even to speak with anyone. The next morning, she was buried. To understand what happened next, we must understand the traditions of the Tewa when a person leaves this world for the next one:

> For four days after death, every soul wanders in and around its village and seeks forgiveness from those whom it may have wronged in life. It is a time of unease for the living, since the soul may appear in the form of a wind, a disembodied voice, a dream, or even in human shape. To prevent such a visitation, the villagers go to the dead person before burial and utter a soft prayer of forgiveness. And on the fourth day after death, the relatives gather to perform a ceremony releasing the soul into the spirit world, from which it will never return.[67]

But Deer Hunter refused to follow this pattern, and instead became absorbed with the idea that during the four-day period he might see her before the ceremony of release. He began lingering about the outskirts of village and then venturing further and further into the surrounding fields day and night, in hopes of encountering White Corn Maiden one more time.

Then, at sundown on the fourth day, while the family members and others were gathering in the village in preparation for the final ceremony of release, and Deer Hunter was wandering far afield in the fading light, he saw a low fire burning amongst the bushes.

In breathless anticipation he walked towards it, and there he found his wife, "as beautiful as she was in life and dressed in all her finery, combing her long hair with a cactus brush in preparation for the last journey."[68] Deer Hunter fell at her feet and between great sobs of grief begged her to stay with him, and not to depart forever into the other world.

But White Corn Maiden refused, telling him she could not stay, for it would anger the spirits and go against the nature of things, and that besides, she soon would no longer be beautiful and Deer Hunter would soon regret keeping her amongst the living where she did not belong.

Deer Hunter protested that he would never reject her, that their love was too strong to ever let them part, and he continued to plead with her not to leave him alone. Finally, White Corn Maiden gave in to his pleas, but told him that she would hold Deer Hunter to his word.

When the villagers, who were already holding the procession towards the place where they would perform the final farewell and release for the departed woman, saw Deer Hunter approaching out of the twilight, and saw White Corn Maiden following him back to the village, they were filled with dread, and began pleading with him to come back to his senses and release his wife. But Deer Hunter refused to listen.

The aftermath of this decision was horrifying. The couple returned to their former home, but soon Deer Hunter began to notice the rapid changes coming over his wife, as she took on more and more of the look of the dead. At first, they continued to sleep in the same place, but Deer Hunter turned his back on his wife. Soon, however, he began to sit up on the roof all night in an attempt to get away from her, but she would always come and join him up there. The villagers could see them up on the roof all night long, silhouetted against the night sky.

Later, Deer Hunter began to try to stay even further from his wife, and now the people would see him running through the fields, pursued by the grim figure of White Corn Maiden, now reduced to a terrifying bony apparition.

Things were very much out of harmony throughout the entire village, because of the disruptive effect that the couple had on all the men, women and children during this time. But then, one misty morning, a tall and powerful figure, dressed all in white buckskin robes and carrying a tremendous bow in one hand, appeared in the center of the village. There he stood, in imposing silence and dignity, while all the villagers wondered who he could be – although they immediately sensed that he had come from the realm of the gods, and that he was here to rectify the horrible situation that had been caused by Deer Hunter's reckless choice.

Still standing at the center of the village, the visitor suddenly called forth in a commanding voice, for Deer Hunter and White Corn Maiden. So powerful was the authority in his tone that it was heard in every home in the village. And soon, the people saw that Deer Hunter and his wife were quietly approaching, in obedience to the summons from the mighty visitor.

The Tewa tell what happened next:

> The awe-inspiring figure told the couple that he had been sent from the spirit world because they, Deer Hunter and White Corn Maiden, had violated their people's traditions and angered the spirits; that because they had been so selfish, they had brought grief and near-disaster to the village. "Since you insist on being together," he said, "you shall have your wish. You will chase one another forever across the sky, as visible reminders that your people must live according to tradition if they are to survive."[69]

The visitor from the spirit world then reached into his quiver on his back, where he carried the two largest arrows that had ever been seen by any of the people. Drawing them forth, he placed Deer Hunter on one arrow, and shot it towards the west, and then did the same with White Corn Maiden on the second arrow.

That very evening, the people of the Tewa noticed two new stars, low in the western horizon, one of them very bright, and one much dimmer: it was Deer Hunter and White Corn Maiden. White Corn Maiden, having already been dead for some time, was the dimmer of the two. And so, the two will be forever together in the heavens, chasing one another through the starry fields, a reminder to all of the events and the lessons of their tragic love.

Once again, we have a story with explicit references to celestial connections, and some of the analysis from previous discussions of Star Myths may suggest which celestial figures can be identified as actors in this moving story from the Tewa people.

In the interpretation of this story offered in the first edition of this volume, I suggested that the now-familiar constellations of Boötes and Virgo play the lead characters of Deer Hunter and White Corn Maiden. There are certainly some details in the story which suggest that Deer Hunter might be associated with the constellation Boötes, particularly when he "turns his back" on his deceased wife, and later goes up to sit on the roof. Both of these descriptions seem to fit the outline of the constellation Boötes.

However, it is not completely certain that Virgo plays the role of White Corn Maiden -- based upon additional analysis on other myths in the period since the first edition to this volume was published, I have seen that the constellation Sagittarius quite often plays the role of a beautiful woman in various myths -- and note that in this story we are told that Deer Hunter first encounters his now-deceased wife beside a fire, combing her hair. These details may point to an identification of White Corn Maiden with the constellation Sagittarius, located (as we have already seen) beside the widest and brightest part of the Milky Way band, often envisioned in myth as a fire. Note that the outline of Sagittarius features a line rising up from the head, like a "plume" or possibly a comb. Another possibility is that the nearby arc of the Southern Crown plays the role of the comb mentioned in the story:

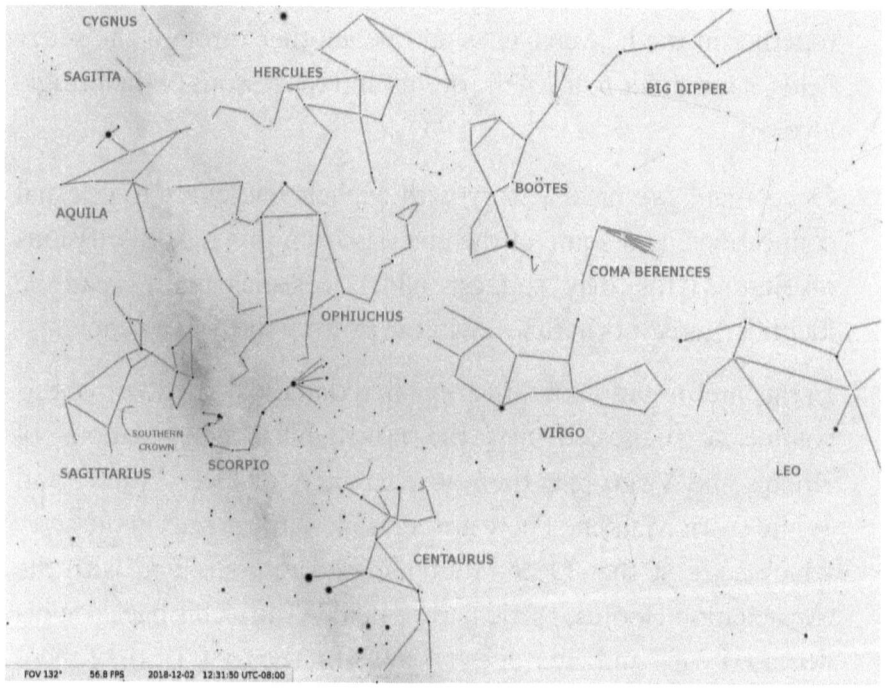

It is also possible (and there is precedent for this interpretation in other myths) to argue that Sagittarius plays White Corn Maiden when she is first seen by Deer Hunter, combing her hair by the fire, but that later when she turns skeletal she becomes associated with Scorpio.

Note that Boötes can be said to be "turning its back" towards Sagittarius (and towards Scorpio) even more so than towards Virgo. However, I now believe that the part of the story which mentions Deer Hunter going "up on the roof" may well indicate the constellation Hercules, since the outline of Ophiuchus can be shown to play the role of a tent, a house, a booth, or other similar shelter in many other Star Myths, and since Hercules is positioned immediately above the peeaked "roof" of the constellation Ophiuchus.

There is a very distinctive example of another sacred story from a completely different quarter of the globe which features a male figure who goes "up on the roof" and who can be shown to be associated with the constellation Hercules atop Ophiuchus, and who is amorously involved with a female figure associated with Sagittarius: the story of David and Bathsheba recounted in the Hebrew scriptures, beginning in 2 Samuel chapter 11.

The celestial foundations of the episode in which "David arose from off his bed, and walked upon the roof of the king's house: and from the roof he saw a woman washing herself; and the woman was very beautiful to look upon" (2 Samuel 11: 2) are examined in more detail in *Star Myths of the World, Volume Three* (*Star Myths of the Bible*).[70] For now, suffice it to say that the evidence connecting the figure of David to the constellation Hercules in the sky is quite abundant, and the evidence supporting the identification of Bathsheba at her bath with Sagittarius at the edge of the widest and brightest part of the Milky Way is also compelling.

There are many other myths in which a female figure described as being in the act of bathing can be associated with Sagittarius beside this widest part of the Milky Way (the bulge which we now believe to be the Galactic Core or Galactic Center of our own galaxy). Some of these include the story of Artemis when she is surprised at her bath by the hapless youth Actaeon, or the story of Aphrodite when she retreats to her grotto in Cyprus after the embarrassing affair in which she is caught in bed with Ares.

Besides the significant episode of David and Bathsheba, there are many other myths which support a connection between the constellations Hercules and Sagittarius, in which the two are lovers (thus supporting a similar interpretation for the story of Deer Hunter and White Corn Maiden, when Deer Hunter goes up onto the roof to escape his wife). For example, many of the amorous affairs involving the god Zeus and either a mortal woman or a reluctant nymph can be shown to involve Hercules (the constellation with which the god Zeus is most often associated, as discussed in *Star Myths of the World, Volume Two*) and Sagittarius (playing the object of the Thunder-god's amorous attentions).

For instance, in the story of Leda and the Swan, I would argue that when Zeus takes on the form of a swan in order to effect a liaison with Leda, he is envisioned as moving into the nearby constellation of Cygnus, located almost directly adjacent to Hercules and positioned to be flying downwards through the Milky Way towards Sagittarius below. Similarly, when the god turns into a shower of gold in order to descend upon Danae, this episode almost certainly envisions Zeus taking on the form of the Milky Way band itself, which runs just past the constellation Hercules, in order to reach the mortal woman and object of his desire.

There is another "Hercules - Sagittarius" example in the scene in the Odyssey involving the homecoming of Odysseus, after the long-suffering hero has slain the suitors in his hall, when Odysseus and Penelope are finally together, but she still wants to test the stranger, to make sure that it is really her long-lost husband. In Book 23 of the Odyssey, the poet describes Penelope as positioning herself "in the light of the fire" while Odysseus sits "against a tall pillar, looking down," waiting to see what his wife will say to him (Book 23, lines 100 - 107).[71]

Clearly, this scene can also be interpreted as describing Sagittarius (representing Penelope, positioned "in the light of the fire") and Hercules (the constellation with which Odysseus himself can be seen to be most-often associated, as discussed in many examples in *Star Myths of the World, Volume Two*). The description of Odysseus seated "against a tall pillar, looking down" is a good description of the constellation Hercules, situated adjacent to the tall pillar of the Milky Way galaxy, and looking downward (see the star charts). This interpretation of the Odysseus-and-Penelope scene is discussed in detail in *Star Myths of the World, Volume Two*.[72]

All of these connections make an extremely compelling case that Deer Hunter in this context is associated with the constellation Hercules, and White Corn Maiden with Sagittarius (or, after she becomes more skeletal, with Scorpio – a constellation which plays a person turned into a skeleton in other myths from around the world, including the story of Izanagi and Izanami from the Kojiki of ancient Japan, examined in *Astrotheology for Life*). They also make a very compelling case for the probability of some sort of connection between the world's ancient myths and scriptures, perhaps being descended from some now-forgotten common source of even greater antiquity.

There is even yet another detail from the Odyssey which may be pertinent to our interpretation of this legend of Deer Hunter and White Corn Maiden, and that is the fact that when Odysseus climbs up a rugged promontory to spy out the palace of Circe, he encounters a "large, lofty-horned stag" on his way back down, which he then spears through the back (Odyssey Book 10, lines 160 - 180).[73]

Star Myths of the World, Volume Two argues that this encounter describes Odysseus (associated with the constellation Hercules) climbing a rugged outcropping associated with the constellation Ophiuchus (directly below Hercules) and meeting the stag (associated with Centaurus) on his way back down.[74] The presence of another myth in which a Hercules-figure can be positively identified as slaying a deer makes a very strong argument that Deer Hunter in this Pueblo myth may also be associated with the constellation Hercules.

In the first edition of Volume One, I presented some arguments that White Corn Maiden might be associated with Virgo, due to the part of the story in which Deer Hunter first encounters his deceased wife next to a small fire, combing her hair. I argued that, because the fiery sun passes through Virgo at the time of fall equinox (the crossing-point down to the lower half of the year), this detail could associate White Corn Maiden with that zodiac sign.

However, as the discussion above should make clear, I now think it more likely that White Corn Maiden is associated with the constellation Sagittarius, who plays the beloved of a Hercules-figure in many other sacred stories from other cultures as well. If so, then the description of White Corn Maiden standing beside a fire would refer again to that widest part of the Milky Way band.

This constellation, rather than indicating the initial plunge down into the lower half of the year (signifying the plunge into the incarnate life) is positioned at the lowest point on that downward cycle -- the great "turning point" of the year, at the winter solstice.

As I argue in *Star Myths of the Bible*, the shameful affair of David's sleeping with Bathsheba and then conspiring to murder her husband certainly marks a low-point in the David cycle of stories in the Bible. Similarly, in the Native American story of Deer Hunter and White Corn Maiden, the husband's refusal to let his wife go (against her own wishes) can be seen as representative of our own love of and obsession with the physical nature during this incarnate life, which is associated in the myths by the *descending part of the annual cycle* in which the hours of daylight grow shorter and shorter, and the hours of darkness grow longer and longer, on the way down to that very lowest point of winter solstice, where at last there will be a realization and a turning (as there is with Deer Hunter, eventually, as well).

After the couple had disrupted the natural order of the ways of the Pueblo for long enough, the imposing visitor from the spirit world appears, standing in the center of the village. He is described as tall and dignified, wearing a brilliant outfit of white buckskin, and one of his main characteristics is his standing position, as well as the fact that he carries an enormous bow and a quiver with two long, straight arrows.

This figure is almost certainly the towering constellation of Orion, who stands with feet planted squarely apart, and who contains the highest percentage of bright stars to overall stars of any constellation in the night sky, which could explain the gleaming white robes of the spirit-world visitor in the story.

Orion carries a mighty bow, which figures in many myths in which a character is played by this well-known constellation. The two arrows, however, are very likely the two parallel lines formed by the nearby constellation of Gemini, the Twins, who are located close to Orion over the shoulder from which he would be expected to sling his quiver, opposite from the arm that is extended and holding the bow.

We can be fairly certain that the Twins are the two arrows, because after commanding Deer Hunter and White Corn Maiden to come to him, the unearthly visitor launches them into the western sky upon one arrow apiece, where they become two stars, one brighter than the other. The most distinctive feature of the two Twins, of course, are their two brightest stars which form the heads of each of the Twins, and in fact give the characters of the two Twins their mythical names in Greek myth: Castor and Pollux (or Polydeuces). One of them (Pollux) is noticeably brighter than the other (Castor is dimmer).

In the Greek myths, the dimmer second-magnitude star Castor was the mortal of the two twins, while brilliant first-magnitude Pollux was immortal. This detail is paralleled in the Tewa myth, in which the brighter star is associated with Deer Hunter, and the dimmer with White Corn Maiden, who was already deceased when placed into the sky. Also, it is no doubt significant that the star Castor is white in color, even though dimmer than Pollux (which has a yellowish hue) – which may help explain the maiden's name in this memorable story of the O'ke Oweenge.

The pattern of a *mortal* and an *immortal* twin seen in the Castor and Pollux story and echoed in the Tewa legend in the pattern of a living husband and a corpse wife is a dominant mythical theme found around the globe. I am convinced that the world's ancient myths use powerful metaphorical stories in order to convey spiritual truths to our understanding -- truths which may be easiest for us to grasp or to absorb when they are presented for us in this esoteric manner.

In the ancient Greek myth of the Gemini twins Castor and Pollux (or Castor and Polydeuces), the mortal twin eventually dies and the divine twin must venture down to the underworld in order to rescue his mortal brother.

Far from being "just" a story about a fantastical and improbable situation about twin brothers one of whom is mortal and one immortal, this myth pictures *our own* situation in this incarnate life, in which we ourselves simultaneously have a mortal, physical nature and also an immortal, spiritual nature. At first, when we are born into this physical universe, we are immersed in and identify with our physical, mortal aspect -- to the point that we seem to be completely disconnected from our immortal, spiritual nature. But, like the story in which the divine twin Pollux must descend into the underworld in order to rescue his mortal brother Castor, the myths illustrate that our own "divine twin" or Higher Self is actively seeking to lift us up from our state of ignorance and illusion.

This pattern will be seen again and again in the myths of the world, from the story of Gilgamesh and Enkidu (discussed later in this volume) to the story of Jesus and the disciple named Thomas Didymus (Thomas the Twin), which is examined in some detail in *Star Myths of the World, Volume Three*.

In this Tewa legend of Deer Hunter and White Corn Maiden, I believe that a very similar lesson is being presented for our understanding. In the marriage of the living husband to a corpse bride we see a picture of our own incarnate condition, in which our spiritual nature is "married" to a mortal physical nature – a physical nature which will eventually die and rot away, despite its great beauty and many wonderful aspects. It is a mistake to become too enthralled with our physical self, to the point that we neglect or deny the spiritual nature.

That this is a constant temptation in this incarnate life is amply illustrated by the many stories in which the negative effects of such an imbalance are illustrated, such as the episode in the Odyssey in which the companions of Odysseus are turned into swine, or the story of the prodigal son in the New Testament in which the younger brother finds himself longing to eat husks at the trough with the pigs.

I would argue that this story from the nation of the O'ke Oweenge is trying to tell us much the same thing -- that we must not become overly enamored with the physical and material aspect of this simultaneously physical-and-spiritual world in which we find ourselves, to the point that we become unbalanced and lose our way.

154

Selections from the Popol Vuh

The Popol Vuh of the K'iche' (or Quiché) Maya (literally, the "Forest Maya," whose civilization was centered in the western highlands of what is today Guatemala) is perhaps the most undiluted sacred text to survive the incredibly vicious mass-elimination of written scriptures from the civilizations that existed in Central and South America prior to the arrival of Europeans in the fifteenth and especially the sixteenth centuries AD.

Like the other ancient scriptures and sacred traditions preserved by the world's different cultures on different continents, the Popol Vuh contains profound wisdom, operating on many levels at the same time, and can profitably serve as a bottomless pool into whose depths one can plunge for an entire lifetime (or many lifetimes) without ever reaching the end of its wonders. And, as with other ancient myths, scriptures and sacred stories from other cultures around the world, the Popol Vuh employs metaphor in order to convey its wisdom to our understanding -- metaphor which can be shown to be celestial in nature.

As with the other myth-traditions addressed in this volume and the other volumes of the series, no book can do justice to the vast landscapes of myth preserved among the cultures of the Americas -- and certainly no single book can do justice to the esoteric wisdom preserved in the Popol Vuh, even if that book focused exclusively on the Popol Vuh and devoted hundreds and hundreds of pages to exploring its metaphors and figures. Like any of the other ancient sacred traditions and texts, a multi-volume series could easily be dedicated to examining the celestial metaphors contained in the events described in the text of the Popol Vuh and their possible esoteric message for our lives, without ever exhausting the material available for study and analysis. Thus, the examination here will necessarily be very limited, with the goal of establishing the undeniable celestial aspects present in this surviving sacred scripture of the continents of the Americas.

The name of this sacred text translates literally to the "House" or "Sleeping Mat" (*Popol*) of the *Vuh* (pronounced "wuj" or "wukh"), meaning "book" in the form of a codex painted on deer skin or bark-paper, according to the preface to his excellent 2007 translation and commentary upon the Popol Vuh by Professor Allen J. Christenson.[75] Another translator, in the introduction to his revised edition of his 1986 translation in which he incorporates the ancient knowledge preserved among the modern-day Quiché Maya, Professor Dennis Tedlock (1939 - 2016) notes that:

> The lords of Quiché consulted their book when they sat in council, and their name for it was Popol Vuh or "Council Book." Because they obtained the book (or some section of it) on a pilgrimage that took them down from the highlands to the Atlantic shore, they called it "The Light That Came from Beside the Sea." Because the book told of events that happened before the first true dawn, and of a time when their ancestors hid themselves and the stones that contained the spirit familiars of their gods in forests, they also called it "Our Place in the Shadows." And because it told of the rise of the morning star and the sun and moon, and foretold the rise and radiant splendor of the Quiché lords, they called it "The Dawn of Life."[76]

The text itself was written down by anonymous members of the ruling lineages of the Quichés after the Spanish had already taken over the Maya kingdom in 1524 by a combination of treachery, murder, and brutal terrorization of the populace, accompanied by the wholesale burning of the precious Maya sacred texts and records at the hands of the priests. During the subsequent years, the European conquerors also set about destroying the knowledge of the sophisticated writing system of the Maya.

In the preface to his 2007 translation and commentary, Allen J. Christenson explains that the authors who wrote the version that we have today probably wrote it down between the years 1554 and 1558, and did so based on their knowledge of the ancient Popol Vuh, all copies of which had by then been lost or destroyed in the purges, during the early decades of which the possession of any Maya texts was punishable by death at the direction of the invaders.

And yet, unlike the other texts from that culture which survived but not without being diluted with European additions or emendations, Christenson explains that the anonymous authors of the Popol Vuh were traditionalists, "in the sense that they recorded the history and theology of the ancient highland Maya people without adding material from European sources."[77] Those who wrote it down, he writes, "were most likely members of the Quiché nobility who may have retained some Precolumbian manuscripts from the royal archives that survived the Conquest."[78]

The text itself contains far more characters and events than can be examined in this volume, but it can be safely stated that each episode fairly bursts with celestial content that will be familiar from our examination thus far of other myths from other cultures around the world. We will examine just a few of them here. The parallels in some cases are striking: in fact, the parallels to episodes in the Hebrew scriptures in some cases are remarkable.

But lest the reader immediately assume that any parallels to Biblical episodes must be a product of imitation of the new religion that was after 1524 forced upon the Maya at the point of a sword, there are other parallels which we will see relate to details in myths from other cultures that are very unlikely (or downright impossible) to have been "borrowed" from the European invaders.

Interestingly enough, the tradition of the Maya themselves held that the original of the Popol Vuh had been brought from across the sea – across the sea from the east, that is from across the Atlantic – in remote ancient times, by representatives of a people who lived across that sea, a people the Maya called the *Tulan*.[79]

The linguistic similarities in that word to the name of the fabled "lost city of *Atlantis*," discussed by Plato and attributed to an account given by priests of Egypt, are undeniable, even if they are dismissed by those who doubt the two words could share any commonality, and whose historical paradigm prevents them from even considering the possibility.

While the similarity between *Tulan* and *Atlantis* may be coincidental, it is notable that both refer to some dimly-remembered civilization "across the sea." I have argued at some length in my 2014 book *The Undying Stars* that the account in the famous *Bibliotheca historica* of Diodorus Siculus, probably written between 60 BC and 30 BC, of "an island of considerable size" which "lies out in the deep off Libya" (Libya being a word used to describe a portion of the known continent of Africa), "a voyage of a number of days to the west," almost certainly describes the continents of the Americas, and that refugees from severe persecution in the centuries we call the 2nd and 3rd centuries AD (and possibly later) may have fled from the Mediterranean to the Americas.[80]

It is equally possible (and, indeed, I think more likely) that the ancient wisdom traditions passed down through the generations of the Maya and the other cultures of the Americas share a *common, even more ancient* source with the ancient wisdom traditions preserved in Europe and Africa and the other continents of the world, and were not the product of contact during the period of conventionally known history. There is abundant evidence to conclude that this ancient celestial system predates even the most ancient texts of the civilizations of ancient Egypt and ancient Babylonia -- and that indeed the system may have been in place by the time that the stones of Göbekli Tepe were made, and the entire massive complex of that site in modern-day Turkey appears to have been deliberately buried no later than 8000 BC.[81]

It is possible that all of the later civilizations known to conventional history were produced thousands of years after the catastrophic destruction of whatever culture or cultures created the original patterns of celestial myth, and that the system was preserved in some form by these various survivors and incorporated into their sacred traditions without any later contact or sharing required. If so, then whoever came from the east across the Atlantic may have done so long before the rise of the cultures in the eastern hemisphere known to conventional history. All of them may have preserved memories and traditions passed down for generations regarding that lost previous Age of remote antiquity, and the term used for this lost Age may have turned into the "Atlantis" mentioned by Plato and the "Tulan" described by the Maya, without any later contact between the hemispheres (although there is certainly evidence for later contact between the hemispheres prior to Columbus or the vikings, this does not mean that the myths or that ancient terms such as "Atlantis" were brought to the Americas by travelers from the other hemisphere).

In any case, even if the linguistic similarity between *Tulan* and *Atlantis* is dismissed as coincidental, the sheer number of similarities between myths using the same celestial metaphors shown so far – many more of which can be demonstrated in the events described in the Popol Vuh – cannot be so easily dismissed.

In addition, there are many other linguistic similarities in words found in the New World which make the *Tulan – Atlantis* similarity more difficult to simply wave off. There is the fact that several tribes of North America used the name *Ta-Iowa* or some variation of it to describe a supreme deity or divinity: the name in fact survives in the name of one of the fifty states of the united states. The linguistic similarity to the divine name of *Yahweh* or *Jehovah* found in the Hebrew scriptures is impossible to deny.

And there are some names used in the Popol Vuh which appear to have similar counterparts in Mediterranean sacred literature. For instance, some researchers have noted that the name Q'ukumatz (or Gucumatz) for the great feathered-serpent deity described in the Popol Vuh has remarkable similarity to the name of the central semi-divine hero-figure of the Gilgamesh series of epics from ancient Mesopotamia (*Gilgamesh* : *Gucumatz*).[82]

And, in the lineage of ruling houses of the Maya, given in the Popol Vuh, the "grandfathers" or first progenitors of two of the groups of great houses share the name *Balam*, a name which has clear affinity with the sun-deity *Baal* of the eastern Mediterranean, or *Bel* of western Europe, or the *Baalim* described in the Hebrew scriptures (a plural form, which means "the Baals").[83]

Interestingly enough, the "grandfather" or first progenitor of a third group of ancient "great houses" (distinct from those descended from the two Balams) bore the name *Mahucutah*, which while not necessarily linguistically related to *Methuselah*, has the same number of syllables and certainly bears a rather noteworthy similarity to it.

But to set these parallels aside, while still noting them as worthy of further consideration, we will see undeniable evidence in the text itself that the figures and episodes preserved in the Popol Vuh are built upon the same ancient foundations which support the other sacred myths found around the world. Below we will summarize some of these characters and events from the Maya Council Book, and then we will examine a small sampling of the evidence which shows that this sacred text is conveying its wisdom through the use of celestial metaphor.

Professor Allen J. Christenson of Brigham Young University, who lived among the modern-day Quiché for many years as an ethnographer and translator, recounts in the introduction to his translation of the Popol Vuh the reverence with which the Quiché treat the words of their ancestors. He explains:

> While working as an ethnographer and translator in the Guatemalan highlands, I collaborated with a number of Maya shaman-priests called *aj q'ijab'* (they of days, or daykeepers). Prior to reading the words of ancient Maya manuscripts like the *Popol Vuh*, it was customeary for one of them, don Vicente de León Abac of Momostenango, to first purify my xeroxed copy of the text by waving copal incense smoke over it and asking forgiveness of the ancestors who had written the original for disturbing them. When I asked why he did this, he replied that to read the thoughts of

ancient ancestors is to make their spirits present in the room and give them a living voice. Such power must be approached with great seriousness, and all care taken to be faithful to their original ideas in any transcription or translation. At the end of our work sessions, he politely dismissed the gods and ancestors involved in that day's reading with his thanks and asked pardon for any offense we might have given.[84]

This attitude, which has survived among a people whose connection to their ancient traditions was violently attacked about five hundred years ago, may well be representative of the reverence with which sacred words were once held in other cultures around the world, where connections with the ancient traditions were interrupted thousands of years before rather than hundreds. Either way, it should serve as a warning to us to approach the ancient sacred stories with proper respect and frame of mind, and to realize how precious the words -- and living voice -- of our ancestors should be in our lives to this day.

The narrative of the Popol Vuh begins with the creation account, presided over by three pairs of gods, identified as the Framer and the Shaper (one pair), Sovereign and Quetzal Serpent (another pair), and Xmucane and Xpiyacoc (a third pair). Later in the account, another god is introduced, named Heart of Sky, who appears to be a triple god: the text tells us that he is also called Huracan, and declares: "First is Thunderbolt Huracan, second is Youngest Thunderbolt, and third is Sudden Thunderbolt. These three together are Heart of Sky."[85]

Regarding the importance of the deity Heart of Sky, Professor Christenson tells us:

U K'ux Kaj (Heart of Sky -- also called Huracan) appears to be the principal god in the *Popol Vuh* account. He is the only deity to appear in every phase of the creation, as well as throughout the mythologic and historical portions of the text. K'ux refers to the heart as the source of the "vital spirit" of a thing, or that which gives it life. According to Coto's dictionary, it is also believed to be the center of thought and imagination. This deity, therefore, combines the powers of life and creativity, which are believed to exist in the midst of the heavens. During each creative period, Heart of Sky is the deity who first conceives the idea of what is to be formed. Other deities then carry out his will by giving it material expression.[86]

The fact that Heart of Sky is also named Huracan, and that he is explicitly identified with the thunderbolt is extremely significant, and will be seen to have important parallels to other deities around the globe who are associated with the same part of the heavens. Thunderbolt-weilding gods are almost exclusively associated with the constellation Hercules in the myths I have examined from various cultures, including the god Zeus of ancient Greece, Jove of the ancient Latins, Thor of the ancient Norse, Indra of ancient India, and Jehovah or Yahweh of the Bible.

Below is an image from the oldest surviving Maya book, dating to the period between AD 1200 and AD 1345, and known today as the Dresden Codex because it was taken to Europe at some point and found its way to Vienna, possibly being sent as a gift or tribute by Hernán Cortés to Charles V during the 1500s, and was later purchased by the librarian of the Royal Library in Dresden (in modern-day Germany), where it remains to this day -- the library now having been renamed the Saxon State and University

Library Dresden. The Dresden Codex is a Maya text, thought to have originated among the Maya of the Yucatán area, and it contains hieroglyphic writing and illustrations. The text itself covers astronomical tables, local histories, and a Flood account.

The image below, from the second page of the codex, shows a deity wielding a thunderbolt, and depicted in the characteristic "deep knee bend" posture that indicates the constellation Hercules in the night sky. The similarities to other depictions of Hercules-figures in myth from other cultures around the globe is unmistakable -- see for example the depiction of Zeus battling Typhon on an ancient Greek vase, in which the body position is nearly identical, and the thunderbolts themselves are also remarkably similar:

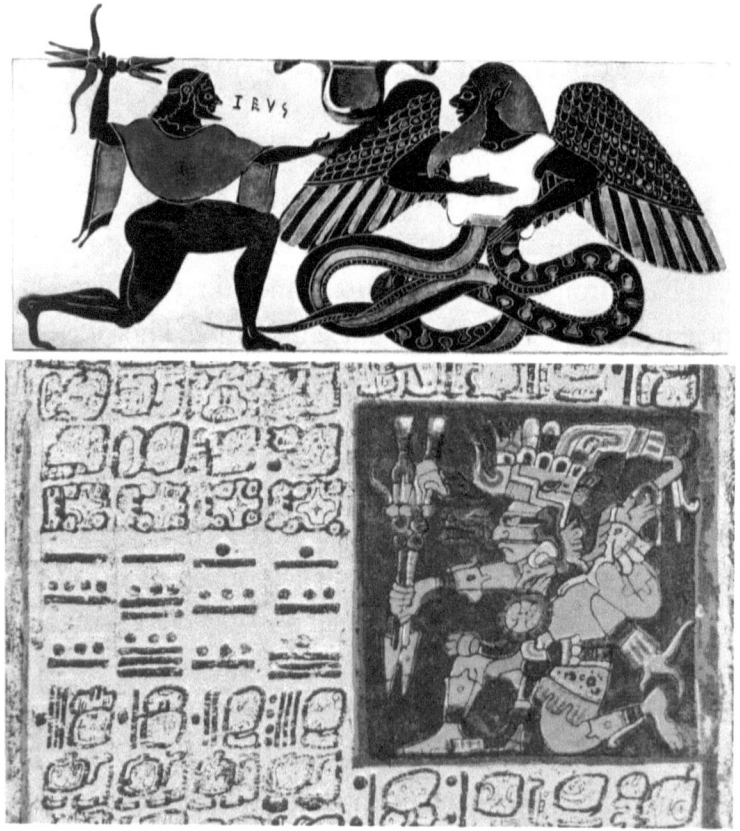

The similarities of the posture of both Zeus and the thunderbolt-wielding Huracan to the outline of the constellation Hercules should be immediately apparent at this point. Below, the image from the Dresden Codex is juxtaposed with the stars of Hercules. Despite the fact that the artist responsible for the artwork in the Maya text has reversed the direction that the god is facing (not uncommon in other artwork from other cultures as well), the connection to the constellation is undeniable:

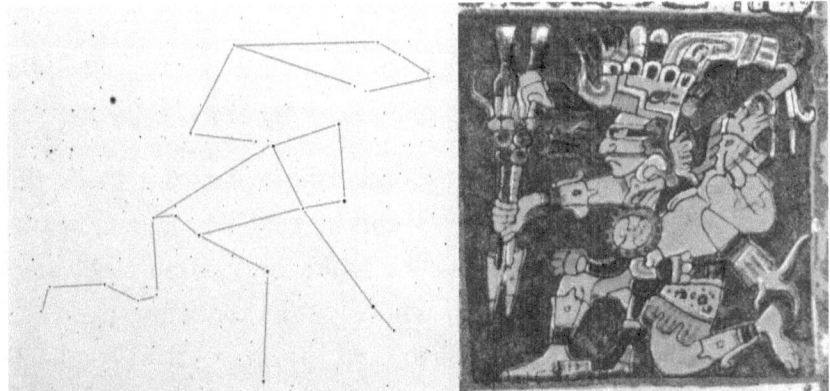

Allen Christenson confirms that the name Huracan (*Juraqan*) literally means "one leg."[87] It is possible that Huracan is related in some way to the figure of the god K'awil or K'awiil of the Maya, who was depicted with one human leg and one serpentine leg: note in the star-chart above showing the outline of Hercules that the rear leg (the deeply-bent leg) could be envisioned as being serpentine in nature.

Turning now to the other deities described by the Popol Vuh as being involved in the creation account, we come to Xpiyacoc and Xmucane. These two are called by many names and epithets: the Patriarch and the Midwife, the Protector and the Shelterer, Great White Peccary and Coati, among many other titles (usually given in pairs, with one title referring to Xpiyacoc and one to Xmucane).

The fact that the goddess Xmucane is called "Coati," after the long-nosed, ring-tailed, jungle-dwelling coatimundi (who are members of the Procyonidae family along with racoons, ringtails, and kinkajous), is noteworthy. Where have we seen a myth in which the woman is given a description that relates to a similarly pointy-nosed animal? And what could this fact tell us about the possible celestial identity of the creator goddess of the Popol Vuh? These two primary deities are also referred to as *She Who Has Borne Children*, and *He Who Has Begotten Sons*.

These characteristics -- the fact that she is referred to as the goddess who has borne children, and that she has characteristics of a coati -- indicate that Xmucane is almost certainly associated with the constellation Virgo, whose outline is suggestive of a woman in the act of giving birth, and the shape of whose head (long, and tapering to a point) gave rise to the description in the Australian myth of the woman as a "bandicoot woman."

As for the identity of Xpiyacoc, also known as He Who Has Begotten Sons, it is less easy to identify him for certain, although we would suspect that his identity is to be found among the constellations most often paired with Virgo as a consort: Boötes, Hercules, or (less frequently) Ophiuchus. Since we can already be quite confident that the constellation Hercules represents the god Heart of Sky, it is probably safe to assume that Xpiyacoc is associated with Boötes.

It is noteworthy that he is referred to by the name Great White Peccary in the Popol Vuh. A peccary (also called a javelina) is a pig-like animal, with short straight tusks, found throughout the Americas. In later volumes, we will see that the constellation

Cetus the Whale will sometimes play the role of a boar in ancient myth, and so it is possible that Xpiyacoc is associated with Cetus, based on this association found in other myths.

However, Cetus is not particularly close to Virgo in the heavens and is not commonly connected with Virgo as a consort in any myth I have encounted thus far. I believe an identification of Xpiyacoc with Boötes is much more likely, not only based on the proximity to Virgo and association as her lover in many other myths, but also from the fact that the outline of Boötes features an outsized head with a long pipe-feature protruding from it, which could be envisioned as a tusk.

Below are images of a peccary (top) and coati (bottom):

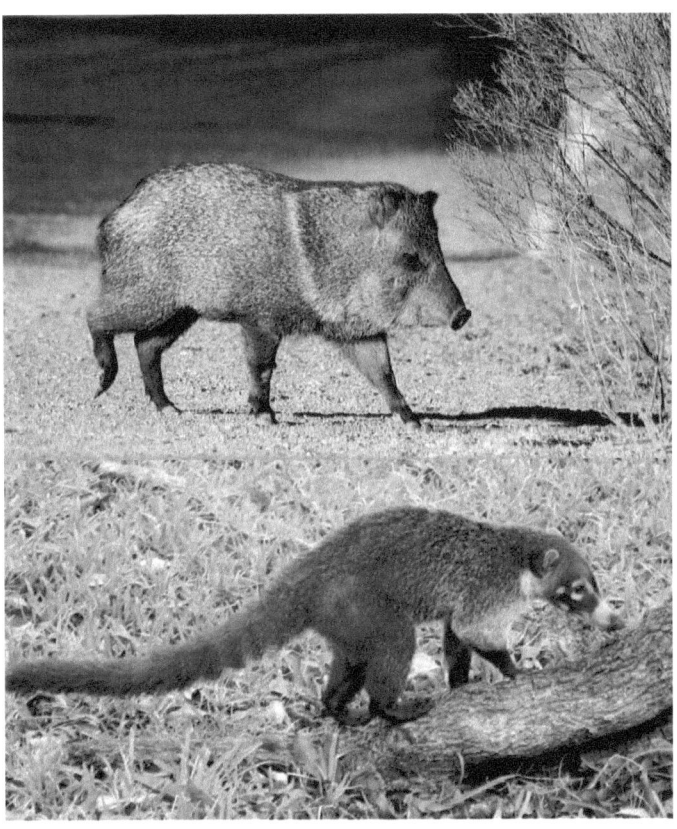

And below, for ease of comparison, are the constellations Boötes and Virgo:

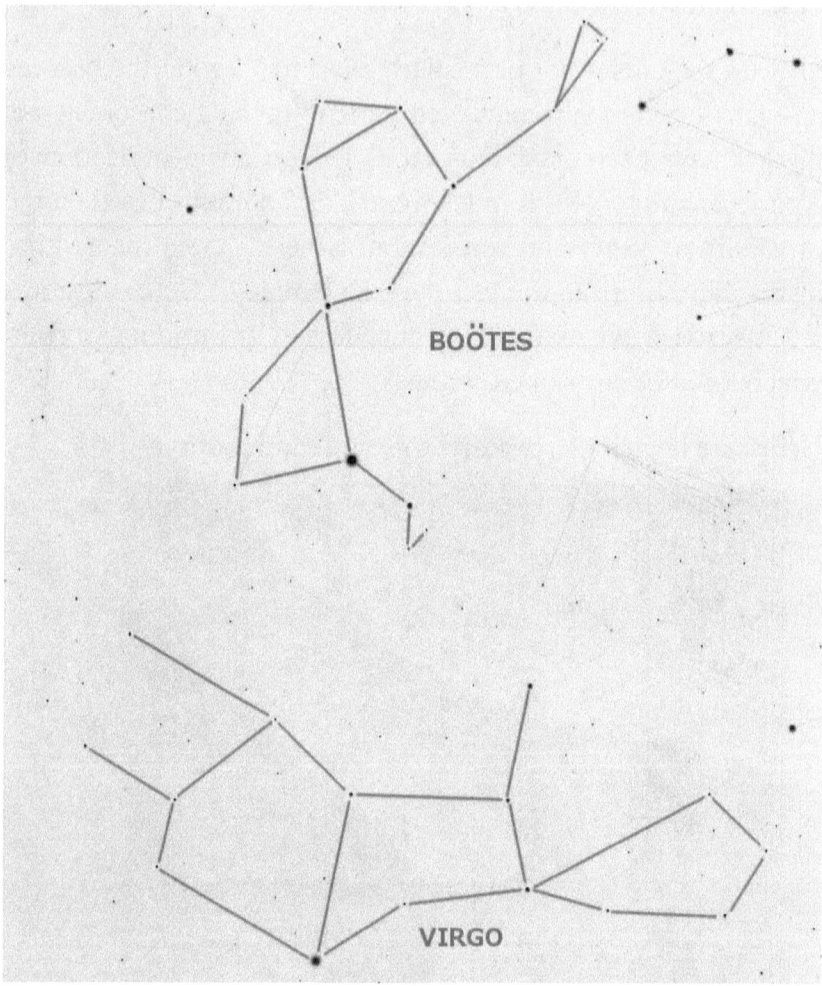

The gods who participate in the creation story in the Popol Vuh, besides Xpiyacoc and Xmucane and the deity Heart of Sky include Sovereign (*Tepew*) and Quetzal Serpent (*Q'ukumatz*). Of these deities, Professor Christenson tells us (beginning with Sovereign):

Tepew (Sovereign) is one of several words in the Popol Vuh that were borrowed from the central Mexican group of languages, Nahua, variants of which were spoken by both the epi-Toltec and Aztec nations. This word is the Quiché form of the Nahua tepeuh, meaning "conqueror" or "majesty" (Campbell 1970, 4). Coto and Basseta record that in the Colonial era, the Quichés recognized the word as referring to "majesty, dignity, lordship, power." Tedlock and Recinos translate the word as "sovereign," which I prefer to the more descriptive "majesty" used by Edmonson.[88]

And of Quetzal Serpent (translated by others as "Feathered Serpent" or "Plumed Serpent"), he writes:

Q'ukumatz may be translated as "Quetzal Serpent" or, less accurately, as "Feathered Serpent." Q'uq' refers to the quetzal bird, *Paromacrus mocinno,* one of the most beatufiul birds in the world. It inhabits the cloud forests of southern Mesoamerica between 3,000 and 4,000 feet in elevation. Both male and female have brilliantly colored iridescent blue/green feathers on their wings, tail, and crest, while their breasts are a bright crimson. The shade of blue or green depends on the angle of light striking its feathers. The male quetzal's tail feathers were highly prized by Maya royalty for their beauty and size, often reaching three feet in length. The unique coloration of the bird carried profound religious significance for the Maya. Its predominant blue/green feathers represented sky and vegetation, both symbols of life. Its red breast represented fire, the force that quickens life. Kumat is a general term for "snake" or "serpent." The serpent was a common Maya symbol for regeneration or rebirth because of its tendency to periodically shed its skin to reveal a newer and brighter one. The combination of an avian lord of the skies with a serpentine lord of the earth and underworld gave this god power over all levels of the Maya universe. He is undoubtedly related to the well-known god Quetzalcoatl (Nahua for "Quetzal Serpent") worshiped by the Aztecs of Central Mexico.[89]

Note that in the 1985 translation of the Popol Vuh, by the late Professor Dennis Tedlock of State University of New York, Buffalo, the deities named Sovereign and Plumed Serpent are treated as a single entity, Sovereign Plumed Serpent. It is certainly possible that one constellation may simultanesouly play the role of both Sovereign and Plumed Serpent, just as I believe that the constellation Hercules plays the role of Heart of Sky who is who is simultaneously the three-fold deities Thunderbolt Huracan, Youngest Thunderbolt, and Sudden Thunderbolt.

In the first edition of this volume, I argued that Quetzal Serpent might be associated in the heavens with the long sinuous form of the constellation Hydra, which is seen in the heavens as a serpent, with the constellation Corvus the Crow on its back to combine the aspects of a bird and a snake.

However, with the benefit of having looked at many additional myths since the publication of that first edition of Volume One in 2015, I believe it is possible to suggest some other celestial connections for the identity of this extremely important Maya deity (who is also undoubtedly related to the Aztec deity Quetzalcoatl, as argued above by Allen Christenson).

One important clue which we find mentioned more than once in the text of the Popol Vuh itself is the fact that when the world is created, Heart of Sky consults with Sovereign Plumed Serpent (or Sovereign and Quetzal Serpent). Here is the Maya text, as translated by Allen Christenson:

Then came his world. Heart of Sky arrived here with Sovereign and Quetzal Serpent in the darkness, in the night. He spoke with Sovereign and Quetzal Serpent. They talked together then. They thought and they pondered. They reached an accord, bringing together their words and their thoughts. Then they gave birth, heartening one another. Beneath the light, they gave birth to humanity. They arranged for germination and creation of the trees and the bushes, the germination of all life and creation, in the darkness and in the night, by Heart of Sky, who is called Huracan.[90]

Since we have already identified Heart of Sky, who is called Huracan, with the constellation Hercules in the heavens, we can ask ourselves which heavenly figure Hercules would most appear to be speaking with, and the answer is unequivocally the constellation Ophiuchus, located immediately below Hercules, and towards which Hercules appears to be bending down, perhaps in order to converse.

From this alone, we might begin to suspect that the constellation Ophiuchus -- which indeed has a serpent as part of the figure in the sky -- might be associated with Sovereign, with Quetzal Serpent, or with both.

Another clue is the description of creation which ensues after Heart of Sky and Sovereign and Quetzal Serpent converse. We are told that they "called forth mountains out of water," and that "the waterways were divided, their branches coursing among the mountains."[91] As we will see when examining myths in later volumes (particularly in *Star Myths of the World, Volume Two; Myths of Ancient Greece*), the constellation Ophiuchus will often play the role of a mountain in world myth, and it appears that the many-headed form of Scorpio just beneath Ophiuchus was often envisioned as streams pouring down at the base of Ophiuchus (see for instance the discussion of the celestial identity of the grotto of Calypso in the chapters on the Odyssey).[92]

Below is a star-chart showing the relative positions of Hercules and Ophiuchus. Note how Hercules could be envisioned as bending down to conspire together with Ophiuchus, as Heart of Sky and Sovereign and Quetzal Serpent are said to do in the text:

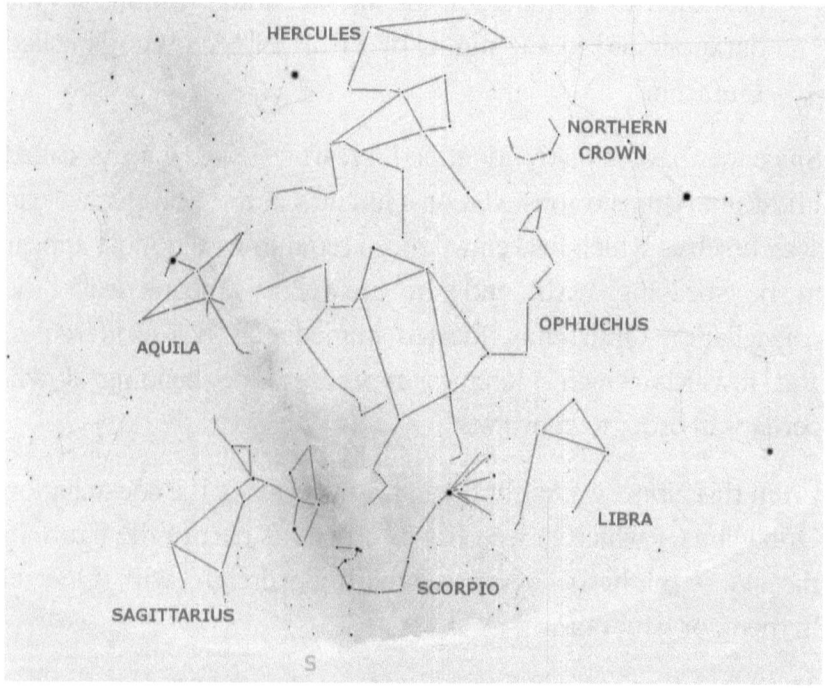

In another passage in the Popol Vuh, an apparently historical figure named Plumed Serpent is described as holding the offices of *Keeper of the Mat* and *Keeper of the Reception House Mat* in the fourth generation of Quiché lords (Allen Christenson translates as "Ah Pop" and "Ah Pop of the Reception House").[93]

The outline of Ophiuchus itself is house-like in appearance, and we have already had occasion to see Ophiuchus playing the role of a house in certain myths examined previously (such as the story of Deer Hunter, up on the roof). It is possible that this detail helps confirm a connection between the figure of Quetzal Serpent and the constellation Ophiuchus.

In the same passage describing the (ostensibly historical) Plumed Serpent who serves as Keeper of the Mat and Keeper of the Reception House Mat in the fourth generation of Quiché lords, we are told that this Plumed Serpent can undergo transformations:

> In one transformation he would rise up into the sky, and in another transformation he would go down to Xibalba. In another transformation he would be a serpent, truly becoming a serpent. In another transformation he would make himself into an eagle; and in another transformation into a jaguar. Truly his appearance would be that of an eagle and of a jaguar. In another transformation he would become a pool of blood. Mere pooled blood he would become. Truly he was an enchanted lord in his essence.[94]

I think it is very likely that Plumed Serpent or Quetzal Serpent is associated with Ophiuchus in the heavens. These transformations can be seen as referring to constellations near to Ophiuchus in the sky, particularly the eagle (Aquila, immediately adjacent to Ophiuchus) and the pool of blood (probably the widest portion of the Milky Way band, visible between the bow of Sagittarius and the knee of the lead leg of Ophiuchus in the star-chart on the previous page). The transformation into a serpent should also be obvious enough, since Ophiuchus holds a serpent which stretches out to either side of the central body of the constellation.

The transformation into a jaguar is more difficult to identify dogmatically, but it is possible that Scorpio (just below Ophiuchus). We have already seen a myth from Africa in which it appears that Scorpio plays the role of a *leopard* who is crushed beneath an upturned mortar (Ophiuchus). In other myths to be examined in later volumes of this series, we will see that Scorpio plays the role of a crouching dog in more than one myth (including as the dog Cerberus, who crouches at the gates of the Underworld in the myths of ancient Greece -- the gates of the Underworld being associated with the doorway-shaped central body of Ophiuchus, which could also explain why this passage from the Popol Vuh describes Plumed Serpent in his transformations going down to Xibalba).

On the right side (as we face it) of the image on the following page is an illustration from the Dresden Codex, a hand-drawn copy of which is included in the 1996 edition of Dennis Tedlock's translation of Popol Vuh, on page 64, and identified as a depiction of Sovereign Plumed Serpent.

The caption beside the illustration in the Tedlock translation reads:

> Sovereign Plumed Serpent: Here he is seated, holding a snake in his hand. On his back he wears a quetzal bird, with its head behind his, its wings at the level of his shoulders, and its tail hanging down to the ground. From the Dresden Codex.[95]

When I saw this image of a deity with a quetzal perched on his shoulder, its head at the same level as the god's head and immediately behind it, I was immediately reminded of the image of the statue of King Chephren (or Khafre) of ancient Egypt, which was included on page 469 of the first edition of this volme of Star Myths (on the very last page of the book, in fact), which shows the falcon-god Horus behind the head of the king. I have juxtaposed that image from ancient Egypt with the depiction of Sovereign Plumed Serpent in the Dresden Codex, below. I believe that the figure of the falcon-god behind the head of the king conveys the idea of the divine nature, the Higher Self, to whom we have access in this life and with whom we should be reconnecting and reintegrating during our earthly sojourn:

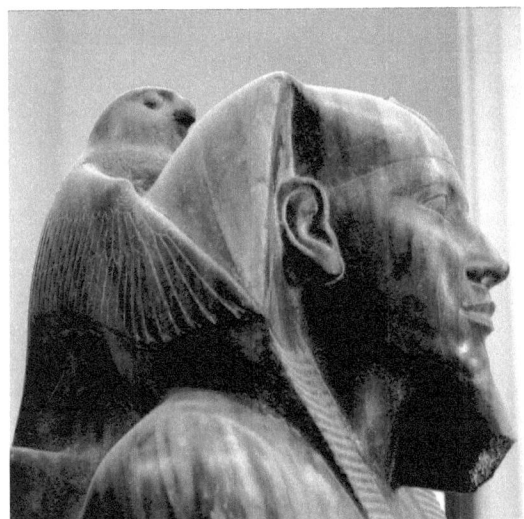 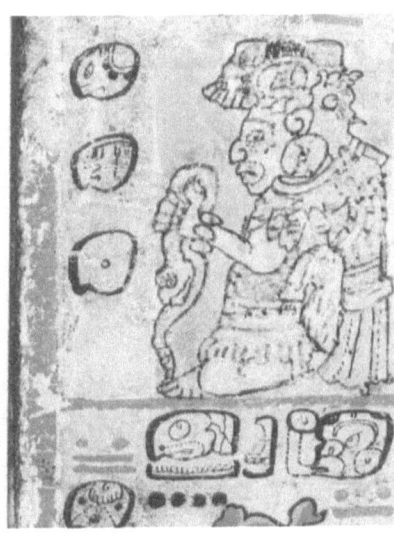

Note that the figure of Sovereign Plumed Serpent in the Maya codex is holding a serpent in one hand, and the bird is peeking over his shoulder on the opposite side: this could indicate that the Maya envisioned the western (head-end) of the line of stars held by Ophiuchus as the *Quetzal part* of the deity, and the eastern (tail-end) as the *serpent part* of the deity.

Below is the same image of the figure from the Dresden Codex identified as Sovereign Plumed Serpent in the 1996 Revised Edition of Dennis Tedlock's translation of Popol Vuh. This time, Ophiuchus has been juxtaposed to show how the "tail-side" of the serpent held by the constellation (on the left as we face the page, and on the east as we face the constellation in the sky) corresponds to the limp rattlesnake held by the figure in the codex image, and likewise how the "head-end" of the serpent held by the constellation (on the right as we face the page, and on the west as we face the constellation in the sky) corresponds to the bird peering over the shoulder of the deity:

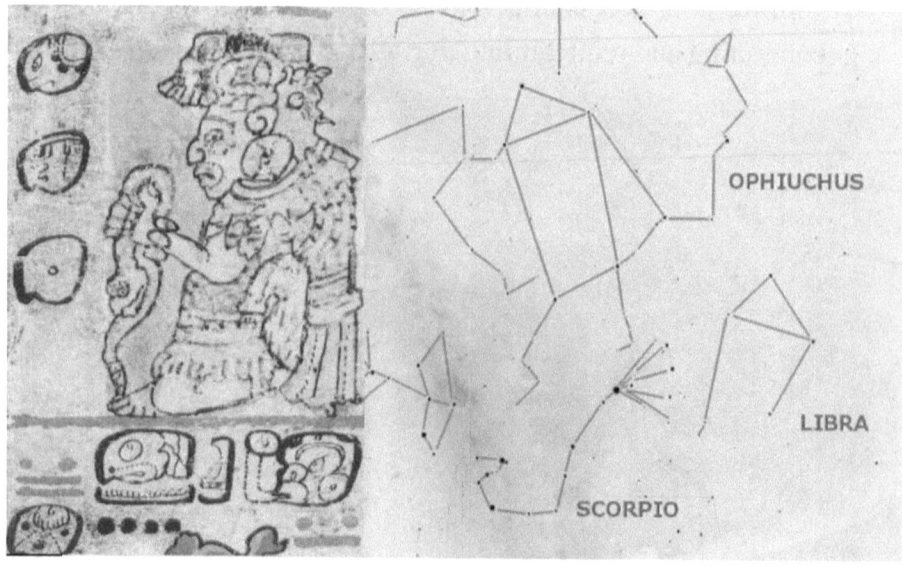

That western, head-end side of the serpent held by Ophiuchus shows up in myth in many different guises, including as a wine goblet or wine-cup, as a pomegranate or other fruit, as a bunch of grapes, and even as the owl who sometimes accompanies the goddess Athena in Greek myth. Thus, I believe it is highly likely that this same celestial feature may have been interpreted as a quetzal or even as a Quetzal Serpent in the figures of Sovereign and Quetzal Serpent of the Popol Vuh.

As noted by Allen Christenson in a quotation cited earlier, there are undeniable parallels between the figure of Q'ukumatz (whose name means Quetzal Serpent in the language of the Maya) and the Aztec deity known as Quetzalcoatl (whose name means the

176

same thing in the Nahua language). As Graham Hancock has extensively documented in his groundbreaking 1995 book *Fingerprints of the Gods*, the figure of Quetzalcoatl played an absolutely central role in the sacred traditions of Central America, and apparently among the civilizations of South America as well, where he was known as Viracocha, whose name means "Foam of the Sea." Indeed, Graham Hancock argues that the same figure takes on all of the following names in various Mesoamerican and South American cultures: Quetzalcoatl, Viracocha, Kukulkan, Gucumatz, Con, Kon Tiki, Tupaca, and many others.[96]

While Graham Hancock in that volume argues that this benevolent figure, who is described as coming from the sea and imparting many civilizing technologies and principles to the people, may have been an actual person, possibly coming from the cultures of the eastern hemisphere in ancient times, and while it is certainly possible that such a figure did exist due to the evidence that trans-oceanic communication did indeed take place during ancient times and continuing up through the centuries prior to Columbus, I believe that in all the descriptions of this mysterious figure we can see clear signs of association with the constellation Ophiuchus as it appears in the sky and as it manifests in other myths from around the world. Thus, if indeed some historical figure came from the eastern hemisphere in ancient times as proposed in *Fingerprints of the Gods*, I would argue that this individual (or individuals) was consciously emulating *aspects and characteristics of Ophiuchus-figures* found in other world traditions, right down to the choice of clothing (long robes and sandals, suggested by the outline of the constellation itself).

Note that the very name Viracocha ("Foam of the Sea") is indicative of the constellation Ophiuchus, which stands beside the column of the Milky Way and in fact has one foot (on the left

177

as we face the star-charts) within the starry path of the Milky Way itself. The Milky Way can be conclusively shown to have been envisioned as the foamy verge of the sea in many ancient myths, including throughout the Iliad (as discussed in *Star Myths of the World, Volume Two*). We will see the Milky Way playing the foam of the sea in the Maui story that is examined later in this volume as well.

Graham Hancock cites accounts which refer to this figure of Viracocha or Quetzalcoatl as a "wise instructor" who:

> came from across the sea in a boat that moved by itself without paddles. He was a tall, bearded white man who taught people to use fire for cooking. He also built houses and showed couples that they could live together as husband and wife; and since people often quarreled in those days, he taught them to live in peace.[97]

These traits can all be identified with the figure of Ophiuchus in the heavens and in other myth-systems from around the world. Note that Ophiuchus is located immediately adjacent to the Milky Way band and indeed to the widest and brightest portion of the galaxy (the Galactic Core or Galactic Center), which was often associated with fire in the myths of the world. Here, Quetzalcoatl is being described as giving the people fire, teaching them to use fire for cooking, in common with other myths we have examined previously regarding the origin of fire. He is also described as building houses, and we can easily find dozens of myths from many different cultures in which the outline of the central portion of the Ophiuchus constellation is associated with a house or a shelter. He is also described as showing the people that they could live together as husband and wife, and this may have to do with the fact that Ophiuchus is located immediately adjacent to the constellations of Virgo and Boötes, who are described as a husband and wife in numerous myths.

The description of this benevolent figure coming from across the sea in a boat that moves by itself with no paddles could of course be describing an ocean-crossing ship with sails, but it is also easily explained as a celestial metaphor: the figure of Ophiuchus standing directly above Scorpio appears in many myths as a human figure in a boat or ship. We will see in *Star Myths of the World, Volume Two*, on Greek mythology, that Odysseus tied to his ship's mast as he passes by the Sirens is a figuring in myth of Ophiuchus above Scorpio (with Cygnus and Aquila likely playing the role of the Sirens, possibly joined by Sagittarius below). And we will see in *Star Myths of the World, Volume Four*, on Norse mythology, that the towering figure of Ophiuchus will often appear in Norse myth as a jotun, and sometimes as a jotun standing in a boat.

Finally, we see that in the above passage, Quetzalcoatl is described as a peacemaker, teaching the people not to quarrel but rather to live in peace. Other sources cited by Graham Hancock in *Fingerprints of the Gods* declare that this benevolent figure "condemned sacrifices, except of fruits and flowers, and was known as the god of peace."[98]

This description is consistent with other benevolent figures who can be shown to be associated with this same important constellation in other myth-systems, including Dionysus in Greek myth, Baldr in Norse myth, and perhaps most especially Christ in the New Testament. In my examinations of all of these figures, I found abundant evidence linking them to the figure of Ophiuchus. The fact that many of the characteristics ascribed to Viracocha or Quetzalcoatl have a "Christ-like" sound to them is not surprising, if both are associated with Ophiuchus in the heavens, and if the characteristics ascribed to Ophiuchus in that ancient system (which appears to be remembered in the various myths of the world) involved the bringing of civilizing technologies, the promulgation of peaceful virtues, and the end of the sacrifice of animals (or indeed of humans).

The traditions cited in numerous sources which describe Viracocha or Quetzalcoatl as a tall, slender, bearded man of pale complexion, wearing long robes and sandals, need not necessarily describe a visitor from the eastern hemisphere of European ancestry. Indeed, celestial figures are often described in world myth as being garbed in dazzling white, as we saw in the story of Deer Hunter and White Corn Maiden, when the mysterious silent visitor arrived in the village. It is not surprising that figures associated with the stars of the heavens would be described at times as dazzlingly white. Even in Norse myth, Baldr (who is undoubtedly associated with Ophiuchus, as I demonstrate in *Star Myths of the World, Volume Four*) is specifically described as dazzlingly white in the surviving original texts.

Note that Ophiuchus often plays the role of an angel in the Biblical scriptures, and these too are traditionally understood to be dazzling beings of light, arrayed in glorious white robes. In *Star Myths of the World, Volume Three (Star Myths of the Bible)*, I discuss at some length the angel described in Revelation chapter 10, who holds a little book and has his right foot in the sea, and his left foot on dry ground. This angel can definitely be identified as an Ophiuchus figure: the constellation clearly has its right foot planted in the Milky Way (in the sea), while its left foot is not in the Milky Way (hence on dry ground).[99]

Continuing with just a few more examples from the Popol Vuh (although by now it should be quite apparent that this sacred text is based on the same celestial system which informs the other myths, scriptures and sacred stories around the globe), we cannot leave our examination without some discussion of the figures of the Hero Twins, whose exploits and adventures dominate much of the narrative after the creation portion of the text is complete. These two twins are named Hunahpu and Xbalanque, and they are first introduced in a story in which they defeat a great bird-entity named Seven Macaw.

The Hero Twins are the children of another twin, One Hunahpu (whose twin brother is named Seven Hunahpu). One Hunahpu is defeated in a ball game in the land of the dead, Xibalba, by the lords of death, and loses his head. He is later restored, in an episode with some parallels to the Osiris myth, by his sons Hunahpu and Xbalanque. The head of One Hunahpu is hung in a tree, where it becomes indistinguishable from a calabash. A maiden named Blood Moon, daughter of a lord named Blood Gatherer, hears about this unusual calabash head, and comes to see it, and she is impregnated by the saliva which the head spits into the palm of her hand -- she later gives birth to the Hero Twins (an "immaculate conception" and virgin birth: we will see additional examples of this same pattern later in this volume).

I believe it is quite probable that the calabash which is hung up in the tree is once again the circlet at the "head-end" of the "serpent" held by the constellation Ophiuchus, towards which Virgo can be envisioned as reaching out her arm (the outstretched arm being a distinctive characteristic of the constellation Virgo). Other possibilities for the identity of the calabash head include the arc of Corona Borealis (which Hercules-figures are described as hanging from the rafters in some other myths we will examine) or even the large somewhat bulbous head of the constellation Boötes – but I am most inclined towards the "head-end" of the serpent of Ophiuchus because it is described in other myths as a fruit in the Underworld (such as the pomegranate which Persephone eats in Hades, in the Greek myth).

The text of the Popol Vuh specifically says that the maiden Blood Moon reached out her right hand towards the calabash skull (in fact, the text reveals that the head directs her to reach out her hand, and then it tells us that she does so, after which the bone spits out its saliva, to land squarely in her hand).[100] It is also possible that the figure of Coma Berenices represents the spit from the calabash head which lands in the hand of the maiden.

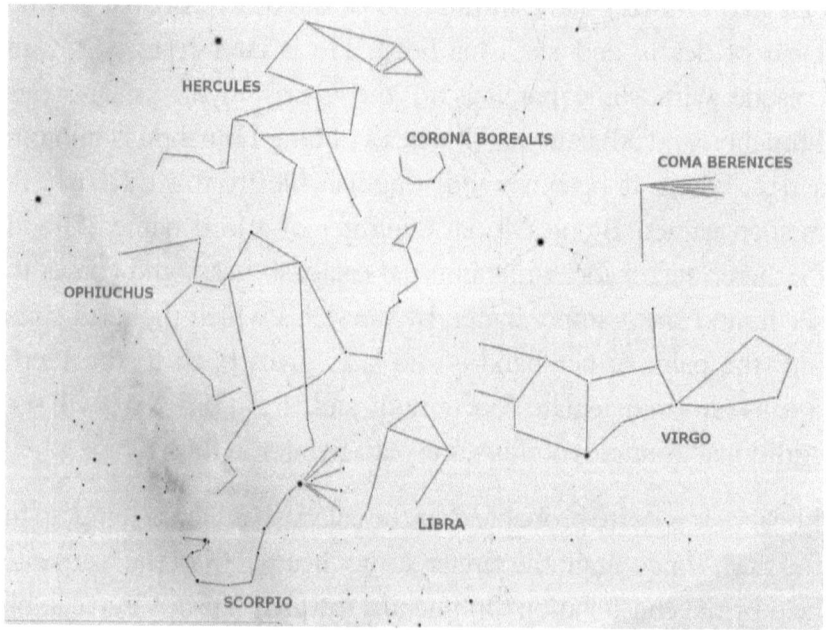

Following the creation account in the Popol Vuh, the first exploits of the Hero Twins which are recounted are their defeat of the powerful but arrogant being named Seven Macaw, and later his two sons Zipacna and Earthquake (Cabracan).

The text tells us that there was once a great nance tree – a tropical fruit tree (*Byrosinima crassifolia*) bearing fruit about the size of a cherry. A prideful bird-lord, named Seven Macaw, would ascend the tree each day to knock down some of its fruit for his food. He had precious stones for eyes and teeth, and metal discs around them, which made him very handsome. Seven Macaw declares that he is the sun, although the text then tells us that "Seven Macaw was not truly the sun, but he puffed himself up in this way because of his plumage and his gold and his silver."[101]

The Popol Vuh says that, being gods, Hunahpu and Xbalanque were troubled at the arrogance of Seven Macaw and "saw evil in this prideful one who acted according to his own desires before the face of Heart of Sky."[102] They note that in some way, the riches over which Seven Macaw keeps watch (including jade, gold, silver, jewels, and other "glittering things") will in some way make it impossible to create humanity, because "people cannot be created where only gold and silver are glory."[103]

Allen Christenson, in a footnote, points out that this speech by the Hero Twins in the Popol Vuh indicates that "the twin heroes Hunahpu and Xbalanque did not act alone or without authority" when they set out to defeat Seven Macaw and his sons: "All their actions were first ordained by the god Heart of Sky, and were carried out under his direction."[104]

The Hero Twins hid themselves in the leaves beneath the tree, and when Seven Macaw perched on the nance tree, Hunahpu shot him in the jaw with his blowgun (Hunahpu's name may mean "Master of the Blowgun" or "Blowgun Hunter" as explained in a footnote by Professor Christenson).[105] In great pain, Seven Macaw sailed down to alight on the ground, where Hunahpu ran out to seize the bird-lord, but Seven Macaw instead seized Hunahpu's arm in his powerful beak, and wrenched the arm off at the shoulder! Then he took the arm home to his wife and hung it up over the fire.

But, Seven Macaw was in great pain, and he complained to his wife of the two evil beings who had shot him in the jaw.

Meanwhile, the twins went to see the Grandfather and Grandmother (Xpiyacoc and Xmucane again, who are the grandparents of the Hero Twins), Grandfather being described as bent over with age, and Grandmother faint with weakness, and asked for their help in retrieving the arm of Hunahpu and avenging themselves upon Seven Macaw. They proposed that if Grandmother and Grandfather came with them, Seven Macaw would be less suspicious, and then Grandmother and Grandfather could say that the two boys could remove worms from teeth, and thus bring comfort to Seven Macaw's aching jaw.

And this is just what happened. As they approached, Seven Macaw let off from his crying over his damaged jaw and aching teeth, and asked from whence the aged travelers came, and if it was their children who were accompanying them (meaning the twins).

Grandmother and Grandfather told Seven Macaw that the twins were their grandchildren, and that the specialty of the group was the removal of worms from teeth, and the remedy of ailments of the eyes. This got Seven Macaw's attention, as the Hero Twins had intended, and he asked for their medical treatment. The visitors removed his teeth, and replaced them with "mere shiny white grains of maize, and immediately his face fell. No longer did he appear as a lord."[106] Then they removed his eyes as well, made up as they were of precious metal, and after that Seven Macaw's pride was taken away, and he could just stare vacantly.

Eventually, Seven Macaw died, as did his wife, and Hunahpu was able to get his arm back again, which he replaced in its socket -- and soon it was as good as new.

The celestial foundations of this famous episode from the Popol Vuh are fairly self-evident. Allen Christenson notes that "the shooting of a bird deity by twin boys armed with blowguns is a frequent subject of Maya art at least as far back as the Early Classic period (AD 200 - 600), indicating that the theological foundation of this incident is of great antiquity."[107]

Below is one such representation, found on a Maya vase from that period, and showing a blowgunner aiming at an eagle-like bird in a tree. Other well-known representations reminiscent of this same incident include the carving on Steles 2 and 25 at Izapa, thought by most scholars to date back to the period of 300 BC to 100 BC, although some argue that they could have been as late as AD 250.

This vase showing a blowgunner and a bird was photographed by the famous photographer of Maya ceramic artwork Justin Kerr, and is designated as vase number K1226. This is my own drawing of what is depicted on that vase:

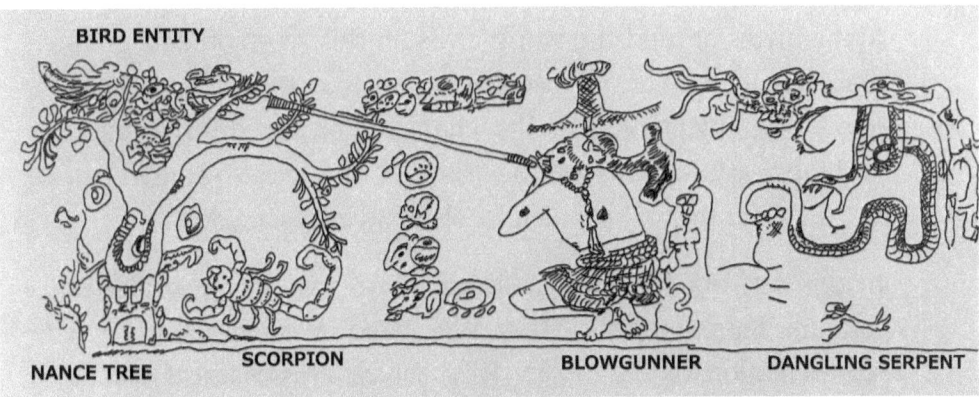

BIRD ENTITY

NANCE TREE   SCORPION   BLOWGUNNER   DANGLING SERPENT

I have named some of the elements present in the artwork for ease of reference. Starting from the left as we face it we see a tree, which I have called the "Nance Tree," and in a fork in the trunk we see a bird-entity with spread-eagled wings. At the base of the tree and to the left as we face the image we see a very obvioius scorpion. Continuing to the right, we see a crouching human figure aiming a very long blowgun towards the bird-entity in the tree: I have labeled him "Blowgunner." Finally, to the right of the blowgunner as we face the image we see a dangling serpent which appears to be a rattlesnake, based on the rattles at the end of its tail, opening its mouth wide to reveal fangs and a long forked tongue.

That the scene on this ancient piece of Maya artwork is celestial in nature should be self-evident: the enormous scorpion at the base of a tree containing a spread-eagled bird-entity is a clear giveaway to anyone who has become familiar with the constellations of the heavens and their frequent appearance in ancient myth and sacred artwork. The constellation Scorpio dominates the night sky during the summer months (summer for the northern hemisphere), and it is positioned at the base of the brightest portion of the Milky Way band, which stretches above it like a great tree, containing an Eagle: the constellation Aquila.

Many myths around the world envision this scorpion as a great dragon, curled up at the base of a mighty tree: we will find one in the Norse mythology, in the character of the dread dragon Nidhogg, who gnaws at the roots of the great World-Tree, Yggdrasil (at the top of which we also find a great eagle).

In this artwork from a Classic-era Maya vase, the tree almost certainly represents the Milky Way band. We may even see a representation of the "Dark Rift" which crosses the Galactic

Center, envisioned as a kind of oval-shaped knot in the widest part of the trunk, just above the face-like feature that the ancient artist has included at the foot of the tree.

Note that the scorpion in the artwork appears reversed compared to the direction that the constellation Scorpio faces in the sky (again, this is not uncommon in such artwork worldwide).

Based on this observation, we might then suspect that the figure of the rattlesnake which I have labeled "Dangling Serpent" might in fact correspond to the serpent of Ophiuchus, which is to the left of the scorpion on the vase artwork but to the right (the west) as we face the constellations in the heavens:

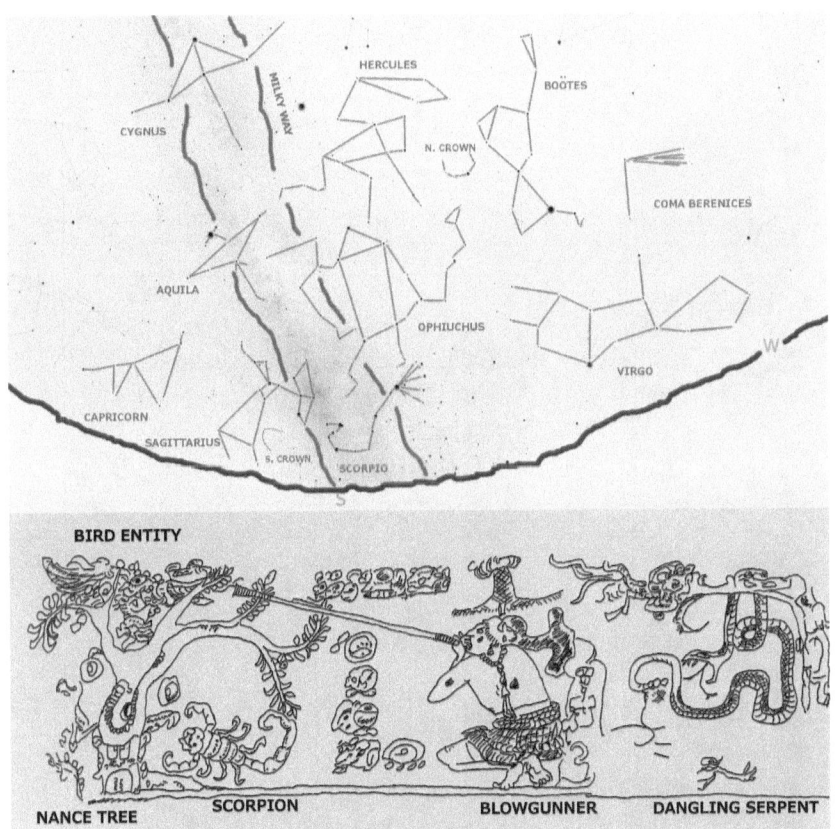

Below is another juxtaposition of the Maya vase artwork and the stars as we see them (from the perspective of a viewer in the northern hemisphere, facing south). This time, I have flipped horizontally the artwork on the vase, so that the scorpion's stinger is on the left, just as the stinger of Scorpio in the night sky points left (east) as we face south. I have also continued the artwork in a "wrapping" fashion, because on the vase itself the artwork wraps in a continuous loop: thus, the "Dangling Serpent" on the left edge of the drawing on the previous page is also next to the "Nance Tree" on the vase itself, just as Ophiuchus is next to the Milky Way in the heavens:

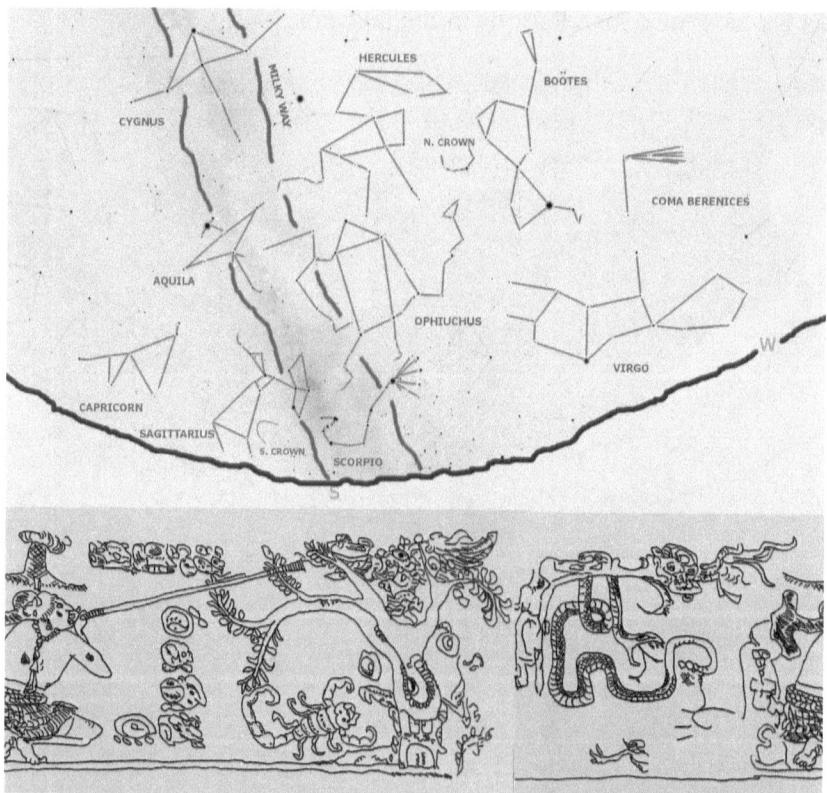

Understanding that this artwork wraps all the way around the original vase helps us understand that the figure of the

Blowgunner himself is actually next to the figure of the Dangling Serpent (which serpent, I argue, corresponds to Ophiuchus): that means that the Blowgunner is in the proper location and facing in the correct direction to correspond to the constellation Boötes in the heavens. Notice that Boötes, of course, has a distinctive "pipe" feature protruding from his mouth, which makes it very probable that Boötes was envisioned as a Blowgunner in the ancient Maya myths. Note also that the Blowgunner in the vase artwork is depicted in a crouching posture, very much corresponding to the outline of Boötes (especially once we notice that the artwork on the vase is "reversed" from the way we would expect to see the constellations in the night sky).

Below is a close-up of the depiction of the Blowgunner from the ancient Maya vase, flipped horizontally, in comparison to the outline of Boötes:

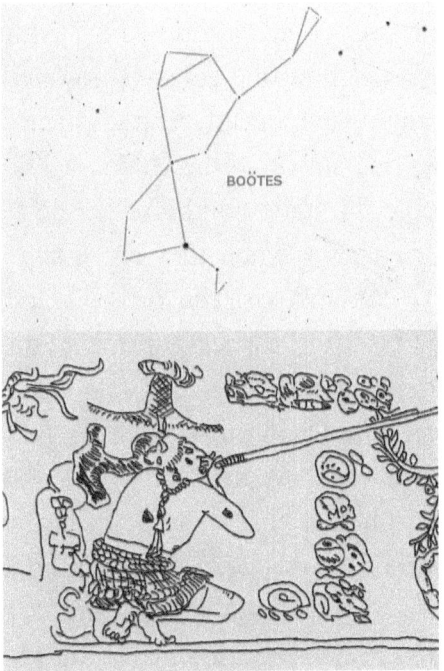

Based on the above analysis, and the fact that the name Hunahpu itself may translate directly to "Master of the Blowgun" or "Blowgun Hunter," as well as the fact that the Popol Vuh explicitly tells us that it is Hunahpu who fires the shot with the blowgun that strikes Seven Macaw, I would be fairly confident in identifying Hunahpu with the figure of Boötes in the heavens.

The identity of Xbalanque is somewhat more ambiguous. I would guess that he is most likely associated with Ophiuchus, since Ophiuchus and Boötes could both be envisioned as being birthed by the same mother (Virgo). Indeed, we will see in our analysis of Biblical scriptures in *Star Myths of the World, Volume Three* that the twins Jacob and Esau are probably identified with Scorpio and Ophiuchus (respectively).

Most likely, however, is an interpretation in which the Hero Twins Hunahpu and Xbalanque "move through" many different constellations during their various adventures. This pattern of taking on the characteristics of first one constellation and then another is very common among important central characters in myth-cycles, such as Moses or Samson in the Bible, or Dionysus or Achilles in ancient Greece. Hunahpu and Xbalanque take on many different disguises, especially when they are going down into the realm of Xibalba to contend with the lords of death, and thus I believe that they take on aspects of many different constellations in turn. At one point, they each lose their head (often a characteristic of Aquarius figures, such as John the Baptist in the New Testament). At another point, they are described as being bound (often a characteristic of Sagittarius figures, such as Joseph in the Genesis account, when he is sold into slavery and taken to Egypt). In some ancient artwork, Hunahpu is even depicted in disguise as a thunderbolt-god.

It should be very evident that the figure of Seven Macaw himself corresponds to one of the two "great birds" of the Milky Way, Aquila and Cygnus, and the details of the story almost certainly indicates Aquila the Eagle, who is located not far above Scorpio and Sagittarius, just beside Ophiuchus. Aquila indeed possesses a great staring "eye" -- the bright star Altair (Cygnus the Swan does not have a very bright star in the head of the constellation the way that Aquila does).

Also mentioned in the text although not cited in the summary above is the wife of Seven Macaw, named Chimalmat. In a note commenting upon this name, Allen Christenson writes:

> Chimalmat is almost certainly derived from the Nahuatl *chimalmatl*, meaning "shield bearer," a fairly common name for female deities. In Aztec legend, she was the mother of the Toltec priest-ruler Ce Acatl Topiltzin Quetzalcoatl. Chimalmat is also one of the names for the mother of the Aztecs' patron god, Huitzilopochtli, as well as the female bearer of cult objects in Aztec migration accounts. Alternatively, the name may be Quiché in origin, consisting of *chi* (preposition "at, in, to, on, from, etc.) and *malmat* (Basseta: to walk in hast) or *malmot* (Coto: "to appear unexpectedly," particularly with regard to a phantasm).[108]

If, as Allen Christenson suspects, this name is related to the Nahuatl word *chimalmatl* or "shield bearer," then this would indicated that the wife of Seven Macaw is associated with Ophiuchus, a constellation immediately adjacent to Aquila (and thus they are envisioned here as a married couple) and one which is envisioned as bearing a great shield in many world myths from other cultures as well. We will see in *Star Myths of the World*,

Volume Two that the goddess Athena can be confidently identified with the constellation Ophiuchus.

Also, in 2017, a very finely-carved gemstone was uncovered in a previously-undisturbed tomb in Pylos (on the western edge of the Peloponnese, in modern-day Greece). The tomb, dubbed the Tomb of the Griffin Warrior, was dated to around 1500 BC (the Mycenaean period), and many of the over 3,000 artifacts discovered within are thought to be of Minoan origin or at least inspired by Minoan art and capabilities.

The gemstone in question, which has been called the Pylos Combat Agate, was revealed to the world in November of 2017, after the millennia of mineral encrustation and grime had been carefully removed, and when I saw images of it, I immediately recognized the combat scene in the artwork on the gem as celestially inspired. The scene features a triumphant warrior at the top, stabbing downwards with a sword into a spearman just beneath, who bears an enormous shield (somewhat dented by combat). The details in these two figures can be confidently shown to indicate the constellations Hercules (triumphant warrior above, stabbing downwards) and Ophiuchus (shield-bearing spearman below, about to receive a fatal wound from the Hercules-figure).

On the ground beneath lies a third warrior, already dead, his arm over his head in a gesture similar to that found in other, later artwork that indiceates the constellation Sagittarius (while the position of his legs and up-thrust knee may indicate the forward half of the constellation Scorpio – both Scorpio and Sagittarius of course being located below Ophiuchus).

On the following page is an illustration of the Pylos Combat Agate, showing the three and their relationship to the stars:

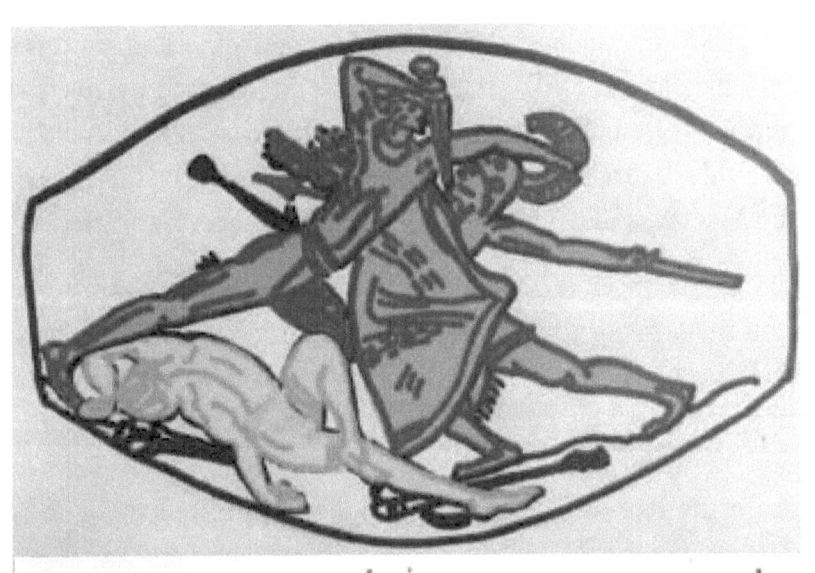

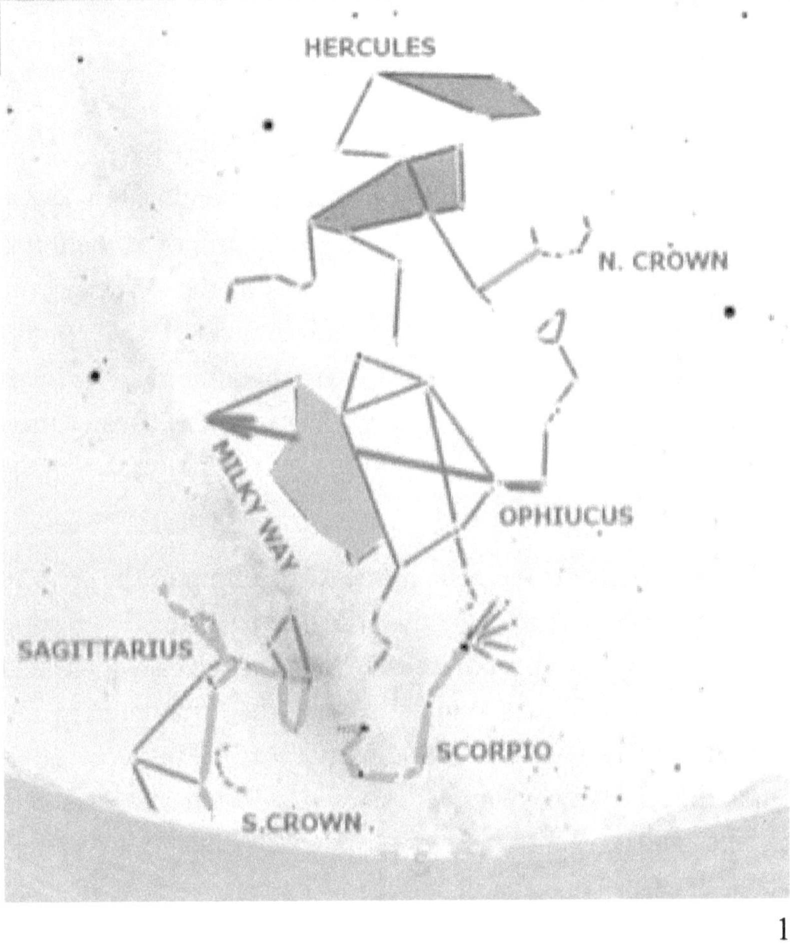

HERCULES

N. CROWN

OPHIUCUS

MILKY WAY

SAGITTARIUS

SCORPIO

S. CROWN

193

In other words, an abundance of evidence from other cultures exists which indicates that the outline of Ophiuchus in the ancient system was often associated with the bearing of a great shield. I believe this is very relevant in the case of Chimalmat, the wife of Seven Macaw, and helps to identify her with that constellation.

When Hunahpu and Xbalanque first attack Seven Macaw, he rips off the arm of Hunahpu and takes it home to his wife, where Seven Macaw then hangs it up over the fire. Having examined many other Star Myths around the world, I am confident that the angled outline of Coma Berenices (or Berenice's Hair) appears at times in the role of a severed arm, still spraying blood (there is another story, from China, that we will examine later in which this connection is also quite apparent, which helps to confirm this interpretation of the severed arm in the Popol Vuh).

The fact that the severed arm is "hung up" high over the fire in the Maya myth also helps us to confirm that our identification of the constellation Coma Berenices as the severed arm of Hunahpu is correct: Coma Berenices is very "high up" in the sky (near the north celestial pole), and we will see another myth in which one of the small constellations flanking Boötes (this time the Northern Crown or Corona Borealis, just in front of the constellation Hercules) is described as being "hung up in the rafters over the fire."

Another important detail given in the text relating to the story of the defeat of Seven Macaw by the Hero Twins is the description of Grandmother and Grandfather, who are specifically identified in this episode as Great White Peccary (the Grandfather) and Great White Coati (the Grandmother). The fact that Grandfather in this passage is described as being hunched over with age, and Grandmother described as being "faint," helps confirm our previous analysis which argued that Great White Peccary was probably associated with the constellation Boötes (which appears to be hunched over, as you can see in the star diagrams on pages 189 and 190) and Great White Coati was associated with Virgo (also called She Who Has Borne Children, because Virgo goes across the heavens as if *on her back*, as if having just given birth -- which is probably why she is described as being ready to faint or as having fainted in this later passage).

As stated at the outset of this chapter, we will not be able to explore all of the celestial aspects of the stories in the Popol Vuh in a single volume. The conflict between the Hero Twins and the two sons of Seven Macaw, Zipacna and Earthquake, are clearly celestial, as are many of the events in the contests between the twins and the lords of the underworld realm of Xibalba.

The great ball court, where games of life and death are played out, is almost certainly seen in the heavens in the Great Square of Pegasus. Losers of these ball games typically lose their head -- and we can see the figure of Andromeda, splayed out at one edge of the Great Square, seemingly without a head:

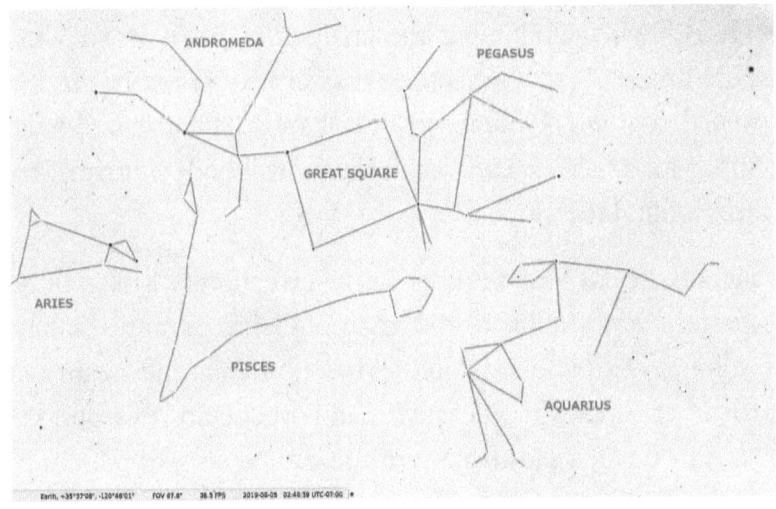

We can be fairly certain that Andromeda was sometimes envisioned as a figure who is losing her head or who has lost her head, because in the Greek myth of Perseus and the Gorgons, when Perseus beheads Medusa, the winged horse Pegasus flies out of the neck of Medusa after Perseus severs her head. In the night sky, we can see Pegasus apparently "flying upwards" out of the neck of Andromeda.

The sacred myths contained in the Popol Vuh may seem difficult to approach at first, but once we begin to understand that they are speaking a celestial language, in common with the world's other ancient myths, we can begin to hear the message that they have for us.

In common with other patterns found across many myth-systems from various cultures, the myths of the Popol Vuh feature semi-divine twins, who are able to overcome almost any adversity when they integrate their powers (unlike the twins who come before them, and who fall into the traps laid by the lords of Xibalba).

As with many other ancient myths around the world, the Popol Vuh features a trip to the Underworld, which ends in triumph for the Hero Twins. Following the analysis of Alvin Boyd Kuhn, presented most clearly in his 1940 masterpiece, *Lost Light*, I am convinced that the Underworld itself most often features as a metaphor for *this incarnate life* in the mortal body in myths from cultures around the globe.[109]

Finally, the Popol Vuh features the resurrection of a slain father, in a pattern very similar to the myth of Osiris examined later in this volume -- a pattern which shows up again and again with numerous variations in other myths and other cultures around the globe. As we will see, this pattern too can be seen to picture our condition in this incarnate life, cast down into a body of death, crossing through this "lower realm" of matter, but restored to life by the divine twin, the product of the second (or spiritual) birth, often described as a kind of "immaculate conception" to distinguish it from the physical conception that led to our first (and physical) birth -- as it is in the Popol Vuh, with the conception of the Hero Twins by spittle in the hand of Blood Moon, rather than by sexual intercourse.

The analysis offered above should demonstrate that the details in the Popol Vuh were not "borrowed" or "imported" from Christian contact by the anonymous elders who were seeking to preserve their civilization's ancient sacred stories. Many of the connections described above would have been completely unknown to Christians living in previous centuries. Many of the connections are to other non-Christian myths, from cultures as far away as ancient Greece or ancient China. And we would certainly not be expected to buy an argument that the "immaculate conception" of the Hero Twins by Blood Moon (by the action of the calabash skull spitting into her hand) was imported or borrowed in any way from the gospels, despite the fact that they share a similar mythical pattern of conception without sexual intercourse.

The layers of meaning in the Popol Vuh, and the wisdom that it can offer us, are bottomless in their depth, as with the other ancient myths given as a precious inheritance to the many nations of the world. It is impossible to plumb them in any great thoroughness in this volume, which is intended more as a survey of many different myth-systems, with a purpose of establishing the evidence that they are all connected by virtue of a common foundation, in the language of the stars.

It is hoped that the more we begin to understand that language, the more we can appreciate their beauty and wisdom, and the more readily we can approach them, and reverently listen to them, to hear what they have to tell us, for our benefit and blessing in this life.

Star Myths of the Pacific: the Maui Cycle

The cultures of the vast expanse of the Pacific Ocean inhabit a region that is larger in total area than that occupied by any other single people-group found anywhere else on our planet. Within this vast expanse, the cultures of the people who live on the countless islands and atolls have generally been categorized as belonging to three main cultural divisions, with many distinctions but also many shared cultural details -- including some shared mythology.

The islands known as Polynesia, whose myths we will be primarily exploring in this chapter, are located within a great triangle of the Pacific Ocean which has as its three corners the Hawaiian Islands at the north apex, the islands of New Zealand or Aotearoa in the southwest corner of the triangle, and the mysterious island of Rapa Nui or Easter Island in the southeast corner of the great triangle.

The other major groupings of islands and cultures in the Pacific, lying closer to Asia and Australia than the islands of the Polynesian cultures have been given the names Micronesia and Melanesia, with the islands of Micronesia stretching in a band to the north of the islands of Melanesia, and primarily consisting of tiny atolls (hence the name Micronesia) as opposed to the much larger islands of Melanesia, which includes in its westernmost section the enormous island of New Guinea, just north of Australia.

It is difficult to truly grasp the enormous distances over which the islands of the cultures of Polynesia are scattered within the great breadth of the Pacific Ocean. The islands of Aotearoa (New Zealand) are as far away from the islands of Hawai'i as . . . well, the distance may surprise you. The straight-line distance from Hilo, Hawaii to Wellington, New Zealand is about 4,632 miles. From San Francisco to New York City is only 2,565 miles; from San Francisco to Caracas, Venezuela is much further but still only 3,905 miles. From Lisbon, one of the most western points on the European continent, to Moscow is 2,427 miles. From Lisbon to Kabul, Afghanistan is 4,215 miles – getting closer to the distance between Hawai'i and Aotearoa, but still not there. From Cairo in Egypt to Cape Town near the southern point of Africa is 4,499 miles. From Moscow to Beijing is only 3,600 miles; from Moscow to Hong Kong is 4,430 miles. So far, the distance between Hilo and Wellington is still farther than all these distances. From New York City across the ocean to Dublin, Ireland is 3,178 miles; to Paris it would be 3,627 miles; to Prague from New York City is still only 4,083 miles; and to Helsinki in Finland is 4,112 miles. From New York City to Moscow we finally get about to the distance between Hawai'i and Aotearoa: that straight-line distance is about 4,666 miles, or about 34 miles further than the distance from Hilo to Wellington.

And yet across these islands there existed cultures sharing a common language (with distinct dialects which may have diverged over the centuries) and a common set of myths. Thor Heyerdahl wrote that, "Such a distribution of a single people [. . .] is unique in the history of man."[110]

Within the pantheon of gods and goddesses, myths and legends preserved among the cultures of the Pacific, we will focus here on the stories surrounding the great culture-hero Maui, whose name is known throughout the cultures of Polynesia (with few exceptions, and in those exceptions the hero himself is still known, albeit by his title Tikitiki-a-Taranga, his first name having somehow been obscured), and even into some of the islands of

Micronesia and to a much lesser extent Melanesia as well.[111] The incredible extent of this deity's reach is detailed in an important 1949 work by Dr. Katharine Luomala (1907 - 1992) entitled *Maui of a Thousand Tricks: His Oceanic and European Biographers.*

As can be said for all the other myth-systems surveyed in this and other volumes of this series, the number of episodes in what Katherine Luomala calls "the vast myth-complex associated with the name of Maui" deserve an entire separate volume of their own (or series of volumes), in order to examine and discuss in detail their abundant celestial references, as well as their many undeniable points of harmony with other myths from around the world.[112]

Further, there are significant variations in the accounts of the many different episodes in the Maui cycle of myths, not just from one island to another across the vast area described above but even within accounts given on the same island, such that the number of exploits to investigate in the career of this amazing demigod is staggering indeed.

Keeping with the scope of this series, the treatment here will be by way of an introduction and very broad overview, with a goal of demonstrating beyond reasonable doubt that the inherited mythology of the cultures of the Pacific, no less than those of other cultures around the globe, share the very same celestial foundation which we have been finding at the bedrock layer of all the other myths we have examined thus far, and which will be examined in the subsequent volumes.

Katharine Luomala notes that Captain Cook (1728 - 1779) was the first European to mention the name of Maui in a written record, in his journal from June 28 of 1769, in which he spelled the name *Mahuwe* indicating three syllables.[113] Notably, Cook uses this name in conjunction with an effigy figure representing the demigod, which apparently had multiple heads (or knobs representing heads, as Katharine Luomala interprets it) -- some versions of the Maui story telling us that he was born with eight heads, an important celestial clue.

The exploits of Maui include raising islands out of the ocean with his fish-hook, raising the heavens so that there will be enough room for men and women to live on earth, stealing fire from the gods to give to humanity, and teaching them how to cook their food instead of eating it raw, slowing down the pace of the sun's journey across the sky so that there will be enough time in the day for the people to cook their food and accomplish other necessary tasks, introducing the sweet potato or *kumara* (a staple food in the Polynesian diet), slaying various terrifying monsters, and descending to the Underworld of his own accord and returning again -- among other adventures and accomplishments.

The story of Maui's birth has many variations, but in most of them he is described as being thrown away by his parents -- in some versions, because the infant has eight heads! One of the earliest European chroniclers of the Maui cycle of myths was George Grey (1812 - 1898), twice governor of New Zealand, who took it upon himself to learn the Maori language and to convince Maori chieftains to recount their traditions and sacred stories to him for preservation in writing. One of his major sources, unacknowledged, was Wiremu Maihi Te Rangikaheke (1815 - 1896), who will be discussed presently.[114]

Grey's account of the Maui cycle of myths, reprinted in Katharine Luomala's 1949 text, has Maui recounting some of the aspects of his birth back to his mother, Taranga (who in this particular telling does not initially recognize him as one of her sons, the older four of whom are named Maui-taha, Maui-roto, Maui-pae, and Maui-waho) as follows:

> "I knew I was born at the side of the sea, and was thrown by you into the foam of the surf, after you had wrapped me up in a tuft of your hair, which you cut off for the purpose. Then the sea-weed formed and fashioned me, as caught in its long tangles the ever-heaving surges of the sea rolled me, folded as I was in them, from side to side. At length the breezes and squalls which blew from the ocean drifted me on shore again, and the soft jelly-fish of the long sandy beaches rolled themselves round me to protect me. Then again myriads of flies alighted on me to buzz about me and lay their eggs, that maggots might eat me, and flocks of birds collected round me to peck me to pieces. But, at that moment, appeared there also my great ancestor Tama-nui-ki-te-Rangi. He saw the flies and the birds collected in clusters and flocks above the jelly-fish. The old man ran, as fast as he could, and stripped off the encircling jelly-fish. Behold, within there lay a human being. Then he caught me up and carried me to his house, he hung me up in the roof that I might feel the warm smoke and the heat of the fire. Thus I was saved alive by the kindness of that old man."[115]

This account preserves certain details of the story that are found in accounts given on many other islands, especially the fact that Maui was wrapped in a tuft of hair cut off by his mother and then cast into the sea-foam, where he was found by his formidable grandfather Tama-nui-ki-te-Rangi and rescued. His grandfather hoists baby Maui up and suspends him in the rafters to dry by the heat of the fire in his dwelling.

This episode is extremely revealing in terms of recognizing beyond any doubt the celestial nature of the Maui myths of

Polynesia and connecting them with other myths from around the world which use the same underlying constellations but clothe them in different storyline details.

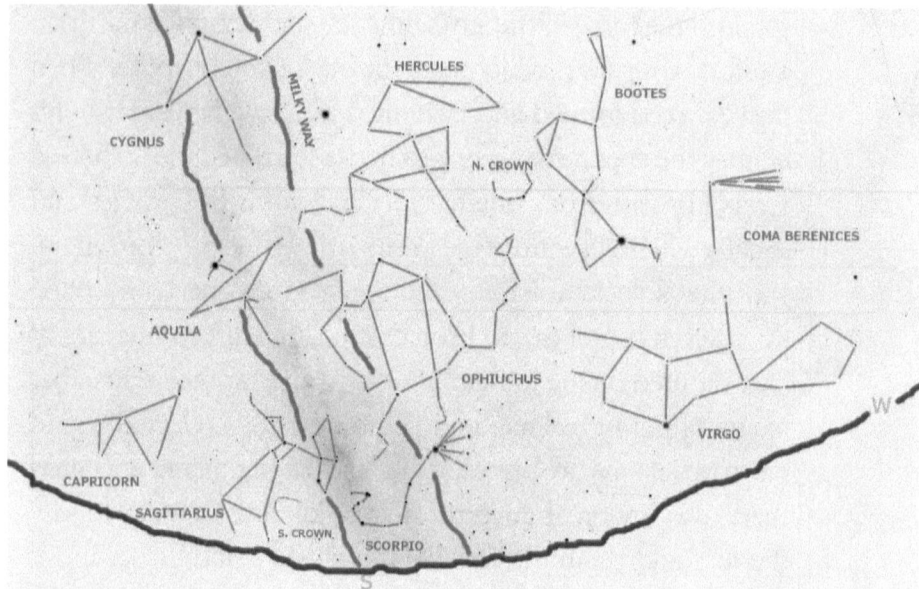

Above we see a now-familiar and very mythologically-important section of the night sky. Focus first on the constellation Virgo, at the right (west) of the image as we face the page. I would argue that we can confidently identify Virgo as being Maui's mother, Taranga: we have previously noted that Virgo can be envisioned as giving birth to constellations such as Ophiuchus and Scorpio, and in this myth of Maui in which the infant Maui is described as being cast into the sea-foam, we can see that the Milky Way is once again playing the foam of the ocean's verge, where baby Maui will be found after he is born.

The fact that in some versions of the story (including some cited by Katharine Luomala in her 1949 text) the baby Maui is said to have had *eight heads* indicates that he is associated at least in some parts of his myth with the outline of the constellation

Scorpio, which was commonly envisioned in various ancient myths from around the globe as having multiple heads -- sometimes three heads, sometimes seven, eight or nine. Note that Scorpio is located within the band of the Milky Way itself: hence, in the "foam of the sea" where baby Maui says he was found by his own respected ancestor Tama.

Note that in this account, Maui joins a host of other well-known infants in ancient myth who are cast into the waters -- virtually all of whom, I would argue, are based upon a few constellations in the same portion of the night sky. These cast-adrift infants include of course Moses in the Genesis account, the legendary king Sargon of Akkad, and the leech-child Hiruko (whose story will be examined later in this volume).

It is also notable that in many versions of the story, the cast-off infant Maui is described as a blood-clot, a miscarriage, or an abortion -- which recalls the story of Rabbit Boy from the White River Sioux, examined in a previous chapter. Katharine Luomala explains that the fact that baby Maui was later doted upon by his mother (to the point that his older brothers become jealous) and given a ceremonial ritual of purification and baptism by his father may have been seen as responsible for having:

> altered the character of Maui from what it would have been had he developed like an ordinary blood clot or miscarriage. The spirit of such an object is shunned by both men and supernatural beings, lives to itself, broods over its lack of affection and status, and thinks up mischief to annoy villagers and their gods. Maui was saved from such an extreme psychology by his parents' prayers and ceremonies.[116]

We shall have occasion to briefly examine this subject of Maui's baptism presently.

The detail of Maui's mother cutting off her own hair in which to wrap the infant almost certainly relates to the constellation Coma Berenices, held aloft above the constellation Virgo in the heavens. This constellation plays the role of the cut-off hair of an important female personage or deity in many myths and stories around the globe, including the hair of Sif (wife of Thor) in the Norse myths.

The very name of the constellation, Coma Berenices (or Berenice's Hair) is attributed to a story about a queen who cuts off her hair, as related by H. A. Rey in his book on the stars:

> This constellation owes its name to a theft: Berenice was an Egyptian queen (3rd century BC) who sacrificed her hair to thank Venus for a victory her husband had won in a war. The hair was stolen from the temple but the priests in charge convinced the disconsolate queen that Zeus himself had taken the locks and put them in the sky as a constellation.[17]

I believe the oldest source for this particular story about Berenice's Hair may be the *Catasterismi* attributed to Eratosthenes (although probably not really written by him at all, but rather a product of the much later 1st century AD). The story of course is almost certainly mythical: the main point of recounting it here is to provide definitive evidence that the constellation Coma Berenices is associated with the *cutting off* of long locks of hair.

Thus Maui's most-common name (among many other epithets and aliases), Maui-tikitiki-a-Taranga or "Maui-topknot-of-Taranga," probably originates in the stars of Coma Berenices, seen as the topknot his mother cuts off when she casts him into the sea-foam. The constellation Sagittarius has a distinctive "plume" or line of stars rising from the back corner of its head, which could be envisioned as a topknot and which could represent his mother's or Maui's own topknot, if the deity is sometimes associated with Sagittarius. As we will see, Maui (like so many other central figures in world myth) will "move through" more than one constellation in his various episodes and exploits (only some of which we will have occasion to examine in this volume).

The seabirds that wish to peck out the flesh of baby Maui when he is abandoned in the seafoam are probably to be identified with Aquila and Cygnus, flying directly above. The flies who want to lay eggs on him so that their maggots can eat his flesh are more difficult to identify, but may be associated with the insect-like outline of the brightest stars of Sagittarius, commonly referred to as "the Teapot" in modern usage, and which very much resemble a grasshopper or locust (and will appear in this role in many myths and scriptures to be examined later). The outline of Scorpio itself can also be shown to be associated with worms and maggots in various myths from around the globe, and thus virtually all of the details of the Maui cast-adrift story recounted above can be seen to have celestial associations.

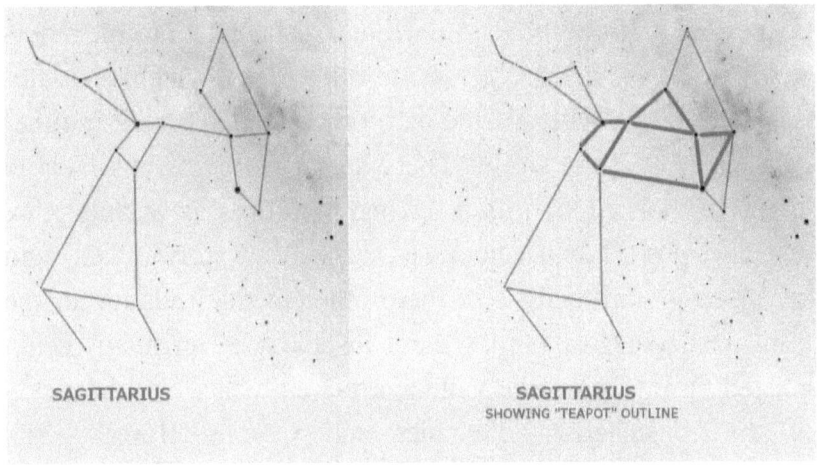

SAGITTARIUS

SAGITTARIUS
SHOWING "TEAPOT" OUTLINE

Above is a diagram of the stars of Sagittarius, first as outlined by H. A. Rey (on the left) and then with the brightest stars connected to show the outline of "the Teapot" asterism. This bright grouping of stars in the Sagittarius constellation can easily be envisioned as a locust-like insect, as shown in the additional outline below (which adds antennae to the top of the head of the "locust," on the upper left as we face the page, as well as an additional segment to the "hind foot" of the insect, on the lower right as we face the image):

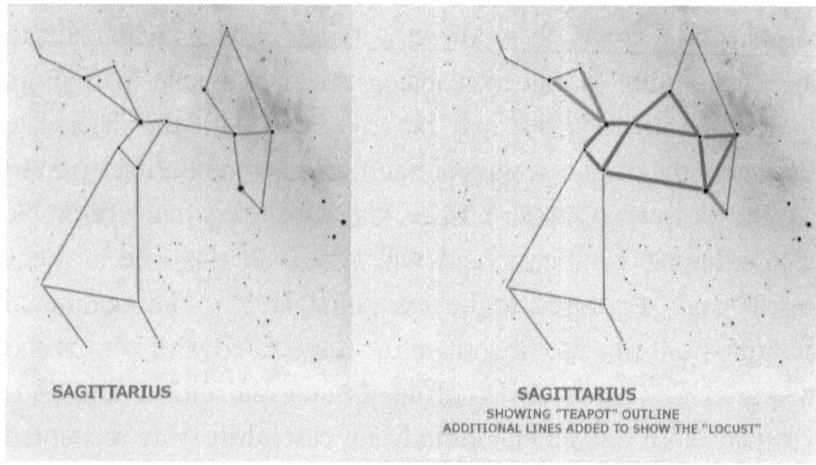

SAGITTARIUS

SAGITTARIUS
SHOWING "TEAPOT" OUTLINE
ADDITIONAL LINES ADDED TO SHOW THE "LOCUST"

When Maui's grandfather Tama-nui-ki-te-Rangi rescues the helpless infant from the sea-foam, and hoists him up to the rafters to dry off and warm up, he is performing an act which associates this myth of the wide Pacific with other Star Myths from other cultures around the world. There are many myths in which an infant is "hoisted up" or "snatched up" by a powerful figure (usually a powerful male figure, as in this Maui story as well), and my research and analysis of these other myths leads me to the firmly-held conclusion that these instances of an infant being hoisted up by a powerful male figure are mythical embodiments of the constellations Hercules and Corona Borealis (the Northern Crown).

The constellation Corona Borealis or the Northern Crown is positioned directly in front of the figure of the constellation Hercules in the night sky -- in such a location that the "lower hand" of Hercules can be envisioned as reaching out and grasping the arc of the Northern Crown. In some ancient artwork, this is depicted as the Hercules-figure either reaching out towards or actually grasping an arc-shaped helmet crest on a defeated enemy, as in the examples below:

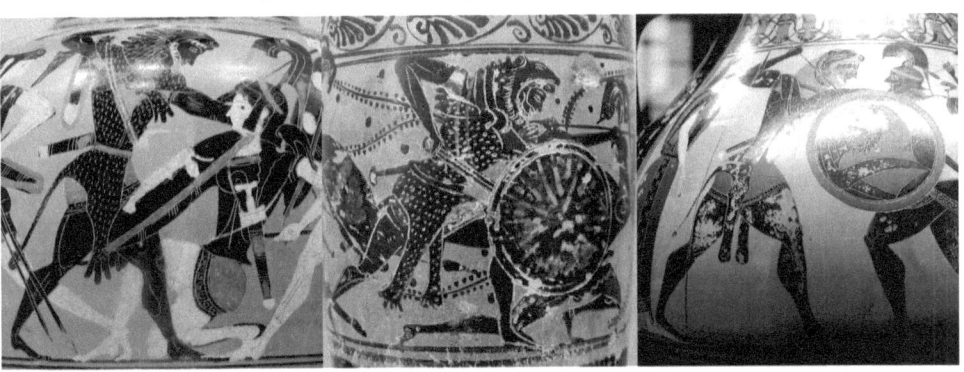

Each of the above images is from a different ancient Greek vase, and each shows a figure who is obviously Heracles (the Greek hero who is more commonly known to us today by the Latin version of his name: *Hercules*). In each case he is depicted in the general outline and posture of the *constellation* Hercules in the night sky, brandishing a sword in his right hand (the left side of the image as we face it) and reaches out with his other hand, just as the constellation appears to do in the night sky. In each case, his other hand (his left hand, on the right-side of Heracles as we face the images) reaches out towards the arc-shaped crest of his opponent's helmet -- and in the rightmost two vases, he is actually depicted grasping the base of the arc-shaped crest (a little difficult to see, but he is indeed grasping the crests -- the interested reader can follow the links in the *Image Credits* section at the back of this volume and zoom-in on the originals to verify if desired).

Chapter Eleven

This action shows one way in which the constellation Hercules was envisioned in ancient times -- reaching out to grasp the arc of the Northern Crown, which in this case is envisioned as the arc of a helmet-crest. Note that in the Pylos Combat Agate, newly discovered in 2017 after lying beneath the ground for around 3,500 years, the triumphant "swordsman" warrior is similarly grasping the arc-shaped crest of his opponent's helmet.

The star-chart below shows the outline of the constellation Hercules, and its proximity to Corona Borealis. An added line, which is not usually imagined or envisioned but which was obviously envisioned at times by those who gave us the ancient myths, has been added to show how Hercules could be imagined to be reaching out to grasp the Northern Crown:

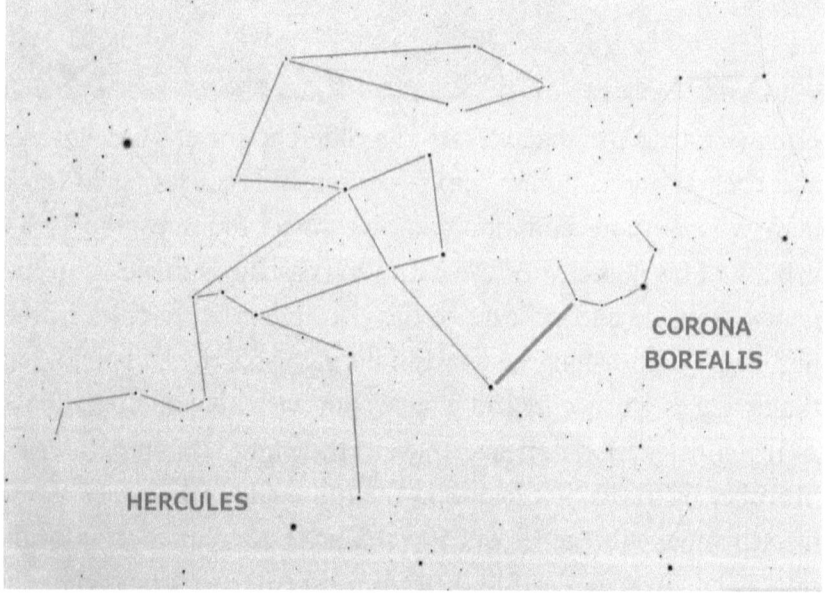

The Northern Crown can be envisioned as the arc-shaped crest of a helmet, as in the images on the page opposite, but it could also be imagined as many other curved or arc-shaped items. In the image below, on the following page, we see another ancient vase depicting the Greek hero Heracles, and this time he is reaching out to grasp a different curved object which can also be associated with Corona Borealis: the curved horn of a bull-faced god (the deity facing Heracles in this particular piece of ancient pottery is usually identified as the horned god Achelous, an important being who is discussed at some length in my 2014 book *The Undying Stars*).

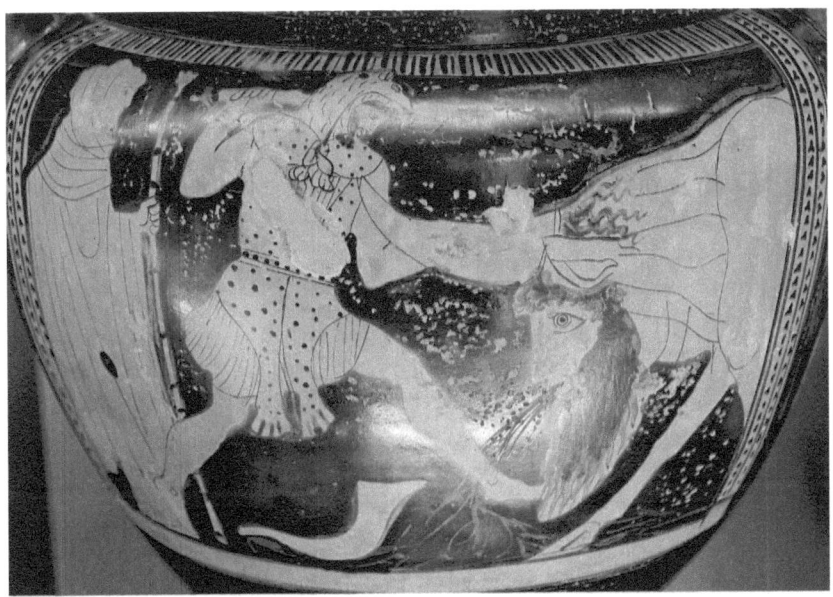

Here once again we see the hero Heracles depicted in a posture strongly reminiscent of the outline of the constellation Hercules in the night sky: his club is raised over his shoulders, pointing forward, in his right hand (on the left as we face the image), and his legs are positioned in the distinctive "lunging" position characteristic of the constellation itself. The hero's head is made to appear more "square-shaped" by virtue of a square beard (characteristic of many Hercules-figures in ancient myth) and the distinctive lion-garment with head-dress worn by the hero in most ancient depictions. Once again, his "lower hand" (the hero's left)

is reaching forward to grasp an arc-shaped object: in this case, envisioned as a great curving horn on the head of the deity.

The above analysis and examples from ancient artwork should establish beyond any debate that the figure of the constellation Hercules in the heavens was sometimes envisioned as grasping the arc of the Northern Crown (Corona Borealis), and that this arc-shaped constellation could be and was envisioned as a variety of different items or objects.

What may seem less than obvious is the fact that this arc-shaped constellation of the Northern Crown could be, and demonstrably was, envisioned as an *arching baby* in many different myth examples from widely-distributed cultures around the globe. The account of Maui being pulled from the sea-foam by his powerful ancestor Tama-nui-ki-te-Rangi is one of them.

In the Maori account recorded by George Grey in the 1800s, Maui's ancestor Tama pulls the baby from the sea-foam and hangs him up to dry among the rafters at the roof of his house, above the fire and smoke, in order to warm little Maui. If you turn back again to the star-chart on page 204, you will see that the constellation Hercules is positioned high up and adjacent to the smoky column of the Milky Way band, near the "roof" shape at the top of Ophiuchus (and also near to the "roof" of the dome of the heavens, the north celestial pole around which all the stars appear to turn). Just in front of Hercules, and not far from the "roof" shape atop Ophiuchus, you can see the dazzling arc of the Northern Crown, representing baby Maui, pulled from the sea-foam by his powerful ancestor Tama, represented by the constellation Hercules.

There are other examples in world myth in which an infant (associated with the Northern Crown) is hoisted up by a powerful male figure associated with the constellation Hercules. The first such example that I ever noticed is found in the Old Testament book of 2 Kings, in chapter 3, during the famous episode which has come to be known as the "Judgment of Solomon," in which the wise king directs a swordsman to cut a living infant in half. This episode is examined in some detail in *Star Myths of the World, Volume Three*.

Another example is the story of the baptism of Achilles (or the "failed baptism" of Achilles), in which the hero's immortal mother Thetis (one of the Naiads) attempts to make her child invulnerable, either by holding him over a sacred fire (in some accounts) or by dipping him in the River Styx (in other versions of the story). In some of these stories, the mortal father of Achilles sees this taking place and, horrified, pulls the infant out of the fire.

Yet another variation on the same pattern, which can be shown to be based on the same stars, can be found in the text of the New Testament book called the Revelation of John (one of many different Revelation or Apocalypse texts, and the only one which was included in the canonical New Testament, although others survived in the Nag Hammadi library of Gnostic texts which were discovered in Egypt in the 20th century). In the twelfth chapter of the Revelation of John, the text describes a woman in travail, about to give birth (Revelation 12: 1 - 2) and before her a great red dragon with seven heads, waiting to devour her child as soon as it is born (Revelation 12: 3 - 4). These figures once again describe the constellations Virgo (the woman in travail, laboring to give birth) and the constellation Scorpio (the red dragon, crouching before the woman and preparing to devour the child as soon as it is delivered: the seven heads of the dragon represent the multiple heads frequently envisioned on the constellation Scorpio, just as Maui is sometimes described as being born with eight heads).

Revelation 12: 5 tells us that when the woman does give birth, she brings forth a man child, but the baby is not devoured by the dragon. Instead, it is "caught up unto God, and to his throne." This verse describes yet another episode in ancient myth and scripture in which an infant is described as being "caught up" by a powerful male figure -- in this case, the constellation Hercules takes on the identity of God on his throne (and indeed, as we will see in Volume Three of this series, the God of the Bible is almost exclusively associated with the figure of the constellation Hercules, both in the Old Testament scriptures and the New).

This passage is powerful confirmation of the argument that the world's myths -- even from cultures far removed from one another -- are built upon a common foundation of celestial metaphor, in which very specific patterns are shared which would not be likely to have simply arisen independently of one another.

There are some who might argue that it is not too surprising to find myths built upon celestial metaphor in cultures far removed from one another geographically: after all, they reason, the stars are visible around the globe, and thus it is only natural to assume that myths in various places might use the same stars.

The counter to this argument is, first, that it is not at all self-evident or inevitable to assume that different cultures will choose to base their myths on celestial metaphor. Such a move is rather surprising. Very few people today are even aware that the world's myths are based on celestial metaphor. If you were to tell a member of a literalist Christian denomination that the stories and characters in the Bible are based on celestial metaphor, you would not be likely to receive the reply, "Well, that's obvious!"

Thus, to find not just one culture on our planet but *virtually all of them* using a system of celestial metaphor as the basis and foundation for their myths and sacred stories is not only not a "natural" or "obvious" development: it is downright astonishing.

Far more astonishing, however, is to realize that not only is virtually every culture using a type of celestial metaphor as the basis or foundation for their ancient myths, but to discover that they are all using variations of *the same system*, with the same way of envisioning the constellations, and with many shared associations for specific constellations spanning myths and cultures far removed from one another. This episode of Maui being hoisted from the sea-foam by his powerful grandfather is one of the most significant examples that refutes the counter-argument cited above.

One might argue that the arc of stars which forms the constellation we call Corona Borealis (the Northern Crown) would be identified as a distinct constellation by many different cultures, completely independent of one another. It is, in fact, a brilliant and very visible little constellation. We might even admit that this brilliant little semi-circle could be independently envisioned as *a crown* in multiple different cultures, without much difficulty. It could also be envisioned as *a necklace* in the myths of different cultures without arousing too much suspicion: one could argue that different cultures could naturally envision Corona Borealis as a necklace, completely independently of one another. And indeed, Corona Borealis does show up as a necklace in more than one world myth from more than one culture, and it does show up as a crown in more than one as well.

However, it is not at all inherently obvious or intuitive that the Northern Crown would be envisioned as *an infant*, hoisted up into the air by a powerful Hercules-figure. The reader is invited to go back to the star-chart on page 210 showing the outline of Hercules and the Northern Crown, and consider whether or not the stars of Corona Borealis resemble an infant, or whether seeing that little arc as a baby would be the first thing that springs to mind. It is certainly not a metaphor that we would expect to find arising independently in cultures far removed from one another, with as little in common as the cultures that produced the Old Testament scriptures and the Maui stories of Polynesia, for example.

And yet, as we have just seen, this situation is exactly what we do find -- and the more myths from cultures around the world that we examine, the more numerous the examples become and the more compelling the evidence that the world's myths are, as the authors of *Hamlet's Mill* put it in their evocative metaphor, the remains of a "great world-wide archaic construction" whose origin and full operational purpose are now "no longer understood," even if on occasion "its original themes could flash out again, preserved almost intact."[118] Even so (the authors say) these flashes still constitute mere "tantalizing fragments of a lost whole."[119]

Even from the little bit we have explored thus far of the Maui myth-cycle we can see that the same world-wide system underlies and informs the episodes describing Maui's life. Let's examine a few more examples whose celestial foundations are also fairly self-evident, in order to confirm beyond any doubt that even here, among the islands scattered like tiny jewels in the seemingly endless expanse of the broad Pacific, on the entire other side of the globe from the home of the Greek myths or the Norse myths or the Bible stories, the same celestial language is being "spoken" in the ancient inherited stories.

Returning to the account given by George Grey, we discover that young Maui was reunited with his mother when he had grown a little bigger, slipping in and being taken home among his older brothers after a big gathering and dance. He soon found that his mother would disappear each morning just as the sun arose (perhaps a reasonable characteristic for her to have, if she is indeed a heavenly constellation), and so Maui determined to know where she went each dawn, and to find the dwelling place of his mother and father, wherever it might be.

So one night, while she was sleeping, Maui took all his mother's clothes and hid them, and then during the same night, he stopped up all the chinks in the walls of their dwelling so that no sunlight could come in, and his mother overslept. When she finally awoke with a start, she was terribly distraught at being so badly deceived, and Maui was able to watch her go to a place in the ground where she pulled up some reeds or tall grass and disappeared down a hole into the underworld, pulling the grasses back over the hole as she did so.

Armed with this knowledge, Maui was able to pull up the cover of the opening to the invisible world, and descend into the underworld himself. In order to do so, he transformed himself into a pigeon and flew down the long narrow descending passageway, so narrow that he had to dip his wings to fit as he flew downwards (this narrative continues to follow the version recorded by George Grey in the 1800s). Which constellation might represent Maui, in the form of a bird, flying down a long narrow passageway?

An interesting and important detail, preserved in the accounts recorded by George Grey in Aotearoa, is that Maui's transformation into a bird (described as a "pigeon" in Grey's account and no doubt referring to the wood pigeon or *kereru* of those islands, a large and beautifully feathered bird which in general appearance is nothing like the birds called "pigeon" in North America), is that this particular transformation is presented as being accomplished in conjunction with the *wearing of some of the items of clothing* which Maui had stolen from his mother.

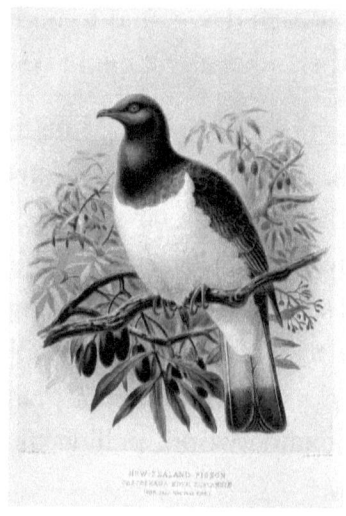

Grey's account tells us that:

> when he first appeared to his relatives in their house of singing and dancing, he had on that occasion transformed himself into the likeness of all manner of birds, of every bird in the world. Yet no single form that he then assumed had pleased his brothers. But now when he showed himself to them, transformed into the very semblance of a pigeon, his brothers said, "Ah, now indeed, oh, brother, you do look very well indeed, very beautiful, very beautiful, much more beautiful than you looked in any of the other forms which you assumed, and then changed from when you first discovered yourself to us."

What made him now look so well in the shape he had
assumed was the belt of his mother, and her apron, which he
had stolen from her while she was asleep in the house. The
very thing which looked so white upon the breast of the
pigeon was his mother's broad belt. He also had on her little
apron of burnished hair from the tail of a dog. The fastening
of her belt was what formed the beautiful black feathers on
his throat.[120]

Having now examined many more myths from around the globe
in fairly minute detail since the date of writing the first edition of
this volume, I can state with some confidence that this episode in
which Maui finds a hole in the ground leading to another world,
by way of a long and narrow passageway which he flies down in
the form of a wood pigeon corresponds to the Milky Way band,
through which the beautiful constellation of Cygnus can be seen
to be flying in the heavens.

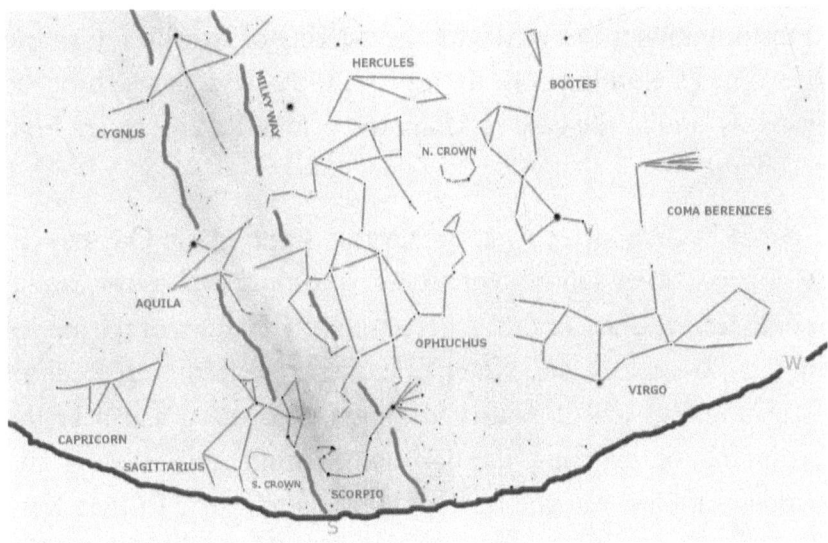

What is intriguing to note is that in the fifth book (or chapter) of
the Odyssey of ancient Greece, the goddess Leucotheia

(sometimes also spelled Leucothea) comes to Odysseus, taking on the form of a sea-bird as she does so. She comes to Odysseus in order to save him as he attempts to sail away from the island of Ogygia on a self-made raft across the open ocean, and he is in need of her help because his raft will be dashed to pieces by the wrath of Poseidon, who has unleashed his storms and mighty waves to thwart the homeward-bound protagonist.

In the story, the goddess changes from a bird form to that of a human woman, and *gives Odysseus her sash to wear* for protection, instructing him to remove all his other clothing and wear only this sash, and then to abandon the bits of demolished raft and dive into the sea.

Volume Two explains that in that story, Leucotheia descending to save Odysseus while in the form of a bird is almost certainly Cygnus as well. It is very interesting that these two traditions, on opposite sides of the world, associate episodes involving transformation into a bird with the wearing of an article or article of women's clothing -- in the case of Odysseus, the sash of the goddess, and in the case of Maui, the belt and apron stolen from his mother.

I noted in the Odysseus story that this scene in the Odyssey (as with many other subsequent scenes, including the "foot-washing scene" near the end of the epic) parallels the pattern of the stories in the gospels of the New Testament, with this descent of Leucotheia to tell Odysseus to plunge into the ocean near the beginning of his long journey home being a parallel of the baptism of Christ at the beginning of his ministry. In that New Testament episode, Christ is almost invariably depicted by artists as wearing only a sash around his waist -- and what is more, there is usually included in these depictions the form of a dove (the

Holy Spirit) descending through clouds and sky above his head. These clouds and sky are usually painted in a way that resembles the column of the Milky Way in the heavens. I would argue that in these accounts, the figure with the sash around his waist corresponds to Ophiuchus (the "serpent-halves" on either side of the constellation's central body being the "sash"), and the figure of the goddess in the form of a sea-bird (or the figure of the Holy Spirit in the form of a dove) is seen in the constellation Cygnus, descending through the Milky Way.

I would also point out that the later medieval romance of *Gawaine and the Green Knight* is also undoubtedly connected to the same ancient theme. In that story, the hero must wear a woman's girdle, given to him by the beautiful Lady Bertilak (the wife of his host at a castle where he stops during his quest to find the Green Knight), which will protect him from harm -- much like the sash given to Odysseus in the Odyssey by the goddess. In this story too, Gawaine is almost certainly seen in the outline of Ophiuchus -- and just over his head (in the night sky) we see the menacing form of Hercules brandishing his powerful weapon. Hercules, of course, plays the role of the Green Knight in that story, and we have already examined the evidence that the great weapon of Hercules can be envisioned as an axe, in our discussion of the god Shango or Xango of the Yoruba nation in Africa.

In this Maui account, not all of the other aspects of the story are present, but it is certainly interesting that in his transformation into a bird associated with the constellation Cygnus, Maui is expressly described as wearing the belt and apron of a woman - an echo perhaps of the elements found around the world in related myths, and a hint that they all may be descended from some common but very remote ancient source.

Continuing with the account from Aotearoa recorded by George Grey in the 1800s, we are told that after Maui in the form of a bird speeds down the narrow cave-like corridor leading to the other world, he reaches nearly to the bottom and then flies along until he gets to a place where the cave widened:

> Again, because the cave was so narrow, he dipped first one wing and then the other, but the cave now widened, and he dashed straight on.

> At last he saw a party of people coming along under a grove of trees. They were manapau trees. Flying on, he perched upon the top of one of these trees, under which the people had seated themselves. When he saw his mother lying down on the grass by the side of her husband, he guessed at once who they were. He thought, "Ah! there sit my father and mother right under me."[121]

Maui as a bird uses his beak to throw berries at his father and mother, and all the people begin to throw stones at the bird, trying to hit it, but Maui only allows his father to hit him, "exactly upon his left leg," and he falls to the ground.

When the people run up to him, he turns into a man, and everyone is frightened and astonished, but Maui's mother recognizes him and recounts again the story of his birth, how she prematurely gave birth to him as she was wandering along the shore of the sea, and how she cut off her locks of long hair to bound him up in them, throwing him into the foam of the sea, where he would be found by his ancestor Tama-nui-ki-te-Rangi.

I'm not sure what celestial detail might be indicated by the detail in the story that says Maui's father hit him with a stone in the left leg, but it is quite likely that Maui in the form of a bird, alighting in the manapau tree corresponds again to the outline of Aquila the Eagle. From here, he can see his mother (described as "lying down on the grass" -- no doubt indicating Virgo) and his father (about whom I do not believe we have sufficient detail to make a precise identification, although presently his father will take Maui and baptize him, which probably indicates an association of his father with the constellation Hercules at this juncture).

The cave corridor down which Maui speeds into the other realm, as mentioned before, is undoubtedly the column of the Milky Way, and as we see in the account as preserved by Grey, it widens near the bottom (just as the actual band of the Milky Way widens in the region between Scorpio, Sagittarius, and Ophiuchus).

Another potentially important detail is preserved in George Grey's record, when Maui's mother just after recounting the story of his birth asks Maui:

> "Where do you come from? From the westward?" And he answered, "No." "From the northeast then?" "No." "From the southeast then?" "No." "Was it the wind which blows upon me, which brought you here to me then?" When she asked this, he opened his mouth and answered, "Yes." She cried out, "Oh, this then is indeed my child."[122]

We have already had occasion to examine the fact, confirmed by abundant evidence found in myths around the globe, that the constellation Hercules -- in addition to being envisioned as a powerful human shape brandishing a weapon overhead -- can also be envisioned as a central disc (or square) with whirling arms radiating from the central element, becoming in some myths a whirlwind, in other myths a whirlpool, and associating the constellation Hercules with wind, rain, and storms (note that Zeus and Jove are storm-gods, associated beyond any doubt with the constellation Hercules, as is Thor in the Norse mythology, Indra in the myths of ancient India, Huracan of the Maya, and even Jehovah or Yahweh in the Hebrew scriptures).

Thus, when asked by his mother Taranga from which direction he has come back to her, Maui answers affirmatively when she asks if he comes *from the wind* which blows upon her -- indicating according to this analysis that he comes from the direction of Hercules, higher up in the Milky Way. This exchange may also indicate that Maui is in some cases associated with Ophiuchus (in addition to being associated with Scorpio), the constellation directly below Hercules and in many myths envisioned as being the "descendant" of the constellation Hercules (just as Solomon, associated with Ophiuchus, is the direct descendant of David, associated with Hercules in the Old Testament, and as Jesus, associated with Ophiuchus, is the Son of God, who is associated with the constellation Hercules, as discussed in *Star Myths of the World, Volume Three*). This analysis would bolster the suspicion that Maui's father is associated with the constellation Hercules, just as his more distant ancestor (possibly grandfather), Tama-nui-ki-te-Rangi is also associated with Hercules.

After Maui gives this answer to his mother, she goes on to declare of her child:

> "By the winds and storms and wave-uplifting gales he was fashioned and became a human being. Welcome, oh my child, welcome. By you shall hereafter be climbed the threshold of the house of your great ancestor Hine-nui-te-po, and death shall thenceforth have no power over man."[118]

These descriptions can all be interpreted as having celestial associations. The declaration that by him the "threshold of the house" of his ancestor Hine-nui-te-po (goddess of night and death) shall be climbed is almost certainly a reference to the same constellation Ophiuchus, this time in its role as the "house of death." In *Star Myths of the World, Volume Two*, we will see evidence that the outline of Ophiuchus was seen as the gates of the realm of death in Greek mythology as well. We can see that the constellation Scorpio, which can be positively associated with Maui, reaches up or "climbs towards" the very "threshold" of the house-shape of Ophiuchus.

As Katharine Luomala notes, this prophecy by Maui's mother creates dramatic tension in the Maui cycle, because the next thing that happens is the baptism of Maui by his father -- and in this baptism we are told that, due to haste, his father mistakenly skipped over some of the prayers in the baptismal ritual (in some accounts, his father fails to mention the name of one of the gods).[119] Because of this omission, the father realizes, "He knew that the gods would be certain to punish this fault by causing Maui to die," as the account recorded by George Grey informs us.[120]

This pattern of a "failed baptism" may seem to be an importation based on contact with Christianity, but I believe this assumption is mistaken, because we have other "failed baptism" episodes in other myth-systems, including the famous example of Achilles to whom we have already alluded. The immortal mother of Achilles, the Naiad Thetis, took steps to ensure her son's immortality (either dipping him in the River Styx, or into a special fire that would render him immortal), but in some versions of the story this baptism is foiled by the agency of the child's mortal father (who is horrified to find his son in the fire and hoists him out).

And sure enough, the Maui cylce of stories do tell of the great demigod's ultimate death. The episode involves Maui attempting to destroy the power of death by crawling through the body of Hine-nui-te-po in the reverse direction that a baby would come out the birth canal, entering her vagina and eventually coming out her mouth, thus killing the goddess and reversing the power of death by his reverse progress.

In some versions of this myth such as that given by Hoani Te Whatahoro (1841 - 1923), Maui transforms himself into a worm (*noke*) in order to enter Hine-nui-te-po in the opposite direction of a birth.[121] This detail should establish without much controversy the celestial figures involved in this episode: Maui is associated with Scorpio and the sleeping Hine-nui-te-po with Virgo, and the myth is reversing the usual order in which Virgo is envisioned as giving birth to figures such as Scorpio or Ophiuchus.

Before he begins his attempt to defeat the power of the goddess of death, Maui strictly warns his bird-companions not to laugh when they see him wriggling into the body of Hine-nui-te-po, although he says that when they see Maui emerging from her mouth at the end of his journey then it will be safe to laugh.

The orators of the legend tell us, however, that the sight of Maui beginning this attempt causes all the birds present to screw up their cheeks as hard as they can to prevent themselves from laughing, and the little wagtail bird, Tiwakawaka, could not contain himself. He lets out a clear chattering laugh, awakening the goddess of night, who feels the wriggling of worms within her and either strangles Maui or snaps him in half with her vagina.

According to the account of Te Rangikaheke, who was one of George Grey's main (but unattributed) sources for the Arawa region, Hine-nui-te-po was able to cut Maui in half because her vagina is lined with sharp teeth of obsidian.

David Roy Simmons (1930 - 2015) of the Otago Museum in Dunedin, writing in the *Journal of the Polynesian Society* in 1965 notes that Te Rangikaheke, also known as William Marsh or Wiremu Maihi, "was a principal chief of Ngati Rangiwewehi tribe of the Rotorua district, and the son of a celebrated priest."[122] He wrote hundreds of manuscripts, many in his own hand, some in English and some in Maori, and he must be considered one of the most important sources we have for Maori mythology, and given the highest authority.

Thus ended the life of the great hero, trickster, and benefactor of humanity, Maui-tikitiki-a-Taranga. The celestial identity of Tiwakawaka, the wagtail, is almost certainly to be found in the constellation Corvus the Crow, a distinctive little constellation with a clearly-visible tail, who is positioned in the sky in such a way as to be looking directly at Virgo's brightest star, Spica, which is located at her hip, and beyond that, her genital region.

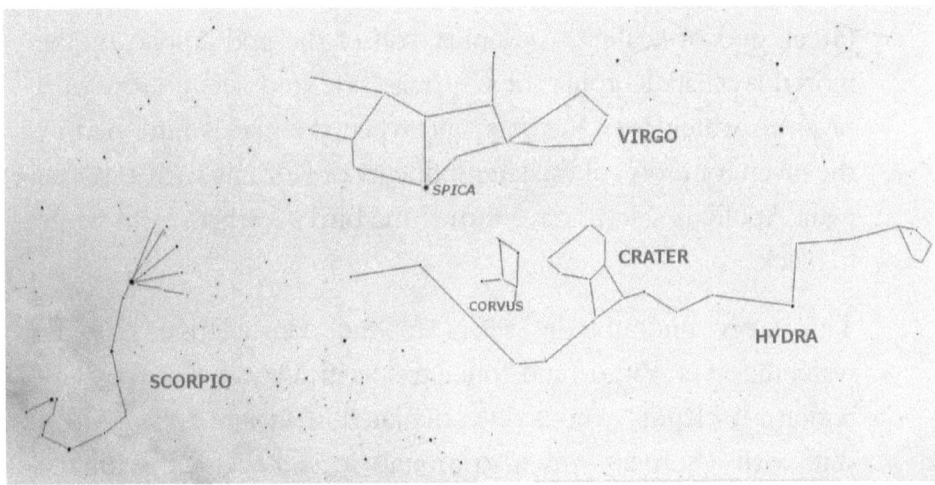

The star-chart on the preceding page outlines Corvus as suggested by H. A. Rey. However, when I go out to look at the stars, I usually envision Corvus as shown below. Here, the focus is zoomed-in further in order to show all the stars of this charming little constellation, a constellation I'm convinced plays the role of the irrepressible little Tiwakawaka in the myth:

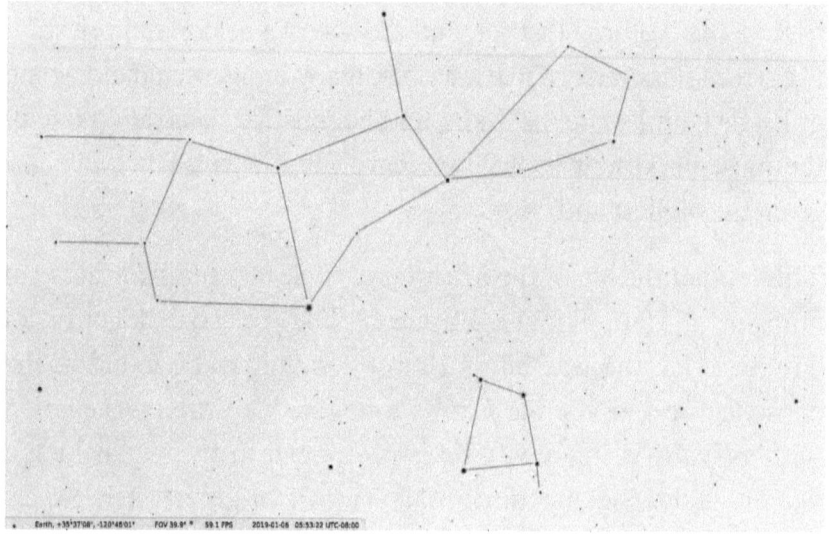

Note that in some of the myths surrounding the birth of the Greek god of healing, Asclepius, son of the god Apollo by the mortal woman Koronis (or Coronis), the god sets a crow or a raven to watch over Koronis, and when the god is informed by the raven (or crow) of the later infidelity of Koronis with a mortal man, Apollo is said to have turned the bird's feathers from white to black.

This story undoubtedly refers to the constellation Corvus, watching over Virgo (and looking specifically towards her lap-region). Asclepius, who is often depicted in ancient art holding a staff with a serpent entwined around it, is associated with the constellation Ophiuchus, as I discuss in an endnote to *Star Myths of the World, Volume Three.*[123] Ophiuchus, of course, is positioned in such a way that Virgo can be envisioned as giving birth to Ophiuchus (as Koronis gives birth to Asclepius). Ophiuchus is also positioned directly beneath Hercules -- and the myths tell us that Zeus eventually ended the mortal life of Asclepius with a thunderbolt (because Asclepius's power to heal people meant that soon no mortal would any longer have to fear death). Asclepius later became a god after Zeus slew him with the thunderbolt-weapon; the positioning of Hercules over Ophiuchus in the heavens almost certainly accounts for this detail in the myths of ancient Greece.

Note the parallels to the story of Maui and Hine-nui-te-po. In both cases, the theme of the myth involves putting an end to the power of death over humanity -- and in each case, this hoped-for outcome is thwarted. Also, in each myth, the constellation Corvus plays a prominent role, which is an intriguing parallel between two ancient myths found literally on the opposite ends of the earth.

There are many more exploits of the great demigod Maui of the Pacific which could be profitably explored for celestial content, but the extended discussion above should establish beyond reasonable doubt that the myths of the cultures found on the islands of Oceania are connected to the myths of other cultures around the globe by the same coded language of metaphor.

Before leaving the Maui cycle of myths, however, let us pause to briefly examine the story of Maui's fishing, which is one of his most widely-celebrated exploits. Katharine Luomala in her 1949 text on the demigod catalogs some of the innumerable cultures situated on islands which Maui is said to have fished up from the depths of the Pacific.

In the account recorded by George Grey, Maui's brothers don't want him to go out fishing with them, so he must stowaway on their boat and only show himself after they have already left the shore and headed out towards the fishing grounds. As noted in the original edition of this volume, in some versions of this story (although not in the George Grey account), Maui takes on the shape of an insect, hiding underneath the floor mats of the boat in order to stow away.

Once he does appear to his brothers, they first want to turn back, but Maui makes the shore recede into the distance, so they have to take their borther with them. In this myth, every time Maui's brothers want to stop and fish, Maui urges them to go further out into the ocean -- a pattern which almost exactly parallels the account of Thor's fishing-trip with the jotun Hymir, with which this episode in the life of Maui shares many parallels. I discuss the famous fishing-trip of Thor in *Star Myths of the World, Volume Four* -- and I believe the two myths are based upon the same constellations in the heavens, despite being found in cultures located so far apart on our planet.

When the brothers have finally paddled all the way out to the open sea, Maui consents to stop the boat, and they let down their hooks. Maui's brothers quickly fill the canoe with fish, and suggest turning back, but now Maui says he will let down his own hook. Here is the account as recorded by George Grey:

> Maui then asked his brothers to give him a little bait to bait his hook. But they replied, "We will not give you any of our bait." So he doubled his fist and struck his nose violently, and the blood gushed out, and he smeared his hook with his own blood for bait. Then he cast it into the sea, and it sank down, till it reached to the small carved figure on the roof of a house

at the bottom of the sea. Passing by the figure, it descended along the outside carved rafters of the roof, and fell in at the doorway of the house, and the hook of Maui-tikitiki-o-Taranga caught first in the sill of the doorway.

Then, feeling something on his hook, he began to haul in his line. Ah! Ah! there ascended on his hook the house of that fellow Tonga-nui [grandson of Tangaroa, god of the ocean]. It came up, up. And as it rose high, oh, dear! how his hook was strained with its great weight. And then there came gurgling up foam and bubbles from the earth, as of an island emerging from the water. His brothers opened their mouths and cried aloud.[124]

The land Maui fihses up in the above description becomes the islands of Aotearoa. Other people on other islands of the Pacific also attribute to Maui the feat of having fished up their islands out of the depths.

I believe that we can associate this story with the same constellations as those which form the foundation for the fishing-trip of Thor with Hymir. As demonstrated in some detail in Volume Four of this series, Thor is undoubtedly associated with the constellation Hercules, and in this episode when Maui is fishing, I believe that Maui is associated with Hercules as well. It is even possible that the description of Maui punching himself in the face to get blood for his hook is somehow associated with the positions of the arms of Hercules, perhaps in conjunction with the arc-shaped Corona Borealis, although of this I am far from certain. It must be admitted that this particular method of baiting his hook could possibly be associated with the outline of Aquarius, from whose pitcher, held in a bent arm, streams of liquid flow downwards (and below whom is the Southern Fish).

What is certain is that the description of the fishing hook of Maui descending down, down into the depths until it passes by the house at the bottom of the ocean, belonging to the grandson of the ocean-god, can be seen as describing the hook of Maui descending past the house-shaped constellation of Ophiuchus, directly below Hercules, until it rests at the sill of the doorway of the structure.

As explained in the first edition of this volume, I believe it is fairly well established that the great fish-hook of Maui is associated with the hook-shaped constellation Scorpio itself, which is found just below Ophiuchus (and indeed can be said to rest at the "sill of the doorway" of Ophiuchus). Note that the hook-shaped pendants which are carved out of whalebone and out of greenstone among the various cultures of the Pacific islands from New Zealand to Hawaii are shaped in a way which is very much evocative of the sinuous shape of Scorpio, and of the barbed tail of that constellation.

Thus, it can be fairly confidently shown that the fishing-trips of both Thor and of Maui involve the constellations Hercules, Ophiuchus, and Scorpio, and envision a fishing-line being dropped from Hercules down to Scorpio. In the story of Thor's fishing, the thunder-god dredges up the mighty Midgard Serpent itself. In the story of Maui's fishing, the great culture-hero dredges up the islands upon which people will later live. In both cases, the others in the boat (Hymir, in the Norse myth, and Maui's brother in the Maui myth) are terrified.

This analysis reveals that Maui, in common with other important figures at the center of an entire "cycle" of myths (such as Moses and Samson in the Hebrew Bible, or Dionysus in the myths of ancient Greece) is not associated with a single constellation but "moves through" more than one constellation, as necessary for his many various exploits and adventures.

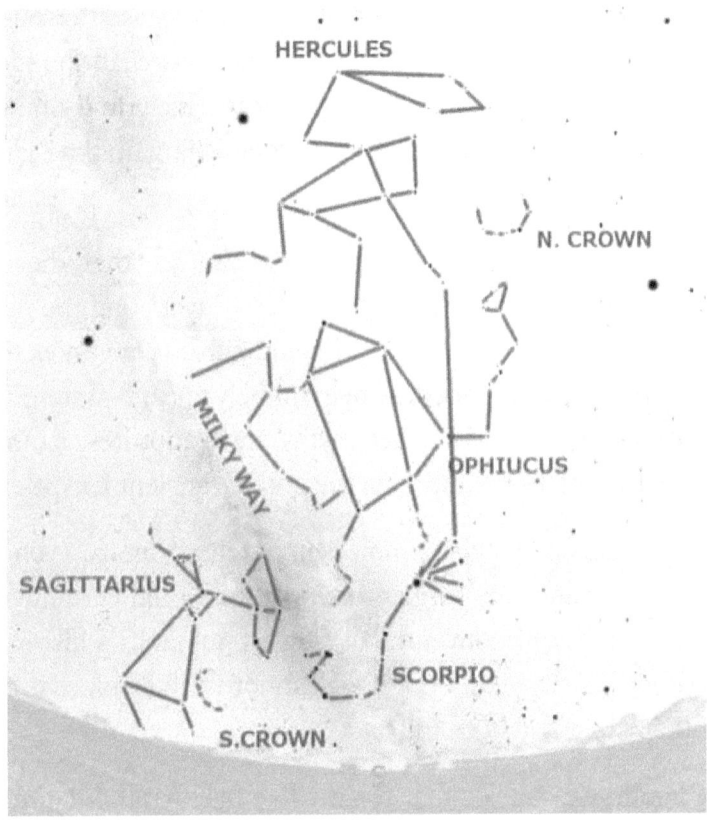

It is very notable to find Maui being associated with the constellation Hercules, because (as Katharine Luomala points out in her encyclopedic study of the hero) Maui is often depicted in artwork such as carvings and totems with his tongue sticking out in a fierce facial grimace, with staring eyes.[125] This facial expression seems somehow to have been associated with Hercules-figures, as discussed at some length in *Star Myths of the World, Volume Two.*

Indeed, figures such as the lion-headed god Bes of ancient Egypt, and the staring Gorgons depicted on ancient Greek and Etruscan pottery, show this same protruding tongue and staring eyes expression -- and I believe it can be convincingly demonstrated that the god Bes and the Gorgon sisters (who chase Perseus after Medusa is slain) are all associated with the constellation Hercules, as is Maui in at least some of his exploits (including one of his most widely-remembered exploits, that of fishing up the islands of the Pacific).

From all these pieces of evidence, we can see that the myths which survived right up until the modern day among the peoples of the vast expanse of the broad Pacific preserve a connection to an extremely ancient system -- an extremely ancient system which also informs the world's other myths and scriptures, to include the stories of the Bible and even the gods of ancient Egypt.

The implications of this commonality are enormous, even if we cannot at present fully explain them. They would certainly seem to indicate that our conventional view of humanity's history is in need of radical revision, even if we cannot yet fully piece together what that revision will entail.

Once again, we can see that the myths of yet another culture are based on the motions of actors in the infinite realm of the heavens. Once again, I would argue that this may indicate that these myths are dealing with truths regarding the infinite realm -- a realm we cannot ordinarily see, and which is thus made "visible" to our understanding through inspired stories which can convey truths which would be difficult for us to grasp any other way (just as Mr. Miyagi used "wax-on, wax-off" to help Daniel-san grasp teachings which the young man would otherwise have had difficulty comprehending, in the first *Karate Kid* movie).

In the episodes we have discussed above, we can sense that in some way, these adventures of Maui are not only about a great god who came down to live among men and women – they are in some way illustrative of our own lives in this incarnate state. We each like Maui are doomed one day to die, but also like him we are imbued with a divine spark which others do not always recognize.

Indeed, in some way we are like Maui's brothers, who often play a role in the Maui stories similar to the role of Doubting Thomas in the gospels: unappreciative of the true nature of their divine brother, and his power to transform the world.

When we begin to accept the truths that the world's ancient myths are trying to convey to us through powerful illustrations and drama, and begin to incorporate them into the way we live and act and think as we go through this incarnate life, we too can begin to overcome obstacles and raise up new creations that others haven't even imagined, like Maui fishing up new islands from beneath the waves.

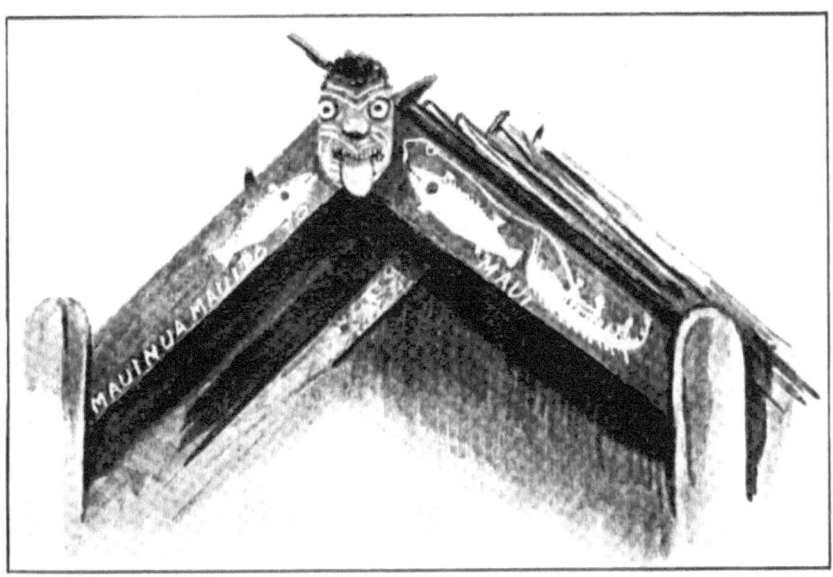

The Fishing of Maui. (From an old house at Whakato.)

The Menri fire myth of Stag and Woodpecker

Having examined at some length the evidence that the myths of the cultures across the broad Pacific are positively members of the same myth-system operating world-wide, let us continue westward past the islands of Melanesia to the Malay Peninsula which stretches down towards Australia and divides the seas at the westernmost edge of the Pacific from the next vast expanse of waters, the Indian Ocean (and Andaman Sea, at the northeastern edge of the Indian Ocean). In this chapter we will briefly examine the fire-origin myth of the Menri people, part of the Semang of the Malay Peninsula, which is today divided between the countries of Thailand and Malaysia.

In the already-mentioned collection of myths entitled *Myths of the Origin of Fire* (1930) by James Frazer, we learn that when the Menri first came into contact with the Malay people, the Malays had fire but the Menri did not.[126] The Malays would gather in a circle around a red flower, the *gantang* or *gantogn*, and warm their hands from it. However, when the "red flower" kindled a blaze in the nearby *lalang* grass, which soon raged out of control, the Menri fled in fear back into the forest, for they knew nothing of this strange and mysterious thing called fire.

The Menri wisdom-keepers tell us that the Stag, seeing the blaze, decided to take some back with him to his home, and so he acquired a firebrand that had been lit by the raging grassfire. He carried it back to his home to serve his needs, but when he went out to work during the day, he placed the brand high up in his hut (or on top of his hut) so that no one could steal it.

But, someone did steal it! The crafty Woodpecker, who was watching the entire proceeding, saw where Stag had placed the firebrand. As soon as the Stag had left, Woodpecker flew up and retrieved the fire, and brought it to the Menri people, telling them that this indeed was fire, and that they should guard it carefully.

Woodpecker also warned the people that the Stag was probably following him, and that he would soon arrive to try to take back his firebrand. He advised that two men should take spears, and when Stag arrived, they should defend themselves with them.

Sure enough, the Stag soon appeared to fetch his fire, and immediately two men with spears attacked. They drove their spears into the head of the animal, who turned around in pain and disappeared again into the deep forest. Up until that time, the Stag had no horns. Afterwards, however, he bore the spears upon his head which became his impressive antlers – but he had lost the gift of fire.

We have encountered a fire-myth in which a Stag steals fire previously, in the Catloltq story of the Old Man and his Daughter, from the Native Americans of the Pacific Northwest living on what is today called Vancouver Island. The center of Vancouver Island sits at around 125° west longitude and over 49° north latitude, while the center of the southern Malay Peninsula sits at around 102° east longitude and only about 4° north latitude (the southernmost tip of the peninsula, near modern-day Singapore, is just over 1° north of the equator line). Clearly, these origin-of-fire myths involving a Stag as the primary agent come from cultures separated by an enormous distance.

The authors of *Hamlet's Mill* take note of the mysterious importance of the symbol of the Stag in myths around the world, and the role of the Stag in bringing fire to mortal men and women. They see evidence that the Stag is somehow related to the archetypal figures associated in the descendants of the cultures of the Mediterranean and western Europe with Kronos and Prometheus, saying:

> For the stag has stood for a long time for Kronos. In the Hindu tradition he is Yama who has been met before as Yama Agastya, and who, "following the course of the great rivers, discovered the way for many." The stag is spread far and wide in the archaic world, with the same connotations. And he is the archaic Prometheus-Kronos, "you who consume all and increase it again by the unlimited order of the Aion, wily-minded, you of crooked counsel, venerable Prometheus." In Greek, *semnē Prometheu.* It leaves no doubts.[127]

Later, in an appendix, the authors of *Hamlet's Mill* investigate further to try to understand how the Stag could be connected in myth to the figures of Kronos and of Prometheus, and they note that in the *Hieroglyphica* attributed to Horapollo, we are told that "A Stag's horns grow out every year: A picture of them means a long space of time."[128] Hence, they speculate, the possible connection between the figure of the Stag and the god of the Aion, Kronos -- who is also associated with the fire-bringer, Prometheus.

And, the authors of *Hamlet's Mill* cite yet another myth, also from the Indigenous First Nations of the Pacific Northwest and also apparently noted by Frazer in another writing where he draws parallels to the Gigantomachy of ancient Greek myth, which features a dancing stag and a figure named Son of Woodpecker who shoots his bow to build a bridge of arrows to heaven, although strangely they do not seem to mention this Menri story recorded by Frazer from half a world away in the Malay Peninsula.[129] The emergence of the same pattern in myth in such disparate locations would certainly seem to point to a need for an explanation beyond "mere coincidence" or "independent development" of the same theme involving the same mythical figures enacting the same drama of stealing fire.

Readers who have followed along with the celestial analysis of the myths thus far should have little difficulty in identifying the constellation most likely to play the role of the fire-stealing Stag in this Menri myth. I'm convinced it is the same constellation which plays the role of Stags in other myths: Centaurus.

We've already seen that the outline of Centaurus can be envisioned not only as a centaur (a combination of a human and a horse) but also as a great deer with spreading antlers -- and note also that Centaurus is located along the Milky Way, in the vicinity of the brightest and widest portion of the Milky Way band, and that the Milky Way plays the role of a column of fire and of smoke in many ancient myths and scriptures.

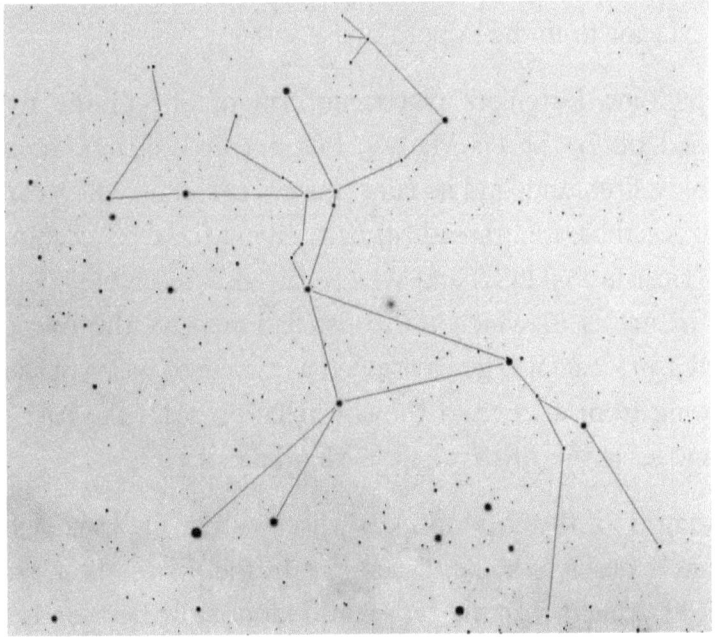

Note that the feet of the Stag are positioned within the band of the Milky Way, and that these "feet" contain the brightest stars of the constellation – including the famous star Alpha Centauri, the brightest star in the constellation of the Centaur, one of the three brightest fixed stars in the heavens from our vantage point on earth, and thought to be the closest star system to us in the galaxy, at just 4.37 light years away. You can imagine the Stag stealing the fire from the conflagration in the *lalang* grass: perhaps holding it in one of his forefeet, perhaps represented by the bright star Alpha Centauri.

The Stag proceeds to hang the firebrand up in his hut (or place it on the top of his hut) in order to prevent anyone from stealing it. As already argued previously, I think it likely that the "hut" in this case may be played by the constellation Ophiuchus, and I would also strongly suspect that the firebrand can be seen in the constellation Coma Berenices, which we have already seen being placed high up over a fire in the story of the Hero Twins and Seven Macaw from the Popol Vuh.

There, Coma Berenices played an arm of one of the twins, wrenched off by Seven Macaw, but it could also be seen to resemble a firebrand, and its faint clusters of stars -- which can be seen to resemble fine threads of hair, giving the constellation its name "Berenice's Hair," and which can also resemble spurting blood in myths in which the constellation plays the role of a severed arm – can also be envisioned as flames or wisps of smoke emanating from a torch, if the constellation plays the role of a firebrand, as in this myth from the Menri people.

The identity of the Woodpecker who sees the firebrand where Stag hid it deserves some discussion. In the first edition of this volume, I argued that the bird can undoubtedly be seen in the constellation Corvus the Crow, which appears to be gazing in the direction of Virgo (as discussed in the previous chapter) -- and if we extend the line of its gaze that would have Corvus looking towards the top of the "hut" of Ophiuchus and the firebrand hidden by the Stag.

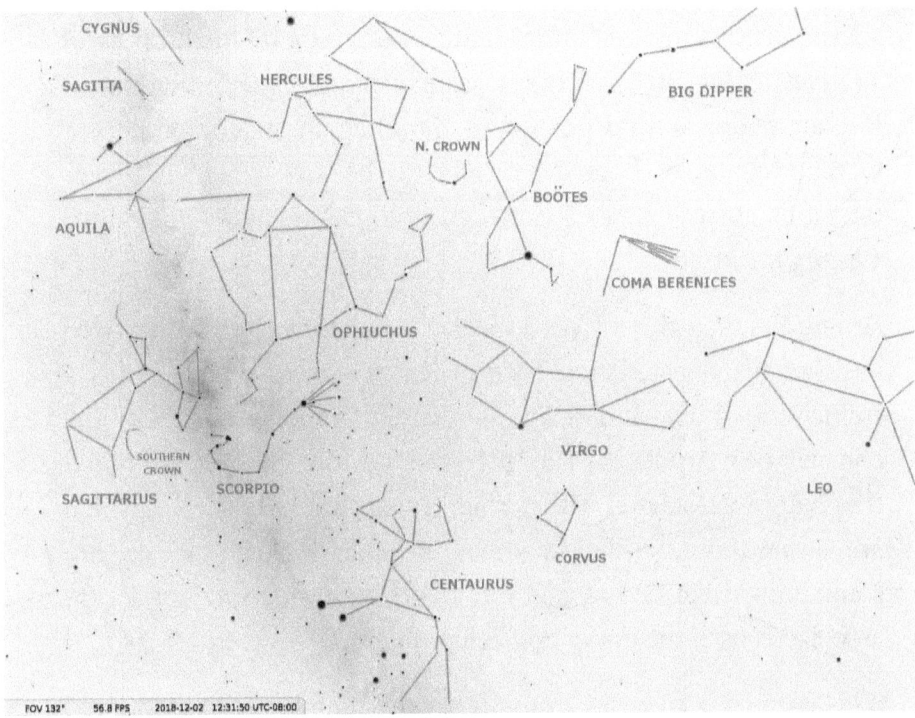

Upon further reflection, however, and with the benefit of nearly five more years of studying the connections between myths and stars since the writing of that first edition, I would offer the possibility that this prolific Woodpecker of myth, found in fire-stealing stories stretched across the globe, might be associated with the outline of Aquila the Eagle. Note first that woodpeckers (including those found in the Malay Peninsula, as well as those of the forests in the Pacific Northwest in the Americas) are crested birds, with a pointed tuft of feathers projecting behind the head opposite to the bill, and that Aquila can certainly be envisioned as a crested bird as well and thus as a Woodpecker!

In addition, we have the citation in *Hamlet's Mill* of a myth "from the Northwest" in which a Son of Woodpecker shoots his bow and creates a bridge to heaven with his arrows.[130] The specific source for this myth is unfortunately not given by the authors of *Hamlet's Mill*, although they note that James Frazer mentions it in conjunction with a parallel to the Giagantomachy of ancient Greece (again, without a footnote to the text in which Frazer cites this story -- it does not appear to be in his *Myths of the Origin of Fire*).

A figure named Son of Woodpecker who shoots a bow may well indicate the constellation Sagittarius, which of course holds a tremendous bow, and which is located *immediately below* the constellation Aquila the Eagle. In the previous chapter, we noted that figures associated with certain constellations in the sky which are located directly below other constellations in the sky are sometimes described in myth as being *descended from* a figure associated with the upper constellation.

This pattern is true, for example, in the figures of Solomon and David in the Old Testament: as we will discuss at length in *Star Myths of the World, Volume Three* (*Star Myths of the Bible*), King David can be positively identified with the figure of Hercules in many of the scriptural stories about him, while Solomon can be confidently identified as corresponding to the heavenly figure of Ophiuchus. The constellation Ophiuchus is located immediately below the constellation Hercules: hence, David is the father of Solomon, and Solomon is *descended from* David.

Similarly, if we find a myth in which a figure who is designated as Son of Woodpecker is shooting a bow, this may well indicate that Woodpecker figures in myth are associated with Aquila, rather than with Corvus, because Sagittarius is located directly beneath Aquila.

Returning to the Menri story, it is also likely that the spearmen in this myth who drive off the Stag by sticking him in the head with their spears (thus giving the Stag horns, although he loses possession of the fire) can be identified with the figure of Ophiuchus. In many myths, Ophiuchus-figures are described as carrying a mighty spear, and at times as carrying two spears. Note that Ophiuchus is located above Centaurus in the star-chart on the preceding page.

As stated before when exploring the celestial aspects of the "fire-stealing" myths found in cultures around the world, I am convinced that these stories are intended to convey an esoteric and primarily spiritual message, rather than having to do with the supposed origin of actual fire among men and women. Note that virtually all of those fire-myths examined in this volume have involved constellations in the vicinity of the widest and brightest part of the Milky Way galaxy, which we believe to be the Galactic Core -- constellations such as Sagittarius, Ophiuchus, Aquila, and Centaurus.

These constellations indicate the region of the annual cycle in the vicinity of the "great-turning point" of the year, when the sun's southward progress towards the low-point of winter solstice will finally stop and turn back northward again, symbolizing a reversal in our own downward motion into carnality and our own "second birth," when we realize that we are not just the sum of our physical nature and begin to reconnect with our spiritual nature and our Higher Self, and begin to re-integrate with our own "divine spark." I believe that the constellations found in various myths were imbued with coded significance in conjunction with the great heavenly cycles, including this great annual cycle in which the great winter solstice turning-point of the year signified rebirth and the elevation of the spiritual nature, which is envisioned as being "cast-down" into matter at the point of the autumnal equinox (in the vicinity of Virgo).

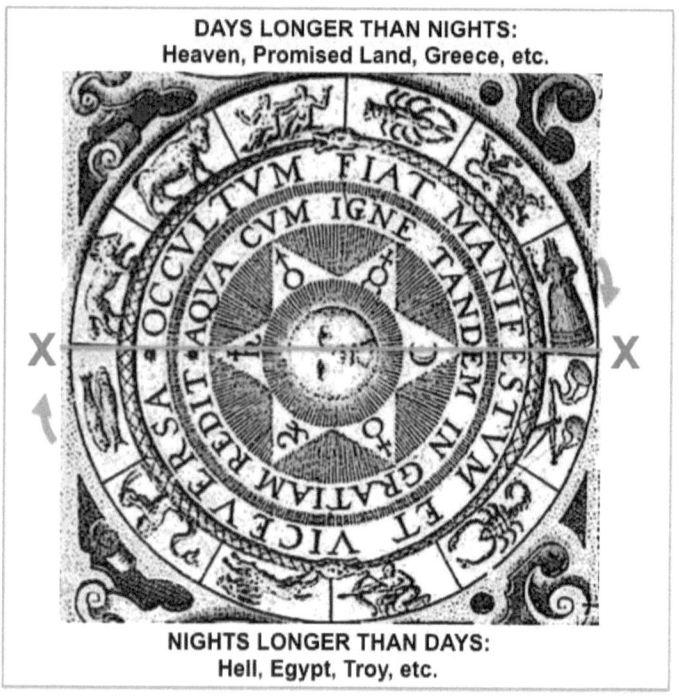

DAYS LONGER THAN NIGHTS:
Heaven, Promised Land, Greece, etc.

NIGHTS LONGER THAN DAYS:
Hell, Egypt, Troy, etc.

In a lecture entitled *Easter: the Birthday of the Gods,* Alvin Boyd Kuhn lays out this ancient esoteric system in which the turnings of the great annual cycle were envisioned as illustrative of the experiences of our own human souls, which originate in the realm of pure spirit (the upper half of the wheel, and indeed at the highest point of summer solstice, located at the 12 o'clock position of the zodiac diagram shown above) and which then plunge down into the incarnate experience at the point of fall equinox (located at the 3 o'clock position in the zodiac diagram shown above). Of the downward plunge into matter, enroute to the great turning point at winter solstice, Kuhn says:

> Then on past September, like any seed sown in the soil, the soul entity sinks its roots deeper and deeper into matter, for at its later stages of growth it must be able to utilize the energy of matter's atomic force to effectuate its ends for its own spiritual aggrandizement. It is itself to be lifted up to heights of cosmic consciousness, but no more can an oak exalt its majestic form to highest reaches without the dynamic energization received from the earth at its feet can soul rise up above body without drawing forth the strength of the body's dynamo of power. Down, down it descends then through the October, November and December path of the sun, until it stands at the nadir of its descent on December 21.
>
> Here it has reached the turning-point, at which the energies that were stored potentially in its seed form will feel the first touch of quickening power and will begin to stir into activity. At the winter solstice of the cycle the process of involution of spirit into matter comes to a stand-still -- just what the solstice means in relation to the sun -- and while apparently stationary in its deep lodgment in matter, like moving water locked up in winter's ice, it is slowly making the turn as on a pivot from outward and downward to movement at first tangential, then more directly upward to its high point in spirit home. So the winter solstice signalizes the end of "death" and the rebirth of life in a new generation.[31]

This insight of Alvin Boyd Kuhn is of tremendous significance, and I am convinced that he has correctly deciphered part of the language of the ancient wisdom. While most other analysts believe that when ancient myths speak of "death" and of "the land of the dead" they are referring to the afterlife, the above analysis by Alvin Boyd Kuhn (which he develops at great length in other writings, and especially in his masterpiece, *Lost Light*) implies that when myths refer to the state of death they are usually referring to *this incarnate life*, into which we plunge at the point of fall equinox and in whose clutches we become more and more tightly gripped as we descend towards that great turning-point. It is at the great turning-point that we begin to awaken to our true divine and spiritual nature, where the seed that has been buried in the earth as if dead (to use the metaphor employed in the quotation above by Kuhn) begins to sprout forth towards new life.

Kuhn masterfully perceived that the world's ancient wisdom envisioned and described this cycle of descent (and first birth) and then regeneration (and second birth) using the great cycle of the annual wheel, and the four great division points of the year: summer solstice, autumnal equinox, winter solstice, and spring equinox. What he does not appear to have noticed is that the *figures in the myths themselves* are also associated with specific constellations, and can thus be employed to indicate positions within that great cycle with even greater precision than is permitted with the rough "quartering" of the year between the four cardinal points of the solstices and equinoxes.

Indeed, as will be demonstrated in more detail in Volume Two of this series, and particularly in the examination of the Odyssey, this added understanding enables us to see motions which go beyond the great circle of the year, because by employing the figure of the Milky Way (which of course is not a constellation itself but rather a great band which encircles the entire heavens, and which runs like a shining column from the lowest point on the zodiac wheel up to the highest point), the ancient myths can speak of the elevation of our spirit along a path that makes a kind of "short-cut" across the center of the zodiac wheel. There is some indication that the fiery path of the Milky Way was envisioned as the proper path for our spiritual elevation and integration, rather than forever following the endless turning of the four stations on the outside of the wheel.

Thus, I believe that these ancient myths involving the origin of fire, and employing figures associated with the constellations near the lowest point on the zodiac wheel, and the great fiery path of the Milky Way itself, are treating esoteric subjects of the absolute utmost importance to our lives to this very day. And, it is perhaps also highly noteworthy that this place of spiritual rebirth is associated by the myths with the region surrounding the Galactic Center itself, where we now believe that stars are born.

These are not "primitive" stories, as they were often patronizingly described by scholars in previous decades and centuries. They are part of the precious inheritance of the human race, imparted in remote antiquity from a source and by a method which is no longer known. This knowledge has tremendous implications for our understanding of our own past, and our understanding of the world as it is in this very moment, at this perilous juncture in human history.

Star Myths of Ancient Egypt

We have now in our survey of world Star Myths traveled across great geographical distances, exploring myths from cultures found on the continents of Australia and Africa and the Americas. On this journey, we have embarked across the Pacific Ocean, examining some of the many myths surrounding the figure of Maui, whose exploits are recounted from the Hawaiian Islands to the Society Islands (Tahiti and Borabora and Raiatea) to the Tuamotus and on to Aotearoa (New Zealand), up through Micronesia as far as the Carolines, and even through parts of Melanesia. We have continued even beyond those islands to the Malay Peninsula and examined a myth of the Menri people, on the land that borders the Andaman Sea and the northern reaches of the Indian Ocean.

In all of these investigations, we have found evidence that the ancient myths of all of these disparate cultures bear evidence of belonging to a great worldwide system, speaking a common celestial language, in which the figures and episodes of the myths can be traced to specific constellations in the night sky: constellations which are often imbued with similar characteristics, personalities, and powers, and constellations whose esoteric meaning and message appear to share many commonalities even in cultures separated by vast distances -- even separated by half the distance around the globe.

Now, having traversed great gulfs of ocean and mountain ranges and jungles, we will turn our journey of exploration in a new direction, and travel back across enormous gulfs of time, back to the earliest civilizations known to conventional history, exploring the myths of ancient Egypt, and ancient Mesopotamia, of ancient

India, and ancient China. We will seek to determine whether it can be said that the myths of these ancient cultures were also based on celestial metaphor, and if they appear to have been using the same system that we have found to be in operation in the myths of Australia and Africa and the Americas and Oceania -- and which, as explored in detail in subsequent volumes of this series, we can show to have formed the foundation of the myths of ancient Greece, and the myths of the Norse, and the stories found in the scriptures that we call the Bible, stretching from Genesis all the way to the book of the Revelation of John.

We will first travel back to the awe-inspiring civilization of ancient Egypt, one of the oldest civilizations known to us today, whose art and architecture, even after the impact of thousands of years, can still take one's breath away.

And yet, despite the wealth of artwork and architecture to survive the ravages of the passing millennia, much of the mythology of ancient Egypt remains at least partially shrouded in mystery.

Writing in 1819, three years before Champollion's breakthrough with the Rosetta Stone began to unlock the writing system of the Egyptian hieroglyphs which had been forgotten since antiquity, James Cowles Prichard (1786 - 1848) points out that although the accounts of the ancient Greek and Roman writers (and also some Egyptian writers, from the later Ptolelmaic period) discussing the gods and goddesses of Egypt have survived, even "Hecataeus and Herodotus, who travelled in Egypt during the period when its native hierarchy still flourished, saw only the outward form of its mythology, or have studiously concealed their knowledge of its recondite sense."[132]

For example, Prichard notes that Herodotus describes the Egyptians as having had three successive series of gods, the oldest set of which were eight in number, but he only mentions two of them by name (whom he equates to the Greek deities Pan and Latona), followed by two sets of deities numbering twelve each, which he (in common with virtually every other ancient author) saw as having direct correspondences to the gods and goddesses of Greece.[133]

One can only imagine the excitement that gripped the world (and in particular the scholarly world) during the years following the discovery by a Napoleonic officer in 1799 of the fragment of an ancient stele which has come to be called Rosetta Stone, containing an identical proclamation written in Greek, Demotic, and classic ancient Egyptian hieroglyphics. Now at last, it was hoped, the ability to read hieroglyphics would be resurrected after so many centuries, and the mysterious texts which adorned so many ancient monuments would at last give up their secrets!

After some years of work, the young genius Jean-François Champollion (1790 - 1832), whose efforts to decipher Egyptian hieroglyphics began in 1820, produced a breakthrough in 1822, when he realized that the hieroglyphs themselves could function both as logographs (somewhat akin to Chinese characters) and as phonetic symbols (like our western alphabet), an insight which had eluded others on the same quest. Over the next several years, Champollion and other scholars made great advances in their ability to read ancient Egyptian texts.

As Geraldine Harris Pinch of the Faculty of Oriental Studies at the University of Oxford explains, those hoping to find in the hieroglyphs some comprehensive text that would explain the ancient beliefs of the Egyptian civilization were doomed to disappointment:

> It soon became clear that Ancient Egyptian religion had not been centred on a single holy book comparable with the Bible or the Koran. There were plenty of hymns and formulaic prayers but few texts that Europeans would classify as theology or philosophy. The vast majority of temple inscriptions proved to be about kings making standard offerings to gods. No collection of national myths and few long narratives of any kind were recovered. Such mythical narratives as did survive were mainly embedded in collections of funerary texts aimed at easing the transition into the afterlife or in magical spells for use in daily life. A relatively small number of mythical themes occurred over and over again in such sources.[134]

Writing near the end of the century which had witnessed Champollion's breakthrough in deciphering the hieroglyphs, Max Müller (1823 - 1900), also an Oxford professor, declared in his preface to his text on *Egyptian Mythology*: "As yet an exhaustive description of this religion could scarcely be written."[135]

He noted that although the Egyptians clearly perceived a great pantheon of gods and goddesses, nevertheless:

> Of most gods we know no myths, an ignorance which is not due to accidental loss of information, as some Egyptologists thought, but to the fact that the deities in question really possessed no mythology."[136]

Of course, just because we do not have extensive texts detailing their characteristics and exploits does not necessarily mean that the majority of deities of ancient Egypt "possessed no mythology." It is certainly possible that exploits and aspects of these gods and goddesses were known and preserved by methods other than the texts that have survived.

It is also possible, and I believe fairly likely, that many of the different gods and goddesses depicted in the artwork of ancient Egypt and known to us by their names (even if not accompanied by mythological accounts which can help us to know more about their aspects than we have been able to deduce from the clues that we have at our disposal) might be aspects or avatars of other Egyptian deities, in much the same way that the gods and goddesses of ancient India manifest avatars, which we will have occasion to discuss later in this volume.

As will be demonstrated, I believe it can be shown that the avatars of certain gods of India derive from constellations nearby in the heavens to the primary constellation of that same god or goddess -- and the same may hold true for the gods of ancient Egypt, although at this point it is difficult to know for certain. If so, then perhaps part of the reason why we do not have extensive "mythologies" about all of the different gods and goddesses may relate to the fact that, as avatars or variants of gods about whom more was already known, not as much needed to be said about some of the deities upon whose exploits and characteristics the hieroglyphic record remains largely silent.

Even about some of the more central deities, the hieroglyphic texts seem to assume knowledge on the part of the reader, and thus even though the god we call Osiris is mentioned in some of the earliest known texts to survive from any civilization on the planet, the so-called Pyramid Texts carved upon the inner walls of the pyramids constructed during the reign of the Fourth and Fifth Dynasty kings and queens, beginning with Unas (or Unis) who reigned from approximately 2353 BC to 2323 BC (over 4,300 years ago), we will rely on the admittedly imperfect and much later outline of the Osiris myth provided to us by the historian and philosopher Plutarch of Chaeronea, who lived from AD 46 to about AD 120.

However, even without a comprehensive text in which we can find detailed accounts and written clues concerning exploits and adventures of all the various deities of ancient Egypt, what we do have are utterances and declarations in texts such as the Pyramid Texts, the later Coffin Texts, the variations on the Book of Coming Forth by Day, which was called the "Book of the Dead" in the 1800s by Prussian Egyptologist Karl Richard Lepsius (1810 - 1884), and other texts which provide us with brief glimpses and details, if not with an extensive narrative. With these, and with what we can learn from statues and other artwork depicting the deities, we still have access to enough knowledge about Egyptian gods and goddesses to make some definitive connections to the constellations of the heavenly realm, and to demonstrate that the same ancient system which we have found underlying the myths of so many other regions of the globe can also be found informing the spiritual wisdom of this mysterious ancient culture.

We will first briefly discuss some of the gods and goddesses of ancient Egypt, about whom we can deduce enough information to make connections to the worldwide celestial system, and then we will move into a more extensive examination of the mythology surrounding Isis, Osiris, Horus, and Set.

Before diving in, it is worthwhile to point out that the very pronunciation of ancient Egyptian words is largely unknown to us today in many cases, because the Egyptian writing does not include most vowels. Speakers of the actual language would have had little difficulty deciphering what was written, but we ourselves are often without enough information to actually recreate the pronunciation that a word would have had in the original tongue. Max Müller provides the analogy of the common abbreviation "st" in English, which we use when addressing a letter as a short-hand for the word "street," but the abbreviation as written does not give sufficient information for someone to determine the sound of the word "street" if they did not know the word that was indicated by the two consonantal letters themselves.[137] Indeed, although Müller himself does not point this out, the same abbreviation used in a different context would indicate a completely different-sounding word, "saint," and a native speaker of English would have little difficulty knowing when "st" means "street" and when it means "saint," but the letters themselves do not give any clues as to how to pronounce either word.

"A great part of the Egyptian vocabulary is known only in this way," Müller explains, "and in many instances we must make the words pronouceable by arbitrarily assigning vowel sounds, etc. to them."[138]

The situation has not really changed in the more than 100 years since Müller wrote those words. Indeed, in a much more recent text on *Egypt and the Egyptians*, by Douglas J. Brewer of the University of Illinois and Emily Teeter of the University of Chicago, the second edition of which was published in 2007 and which is presently in use as a textbook in some college courses on Egypt, a very similar example to that employed by Professor Müller is employed, when the authors explain that "when reading the classified advertisements in a newspaper, anyone who has shopped for an automobile can recognize and read the seller's abbreviation: 2003 Ford, red, 2dr, exc. cond., v-6, lw ml, ask. 4K obo, will neg."[139]

Of course, the advent of free online advertising sites has by now nearly obliterated the classified advertisement section of newspapers (along with the business model of most print newspapers themselves), so that in a few more years or decades the above example may become unreadable to younger generations, but the point the authors make is that while such a system is understandable to those versed in it, "such a system poses a problem for scholars trying to vocalize ancient Egyptian words written in hieroglyphs because no one knows with certainty how they were pronounced."[140]

Professors Brewer and Teeter do point out that we have some clues regarding the ancient pronunciation, based on the Coptic language which descends from earlier forms of Egyptian, as well as from ancient transcription of Egyptian words into Greek, Akkadian, and other versions, which enable some reconstruction of the original, but the general uncertainty means that we cannot be dogmatic about most of the original pronunciations of the names of gods and goddesses mentioned below -- and also helps to explain why some names have been rendered with different spellings during different decades or by different authors.

The first of the gods of ancient Egypt we will discuss is the god Atum (also sometimes written as Tum, Tem, or Temu, for reasons just described). In the creation account of the ancient city of On (or Heliopolis), in lower Egypt near modern Cairo, Atum is described as being the first god to emerge from the watery emptiness of Nu (*nw*, also written as Nun, Nenu, or Nunu) in the beginning. There are other creation accounts from other cultural centers in ancient Egypt, such as Memphis, Thebes, and

Hermopolis -- and these accounts and the main gods who are described in them are sometimes referred to as the "Memphite theology" or the "Theban theology," etc. Atum is the primordial god described in the theology of On or Heliopolis, while Ptah is the primordial god of the Memphite theology, and Amun of the Theban.

The Heliopolitan theology describes Atum emerging from the primordial emptiness and standing upon the Benben, a triangular or pyramidal stone which also emerges from the primordial waters. This description sounds very much like a description of the constellations Hercules and Ophiuchus, with Hercules being positioned directly above and indeed "standing upon" the triangular shape at the top of the constellation Ophiuchus, which could very easily be seen as representative of the pyramidal Benben stone.

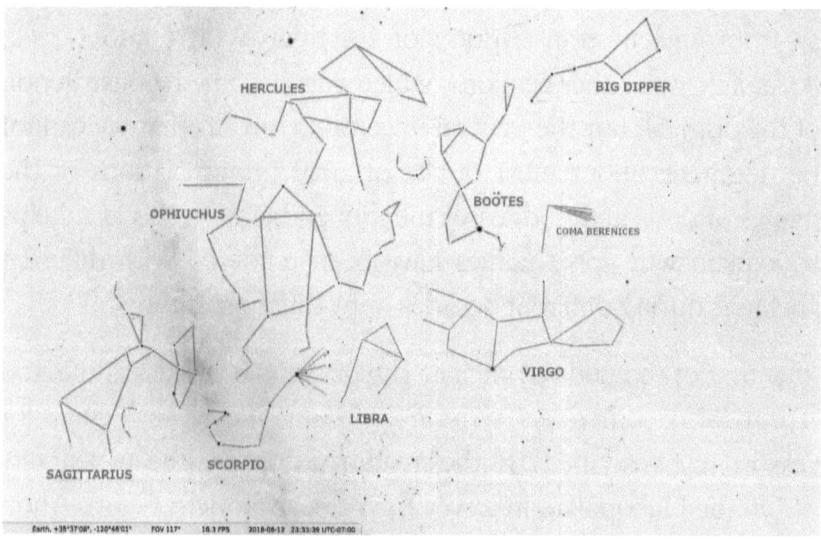

Professor Geraldine Pinch informs us that: "The name Atum comes from a word meaning completeness or totality. The potential for all life was contained within Atum."[141]

Because he personifies totality, Atum could generate other gods without the presence of any other -- and thus the ancient texts describe Atum bringing forth the next two deities by the process of masturbation.

Utterances or spells in the Pyramid Texts and the Coffin Texts inform us that Atum took his own semen and spat it out to create the god Shu (god of air) and the goddess Tefnut (goddess of moisture and dew).

The Pyramid Texts, Coffin Texts, and Book of Coming Forth by Day (also called the Book of the Dead, and in previoius centuries often referred to as "The Ritual") consist primarily of passages which begin with the Egyptian words meaning "to speak with the mouth," and are hence called "utterances" or "spells." Utterance 527 of the Pyramid Texts declares:

> To say: Atum created by his masturbation in Heliopolis.
> He put his phallus in his fist,
> to excite desire thereby.
> The twins were born, Shu and Tefnut [. . .][42]

This passage is graphically clear. However, students will often read that Atum created Shu and Tefnut by his spittle instead (or, in some cases, will read that Atum is sometimes described as creating by masturbation, and sometimes by spittle). Indeed, the spells in the Pyramid Texts and other texts sometimes seem to contradict each other, and other texts declare that Atum "sneezed" out or "spat" out Shu and Tefnut, but as Professor of Egyptology of the University of Leuven in Brussels, Harco Willems, explains in his book *The Coffin of Heqata*, commenting on Spell 77 of the Coffin Texts (which recounts this act), "reference is not made to Atum's spittle, but to his seed, which, after its ejaculation, entered his mouth, whence Shu and Tefnut were spat out."[43]

Geraldine Pinch says that Atum "masturbated and impregnated himself with his own semen to produce the divine siblings Shu and Tefnut" and that "In the act of creation, Atum was shown in human form holding or sucking his erect penis."[44]

The stars of the constellation Hercules could be connected with only very slight modification to envision this action of creation:

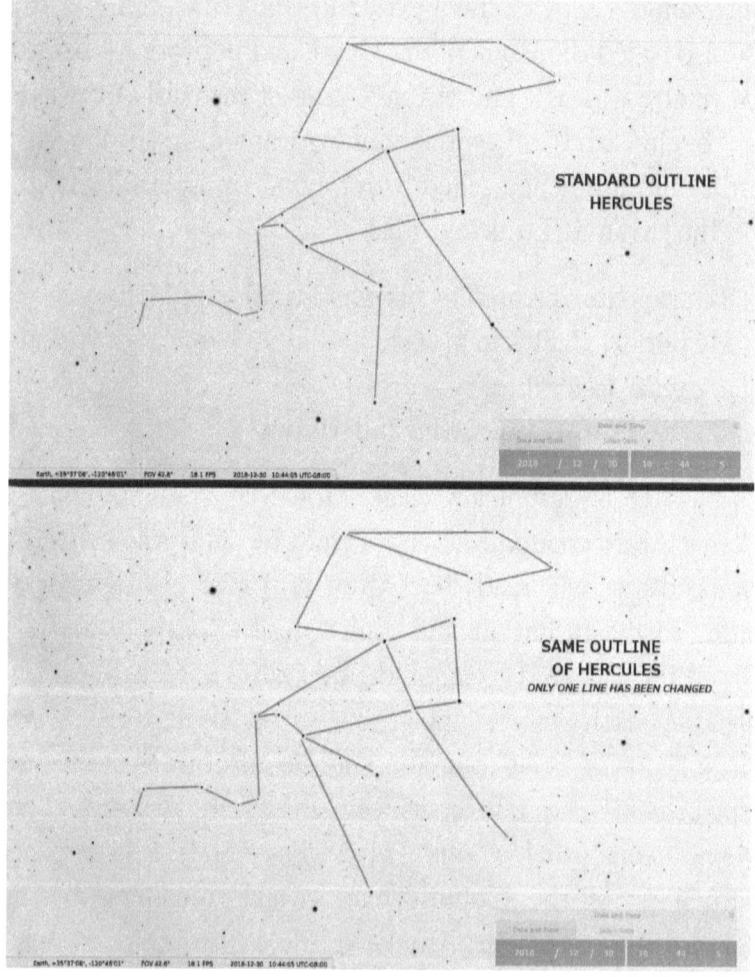

In the star-chart above, only one connecting line has been changed, but the interpretation of the outline is obviously much different. It does not take much imagination to realize that the downward-reaching arm of the constellation could also be altered to envision the act of self-creation described in the ancient Egyptian utterances (alternately, the line of the phallus envisioned in the second chart above could be extended to the current location of the downward-reaching hand, probably to the second-to-last star in that downward arm, rather than to the star at the very end of the lower arm as drawn).

The above analysis illustrates a phenomenon common in ancient mythology from many cultures: extremely frank and sometimes graphic sexual themes are sometimes described, some of them very jarring to modern readers (especially those who have grown up with some exposure to the myths, but with the more graphic sexual content expurgated or altered). As it turns out, I believe that most if not all of the content in mythology that can seem shocking or unnerving can be shown to have a celestial explanation, and thus to be yet another example of the operation of the ancient system of metaphor. The ancients were not shy about using metaphors relating to virtually all aspects of life, including sexual aspects, and I believe that there are esoteric and spiritual teachings underlying virtually everything preserved in the widom of the ancient myths.

Thus, Atum sneezes out or spits out the god Shu and the goddess Tefnut. Note in this description that we find something of a parallel to the Maya myth preserved in the Popol Vuh, in which the Hero Twins are generated by the act of spitting as well (although in that case, it is the calabash head of their father who spits into the hand of Blood Maiden, thus making her pregnant).

When we examined that myth in a previous chapter, we suggested a possible celestial foundation for that story as well.

This act of creation by Atum has an even more direct parallel, I would argue, to the well-known myth of the birth of Athena from the head of Zeus, in the mythology of ancient Greece. In *Star Myths of the World, Volume Two* we will see abundant evidence which argues that the goddess Athena is associated with the tall, spear-bearing (and often shield-bearing) form of the constellation Ophiuchus, located directly below the constellation Hercules (a constellation which can be difinitively associated with the god Zeus, wielder of the thunderbolt). This myth of the birth of Athena is another example in which a figure associated with a constellation *below* another in the heavens is said in myth to be *descended* from that constellation directly above.

In the myth of Atum's creation of Shu and Tefnut, Shu is ejected from the nose or mouth of Atum -- and I believe that Shu (who is usually depicted as standing, with two upraised arms) can be associated with the same constellation of Ophiuchus. The downward-reaching arm of the constellation Hercules, directly above, can be seen as a line proceeding out of the head of Hercules -- the line indicating the sneezing or spitting-out by Atum which brings Shu into being.

I believe that Shu can be identified with Ophiuchus, and that his sister Tefnut (associated with the moisture and dew which inhabits the air and which comes down from heaven) is most likely associated with the Milky Way itself.

The star-chart on the following page shows the events and heavenly actors of the discussion thus far: Atum is associated with the figure of Hercules, who is standing above the pyramid-shaped Benben stone just below. Because he is complete in himself, he can create by himself, without any other, and does so in the process described above. He spits out the god Shu, seen directly below and associated with the constellation Hercules. The goddess Tefnut may well be associated with the Milky Way, immediately adjacent to Ophiuchus (Shu):

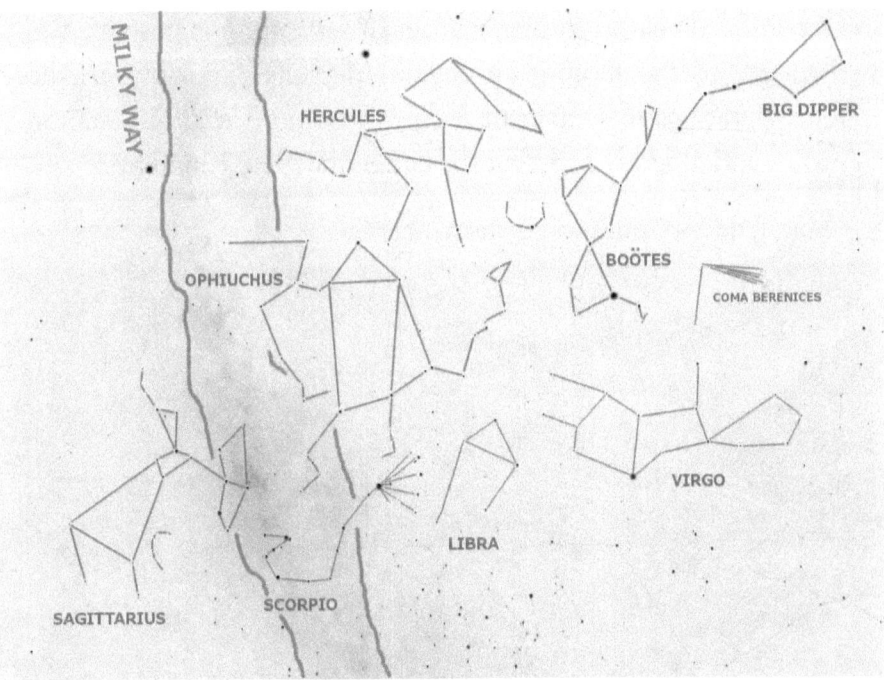

Professor Geraldine Pinch explains that Shu and Tefnut, once separated from their father Atum,

> came together in the first sexual union of male and female. Tefnut then gave birth to another pair of deities, a son Geb, who was associated with the earth, and a daughter Nut, who was associated with the sky. Geb and Nut embraced each other so ardently that there was no room between them for anything to exist. Nut conceived children but could not or would not give birth to them. Geb and Nut seemed to want

to become one, reversing the movement toward diversity. If creation was to continue, another separation was necessary.[145]

This embrace of earth and sky also threatened to crush out any space where life could exist, and thus to remedy the situation, their father Shu separated Geb (the earth) and Nut (the sky). Geraldine Pinch notes that this act of separation is described in Spell 76 of the Coffin Texts, and depicted in many artistic representations from ancient Egypt, "first portrayed in detail on coffins and funerary papyri at the end of the New Kingdom."[146]

One such representation is shown below:

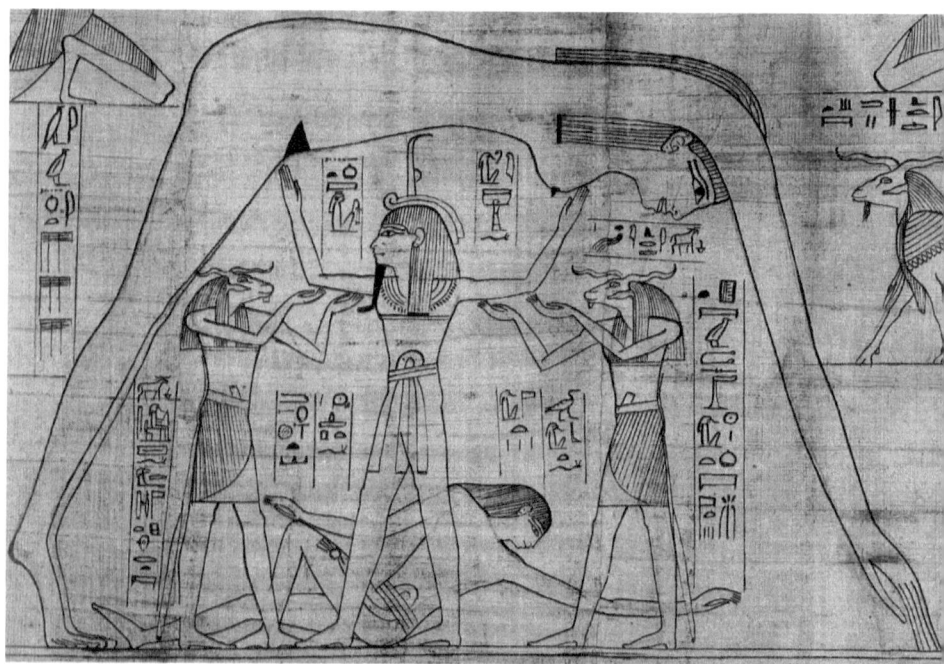

Here we see the god Shu, with his upraised arms, separating the sky goddess Nut (above) and the earth god Geb (below, reclining semi-supine, stretching one hand forward). Professor Pinch explains that, "Shu created a space between earth and sky in which creatures could breathe the air that gives life."[147]

Because we have already analyzed some evidence which suggests that Shu with his upraised arms is associated with the constellation Ophiuchus, the celestial correspondences in this famous scene from ancient Egyptian myth almost leap out at us.

In the above scene, the constellation Hercules is now the sky goddess, Nut. If we simply do not imagine lines connecting the stars of the "forward leg" of the outline of Hercules, the outline which remains will be seen to resemble the posture of Nut very satisfactorily. Note that it is not at all uncommon for the same constellation to play a male figure in one episode of myth and a female figure in another episode -- or even within the same episode. We have already mentioned that the constellation Hercules almost certainly plays the role of the Gorgon sisters of Medusa in Greek myth (who are, of course, female entities).

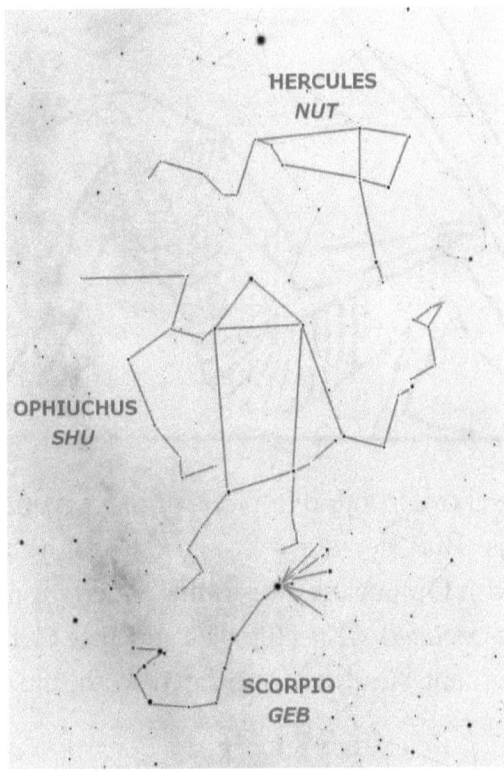

Note that the sprawled-out body posture in which Geb is invariably portrayed by the ancient artists indicates an association with the constellation Scorpio: the body-angle of the god of earth and of the outline of the constellation in the sky are nearly identical. Additionally, we know that Geb was sometimes described as the father of serpents, and that he was also sometimes depicted with a serpent-head. These attributes, in conjunction with the clear celestial correspondences seen in the recurring artistic depictions of Shu separating Nut and Geb, should confirm the association of the earth god with the constellation Scorpio.

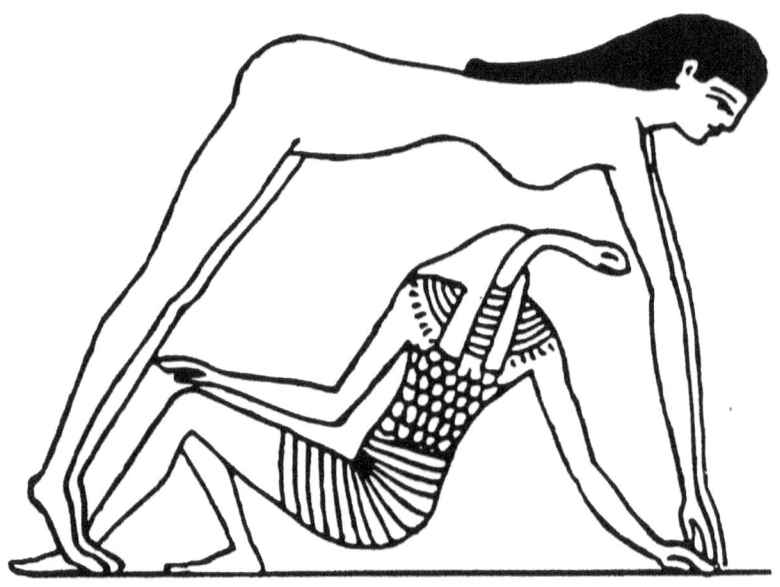

The drawing above is found in *Gods of the Egyptians* (1904), by E. A. Wallis Budge (1857 - 1934). Although it omits Shu (associated with Ophiuchus), it is quite evident from the outlines that Nut is associated with Hercules and that Geb (shown this time with serpent head) is associated with the constellation Scorpio.

It is very noteworthy that, as Budge explains: "According to one myth Nut gave birth to her son the Sun-god daily, and passing over her body he arrived at her mouth, into which he disappeared, and passing through her body he was reborn the following morning."[48] This direction of progress would seem to mirror that attempted by Maui in the Pacific myth examined earlier (which led to Maui's death).

It is also most intriguing to note the similarities between this scene of Shu standing between Geb and Nut, and the scene on the recently-discovered Pylos Combat Agate -- particularly the general postures of Geb (in the Egyptian scene) and the "slain warrior" (at the bottom of the Pylos Agate scene). While I believe both scenes are based upon the same three constellations (Hercules above, Ophiuchus in the middle, and Scorpio at the bottom), it is possible that the Pylos scene also incorporates aspects of Sagittarius. The slain warrior in the Pylos scene is facing in the other direction as that faced by Geb in the Egyptian artwork, and has one arm draped over his head in an attitude characteristic of other Sagittarius-based artwork in later paintings (and no doubt inspired by the "plume" of stars that appear over the head of the constellation Sagittarius in the sky).

Nevertheless, the slain warrior in the Pylos Combat Agate scene has one leg stretched out, in much the same way that Geb extends one arm in the Egyptian depictions of the scene of Geb, Shu and Nut (see again the drawing on page 193).

One other noteworthy detail in the above identification of Geb with the figure of Scorpio is the confirmation that it gives us for the previous assertion that constellations below another constellation will sometimes be described in myth as being descended from the constellation above: Geb (Scorpio) is the son of Shu (Ophiuchus), and Scorpio is located directly beneath the feet of Ophiuchus. However, we also see in this myth that Nut, who is the daughter of Shu, is associated with a constellation directly above Ophiuchus -- so apparently this analogy of genealogical descent can sometimes be seen to go "back upwards" in myth! We will have occasion to see a similar phenomenon with one of Geb's sons by Nut, the god Osiris, who can be shown to have connections to the constellation Ophiuchus as well.

Returning to the figure of Atum, readers with some background in Egyptian mythology may be aware of the fact that this all-encompassing creator god, whose very name signifies completeness and totality, is also identified with the sun-god Ra (or Re), and that his name is often given as Atum-Ra or as Ra-Atum.

Geraldine Pinch notes that, in addition to the Hand of Atum (with which he had given birth to Shu and Tefnut) and which was personified as an independent goddess, the Eye of Atum was also personified as an independent goddess "who was both the daughter and the consort of the creator."[49]

My interpretation of the celestial origin of this detail is that the constellation Hercules can be seen to be reaching downward with its lower arm (indeed, with the Hand of Atum) towards the "head-end" of the serpent held by Ophiuchus -- and the small triangular or diamond-shaped circlet at the top of this side of the Ophiuchus-serpent (the west side of the serpent) can be envisioned as reminiscent of a disembodied eye. The star-chart on the opposite shows the constellation Hercules (associated with Atum) reaching towards the eye-shaped "serpent-head" of the serpent held by Ophiuchus.

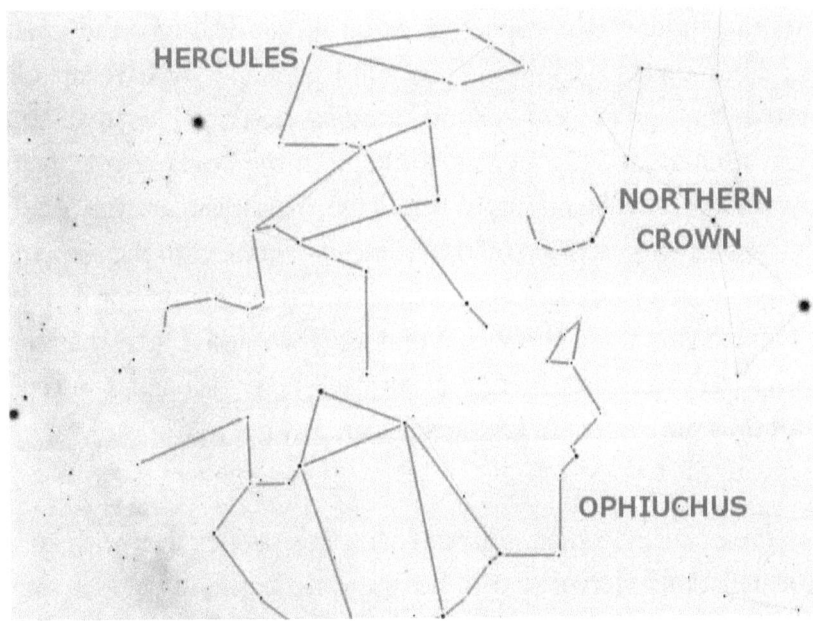

We will see presently that the great god Amun, closely associated with the so-called "Theban theology" of Thebes (*Waset*, or the "City of the Scepter" to the ancient Egyptians) in Upper Egypt, within the modern-day city of Luxor, was also closely associated with Ra and the solar disc, and was often referred to as Amun-Ra. I am convinced that the "radiating" or "whirling" form of the constellation Hercules was also associated with the winged sun symbol found in ancient cultures such as those of Egypt and also of Mesopotamia, and this is another possible explanation for the identification of Atum and Amun with the solar god Ra.

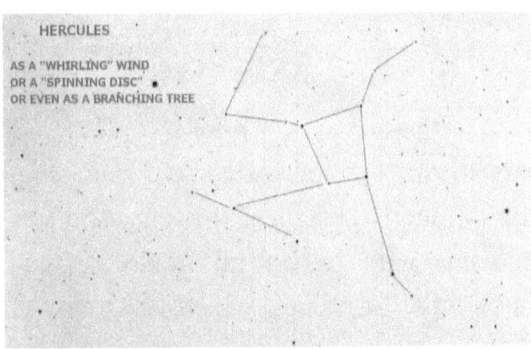

Another noteworthy aspect of Atum is his defeat of the great serpent-monster Apophis (or *Apep* in Egyptian). We have already noted that great serpents or dragons described as dwelling beneath a great tree (such as Nidhogg in the Norse myths, who dwells beneath the mighty World Tree, Yggdrasil) are very often associated with Scorpio (and in some instances, with the serpent-human form of Ophiuchus, or with a combination of Scorpio and Ophiuchus -- we will see in Volumes Two and Three that the "whirling" outline of Hercules can itself be envisioned as a tree, and thus the serpent of Ophiuchus can play the role of the dragon beneath the tree as well).

A great many other figures who are associated with the constellation Hercules can be seen to battle great serpent-monsters in world myth. Zeus battles and defeats the great fire-breathing monster Typhon, for example -- we earlier saw an image from a piece of ancient Greek pottery which shows Zeus (in characteristic Hercules-constellation outline, and raising his thunderbolt weapon) confronting Typhon:

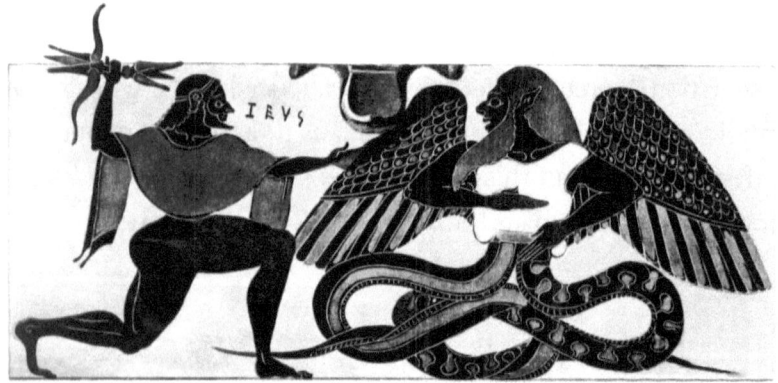

Note that in this image, Typhon is depicted as having a human torso flanked by symmetrical wings: this corresponds, I would argue, to Ophiuchus with its central "torso" framed by two symmetrical shapes (the "serpent") which this artist appears to have envisioned as two wings. Below the human torso of Typhon in this artwork, the monster consists of entwined serpents -- these correspond to the serpentine form of Scorpio, directly below Ophiuchus, or indicate again the serpent-halves on either side.

Other figures who can most certainly be seen to be associated with the constellation Hercules in the heavens and who fight serpentine monsters include the hero Heracles himself, who of course battles the nine-headed Hydra. This episode in the myths of ancient Greece is almost undoubtedly based on an envisioned battle between Hercules (the hero Heracles in the myth, obviously) and Scorpio (upon which constellation the multi-headed Hydra is based).

Also, as discussed in *Star Myths of the World, Volume Four*, the god Thor of Norse myth is identified in the heavens with the same powerful constellation Hercules. The nemesis of Thor, of course, is the powerful Midgard Serpent. Also mentioned in the discussion of Thor's battle with the Midgard Serpent are the parallels to Marduk's defeat of Tiamat (Marduk is a Babylonian god who was associated with the planet Jupiter, as are other deities corresponding to the constellation Hercules such as Jove and Zeus).[150]

It is also possible to argue that Jah or Jehovah of the Bible is described as defeating a similar monster, described as Leviathan in Isaiah 27 (verse 1) and in Psalm 74 (particularly verses 13 and 14). And, as the analysis in *Star Myths of the World, Volume Three* makes abundantly clear, the God of the Bible is frequently associated with the constellation Hercules.

From all of these points of correspondence, we can see some basis for asserting that the god Atum of ancient Egypt, the god whose name means "completeness or totality," and who creates from within his own completeness, out of the primordial chaos, has certain parallels to the God of the Bible, as well as to other immanent gods of other cultures, including Zeus and Jove -- all of whom are associated with the same powerful constellation which we call Hercules.

The deities who are described as the children of Geb and Nut, Osiris, Isis, Set and Nephthys, will be discussed in more detail presently, during the exploration of the celestial aspects of the Isis and Osiris cycle of myths, and of their son Horus. Before we do, however, let us explore some of the other gods and goddesses of ancient Egypt, while realizing that (once again) the subject of Egyptian mythology could easily fill an entire multi-volume series of books and we will thus have to select only a few to discuss here.

We have seen that the god Atum bears a name which indicates completeness and totality, and thus is the god behind all the others, out of whom the rest all proceed. This same principle is described in the so-called Memphite theology in conjunction with the god Ptah, and in the Theban theology in conjunction with the god Amun.

In the Memphite theology, the god Ptah creates through the act of speaking. Geraldine Pinch notes that the apparent contrast with the graphic act of creation described above for Atum was actually reconciled at least conceptually by ancient Egyptian texts themselves which metaphorically equate the issuance of the words of creation from the mouth of Ptah with the issuance of the semen of creation from the mouth of Atum:

> The Memphite theology restates the myth by using link words centred on the mouth. Atum used his mouth as a womb but the parts of the mouth could also represent the power of divine speech. The Egyptians believed that the

intelligence controlling the body was located in the heart. In the Memphite Theology, Ptah is said to bring deities, people, and animals into being by devising them in his heart and naming them with his tongue.[151]

In other words, the more graphic creation story can be understood to be metaphorical, and to illustrate that the words of the creator, who encompasses totality, are literally "pregnant" with power and generative force.

The god Ptah (judging from later texts and artwork) came to be associated with both Sokar (a god depicted as "a human or hawk head emerging from a mound or chest" or as "a shrouded hawk or as a hawk-headed man or mummy").[152] A "shroud" as used here signifies a wrapping for a dead body: depictions of Sokar are very much reminiscent of depictions of Osiris, who is also envisioned as wearing a shroud or being wrapped as a mummy, and indeed Sokar appears to have been associated with Osiris as well, to the point that many scholars of Egyptian myth will refer to the three as *Ptah-Sokar-Osiris.*

The symbology of a hawk-head or a hawk-headed man emerging from a chest or mound, as Sokar's symbology is described above by Professor Geraldine Pinch, suggests once again a combination of the constellations Hercules and Ophiuchus, just as we have previously discussed in conjunction with Atum standing upon the pyramidal Benben. The outline of Ophiuchus suggests both a chest (the long rectangular central section of the constellation) and a mound (the triangle atop the tall rectangle).

Additionally, as we have already seen in some previous discussions, the outline of Ophiuchus can also be interpreted as suggesting a "shroud" or even "mummy wrappings" -- the two "serpent-halves" on either side of the central body being envisioned in many myths as a sash or other "winding"-type garment (see the previous discussion on the "baptism of Odysseus" in which he is given a sash by a benevolent goddess, which is akin to the sash or girdle given to Gawaine by a beautiful lady to protect him from the axe of the Green Knight).

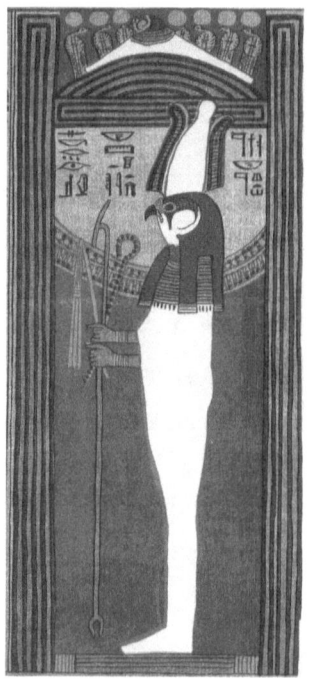

The symbology of a "hawk-headed" human figure could suggest the constellation Hercules again: we will see later that the god Horus may have been associated with the constellation Hercules as well. Thus Sokar, who combines a tall, narrow anthropomorphic body with a hawk's head at the top may well represent a combination of Ophiuchus (a tall, narrow anthropomorphic figure wrapped in a shroud or in mummy-windings) and Hercules (the hawk's head at the top of the god's shoulders). This identification is by no means definitive, but it is certainly possible. The outline of Hercules has a distinctively square-shaped head, and as can be seen in the image above the hawk- or falcon-head of deities such as Sokar and Horus are also fairly square in their outline.

Ptah himself is usually depicted in ancient Egyptian art as an anthropomorphic figure, without enough distinctive detail to associate with any specific constellation with absolute certainty. There is, however, one distinctive feature of Ptah depicted in many, although by no means all, of his representations in ancient art (including wall-reliefs, paintings, and statuary), and that is the god's distinctive and very large "side-lock." The sidelock was a symbol of youth (worn by children), but it was also the distinctive hairstyle of the priests of Ptah at Memphis, and the god is also sometimes shown with a sidelock.

Below are two images of a sidelock -- these are actually of the god Khonsu because public-domain images of Ptah with sidelock are more difficult to find. However, when Ptah is depicted with sidelock, he looks nearly identical to these images, except that he wears the straight beard instead of the curved beard shown below.

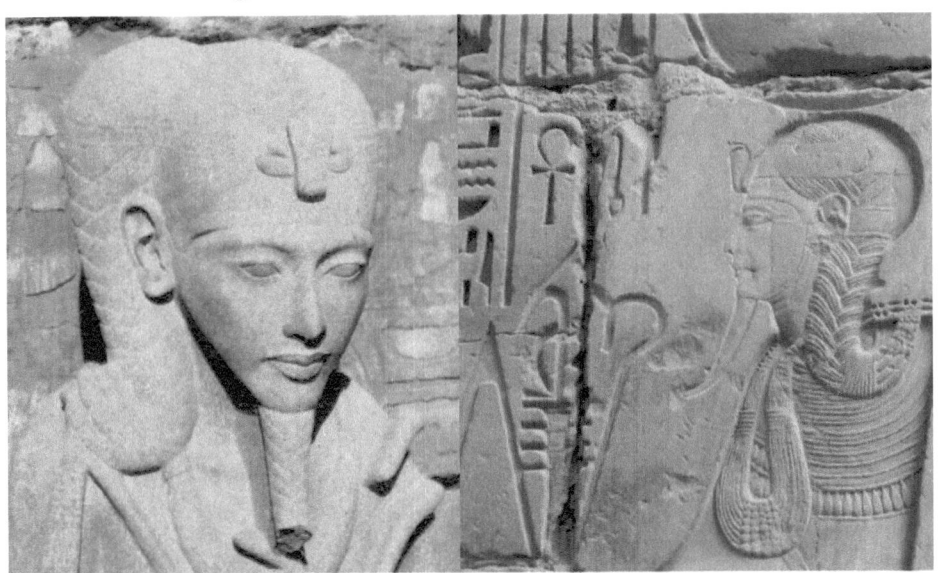

Chapter Thirteen

It is difficult to argue with certainty that the sidelock relates to a specific celestial outline: numerous constellations have features which could *possibly* relate to a sidelock, among them Sagittarius (which has a distinctive upright "plume" from the top of the head, which is not really the same as a sidelock) and also Boötes (which has a "pipe" which is again possible but not an exact match). Another possibility is Ophiuchus, and the "tail-end" of the serpent, but again this is not a slam-dunk for a sidelock either.

However, I think that it is very likely that Ptah (as well as possibly Khonsu, who also wears a sidelock) is actually associated with the constellation Hercules, just as we have already seen Atum being associated with Hercules. If we look at the shape of the heavy sidelock shown in the previous image, with its "upward curve" or "curl" at the bottom of the lock, we can see such a feature in the outline of the constellation Hercules itself. Indeed, based on the thickness of the sidelocks pictured, we could argue that the entire "upraised arm" (the arm brandishing a weapon) could be envisioned as a sidelock, or at least the part of it leading up to the weapon itself (the outline of the weapon itself would then be ignored).

Additionally, upon close examination of the stars of Hercules, we see that there is in fact a set of stars, not extremely bright but certainly visible (and indeed as bright as some of the stars which are included in the outline of the constellation, such as some of the stars in the upraised weapon), which actually make a very convincing little "sidelock" emanating from the lower corner of the head (at the same place that the mighty "upraised arm" emanates from the constellation, but forming a much tighter little "curl" than the upraised arm itself).

These stars are shown in the closeup of the constellation Hercules on the following page:

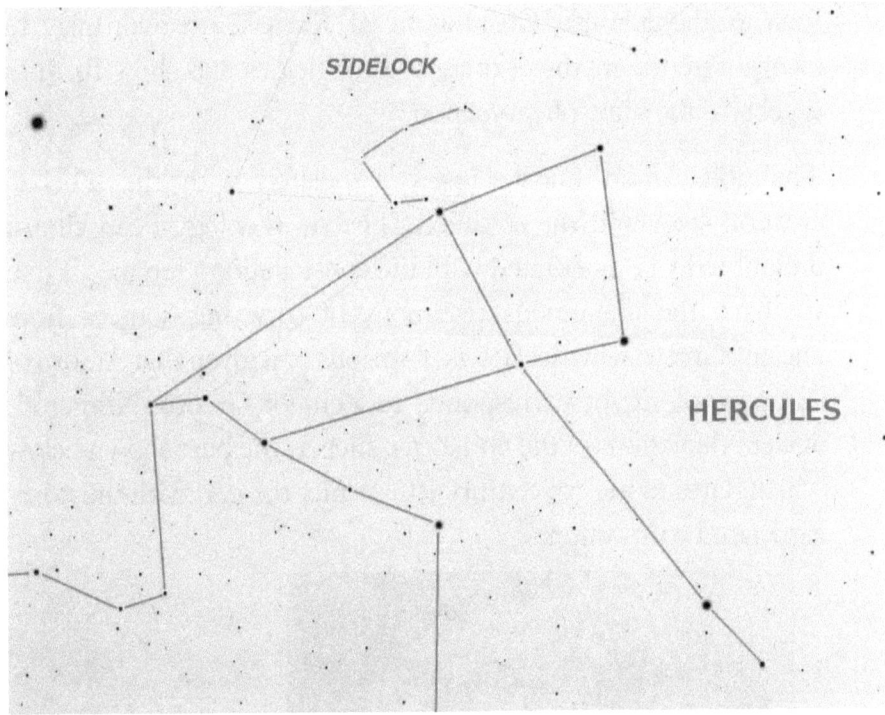

In other words, I would argue that the "Memphite theology" and the "Heliopolitan theology" are actually describing creator deities who are based on *the same* important constellation in the night sky: the constellation Hercules.

Indeed, I would also argue that the creator god Amun, at the center of the "Theban theology" is also associated with the same constellation -- and thus it is perhaps possible to argue that all three are in a sense "avatars" of one another, or if not precisely avatars then different manifestations or personifications of the same divine concept.

Speaking of Khonsu, who is also described as a creator deity in a text known as "the Khonsu Cosmogony," and who could also be associated with the constellation Hercules according to my analysis, Professor Geraldine Pinch writes, "Texts of this type, such as the Khonsu Cosmogony at Karnak, use wordplay to incorporate the myths of other creator deities and show them as aspects of the same phenomenon."[53]

The god Amun (most closely associated with the Theban creation story and the so-called "Theban theology") can almost undoubtedly be associated with the constellation Hercules. First, we have the unanimous testimony of surviving sources from ancient Greece who declare as if obvious or a given that Amon (or Ammon) of Egypt corresponds to Zeus of Greece. Numerous ancient depictions of the god Zeus, such as the bust shown below which dates to the 5th century BC, depict the god with the horns associated with Amun:

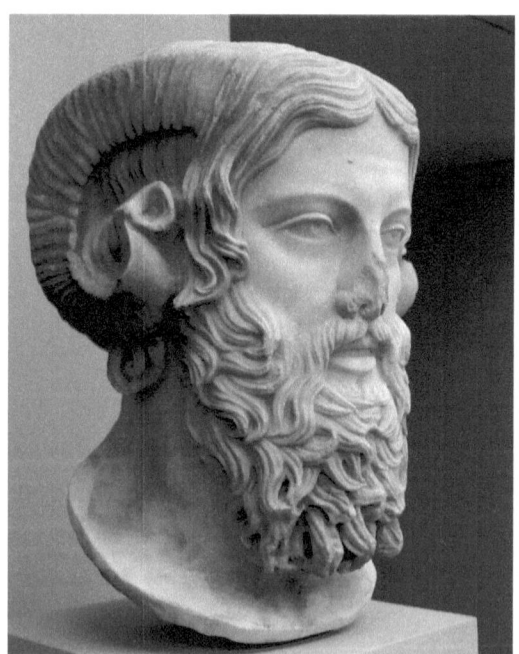

Note that the stars in the constellation Hercules which I argue could have been envisioned as a "sidelock" could aslo be envisioned as a curling ram's horn!

As will be demonstrated by examples given in *Star Myths of the World, Volume Two* (*Myths of Ancient Greece*), Zeus is associated with the constellation Hercules in the heavens.

As a sort of confirmation that the constellation Hercules may have in some cases been envisioned as having "ram's horns" (at least in the mythology of ancient Egypt), it is very noteworthy that the ram-headed god Khnum was described as a creator god who created by shaping at the potter's wheel. Geraldine Pinch writes:

> Two deities, Ptah and Khnum, were sometimes credited with physically "fashioning" the world and its inhabitants. [. . .] The shaping of royal bodies was a task more usually attributed to Khnum. Khnum was represented by a ram, an animal renowned for aggressive virility. He was sometimes described as "begetting" the gods, but as a creator he was usually celebrated as the divine craftsman who "formed everything" on his potter's wheel.[154]

Note that the ram's horns of Khnum are sometimes depicted in a manner most reminiscent of the shape of the sidelock shown earlier:

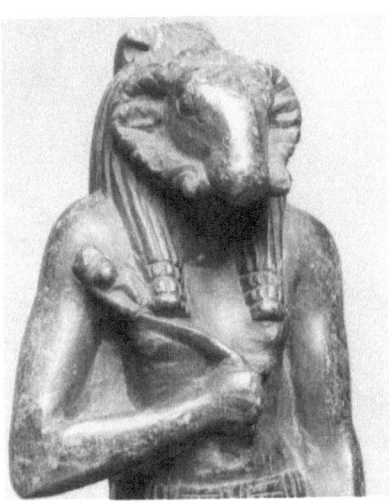

The fact that the ram-headed god Khnum is envisioned as fashioning everything on his potter's wheel is very significant, because it can also be seen as helping to confirm the identification of Khnum with the constellation Hercules. The figure of Hercules can be seen to be "reaching downwards" towards the little circlet or triangle at the top of the "head-end" serpent-half of Ophiuchus.

This shape is envisioned in the myths in many different ways -- not only as the head of a serpent held by Ophiuchus, but also as a wine-goblet, or as a fruit such as a pomegranate or even as a strawberry (in a Native American myth with strong parallels to the story of Orpheus and Eurydice of ancient Greece, discussed in *Astrotheology for Life*), and here in the description of Khnum creating all things at his potter's wheel we see the same feature of Ophiuchus being envisioned as the spinning potter's wheel itself, towards which Khnum (associated with Hercules) is reaching. Below is a line drawing of Khnum at the wheel, to show the how the wheel was envisioned as being a small disc atop a post, alongside an actual wall-painting from Dendera showing a similar scene with Khnum at the wheel:

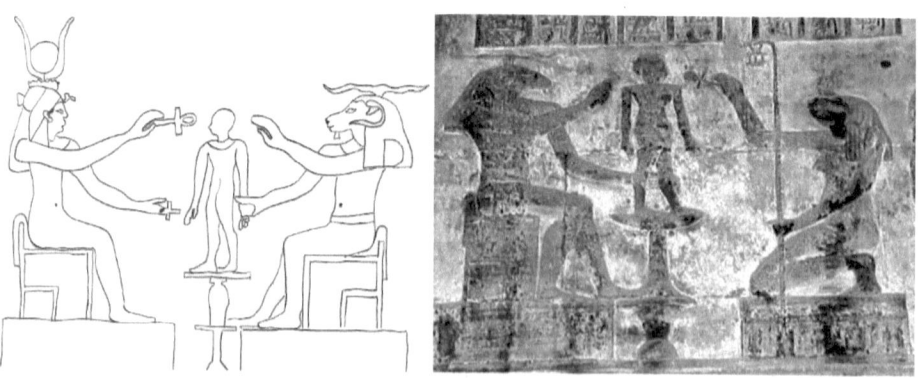

Note that the shape of the wheel upon its vertical axle very much resembles the shape of the top of the "head-end" of the serpent held by Ophiuchus, and towards which Hercules is reaching:

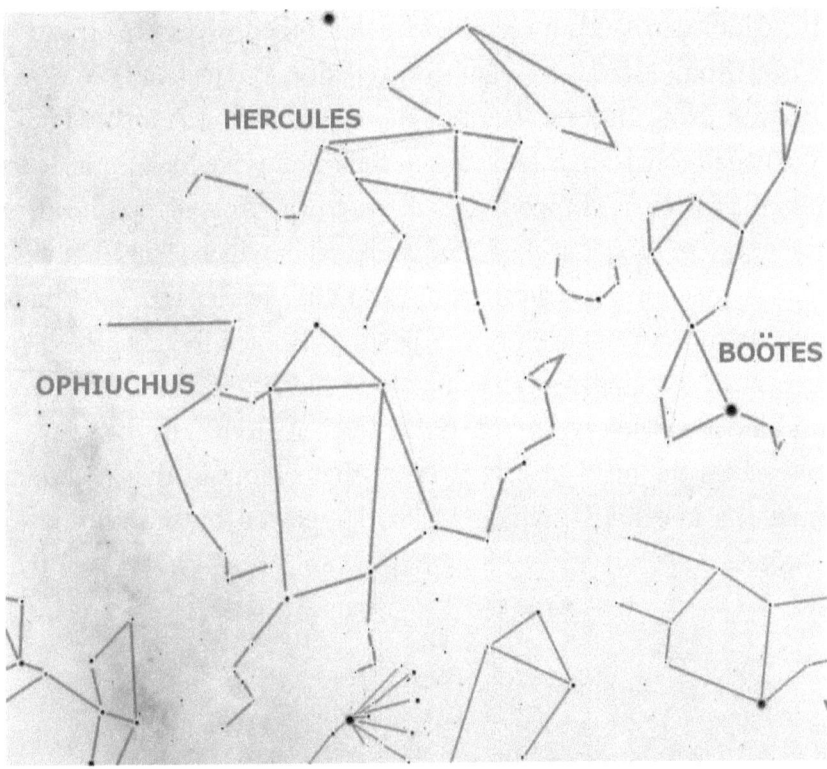

Can you see that the constellation Hercules in the sky can be envisioned as a potter, and indeed as a potter using his leg to vigorously turn the wheel? The wheel itself is represented by the small triangular shape atop the "axle" emanating from the right or western side of Ophiuchus. The lower hand of Hercules reaches down towards this small triangle on a post (the turning wheel atop its axle).

Note that in the image on the previous page, showing the wall-relief at Dendera (at right as we look at the page), Khnum is working at the potter's wheel and opposite him on the other side of the wheel is the frog-headed goddess, Heqet (or Heket). Heqet was sometimes described as the goddess who breathed life into the creations that Khnum fashioned on his wheel.

If we look across from Hercules, at the "other side" of the potter's wheel from Hercules, what constellation do we find? We see Boötes. Note that the head of this constellation is rather large. We usually envision it as facing to the right as we look at the star-chart. However, compare the shape to the frog-shaped head of the goddess Heqet in the Dendera panel in which she is depicted across the potter's wheel from Khnum: clearly, the Egyptians appear to have envisioned the head of Boötes in this case as a frog-head, looking upwards and to the left as we face the chart, and indeed when we think of the head of Boötes in this way, it resembles the head of a frog. Note that Heqet in that Dendera image is kneeling -- which is also suggested by the outline of Boötes:

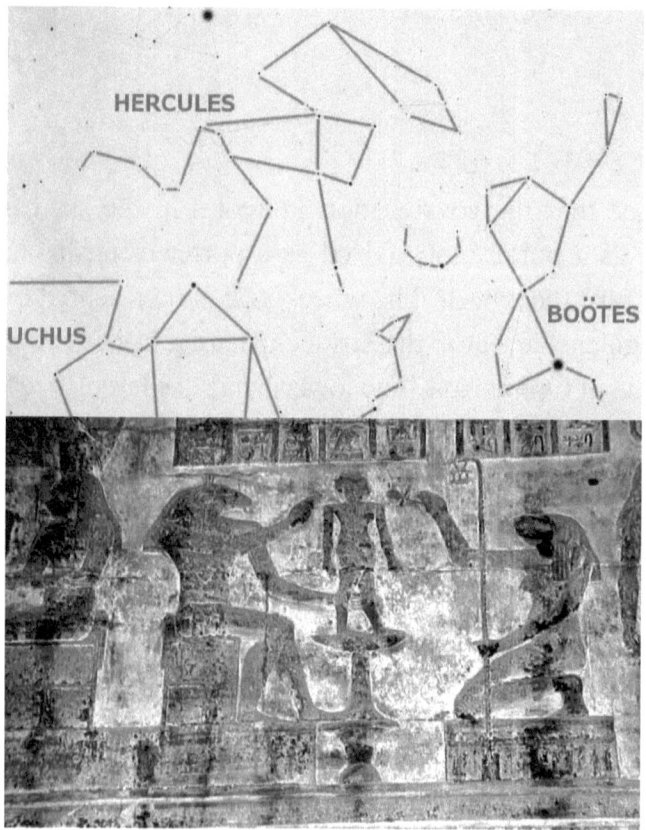

Note that the goddess Heqet in the Dendera panel is depicted as carrying a tall staff, with what may be a lantern at the top. Whatever is depicted atop this staff, it is very likely that this staff can be seen in the sky as part of the constellation Boötes, in the tall pipe with small triangular shape at the top (or a "curving-over" top, if you don't imagine the third side of the triangle -- note how this curving-over shape is also seen in the staff of Heqet as depicted at Dendera).

Note also that in the line-drawing on page 278, which also depicts a scene from a different building at Dendera, Khnum is not accompanied by Heqet but instead by a goddess who appears to be Hathor (see the tall horns in her headdress). Heqet and Hathor were associated in some ancient inscriptions, and both were goddesses who presided *over* childbirth (can you guess why? look *just below* the constellation Boötes and you will find the constellation Virgo, on her back with her legs raised and apart). The fact that Hathor is depicted "across the potter's wheel" from Khnum is a strong indication that Hathor, too, was associated with the constellation Boötes. Hathor is sometimes depicted with a cow's head -- and I would thus venture to guess that the head of Boötes was alternately envisioned by the ancient Egyptians as the head of a cow (in the case of Hathor), rather than as the head of a frog (in the case of Heqet).

The above analysis of the likely association of Hathor with Boötes and Heqet with Boötes helps to confirm the identification of the potter's wheel with the small triangle atop the western "serpent-half" of Ophiuchus, and thus to also confirm the association of Khnum (the ram-headed and ram-horned god) with Hercules -- and thereby to likewise confirm the association of Amun (who is sometimes depicted with ram's horns, and who is also associated by the ancients with the god Zeus of the Greeks, who is also sometimes depicted with ram's horns) with the constellation Hercules as well! The supporting evidence, in other words, is quite compelling (and, I would argue, conclusive).

Note also the fact that the God of the Bible can be clearly seen to be associated with the constellation Hercules in many instances (some of them discussed in *Star Myths of the World, Volume Three*). Students of the Bible should not have to be told that God is explicitly described as a potter at the wheel in many scriptural passages. Specific passages likening the LORD to a *potter* and his people to the *clay* are to be found in Isaiah, Jeremiah, Lamentations, Zechariah, Romans, and the book of Revelation.

These very clear "celestial metaphor" connections echo or harmonize with the very clear thematic parallels between the creation accounts in the various ancient Egyptian accounts and the Genesis account. I believe it can be shown that all of them are closely related, and appear to revolve around the same set of specific constellations in the heavens.

Returning to the god Amun of ancient Egypt, we can be fairly confident that he was associated with the constellation Hercules not only by the witness of ancient sources who virtually unanimously assert that this god of Egypt corresponds to Zeus or Jove (including surviving texts from Herodotus, who lived from about 484 BC to 425 BC; Manetho, who was an Egyptian priest of Ptolemaic Egypt, thought to have lived in either the fourth or third centuries BC; and from later sources such as Diodorus Siculus, who wrote during the first century BC, sometime between the years 60 BC and 30 BC), but also by ancient artwork such as the image below from a surviving temple of the Ptolemaic period of ancient Egypt, showing Amun-Ra in an outline that we should now be able to recognize as corresponding to the constellation Hercules:

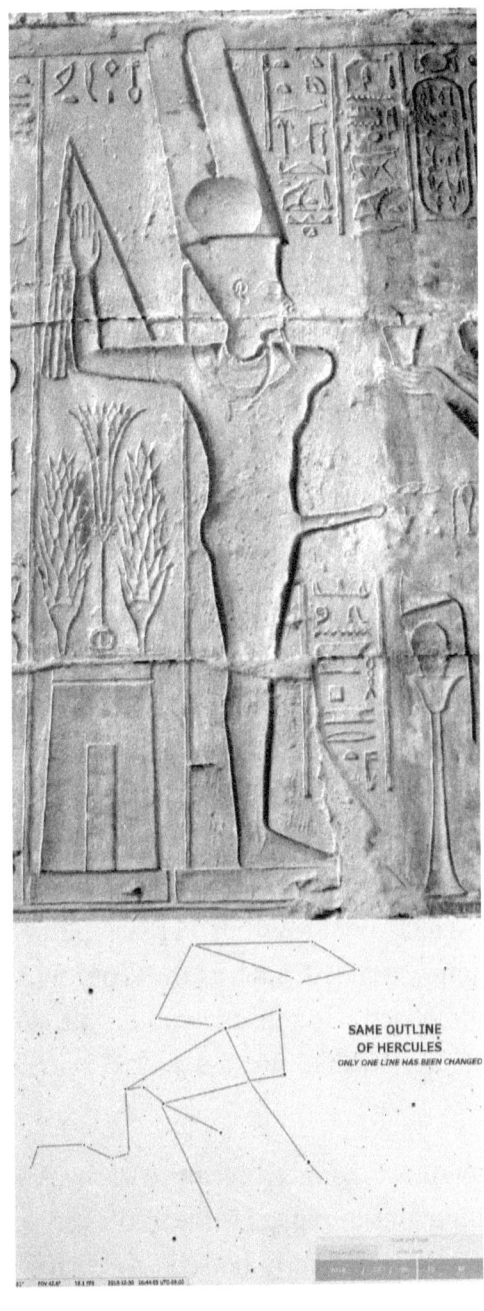

SAME OUTLINE
OF HERCULES
ONLY ONE LINE HAS BEEN CHANGED

The correspondences of the ancient artwork depicting the god Amun-Ra and the outline of Hercules should be fairly obvious. We see, for instance, the upraised arm, bent at an angle which is suggestive of the constellation in the night sky (the arm of Hercules which is often envisioned as brandishing a weapon). We see the square-shaped head: in the case of the preceding artwork, it is the headgear which the god is depicted as wearing which is square-topped in shape, corresponding to the square-shaped head of the constellation in the heavens.

Note also that in the depiction of Amun-Ra, above the square-topped headgear there are two very tall plumes, which also terminate in a rather flat top, as if the god is wearing a tall rectangle atop his already square-shaped headgear. This "tall rectangular hat" on a Hercules-associated deity is significant, because the depictions of the god Tiki in the Pacific region also regularly feature a very high and rectangular-shaped head, or some sort of tall rectangular hat, thus indicating a correspondence to the constellation Hercules (we can be confident that Amun-Ra is associated with the constellation Hercules, and since Amun-Ra is also depicted with tall rectangular headgear, we can be confident that the Tiki depictions with tall rectangular heads or headgear also indicate Hercules -- which confirms our earlier suggestion that figures with the tongue extended, such as the Gorgons in ancient Greece, and the lion-headed Bes in ancient Egypt, and also the Tiki depictions in the Pacific, are associated with the constellation Hercules).

Of course, the most distinctive feature of the Amun-Ra depiction in the foregoing ancient image is the god's very long, erect phallus. This feature can very clearly be seen to correspond to the "first segment" of the "forward leg" of the outline of Hercules, as seen in the star-chart depicted below the ancient Egyptian depiction of the god. Indeed, the proportional length of the phallus in the ancient Egyptian artwork appears to correspond to the suggestion from the constellation in the sky, as opposed to the proportions of an actual male member in human anatomy.

This analysis gives rather striking confirmation that Amun, as with Atum and Ptah (as well as Khnum, and also apparently Khonsu) can be associated with the outline of Hercules in the infinite heavens above. In one sense, it is as if all of these central deities are "avatars" of the same power, who inhabits the Invisible Realm and whose characteristics can be "seen" (or at least analogized) through an understanding of the *aspects associated with Hercules-figures* in myth (figures who include Zeus and Jove of ancient Greece and Rome, as well as Jehovah or Yahweh of the Bible).

The fact that Amun was understood by the ancient Egyptians to be the invisible god, the hidden god, underscores an important truth about the ancient system of myth: these myths are a way of conveying to our hearts an understanding of the reality of the Invisible Realm, and the invisible powers, which we *cannot* see. They use representations from the heavens, which we can see, in order to help us to understand profound concepts which we cannot actually see with our eyes. Whoever gave us this incredibly ancient system had to find something in the visible realm which could be used to convey in powerful metaphoric form the truths about the Invisible Realm.

In *Moby Dick* (1851), Herman Melville (1819 - 1891) employed the most expansive canvas he could find in order to treat themes of great profundity and import -- and he found it, in the world's vast ocean expanse and terrifying depths, and in the mighty cetaceans which plumb the mysterious expanse of that watery abyss.

The Star Myths of the world employ a canvas even more awe-inspiring than that: the silent, cycling expanse of the heavens. It is a metaphorical field perfectly suited for conveying to us the realities of the infinite realm, because the ocean of the heavens is in fact *truly infinite* in its depth. When we gaze into the night sky, we truly are staring into infinity.

Thus, although the god Amun is associated with the outline of Hercules, the outline of this constellation is *not* the god Amun. The god Amun of ancient Egypt is the invisible god, the universal god. Plutarch says of Amun, citing the above-mentioned Manetho, that his name means "concealed."[155] He goes on to say, speaking of the Egyptians, that:

> When they, therefore, address the supreme god, whom they believe to be the same as the Universe, as if he were invisible and concealed, and implore him to make himself visible and manifest to them, they use the word "Amoun;" so great, then, was the circumspection of the Egyptians in their wisdom touching all that had to do with their gods.[156]

Thus, we see that a wide variety of evidence argues that attributes and characteristics of the invisible god Amun were conveyed in this ancient system through association with the constellation Hercules, in common with many other gods with similar characteristics in the myths of the world, including Zeus, Jove, Huracan, Tama-nui-ki-te-Rangi, Thor, and Jah -- and also in common with other immanent gods described in the ancient Egyptian system including Atum and Ptah and Khnum.

Let's briefly explore a few other related pieces of evidence from Egypt which help to confirm the argument that the ancient system running through so many other myths from so many other cultures in so many other parts of the world can also be seen to be operating in Egypt, and which will also help to illuminate important themes present in the myths of that ancient culture, before turning to an examination of the Osiris and Isis cycle.

Let's first briefly examine the imagery of the divine boat or barque, which is depicted in ancient artwork carrying various gods and goddesses. Professor Emily Teeter, of the University of Chicago (mentioned previously) has written that:

> Reflecting the importance of boats in daily life, the gods of the Egyptians were said to be transported in celestial barques. From the Early Dynastic Period onward, an image of the deity would regularly be carried from the temple sanctuary in a model boat by priests in procession, either on a visit to another temple or on a circumambulation of the deity's own sanctuary.[157]

It can be demonstrated from examples found in many Star Myths from other cultures that the shape of the constellation Scorpio can be envisioned as resembling a boat or an ocean-going ship, with its upturned prow and tail, and the sacred barques depicted in ancient Egyptian artwork and preserved in numerous archaeological sites from the ancient period certainly resemble this shape. This same shape is also present in the classic outline of the Viking ships (and we find clear evidence of Norse myths in which Scorpio plays a boat or a ship), and in the outline of ships from ancient Greece (both those found in ancient artwork and preserved at the bottom of the Black Sea, for instance), with their high prow and stern portions and relatively flatter central sections.

In these other Star Myths, and particularly those examined in *Star Myths of the World, Volume Four (Norse Mythology)*, the occupant of the boat or ship is often envisioned as corresponding to the figure of Ophiuchus, and sometimes Ophiuchus and Hercules together (such as in the famous fishing-expedition undertaken by Hymir and Thor) -- and I believe that this holds true in ancient Egypt in many cases as well.

The image below is fairly representative, and is taken from a version of the Book of the Amduat (also known as the Book of What is in the Underworld, and the Book of the Hidden Chamber), which shows the progress of the solar barque during the twelve hours of the night (the ancient Egyptians appear to have always given twelve hours to period of daylight and twelve hours to period of darkness, but those hours would become longer or shorter depending on whether earth was in the part of the year when night was longer than day or the part of the year when day was longer than night). This particular detail from an Amduat scroll shows the "Eleventh Hour" of the night -- the solar barque (containing the god Khnum) is shown being pulled along through the realm of the Duat:

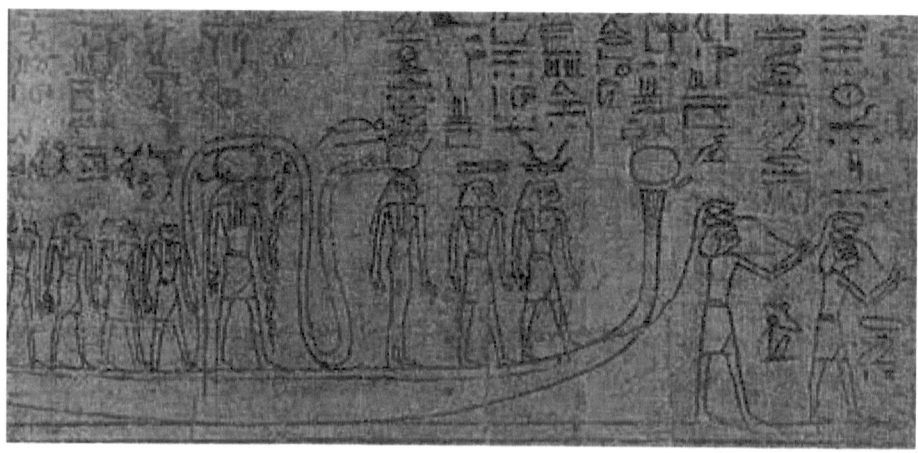

In the image, Khnum can be seen, holding a staff which itself is in the form of a serpent, and at the same time Khnum is surrounded by a serpent which arches up over his head, drops back down to make a complete "bell-shape" or "upside-down U" over the god, and then rears back up with its "serpent-head" almost as high as the top of the arched back.

I would argue that this "dome-shaped" serpent enclosure can be confidently associated with the constellation Ophiuchus, which is envisioned as "standing in the boat formed by Scorpio" in so many other Star Myths from around the globe. Ophiuchus, of course, is a constellation associated with a serpent, and indeed a constellation which consists of a "central body" (the "bell shape" or "upside-down U" shape in the ancient Egyptian artwork) with a serpent protruding on either side, and with its "serpent-head" side rearing up to about the same height as the top of the central body, just as in the ancient artwork.

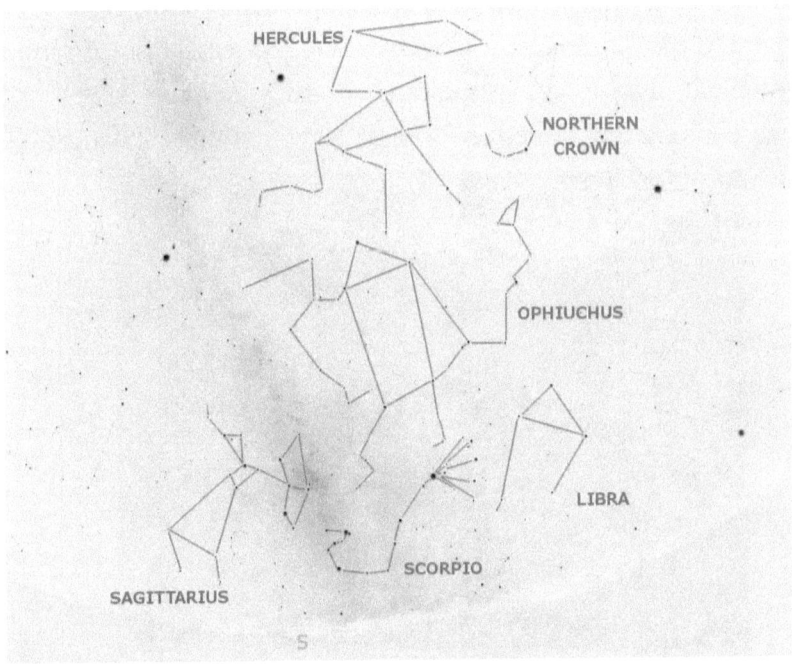

We have already examined evidence that the god Khnum is associated with the constellation Hercules, above Ophiuchus, and in the above artwork (in which Khnum holds a serpent-like staff) it can be seen that he is associated with Ophiuchus as well. Indeed, the gods Atum-Ra and Amun-Ra are also closely associated with the celestial barque or the solar barque, and frequently depicted in it in ancient Egyptian art as well.

Geraldine Pinch writes that, "Khepri, the young sun of dawn, often formed a pair with Ra-Atum, the old sun of evening. The Night Boat of the sun was associated with Atum and the Day Boat with Khepri."[158] Khepri, the scarab god, may well be envisioned in the stars of the constellation Ophiuchus as well. I have previously written extensively about my belief that the scarab symbol of ancient Egypt is associated with the constellation Cancer, located near the "top of the year" at summer solstice, but the fact that Khepri is closely associated with the solar barque indicates that the central shape of Ophiuchus may well have suggested the scarab also -- even the "winged scarab" so common in ancient Egyptian symbology, if the "serpent-halves" of Ophiuchus are envisioned as forming two outstretched wings:

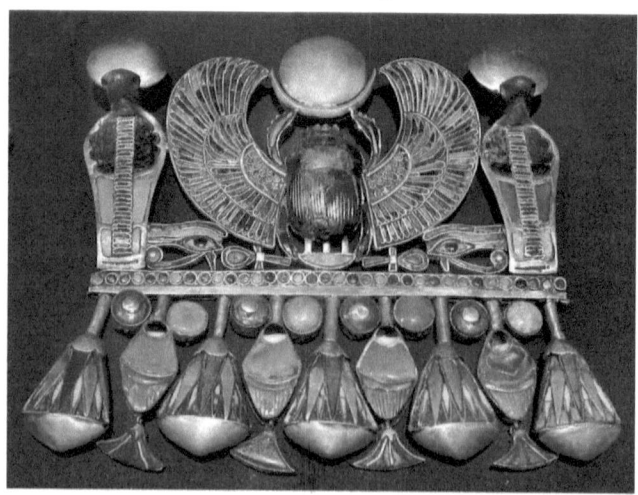

The image above shows jewelry from the tomb of Tutankhamun featuring a winged scarab, holding up a solar disc. The winged scarab is flanked by two uraeus serpents, which may reinforce the alleged Ophiuchus association. Note that, like the body of the scarab itself, the outline of the central body of the constellation Ophiuchus can be seen as having a smaller "upper section" above a larger "lower section." In the image below, I've marked these as "A" and "B" on both the scarab image and the Ophiuchus outline:

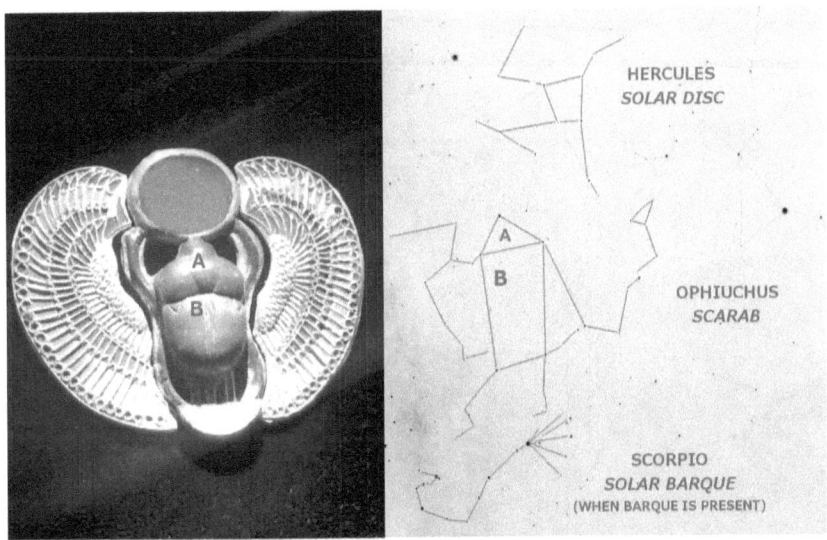

The "serpent-halves" of Ophiuchus, flanking the central body on either side, form the "upraised arms" of the scarab, and in some cases can be envisioned as the upward-curving wings (for the "winged scarab" symbol). Note that the scarab in both of the above images (particularly the one on this page) shows only four legs -- and these correspond to the two "serpent-halves" of the constellation (forming the upper legs, or "upraised arms") and the two "legs" of Ophiuchus (the bottom two legs of the scarab).

In the above two diagrams, the scarab is not depicted above a stylized celestial boat or barque – but such depictions of the scarab are in fact quite common, and almost certainly provide additional confirmation that we are correct in associating these scarabs with the constellation Ophiuchus: the celestial barque below the scarab is representative of the constellation Scorpio. Below is another scarab, this time from a magnificent necklace found in the tomb of Tutankhamun, depicting a scarab above a celestial barque:

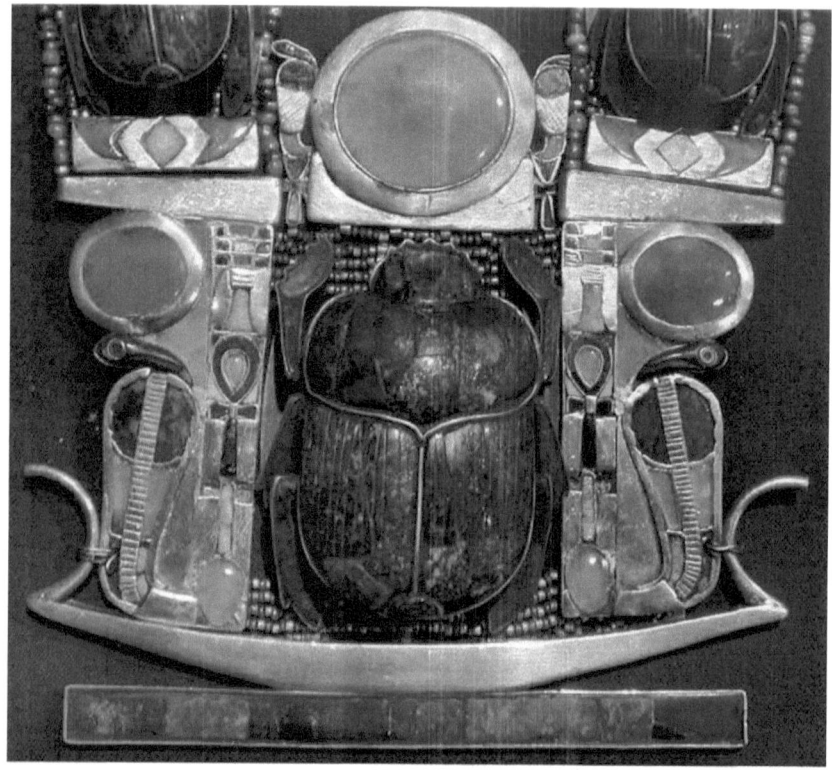

Once again, note the uraeus serpents flanking the scarab on either side. Note also the solar disc above the scarab itself – just as Hercules is above Ophiuchus. In the star-chart on the previous page, I show Hercules in the constellation's alternate way of being envisioned in Star Myths from around the world: as a whirling disc. I am convinced that the fact that Hercules can appear as a disc with rays emanating from it corresponds to the common symbology found not only in Egypt but in many other cultures (including ancient Mesopotamian cultures) depicting the sun as a disc with rays emanating from it, or wings emanating from its sides, or some similar version of these well-known godlike solar discs.

Confirmation that the "winged sun" corresponds to the "whirling form" of the constellation Hercules comes from many sources. The images below are from ancient Assyria, and we will examine the Star Myths of the ancient Mediterranean in a later chapter, but they provide very solid evidence that the winged sun corresponds to the constellation Hercules:

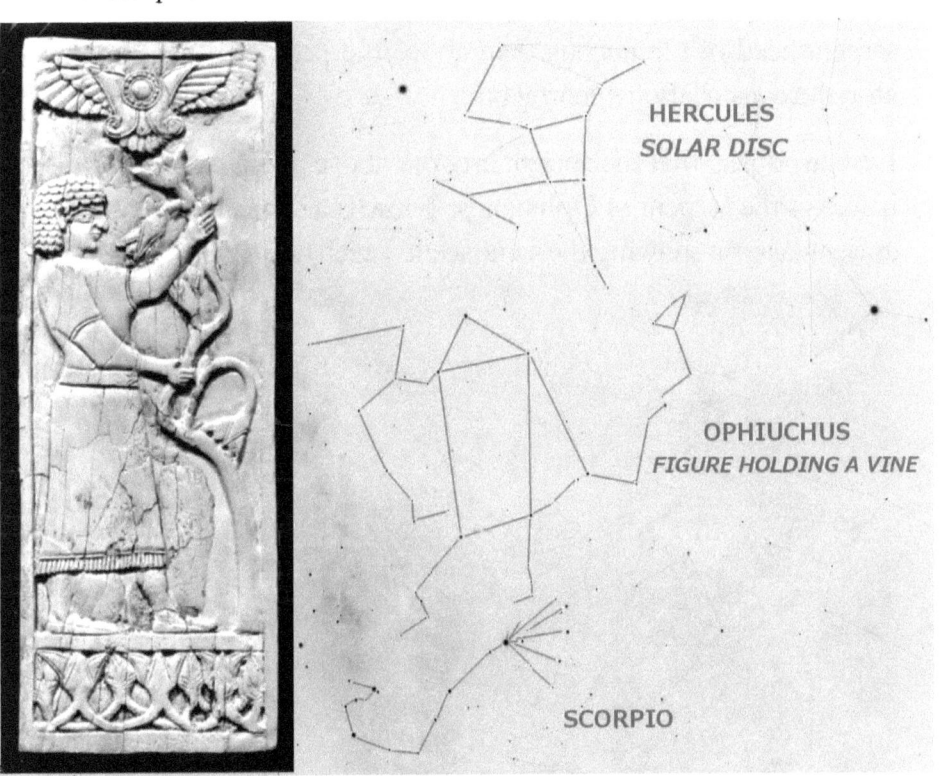

In the ancient artwork shown above, from Assyria, we see a youth in a fairly long tunic grasping a large flowering vine -- and above him a winged solar-disc. By this point, it should be obvious to the reader that this youth corresponds to Ophiuchus, with the

293

flowering vine (possibly a great lotus-plant) corresponding to the "head-end" of the "serpent" held by the constellation (the right half of the serpent held by Ophiuchus, as we face the star-chart shown above, which is to say the west side of the constellation). The long tunic of the youth corresponds to the outline seen in the central body of the constellation Ophiuchus in the heavens. The solar disc above the youth is in the exact right spot to correspond to the "whirling form" of the constellation Hercules: it is more above the topmost lotus-flower (the "serpent-head" feature of the constellation) than it is above the head of the youth, just as the central "disc" of the constellation Hercules is more above the serpent-head of Ophiuchus than above the peak of the triangle atop the constellation's central body.

Lest any object that the ancient artwork above doesn't show *both* halves of the serpent of Ophiuchus, below is a similar panel from ancient Assyria showing the same scene which does:

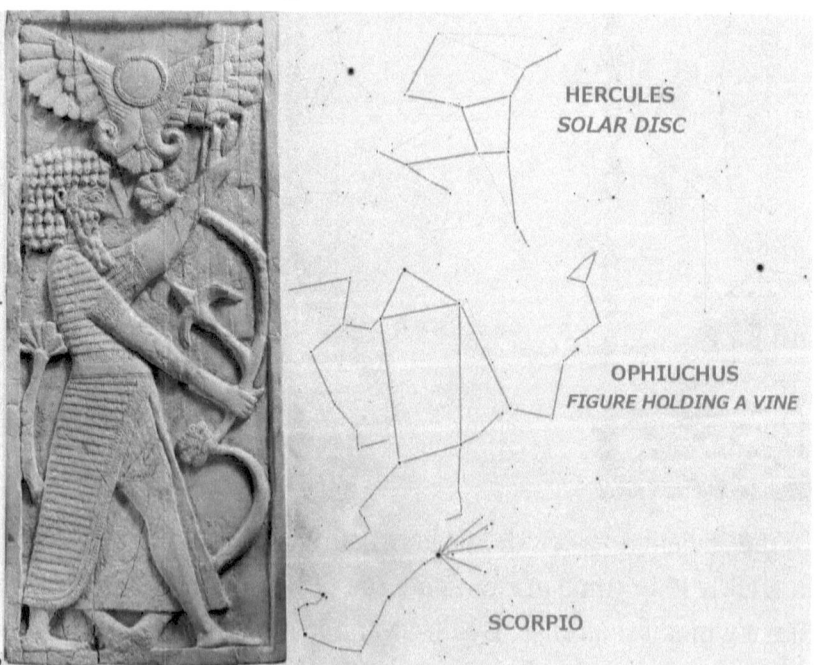

HERCULES
SOLAR DISC

OPHIUCHUS
FIGURE HOLDING A VINE

SCORPIO

Note that in the figure above, the man holding the vine is wearing a similarly long tunic or skirt, corresponding to the length of the central body of Ophiuchus above the visible feet of the constellation. The winged solar disc is positioned similarly to the position in the previous image, above the topmost flower of the vine and basically nestled above the space between that topmost flower and the head of the man holding the vine (just as the whirling form of Hercules is nestled into a similar space above the "serpent-head" on the west side of Ophiuchus and the topmost point of the triangular section above the constellation's central body). As noted previously, this image features part of the branching vine going towards the other side of the man's body, corresponding to the part of the "serpent" held by Ophiuchus which is on the east side of the constellation's central body (the serpent-half on the left as we face the star-chart depicted above).

An intriguing detail in this second Assyrian panel, different from the panel shown just before, is the fact that the man holding the vine in this second panel is really only grasping the vine with his lower hand (very similar to the outline of the constellation as drawn by H. A. Rey and shown in the star-chart above). His upper hand, instead of holding the vine higher up, appears to be offering an egg-shaped stone (or even an egg) towards the direction of the solar disc, or at least towards the heavens.

These panels should decisively establish the fact that in the ancient system, the winged sun corresponds to the constellation of Hercules -- and in particular the constellation Hercules when envisioned in "whirling" form, with the square-shaped "head" of the constellation forming a central disc, and the other stars envisioned as radiating lines coming out from the central figure.

In ancient Egyptian art and iconography, the winged solar disc symbol is not uncommon. Below is an image from a funerary stele from Egypt during the Roman period, dating to the 1st or 2nd century AD, showing a winged sun disc:

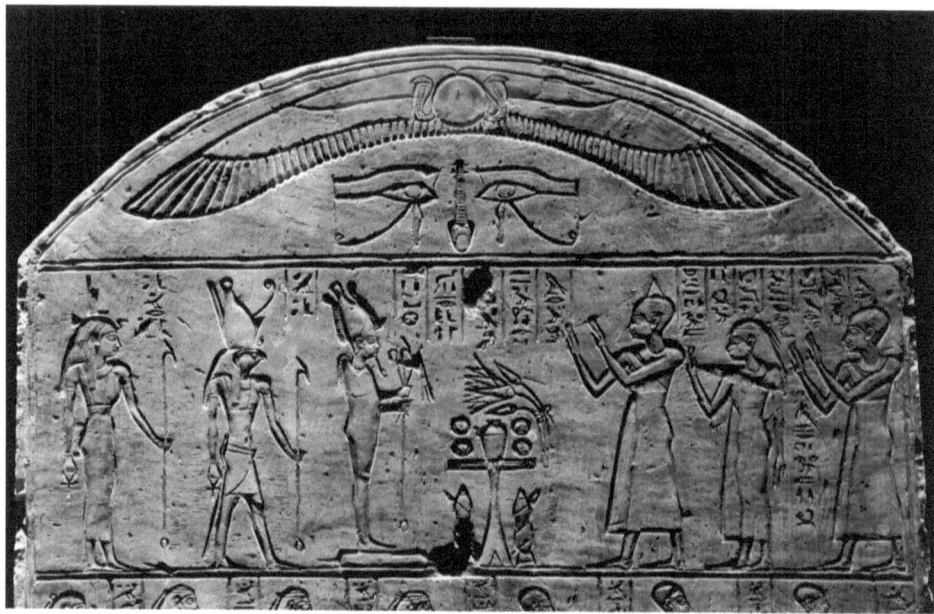

Note that the figure of the god Osiris is now occupying the position that was occupied in the previoius artwork from Assyria by the figures holding the vines -- in other words, in the position corresponding to the constellation Ophiuchus. The vine itself has now been replaced by an offering table, the shape of which is very reminiscent of the shape seen previously in the potter's wheel of the god Khnum, which we argued would also correspond to the "head-end" of the "serpent-half" held by the constellation Ophiuchus. Directly above the piece of pottery on the table we see a stylized lotus plant, which of course recalls the association of the lotus-flower with this same portion of the Ophiuchus constellation that we saw in the previous two images from ancient Assyria.

The above analysis should confirm that the solar disc seen in ancient Egyptian artwork was also associated with the figure of Hercules, and thus explain why deities such as Atum and Amun (who are also associated with the constellation Hercules) also manifest as the god Ra (or Re), associated with the solar disc.

Perhaps more common than depictions of the winged solar disc in ancient Egyptian iconography is the solar disc with rays emanating downwards, which corresponds equally to the very same "whirling form" of the constellation Hercules in the heavens. Below we see artwork from the period of Akhenaten, showing the solar disc (called the Aten) pouring out rays upon the royal figures, each ray terminating in a blessing hand:

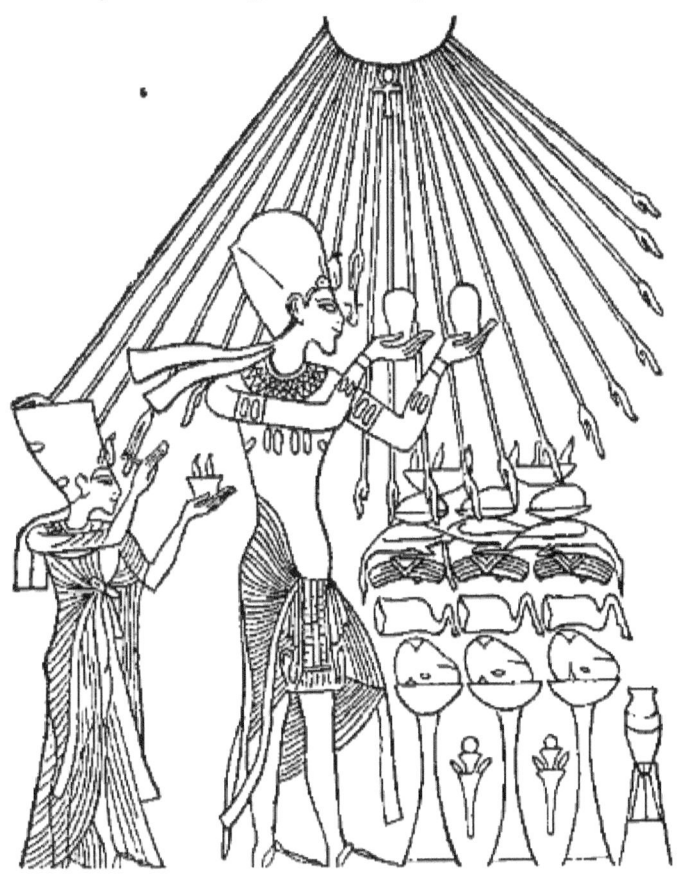

Much has been made of the historical evidence that Akhenaten (who had originally taken or been given the royal name Amenhotep IV) replaced the worship of the traditional gods and the central place of Amen or Amun with the veneration of the solar disc shown above, known as the Aten. In *Egypt and the Egptians*, Professors Brewer and Teeter write:

> The worship of the traditional pantheon was abandoned in favor of the worship of the sun and its life-giving light, initially in the form of Ra-Horakhty and then, by year 3 or 4 of his reign, in an entirely new form: the globe or disk of the sun, whose rays terminated with tiny human hands. The Aten's names were encircled by a cartouche, formerly a prerogative of kings and queens. In the new decorative program, only the king and the royal family were centered under the rays of the sun, and they were the sole communicants with the god. At the same time, the king changed his name from Amunhotep IV ("Amun is Satisfied") to Akhenaten (perhaps "The One who is beneficial to the Aten"). In year 5, Akhenaten moved the administrative capital to Tell el Amarna, a spot in Middle Egypt which was, according to the boundary stones, "dedicated to no other god." There an entirely new city was built, surrounded by the homes of the administrators and courtiers who were obliged to follow the king. Between years 8 and 12 of the reign, the worship of all other gods was officially forbidden, and in an effort to enforce this new theology, the names of the other gods were hammered from statues and the temple walls.[159]

What is fascinating about the above analysis is that, whatever was going on during the reign of Akhenaten (king from 1353 BC to 1336 BC) and wherever these radical changes originated (whether in his own mind or from some other source), it appears that the symbology adopted (including for the Aten disc) still conforms to the symbology of the ancient world-wide system of celestial metaphor we have been examining, and which can be shown to underlie the iconography of the traditional pantheon whose worship was suppressed during the Amarna period.

In the drawing of Akhenaten and Nefertiti beneath the Aten shown on page 297, for example, it should be quite evident that Akhenaten himself is depicted in very much the same position as that occupied by each of the individuals holding the vine in the two panels from ancient Assyria shown previously -- that is to say, in the position of the constellation Ophiuchus. In this case, his upraised hands (in the position of offering and worship) almost certainly correspond to the western serpent-half (the "head-end" of the serpent) of Ophiuchus -- or perhaps to both serpent-halves, one hand for each, although this seems less likely.

Note that the Aten disc is positioned almost exactly as noted previously, in the two images from ancient Assyria and in the winged-disc from Egypt seen on the funerary stele. Once again, the disc itself is nestled into the space above the "V" formed by the outermost upraised arm and the top of the king's head -- just as the square central "head" of the constellation Hercules is located in the space above the "V" formed by the western serpent-head and the top of the triangular crown of the central body of Ophiuchus.

Indeed, it is even possible to make the argument that Akhenaten's queen, Nefertiti (thought to have lived from about 1370 BC to about 1330 BC) is depicted in the artwork shown as standing in a position which would associate her with the constellation Sagittarius, which is adjacent to and slightly below Ophiuchus in the heavens, and which is a constellation often associated with powerful and beautiful female figures (both divine and mortal) in the ancient myths of the world.

Note too that Akhenaten in the illustration is depicted wearing a rather long tunic, very much the length of those worn by each figure in the two Assyrian examples shown previously, which reveals about as much of his legs below as would correspond to the length of the legs of Ophiuchus below the long "rectangle" of the central body of the constellation. Nefertiti, on the other hand, is shown wearing a full-length dress, which corresponds again to the outline of the constellation Sagittarius:

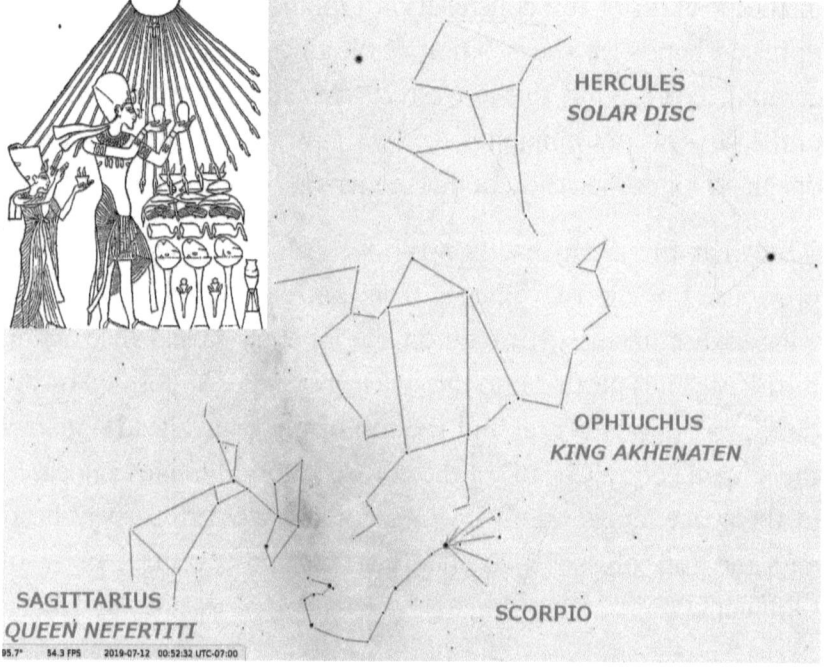

Of course, one might argue that the length of the garments of the king and queen in the ancient artwork from the Amarna period corresponds to the length of garments worn by men and women in that culture at that time, and any correspondence of those lengths to the outlines of the constellations Ophiuchus and Sagittarius in the sky is "mere coincidence" – but is it not also possible that the garments worn by kings and queens in that ancient culture were deliberately patterned to evoke the heavenly figures of Ophiuchus and Sagittarius (perhaps following some ancient tradition handed down for centuries, its source long forgotten)? The same question could perhaps be asked regarding the headgear of the kings and queens of ancient cultures as well.

The Amarna period of the reign of Akhenaten and the deliberate suppression of the traditional pantheon is certainly a noteworthy subject for deep consideration. Does it indicate that the ancient Egyptians were not actually aware that the manifestations of the deities were patterned on the constellations of the stars? Or does it represent an attempt to re-define the aspects of the powers who were "seen" in those same constellations in the heavens (using the same constellations, but re-assigning the attributes of *the powers behind* those visible representations)?

It is perhaps difficult or impossible to know at this point in history, nearly 3,400 years after the beginning of the reign of Akhenaten in Egypt. But the questions remain relevant to this very day, because we have seen a very similar attempt to "wipe out" or denigrate the old gods, based upon a strict interpretation of a new deity, in the Christian period that started during the centuries we refer to as the second and third centuries AD (or CE) and continuing to this day. This attempt to eradicate all other deities is remarkable, given the fact that the stories and figures in the scriptures of the Bible (to include the figure of the central deity Jah or Jehovah or Yahweh) can also be shown to be based on the very same system of celestial metaphor which underlies all the other ancient myths and scriptures around the globe!

The above discussion reveals how vitally important an understanding of the ancient system of celestial metaphor should be considered for any comprehensive study of ancient history. In fact, I would argue that without incorporating an awareness of this worldwide celestial system, we cannot hope to arrive at an accurate understanding of what was going on, and will be prone to making egregious errors of interpretation.

The authors of *Hamlet's Mill* allude to just such type of misinterpretation on the part of scholars who refuse to consider the possibility that ancient symbology from cultures such as Egypt might reflect celestial realities rather than historical or political events, bemoaning the fact that, for example, "the specialists insist upon calling the celestial churn 'a symbol of uniting the two lands' [. . .]."[160] In that case, they are discussing artwork which they believe has to do with the ages-long motion ("churning") of the precession of the equinoxes, and which ancient myth and symbol allegorizes in some instances as a great heavenly (and earthly) battle between opposing forces, but which historians insist on literalizing, for instance by seeing such symbology as representative of the political unification of Upper Egypt and Lower Egypt.

Another example which could be offered, although not discussed in *Hamlet's Mill*, are the fairly common depictions in Egyptian artwork showing a king subduing his enemies, or even executing captive enemies, in which the artwork can be seen to draw on celestial symbology. These scenes are so common down through the centuries that they have been given a special name: "smiting scenes."[161]

One extremely early example, shown on the opposite page, comes from an ivory seal of king Den of the First Dynasty, who is thought to have reigned from about 2970 BC to about 2928 BC. This smiting scene from the time of Den, and virtually all the other smiting scenes to come after it down through the millennia, can be shown to be based upon specific stars in the heavens -- possibly upon the outlines of the important constellations Orion and the River Eridanus:

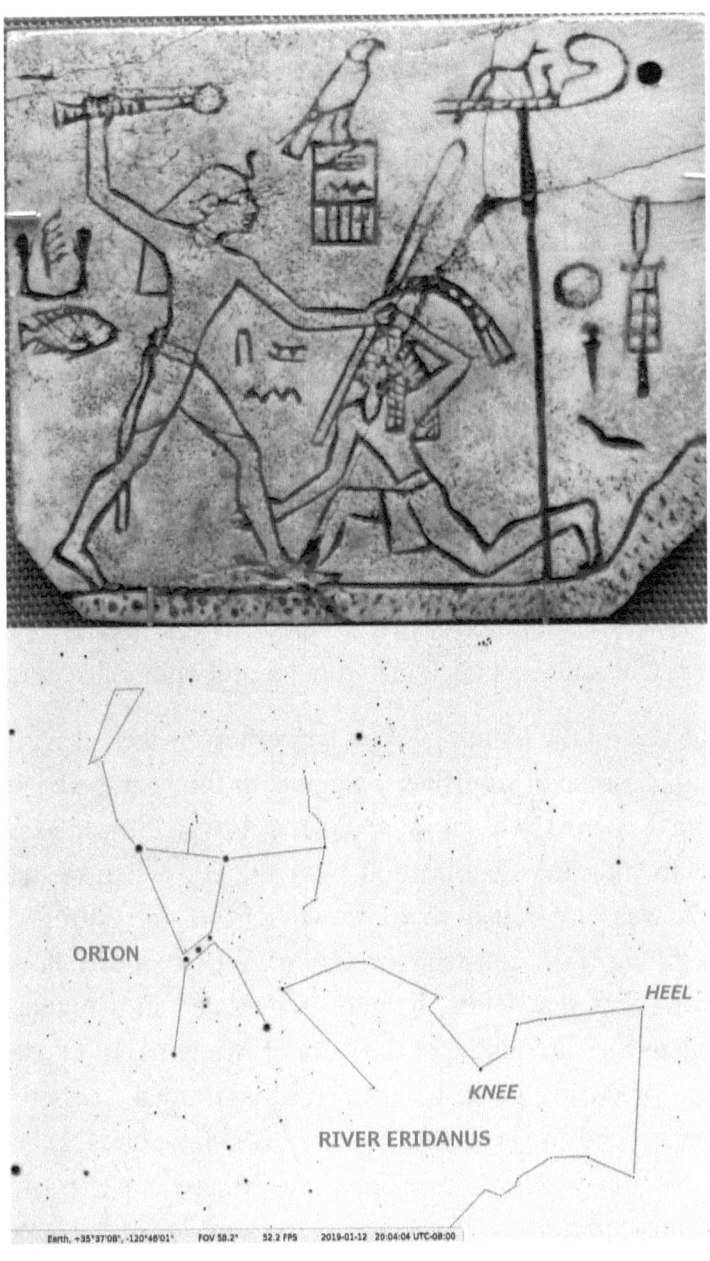

In the image shown above, we see the representation of the king, striding forward with his arm raised nearly upright, and apparently preparing to smite a defeated enemy, who is shown grasping the lower part of the king's forward leg. Below the seal of Den are the stars of the constellation Orion, who also appears to be "striding forward" in the sky, and who raises one hand over his shoulder, such that it is nearly vertical, in manner very suggestive of the scene in the ancient seal artwork.

A possible clue in the artwork which points to this region of the sky, according to my analysis, is the fact that the vanquished opponent is grasping the forward leg of the king: this is very suggestive of the stars of the constellation Eridanus, which is an extremely long "river of stars" which originates at a point very close to the forward leg of the constellation Orion, near the bright star Rigel. Indeed, many ancient myths describe water or other liquid flowing from the foot of an Orion-figure (such as the story about the defeat of the bronze automaton Talos in ancient Greek myth, who is defeated when a screw in his heel is removed, allowing his animating ichor to run out and immobilize the giant).

In the case of the "smiting scene" pattern from ancient Egypt, the twisting course of the River Eridanus in the heavens becomes a defeated enemy (who is grasping the forward lower leg of the king, to indicate identification with the constellation Eridanus which was envisioned to be flowing from the bottom of the forward leg of the constellation Orion). We can see in the ancient artwork that the defeated figure is depicted in a manner very suggestive of the outline of the stars of Eridanus. In my diagram on the preceding page, I have placed additional labels to show where a bend in the stars of Eridanus corresponds to the rear knee of the vanquished enemy, and where a sharp angle in Eridanus corresponds to the heel of the same leg of the opponent.

It should be noted here that it is also quite likely that many "smiting scenes" embody yet another manifestation of a Hercules and Ophiuchus scene. Surviving art from ancient Greece reveal *many* scenes depicting Heracles subduing a kneeling opponent and grasping a curved helmet-crest, similar to the Egyptian smiting scenes (the Pylos Agate art also follows the pattern, and even the description of Moses "smiting the rock" in Exodus). In the King Den seal, I think more clues point to an Orion connection, but in other smiting scenes they point to Hercules. In either case, however, the smiting scene is clearly celestial.

Before concluding with some observations about the celstial aspects of the vitally important myth-cycle involving Isis, Osiris, Horus, Set and others, let us briefly examine one other very significant god: the ibis-headed deity Thoth, the god of writing and learning, wisdom and the moon.

As with virtually all ancient Egyptian names, the original pronunciation of this god's name in the language spoken during the dynastic period is now unknown. The god's name was written in hieroglyphics as a sacred ibis (which itself signified the god Thoth), followed by the "bread loaf" symbol (associated with the "T" sound), followed by the "pair of reeds" symbol (sometimes rendered simply as two parallel lines, inclined, associated with the "Y" sound), and is often rendered into our lettering system as *dhwty*. The name of the god is sometimes reconstructed as *Djehuty, Djeheuty,* or some variant thereof, such as *Tehuti,* in the *Egyptian Hieroglyphic Dictionary* of E. A. Wallis Budge).[162] Writing in the nineteenth century, Max Müller renders the god's name as Thout(i) and adds "(earlier Zhouti, Dhouti)."[163]

In Budge's *Egyptian Hieroglyphic Dictionary,* the author provides various titles and apellations associated with the god found in ancient inscriptions, including "judge of the gods," "master of words of power," "Thoth the ibis," "Thoth the Great," "Thoth the Twice Great," "Thoth, great one of spells," and "Thoth, lord of the divine Word, just scribe of the Company of the Gods."[164]

Thoth is often depicted in ancient Egyptian texts and monuments, writing on a tablet and recording important events, as shown in the examples below (from an 1888 book on Egyptian divinities):

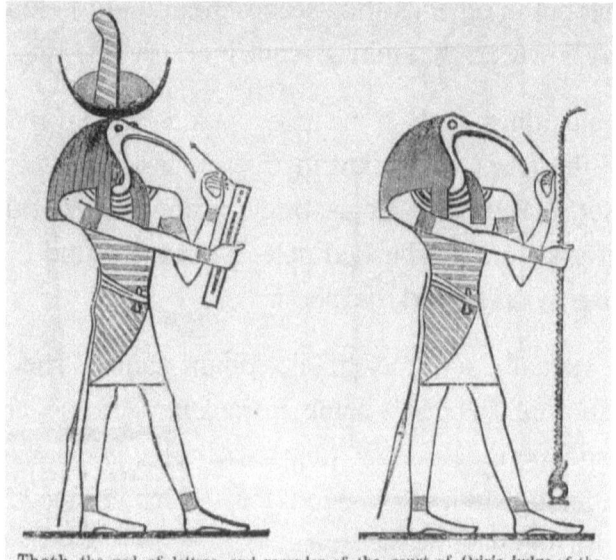

Thoth, the god of letters, and recorder of the court of Osiris, judge of the dead; has an ibis head, sometimes surmounted with a crescent moon and feather; holds a pen and tablet, or pen and palm branch.

All writing was believed to have originated with the god, and thus all the spells in the Pyramid Texts and later versions of these texts come from Thoth.

He is also associated with the heart, according to some ancient sources, including the aforementioned Horapollo (or whoever was the author of the text on hieroglyphs attributed to Horapollo). As James Cowles Prichard remarks, citing Horapollo's *Hieroglyphica*:

306

Horapollo informs us that the Egptians "designate the heart by the emblematical figure of the Ibis; for this animal," he adds, "is intimately connected with Hermes, the president of the heart, and of the reasoning faculty; the form of the Ibis itself bears a congruity to the heart, and this congruity is a circumstance much noted by the Egyptians."[165]

Note that when Horapollo talks about the Egyptian Hermes being the "president of the heart," he is referring to Thoth – the ancient Greek and Roman authors universally assume that the gods of Egypt and the gods of Greece or Rome are the same deities, albeit with different names and some different symbology and iconography between the different cultures, and they associate Thoth with Hermes even as they associate Zeus with Ammon.

Based on the fact that Thoth is the god of writing and the scribe of the gods, I have long suspected that this god is somehow connected with the constellation Hercules, based on my analysis presented in *Star Myths of the World, Volume Three* (*Star Myths of the Bible*) showing that the passages in Exodus which describe the Ten Commandments as having been engraved on the tablets by the very finger of God are describing the constellation Hercules, who appears to be reaching downwards towards the "serpent-head" feature on the western side of Ophiuchus as if to write upon it (the small triangle or circlet atop this half of the serpent being envisioned in this case as a tablet).[166]

Additionally, I also suspected Hercules as the possible celestial identity of this Egyptian god because of the arguments for a linguistic connection between the name of Thoth (or Djehuty) and the figure of David in the Old Testament (an idea I mention in my 2014 book *The Undying Stars*, and which was first put into my mind by some of the arguments of Ralph Ellis, as I noted in *The Undying Stars* -- even though I generally disagree with the fairly "literalistic" and historical interpretations Ralph Ellis puts forth for many of the characters in the Old and New Testaments, characters whom I believe to be celestial and esoteric in nature rather than historical, terrestrial, and literal).[167] The names *Thoth* (or Djehuty) and *David* (or Daoud) have linguistic similarities.

As we will see in the third volume of this series, the figure of David in the scriptures of the Old Testament is associated beyond any doubt with the figure of Hercules in the heavens. This fact has long caused me to suspect that Thoth might also be associated with the same constellation. Indeed, as discussed in *Star Myths of the Bible*, when David writes the treacherous letter which he gives to Bathsheba's husband Uriah, carrying a death sentence for Uriah, David (as the constellation Hercules) is reaching down and writing, in a manner reminiscent of the writing on the tablets of the Ten Commandments, and in a manner reminiscent of Thoth writing upon his tablet.

But how can the constellation Hercules, with its massive square-shaped head, ever be reconciled with the familiar depictions of the Egyptian god Thoth or Djehuty, with his graceful curving neck and ibis head?

The likely solution came to me in a flash one day as I was looking at the stars of the outline of the constellation Hercules, and considering this very question. The portion of the constellation which is usually envisioned as the "upraised arm," the arm of Hercules which is imagined to be brandishing a weapon, such as a great sword or club or thunderbolt, can also be envisioned as the long-necked head of an ibis, as shown in the image on the following page. In the outline of Hercules at top, the only difference from the outline we have been using (the outline that is based on the suggestion of H. A. Rey in his 1952 book) is that the stars of the "lower half" of the weapon brandished by Hercules have been left out. Leaving these out, the "upper arm" of the constellation can be imagined as a large ibis-head:

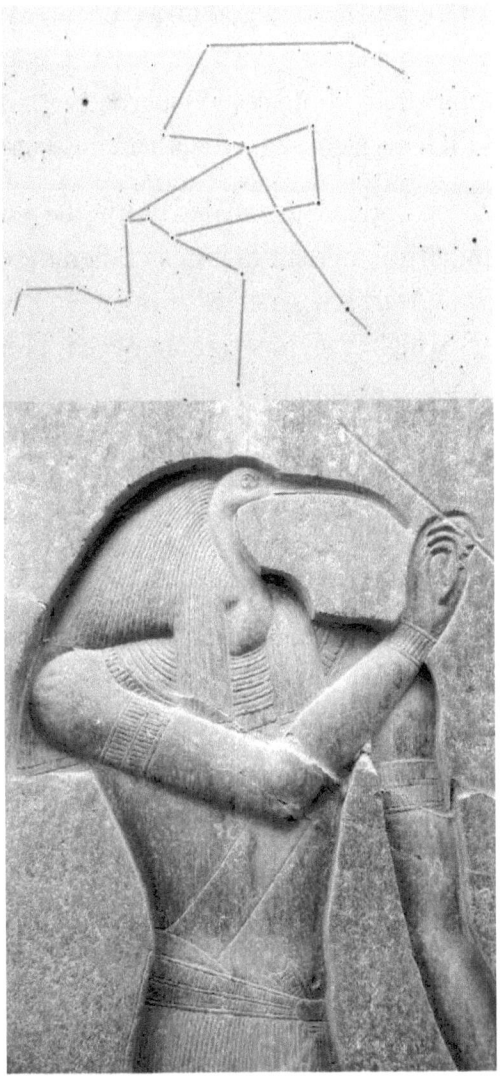

Note that the "ibis-head" version of Hercules shown above makes very minimal changes to the outline we have been using. Various

309

other ways of connecting the stars could be suggested (such as starting from the top corner of the usual stars of the "head" of Hercules, or even incorporating the smaller star we looked at earlier in conjunction with the discussion of the side-lock, for example) which might make the ibis-head seem even more similar to the depiction of the ibis-headed god in ancient artwork, but the above suggestion demonstrates with the least alteration to the outline the possibility that Thoth could have been associated with the constellation Hercules, envisioned with an ibis-head.

If the god Thoth is indeed associated with the constellation Hercules (as I am fairly confident that he is), then the association of this god with *the heart* resonates with other Star Myths from other cultures in which the juncture between Hercules and Ophiuchus was associated with the heart.

For example, as discussed in *Star Myths of the World, Volume Three (Star Myths of the Bible)*, when the LORD meets Solomon in a dream, in I Kings 3, and Solomon asks for wisdom, God is pleased with this request by the king, and says to Solomon: "I have given thee a wise and an understanding heart" -- a declaration which I believe we can see enacted for us in the night sky over our heads, if we look at the constellation Hercules (with whom the LORD is invariably associated in the scriptures) reaching down to place a "heart" in the upraised hand of Ophiuchus (i.e., the triangular "serpent-head" of the constellation Ophiuchus, with whom the figure of Solomon can be shown to be associated: this triangular shape was seen as a heart in ancient myths, including in the Mahabharata of ancient India which we will examine later in this volume). In other words, God is giving a wise and understanding heart to Solomon, and this gesture is envisioned in the relative positions of Hercules and Ophiuchus.

We can also find other passages in the Bible, such as in the book of Jeremiah chapter 31 and verse 33, in which the LORD declares he will write his law upon the hearts of his people, and I believe that this declaration is founded upon the ancient system of celestial metaphor which clearly associates the leaning-forward and downward-reaching posture of the constellation Hercules, extending an arm towards the upraised "serpent-head" section of the constellation Ophiuchus, as having to do with writing (on the part of Hercules) and a heart (the feature atop the western "serpent-half" of Ophiuchus).

Thus, I believe that we can with some confidence connect Thoth, the god of writing and also of the heart, with the constellation Hercules in the heavens -- an association which helps explain the reverence with which this god was held in ancient Egypt.

From the above analysis, we can see that the correspondences between the myths of ancient Egypt and the accounts in the scriptures collected into what we call the Old and New Testaments of the Bible are remarkably strong -- even to the point of linguistic parallels between names (such as that between the name of the god Djehuty and the name of David), as well as strong parallels between the creation accounts, and between the characteristics of the immanent, invisible, all-encompassing divinity whose aspects are made visible to us through the characteristics associated with the constellation Hercules in the heavens.

There is even further evidence for making an association between the god Thoth and the constellation Hercules, and that is the well-established fact that Thoth also had a baboon form or avatar, in which form he would sometimes be depicted in ancient artwork. We will see later in this volume that there is evidence from from India (Hanuman) that the constellation Hercules was sometimes envisioned as an ape or monkey. Apes and monkeys typically have a rather square-shaped head, sometimes with a "beard" or "ruff" which resembles the square beard found on other Hercules-related figures (including the square full beard shown on the god Zeus, and also on the hero Heracles himself, as well as on the depictions of Gorgons in Greek myth, whose fringe of serpents was often drawn in a manner resembling a beard or ruff, and who can be confidently connected to the constellation Hercules as well, according to my analysis). The fact that Thoth also has a baboon form or avatar helps to confirm the connection of this god with that constellation.

We will conclude our survey of the celestial aspects of the ancient Egyptian spiritual tradition with an examination of another important myth-cycle, and one whose parallels to the gospel cycle of stories in particular have for many decades received much scholarly attention: the mythology surrounding the dying god Osiris, and the efforts of the goddess Isis and their son Horus to bring about the god's restoration and resurrection.

The similarities of the Osiris myth to the mysteries described in the gospel accounts are so close and so significant that it is entirely possible that the common name for the scriptures which describe the Christ cycle – that is to say, the "New Testament" – is a misnomer. Indeed, instead of speaking of an "Old Testament" and a "New Testament," it might be more appropriate to speak of an "Old Testament" and a "Really Old Testament."

Gerald Massey (1828 - 1907) has argued that in speaking of the mysteries of the Christ (in epistles and teachings which likely predate the publication of the canonical gospel narratives which today are contained in the books of Matthew, Mark, Luke and

John), the figure known to us as Paul was actually divulging mysteries which had been kept secret since the earliest days of ancient Egypt, if not for even longer than that.

In an essay entitled *Paul the Gnostic Opponent of Peter, not an Apostle of Historic Christianity,* Massey points to very explicit verses in Paul's letters in which the writer basically asserts that this is exactly what he is doing. For instance, Massey points to the verse in Paul's epistle to the Romans in which he references "the revelation of the mystery, which was kept secret since the world began," but which Paul is obviously teaching openly (Romans 16: 25).

Massey declares: "The fact is that Paul was a publisher of the ancient mysteries; that was why his enemies strove to kill him. He openly promulgated the Gnosis that had always been kept secret."[168] Other verses Massey cites include 1 Corinthians 2: 7 - 8, in which Paul writes that he speaks of "the wisdom of God in a mystery, even the hidden wisdom, which God ordained before the world unto our glory; which none of the princes of this world knew," and also Ephesians 3: 5, in which Paul calls his teaching of the mystery: that "which in other ages was not made known unto the sons of men."

The Christ cycle, of course, is not identical to the Osiris cycle, but the parallels are self-evident, and have been remarked upon by many commentators and analysts down through the centuries. I am convinced that (like most of the other Star Myths of the world) they were intended to convey very much the same esoteric wisdom, even if the superficial details used to "give shape" to the teachings about invisible things differ.

A metaphor that I have used in the past to try to explain this concept is the idea of "invisible furniture," which we cannot see, but which can be draped over with sheets or blankets or tapestries in order to reveal the underlying shapes of the invisible doctrines. These tapestries or draperies (the myth-systems found around the world) can vary greatly in their outward appearance. Some are richly embroidered, others are gauzy and almost transparent, while others are rough and rather coarse on their exterior. The shapes underneath remain the same, but the myth-coverings that allow us to see the invisible forms will vary tremendously.

The designs and outward appearance of the Egyptian myths, however, have much in common with the patterns found in the Bible stories, and although their "feel" might initially seem to differ, it is likely that they branched apart much more recently than did some of the other myths found in other cultures around the globe.

Writing about the Osiris cycle of myths, Professor Robert Ritner of the University of Chicago has said:

> Few Egyptian myths are as well known, or have had such an impact on Western speculation, as the cycle of tales regarding the salvation deities Isis and Osiris. References to the actions of these gods abound in surviving Egyptian hymns, prayers and funerary literature, yet perhaps because their story was so familiar to a native audience, it is the Greek adaptation of Plutarch (*De Iside et Osiride*) that preserves the longest exposition of their myth, composed some 2,500 years after the formation of the cult.[169]

It is true that the surviving texts, such as those in the Pyramid Texts (the most ancient extended texts we know of to date, going back to earlier than 2300 BC, as mentioned previously) do mention Osiris frequently, and assume such a level of familiarity in the reader that they do not give a comprehensive outline of the entire cycle, but this may not be because, as Dr. Ritner puts it, "because their story was so familiar to a native audience," but instead because the story was a profound mystery, not expounded in all its detail but kept secret, the antiquity and secrecy of which can be inferred from the passages from the epistles of Paul cited above, regarding the antiquity and secrecy of the related mystery of the Christ.

The philosopher and historian Plutarch of Chaeronea, mentioned previously, who lived from around AD 46 to around AD 120 in the region of Beoetia in Greece, was an initiate into ancient *mysteria*, and served for many years as a priest of Apollo at the temple of Delphi.

In a text entitled *Of Isis and Osiris, or of the Ancient Religion and Philosophy of Egypt* (originally *De Iside et Osiride* in Latin), included in Plutarch's *Moralia* (or *Morals*), he gives an account which is valuable for giving a fairly comprehensive overview of the Osiris cycle, and for the fact that during Plutarch's day there were still priests and priestesses of Egypt who could be expected to be recipients of the stream of that civilization's ancient sacred knowledge.

While it is clear enough that the version delivered by Plutarch is a product of his era and no doubt contains some importations of traditions related to Greek myth, it is probably safe to use his *Of Isis and Osiris* for the broad outline of the general myth, which we will examine for its celestial components.

Plutarch tells us that Osiris was born on the first of the five "intercalary" days added to the three hundred sixty days of the year (according to legend, the addition of these days was accomplished by the god Thoth), and that his brothers and sisters

315

Horus the Elder, Set (whom ancient classical-era writers including Plutarch identified with the monster Typhon who was pinned under Mount Aetna by Zeus), Isis and Nephthys were born on the other four intercalary days, in that order (one per day).

Osiris, like Q'ukumatz of the Maya and Quetzalcoatl of the Aztec and Viracocha of the Inca, was a civilizing deity. Plutarch tells us that:

> One of the first acts related of Osiris in his reign was to deliver the Egyptians from their destitute and brutish manner of living. This he did by showing them the fruits of cultivation, by giving them laws, and by teaching them to honour the gods. Later he travelled over the whole earth civilizing it without the slightest need of arms, but most of the peoples he won over to his way by the charm of his persuasive discourse combined with song and all manner of music. [170]

This activity on the part of Osiris, going around the world and dwelling among humanity to teach them peaceful and civilizing arts, is a common element in many mythologies around the world, usually associated with a lost Golden Age. The civilizing deity who dwells among humanity often displays what we could call "Osirian" characteristics (or "Saturnian" characteristics, as the Latin deity Saturn follows the same pattern), one of these being that the Golden Age ends when the deity is eventually slain or driven away, to sleep in an underworld of some sort, sometimes in a cave beneath the sea as is the case with Saturn of the Latin myths, or in the underworld realm as is the case with Osiris.

Plutarch tells us that while Osiris is away on his worldwide civilizing tour, his treacherous brother Set plans a trap to kill Osiris, and that this plot was hatched with seventy-two co-

conspirators. Having secretly measured his brother's body at some time previous, Set constructs a beautiful sarcophagus-like chest, richly ornamented. Then, when a great festival was taking place after Osiris returned, Set calls for this chest to be brought into the scene of the festivities. Plutarch tells us (referring, as always in Plutarch's texts, to *Set* as "Typhon"):

> The company was much pleased at the sight of it and admired it greatly, whereupon Typhon jestingly promised to present it to the man who should find the chest to be exactly his length when he lay down in it. They all tried it in turn, but no one fitted it; then Osiris got into it and lay down, and those who were in the plot ran to it and slammed down the lid, which they fastened by nails from the outside and also by using molten lead. Then they carried the chest to the river and sent it on its way to the sea through the Tanitic Mouth [one of the outlets of the Nile Delta, near ancient Tanis]. Wherefore the Egyptians even to this day name this mouth the hateful and execrable. Such is the tradition. They say also that the date on which this deed was done was the seventeenth day of Athyr [November 13, according to the footnote in the Loeb edition of 1936], when the sun passes through the Scorpion, and in the twenty-eighth year of the reign of Osiris; but some say that these are the years of his life and not of his reign.[71]

Plutarch then tells us that the first to learn of this dreadful murder were certain "Pans and satyrs," a point also confirmed by the accounts of Herodotus and of Diodorus Siculus, and that when these brought the news to humanity, the ensuing reaction gave rise to the term "panic," after the name Pan (which also gives us the word "pandemonium").

317

Plutarch recounts that the goddess Isis, the beautiful consort of Osiris, upon hearing of the death of her beloved husband, immediately cut off one of the tresses of her hair. She then wandered everywhere in search of news as to where the casket bearing the body of Osiris could have gone. Eventually, she met some little children, who had seen the seventy-two henchmen of Set launching the coffin down the river and into the sea.

In the meantime, we learn that the sea eventually cast the sarcophagus with Osiris upon the shore near the land of Byblus, amongst a clump of heather, which eventually grew up into a great and massive vine or even a tree trunk (sometimes described in other accounts as a tamarisk tree), completely enclosing the casket and hiding it from view.

Here is the account as given by Plutarch and translated into English by Frank Cole Babbitt (1867 - 1935) of Trinity College in Hartford, Connecticut:

> Thereafter Isis, as they relate, learned that the chest had been cast up by the sea near the land of Byblus and that the waves had gently set it down in the midst of a clump of heather. The heather in a short time ran up into a very beautiful and massive stock, and enfolded and embraced the chest with its growth and concealed it within its trunk. The king of the country admired the great size of the plant, and cut off the portion that enfolded the chest (which was now hidden from sight), and used it as a pillar to support the roof of his house. These facts, they say, Isis ascertained by the divine ispiration of Rumour, and came to Byblus and sat down by a spring, all dejection and tears; she exchanged no word with anybody, save only that she welcomed the queen's maidservants and treated them with great amiability, plaiting

their hair for them and imparting to their persons a wondrous fragrance from her own body. But when the queen observed her maidservants, a longing came upon her for the unknown woman and for such hairdressing and for a body fragrant with ambrosia. Thus it happened that Isis was sent for and became so intimate with the queen that the queen made her the nurse of her baby. They say that the king's name was Malcander; the queen's name some say was Astarte, others Saosis, and still others Nemanus, which the Greeks would call Athenais.[172]

After being brought to the palace as a nurse, Isis (we are told) nursed the baby by giving it her finger to suck – certainly a possible celestial clue. She also (each night, after the palace had gone to sleep) held the baby over a fire – a motif we have seen before and will see again – in order to "burn away" its mortality and give it the gift of immortality.

Further, she would turn herself into a swallow and dart about the pillar that held up the roof – the pillar enclosing the casket containing the body of Osiris – uttering a wailing cry of lamentation as she did so.

One night, the queen secretly observed the supposed nursemaid of her baby. The mother was horrified to see Isis suspending the child over the fire in order to give it immortality. She rushed in and with a loud cry of terror snatched the baby away . . . and in doing so, deprived it of its immortality. Again, this important motif is one that we have already observed in the Maui cycle of myths – from the islands of the Pacific on the other side of the globe – and it is one that manifests over and over in mythology in many cultures.

The goddess then revealed herself to be Isis, and asked for the pillar containing the casket. Of course, the king and queen of Byblus were over-awed by the presence of the great goddess, and immediately granted her request. Isis easily removed the pillar, as well as the thick folds of wood that had grown around the sarcophagus containing her beloved Osiris.

Then, Plutarch passes on the detail that Isis wrapped up the old wood that had enclosed the coffin in a linen cloth, and poured perfume over it, and left it with the rulers of Byblus. Plutarch relates that "the people of Byblus venerate this wood" and its cloth to this day.[173]

Taking the sarcophagus itself, Isis departed by boat. She came to a swampy place and, finding a lonely island, disembarked in the night to open the casket, where she could embrace her slain husband and weep over him and caress his face. Then, she hid the casket amongst the reeds and went in search of her son Horus, according to Plutarch's account.

However, Plutarch tells us, Set happened to be out in the swamps hunting by the light of the moon, and later that same evening he happened upon the hidden casket – which he immediately recognized. Opening it up, he found the body of Osiris and cut it into fourteen pieces, and scattered them through the swamps and up and down the Nile.

Horrified, Isis commenced a long and sorrowful search for the dismembered parts of her husband's body, sailing through the swamps in a boat of papyrus. Eventually, she found thirteen out of the fourteen parts, and held a ritual funeral for each one as it was recovered. For this reason, Plutarch tells us, "there are many so-called tombs of Osiris in Egypt" (Plutarch also says that the purpose of the multiple tombs might have been to try to deceive

Set and make it more difficult for him to ever find and desecrate the body of Osiris again).[174]

The traditions are fairly consistent that the one piece of the dismembered body that Isis was unable to locate was "the male member, for the reason that this had been at once tossed into the river, and the lepidotus, the sea-bream, and the pike had fed upon it; and it is from these very fishes the Egyptians are most scrupulous in abstaining."[175] Isis made a replica of this missing piece instead and consecrated it for worship and for ritual festivals (we will see a parallel in India with the Shiva lingam).

The recovery of the pillar containing the casket and corpse of Osiris is depicted in ancient Egyptian art, often using a special symbol associated with Osiris which is known as the Djed Column (also translated as "Tat" by earlier generations of scholars of ancient Egypt).

While it is true that this account of the story of Isis and Osiris, and the treachery of their brother Set, was not recorded in this particular form until the late first or early second century AD (the actual date of composition of Plutarch's *Moralia* being a subject of debate among scholars, but generally thought to have been sometime between AD 92 amd AD 106), there are plenty of references to Isis and Osiris and Set in much earlier texts, as well as artwork from Egypt which confirms some of the details of Plutarch's account.[176]

For instance, the image on the following page comes from temples at Abydos erected during the reign of Seti I, the son of Ramesses I and the father of Ramesses II, and it depicts Isis receiving the pillar containing the casket and body of Osiris from the king of Byblos. Seti I was king from 1290 BC to 1279 BC. Thus, this depcition from the time of Seti provides strong confirmation for some of the aspects of the Osiris myth as recorded by Plutarch, fully fourteen centuries later.

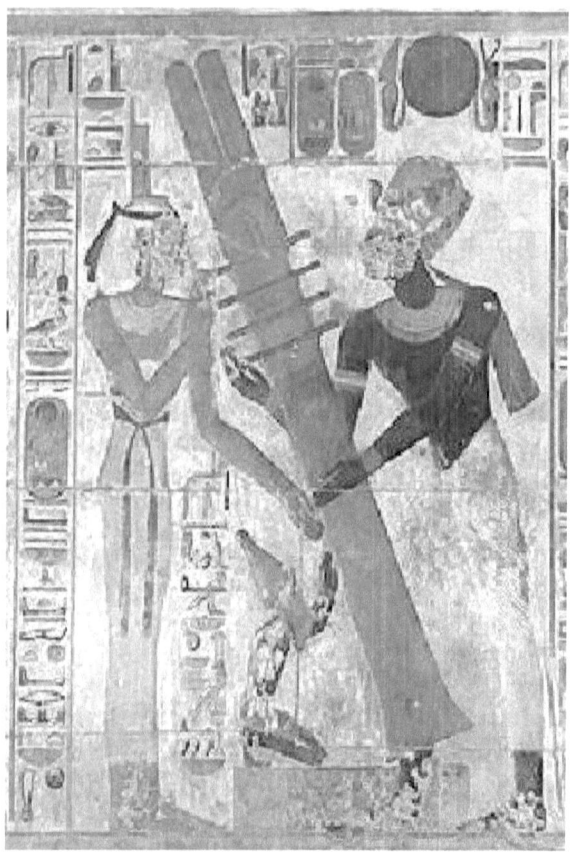

In the image, the pillar is depicted as a Djed column, an extremely important symbol in ancient Egyptian culture, associated with the backbone of Osiris. The horizontal bars near the top portion of the pillar are characteristic of depictions of the Djed, and are suggestive of the vertebrae of a human body. In *Handbook of Egyptian Mythology*, Geraldine Pinch writes that, "By the New Kingdom, the *djed* was closely associated with the mythology of Osiris. The taboo subject of the murder of Osiris could be alluded to by saying that Seth had 'laid the *djed* on its side.'"[177]

I believe that we have enough evidence in the material cited thus far to draw some conclusions regarding the celestial foundations of some of the figures and events in the Osiris cycle to this point. Let's discuss those before moving on to the arrival of the god Horus and his contending with Set.

While there are numerous reasons to assume that Osiris is associated primarily with the constellation Orion, and while this is the primary tack which I followed in the first edition of this volume, after some additional years of study of this ancient system (primarily during the research and writing of the subsequent books published since that first edition), I now believe that the mythological evidence for associating the god with Ophiuchus is very strong.

It is certainly possible that Osiris is associated with *both* Orion and with Ophiuchus: important figures in myth are not infrequently seen to "move" through different constellations, and a pairing of Orion and Ophiuchus is not at all unknown from other Star Myths around the world. Indeed, in *Star Myths of the World, Volume Two*, I argue that Prometheus may be associated with Orion (primarily in his role as bringer of fire to mortal men and women) and also with Ophiuchus (particularly when he is bound and tormented). If Osiris is also associated with both of these constellations, that would be a most intriguing parallel, since both Prometheus and Osiris play a role as beneficient "civilizing" figures who are later "bound" (Prometheus to a rock in the Caucusus mountains, where as punishment his liver is gnawed upon by an eagle, and Osiris to the underworld, where he is bound in mummy-clothes and funereal garments).

The arguments for an association between Osiris and Orion are fairly well established. The god Sah (or Sahu), described as the "father of the gods" in utterance 274 of the Pyramid Texts, is associated with the constellation Orion (which constellation scholars believe to have been called by the same name, Sah, by the ancient Egyptians), and utterance 442 of the Pyramid Texts expressly declares:

> Behold, he is come (again) as Sah; behold Osiris is come as Sah, lord of the wine-cellar at the Wag-feast.[78]

In his discussion of ancient Egyptian "star clocks," mathematician and historian of scientific thought Otto E. Neugebauer explains that, although we do not know for certain the identity of each "decan" (or group of stars which would be observed on the eastern horizon just prior to dawn for ten days, until a new decan rose into view during that pre-dawn hour), scholars believe that "Sirius and Orion figured among the decans" and that "Sirius was, so to speak, the ideal prototype for all the other decans."[79]

The illustration on the following page depicts a rectangular star-clock found in the tomb of Seti I. As Professor Neugebauer explains in his book *The Exact Sciences in Antiquity*, we believe that such a clock was read from right to left,[80] into the facing images of the deities representing the decans, as if the reader is having a conversation with the images -- the same way that hieroglyphics are also read, because hieroglyphic texts can be read from left-to-right, right-to-left, or top-to-bottom, but to distinguish between right-to-left and left-to-right one would only need to think of "having a conversation" with the figures in the hieroglyphs.

I've enlarged one section: in the enlarged section of the star-clock, we see a tall goddess, taller than any of the other decans. This figure is thought to have been associated with the star Sirius (or

Sopdet to the ancient Egyptians, translated to *Sothis* by the Greeks):

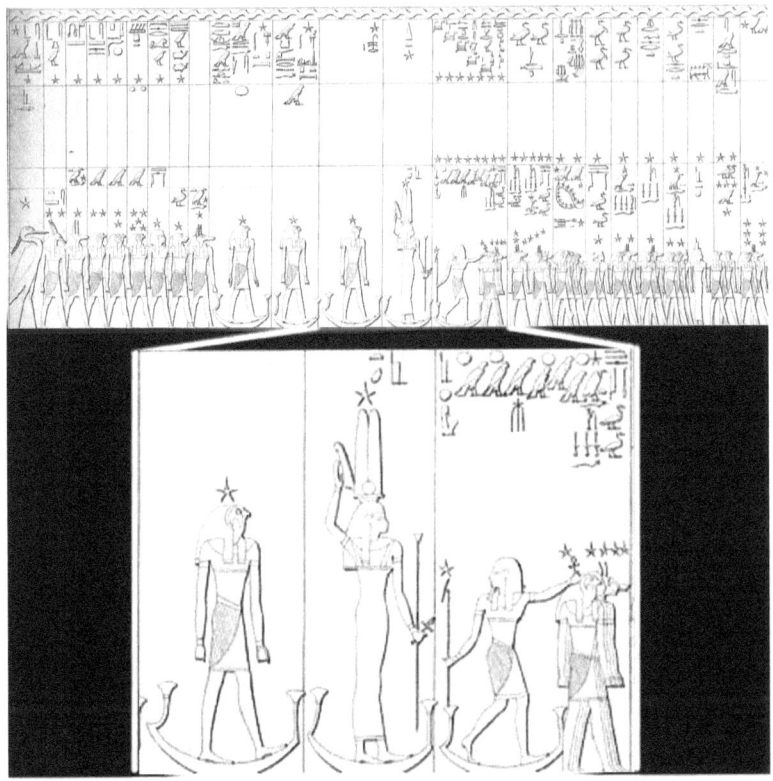

Note the large star over the head of the goddess. Note also the "throne-shaped" symbol in the hieroglyphs just above the star (the right-most hieroglyphic symbol above the goddess). This throne shape is associated with Isis, and is often drawn atop the head of the goddess Isis in surviving artwork from ancient Egypt.

Because the star Sirius (which is the brightest fixed star in our heavens, the only brighter objects being our own sun and the wandering planets) follows the constellation Orion, it makes sense that the "striding" figure just before the goddess would correspond to Orion (since the constellation Orion rises before the star Sirius).

Interestingly enough, if one is not wedded to the interpretation of seeing the star above the tallest decan in the above star-clock as Sirius, then one could make the argument that the striding figure normally interpreted as Orion might instead correspond to the outline of the constellation Ophiuchus. First, the figure has one arm holding a staff (on the left as we face the image), and the other extended and raised with an Ankh symbol protruding from the upper hand. This outline could be interpreted as the constellation Ophiuchus, with the staff corresponding to the "tail-end" of the serpent held by the figure's central body (the eastern side of the constellation) and the upraised arm with Ankh corresponding to the "head-end" of the serpent which is topped by a circlet (the western side of the constellation). Supporting this interpretation is the fact that the figure holding the staff and the Ankh is standing in a sacred boat, which we have already argued can correspond to the shape of Scorpio (and Scorpio is directly beneath Ophiuchus).

But if this interpretation is correct, then what constellation would play the role of the goddess who follows behind the Ophiuchus-figure? I would suggest that she might well correspond to the constellation Sagittarius, which not only has a long dress as seen in the outline in the sky, but also has a "plume" on the left (or eastern) side of the head, corresponding to the upraised arm of the goddess in the star-clock, and the "plume" or "feather" seen protruding towards the left side of the illustration as we face the page. Indeed, this interpretation seems to have much to support it, in terms of the outline of the constellations themselves (and, once again, Ophiuchus rises before Sagittarius, and thus this interpretation works with the direction of the actual star-clock).

However, an objection might be offered that Sagittarius does not have a bright star above its head, as the goddess in the illustration is shown to have a bright star above her head. The counter to this objection is the fact that the bright star Altair, in the constellation Aquila the Eagle, is seen above Sagittarius, and could be the bright star indicated in the star-clock above the figure of the goddess decan, which the ancient sky-watchers would see rising in the east at about the same time that the constellation Sagittarius rises.

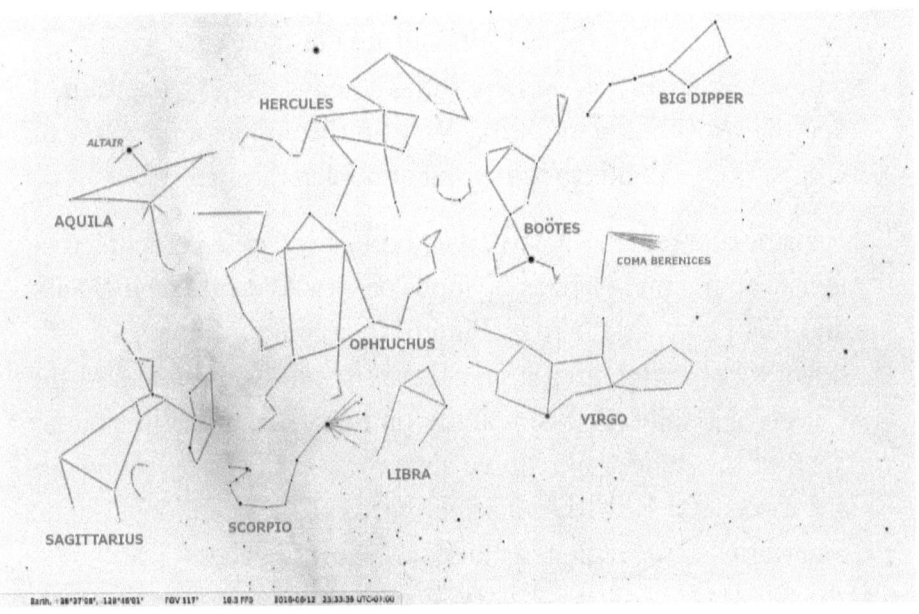

If so, it would argue that the goddess Isis may sometimes be associated with the constellation Sagittarius, a conclusion which I believe to be supported by passages in Plutarch's account, particularly the part in which Plutarch tells us that the goddess was looking for the casket containing the body of Osiris and ascertained that it was in Byblus (or Byblos). Plutarch writes:

> These facts, they say, Isis ascertained by the divine ispiration of Rumour, and came to Byblus and sat down by a spring, all

dejection and tears; she exchanged no word with anybody, save only that she welcomed the queen's maidservants and treated them with great amiability, plaiting their hair for them and imparting to their persons a wondrous fragrance from her own body.[181]

The description of the goddess sitting down *by a spring* resonates with myths we have examined over and over in other cultures, in which a goddess or other female figure is described beside a pool, a spring, or a secluded grotto: the goddess (or princess, such as in the case of Nausicaa in the Odyssey) in these cases is invariably associated with the constellation Sagittarius, and the widening in the Milky Way (in the region of the Galactic Center) corresponds to the spring or pool in the myth.

In many of these Star Myths, the goddess will be accompanied by female attendants, such as Nymphs or Graces or mortal maidens, and this is the case here in Plutarch's account in which Isis sits down by a spring, and is met there by the maidservants of the Queen of Byblos. As we will see on many occasions in Volume Two of this series (and Three also) these maidens or attendants are associated with the multiple heads of Scorpio, adjacent to Sagittarius in the region of the "pool" of the Galactic Core.

Thus, I now believe that a very strong argument can be made for an association of Isis and Osiris with the constellations Sagittarius and Ophiuchus, even if there is other evidence (argued by Egyptologists going back for more than a century) for an association between the pair Isis and Osiris and the pairing of the star Sirius as it follows the constellation Orion (on the entire other side of the heavens from Sagittarius - Ophiuchus).

Certainly I do not disagree that the ancient texts appear to make explicit an association between Osiris and Orion and between

Isis and Sirius. In addition to texts cited earlier, there is a passage in chapter 44 of the Book of the Dead which declares:

> I am Osiris, brother of Isis. I am Orion. I am Anubis. I am Horus. I am Tem.[182]

And in an ancient text called the *Lamentations of Isis and Nephthys*, we read lines in which Isis is speaking to the god An and says (as translated by Budge):

> Thy divine emanation glorified Sahu in the heavens, rising and setting each day. And I am like Septet (i.e. Sirius) behind thee, and I go not away from thee.[183]

Additionally, we can find many instances of artwork in which Osiris is portrayed upon a bier or couch – often indicating that he has been slain and sometimes in the form of a mummy. Notably, however, in some of the depictions of Osiris upon a couch, he is depicted in a "striding" posture reminiscent of the constellation Orion, even though such a posture would be most unnatural for someone to adopt while lying on a couch:

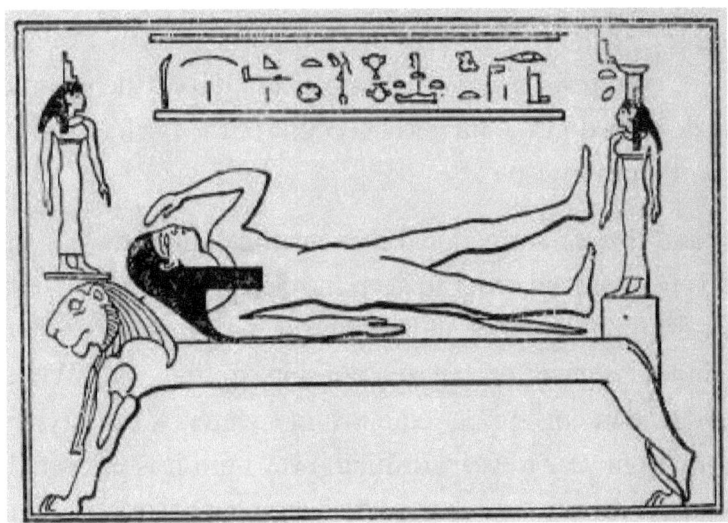

The authors of *Hamlet's Mill* associate the story of Osiris, Isis and Set with the implacable motion of precession, which over the course of centuries appears to "delay" or "hold back" the background of stars such that the stars and constellations which would be expected to be at a specific place in the heavens on a specific date each year will be slightly below their expected location. This delaying action is very gradual: a star will only be one degree of arc distance (or about the width of your pinky finger, when held at arm's distance from your face) after seventy-two years, and its delayed location will be relative to its location in the sky on that particular day and time seventy-two years earlier, not relative to its location the night before.

Because the earth does not orbit the sun in an even number of days (its rotations on its axis do not evenly match up with the amount of time it takes for the planet to come back to the exact same point on its orbital path that it occupied a year before), calendar systems which count days always have some "slippage." This slippage is why the Gregorian system we use today needs to add a "leap day" every four years (except on years ending in two zeroes), and it is also why the ancient Egyptians (and other ancient cultures) had to add "intercalary days," such as the five days described in the mythical account of the birth of Osiris and his brothers and sisters.

The addition of correctional days such as our extra day in leap year is necessary in order to keep the calendar dates from drifting away from the solstices and equinoxes which indicate where we are in our actual orbital relationship to the sun. While the calendar date of spring equinox or winter solstice will vary slightly from year to year (drifting away until it is corrected by a leap year), when we reach the actual moment of spring equinox or winter solstice, we are in fact back at the exact same point in our orbit relative to the sun that we were on the previous spring equinox or winter solstice the year prior.

Thus, calendar date slippage aside, we can use the position of the stars in the heavens at the equinoxes and solstices to observe the slow, ages-long "delaying action" of precession. We know that the ancients did use the solstices and equinoxes for just such observations, and that the two solstices and two equinoxes were imbued with spiritual significance in the ancient worldwide metaphor system underlying the Star Myths, as discussed previously.

In particular, the location of the stars in the hours just prior to the sunrise on the spring equinox have been used to describe the progress of the precessional cycle. As we go through the year, the sun can be seen to "move through" the zodiac constellations as we go around the sun. In other words, as we make our way around our orbit, the line drawn from the earth towards the sun and on beyond it to the background of stars that would be visible on the other side of the sun (if not washed out by the sun's brilliance) will change from month to month as we progress around.

Think of a circular train-track going around the sun, with a forest on the outside of the track upon whose trees at regular intervals are affixed signs bearing images of the different constellations of the zodiac: if someone sitting in a train going around this circular track pointed a powerful laser-pointer at the sun as they rode in a big circle around the sun in the middle, extending the beam of the laser-pointer past the sun would point to the successive images of the zodiac constellations *on the other side of the sun* as the train went all the way around, coming to a new constellation-image every one-twelfth of the way around the track. This set of stars on the *far side* of the sun (in a line from earth as we travel around the orbital track) can be thought of as the constellation that the sun is "occupying" at any given part of the year.

Even though we cannot see the stars during the day, we can determine which stars are the background stars for the sun at any time of year, through a variety of different methods. One easy method is simply to observe the eastern horizon just before sunrise, when it is still dark enough to see which stars are just above the horizon as the sky begins to lighten due to the sun's approach. By observing which stars are visible before the sun causes the sky to become so light that the stars are no longer visible, it is possible to know which constellation the sun is "in" on any given morning. As we go through the year, the sun will move through the different zodiac constellations, at a rate of about one per month (since there are traditionally twelve zodiac constellations, with somewhat even spacing, such that the sun will move through about one per month).

For the past two thousand years, the sun has been occupying the constellation of Pisces at the time of spring equinox each year -- but because the motion of precession "delays" the background of stars by a very small amount (only one degree every seventy-two years), Pisces has been progressively "held down" a tiny bit more each year (only enough to add up to one degree after seventy-two years), such that we are now in the period of transition when the sun is in the space between Pisces and the preceding zodiac constellation, Aquarius, on the important morning of spring equinox (and at this point, the sun is much closer to Aquarius on that morning than to Pisces).

Because the twelve zodiac constellations divide up a 360-degree circle between them, they can each be said to occupy approximately 30 arc-degrees of that circle (360 divided by 12). If the delaying motion of precession only "holds back" the background of stars by a single degree every 72 years, then at that rate it would take 2,160 years (or 72 degrees per year multiplied by 30 degrees per zodiac section or "house") for the delaying action to "hold down" a zodiac constellation to the point that the sun will occupy the *preceding* constellation on a specific designated point on our orbit (such as the specific morning of spring equinox prior to sunrise).

This delaying action has now almost held back the constellation of Pisces to the point that we can say we are no longer in the "Age of Pisces" (when the sun is located in Pisces on the spring equinox) and have transitioned to the "Age of Aquarius" (when Aquarius will be the background of stars on spring equinox instead of Pisces).

Note that this ages-long cycle of precession was imbued with tremendous spiritual significance in the ancient system of celestial metaphor which we are exploring in these volumes. If you think back to the image of a circular train-track going around a central sun, with images of the zodiac constellations arranged on the outside of the track, a person riding around the circular track and pointing a powerful laser-pointer at the sun and *on through* to the "background" constellation on the *other side* would reasonably expect to see the *same constellation* on the other side every time the train got back to a recognizable point on the track. When the train gets to the "nine o'clock" position on the track, for instance (looking down at the circular track from above, and designating points on the circle starting from a twelve o'clock point and moving all the way around), the person in the train with the laser-pointer would expect the pointer to point to the same constellation "behind the sun" that the laser-pointer hit the previous time that the train reached the "nine o'clock" position on the circular track. However, if (after thousands of laps around the track) the laser-pointer ended up pointing past the central sun to a *different* constellation on the other side, even though the train was located at the same point on the track (such as the nine o'clock point on the track), that would be quite surprising! It could be interpreted as meaning that the forest of trees, upon which the signs bearing the images of the constellations are affixed, was somehow "slipping" instead of remaining fixed.

And this is exactly what we observe on our own "track" around the sun, as earth orbits our central star. The seemingly "fixed" background of stars is actually "slipping" such that the arrival of the constellations in their expected locations at their expected times (such as when we reach the "nine o'clock" position of the spring equinox, or the "three o'clock" position of fall equinox, or the six o'clock" position of winter solstice) will be delayed. This delaying action will be very slight -- only a single degree every 72 years -- but after about 2,160 years the delay will be enough that an entirely different constellation will have "usurped" the position of the expected zodiac constellation on the specified day.

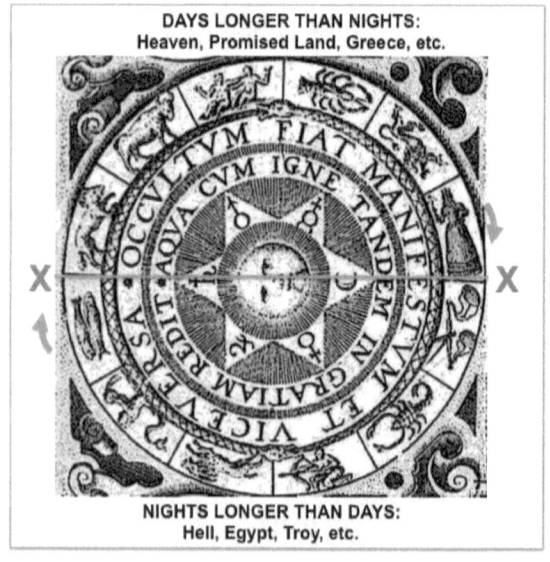

DAYS LONGER THAN NIGHTS:
Heaven, Promised Land, Greece, etc.

NIGHTS LONGER THAN DAYS:
Hell, Egypt, Troy, etc.

The zodiac constellation in which the sun was located on spring equinox, prior to the Age in which the sun was located in Pisces, was the constellation Aries the Ram. After approximately 2,160 years of precession's delaying action, Aries was *held back* so much that the sun occupied Pisces on the important spring equinox instead of occupying Aries. However, prior to Aries, there was yet another set of background stars on the date of the spring equinox each year: the constellation Taurus. After about 2,160 years of precession's delaying action, Taurus was held back so much that the sun was in Aries (which, as you can see in the diagram above, *precedes* Taurus in the cycle) on that spring equinox morning, instead of in Taurus.

And yet, even Taurus was in a sense a "usurper" from the *previous* constellation in which the sun had been located on spring equinox, in the previous age. On the wheel above, we see that Taurus precedes Gemini -- which means that in the Age prior to the Age in which Taurus became the background stars for the sun on the spring equinox, the background stars for the sun on the spring equinox were the stars of Gemini, rather than Taurus.

Gemini in the sky is located just above the lower (or trailing) shoulder of Orion as Orion crosses the sky, such that the constellations rise roughly at the same time. Orion is much more distinctive and visible than Gemini. Thus, during the Age of Gemini, the leading edge of the massive form of the constellation Orion would be peeking over the eastern horizon before dawn on the significant morning of the spring equinox (because the sun was located in Gemini on the spring equinox day each year, during the Age of Gemini). However, precession's inexorable (if very gradual) delaying action would over the years seem to "hold down" Orion beneath the horizon on the spring equinox morning -- a tiny bit more each year (but only enough to hold the stars back by a single degree every 72 years). Thus, after about 2,160 years of this delaying action, Orion (and Gemini) would be delayed so much that they would be held down completely at sunrise on spring equinox each year, and the sun would have moved into a different set of background stars: the preceding constellation of Taurus, which precedes Gemini in the zodiac wheel.

The authors of *Hamlet's Mill* recognize that this motion of precession was understood by the ancients, and included in their myths. Its significance in the ancient system was so great, de Santillana and von Dechend perceive, that the ancients saw the motion of precession as "a great cycle which could affect humanity as a whole."[184] Referring to this ancient understanding of precession, de Santillana and von Dechend write:

> They believed that the sliding of the sun along the equinoctial point affected the frame of the cosmos and determined a succession of world-ages under different zodiacal signs. They had found a large peg on which to hang their thoughts about cosmic time, which brought all things in fateful order.[185]

Without precisely spelling out how the action described by the myth itself might embody this precessional motion, the authors of *Hamlet's Mill* nevertheless perceive that the pattern in the Osiris myths (in which the god is slain and sent to sleep in the underworld) somehow relates to the great cycle of precession, as do many other myths which exhibit the same pattern.

Indeed, in this category of Osiris-like myths they also include the outline of the story of Hamlet, which Shakespeare appears to have derived from a series of northern European myths involving a figure known as *Amleth* or (as Saxo Grammaticus, who lived from AD 1150 to AD 1216, calls him) *Amlethus*.[186] Note the astonishing parallels in the Hamlet story to the plot of the Osiris myth as described thus far: the rightful king is slain by his jealous brother (in the case of Osiris, the brother is Set, and in the case of old King Hamlet, the brother is Claudius). The son of the slain king must restore order (in the case of the myth of Isis and Osiris, their son is the god Horus, while in the case of the Hamlet story it is young Hamlet, called Amleth in the older source material).

Although they clearly perceived connections between the world's myths (and the patterns which surface again and again, in culture after culture around the world) with the motions of the stars, the authors of *Hamlet's Mill* never explicitly lay out the mechanisms by which the heavenly motions relate point-by-point to the mtyhs themselves.

However, building on the foundations which de Santillana and von Dechend had begun, Jane B. Sellers suggested a way to make explicit the connections which the authors of *Hamlet's Mill* had only implied. In a book published in 1992 (23 years after the publication of *Hamlet's Mill*) and entitled *The Death of Gods in Ancient Egypt: A Study of the Threshold of Myth and the Frame of Time* (in a clear nod to the earlier book by de Santillana and von Dechend, the complete name of which was *Hamlet's Mill: An essay on myth and the frame of time*), Jane B. Sellers explains that the failure of Orion to appear above the horizon on the expected day, due to the delaying action of precession, translated in ancient myth into the murder of the god Osiris by his brother Set and his henchmen.

She writes:

> I am convinced that if the death of Osiris is to be found in the movements of the constellation Orion, it lies in something greater than Orion's seasonal absence resulting from the

regular movements of the sky. The texts indicate a mild acceptance of such a disappearance:

> *In your name of Dweller in Orion, with a season in the sky and a season on earth, O Osiris.*
>
> (The Egyptian Pyramid Texts)

I believe the traumatic event to have been the dreaded failure of any of Orion's stars, on the specific date of balance, to reappear in the east after the constellation's seasonal absence. As a result of precession over the millennia, fewer of Orion's stars had been visible before sunrise on that morning, and finally there were none. This is the loss commemorated in myth and ritual; the loss repeated every two thousand years, although the hero's identity changes; the loss that is echoed later in the mournful dirge, 'The Great God Pan is Dead.'[187]

Note how well the mechanism elucidated by Jane B. Sellers fits the details of the death of Osiris story: the rightful ruler (the constellation whose rising marks the "specific date of balance," by which Sellers means the date of equinox, and in this case the spring equinox) is displaced by a usurper -- and indeed is "held down" beneath the horizon as if being drowned by the constellation who wants to take over the throne.

Not only that, but as Jane B. Sellers points out, Plutarch has included a detail in his account which appears to scream out its recognition of a connection to the motion of precession: when Set ambushes his brother Osiris, imprisoning him in a coffin which he then floats out to sea, Set does so with the assistance of *seventy-two henchmen!*[188]

This number, Sellers notes, is a specifically *precessional* number: it represents the approximate amount of time, in years, needed for the action of precession at the present rate to delay the background of stars by one single degree, from one year to the next. Other "precessional numbers" (also pointed out by de Santillana and von Dechend, following observations by some earlier scholars of myth) appear over and over in myths around the world, all related to 72, including 108 (which is 72 plus half of 72), 216 (which is 72 times 3, and which points to 2,160 which is the number of years that precession would require to delay the sky enough to move the sun into a new zodiac constellation on a specified day of the year, including the dates of the equinoxes and solstices), 432 (which is 216 doubled, or 72 times 6), and other multiples of these same numbers (usually powers of ten, such that 108 might appear as 108,000 and 432 might appear as 432,000).[189]

I am certain that the Jane B. Sellers (and the authors of *Hamlet's Mill* before her, as far as their argument goes) have made a correct connection between the inexorable grinding of precession and the myths involving the death of gods such as Osiris. As they perceive and explain, the failure of the stars to rise at their appointed time was equated (by the worldwide myth system) to a great "dislocation." (Note that this system is of such antiquity that it clearly *predates* the Pyramid Texts, which are replete with references to Osiris and which were inscribed before 2300 BC).

This theme of "dislocation" will surface again and again in the Star Myths of the world. It is seen in the Osiris myth in the slaying of the rightful king by the treacherous actions of Set and his henchmen. It is seen in the Odysseus myth in the dislocation of Odysseus during his exile on Ogygia, away from his proper roles and responsibilities, while 108 suitors (another precessional number) devour his livestock and connive to sleep with his wife, murder his son, and become king in his place (just as Set conspired to become king in the place of Osiris). It is seen in the stark description of Ragnarok in the Norse myths, when the forces of destruction burst through their boundaries and unleash fire and slaughter upon the Norse worlds, and the slain heroes of Valhalla march forth to do battle through the 540 doors of the great hall, each of which can accommodate 800 warriors marching abreast (for a total of 432,000 warriors, which again is a precessional number, as noted in both *Hamlet's Mill* and *Death of Gods in Ancient Egypt*).[190]

For all of the reasons given above, I thus am comfortable conceding that Osiris may well have connections to the constellation Orion, which constellation was "held down" by the motion of precession at the end of the Age of Gemini, before the Age of Taurus -- at a date of tremendous antiquity. The authors of *Hamlet's Mill* imply that the Age of Gemini may have been the Golden Age.

For this identification of the Age of Gemini with the Golden Age they supply a variety of good arguments, including the alignment of the band of the Milky Way with the equinoxes during the Age of Gemini, as well as their argument that the fall of Phaëthon who drove his father's sun-chariot appears to have been associated with the end of the Golden Age, (note that Auriga the Charioteer is also grouped along with Gemini and Orion and would thus have "plunged into the earth" during the same epoch in which Gemini failed to appear on the appointed date of spring equinox, when Orion was being held beneath the horizon as well).[191]

These arguments, in addition to the actual ancient texts which appear to declare an identification of Osiris with Orion, make a strong case for the association of the god with that figure in the infinite realm of the night skies. *And yet*, in addition to all these lines of reasoning, we have some fairly clear evidence in the myths themselves and in the iconography which has survived the millennia and come down to us from ancient Egypt, to associate the god Osiris with the constellation Ophiuchus as well.

First, in the passages we've been examining from Plutarch's account of the Isis and Osiris myth-cycle, the casket containing the body of the slain god is described as coming to rest beside the shores of the sea:

> Thereafter Isis, as they relate, learned that the chest had been cast up by the sea near the land of Byblus and that the waves had gently set it down in the midst of a clump of heather. The heather in a short time ran up into a very beautiful and massive stock, and enfolded and embraced the chest with its growth and concealed it within its trunk. The king of the country admired the great size of the plant, and cut off the portion that enfolded the chest (which was now hidden from sight), and used it as a pillar to support the roof of his house.[192]

We have now seen in previous Star Myths from other cultures that the constellation Ophiuchus is situated adjacent to the brightest portion of the Milky Way band, which often appears in ancient myth as the line of the sea-shore where the foam of the waves laps up over the sand. The text describes the chest containing the god coming to rest "in the midst of a clump of heather" which soon grows up "into a very beautiful and massive stock" (a "stock" being another word for a trunk of a tree) which enfolds the casket within its woody growth.

Note that there are a number of shrubs and trees which go by the name of "heather" today, but that the genus *Erica* described by Pliny the Elder (AD 23 - AD 79) in his *Naturalis Historia* includes some species which can grow over 20 feet tall.

I would argue that the above description by Plutarch, of the heather "running up" and enfolding the chest of Osiris with its trunk, has strong parallels with other descriptions found in other Star Myths relating to the constellation Ophiuchus when envisioned as a branching tree with a solid trunk (such as, for example, the description of the branching olive tree in which Odysseus makes a snug place to sleep for the night, after washing up on the shore of the land of the Phaeacians in the Odyssey, discussed in *Star Myths of the World, Volume Two*).

In the case of the Osiris myth as related by Plutarch, I'm convinced that the central rectangular portion of the constellation represents the casket containing the murdered Osiris, while the two "branches" which are normally envisioned as the "serpent-halves" represent the spreading branches of the tree which has grown up around the coffin of the god.

The text from Plutarch explains that the King of Byblus (or Byblos) admired this heather tree with its massive trunk, and cut it down in order to *support his roof.* This description suggests that the ancient mythgivers here envision the rectangular portion of Ophiuchus as the *chest* of Osiris (now engulfed by the trunk of the tree), while the triangular portion of the constellation (just above the rectangle) is seen as the *roof* of the palace of the King of Byblus, now supported by the coffin in the tree.

The diagram of the following page shows the interpretation, in which Ophiuchus represents the chest containing the god, engulfed by the heather, and used as a pillar to hold up the roof:

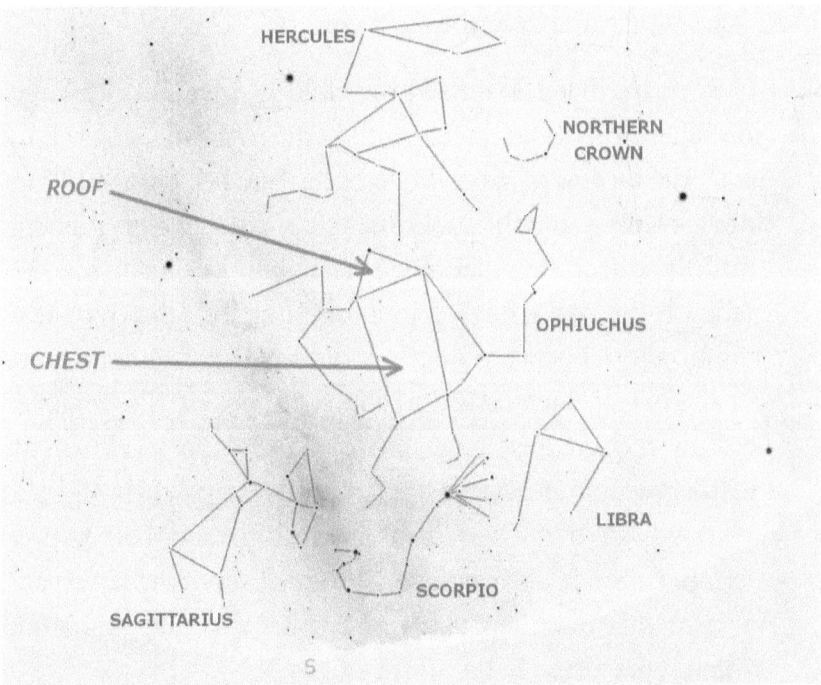

In the above star-chart, we see the triangular roof above the chest containing Osiris, which holds up the roof. I would propose that the King of Byblus is probably associated with the constellation Hercules in this instance -- the constellation Hercules often playing the role of a king in various Star Myths discussed in this series.

Hercules probably plays the King of Byblus when giving the pillar to Isis -- but when the Queen of Byblus cries out in fear upon seeing her baby in the fire (where Isis had placed the baby to try to make it immortal), this incident as related by Plutarch is obviously reminiscent of other episodes in which we see "infants snatched up" and which also certainly involve Hercules reaching out towards the Northern Crown, which in these cases is envisioned as an arching baby.

Here is how Plutarch describes that episode:

> They relate that Isis nursed the child by giving it her finger to suck instead of her breast, and in the night she would burn away the mortal portions of its body. She herself would turn into a swallow and flit about the pillar with a wailing lament, until the queen who had been watching, when she saw her babe on fire, gave forth a loud cry and thus deprived it of immortality. Then the goddess disclosed herself and asked for the pillar which served to support the roof. She removed it with the greatest ease and cut away the wood of the heather which surrounded the chest; then, when she had wrapped up the wood in a linen cloth and had poured perfume upon it, she entrusted it to the care of the kings; and even to this day the people of Byblus venerate this wood which is preserved in the shrine of Isis.[193]

Although Plutarch's account does not explicitly describe the queen herself as snatching the babe from the fire, the parallels to the story of the failed baptism of Achilles -- and the story of the rescue of baby Maui -- should be self-evident. I would certainly include this example from Plutarch, in which the child of the King and Queen of Byblus is deprived of the immortality which Isis intended to bestow upon the babe, as another example of the "failed baptism" pattern found in Star Myths worldwide. Perhaps the Queen of Byblus herself was actually envisioned as pulling the infant from the fire, in which case she too would probably be associated with the outline of Hercules.

Below is artwork from the late 1700s AD, showing Thetis (the mother of Achilles) dipping the infant into the river Styx in order to confer immortality upon the parts of the baby that the waters touched:

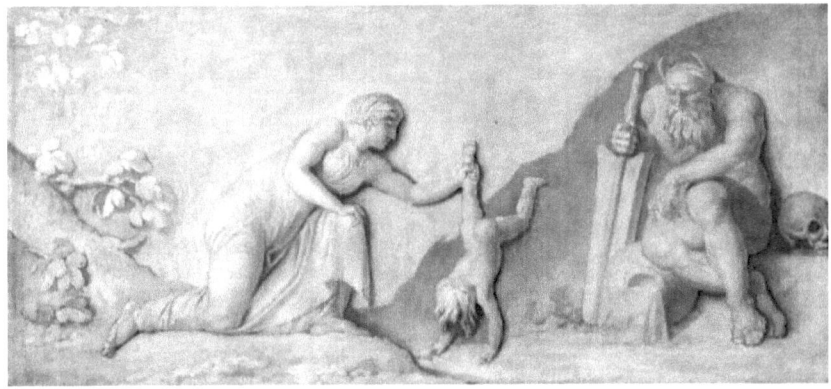

The parallels to the constellations should at this point be self-evident (Thetis corresponds to Hercules, and the arching baby Achilles to the arc of the Northern Crown).

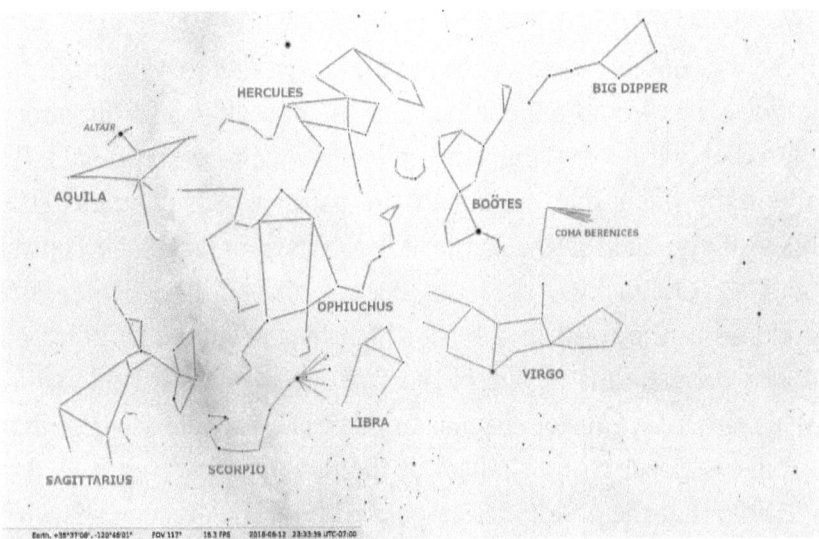

In the above chart you can also see how the form of the serpent held by the constellation Ophiuchus, usually referred to as the two "serpent-halves" on either side of the constellation's central body and discussed in many previous myths we've examined from other cultures, plays the role of the "branching heather tree" that surrounds the chest containing the body of the god.

In the passage cited above, we find an added detail explaining that Isis gave the wooden chest to the King and Queen of Byblus, after *wrapping it in linen* and anointing it with perfume. Plutarch implies that this linen-wrapped wood could still be seen in the shrine of Isis (presumably in Byblus or Byblos) in his day: I would argue that we can see the wood wrapped in linen to *this* day, if we go out on a clear night during the months of the year that Ophiuchus is visible.

There, on either side of the central "casket" we see the twisting, winding "serpent-halves," which can also be envisioned as the linen wrappings of the coffin (just as we earlier saw them playing the winding-sheet or shroud of Sokar: see pages 271 - 272).

It is also notable that in the myth, according to Plutarch, the goddess Isis would take on the form of a swallow and "flit about the pillar with a wailing lament" (meaning that she would flit about the pillar that contained the coffin which contained the body of the slain god). If the pillar corresponds to the central body of Ophiuchus (as I am certain that it does), then the goddess in the form of a bird which flies around this pillar no doubt corresponds to one of the two "great birds" of the Milky Way, either Cygnus or Aquila. In this case, I would suggest that Aquila is closer to the "pillar" of Ophiuchus, although it is also possible that the goddess is associated with the graceful shape of Cygnus the Swan.

As we saw in the artwork from Abydos shown earlier (page 322), in which Isis receives the pillar from the King of Byblus, the column itself was explicitly linked to the Djed symbol, and shown with the characteristic parallel segments which represent the vertebrae (the Djed column itself being identified with the backbone of Osiris).

Thus, we have in this myth -- and in the evidence supporting an association between Osiris and Ophiuchus, as well as between the *pillar* containing Osiris and Ophiuchus, and between this pillar and the Djed column -- support for an identification between the Djed itself and Ophiuchus.

The Djed, in fact, was sometimes depicted in ancient Egyptian iconography in ways which reinforce this association with the constellation Ophiuchus, such as in the illustration below from the exquisitely illustrated version of the Book of Going Forth by Day (aka the Book of the Dead) belonging to the scribe Ani of Thebes, and buried with him in his tomb, believed to date to about 1250 BC:

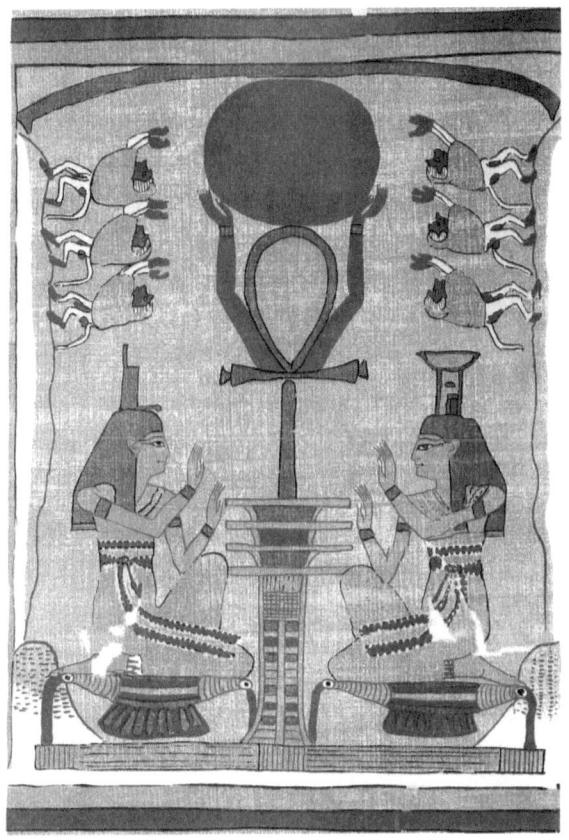

In that illustration, we see a Djed column supporting an Ankh cross (also known as the *crux ansata* in Latin, which means "cross with a handle") with upraised arms supporting a solar disc. The Djed and Ankh are flanked by the goddesses Isis (on the left as we face the image) and Nephthys (on the right).

We have already noted that the two serpent-halves of Ophiuchus may appear in ancient Egyptian iconography as upraised arms, particularly when raised-up towards the solar disc (which we argue can almost certainly be shown to correspond to the "whirling" form of the constellation Hercules). We have also noted that Osiris appears in the position corresponding to the constellation Ophiuchus beneath a winged solar disc in the ancient funeral stele on page 296. And, we have noted the frequent presence of Ankh and Djed symbology alongside or in conjunction with the symbol of the sacred Scarab -- and I would argue that this may indicate that *the Djed* (as well as the god Osiris who is associated with the Djed) as well as *the Ankh* and also *the Scarab* are all in some way manifestations of the same symbol in the sky, the constellation Ophiuchus.

That the constellation Ophiuchus could be depicted as the Djed column is fairly self-evident, as the constellation has a tall and rectangular central body. However, an association with the Ankh cross is less obvious. Certainly, the central portion of the constellation can be seen as giving us the outline of the classic cross, if we see the star at the top of the triangular head as the top of the cross, and the horizontal line at the base of the triangle (the top of the rectangle) as the cross-bar. Indeed, as argued in *Star Myths of the World, Part Three*, this constellation almost certainly manifests as the Cross of Calvary in the gospel accounts.

However, this explanation does not easily translate into the Ankh cross, with its hoop or "handle" above, and I cannot say for certain how the Ankh was associated with Ophiuchus, except to point out that the iconography of Egypt just described often associates the Ankh with the Djed as well as with the Scarab.

As already mentioned, it may be that the Ankh was suggested by the "serpent-head" feature of the constellation, rather than by the shape of the central body. However, it is also possible that the part of the constellation that we envision as a triangle atop the rectangle was in some myths envisioned as a dome shape -- there is certainly much evidence that Ophiuchus-figures in myth are often envisioned as wearing a helmet, which is often dome-shaped on top. In any case, I believe we can be very confident that Ophiuchus is associated with the Djed column, as well as with the casket containing the body of Osiris, and also with the slain god himself. The connection to the Ankh appears to be supported by ancient iconography, even if I cannot yet definitively tie the shape of the Ankh to a specific aspect of the constellation itself.

In her *Handbook of Egyptian Mythology*, Professor Geraldine Pinch informs us: "Some early uses of the djed symbol imply that it could be thought of as a pillar holding the sky above the earth."[194] This of course resonates with our earlier discussion of the role of the god Shu, who holds up his daughter the sky-goddess Nut to keep her separated from his son the earth-god Geb (see images on pages 261 and 262). We saw from our analysis that Shu with his upraised arms is also almost certainly associated with the constellation Ophiuchus -- and thus this information that the Djed was anciently envisioned as performing the same function is further indication that we are correct in our indentification of the Djed (and the god Osiris) with Ophiuchus.

The *slaying of Osiris* was symbolically portrayed in the "casting down" of the Djed column, and his *resurrection and restoration* were symbolized by the raising of the Djed back to an upright and triumphant position (as shown in the image from the Papyrus of Ani on page 347).

In his indispensable 1940 book *Lost Light,* Alvin Boyd Kuhn explains the esoteric meaning as it relates to the life of each and every soul who is symbolically "cast down" into this lower realm of incarnation (which Kuhn identifies with the realm of the dead, perceiving that when the world's myths speak of the Underworld, they are usually describing this incarnate life, rather than any condition of the soul after the death of the body). Using an older way of rendering the word *Djed* in English, calling it the "Tat" or the "Tat cross," he writes:

> The cross is a symbol of life, never of death, except as "death" means incarnation. [. . .] The savior is not nailed *on* the tree; he *is* the tree. He unites in himself the horizontal human-animal and the upright divine. And the tree becomes alive; from dead state it flowers out in full leaf. The leaf is the sign of life in a tree. The Egyptians in the autumn threw down the Tat cross, and at the solstice or the equinox of spring, erected it again. The two positions made the cross. The Tat is the backbone of Osiris, the sign of eternal stability. And *Tattu* was the "place of establishing forever."[195]

Elsewhere in the same chapter, Kuhn explains that the "old Egyptian dramatism of throwing down the Tat cross with its face to the ground" illustrates "the soul's fall into matter and death."[196]

Note that Kuhn's brilliant insight not only perceives that the casting down of the Djed represents our descent into this incarnate existence, but also that this descent was associated with the point of fall or autumnal equinox. He also asserts that the Djed would be raised back up again at either "the solstice or the equinox of spring" (referring, I am certain, to the *winter* solstice, where the sun's progress downward is finally arrested and the sun's course makes its great turn back upwards).

Based on our preceding analysis, which finds compelling evidence for associating both the Djed and the god himself with the constellation Ophiuchus, we can be all the more confident that it was at this lowest point (the winter solstice) that the Djed was envisioned as being raised back up again, because Ophiuchus is positioned above and between Scorpio and Sagittarius, near the very lowest point on the sun's journey, and adjacent to the brightest portion of the Milky Way band, which stretches upwards like a vertical column rising up from that great turning-point of the year.

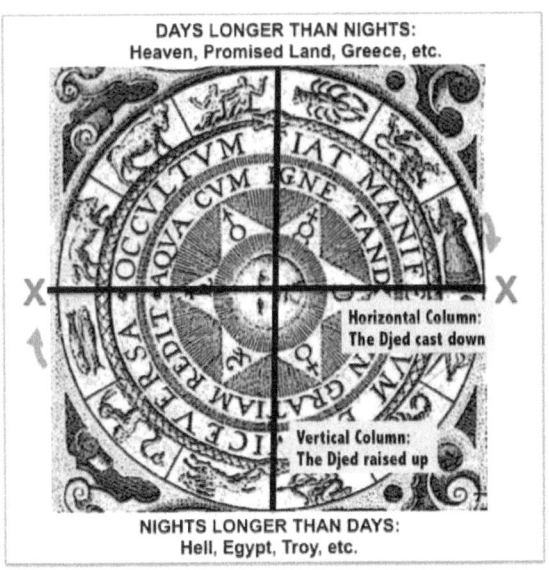

DAYS LONGER THAN NIGHTS:
Heaven, Promised Land, Greece, etc.

Horizontal Column:
The Djed cast down

Vertical Column:
The Djed raised up

NIGHTS LONGER THAN DAYS:
Hell, Egypt, Troy, etc.

Based on Kuhn's explication of the symbology, we can see that the "great cross" of the year created by the two equinoxes and the two solstices helps us to understand this potent ancient metaphor.

The ancient code designates the point of fall equinox as representative of the point on our soul's journey at which we plunge down into the body -- and this is the point at which the Djed is cast down into a horizontal position. It is the point at which we take on a physical body -- and hence, an animal nature, and as Kuhn points out elsewhere, it is the nature of most animals to go about in a horizontal position, and thus the "cast down Djed" is representative of this condition.[197]

But in this incarnate life, although at first we may not perceive it, we are actually "crossed" in that we are always possessed of a spiritual nature, even while we have been "cast down" into a physical form. And, after plunging down deep into entanglement with all that is material and physical, we reach a "turning point" (associated in the language of the myths with the turning point of the year at the winter solstice), where our connection with our true divine nature is restored -- and the Djed is raised back up.

Thus, the line between the lowest point of the year (winter solstice) and the highest point of the year (at summer solstice) creates a "vertical line" on the great wheel of the sun's annual cycle, which forms a cross with the "horizontal line" which connects the two equinoxes. This vertical column stretching upwards from the lowest point in the cycle to the highest was symbolized in the Djed column *raised back up* -- and appears to have been associated in many, many mythologies around the globe with the mysterious figure of Ophiuchus.

Ophiuchus plays the god who is slain -- and who is representative in his underworld situation of our own condition in this mortal life. We ourselves, the myths are illustrating, have a divine nature, but we have been "cast down" into the underworld of this incarnate life, where our condition is analogous to that of the god who is slain.

Note that not only Osiris in ancient Egypt but also Christ in the gospels, Baldr in the Norse myths (as well as his father Odin himself, when he hangs on the Tree), Dionysus in ancient Greece, and even Quetzalcoatl the god who came and dwelt among mortals, can all be identified with the figure of Ophiuchus in the heavens -- and in all of their stories I would argue that the same powerful truths are being illustrated for our deeper understanding.

This re-establishment of the vertical connection -- the connection to the Higher Self, the spiritual nature, the realm of the gods -- is described metaphorically in the myths as the *second birth*, the spiritual birth, and the connection with the Divine Twin.

In the myth-cycle of Isis and Osiris, it is depicted in the birth of Horus, from the union of the goddess with her husband (after he has already descended to the underworld of the dead, representative of the fact that this second birth occurs when we have already sunk into the incarnate condition). It is Horus who will restore his father, and battle with and defeat Set, the slayer of Osiris.

The identity of the goddess Isis bears some discussion before examining the likely identities of Horus and Set. We have already argued that Isis is likely associated with the constellation Sagittarius when the goddess goes to Byblus and meets beside a spring with the maidservants of the queen. We have also seen that when she takes the form of a swallow and flits about the pillar made from the tree that has grown about the coffin of Osiris, the goddess is likely associated with either Aquila or Cygnus (probably Aquila in this case, since closer to Ophiuchus).

However, when Isis first learns of the murder of Osiris by the actions of Set and his henchmen, Plutarch relates that "Isis, when the tidings reached her, at once cut off one of her tresses and put on a garment of mourning [. . .]."[198] This part of the story, whether added in later centuries or whether an authentic detail from the earliest dynasties of Egypt (or before) almost certainly indicates an association between the goddess and the constellation Virgo. As we have already discussed in previous myths, the constellation Coma Berenices is located directly above the "outstretched arm" of the constellation Virgo, and is associated in myths from around the globe with the cutting off of the hair of a female figure who is associated with Virgo.

There are other reasons to conclude that Isis is often associated with the constellation Virgo, one of the most important of these being the numerous artistic representations (in wall reliefs and paintings as well as in statuary) of the goddess seated and holding the child Horus in her lap at the end of her outstretched arm:

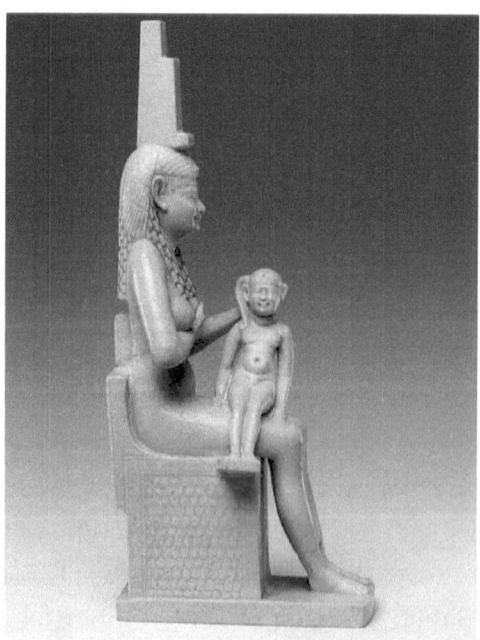

These depictions can be seen to be based on the form of the constellation Virgo, which can be envisioned as being in a seated posture, and which has a relatively bright star at the end of the constellation's distinctive outstretched arm, marked by the star Vindemiatrix. There is ample evidence to suggest that this star was seen in ancient myth as indicative of the baby held upon the lap of the goddess (see the location of the child in the statue above, from the fourth century BC). These scenes of Isis and Horus, as many other commentators in previous decades and centuries have noted, share a very similar pattern to the Madonna scenes of the Virgin Mary and the Christ child, and that is because (I am convinced) both scenes are patterned upon *the same stars.*

Additionally, the scenes of Isis receiving the body of the slain Osiris and those of Mary receiving the body of the Christ after the Crucifixion also show many similarities:

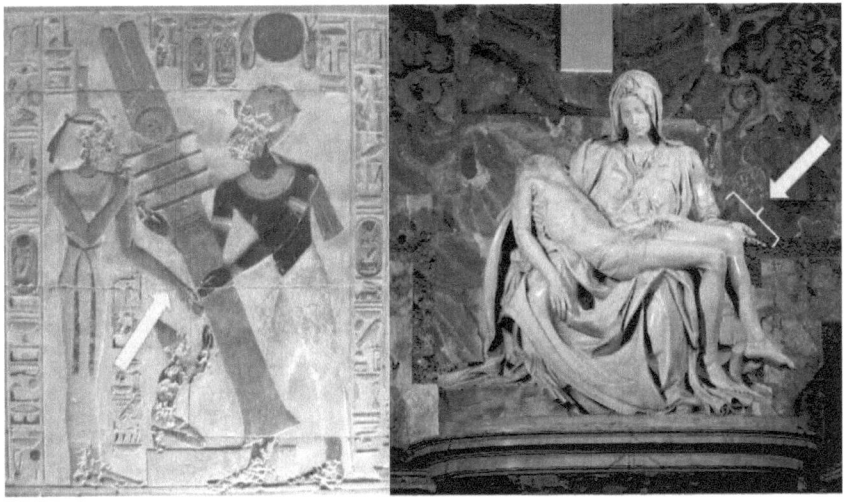

Above we see the same image from Abydos shown previously, of Isis receiving the Djed pillar with Osiris, juxtaposed with the Pietá by Michelangelo showing Mary with the body of Jesus. In both scenes, the "outstretched arm" (distinctive to Virgo) is emphasized by the artist.

355

Thus, we see that the goddess Isis, like other very important figures in any body of myth from different cultures around the globe, "moves through" different constellations in accordance with her different roles or situations in different exploits and accomplishments. This fact alone should indicate to us that the gods and goddesses of myth are *not the same* as the constellations themselves: the deities inhabit an Invisible Realm, not visible to us in what we might call "ordinary reality" (this term implies that in certain altered states, we can see things which may also be classified as part of "reality" but of a part of reality which we do not ordinarily perceive).

The myths help us to "see" or "perceive" or learn lessons from and about the reality which is beyond our ordinary reality, and generally invisible to us in ordinary reality, but which are, nonetheless, very real. They do this by illustrating aspects of the reality that is beyond our ordinary vision, and they choose to illustrate these aspects of the Invisible Realm through the most expansive and awe-inspiring "canvas" available within our ordinary vision: the infinite heavens themselves. We should not confuse the powers of the gods of the infinite realm with the visible constellations, but we can perceive and understand aspects of their nature through the characteristics and motions of these visible markers in the heavens, and their meaning within a great "code" or "language" built upon the majestic cycles of the celestial sphere.

The goddess Isis is clearly associated with the constellation Virgo, and thus with the "first birth" of our plunge down into the incarnate condition, but she is also associated with the "second birth," the birth of the divine Horus who restores and revives the slain god of his father Osiris. As such, she appears in the position of the constellation Sagittarius (during her visit to Byblus, in order to retrieve the god who has been slain), Sagittarius being a constellation associated with the "second birth" and with the elevation of the spiritual nature and the restoration of that integration with the divine aspect of our nature, an elevation which in the myths of the world is also associated with the movement upwards through the shining column of the Milky Way (Sagittarius being stationed at the "base" of the very brightest and most impressive portion of this shining band).

She is also associated with the soaring birds of the Milky Way band, who also are most visible during the time of year when the brightest part of the Milky Way is visible in the heavens. We have already suggested that she may be associated with Aquila, when she flits about the pillar containing the slain god, but other iconography (particularly that of the "Winged Isis" manifestation of the goddess) suggests a connection with Cygnus as well:

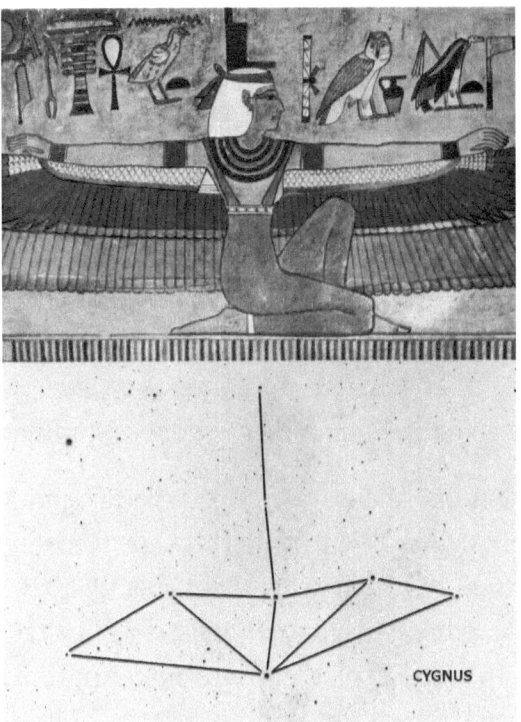

CYGNUS

These associations indicate that the goddess is also closely associated with the *elevation of our spiritual nature* beginning at the great turning-point and proceeding upwards along the Milky Way, as well as with the process of our re-integration with the Higher Self.

Alvin Boyd Kuhn, as usual, has some insightful words on the role of the goddess, who often operates in this capacity in conjunction with the goddess Nephthys (see again the image of the restored Djed from the Papyrus of Ani on page 347, where the Djed-Ankh is flanked by the two goddesses Isis and Nephthys). Discussing the symbology of the "two mothers" who appear in some myths, Kuhn writes:

> Matter is the virgin mother of all life in the aboriginal genesis. All things are generated in the womb of primordial matter, the "old genetrix" of Egyptian mythology. And it is by a consideration of the nature of matter and its evolution that we are able to arrive at the true meaning of the double motherhood of life. For oddly enough, matter is seen to exist in two states, in each of which it becomes mother of life, at two different levels. Primordial matter, the sea of (to us) empty space, is the first mother of all living forms. This is the primal "abyss of the waters" in *Genesis*. The Latin word for "mother" is our very word "matter," with one "t" left out -- *mater*. And how close to *mater* is *water!* And organic structure is the second mother, parent of spiritual mind.

> The ancient books always grouped the two mothers in pairs. They were called "the two mothers" or sometimes the "two divine sisters." Or they were the wife and sister of the God, under the names of Juno, Venus, Isis, Ishtar, Cybele or Mylitta. In old Egypt they were first Apt and Neith; and later Isis and Nephthys. Massey relates Neith to "net," i.e.,

fish-net! Clues to their functions were picked up in the great *Book of the Dead*: "Isis conceived him; Nephthys gave him birth." Or: "Isis bore him; Nephthys suckled him," or reared him. The full sense of these statements was not discerned until they were scrutinized in the light of another key sentence which matched them: "Heaven conceived him; the Tuat brought him forth." With this came the flash of clear insight into the mystery. For that which is to eventuate in the cycles of evolution as divine mind in an organic creature -- man -- is aboriginally conceived by divine ideation in the innermost depths of Cosmic Consciousness, or in the purely noumenal world, or again in the bosom of Infinite Spirit, where Spirit is identical with pure undifferentiated matter. This is mirrored in the Egyptian statement that Isis conceived him. Matter in its invisible, inorganic state was the womb of the first conception. Isis is virgin, i.e., pure matter, or matter sublimated to spiritual tenuity. The Tuat, on the other hand, is really earth, as the type of physical matter, or matter organic, aggregated into substantial forms, called by us physical matter. It is matter as substance, constituted and existent in the visible world in structural forms. Isis was matter subsistent as empty space, and Nephthys was atomic matter, consitutuent of visible structural forms.[199]

What Alvin Boyd Kuhn and others of his generation refer to as the "Tuat" is now more commonly rendered in our letters as the Duat -- the realm of the west in the ancient texts of Egypt which was associated with the descent of the stars out of the clear and crystal realms of their course across the sky and down into the horizon where they descend into the lower and grosser elements of earth and water (where the stars "set" due to the turning of our planet). The Duat is thus identified by most scholars with the "realm of the dead" and the "underworld" -- but, as Kuhn makes clear and supports with many examples and lines of argument, the ancient myths of the world usually mean this incarnate life in the physical realm when describing "the underworld." Thus, as he argues in the passage just cited, it is "down here" in the struggles of the soul through the lower realms of matter that the divine nature is brought forth -- and it is this esoteric and profound teaching which the entire cycle of the Isis and Osiris and Horus myth is impressing upon our understanding.

Let us now briefly turn to the divine child of Isis and Osiris, the god Horus, and his struggles with Set his uncle, before bringing our sojourn through the myths of ancient Egypt to a close for now.

After the murder of Osiris, Set wanted to usurp the throne of Osiris. In a text thought to date to the time of Ramesses V (who reigned for about four years until his death in 1145 BC), entitled "The Contendings of Horus and Seth," one version of the struggle between Horus (aided by his mother Isis) and Set (also written in our letters as *Seth* by some translators) is described. In *Death of Gods in Ancient Egypt*, Jane B. Sellers analyzes this and other ancient texts to advance her argument that these contendings between Set and Horus describe the Age of Taurus (the precessional age following the Age of Gemini, which as we noted above would be the age that ensued after Orion was no longer rising, along with Gemini, on the important date of spring equinox -- his role having been "usurped" by the stars of the constellation Taurus instead).[200]

Sellers thus argues that Set (or Seth) is associated with Taurus, while Horus (his opponent) is associated with the stars of the constellation Scorpio (or *Scorpius*, as some argue the constellation should technically be called, in distinction from the zodiac sign of Scorpio, although following H. A. Rey I myself have always called the constellation Scorpio; Jane Sellers refers to it as Scorpius). She argues that Scorpio, marking the opposite equinox during the Age that the sun was in Taurus on the spring equinox, would be the logical "contender" to Set (or Seth) and that when the nine gods of the Ennead declare that Set and Horus shall rule over equal kingdoms, the myths are describing Set ruling over the spring equinox and Horus over the autumnal, an argument which does appear to have much evidence to support it based on the precessional discussion we have already presented regarding the connection of precessional metaphor and precessional number in accounts of the death of Osiris.[201]

Following arguments first suggested by Virginia Lee Davis, a scholar of ancient Egypt at Yale University, Jane Sellers further argues that when the text of the "Contendings of Horus and Seth" tell us that Horus was given the rule over northern Egypt, and Seth the rule over southern Egypt, that this too supports the connection of Set to Taurus and Horus to Scorpio, in that the forward part of Scorpio emerges on the same side of the Milky Way as the north celestial pole -- thus indicating that Scorpio could "rule" the half of the heavens containing the north celestial pole. Taurus, on the other hand, is situated across the sky from Scorpio and (like nearby Orion) is on the side of the Milky Way band which is opposite from the north celestial pole – thus indicating that Taurus and therefore Set would naturally be described as ruling *southern* Egypt even as Horus was given *northern* Egypt.[202]

These are interesting arguments, and may have some validity, because I am of the opinion that the ancient myths may operate on "several levels at once," with gods being associated (for instance) with specific planets even as we can now demonstrate that they are also clearly associated with specific constellations (the evidence supporting an identification of Zeus or Jove with the constellation Hercules, for example, is simply overwhelming -- but it does not take away the obvious fact that this god is also associated with the planet we call Jupiter, Jupiter being a name for Jove which actually means "Zeus *pater*" or "Jove the Father").

Nevertheless, even if the arguments offered above from Jane B. Sellers and Virginia Lee Davis are correct regarding an "equinoctial" association for Horus and Set and their contendings (each ruling over "half the year" as well as "half the sky" as described), I believe we can also observe some very clear associations of these gods with specific *constellations*, including in the actions described in the "Contendings of Horus and Seth."

One interesting episode in the "Contendings" involves Isis bribing a ferryman for a ride across a river -- the ferryman having been strictly ordered *not* to ferry any woman resembling Isis across, in order to prevent her from influencing the outcome on behalf of her son Horus. She first offers the ferryman a cake as incentive to violate this order and bear her across, which offer he rejects, then a golden signet-ring, which he accepts and ferries her across. I have detailed multiple myths in which the "head-end" of the serpent of Ophiuchus (on the west side of the central body) appears as a cake of some sort in ancient myth (see the discussion in note 99 on pages 740 and 741 of *Star Myths of the Bible*, for instance). The same feature of the constellation also figures as a ring or circlet in many myths (such as in the description of the two spears of Hector, in the Iliad of ancient Greece, for example). Thus, this episode reinforces our analysis from earlier which argues that figures being transported in a boat are often associated with Ophiuchus -- and indicates that when Isis is ferried across the river in this particular episode, she may temporarily "move through" that constellation as well.

A very interesting aspect of that episode in which Isis pays the ferryman to take her across the river is that, when she reaches her destination, she transforms herself into the form of a very beautiful maiden (probably indicated by the constellation Sagittarius), thus attracting the attention of Set. She tells Set that she is the wife of a cattleman, and that together they had a son. She tells him that when her husband died, her son started to tend the cattle, but then a stranger came and took up residence in the stable, threatening to beat her son and take the cattle himself. Set, indignant, asks angrily how it is that the cattle should be given to a stranger, while the son and heir of the dead father is still alive!

Isis then transforms herself into a kite (a type of small hawk) and flies up into the branches of an acacia tree, and from there calls out to Set and declares that his own mouth has just judged him (because, obviously, he is attempting to do something exactly analogous to the thing he has just condemned, in that he wants to usurp the throne of Osiris while Horus the rightful heir lives).

Clearly, those who have read through the explications of so many of the myths described already in this volume will recognize that Isis turning into a kite almost certainly indicates the constellation Aquila. The most intriguing thing about this episode, to me, is the way that it very clearly parallels an incident in the scriptures of the Old Testament, in which the LORD sends Nathan the prophet to accuse King David of unrighteousness in his murder of Uriah in order to take Uriah's wife, Bathsheba.

This incident is found in the text of 2 Samuel chapter 12, and involves Nathan telling a story to the king about a rich man who owns a great flock of sheep, but steals the beloved ewe lamb of his very poor neighbor and slaughters that to make a feast for a visitor, rather than using one of his own sheep. Upon hearing this story, David angrily declares that the man who did this to his neighbor's beloved little ewe lamb shall surely die -- whereupon Nathan turns to David and tells him: "Thou art the man."

During this incident in which Isis takes on the form of a beautiful maiden (likely Sagittarius) and Set calls out to her because he is attracted by her beauty, the text tells us that he stood behind a sycamore tree and called out to her in order to get her to come over to him. This little detail may indicate that Set in this instance is also associated with the constellation Ophiuchus, which is opposite from Sagittarius and which as we have already seen is associated with a branching tree (such as in the description of the chest of Osiris being surrounded by the branching heather-tree, discussed earlier).

This suspicion will be supported by other examples we see in the text of the "Contendings." I am convinced that the god Horus is visible in the heavens in the form of the constellation Hercules, which we have earlier argued to be associated with the hawk-headed god Sokar. If so, then the association of Horus with Hercules and Set with Ophiuchus may be confirmed by one of the most frequently-cited and graphic events in the contendings between the two gods, in which Set is described as stealing the eye (or the eyes) of Horus.

If you look at outlines of the constellations themselves, you can perceive the celestial origin of this aspect of the myth: the constellation Ophiuchus is holding aloft a small eye-shaped outline in one hand (the "serpent-head" on the western side of the central body of Ophiuchus), while the constellation Hercules reaches down towards this same eye-shaped outline: Set (Ophiuchus) has ripped out the eye of Horus (Hercules).

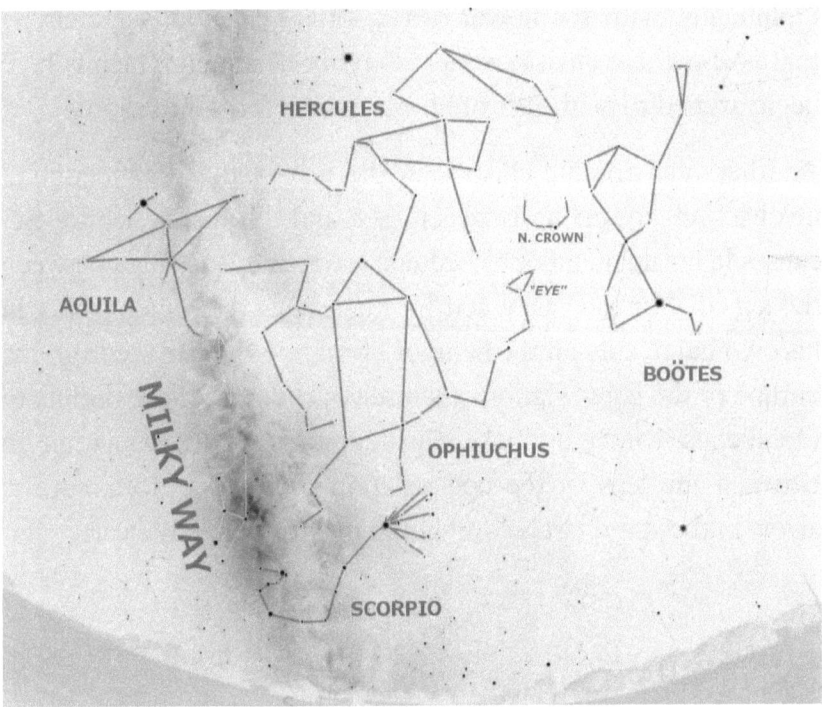

In the text of the "Contendings" it is the goddess Hathor who restores the eyes of Horus (we have already seen some evidence that Hathor may be associated with the constellation Boötes, which is adjacent to the "eye" on the other side of it from Hercules). In other ancient sources, however, we read that it was the god Thoth who heals the eye of Horus -- and this would also tend to support the identification of the eye with the "serpent-head" feature on the constellation Ophiuchus, as we have already made the argument that Thoth is another god associated with the constellation Hercules, and we can see in the heavens that Hercules is reaching down towards this eye. Still further confirmation comes from the line in text of the "Contendings of Horus and Seth" which says that when Set stole the eye of Horus, it grew up into a lotus (the lotus also being associated with this same celestial feature of the western serpent-half held by Ophiuchus, with the flower of the lotus being the same circlet that is elsewhere envisioned as a serpent-head and which is here being argued to be the eye of Horus, which turns into a lotus).

Another very graphic episode in the text of the "Contendings" involves an argument between Set and Horus in which Set causes his male member to become erect, and ejaculates between the legs of Horus (Isis, when Horus reveals the semen of Set in his own hand, cuts off the hand of Horus).[203] We can see from the outline of the constellations themselves the part of the outline of Ophiuchus which undoubtedly figures as Seth ejaculating in between the legs of the constellation Hercules (Horus) -- the arrow in the star-chart below should make it perfectly clear:

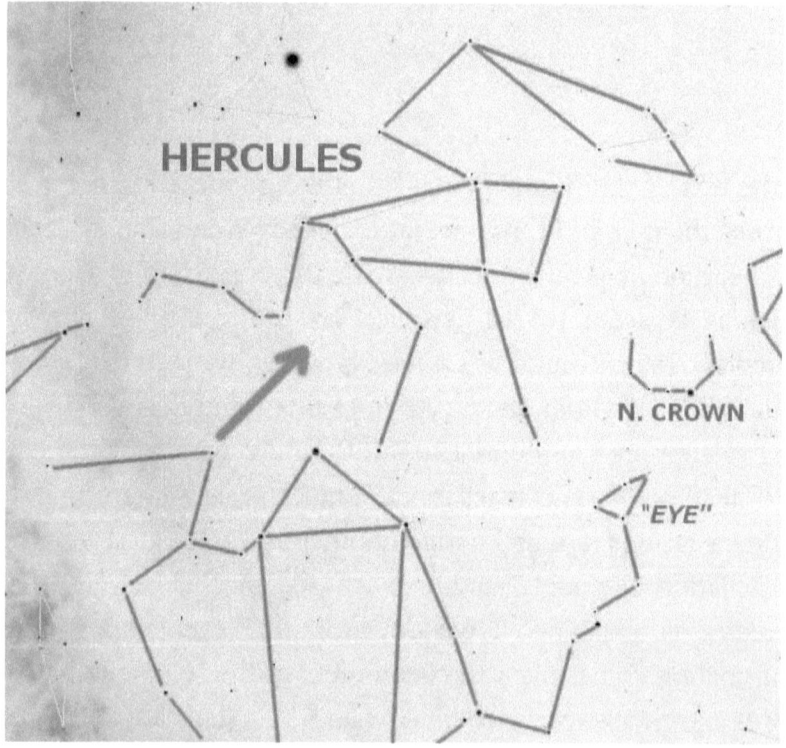

When Isis cuts off the hand of Horus, this incident undoubtedly describes the constellation Coma Berenices, which we have seen playing the role of a severed hand already (in the Popol Vuh of the Maya) and which we will see playing the same role again in myths to be examined later in this volume.

In order to get back at Set, the text of the contendings tell us that Isis then took some fragrant ointment and applied it to the phallus of Horus, causing him to ejaculate into a pot. She then went to Set's garden, found Set's gardener, and asked what kind of vegetable Set likes to eat. Upon being told that he eats only lettuces, Isis applies the semen from the pot onto the lettuce in the garden, which Set consumes according to his daily habit of eating lettuce.[204]

Once again, this graphic and frankly bizarre episode is explainable in terms of celestial content: we have already seen that the constellation Hercules was envisioned in another myth of ancient Egypt as masturbating and ejaculating, in the creation account involving the god Atum. I would argue that this same way of envisioning the constellation Hercules is behind this part of the story of the "Contendings of Horus and Seth." See again the modified outlines of Hercules shown on pages 258 and 283 if in any doubt about this assertion. I would guess that the pot into which he is described as ejaculating may be the bowl-shape of the Northern Crown, and the "lettuces" which Set likes to eat are probably indicated by the "serpent-head" once again, which is located just below the Northern Crown and could also be envisioned as being in the direction that the constellation Hercules would be seen as ejaculating, based on the outline of the stars. If Set is associated with Ophiuchus, as we have already argued, then he may be envisioned as being about to take a bite out of the "lettuce" he is holding in his western hand.

Set then challenges Horus to meet him before the tribunal of the Ennead of gods (the Ennead, a name which means "the Nine," was a grouping of gods of ancient Egypt headed by Geb, the son of Shu and Tefnut, and the father of Osiris).

To this, Horus agrees, and Set tells the assembled gods that he (Set) should be awarded the office of ruler, because he has performed the labor of a male against Horus. At this Horus laughs and tells the gods to call out to Set's semen and see from whence it answers. Apparently because Isis cut off the hand of Horus and cast it away, the semen of Set answers from the water in a marshy area, thus refuting Set's claim.

Then, the text of the "Contendings" tells us, the god Thoth places his hand on the shoulder of Set (a gesture which is consistent with the identification of Thoth with Hercules and Set with Ophiuchus) and calls to the semen of Horus to reveal itself and come out. From within Set, the semen of Horus asks, "From whence shall I come out?" Thoth commands it to come out of the ear of Set, but the semen responds by asking if divine seed should come out of the ear, and Thoth then commands it to instead come out from the top of his head -- and the semen of Horus emerges as a golden solar disc upon Set's head. The text then tells us that, distraught, Set reaches up with his hands to seize the solar disc.[205]

This episode, in which a disc emerges from the head of Set and he reaches up towards it, should cement the connection between Set and Ophiuchus, as we have already seen extensive analysis which identifies the solar disc with the "whirling form" of Hercules, above Ophiuchus -- and seen iconography showing an Ophiuchus-figure reaching with his hands towards the disc above.

After this incident, the Great Ennead declares: "Horus is right, and Set is wrong." Thus, after this and many other episodes in which the two gods contend, Horus prevails over Set and is declared the ruler in place of Osiris, rather than Set.

Some readers may object with the identification of Set with Ophiuchus, since we have just spent some time arguing that Osiris is associated with Ophiuchus. I would reply that Set may primarily be associated with Ophiuchus when he is contending to *take the place* of his brother whom he murdered. Later, when he is put down, he may be associated with the constellation Scorpio, beneath Ophiuchus: it is undeniable that Set was associated with Typhon by the ancient Greeks, and as we have already seen there is evidence that Typhon was associated at least in part with Scorpio. Zeus defeated Typhon by piling Mount Aetna atop the monster -- envisioned in the sky, I would argue, in the mountain-shaped constellation Ophiuchus (which is surmounted by a triangular feature) on top of the constellation Scorpio below. Scorpio plays a role of a dragon-like being in many ancient myths, and the ancient Greeks attributed the eruptions of the volcano of Aetna to the monster Typhon who was still trapped beneath it, belching out venom and smoke and fire. There are many myths in which a figure associated with Scorpio plays the role of an adversary to a figure associated with Ophiuchus, as Set is an adversary to Osiris. Thus, it is possible that Set may be associated with other constellations, including Scorpio, but it should be quite evident from the arguments given above that, at least in the "Contendings of Horus and Seth," the god Set is associated with Ophiuchus.

Additional confirmation for this identification of Set with Ophiuchus is a line in the text of the "Contendings" in which Set declares that he "stands in the prow of the Bark-of-Millions."[206]

369

This description of standing in the sacred barque we have seen to be indicative of Ophiuchus. Likewise, in a text from the temple of Edfu cited by Jane Sellers, we are told that Horus sits down upon "his canopied seat, upon his throne (which was the throne) of Re."[207] This description of the throne or seat of Horus as being "canopied" is characteristic of Ophiuchus, the upper triangle of which causes it to be envisioned as a tent or a canopy in many ancient myths and scriptures. Thus, Ophiuchus is here described as the *seat* or *throne* of Horus, indicating that Horus is associated with Hercules (directly above Ophiuchus). This same canopied throne is also called the throne of the sun-god Re or Ra, again describing Hercules (Ra) above Ophiuchus (the throne).

All of the imagery of the ancient myths, at times seemingly bizarre and disturbing, can be argued to have an esoteric meaning, speaking to us in celestial metaphor of aspects of our own soul's journey, through this incarnate life (and perhaps through cycles of incarnations), on the path of integration with the divine nature, through experiences which we can only attain via the "difficult crossing" of the lower realm.

Horus, the triumphant son of Osiris, is the restorer of the *slain god* -- and the slain god, as Alvin Boyd Kuhn reminds us, is a picture of our own condition in *this mortal life* of the body. Kuhn cites particularly memorable lines in Gerald Massey's translation of the Book of the Dead (properly known, we've noted, as the *Book of Coming Forth by Day*), in which Horus declares that his mission is to restore not only Osiris, but all those who are undergoing the trials of incarnation: "Witness of Eternity is my name, the persistent traveller on the highways of heaven. I am the everlasting one, I am Horus, who steppeth owards through eternity. I, even I, am he who knoweth the paths of heaven. Its breezes blow upon me. I advance whithersoever there lieth a wreck in the field of eternity, and I pilot myself towards the darkness and the sufferings of the deceased ones of Osiris."[208]

In the spells of the Book of Coming Forth by Day, Kuhn notes, the utterances declare that the man or woman must be raised up by taking again the divine aspect that has been temporarily lost or forgotten during the plunge into mortal incarnation.[209] Thus, in the case of the Papyrus of Ani, the name of *Ani* is inserted into the spells, to make it clear that the text is talking about him when it declares that Ani will manifest the characteristics of the various gods and goddesses. In the 1901 translation of the Papyrus of Ani, E. A. Wallis Budge translates chapter 42 (in part) as follows:

> The hair of Osiris Ani, triumphant, is the hair of Nu.
> The face of Osiris Ani, triumphant, is the face of Ra.
> The eyes of Osiris Ani, triumphant, are the eyes of Hathor.
> The ears of Osiris Ani, triumphant, are the ears of Ap-uat.
> The lips of Osiris Ani, triumphant, are the lips of Anpu.
> The teeth of Osiris Ani, triumphant, are the teeth of Serqet.
> The neck of Osiris Ani, triumphant, is the neck of Isis.
> [. . .]
> The backbone of Osiris Ani, triumphant, is the backbone of Set.
> [. . .]
> There is no member of my body which is not the member of some god.
> The god Thoth shieldeth my body altogether, and I am Ra day by day.[210]

Of this process, Alvin Boyd Kuhn comments:

> Here is strong assertion again that man is to summarize in himself the qualities of the whole scale of being, demonimated gods. All their powers and virtue have to be

embodied in man's organic wholeness to make him, like the resuscitated Osiris, "Neb-er-ter, the god entire." Every member of the old Atum, deceased and defunct, had to be fashioned anew in a fresh creation. Like a person recovering from amnesia, he had to recollect his former knowledge, reassemble the component elements of his dismembered integrity.[211]

When we come down to this world, we are disconnected, dislocated, and alienated from the totality of who we really are. The ancient spells of Egypt are intended to restore us to completeness, and to the realization of who we are.

Note that, writing in 1940, Alvin Boyd Kuhn uses the masculine pronoun to refer collectively to men and woman -- all humanity. This convention emphatically does *not* imply that his comments are restricted to men at the exclusion of women: indeed, he explicitly denies this elsewhere, and at one point says "men and women" to ensure that the reader understands. For instance, in one passage in *Lost Light*, Kuhn cites numerous sources to imply that the reconciliation between Set and Horus was also seen as representative of our own reintegration with our forgotten Higher Self and divine nature:

> To Horus it is said: "Thou dost renew thy youth"; and in his rising to life he is declared to make men and women alive. "I went in as a hawk," he sings; "I came out as a phoenix" -- that is, transformed. Says Job: "I shall die in my nest, and I shall multiply my days like the phoenix." "My transformations are those of the double god, Horus-Set" (Ch. 180). He became "the lord of both parts," with the atonement made. Jesus in matter and the Christ in spirit are identical with the two Horus phases.[212]

Thus, as we arrive at the conclusion of our examination of just *some* of the myths of ancient Egypt, we cannot escape the realization that their profound system of spirituality and awakening was established upon the same foundation of celestial code which we have observed operating in the myths of so many other cultures around the globe.

Stories and episodes which would at first seem bizarre and disturbing, if understood only literally, are revealed to be based upon familiar celestial figures, and to fit within an overarching system that is esoteric in nature, conveying deeper truths that have to do with our own soul's journey -- not merely in the afterlife but rather in this mortal experience as we pass through the incarnate condition, on a road which leads through eternity.

The gods and goddesses who dwell in the realm of the infinite, a realm of pure potentiality, are shown to manifest in us -- seemingly "ordinary" men and women. We are led to conclude that we must incorporate the attributes and virtues and powers of the various gods and goddesses not in the *next* life, but rather in this one.

Star Myths of Ancient Mesopotamia

Mesopotamia is a Greek word which literally signifies "middle (between) rivers" and refers to the ancient cultures occupying the land beside and between the Tigris and Euphrates, mighty rivers which run down from the eastern region of modern-day Turkey all the way to the Persian Gulf, creating a rich alluvial plain that became the home of one of the earliest known civilizations.

The rivers would periodically flood and deposit silt over the floodplains -- Professor Harriet Crawford of Cambridge and University College London writes that: "Sites of the fifth millennium have been found under as much as five metres of deposit."[213] Despite the rich soil in much of the region, rainfall is very sparse, thus requiring the innovation of irrigation canals from the freshwater rivers in order to successfully water crops.

Beginning as early as the 1600s but accelerating in the late 1700s and early 1800s, excavation and exploration of the ruins of the ancient Mesopotamian cultures of this region led to the discovery of ancient texts consisting of wedge-shaped (or "cuneiform," from the Latin word *cuneus* or "wedge") writing inscribed upon clay tablets -- and efforts to decipher this unique writing system eventually yielded success in the late 1850s.

At the time, due to the heavy influence of ancient Biblical and ancient Greek sources, researchers assumed that the writing system was the invention of the Babylonian and Assyrian civilizations (which are mentioned frequently in those ancient Hebrew and Greek sources), and had no idea of the existence of an even earlier civlization which had flourished in the region prior to the rise of Assyrian and Babylonian culture, and which would have a tremendous cultural influence on the newcomers who created the Akkadian-speaking Assyrian and Babylonian civiliations.[214]

Akkadian is a Semitic language, but some early scholars in the late 1850s and 1860s began to realize as they studied the cuneiform texts that the writing-system itself did not appear to be designed in a way that is optimal for the transmission of Semitic languages, and contained features not found in other forms of Semitic writing. Writing in 1963, about a hundred years after scholars first began to suspect that this writing-system might have predeated the arrival of speakers of the Semitic Akkadian language-group, Samuel Noah Kramer explains:

> In the Semitic languages the stable element is the consonant, while the vowel is extremely variable. It seemed unnatural, therefore, that the Semites should invent a syllabic system of orthography in which the vowel seemed to be as unchanging as the consonant. The distinction between soft and hard palatals and dentals is a significant feature of the Semitic languages, but the cunieform syllabary did not seem to express this distinction adequately. Then, too, if Semites had invented the cunieform script, it should be possible to trace the syllabic values of the signs to Semitic words. But this was rarely the case; the great majority of the syllabic values for the cuneiform signs seemed to go back to words or elements for which no Semitic equivalent could be found.[215]

Thus, beginning with the Irish-born scholar and clergyman Edward Hincks (1792 - 1866), who along with Henry Creswicke Rawlinson (1810 - 1895) and Julius "Jules" Oppert (1825 - 1905) had complemented one another's efforts and insights to successfully decipher cuneiform in the first place, suspicion began to mount that this writing-system had belonged to some as-yet unknown language-group, prior to the arrival of the Akkadian-speaking people of the area.[216]

After Hincks and Rawlinson tentatively suggested some incorrect hypotheses regarding the identity of these mysterious predecessors, it was Jules Oppert in 1869 who presented a lecture in which, based upon a translation of an inscription referring to the "King of Sumer and Akkad," he suggested that this title referred to a king of two different culture groups inhabiting the same region of Mesopotamia: the Akkadian people (Babylonians and Assyrians) and the Sumerians, who spoke a different and unrelated language, and who were the likely originators of this wedge-shaped form of writing (a contender for the oldest known writing-system of any culture on our planet).[217]

Later discoveries in the 1870s of inscribed statues, stelae, and tablets in the Sumerian language (a "language isolate" with no certain linguistic relatives and no known linguistic descendants among any culture on earth) would prove Oppert's hypothesis correct, and we now understand that the previously completely forgotten Sumerian civilization had flourished in the Mesopotamian region from at least 3000 BC, before the later arrival of the Akkadian-speaking newcomers who would create the civilizations of Babylonia (in the southern part of Mesopotamia) and Assyria (in the northern part of Mesopotamia) beginning around 2000 BC, and supplanting the Sumerians almost completely by about 1800 BC, after a period in which the newcomers absorbed many cultural and linguistic elements from the Sumerians -- including their gods and myths.[218]

Indeed, subsequent investigations of the thousands of ancient clay tablets which have survived, including in the so-called

"Library of Ashurbanibal" (king of the Neo-Syrian Empire, whose royal palace was in Nineveh along the Tigris, in northern or Upper Mesopotamia) reveal that long after the Sumerian language had ceased to be spoken, it was preserved as a sacred language among the scribes of the cultures of Assyria and Babylon, in much the same way that Latin continued to be used as a sacred language among Christian clerics for centuries after Latin ceased to be anyone's mother tongue.

Thus, when examining the mythology of ancient Mesopotamia, it is helpful to understand this history, in order to understand that there are slightly different names applied to the same gods and goddesses and human characters depending on whether we use the Sumerian name or the Akkadian name. The Akkadian names of the ancient Babylonians are more familiar to us today -- we are more likely to recognize the Akkadian name of the goddess *Ishtar*, for example, than the corresponding Sumerian name, which is *Inanna*, and more likely to use the Akkadian name *Gilgamesh* than the Sumerian *Bilgames* or *Bilgamesh*, for the semi-divine hero whose adventures we will examine in this chapter. Where possible, however, this volume will at least introduce both.

In addition to the fact that the modern history of the "rediscovery" of the forgotten culture of Sumer is fascinating and intellectually stimulating in its own right, is also worth the above brief summary of the events leading to its rediscovery because I believe we find ourselves in a very analogous situation today, with regards to the evidence for the existence of a predecessor culture of great spiritual sophistication, predating the earliest civiliations known to us at the present date: a predecessor culture whose existence has been all but completely forgotten, and yet a culture whose existence is indicated by certain anomalous pieces of evidence which can be found in the successor cultures around the world today -- not least of these pieces of evidence being the incredible system of ancient celestial metaphor lying "dormant" beneath the myth-systems of cultures around the globe, which system is the subject of this volume and this series!

Just as the scholars in the 1850s had no inkling that an advanced culture now known to have been called the Sumerians (a word derived from the Akkadian name for them -- surviving tablets written in Sumerian refer to the Sumerians as the *ug sag gig ga* or *sag gig ga*) even existed, and were for the most part not looking for them, the same situation obtains today, with the vast majority of academia completely satisfied of the nonexistence of any influential civilizations prior to the earliest civilizations known to their conventional timelines (including ancient Sumer, ancient Egypt, ancient China, and the ancient Indus-Saraswati civlization), and not even looking for such a possibility.

Indeed, the arguments of those who, somewhat akin to the observations made by the early codebreakers of the cuneiform system, have noticed compelling evidence that points to the existence of some predecessor civilization capable of creating massive and sophisticated monuments on the scale (for example) of Göbekli Tepe have met with not just skepticism but outright hostility from the conventional historians.

Indeed, the present situation even has a parallel in the story of the re-discovery of the existence of the Sumerian civilization, because even after Hincks, Rawlinson, and especially Jules Oppert pointed to the evidence that cuneiform must have been developed by a culture speaking a language completely different from the Semitic languages, Samuel Noah Kramer describes the reaction of a well-known scholar of the day named Joseph Halévy (1827 - 1917), who:

in spite of all the evidence to the contrary, denied the very existence of both the Sumerian people and language. Beginning with the 1870's and for more than three decades thereafter, he published article after article insisting that no people other than the Semites had ever been in possession of Babylonia, and that the so-called Sumerian language was merely an artificial invention of the Semites themselves devised for hieratic and esoteric purposes. For a very brief period he was even supported by several eminent Assyriologists. But all that is now only a matter of historical curiosity; for not long after Oppert's perspicacious conclusions about the non-Semitic people of Babylonia and their language, two excavations were begun in southern Babylonia which put the Sumerians on the map, as it were, with the discovery of statues and steles which revealed their physical features, and innumerable tablets and inscriptions significant for their political history, religion, economy, and literature.[219]

I would suggest that we find ourselves at a very similar juncture in history, one in which the overwhelming evidence for the existence of a presently-unknown "lost civilization" can be seen all around the world, having been ably illuminated by scholars including R.A. Schwaller de Lubicz (1887 - 1961) beginning primarily in the 1940s, the authors of *Hamlet's Mill* as well as John Michell in the 1960s, and picking up steam with later investigators such as John Anthony West (1932 - 2018), Robert Schoch, Graham Hancock, and many others in subsequent decades, and yet the academic establishment (like the "eminent Assyriologists" following the lead of Joseph Halévy starting in the 1870s) are presently digging in their heels and refusing to even consider the possibility that their paradigm is in need of radical revision.

Having established some background regarding the cultures of ancient Mesopotamia, let's now turn to the myths themselves. Once again, the sheer volume of the available material necessitates that only a selection can be examined here. Writing in 1899, early scholar and translator of Mesopotamian mythological tablets Leonard William King (1869 - 1919) noted that the Mesopotamians had literally hundreds of gods. He notes that the largest of the tablets found at the Library of Asshurbanipal at the time King was writing was a tablet consisting of 150 lines arranged in six columns, just about each line containing the different name of a deity (approximately 900 names!).[220]

About many of these gods and goddesses, King admits in the same breath, we still know little to nothing. However, he goes on to say that the ancient scribes did leave us a great volume of inscriptions containing hymns and prayers to various deities, which give us some insight into the attributes of those who are mentioned there, and often the honorific titles added along with the names of deities will yield further insights into the aspects of the god or goddess in question.[221]

And, in addtion to hymns, prayers, titles and attributes, the scribes of ancient Mesopotamia also recorded numerous copies of nearly complete mythical accounts and texts, which constitute a veritable treasure-trove of information with which to explore the divine world of the Sumerian, Assyrian, and Babylonian civilizations. Indeed, scholars now believe that some of these ancient tablets may contain material which must have been formulated as early as 3000 BC, if not even earlier in some cases -- making the written scriptures of ancient Mesopotamia perhaps the oldest extended systematic mythological accounts to survive the ravages of time in any civlization known at this point.

For purposes of our brief survey of the myths of ancient Mesopotamia, I propose we begin by looking at a few aspects of the so-called Babylonian "creation account," known as Enuma Elish (after the first words in that text, which translate to "When the heavens above . . . "), in order to meet a few of the important deities and supernatural figures (and to note some of the widely remarked-upon parallels to the later Genesis creation account, and to similar patterns found in other ancient traditions).

From there, we will transition to an examination of some of the celestial aspects of the most popular myth-cycle from ancient Mesopotamia (at least, most popular among the ancient Mesopotamian scribes themselves, judging by the number of tablets containing aspects of this myth) -- the cycle involving the "twins" Gilgamesh and Enkidu.

We will conclude with a discussion of some of the possible esoteric meaning in these Star Myths of ancient Mesopotamia, in conjunction with which we will briefly examine the "Noah-figures" of Mesopotamian myth, whose names are Ziusudra (Sumerian), and Uta-napishti (introduced at the end of the Gilgamesh cycle), and also a related figure named Atrahasis, who has his own ancient narrative describing his experiences while surviving a cataclysmic flood.

The mythological account to which we today refer as Enuma Elish consists of seven distinct sections, each of which would be inscribed on a single tablet, and hence the work has also been described as the "Seven Tablets of Creation" by the above-mentioned Leonard William King (and which became the title of a translation and discussion of Enuma Elish that he published in 1902), although the action of the epic centers as much on a titanic struggle between the gods as it does on the events of creation itself.

Alexander Heidel (1907 - 1955) who published a translation in 1942 entitled *Babylonian Genesis* and focused on the parallels between the Genesis account and Enuma Elish provides this discussion of the discovery of the tablets and the immediate recognition of the similarities:

> This great epic is recorded on seven clay tablets and covers in all a little over one thousand lines. The first fragments to come to light were discovered by Austen H. Layard, Hormuzd Rassam, and George Smith among the ruins of King Ashurbanipal's (668 - ca. 630 BC) great library at Nineveh between the years 1848 and 1876. During their explorations at Ashur (the old capital of Assyria), from 1902 to 1914, the German excavators unearthed a number of fragments of an Assyrian version of the Babylonian story (especially of Tablets I, VI, and VII) which differs from the latter chiefly in that some copies substitute the name of Ashur, the king of the Assyrian gods, for that of Marduk, the king of the Babylonian deities, and in that they make Lahmu and Lahâmu the parents of Ashur. In 1924 - 1925 two almost complete tablets, I and IV, of a Neo-Babylonian version of the epic were discovered at Kish by the joint expedition of Oxford University and the Field Museum of Chicago. And in 1928 - 1929 the Germans found quite a large Neo-Babylonian fragment of Tablet VII at Uruk (the biblical Erech). Thanks to these discoveries and to purchases of fragments which have been made from dealers in antiquities (the provenance of most of these fragments being uncertain), the epic has been restored almost in its entirety; the only tablet of which a large portion is still wanting is Tablet V.

The first to publish an account of the epic was George Smith, of the British Museum, who in 1875 described in a letter to the Daily *Telegraph* the contents of about twenty fragments of the creation series. In 1876 appeared his book *The Chaldean Account of Genesis*, which contained a translation and discussion of all the pieces which had been identified. All this material was very fragmentary, but the resemblance of its contents to the initial chapters of the Old Testament was unmistakable, and consequently it had an immediate appeal to a much wider circle of students than would otherwise have been the case. Since then this story has been copied and translated by a great many Assyriologists, especially as new tablets or portions of tablets have been found.[222]

Although Enuma Elish is known to us from the later Babylonian and Assyrian tablets, scholars generally agree that the contents originated much earlier, based upon (among other evidence) artwork and inscriptions dating back to the first half of the second millennia BC that appear to indicate events described in the epic. The action described in the seven tablets reveals some broad parallels to the seven days of creation described in the Genesis account, even though the actual events and beings in Enuma Elish are very different on their surface.

For example, mankind is created on the sixth day in the Genesis account (Genesis 1: 26 and following), and the creation of mankind is described in Tablet VI of Enuma Elish -- a notable parallel. However, in Enuma Elish, men and women are created from the blood of the slain deity Kingu, a consort of Tiamat, by Marduk, in order to relieve the burden of toil by the gods (particularly those gods who rebelled against the order of heaven). These types of details give a very different flavor and feel to the

Mesopotamian creation epic, while still preserving parallels which indicate some deep and ancient connection. It is a good example of the very type of similarity which we will notice again and again as we continue our journey through the Star Myths of the world, for instance in Volume Four when we explore the Norse mythology and its undeniable parallels to myths from other cultures, while still displaying a texture and atmosphere uniquely Norse in character.

In the introduction to his presentation of an English version of Enuma Elish, Timothy J. Stephany provides a table based on the parallels delineated by John Romer in *Testament: The Bible and History*, in which the order of events in the Mesopotamian tablets differs at points from the order of events in the six days of the Genesis account, while still revealing the patterns which were immediately apparent to the first modern translators of Enuma Elish in the second half of the nineteenth century.[223] This table of correspondences is shown below:

Genesis Creation	*Generation of gods*	*God of*
Day 1 -- *light from dark*	3 -- *Anshar and Kishar*	*the two semi-spheres*
Day 2 -- *water separation*	1 -- *Apsu and Tiamat*	*the fresh and salt water*
Day 3 -- *dry land*	2 -- *Lahmu and Lahamu*	*the silt-lands*
Day 4 -- *heavens made*	4 -- *Anu*	*the heavens*
Day 5 -- *oceans made*	5 -- *Ea (Nudimmud)*	*the waters*
Day 6 -- *mankind made*	6 -- *Marduk*	*(creator of mankind)*
Day 7 -- *God rests*	(gods relieved from labors)	

The first column of the above table obviously summarizes events from the Genesis creation account, on the seven successive days described. The second column provides a parallel from Enuma Elish, and indicates the "generation" in which the corresponding figures of the ancient Mesopotamian pantheon belong (with the original entities Apsu and Tiamat being the first generation, their first children Lahmu and Lahamu forming the second generation, and so on). Thus, Anshar and Kishar are arranged as a Mesopotamian parallel to the separation of light from dark on the first day of the Genesis account, even though Anshar and Kishar as the offspring of Lahmu and Lahamu belong to the third generation in the Mesopotamian account (indicated with a "3").

Clearly there are some strong parallels, but at the same time we see fundamental differences between the manifestations in ancient Mesopotamia and in the Genesis text. Indeed, although Enuma Elish is frequently referred to as a "creation account," many scholars point out that *creation* actually occupies a relatively small proportion of the action described in the tablets. Alexander Heidel asserts that:

> *Enûma elish* is not primarily a creation story at all. If we were to put together all the lines which treat of creation, including the theogony and even granting that most of the missing portion of Tablet V deals with works of creation, they would cover not even two of the seven tablets but only about as much space as is devoted to Marduk's fifty names in Tablets VI and VII. The brief and meager account of Marduk's acts of creation is in sharp contrast to the circumstantial description of his birth and growth, his preparations for battle, his conquest of Tiâmat and her host, and the elaborate and pompous proclamation and explanation of his fifty names. If the creation of the universe were the prime purpose of the epic, much more emphasis should have been placed on this point.

> As it is, there can be no doubt that, in its present form, *Enûma elish* is first and foremost a literary monument in honor of Marduk as the champion of the gods and the

creator of heaven and earth. Its prime object is to offer cosmological reasons for Marduk's advancement from the position as chief god of Babylon to that of head of the entire Babylonian pantheon. This was achieved by attributing to him the defeat of Tiâmat and the creation and maintenance of the universe. The description of the birth of the gods and of the subsequent struggle between Ea and Apsû and the account of the origin of the universe were added mainly for the purpose of furthering the cause of Marduk; the former was included as the antecedant to Marduk's conflict with Tiâmat and his accession to supreme power among the gods, while the latter, the story of the creation of the universe, was added not so much for the sake of giving an account of how all things came into being, but chiefly because it further served to enhance the glory of Marduk and helped to justify his claim to sovereignty over all things visible and invisible.[224]

The intriguing thing about this assertion is that, while Alexander Heidel almost certainly did not know it, the Mesopotamian god Marduk is undeniably associated with the same constellation Hercules with which the God Jehovah of the Bible texts can also be shown to be undeniably associated.

Thus, this interpretation of the tablets of Enuma Elish as an epic whose primary purpose is to magnify Marduk and justify his ascension to preeminence may indicate an even closer affinity between the Genesis and Mesopotamian accounts, in which the gods and entities of the Mesopotamian story become the non-divinized "light and dark," "firmament that divides the waters above and under the firmament," "dry land and gathered waters called seas," and so forth described in the Genesis story.

I would argue that both versions are describing heavenly events, visible in the celestial realm, whether the waters are divinized and given the names Apsu and Tiamat (divided by the entity known as Mummu) or whether they are called the "waters above the firmament" and the "waters below the firmament," (with the dividing firmament corresponding to the mist-like Mummu of the Babylonian account).

The reader may already suspect my proposed interpretation for the dividing of the "fresh waters" of Apsu from the "salt waters" of Tiamat in the Mesopotamian epic, with Mummu in between them, which parallels the Genesis "firmament" with waters above and below: it almost surely has something to do with the division of the heavens by the ring of the Milky Way band into two halves, one half being "above" the Milky-Way divider -- perhaps, following the arguments of Jane B. Sellers and Virginia Lee Davis that were discussed on pages 361 and 362 of this book, with the "above" half being indicated by the portion of the heavens on the "north-celestial-pole-side" of the Milky Way, and the "below" half being indicated by the heavens on the opposite side of the Milky Way from the north celestial pole.

On the following page is a star-chart representing the entire night sky -- indeed, the entire "celestial sphere." (We can imagine the heavens to be a sphere within which *we* are at the center, from our perspective on earth: a great sphere turning about us every day, with a north celestial pole at the top of the "sphere" and a south celestial pole at the bottom, even though the illusion that it is a turning sphere with a north and south pole is caused by the fact that we ourselves are on a spherical planet which is turning on its axis, creating two axis-points or hubs in the heavens above and below the axis of earth's turning).

387

The chart below is a "projection" in which the apparent sphere has been projected onto a flat rectangular surface: thus, to turn it back into a celestial sphere one would need to roll it into a kind of "tube" by cutting it out of the page and bringing the left and right edges together to form a cylinder. Instead of having the drawing of the stars and Milky Way on the outside of this tube, it would be more accuract to roll it into a tube with the diagrams on the *inside*. Next, one would have to magically "gather" the top edge of the cylinder into a point (the north celestial pole) and same for the bottom edge, creating a sphere out of the cylinder (with all the diagrams on the inside).

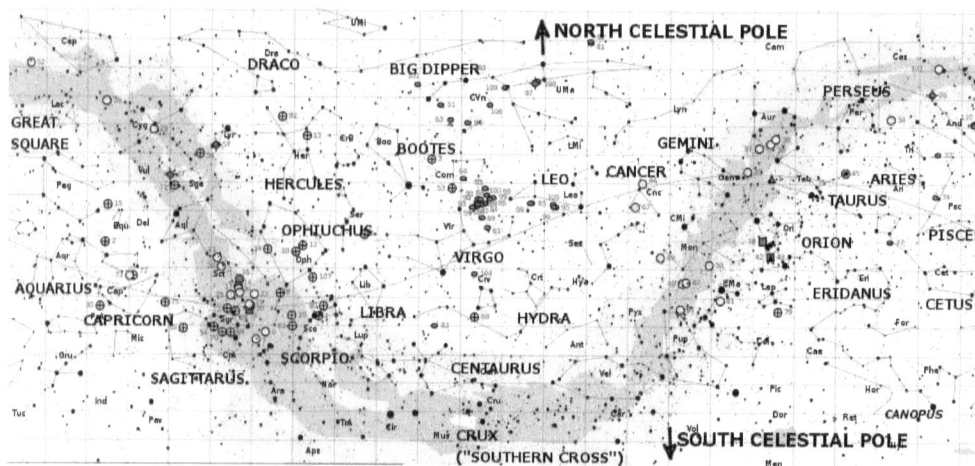

Thus, we see that the "point" of the north celestial pole is actually represented in the rectangular chart above by the entire top edge of the rectangle, and same for the "point" of the south celestial pole by the bottom edge of the chart.

With that explanation out of the way, the reader can now perceive what is meant by "the half of the sky that is above the Milky Way" and the half that is below. The Milky Way band, seen in the chart as a great meandering shaded region, divides the heavens in two. The section containing the north celestial pole would be the "waters above" (or the Apsu, for the Mesopotamians), and the section containing the south celestial pole would be the "waters below" (associated with Tiamat in the Mesopotamian system).

The "firmament" which divides the *waters above* from the *waters below* in the Genesis account would thus correspond to the Milky Way itself -- possibly associated in some way with the minister Mummu in Enuma Elish, whom Alexander Heidel posits might be a kind of mist generated by both bodies of celestial water:

> Apsû was the primeval sweet-water ocean, and Tiâmat the salt-water ocean, while Mummu probably represented the mist rising from the two bodies of water and hovering over them, particularly since in Tablet VII:86 he is brought in direct relation with the clouds."[225]

Thus, in the chart on the previous page, the "waters above" or the Apsu would consist of the "peninsular" shape above the band of the Milky Way, occupying the center of the chart (the unshaded region of sky above the Milky Way, protruding downward from the top of the chart), while the "waters below" or the salt-water of Tiamat would consist of the two unshaded sections on either side of the chart which are below the shaded band of the Milky Way, and which together actually form another triangular "peninsula" protruding upwards from the bottom edge of the chart if you roll the rectangle into a tube by connecting the left and right edges, as suggested earlier (in other words, the "waters below" section would form another peninsula pointing upwards from the southern edge, mirroring the peninsula pointing downwards from the top edge which is visible in the center of this chart).

In reality, however, neither of the regions would resemble a triangular "peninsula" in the sky, since the top and bottom edges of the chart are actually two points in the heavens -- thus, the regions which in the projection resemble peninsulas are seen in the heavens as great hemispherical sections of the sky, coming together along the broad "seam" formed by the band of the Milky Way, one hemisphere containing the north celestial pole and thus designated "above" (although we can never see all of either of the two hemispheres when standing on our planet, because the bulk of earth itself, which we see as the ground below our feet stretching out to the horizon in all directions, gets in our way).

In the preceding chart, I have added labels to indicate the locations of some of the mythologically-important constellations, including all of the zodiac constellations from Aries to Pisces, as well as Hercules, Boötes, Orion, the River Eridanus, Perseus, the Great Square, Cetus the Whale, Draco, Centaurus, and Crux (often called the "Southern Cross").

I've also labeled the Big Dipper (an asterism in the Great Bear), the front two stars of which are known as the "Pointers" because they point in the direction of the north celestial pole (and the star Polaris in the present epoch) -- and in the chart I have added an upward-pointing arrow leading up from these pointer-stars towards the north celestial pole (but remember that in this two-dimensional projection, the "point" of the north celestial pole has been spread out into the *entire upper edge* of the rectangular chart).

The outlines of the constellations in that chart use the conventional system, rather than the system suggested by Rey in 1952, and the observant reader might notice a number of little circles scattered about the chart area, circles which are larger than the stars themselves. These little circles represent areas in the sky containing "Messier objects" (such as nebulae and star clusters, like the Pleiades or the Beehive), because the image that I used to make the diagram is a Messier object chart.

Constellations which are located on the "north-celestial-pole-side" of the Milky Way (the "waters above" the firmament, and the region associated with Apsu in the Mesopotamian system) would thus include Hercules (usually the most powerful figure in any myth-system), Boötes, Ophiuchus, Virgo, and the Twins of Gemini, among others.

Constellations which are located on the "opposite side" of the Milky Way from the north celestial pole would thus include Sagittarius, Capricorn, Aquarius, and Taurus -- but the only figure on the "waters below" side of the Milky Way band who could possibly represent a warrior large and strong enough to challenge a figure associated with the constellation Hercules in the north would be Orion, whose towering form is located just below (south of) the Milky Way band.

The dramatic tension of the Mesopotamian epic arises from the multiplication of gods who are the descendants of the original deities Apsu and Tiamat. The generation born from Apsu and Tiamat, a god named Lahmu and a goddess named Lahamu (the second generation of deities), in turn produces a third generation of deities: a god named Anshar and a goddess named Kishar (the third generation of gods). This generation in turn produces a son Anu, the god born of Anshar and Kishar (Anu belonging to the fourth generation of deities).

Anu himself had a son known as Nudimmud, also known as Ea. This god, known to the speakers of Akkadian as Ea or Nudimmud, corresponds to the god called Enki by the Sumerians. The god Ea (or Nudimmud, or Enki in Sumerian) belongs to the fifth generation of deities. The attributes of Ea-

Nudimmud are not completely known to us, due to damage in the survivng tablets at the lines describing the god's powers, but the portions of the lines which remain intact surrounding his introduction into the text describe him as "Abounding in all wisdom" (Tablet I, line 18) and "exceeding strong" (Tablet I, line 19) and declare that "He had no rival" (Tablet I, line 20).[226]

All of this genealogy occupies only the first 21 lines of the text of Tablet I of Enuma Elish. But in line 22, the dramatic tension is introduced: Apsu and Tiamat are troubled and confused by the commotion created by the multiplying gods. Apsu complains to Tiamat that he can neither rest by day nor be at peace by night -- and declares that he will solve the problem by destroying the source of the commotion. At this, Tiamat is outraged and curses the idea of extinguishing their own offspring, but Apsu and his vizier Mummu are determined to carry out the plan.

The text then tells us that Ea (Nudimmud or Enki), "he who knoweth all," was aware of the intentions of Apsu, and decided to take action.[227] "He went up and beheld their muttering," the tablets declare (Tablet I, line 60), and although the text is somewhat damaged after that, the snippets that remain legible seem to describe an incantation wrought by Ea through which Apsu and Mummu are rendered powerless and taken captive by Ea.[228] As a result, Ea strips Apsu of his crown and his glory, slays him, and takes his place as the leader of the gods.

Tiamat, who had opposed Apsu's plan, is nevertheless enraged at Ea for slaying Apsu and usurping his place, and determined to work out revenge against Ea and those who now side with him. She brings forth eleven kinds of monsters to help her seek her vengeance:

> ➤ "monster-serpents" described as "sharp of tooth and merciless of fang," (Tablet I, lines 114 - 115)²²⁹
> ➤ fierce "monster-vipers" of whom the text says "their bodies reared up and none could withstand their attack" (Tablet I. line 120),²³⁰
> ➤ vipers (Tablet I, line 121),
> ➤ dragons (same line),
> ➤ Lahamu (same line),
> ➤ raging hounds (Tablet I, line 122),
> ➤ scorpion-men (same line),
> ➤ hurricanes (same line),
> ➤ mighty tempests (Tablet I, line 123),
> ➤ fish-men (same line),
> ➤ and rams (same line).

The identity of these monsters brought forth by Tiamat to help her do battle against Ea and his followers are so obviously celestial that we should pause here and examine possible explanations for this entire conflict.

The pattern has very recognizable parallels to the conflicts recorded in ancient Greek myth surrounding the creation and first generations of gods and Titans, of which we read in the Theogony of Hesiod (Hesiod is thought to have lived sometime between the years we call 750 BC and 650 BC). In the Theogony, the sky-father Ouranos and the earth-mother Gaia bear offspring including the "hundred-handed ones" and the enormous but misshapen Cyclopes -- and Ouranos banishes these to the pit of Tartaros, an act which outrages Gaia their mother. When Ouranos and Gaia have additional children, the Titans, Gaia plots revenge against Ouranos, and arms the boldest of the Titans (Kronos, corresponding in many ways to the Latin figure of Saturn) with a flint sickle, with which he ambushes and castrates Ouranos, taking his place. Kronos (Saturn) will later be overthrown in the same way by Zeus (Jupiter or Jove), during a cataclysmic struggle between the upstart Olympian gods and goddesses and the previous generation of Titans -- all of which events can be easily seen to have strong echoes with the events developing in Enuma Elish described thus far.

The celestial aspects of the events described in Hesiod's Theogony are explored in greater depth in *Star Myths of the World, Volume Two* (*Myths of Ancient Greece*). Suffice it to say here that the authors of *Hamlet's Mill* make a strong case that the offense of the Titans, whose very name appears to descend from the Greek word meaning "striver," or "strainer," or "over-reacher," is related to the action of precession, which causes the stars and constellations to overstep their boundaries.[231]

Citing Emil Friedrich Kautzsch (1841 - 1910), authors de Santillana and von Dechend identify the Titans with the angels in the Bible who rebel against God and are consigned to eternal punishment, such as those described in the Book of Enoch chapter 18 in this way:

> "Those stars which roll around over the fire are those who, at rising time, overstepped the orders of God: *they did not rise at their appointed time.* And He was wroth with them, and He bound them for 10,000 years until the time when their sin shall be fulfilled."[232]

In that discussion, the authors of *Hamlet's Mill* argue that not only the Titans, but also the gods in Enuma Elish whose multiplying crowded their progenitors Apsu and Tiamat and disturbed their rest, as well as the Asuras described in the texts of ancient India, as well as the rebel angels in the Bible and related non-canonical texts, fit into this pattern of supernatural figures who were originally benign but whose overstepping of their boundaries initiates a cosmic struggle in numerous world myth-systems.[233]

Now, it should be noted that the motion of precession will not actually change which constellations are situated "above" the Milky Way (that is, to the north-celestial-pole-side) or "below" the Milky Way, but it *will* alter the intersection of those constellations with the four great "boundary markers" of the annual cycle (the solstices and equinoxes), and if the band of the Milky Way is aligned with any pair of solstices or equinoxes, it will alter that intersection as well -- which is precisely what took place when the action of precession brought an end to the Age of Gemini (which the authors of *Hamlet's Mill* seem to identify with the "Golden Age").

Indeed, de Santillana and von Dechend address the fact that precession does not alter the relationship of the constellations to the Milky Way, but that precession will shift the Milky Way even as it shifts the constellations, such that alignments of the Milky Way with the important stations of the year will be disturbed in just the same way that the alignments of constellations with those important dates will also be disturbed. They note that the myths of many cultures describe the Milky Way band as a pathway for souls in between incarnations, and that during the Age of Gemini (when the sun was in Gemini on the spring equinox, and thus in the opposite sign of Sagittarius at fall equinox) the Milky Way would thus have aligned with the two solstices (since the band of the Galaxy passes by Sagittarius on one side of the heavens and Gemini on the other).[234]

Thus, the motion of precession which delayed the constellations and allowed one zodiac sign to periodically "usurp" the sign which had ruled before it *also* disturbed the order which had established the Milky Way (that "path of souls") to stretch like a bridge from one equinox to the other, and thus pushed some constellations on the "Tiamat side" of the Galaxy into the half of the year which is ruled by darkness (the portion that follows the autumnal equinox and contains winter solstice), while bringing some constellations on the "Apsu side" into the half of the year ruled by light (the portion that follows spring equinox and contains summer solstice).

A way to understand this is to look at the zodiac wheel diagram below, showing the signs which the sun would occupy during the Age of Taurus, which ensued *after* the end of the Age of Gemini which preceeded it:

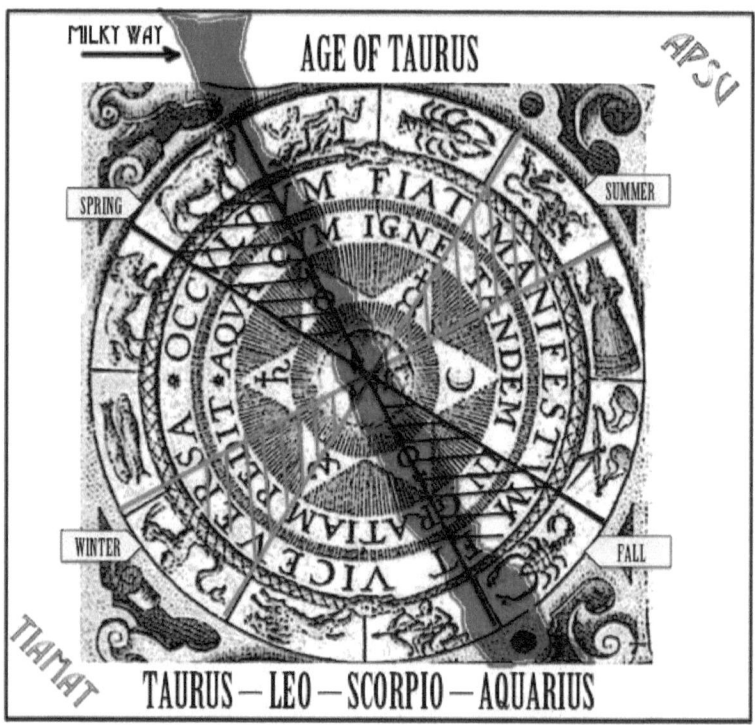

There is a lot going on in that diagram, admittedly, but let's begin with the rather unusual feature I've added to this particular diagram: the Milky Way band itself, rising up between Scorpio and Sagittarius at the bottom-right portion of the zodiac wheel and crossing up towards the intersection of Gemini and Taurus in the upper-left portion of the wheel. This represents the path of the Milky Way in our sky as seen from earth, and the motion of precession *will not alter* that path's location relative to Gemini and Sagittarius.

The constellations which are "above" the Milky Way (that is to say, on the north-celestial-pole-side of the Milky Way) are to the *right* of the Milky Way band on the zodiac wheel drawn here. These include Gemini, Cancer, Leo, Virgo, Libra and Scorpio (most of Scorpio being *within* the Milky Way band, but as Virginia Lee Davis and Jane B. Sellers point out, the very front end of the Scorpion peeks out into the "upper half" of the heavens, or the space on the north-celestial-pole-side of the Galaxy band). These constellations are in the "waters above" or the "Apsu side" of the Milky Way, and hence I have added the label "Apsu" in the upper-right corner of the zodiac diagram, to indicate that these constellations are always going to be located in the region *north* of the Galaxy. If you wish to confirm this labeling, turn back to the whole-sky star-chart on page 388.

Similarly, I have added the label "Tiamat" to the lower-left corner of the zodiac diagram, to indicate that all the constellations from Sagittarius to Aries (left of the Milky Way in the picture above) are located *below* the Galaxy (on the south-celestial-pole-side).

Now, you may want to get up and do a little stretching before tackling this next concept, or take a series of deep breaths.

Ready? The diagram shows a kind of "great cross" indicating the zodiac stations that mark the two equinoxes and two solstices. The shifting of the precessional Ages *will* rotate this great cross in a counter-clockwise manner. The diagram on page 396 and below shows the Age of Taurus, when the spring equinox has moved from Gemini to Taurus, thus shifting that entire "cross" one position counter-clockwise from its previous setting. In doing so, the shift of precession from the Age of Gemini to the Age of Taurus has moved Sagittarius into the half of the year that is "below" the point of fall equinox (whereas previously, Sagittarius itself marked the point of fall equinox -- but now, in the Age of Taurus, Scorpio marks the point of fall equinox, as you can see).

The diagram is reproduced below for your convenience, so you don't have to keep turning back a page to look at it as you read through the explanation:

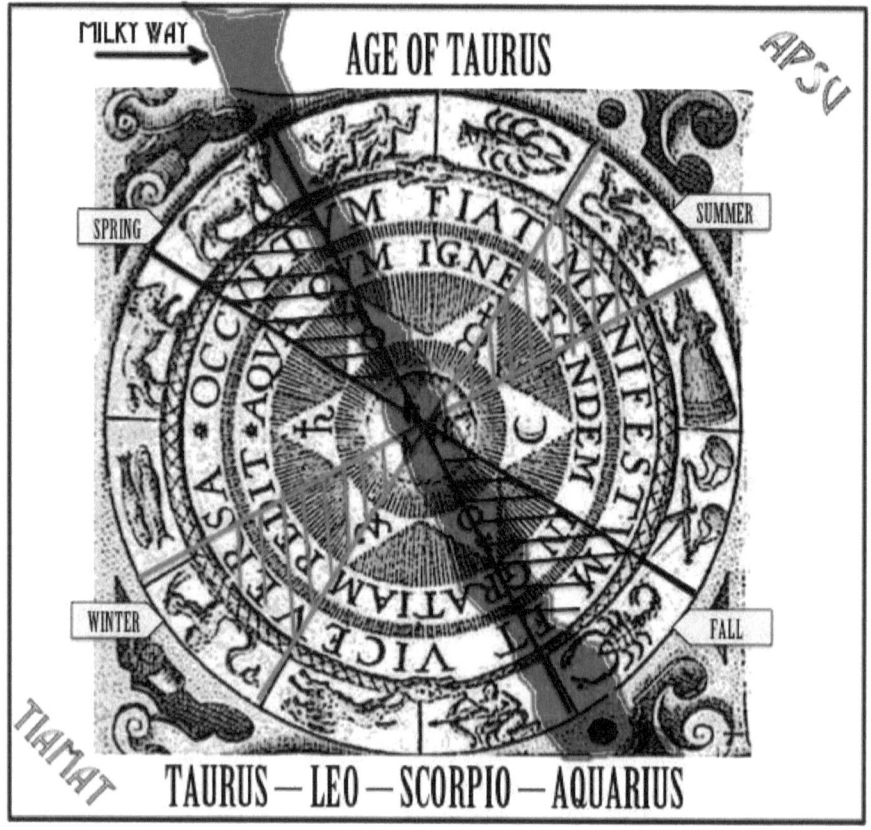

As we can see from the diagram, Sagittarius is a constellation which plays on the "team" of Tiamat. Sagittarius will always be on Team Tiamat -- the motion of precession will not change that. It is located in the heavens on the "lower" side of the Milky Way band, on the side opposite the north celestial pole. However, during the Age of Gemini, Sagittarius was at the point of fall equinox, and after the shifting of precession ended the Golden Age, Sagittarius was now "thrown down" into the *winter* half of the year, because the point of fall equinox slid from Sagittarius into Scorpio.

At the same time, the constellation Gemini (which plays on Team Apsu, being located "above" the Milky Way band) moved fully into the *summer* half of the year. This happened because in the previous Age of Gemini, the constellation Gemini marked the spring equinox, but when the motion of precession caused the spring equinox to slide into Taurus, then Gemini stopped being "on the boundary" and moved fully into the "upper half" of the year. It's as though Team Apsu advanced a player into the summer side of the year, while Team Tiamat simultaneously saw one of its own players sent down into the penalty box of the winter half of the year.

Based on the above analysis, I believe that the authors of *Hamlet's Mill* are correct in their assertion that the "overstepping of boundaries" that disturbed the placidity and rest of Apsu and Tiamat is caused by the motion of precession. Indeed, Apsu does not seem to be at all pleased by the movement of constellations into new halves of the year due to the motion of precession, even if (as suggested above) "Team Apsu" seems to be getting the better of this motion than "Team Tiamat." Instead, he is annoyed at all the moving about, as if to say "confound these pesky deities (constellations) moving around and crowding my space -- I think

I will just destroy them: somebody fetch me my minister, Mummu!" Apsu and Mummu then plot various types of destruction.

Let us next examine the possible celestial identity of the god Ea (Sumerian Enki), who in his unbounded knowledge becomes aware of the awful plan of Apsu and Mummu, and speaks an incantation which robs them of their power, and who then proceeds to take the glory and crown of Apsu for himself.

Below is a Sumerian cylinder-seal showing the god Enki (whom the Babylonians call Ea) among other deities: he is the god with streams of water pouring down from the region of his shoulders, to both the left and the right of him:

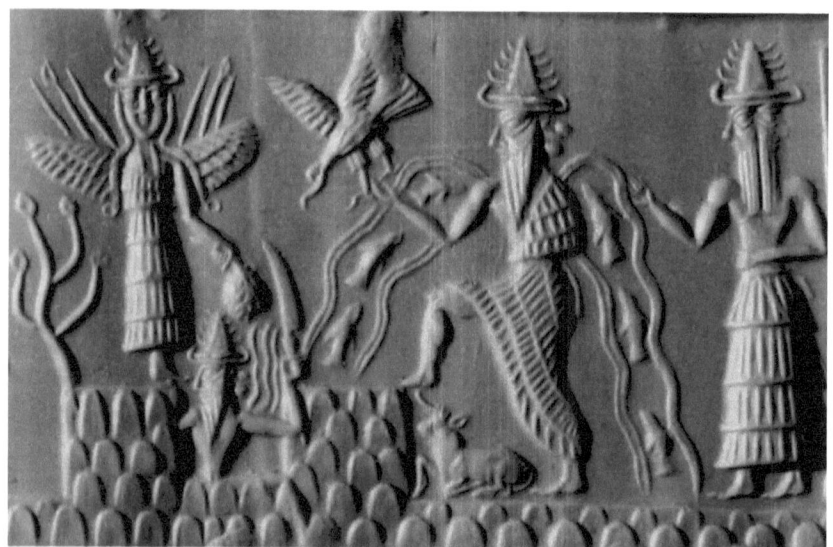

The above image is from an ancient Sumerian cylinder-seal made of hard greenstone, thought to date to around 2300 BC, which is today housed in the British Museum and is known as the "Adda Seal" after the name of the ancient scribe to whom it belonged.

Scholars believe the figures shown include (from left to right):

> ➤ the goddess Inanna (whom the Babylonians call Ishtar),
> who is seen holding a branch of some sort in her
> outstretched hand: this posture and the presence of the
> branch with leaves and fruit clearly indicate an
> association with the constellation Virgo, whose
> outstretched arm reaches towards Coma Berenices -- the
> branch depicted in this ancient seal,
> ➤ the sun-god Shamash (located below Inanna, in the cleft
> of the mountains, cutting his way out with a large knife)
> ➤ an eagle or other large bird accompanying Enki
> ➤ the god Enki himself, who is depicted with one upraised
> hand on the side of the eagle, as well as having two
> streams of water emanating from his shoulders, each
> stream containing three fish
> ➤ the god Umisu, who is the minister or vizier of Enki, and
> who has two faces, one pointing towards the left of the
> image and one pointing towards the right.

The gods and goddess depicted in this ancient seal all wear
helmets with multiple horns, indicating their status as deities. At
first glance, it would seem certain that Enki in this depiction is
associated with Aquarius, a constellation which can be seen to
have an outstretched leg and a bent and upraised arm, nearly
identical to the posture of Enki in the ancient artwork shown here.
Additionally, of course, Aquarius is associated with the pouring-
out of water, and that certainly seems to match the depiction of
the god Enki in this cylinder-seal.

However, this identification may not be as certain as it first
appears. For one thing, Aquarius does not have streams of water
going to *either* side -- wavy lines on *both* sides of a central body
are more characteristic of Ophiuchus than of Aquarius. There are
some figures in ancient myth of other cultures (notably Dionysus)

401

who appear to combine features of Aquarius and Ophiuchus, and it may be the case that Enki, like Dionysus, also combines aspects of both these constellations (the celestial associations of the important god Dionysus of ancient Greece are discussed more extensively in Volume Two of this series).

Addtionally, the constellation Aquarius is not at all close to the constellation Virgo in the heavens, and yet as we have just noted, this cylinder-seal clearly depicts a Virgo-figure in the form of the goddess Inanna, with her outstretched arm holding a branch that is almost certainly indicative of Coma Berenices. Ophiuchus, on the other hand, is adjacent to Virgo and frequently associated with Virgo-figures in various world myths.

Additionally, the constellation Aquila the Eagle is adjacent to Ophiuchus as well, thus adding to the suspicion that Enki in this seal may be associated with Ophiuchus. There is also a constellation known as Delphinus the Dolphin "swimming" along the edge of the Milky Way band, just above the form of Aquila the Eagle -- and thus the presence of fish-shapes within the streams emanating from the god Enki in this seal may indicate a sort of conflation of the two wavy lines of the serpent-half of Ophiuchus (which are envisioned as two streams on either side of the central body of the god, in this image) and the "waters" of the Milky Way, where we find the outline of Delphinus.

The identity of the double-faced vizier Umisu is even more difficult to determine, but it is possible that he may be associated with the constellation Boötes. Remember that in our examination of the myths of ancient Egypt, we saw evidence that the frog-headed goddess Heqet or Heket, who sits across from Khnum during the making of mortal men and women on the potter's wheel, is assocated with the figure of Boötes in the sky, and in that instance Boötes is envisioned as "facing" towards the left (the frog-head is looking to the left). In most other cases, however, Boötes is envisioned as looking towards the right (in the direction of the "pipe" in his mouth, that is). Thus, it could be argued that the constellation Boötes is "double-faced" or "double-facing" -- the constellation can be envisioned as having a face that looks left, and another that looks right as we face the constellation in the sky. Note that if Umisu is associated with Boötes, then this cylinder-seal contains deities associated with Ophiuchus, Virgo, and Boötes -- three constellations which are indeed near one another in the heavens.

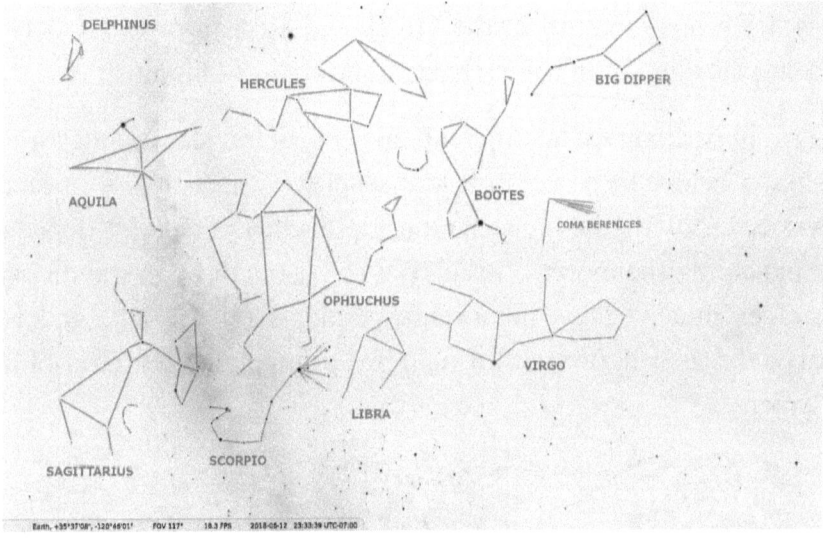

Additionally, as can be seen from the star-chart above, there are reasons to associate Kronos and his flint sickle with the outline of Ophiuchus (although I have previously argued that Kronos might be associated with Orion). Note that the "eastern serpent-half" (on the left side of the central body of Ophiuchus, in the star-chart above) could be seen as resembling a large scythe or sickle -- the very implement with which Kronos is said to have castrated his father the sky-god. Note too that the figure of Hercules is seen directly above this sickle-wielding outline of Ophiuchus, with legs spread apart just above the sickle itself!

If Kronos is indeed associated with Ophiuchus (particularly in his act of emasculating his father and taking over the throne of heaven), then not only would this association help explain the recurring pattern in Greek myth of a god who arises from below (Ophiuchus) to castrate and take over rulership from a god who held it previously (Hercules), but it would also provide additional support for an association between Enki (or Ea) and Ophiuchus. We have already noted that Ea / Enki as *the god who is bold enough to stand up against Apsu* forms a rather direct parallel with Kronos / Saturn in the Greek and Roman myth (Kronos being the only Titan willing to stand up against Ouranos).

The illustration of a different ancient Sumerian cylinder-seal shown below helps confirm our suspicion that Enki is in fact associated with the constellation Ophiuchus. This seal depicts Enki aiding the mortal Ziusudra, who passes through the Flood and eventually gains immortality. Enki is on the left, and is depicted as a figure with a man-like torso above the coils of a serpent:

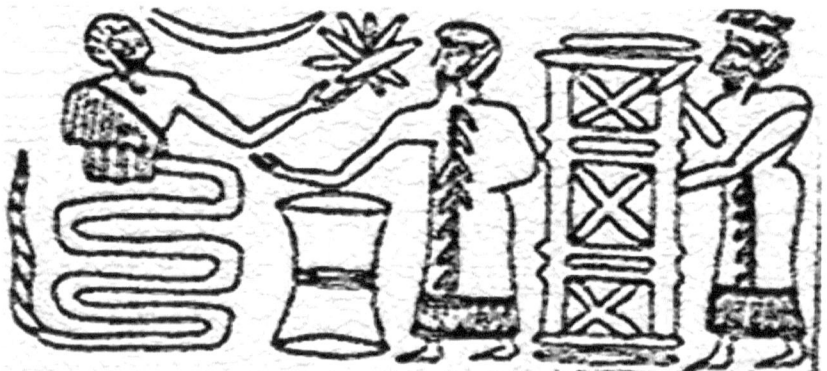

In this ancient cylinder-seal artwork, Ziusudra has an extremely long arm, extended. Enki appears to be handing something to him (some say it is a tablet of some sort, although it also resembles the depictions we've seen in other artwork of *a sun-disc with rays emanating outwards from a central point*).

This depiction of Enki as an entity with human-like torso above a twisting serpent should look familiar: we have previously shown an ancient depiction of Zeus slaying Typhon in which Typhon is depicted in a nearly-identical fashion (see pages 164 and 268 for some discussion, as well as the image below which we've seen on both of those pages):

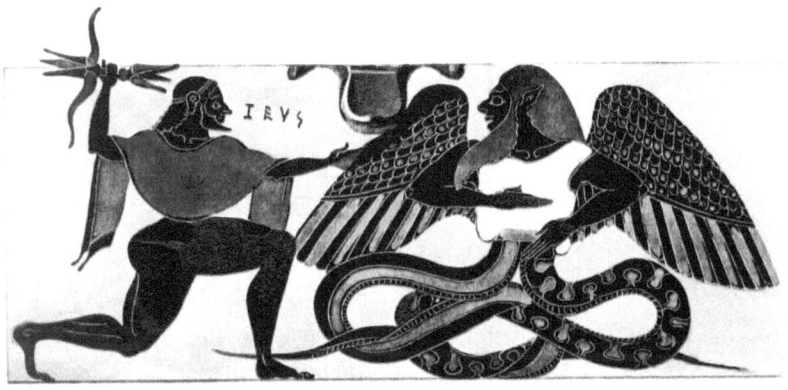

As we've already argued, the posture of Zeus cannot indicate any constellation other than Hercules, while Typhon most likely represents a figure combining aspects of Ophiuchus (the human torso above) and Scorpio (the serpents below), since Ophiuchus is directly above and very close to Scorpio, while Hercules is directly above Ophiuchus. The similarity of iconography between the ancient Sumerian cylinder-seal and the ancient Greek pottery artwork should conclusively demonstrate that Enki is closely associated with Ophiuchus.

Returning to the Sumerian seal on the preceding page, note that the object Enki is offering to Ziusudra is in the correct position celestially to be either a tablet (the small circlet that forms the "serpent's head" on one side of Ophiuchus plays a tablet in other myths we will examine in later volumes) or a solar disc (we have seen that the solar disc depicted above Ophiuchus-figures in other ancient artwork is frequently "offset" slightly and depicted above the *arm* or *hand,* rather than being depicted directly above the *head* of an Ophiuchus-figure: see for example the ancient artwork shown on pages 293, 294 and 297).

The depiction of Ziusudra with an (extremely) extended arm probably indicates an association with the constellation Virgo, at least in this artistic representation. In any case, based on this cylinder-seal depiction of Enki we can confirm our suspicion of an association between Enki (Ea) and Ophiuchus.

Just as Kronos, who usurped the place of his own father, and will eventually be overthrown by his son Zeus (who successfully leads the Olympian gods in a cataclysmic battle against Kronos and the Titans), Ea (Enki) will also be supplanted by his own son, Marduk. And, just as Zeus can be positively identified with the constellation Hercules (for reasons discussed at length in the next volume of this series), Marduk can also be positively identified with the same constellation -- adding yet another layer of resonance between the Enuma Elish account and the counterpart in ancient Greece.

Unlike Zeus, who led a violent assault on the Titans, Marduk replaces Ea as the ruler of heaven by striking a deal -- although the deal involves battling Tiamat and her followers, which does parallel the exploits of Zeus and his battle against the Titans.

The gods call on Marduk (who is the son of Ea and Ea's consort, the goddess Damki or Damkina) after first Ea and then Ea's father Anu (acting under the advice of Anshar, the father of Anu and the grandfather of Ea) approach Tiamat individually to try to placate her, to no avail. In despair, the gods seem at a loss -- until Anshar remembers the might of Marduk, and realizes that Marduk alone could have the power to defeat Tiamat.

When Anshar tells Marduk of their dire situation, Marduk declares that Anshar should have no fear -- Marduk will accomplish whatever Anshar has in his heart (Tablet II, lines 116 - 122). Anshar exults: "Rejoice and be glad; the neck of Tiamat shalt thou swiftly trample underfoot," repeating that formula two times for emphasis (Tablet II, lines 123 - 126).[235]

However, Marduk demands that if he does venture forth to fight Tiamat and save Ea and his allies from Tiamat and her hordes, then Ea shall no longer be king over all the gods but instead Marduk shall be supreme, to destroy and create by his word. As if to demonstrate their sincerity, or to test Marduk's power, the assembled gods "set in their midst a garment," and direct Marduk to command it to vanish, and command it again to reappear -- a miraculous sign which Marduk successfully accomplishes (Tablet IV, lines 21 - 28). Beholding this, all the gods rejoice, pay homage to Marduk, and declare: "Marduk is king!"[236]

Following this display of power, the gods all urge Marduk to go forth and "cut off the life of Tiamat" (Tablet IV, line 31).[237] The lines describing Marduk's preparation for battle with Tiamat, as well as the description of the battle itself, strongly suggest that Marduk (in parallel with many other examples of the "most powerful god" in any pantheon) corresponds to the constellation Hercules.

The text of Tablet IV describes the god arming himself for the confrontation with Tiamat and her eleven categories of monsters. He will also have to face a god named Kingu, who urged Tiamat on in her anger against Ea after the death of Apsu, and who then became her new consort to replace Apsu.

The tablets describe Marduk's preparation as follows:

> 35. He made ready the bow, he chose his weapon,
> 36. He slung a spear upon him and fastened it . . .
> 37. He raised the club, in his right hand he grasped (it)
> 38. He set the lightning in front of him,
> 40. With burning flame he filled his body.
> 41. He made a net to enclose the inward parts of Tiamat,
> 42. The four winds he stationed so that nothing of her might escape;
> 43. The South wind and the North wind and the East wind and the West wind
> 44. He brought near to the net, the gift of his father Anu.
> 45. He created the evil wind, and the tempest, and the hurricane,
> 46. And the fourfold wind, and the sevenfold wind, and the whirlwind, and the wind which had no equal;
> 47. He sent forth the winds which he had created, the seven of them;
> 48. To disturb the inward parts of Tiamat, they followed after him.
> 49. Then the lord raised the thunderbolt, his mighty weapon,
> 50. He mounted the chariot, the storm unequalled for terror,
> 51. He harnessed and yoked unto it four horses,
> 52. Destructive, feroucious, overwhelming, and swift of pace;[238]

This passage is simply bursting with indications that the god Marduk is seen in the heavens in the form of the constellation Hercules. First, there are his weapons, in particular his upraised club (in his right hand) and of course his possession of the thunderbolt -- the weapon which is almost exclusively associated with Hercules-figures in myth, no matter upon which continent the myth is found.

Additionally, there is the inclusion of winds as a weapon of Marduk -- indeed, a veritable panoply of winds, including the whirlwind and the winds of the four directions. Hercules figures, as we have already discussed and as we will continue to see in future volumes of this series, are closely associated with the wind, no doubt due to the "whirling" form of the constellation, which can be seen as having vectors emanating from it in four directions (north, south, east and west) and which is frequently described in myth as a whirlwind.

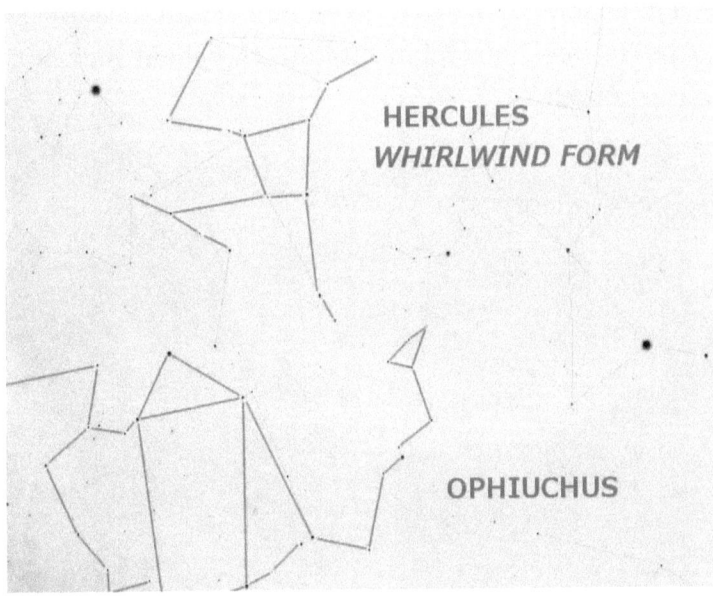

HERCULES
WHIRLWIND FORM

OPHIUCHUS

There is also mention of a net -- and note that in the image above, the same outline of Hercules could be envisioned as a net, ready to descend upon the constellation Ophiuchus. If this assertion seems like "a bit of a stretch" to the skeptical reader, please suspend judgment until reading through *Star Myths of the*

World, Volume Two in its entirety, in which it is argued that the same constellation Hercules functions as the cunning net which Hephaestus rigs above his canopy bed (Ophiuchus playing the role of the bed) in order to entrap his wife Aphrodite during her amorous tryst with the god Ares.[239]

Additionally, there is also the description of Marduk mounting his fearsome chariot -- itself described as a storm -- pulled by four ferocious steeds. We will see evidence again and again in myths from ancient India, ancient Greece, and even the Norse myths that the steeds pulling chariots in myth will often be associated with the four stars of the Big Dipper which make up the "bowl" of the Dipper, with the "handle" stretching back envisioned as the reins. The charioteer of this team is often the constellation Boötes, while the constellation Ophiuchus directly behind Boötes is often the war-cart itself.

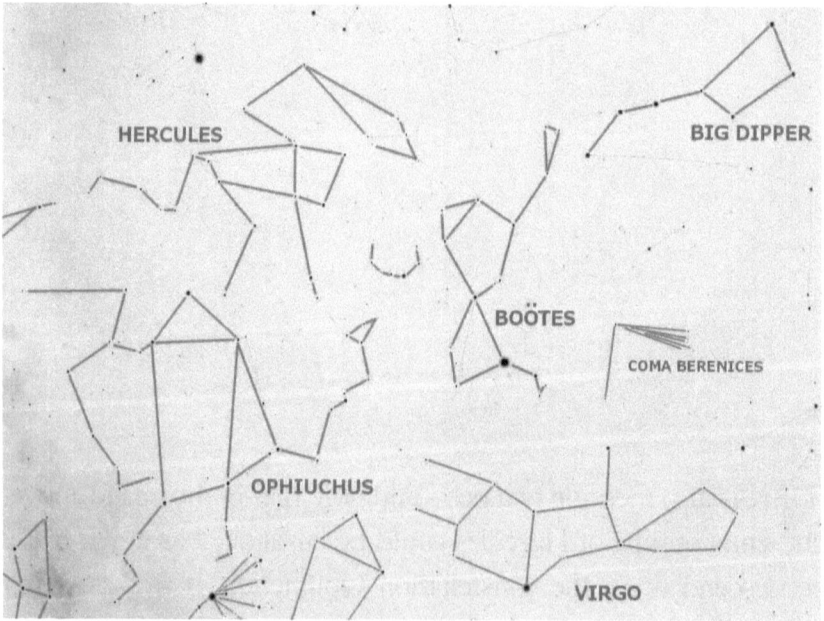

In many cases, the constellation Hercules is included in these "chariot" or "war-cart" scenes.

We will see a Hercules-figure included in the war-cart of Arjuna and Lord Krishna in the Mahabharata, for example, later in this volume. We will also see the god Thor riding in a war-cart in the Norse mythology (explored in Volume Four of this series), and in that case he corresponds very much to Marduk in this description, with the constellation Hercules representing the god Marduk or the god Thor, and the constellation Ophiuchus representing the god's war-cart, while the Big Dipper represents the team hitched to pull the vehicle.

Surviving artwork from ancient Mesopotamia confirms the connections between Marduk and the constellation Hercules in the heavens. Below is an image of a bas-relief found in Mesopotamia, which was excavated and a drawing made during an expedition to the ruins of ancient Nineveh during the first half of the nineteenth century.

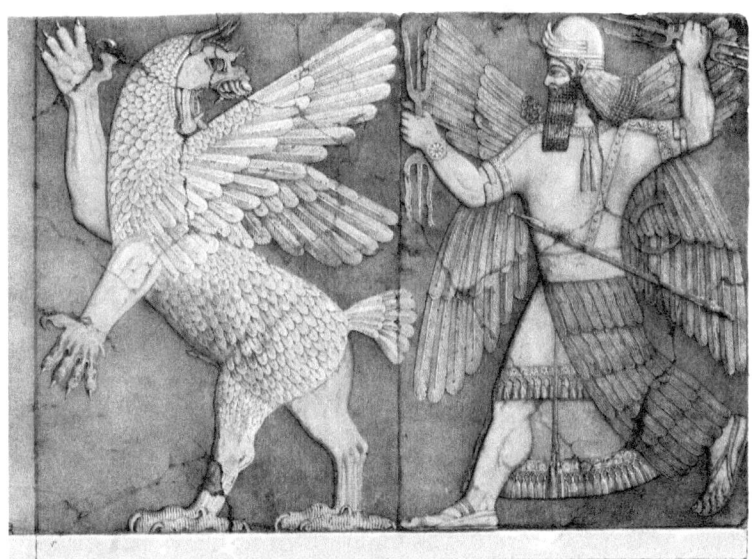

The antorhopomorphic figure at right in the bas-relief undoubtedly displays all the hallmarks of the constellation Hercules: striding posture with rear knee-bend, rear heel raised, full beard, one arm over head, and brandishing thunderbolts. It is now thought that this figure represents Marduk, and the image is usually labeled as such. When the book in which this illustration first appeared was being written, however, for eventual publication in 1853, the cuneiform system of writing had not yet even been deciphered.

Now Marduk goes forth to battle with Tiamat and her army.

The text tells us that Marduk raises his mighty thunderbolt, and addresses the primordial goddess:

> "Thou art become great, thou hast exalted thyself on high [. . .] thou hast followed after evil, and against the gods my fathers thou hast contrived thy wicked plan. Let then thy host be equipped, let thy weapons be girded on! Stand! I and thou, let us join battle!" (Tablet IV, lines 75 - 86).[240]

At this, Tiamat rages, shrieks, shakes and trembles, recites an incantation, and advances towards Marduk, who likewise advances towards her and her host. Then the text of Tablet IV tells us that:

> 95. The lord spread out his net and caught her,
> 96. And the evil wind that was behind (him) he let loose in her face.
> 97. As Tiamat opened her mouth to its full extent,
> 98. He drove in the evil wind, while as yet she had not shut her lips.
> 99. The terrible winds filled her belly,
> 100. And her courage was taken from her, and her mouth she opened wide.
> 101. He seized the spear and burst her belly,
> 102. He severed her inward parts, he pierced (her) heart.

103. He overcame her and cut off her life;

104. He cast down her body and stood upon it.

105. When he had slain Tiamat, the leader,

106. Her might was broken, her host was scattered.

107. And the gods her helpers, who marched by her side,

108. Trembled, and were afraid, and turned back.

110. But they were surrounded, so that they could not escape.

111. He took them captive, he broke their weapons;

112. In the net they were caught and in the snare they sat down.[241]

This battle reveals some parallels with myths from far away cultures, as well as giving us some clues as to the identity of Tiamat herself. While writing *Star Myths of the World, Volume Four*, and researching the chapter on Ragnarok, I was astonished to discover strong evidence of a connection between the fate of the high god Odin in his battle with Fenris Wolf (the Wolf opens his gaping jaws and swallows Odin) and the intricate carved artwork upon the enormous "coffin lid" found in the tomb of the Maya ruler Pakal the Great (who lived from AD 603 - AD 683, and who reigned from AD 615 until his death) discovered within the Pyramid of Inscriptions in Palenque.

The description of the Wolf, Fenris, opening his jaws to swallow Odin and Tiamat opening her mouth to its full extent towards Marduk appears to be a parallel. In *Star Myths of the World, Volume Four (Norse Mythology)*, I present extensive evidence which demonstrates that Odin is strongly associated with the constellation Ophiuchus, and that the jaws of Fenris in this case are envisioned as the two upward-curving "serpent-halves" of Ophiuchus, which appear to be engulfing his body (engulfing the central body-section of the constellation). I also demonstrate that when Odin's son Vidar finally slays the Wolf, in some accounts by stepping on one jaw with his mighty shoe and tearing the Wolf asunder by the jaws, and in other accounts by taking his sword and piercing the heart of the Wolf, Vidar most likely corresponds to the constellation Hercules, directly above Ophiuchus.[242]

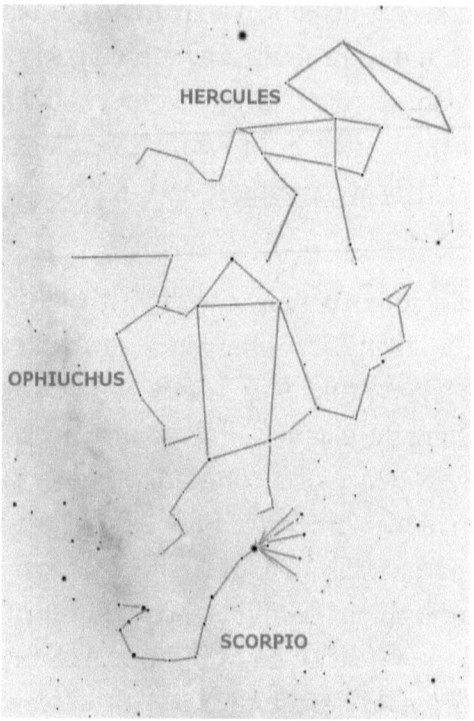

Thus, the parallel between these myths of Fenris and Tiamat (and, as I demonstrate in Volume Four, between the battle with Fenris and the artwork on the famous coffin-lid of Pakal as well) is extremely strong. Note that in the Norse myths, the Ophiuchus-figure of Odin could not defeat the Wolf, but the Hercules-figure of Vidar successfully does slay Fenris. Similarly, in the Babylonian Enuma Elish, the Ophiuchus-figure of Ea cannot prevail against Tiamat, but the Hercules-figure of Marduk successfully does slay her, and in a manner which shares some elements with the accounts of Vidar's defeat of Fenris (including standing upon her, as well as piercing her heart).

We have already mentioned the sending forth of wind and the bearing of the thunderbolt as constituting distinctly Herculean characteristics in the Star Myths found around the world.

The slaying of Tiamat by Marduk also has strong parallels to other myths in which a figure associated with the constellation Hercules battles a monster associated with the constellations below Hercules (Ophiuchus and / or Scorpio), including the battle of Zeus against Typhon mentioned many times previously in this volume.

It is also most noteworthy, as Timothy J. Stephany notes in his edition of Enuma Elish, that the God of the Bible is described more than once as the one who defeats the Leviathan, that crooked serpent, the dragon of the great deep, such as in Isaiah 27: 1 and Psalm 74: 13 - 14.[243] Stephany also points out that in the verses of Isaiah 51: 9 - 10, when the speaker is calling out, "put on strength, O arm of the LORD" the text asks: "Art thou not it that hath cut Rahab, and wounded the dragon? Art thou not it which hath dried the sea, the waters of the great deep; that hath made the depths of the sea a way for the ransomed to pass over?" Stephany notes that not only is the speaker hearkening back to the slaying of a dragon as evidence of the power of the LORD, but the text also uses the Hebrew word *tehom* (translated in the text above as "the great deep"), which appears to be linguistically related to the name of Tiamat (*Tiamat --> tehom*)![244]

This observation by Stephany is very significant, especially in light of the previously-cited assertion from Alexander Heidel in the introduction to his 1942 translation of Enuma Elish, that the epic is not so much a creation account (although it contains a fairly brief creation account) as it is a justification for the elevation of Marduk above all the other deities. The verses in the Old

Testament which hearken back to God's slaying of the Leviathan appear to echo, even if much more faintly, the same justification for his pre-eminence as that offered in Enuma Elish for the pre-eminence of Marduk (his slaying of Tiamat and his defeat of her host).

Stephany also points out that verses in the scriptures of the Old Testament make reference to the LORD's setting of limits, for example limits to the boundaries of the sea, as well appointing the foundations of heaven and earth (such as in Psalms 89: 9 - 11), and that this pattern echoes the boundary-setting activities which Marduk is described as performing after he slays Tiamat and takes her army captive.[245]

The parallels to events in the Bible, in the Greek myths, in the Norse myths, and even to iconography from the Maya period found in the specific details of the battle between Marduk and Tiamat are startling -- but they are explained by the fact that all of these cultures appear to be allegorizing the same region of the sky in very similar ways. The most likely explanation for this wide-ranging phenomenon, in my opinion at this time, is some relationship to a common but now forgotten ancient culture from which this system of celestial metaphor must have originated, and whose echoes down through the centuries testify to its existence, even if today virtually no one in conventional academia is searching for it, or is even aware that they should be.

Having seen what should be considered very strong evidence for the celestial identities of Marduk and Tiamat themselves, let us turn to Tiamat's army. The reader should have immediately noticed that the list of her eleven categories of monstrous allies sounds suspiciously celestial in nature. That list, as translated into English by Leonard William King, can be found on page 393.

Some of the figures mentioned, such as the ram, need no explanation and clearly correspond to familiar constellations (in this case, the zodiac constellation of Aries the Ram). The raging hounds may also be identified with the constellations Canis Major and Canis Minor (although in some myths, as we will see in later volumes, Scorpio plays a hound as well). In other cases, however, more explanation will be helpful in seeing the celestial connection.

The creatures translated by King as "monster-vipers" of whom the text tells us that "their bodies reared up and none could withstand their attack" probably correspond to Scorpio, a constellation which often appears in the role of a serpent (sometimes a many-headed serpent, as in the monstrous hydra which the hero Heracles must battle as one of his twelve labors). The description of "rearing up" is most apt for the outline of this constellation, which indeed appears to be flaring up as if to lunge forward in attack:

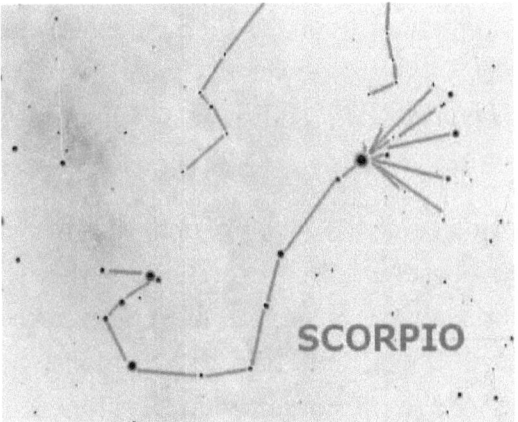

The mention of other "monster-serpents," "vipers," and "dragons" likely refers to other heavenly serpents or dragons, of which there are several, including the constellation Hydra (I believe that Scorpio actually plays the Lernaean Hydra that Heracles must defeat in the myth, rather than the constellation we know as Hydra), the constellation Draco the Dragon, and the serpent held by Ophiuchus.

The categories identified in King's translation as "hurricanes" and "mighty tempests" are most likely connected to the constellation Hercules, as we've already discussed at length. Even though Marduk is of course associated with this same constellation, that does not mean that a myth can "only use a constellation one time" -- it is not at unknown for a constellation to play two different roles in the same myth, much like a movie or a play in which the same actor appears in more than one role without too much disturbance on the part of the audience.

The case of the "scorpion-men" mentioned in Tablet I, line 122 (and multiple times thereafter, as the verses of Enuma Elish are formulaic in nature, with long sections repeating with little variation) is interesting, in that they have echoes with the scorpion-locust-centaurs described in Revelation chapter 9, a fact which was remarked upon by German philologist Franz Boll (1867 - 1924), whose observations were in turn noted by the authors of *Hamlet's Mill* and discussed in Appendix 36 of that text. They write:

> Franz Boll (*Offenbarung,* pp. 69ff.) has recognized in those strange locust-demons of Revelation -- they come out of the well of the abyss -- who resemble horses with human heads, and have wings, and tails of scorpions, the Sagittarius-Centaur of Mesopotamian boundary stones, also to be found on the rectangular zodiac of Dendera.[246]

The "strange locust-demons" referenced by de Santillana and von Dechend in the quotation above are found in the text of Revelation chapter 9, and (as Franz Boll argued in his 1914 work

Aus der Offenbarung Johannis which is German for "On the Epiphany of John," or the "On the Revelation of John") these "locusts" who are also described as having the "power as scorpions" and the "tails like scorpions" (as well as being "like unto horses" and having "faces as the faces of men" and "crowns like gold") can be positively identified with the constellation Sagittarius (along with the nearby constellations of Scorpio, and also the Southern Crown).

Although never fully explained by de Santillana and von Dechend, the "locust-like" horses with the faces of men and crowns of gold and scorpion tails contain clear connections to Sagittarius, Scorpio and Corona Australis (the Southern Crown). First, these locusts are described as emerging from the "smoke" arising from the bottomless pit: a description of the rising column of the Milky Way, the brightest and widest portion of which ascends between Sagittarius and Scorpio. Second, the description as "locusts" refers to Sagittarius, the brightest stars of which form an outline often referred to in modern times as "the Teapot," but which could also be envisioned as a large grasshopper or locust:

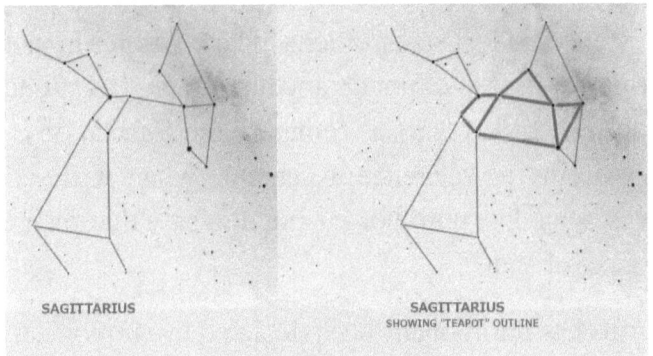

SAGITTARIUS

SAGITTARIUS
SHOWING "TEAPOT" OUTLINE

When envisioned as a "teapot," these bright stars in Sagittarius have a "spout" on the west (the right as we face the chart above) and a "handle" on the east (the left as we face it). A triangular "lid" can be seen on top of the "teapot."

This same "teapot" outline, however, could easily be envisioned instead as a locust or grasshopper, I argue. In that case, the "spout" on the right as well as the "lid" on the top becomes the large, folded rear legs of the insect. The locust faces towards the east (the left, as we face the chart). We could even envision "antennae" coming out of the "head" of the insect in the outline. Below, lines for the "antennae" have been added, as well as a "rear foot" behind one of the folded rear legs of the locust-outline:

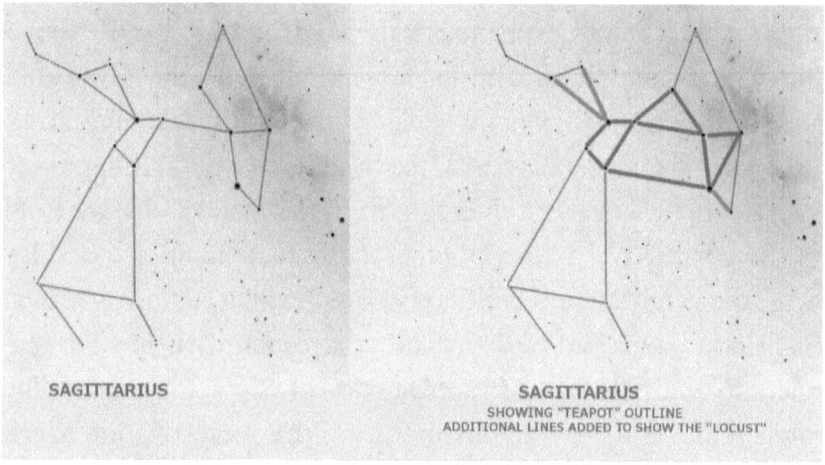

SAGITTARIUS

SAGITTARIUS
SHOWING "TEAPOT" OUTLINE
ADDITIONAL LINES ADDED TO SHOW THE "LOCUST"

This outline makes it clear that Sagittarius is connected to the many instances of locusts or other similar creatures in world myth and scripture -- but does not do anything to help us to understand how Sagittarius also plays a "centaur" (the Revelation 9 passage certainly seems to reference a centaur, when it describes the locusts as being like unto horses, but also says that their faces are "as the faces of men").

Sagittarius has traditionally been depicted in astrological artwork as a centaur-figure, with a human torso down to the waist, below which is the body of a horse. The Sagittarius centaur often holds a bow, which we can understand from the outlines shown above. But how do the outlines of Sagittarius suggested by H. A. Rey, and depicted in most of the illustrations in this series of volumes, give rise to seeing Sagittarius as a centaur?

The answer, I am convinced, is found when we note that there are some faint stars in the constellation Sagittarius which, if connected, create a kind of "tufted tail" as well as an additional "leg" which transforms the constellation's "long skirt" into the body of a horse, with a human torso arising from the long body (and holding a bow):

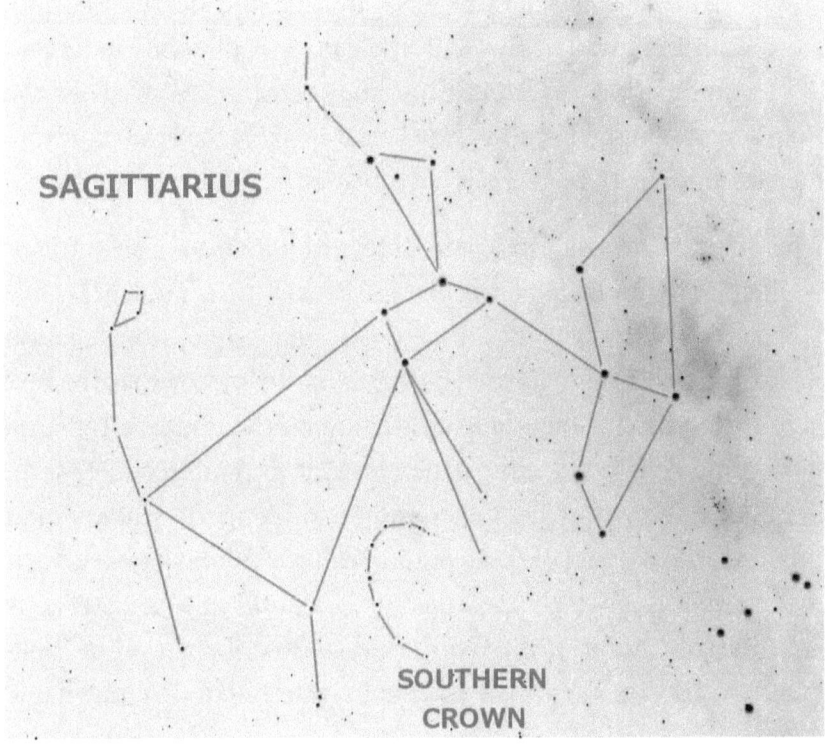

In the above star-chart, additional lines have been added to those suggested by H. A. Rey for the outline of Sagittarius. The addition of two "front legs" transforms the "long skirt" of the more human-shaped outline of the constellation into the long "horse body" of the centaur. Lines have also been drawn to stars which form the "tufted tail" for the animal body of the centaur.

Clearly, Revelation 9 is referring to Sagittarius when it describes creatures which are both "locusts" and "horses with faces as the faces of men" (i.e., both locusts and centaurs). These creatures are also described as having tails of scorpions (referencing Scorpio) and crowns like gold (referencing the Southern Crown, Corona Australis).

Thus, based on the above analysis, I would argue that it is quite probable that the "scorpion-men" described in Enuma Elish are also a mythical combination of Sagittarius and nearby Scorpio. The "scorpion-men" of Revelation 9 can be confidently identified as a combination of Sagittarius and Scorpio (as well as the Southern Crown), and thus I believe it is likely that the scorpion-men brought forth by Tiamat have an identical celestial identity.

The identity of the monster category labeled "Lahamu" or "Lahami" (found in Tablet I, line 121, as well as in Tablet III, line 89, and elsewhere) may relate to the same constellation Sagittarius which we have just examined. It is clear that the text here is describing something distinct from the goddess Lahamu who is named in the first generation of gods descended from Apsu and Tiamat (the generation consisting of Lahmu and Lahamu, the parents of Anshar and Kishar). While not positive, it may be that this word "Lahamu" or "Lahami" in this instance is an Assyrian variant of the word used to describe a kind of "bull-man" or "lion-man" which is usually referred to by the name *Lamassu.*

The following page displays a photograph of a Lamassu from the throne-room of the north-west palace of Nimrud, in upper Mesopotamia. The creature has the body of a lion and the head of a man. Other examples look very similar, but the body is of a bull with the head of a man (the main difference being in the feet of the animal, which are paws in the case of a lion-body and hooves in the case of a bull-body).

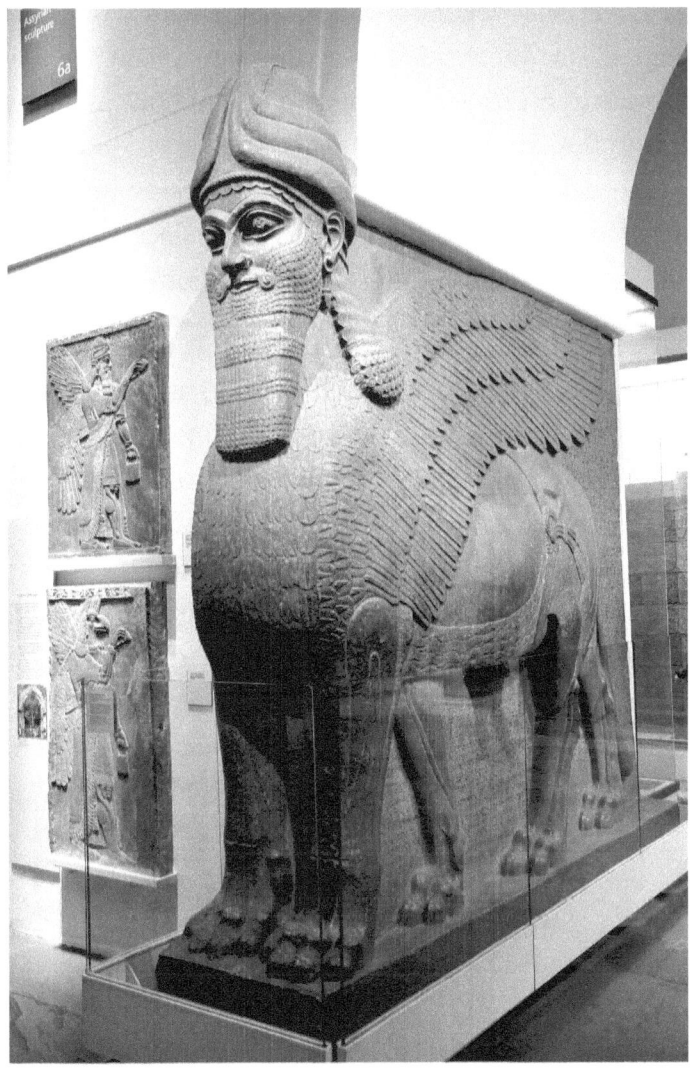

Note that the common feature of both bulls and lions is their possession of a *tufted tail* -- which is why I believe that the Lammasu (of either variety) are associated with the constellation Sagittarius in the heavens. We've just seen that there are stars in the vicinity of Sagittarius which can be connected to make a tufted tail behind a horse-like body, while still retaining the torso and head of a human figure. This aspect of Sagittarius gives rise to the traditional depiction of Sagittarius in artwork as a centaur holding a bow. However, those same stars could just as easily be envisioned as creating a bull-body or a lion-body as they could be envisioned creating a horse-body. Indeed, envisioning a lion-body or a bull-body actually fits the outline of the "tail" of Sagittarius better than does the idea of a horse-body, since the "tuft" of stars causes the tail to be like that of a bull or a lion, rather than like the tail of a horse.

The identity of the "fish-men" is found in the nearby zodiac constellation of Aquarius, a constellation which has a human outline and which is located directly above the constellation of Piscis Austrinus, the Southern Fish (we've already met Aquarius in conjunction with a great fish, in the story of Mirragan and Gurangatch, from the Star Myths of Australia). In addition to being situated above a fish, the outline of Aquarius also features a diamond-shaped head, which I am certain relates to the "fish-mouth" head-dress seen in some ancient Mesopotamian depictions of certain helpers of humanity known as the Apkallu.

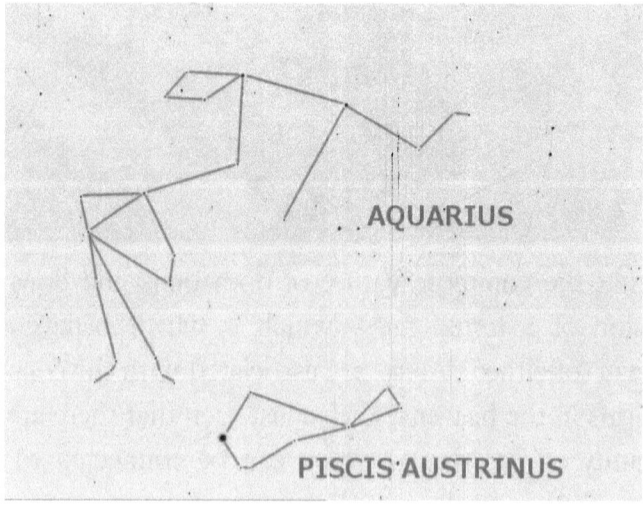

The word *Apkallu* is the Akkadian term; the corresponding word for these beings in Sumerian was *Abgal* and thus the word *Apkallu* is an example of the kind of linguistic borrowing from the Sumerian very common in Akkadian which indicates a long period of co-existence between the cultures and the heavy influence on the later civilizations of Babylonia and Assyria from the culture of the Sumerians. The Apkallu were described as great sages (in more than one ancient tablet they are described as being seven in number, they are often associated with the time before the Deluge, and are often described as being "half-fish").

Note the "fish-headgear" in the artwork below, from ancient Nineveh, as well as the similarity to the "bishop's mitre" headgear still in use to this day -- and compare to the shape of the head of the constellation Aquarius on the preceding page:

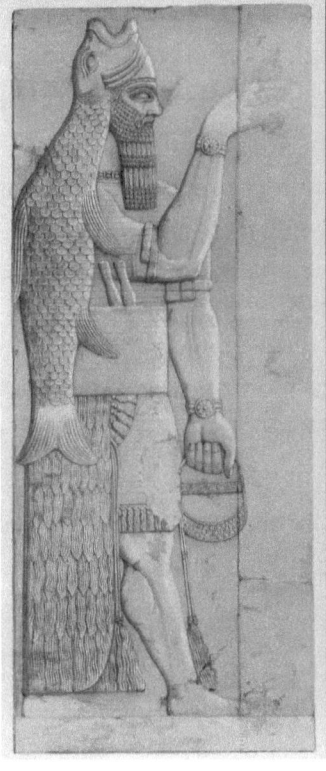
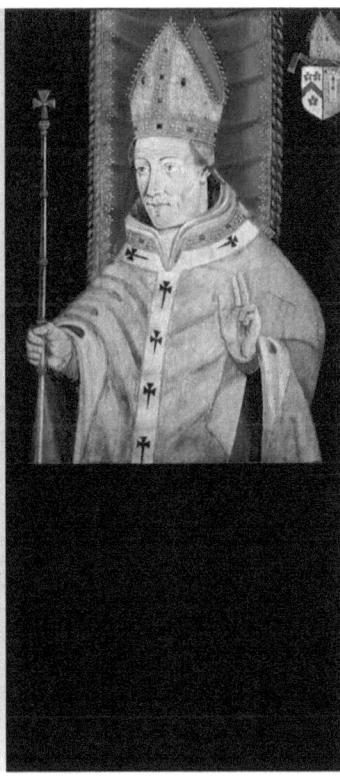

The "fish-man" shown on the previous page is closely associated with the sages described by a priest of Marduk named Berossos, who lived during the age that Alexander the Great conquered Mesopotamia and who sought to preserve the ancient wisdom of his culture during the period when the Hellenistic influence was washing like a flood over the older traditions, a flood which would eventually lead to the discontinuation of the use of cuneiform and the loss of the ability to read the ancient texts for a period of more than two thousand years, until the successful efforts of Hincks, Rawlinson and Oppert in the 19th century AD.

Berossos is thought to have been born in Babylonia between 330 BC and 323 BC. His date of death is unknown. His name in Akkadian was likely *Bel-re-ushu*, meaning "Bel is his shepherd" (Bel or Baal being another name for the god Marduk).[247] Berossos wrote a history of ancient Mesopotamia, from the creation by the gods down through a period closer to the time of Berossos himself, but as no originals of his work have survived, we cannot be exactly sure about the details. We know of his writings only through citations by other writers who consulted his history of Babylon (the *Babyloniaca* of Berossos).

Berossos repeats the creation account which is found in the Enuma Elish (copies of which did survive, on clay tablets, as already noted). In their 1996 edition translating what is known of the works of Berossos (of the Hellenistic period of Babylonia) and Manetho (of Hellenistic Egypt), Gerald P. Verbrugghe and John M. Wickersham note that the creation epic of Enuma Elish was recited in ancient Mesopotamia at the beginning of every new year.[248] However, since much of the action in Enuma Elish takes place prior to the creation of mortal men and women, those events had to be transmitted to humans from some non-human source, and this source, Berossos explains, was Oannes, the first of a line of sages to emerge from the waters of the sea (the Persian Gulf) and teach humanity the creation account of Enuma Elish, as well as civilizing skills including agriculture.[249] Verbrugghe and Wickersham explain that in the first book of his *Babyloniaca*, Berossos recounts the story of:

> how humans learned about what Marduk had done in creating order in the world from Oannes and other similar monsters from the sea. These monsters not only taught humans about creation but gave them the gift of civilization. Oannes and the others who are named in Berossos's text do not appear in ancient Semitic literary texts and are not mentioned with the antediluvian kings in king-lists. They are not, however, Berossos's creations. A late Babylonian tablet found at Uruk mentions these teachers of humans with antediluvian kings: the tablet is based on Sumerian mythology [. . .].[250]

Berossos is a very important source, in that he was deliberately trying to present ancient Babylonian history to a largely Greek-speaking audience, and because he had access to sources and texts which have not survived elsewhere. Recounting the description of Oannes as recorded by Berossos (and cited by surviving writers from antiquity who had access to his work), Verbrugghe and Wickersham write:

> It had the whole body of a fish, but underneath and attached to the head of the fish there was another head, human, and joined to the tail of the fish, feet, like those of a man, and it had a human voice. Its form has been preserved in sculpture to this day. Berossos says that this monster spent its days with men, never eating anything, but teaching men the skills necessary for writing and for doing mathematics and for all

sorts of knowledge: how to build cities, found temples, make laws. It taught men how to determine borders and divide land, also how to plant seeds and then to harvest their fruits and vegetables. In short, it taught men all those things conducive to a settled and civilized life. Since that time nothing further has been discovered.[251]

The description of seven civilizing entities or "Seven Sages" (the first of whom, in the accounts of Berossos, was named Oannes) finds echo in other cultures as well, including ancient India which had accounts of "Seven Rishis" (described, for example, in the Vishnu Purana, Book 2 and chapter 8), and ancient Egypt (where Seven Sages are mentioned in the Edfu Building Texts, inscriptions from a Ptolemaic-era temple, but thought to preserve knowledge and traditions having their origin in much more ancient times).

The name Oannes given by Berossos is generally thought to be a Greek format for the original name Uan or U-an. Many commentators over the decades have remarked upon possible linguistic connections between the name of this watery being and the name of the patriarch who survives the Flood in the text of Genesis, namely *Noah*, whose name may also be linguistically-related to the name of *Uta-napishti* or *Uta-napishtim* or *Utnapishtim*, the survivor of a great Flood described in the Gilgamesh tablets.

The celestial analysis approach to ancient myth offered in this and subsequent volumes opens an additional perspective upon this oft-remarked possible connection between Oannes, Uta-napishtim, and Noah, in that (as we've just seen) the fish-men of ancient Mesopotamia may have been associated with the constellation Aquarius (a "watery figure" in the heavens, and one with a distinctly diamond-shaped head, the shape of which may have given rise to the distinctive "fish-mouth" headgear which is seen in the ancient fish-man artwork from Nineveh and also seen in the shape of the bishop's mitre which is still in use). As will be discussed at length in *Star Myths of the World, Volume Three (Star Myths of the Bible)*, there is abundant evidence that both Noah in the Old Testament and John the Baptist in the New Testament are associated with the celestial figure of Aquarius as well. And, indeed, we can see that there is a likely linguistic connection between the names of *Noah* and *John* (and back in time to the names of *Oannes* or *U-an* and *Uta-napishtim* as well).

If you flip back to the image of the fish-man figure on page 425, you may notice some interesting details, including the fact that the figure depicted in the ancient artwork from a bas-relief in Nineveh appears to be holding something in the upraised hand, and that in his downward-reaching hand he appears to be holding a satchel, or a purse, or a handbag of some sort.

These are important observations. First, we have already noticed that figures from ancient Mesopotamia have been shown in artwork holding a kind of smooth, egg-shaped object in their upraised hand, and we have previously identified these figures with the outline of the constellation Ophiuchus. In particular, we saw an image from ancient Assyria, shown on page 294, holding up a smooth, egg-shaped object in one upraised hand, while also holding a branching vine with the other hand. That image can be confidently associated with the constellation Ophiuchus, as already discussed. The winged solar disc, as well as the similarities to another piece of artwork from ancient Assyria shown on page 293, in which the egg-shaped object is replaced with a lotus-flower atop one of the branching vines, makes the association with Ophiuchus quite certain.

I would argue that this Oannes-figure, who may be holding a similar object in his upraised hand and a satchel in his downward-stretching hand, exhibits some features which also correspond to Ophiuchus, in addtion to the correspondences with Aquarius that we have just been arguing (such as his diamond-shaped head).

Indeed, as it turns out, there is a pattern in ancient myth of figures who can be seen as being associated with Aquarius also being associated with Ophiuchus. For example, in the discussion of John the Baptist found in *Star Myths of the Bible,* plenty of evidence is presented which positively identifies the figure of John the Baptist with Aquarius -- and yet there are also some passages in the Biblical texts which indicate a possible correspondence with Ophiuchus as well (in particular the description of John as wearing raiment of camel's hair with a leathern girdle about his loins, and subsisting on locusts and wild honey).[252]

Similarly, we can confidently identify the figure of Noah in the book of Genesis with the constellation Aquarius, particularly when he plants a vineyard, drinks of the wine, and becomes drunk (in the story of Shem, Ham, and Japheth). However, there are reasons to argue that Noah, too, has some association with the constellation Ophiuchus, particularly when he rides out the great Genesis Flood in the Ark (both the Ark of Noah and the Ark of the Covenant being likely representations of the constellation Ophiuchus in the heavens).

Thus, we see that there appears to have been some kind of ancient understanding of a connection between Aquarius and Ophiuchus in some cases. At this time, I am not positive about the significance of this ancient connection, but I believe the evidence for such a connection is quite abundant. It is possible that such a connection is related to the previously-discussed connection of Apsu with the "waters above" (on the north-celestial-pole-side of the Milky Way ring) and of Tiamat with the "waters below" the Milky Way. Aquarius is a constellation found "below" the Milky Way (on the opposite side from the north celestial pole), while Ophiuchus is situated "above" the Milky Way (on the same side as the north celestial pole).

If so, then the fact that fish-men figures (such as Oannes) are described as coming out of the sea and then going back down to the sea could be related to this "dual identification" with Aquarius and Ophiuchus. When envisioned as corresponding to Aquarius, they are located "below" the Milky Way, in the "salty water" of Tiamat. But the association with Ophiuchus would place them "above" the Milky Way and thus out of the salty deep associated with Tiamat -- just as Oannes is said to have emerged from the sea, but is also said to descend back into the sea every night.

The above interpretation is by no means certain, but it is an intriguing possibility. It is clear that there are remnants of the ancient system which were remembered in ancient history to some degree, and which show up in the myths that have been preserved, even if we now have difficulty deciphering exactly what all these connections were, or their esoteric significance.

The discussion of the implements depicted in the hands of the fish-man brings us to an opportune point to introduce the fraught topic of the *Anunnaki* -- "fraught" (with potential controversy, and thus with some emotional charge for certain readers) because during the second half of the twentieth century in particular, a new type of literalistic interpretation of ancient myth was popularized by certain individuals who may or may not have actually believed the arguments they were advancing. Of course, I myself am open-minded towards alternative theorizing by those who present evidence and argue sincerely -- but it cannot be denied that occasionally, certain individuals will advance arguments that they do not actually believe, for an ulterior motive. Someone who advances such arguments insincerely can properly and accurately be termed a *charlatan.*

During the twentieth century, certain individuals have advanced literalistic explanations for the figures and events described in ancient myths and scriptures, basing their explanations upon the proposed movements of planets racing around outside of known orbits, such as the proposed ancient erratic motions of the planet Venus (in the arguments of Immanuel Velikovsky, 1895 - 1979) or the supposed motions of a supposed "Planet X" or "Nebiru" (in the arguments of Zechariah Sitchin, 1920 - 2010).

These individuals, who may or may not have actually believed the theories that they put forward as if with absolute certainty (often aided by tremendous media attention to help reach massive audiences, particularly in the case of Velikovsky), insisted that the erratic motions of these planets gallivanting around the solar system (sometimes in close proximity to our planet earth) are actually responsible for events described in ancient myth, such as the parting of the Red Sea (in the Biblical text of Exodus), or the later parting of the River Jordan (in the Biblical text of Joshua, supposedly because Venus after making a close pass just in time to part the Red Sea for Moses, swung back around a few years later at the exact proper moment to part the River Jordan for Joshua), and a host of other mythical signs and wonders, which are argued as having taken place in literal, terrestrial history.

In the case of the "theories" of Zechariah Sitchin, the periodic visits of the planet Nebiru also brought the visit of alien beings from that planet to our earth -- beings Sitchin identifies with the deities described in ancient Mesopotamian texts as the Anunnaki (also the *Anunna* in Sumerian, the *Anunnan*, and other variants), whom Sitchin argues to have been literal aliens from another planet.

The best way to refute an incorrect hypothesis is to present another hypothesis which better explains the totality of the evidence. In the case of the theories put forward by Velikovsky and Sitchin (whether sincerely or, as I suspect, possibly insincerely for some other agenda), it is not difficult to propose a hypothesis which fits the available evidence better than their fabrications, because there is absolutely no evidence of planets the size of Venus or the supposed Nebiru / Planet X having made any close passes through the inner solar system during human history or even prehistory -- and in fact there is plenty of evidence to the contrary.

For one thing, the asteroid belt shows no signs of having been disturbed by the passsage of planets the size of Venus or larger at any time in the past several thousand years -- or even at any time in the past several million years. In addition, the ancient records of several cultures (including ancient Egypt and ancient Babylon) indicate that they were watching the orbits of Venus along its present orbit prior to and during the periods that Velikovsky argues that Venus was actually swinging wildly through the solar system between Jupiter and the sun, terrorizing everything in its path and making several loops and curlicues in its travels in order to cause the "events" described in ancient myths and scriptures.

Just as there is no evidence among the physical sciences for planets the size of Venus or Nebiru plowing through the asteroid belt and the inner solar system as proposed by Velikovsky and

Sitchin (and indeed there is plenty of evidence to the contrary), there is also overwhelming evidence (as I have labored to demonstrate thus far in this volume, and will continue to demonstrate in the subsequent volumes in this series) that the ancient myths of the world are *not* describing literal, terrestrial, historical events but rather that they are based upon a system of celestial *metaphor* -- and celestial metaphor based upon the stars and heavenly cycles which we can *still see to this day*.

The reader or scientist comparing the competing explanations for the ancient myths (the explanations of Velikovsky and Sitchin, which propose that the ancient myths are describing literal events, caused by an unhinged planet Venus or by visits from a supposed Planet X and the supposed alien beings who come from that supposed planet, versus the explanation that demonstrates the evidence that the world's ancient myths are based upon a system of metaphor, using the constellations and heavenly cycles, such as the cycle of the year and the cycle of precession) is invited to examine all the evidence and decide for himself or herself which hypothesis appears to fit all of the evidence most satisfactorily.

Setting aside the now widely-popularized interpretation of the identity of the Anunnaki, argued by Sitchin in a series of books beginning in 1976, which argued that the Anunnaki were extraterrestrial beings from the Planet Nebiru who traveled to earth using 1960s-style rocketships in search of gold in order to repair their damaged atmosphere (and who genetically-engineered *homo sapiens* out of some other pre-existing species, in order to be the slaves of the Anunnaki and to mine gold for them), let us briefly discuss the deities identified as the Annunaki in various surviving Mesopotamian texts, including Enuma Elish.

The term *Anunnaki* appears to have undergone some shifts in meaning over the centuries. The term appears to have in some cases referred to the high gods and in other cases to have been applied to a set of gods who were sent down to the underworld. Scottish archaeologist Jane McIntosh defines "Anunnaki" as follows:

> An early Sumerian term for the gods, especially the mass of nameless gods who were first created. By the second millennium, however, the term generally refers more specifically to the gods of earth and the underworld, contrasting with *igigi*.[253]

In the Atrahasis, an early ancient Mesopotamian text recorded on three tablets, the Anunnaki are the supreme gods and the Igigi are deities who serve as their laborers. The text itself has been found on clay tablets dated as far back as 1700 BC, although the source of Atrahasis may have been much earlier.[254] The epic itself is a flood-myth, and we will briefly examine the importance of flood-myth towards the end of this chapter. The story of the Anunnaki appears to have been associated with the flood-narratives of ancient Mesopotamia, of which Atrahasis is a crucial text. Atrahasis recounts the story of the attempt by certain gods (instigated primarily by the war-god Enlil or Ellil, the brother of Ea or Enki) to reduce or eliminate the human population with a flood (and the efforts of Atrahasis, assisted by Enki, to survive the flood, along with his family).

The text of Atrahasis commences as follows:

> When the gods instead of man
> Did the work, bore the loads,
> The gods' load was too great,
> The work too hard, the trouble too much.

> The great Anunnaki made the Igigi
> Carry the worldload sevenfold.[255]

In this older epic, the Anunnaki are clearly superior to and indeed creators of the gods who make up the Igigi -- although some later texts indicate that this relationship was reversed. In Atrahasis, the gods assigned to toil (the Igigi) become fed up with their labors, and hold a demonstration in which they burn all their implements of manual labor.

However, as Assyriologist Gwendolyn Leick has explained in her overview of the Anunna or Anunnaki:

> The term has the general meaning of 'those of princely blood; royal offspring.' It seems to denote a collective of undifferentiated but senior gods, usually counted as fifty (in an older tradition as seven and in the *Enuma eliš* sixty). At some point it may have designated the sum total of the local numina of a city (*a-nun-na-eridu^{ki}-ninnu-bi*, 'The Fifty Anunna of Eridu,' in a hymn from Drehem).

> The Anunna first appear in Sumerian texts in the Ur III period as protective and interceding gods. [. . .] On the other hand they appear very frequently in literary compositions, hymns and prayers, myths and epics of all subsequent periods. Their function in these texts is ambiguous. They are said to have been the offspring of An, or at any rate after the great gods and before the minor deities which were instrumental in the differentiation of the created world and human beings (so for instance in *Enki and Ninmah* or in *Lahar and Ašnan*). They suffered great deprivations before the world was fully organized, they had to eat grass and were always hungry (Lahar and Ashnan) and they were burdened with heavy manual labour (Enki and Ninmah, Atra-hasis; in

the *Enuma Eliš* they built the city of Babylon for Marduk, since he was relieved from working by creating man). [. . .] Marduk also divided the Anunnaki into three hundred 'heavenly' and three hundred 'underworld' Anunnaki (*Enuma eliš*). In other compositions, they have much less clearly defined roles.[256]

It is the discussion of an ancient rebellion, as well as the textual evidence for Anunnaki who have been banished to the underworld by later gods, which causes the authors of *Hamlet's Mill* (and other scholars as well) to see in some aspects of the Anunnaki a parallel to the Titans of ancient Greece, who are later overthrown and sent down to Tartarus by the Olympian gods.

De Santillana and von Dechend see in this pattern (which appears in ancient myth again and again, in many different cultures) a description of the effects of the ages-long action of precession, which causes stars to "overstep their bounds" and which sends some constellations "down to the underworld" (by delaying their rising over a very long period best measured in centuries, and eventually by "holding them down" beneath the horizon on their customary date of rising). Of this pattern, which they see in the Titans of ancient Greece and in the Anunnaki of ancient Mesopotamia, as well as in the Asura of ancient India, the authors of *Hamlet's Mill* explain (beginning specifically with a quotation from Jane Ellen Harrison, 1850 - 1928, regarding the Titans):

> in the case of Jane Harrison who remarked upon the Titans: "They are constantly driven down below the earth to nethermost Tartaros and always reemerging. The very violence and persistence with which they are sent below shows that they belong up above. They rebound like divine

india-rubber balls." It is rather evident that these divine india-rubber balls were not really sent below: what was overthrown were the expired ages together with the names of their respective rulers.[257]

Thus, it is the inexorable turning of the celestial cycles which "imprisons below" the gods or beings who once reigned supreme, and their casting-down is not permanent, but there is always a promised return (as in the case of the figures of Osiris, or Kronos, or Saturn, or even King Arthur, who are banished to an underground or underwater cave, there to sleep away the ages, until the eventual and long-anticipated day of return). This pattern, found in many cultures, helps us to understand the oft-remarked-upon "ambiguity" of the Anunnaki, who in some texts appear to be associated with the gods who reign supreme, and in other texts with the gods who are cast down to the underworld, or who must labor and toil, but who eventually rebel and seek to return to their formerly exalted position, through violence if necessary.

It should be noted that in some texts, the number of the Anunnaki appears to have been seven -- the very same number as the Apkallu, who emerged from the deep in order to help mankind, only to return again to the deep (thus also falling into the same pattern noted above by Jane Ellen Harrison and later by the authors of *Hamlet's Mill*).

On the page opposite is aother bas-relief found at a temple in Nineveh during the ninenteenth century, sometimes thought to represent a category of Apkallu, and other times thought to represent a member of the Anunnaki (and, as we have just noted, in some ways there are parallels between the two groups of beings):

438

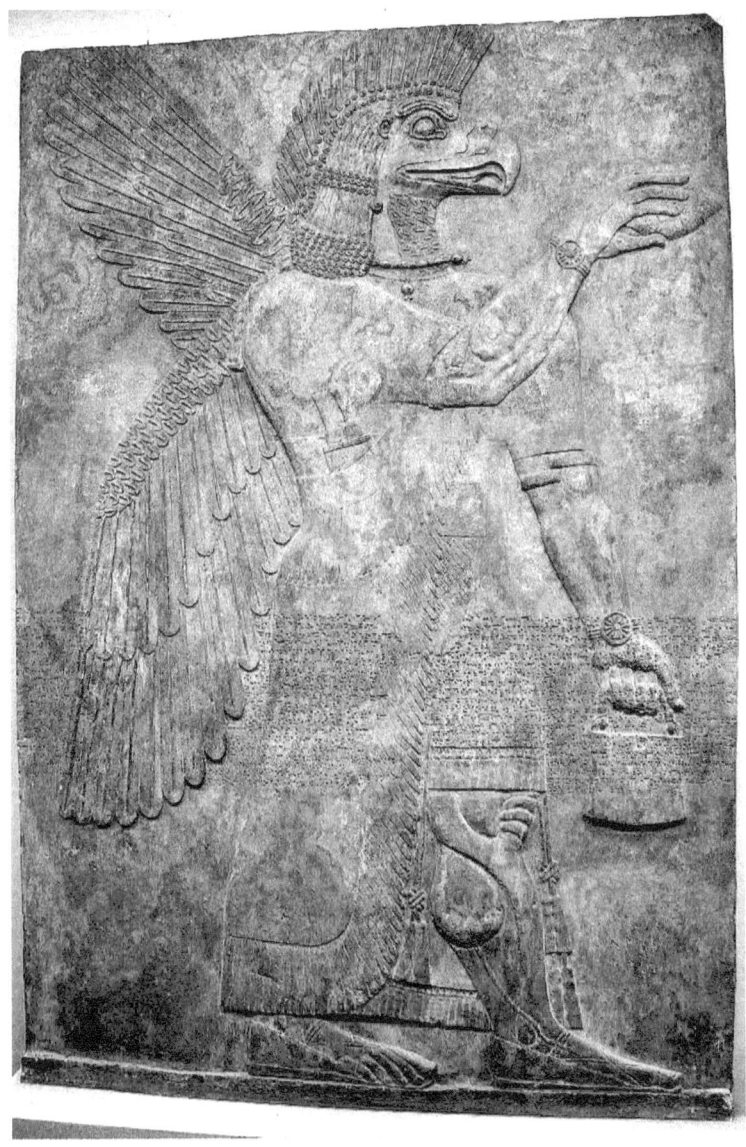

Note that in the image above, the eagle-headed being is holding
up a raised hand which holds an egg-shaped (or pinecone-shaped)
object: we have already established that this upraised hand with
egg-shape almost certainly corresponds to the "head-end" of the
western serpent-half of Ophiuchus, thus indicating that this
winged figure likely corresponds to that constellation in the sky.

439

The figure holds the distinctive "satchel" or "purse" in its lower hand, below the upraised hand holding the pinecone or egg. Now look at the outline of the constellation Ophiuchus, below, to which the outline of the nearby zodiac constellation of Libra has also been added:

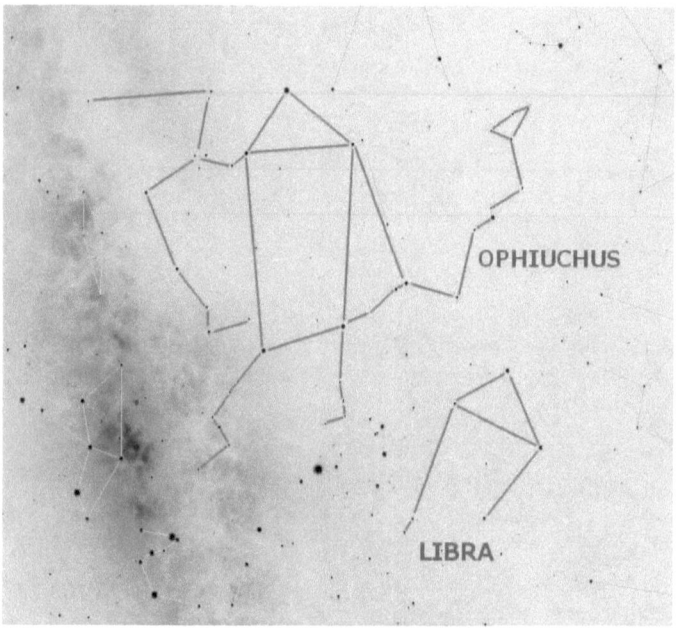

I would argue that the pinecone held in the upper hand definitively identifies this figure (and other ancient Mesopotamian figures holding the same pinecone or egg-shaped object in a raised hand) with Ophiuchus. You can see the "serpent-head" on the right side of the central body of Ophiuchus in the diagram above, corresponding to the egg or pinecone held by the Anunnaki or Apkallu figure in the ancient wall relief.

The double set of wings on the left of the ancient artwork (on the opposite side of the body from the upraised egg or pinecone) would thus correspond to the left half of the serpent of Ophiuchus (on the left of the central body as we face the chart above, which is the east as the constellation is seen in the heavens).

Finally, the all-important "satchel" or "purse" held by this figure (and many others like it found in other ancient Mesopotamian scenes) corresponds to the constellation Libra.

Note that the discovery of an Ophiuchus-figure holding a Libra-shaped implement is not unique among ancient myth: in *Star Myths of the World, Volume Three* (*Star Myths of the Bible*), we will see evidence that Michael the Archangel is also frequently depicted as holding Balances or Scales (associated with Libra), and that Michael himself is associated with Ophiuchus:

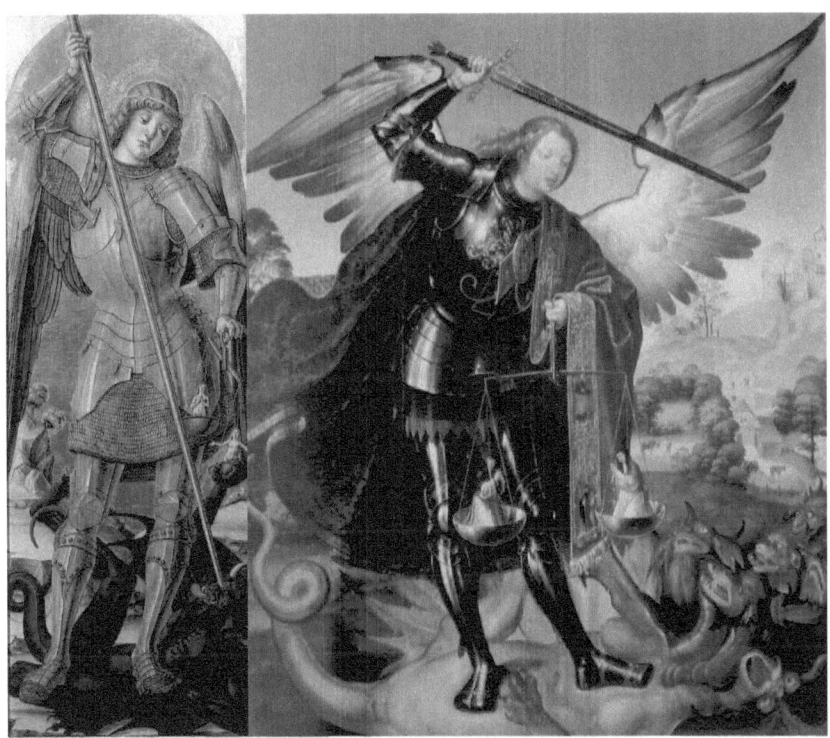

Above we see two depictions of Michael defeating the dragon (an episode described in the canonical book of Revelation, chapter 12). In both cases, we see the Archangel holding a set of Scales in his lower hand (on the right side of his body), just as the figures from ancient Mesopotamia hold a satchel or purse in the same area.

The dragon upon whom the Archangel is standing is of course the constellation Scorpio: Ophiuchus is located immediately above Scorpio in the heavens. This fact confirms the association of Michael the Archangel with Ophiuchus, and thus the fact that *Michael is often depicted holding Scales or Balances as well* indicates precedent for identifiying the "satchel" or "handbag" held by the ancient Ophiuchus-figures of Mesopotamia with the constellation Libra (just as the set of Scales held by Michael is clearly Libra).

Other figures from surviving ancient Mesopotamian artwork are depicted with the same upraised hand holding a pinecone or egg-shaped object, and lower hand holding a satchel or purse -- some of them with anthropomorphic heads rather than animal heads:

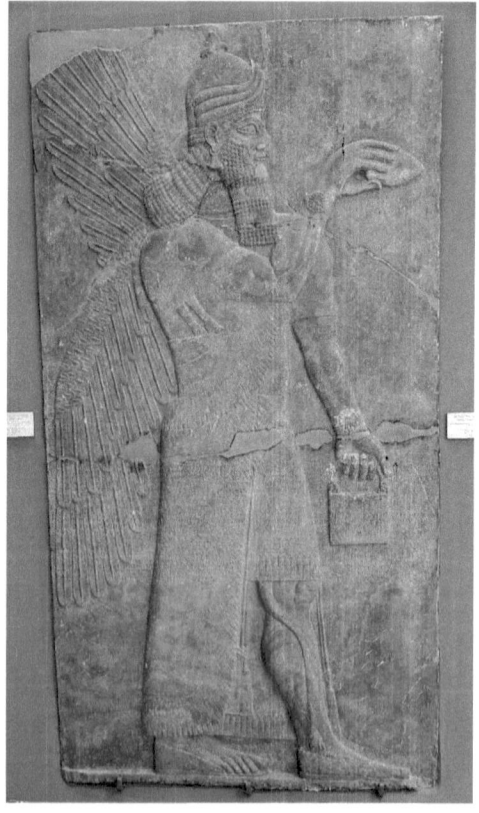

It should be clear that this artwork also corresponds to the outline of the constellation Ophiuchus (note that this figure, too, displays the double-wings on the side opposite the upraised hand and holds the satchel which corresponds to Libra).

Returning to our hypothesis regarding the identity of the portions of the night sky associated with Apsu and with Tiamat, in the "waters above" the Milky Way and the "waters below," respectively, it is possible that the changing status of the gods designated as the Anunnaki (sometimes associated with the high gods who created the Igigi, and other times cast down to the underworld, or split by Marduk between the heavens and the underworld) may have to do with this division above and below the Milky Way, and with the movement of precession which progressively brings some of the constellations in either realm into either the "upper half" or "lower half" of the year (based on the shift of the sun's background stars on the significant station-markers of the year, particularly spring equinox).

The fact that so many pieces of ancient artwork from Mesopotamia depict figures associated with Ophiuchus indicates the significance of this constellation -- a constellation sometimes referred to as the "thirtheenth zodiac sign" due to the fact that the path of the ecliptic (the path that the sun takes through the background of stars in a year, created by the plane of earth's own orbit) does in fact cross through the lower of the two "legs" of the constellation's outline, thus qualifying Ophiuchus as the thirteenth constellation through which the sun appears to travel each year (along with the twelve constellations of the conventional zodiac: Aries, Taurus, Gemini, Cancer, Leo, Virgo, Libra, Scorpio, Sagittarius, Capricorn, Aquarius, and Pisces). Ophiuchus is positioned just above Scorpio, and the leg of

Ophiuchus through which the sun passes projects down into the space between Scorpio and Sagittarius (it is the leg on the left or east), and the sun will thus cross the stars of ths leg of Ophiuchus in between its passage through Scorpio and its entry into Sagittarius:

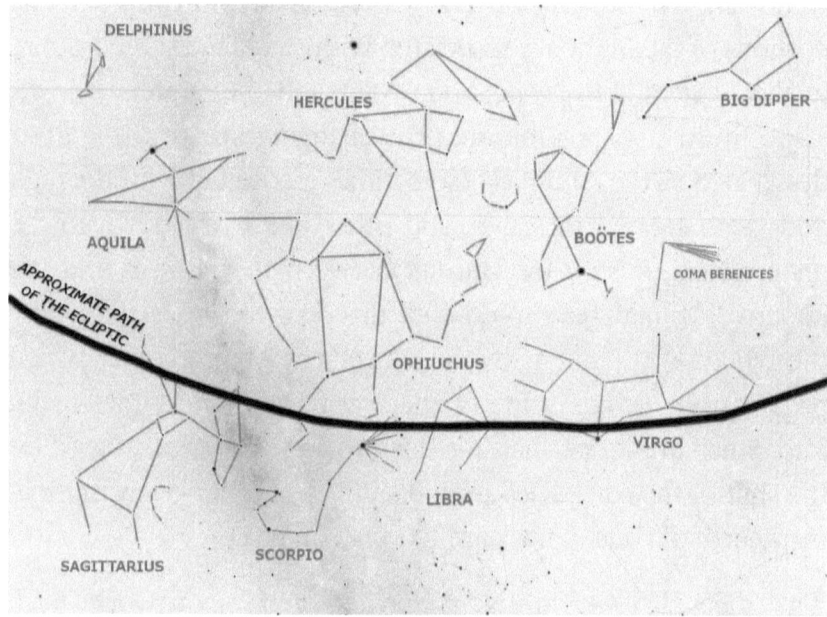

In the star-chart above, the approximate path of the ecliptic has been added. The earth's annual orbit around our sun will cause the sun to "move through" the background stars shown above, beginning on the right side of the chart as we face it and moving towards the left. You can see that our orbit will cause the sun to move through the background stars of Virgo before crossing through the background stars of Libra, then through the topmost part of the zodiac constellation of Scorpio, and then the sun's path will take it just past the "toe" of the first foot of Ophiuchus (the foot directly above the "head" of Scorpio) and then the path will cut right through the second (eastmost or leftmost) leg of Ophiuchus -- the leg that projects down into the space between

Scorpio and Sagittarius. Then, the sun's path will take it onwards towards Sagittarius and on to Capricorn beyond.

Thus, to revisit our earlier discussion about the motion of precession causing Sagittarius to be "plunged" down from its position marking the fall equinox (during the Age of Gemini) to a position which is *after* the fall equinox (and thus in the "lower half" of the year, the winter-solstice half of the year) during the Age of Taurus (see again pages 394 to 399), we can see from the preceding star-chart that such a shift could also be envisioned as plunging Ophiuchus down "below the line" of fall equinox along with Sagittarius (since the shift in precessional ages from the Age of Gemini to the Age of Taurus shifts the constellation marking the important day of fall equinox from Sagittarius into Scorpio). This fact may help to explain the nearly ubiquitous role of Ophiuchus as the constellation associated with figures who go down into the underworld, including Baldr in the Norse myths, Eurydice in the myths of ancient Greece, Osiris in the myths of ancient Egypt, and of course Jesus in the New Testament gospels (among others).

Before concluding this brief examination of the importance of Ophiuchus and the deities designated as the Anunnaki, we should note that in the surviving mythology of ancient Mesopotamia, it is the goddess Ishtar or Inanna who descends into the realm of the dead and returns triumphantly. In a text from the culture of ancient Sumer entitled *Inanna's Descent into the Underworld* (often referred to simply as "Inanna's Descent"), the goddess deliberately goes down to the underworld in order to claim power over that realm as well as the realm of heaven. Her original plan is not, strictly speaking, successful, but she left a "backup plan" with her attendant, Ninshubur, to come find her if she does not return after the appointed three days, and this plan is

445

successful, enabling Inanna to return from the dreaded realm of death. However, when Inanna first travels down into the underworld, clothed in multiple layers of protective garments or articles of jewelry or accessories (nine or seven layers), these layers are successively stripped off of her as she goes through the seven gates of the realm of death, until she arrives naked at the throne of the dread goddess Ereshkigal. Instead of arriving in power, therefore, she arrives in a compromised condition, and is turned into a corpse and hung up on a hook.

Which constellation would most likely represent the goddess Inanna in the underworld, when turned into a corpse and hung up on a hook? Turn back to any of the outlines of Ophiuchus shown in this book, such as that on page 444, and you will see that the "left serpent-half" (the tail-end of the serpent, on the east side of the central body of Ophiuchus) resembles a large hook at the top (we earlier argued that the same tail-half of the serpent might represent the great sickle or scythe of Kronos when he overthrows his father Ouranos -- a connection which I did not notice at first and which is thus slightly different from the interpretation offered in *Star Myths of the World, Volume Two*). This large hook-shaped feature on the left side of the outline of Ophiuchus almost certainly represents the hook upon which Inanna is hoisted in the underworld, and thus Inanna in this situation is associated with the constellation Ophiuchus (i.e., with the central body of the constellation) -- in much the same way as the other figures in world myth who go down into the underworld are associated with Ophiuchus, including Baldr (discussed in Volume Four of this series) and Osiris (discussed in the previous chapter) and Jesus at his Crucifixion, (discussed in Volume Three of this series, *Star Myths of the Bible*).

Indeed, amplifying our understanding of the importance of the figure of Ophiuchus in the myth-pattern of the god or goddess who is banished (at least for a time) to the underworld realm, the Anunnaki are described as being present at this scene of judgment of Inanna, when she is turned into a corpse and hung on the hook, and in fact participate in the judgment of the goddess.

Notably, when Inanna's attendant, Ninshubur, descends to the underworld to rescue Inanna from her predicament (after waiting three days as directed, and then going to various gods for help, and finding compassion only with the god Enki or Ea, who creates two genderless mourners to accompany Ninshubur to the underworld and help her revive Inanna), Ninshubur discovers the goddess Ereshkigal groaning in pain, as if in the throes of labor (childbirth) -- an indication that Ereshkigal probably corresponds to the figure of Virgo, which as we have already seen appears in many myths around the world as a woman in travail (because the constellation appears to be on its back, with legs elevated and apart, as with a woman in the act of delivering a baby).

If Ereshkigal goddess of death is associated with Virgo, then her sister Inanna is likely associated in some instances with Sagittarius, particularly when Inanna dresses in all her divine regalia before descending to the underworld (prior to being turned into a corpse and hung on the hook, in which situation she is associated with Ophiuchus). If so, then these two divine sisters (Ereshkigal and Inanna) fulfill the pattern mentioned previously regarding the "two mothers" or the "two divine sisters" (see extended quotation from Alvin Boyd Kuhn beginning on page 358 of this volume). The first (associated with Virgo) represents our first (physical) birth into a mortal body, destined to perish, while the second (associated with Sagittarius) represents our "second birth" or our "re-birth" -- our spiritual birth, marking the beginning of our spiritual elevation, and our re-integration with our divine nature.

When Ninshubur and the two genderless assistants created by Enki revivify Inanna, and before the goddess departs from the underworld, the Anunna declare that a substitute must be provided to take Inanna's place. The underworld entities suggest one substitute after another (including Inanna's attendant Ninshubur, and Inanna's son Shara), but Inanna refuses to consider any of these possibilities. Instead, continuing on her way back to the land of the living, Inanna selects her husband Dumuzi (also called Dumuzid, and also Tammuz), who far from mourning the apparent death of Inanna was dressed in his finest attire and sitting upon his throne.

Thus, Dumuzi becomes another dying god, although due to the compassion of his sister Geshtinanna, he only spends half of the year in the realm of the dead, Geshtinanna taking his place for the other half of the year. Although the authors of *Hamlet's Mill* argue that "there is doubt" regarding an identification of Dumuzi with Baldr or Osiris, they note the similarity of lamentation described in ancient times among all beings in all worlds at the death of each of these "dying god" figures (a similarity which suggests an association between them).[258] Further, as mentioned in *Star Myths of the World, Volume Four*, it is notable that the wife of the Norse god Baldr is named Nanna (very similar to both Inanna and Geshtinanna, the wife and sister of Dumuzi).[259] The weeping over Tammuz is even mentioned in the text of the book of Ezekiel in the Bible (in Ezekiel 8: 14).

Having discussed almost all of the allies of Tiamat in her battle with Marduk, there remains only to briefly mention the leader of her army -- Kingu, who becomes the consort of Tiamat. I'm not sure that there is enough detail in the texts themselves to be definitive in an identification of Kingu with a specific constellation. In the translation of Enuma Elish by L. W. King, we read (referring to Tiamat) that:

> She hath exalted Kingu; in their midst she hath raised [him] to power.
> To march before the forces, [to lead the host],
> [To] give the battle-signal, to advance [to the attack],
> [To direct] the battle, to control the [fight]. Tablet III, 38 - 41.[260]

I believe that it is at least a strong possibility that this figure, "raised to power" in the midst of *the host of Tiamat*, corresponds to the constellation Orion, if indeed we are correct in identifying the forces of Tiamat with the region "below" the Milky Way band in the heavens (on the south-celestial-pole side of the Milky Way). When first discussing this possibility, and in conjunction with the discussion of the star-chart presented on page 388, we noted that of all the constellations "below the Milky Way," Orion is the largest and most powerful in appearance (as opposed to the constellations "north of the Milky Way" which include the large and powerful-looking constellations Hercules and Ophiuchus, as well as the large but not as powerful-looking Boötes).

After the defeat of Tiamat, when the victorious gods allied with Marduk capture those who aligned themselves with Tiamat, Kingu is put on trial and charged with having incited Tiamat to violence. The gods cut Kingu's arteries and use the blood to fashion mortal men and women: the first people. If Kingu is associated with Orion, the draining of his blood fits a pattern that appears in other Orion-related myths, in which the long stream of the constellation Eridanus (originating near the front (westernmost) leg of Orion, is envisioned as blood or ichor draining from his body. I've found that other figures who are cut up and used to fashion the world may also be associated with Orion, such as Ymir in Norse mythology, and thus the use of Kingu's blood (mixed with earth) to make mankind may be consistent with his association with Orion -- although once again it is not completely certain. Note that in the ancient Mesopotamian myths, the body of Tiamat was also cut up to fashion the earth and its features, and also that in some versions of the creation of men and women, it appears that Marduk uses his own blood (rather than Kingu's) and in these versions Marduk only uses Kingu's bones.[261]

Note also that the text of Enuma Elish, Tablet VI, in recounting Marduk's decision to create mankind, has Marduk give the reason for mankind's creation in his own words:

> 7. "I will create man who shall inhabit [the earth],
> 8. That the service of the gods may be established, and that [their] shrines [may be built.]."[262]

As translator Leonard William King points out in a footnote to these lines in his 1902 translation, "It is interesting to note the reason that is here implied for the creation of mankind, i.e. that the gods may have worshippers."[263] Glaringly absent is any mention of creating men and women so that the gods may have substitutes to go down into the gold mines in order to retrieve gold for the repair of the atmosphere of the supposedly atmosphere-deficient planet Nebiru, as claimed by Sitchin and his followers.

Before moving on from the examination of the celestial metaphor present throughout Enuma Elish, the test to which the gods put Marduk when they invest him with sovereignty in preparation for his battle with Tiamat deserves brief mention. The text as translated by King, from Tablet IV of Enuma Elish, reads:

19. Then set they in their midst a garment,

20. And unto Marduk their first-born they spake:

21. "May thy fate, O lord, be supreme among the gods,

22. To destroy and to create; speak thou the word, and (thy command) shall be fulfilled.

23. Command now and let the garment vanish;

24. And speak the word again and let the garment reappear!"

25. Then he spake with his mouth, and the garment vanished;

26. Again he commanded it, and the garment reappeared.

27. When the gods, his fathers, beheld (the fulfilment of) his word,

28. They rejoiced, and they did homage (unto him, saying), "Marduk is king!"[264]

While there is not really enough detail in this passage to make definitive proclamations about positive celestial foundations for the garment-vanishing (and re-appearing) episode, it is possible to note that in other Star Myths I have examined previously, from other cultures of the world, when a garment is being "spread out" or "set in the midst" of a group, it can in other cases be shown quite convincingly to be associated with the Great Square of Pegasus. For example, in the Genesis account of the drunkenness of Noah, when Noah's sons Shem and Japheth walk backwards with a garment between them, over their shoulders, an abundance of evidence points to an identification of this garment with the Great Square. Thus, I believe it is at least possible that the garment in this "investiture of Marduk" scene may also be associated with the same Great Square.

If you are able to watch the stars cross the sky for yourself throughout the night, on successive nights throughout the year, you will realize that some constellations set when others are rising, and vice versa. While not precisely opposite to one another in the heavens such that their rising and setting are exactly opposite, the constellations of Hercules and Pisces (between whose two Fishes we find the asterism of the Great Square of Pegasus) are offset to such a degree that when Hercules is *rising* from the eastern horizon, the Great Square will have *just set* below the western horizon (as if being "commanded to disappear" by the arrival of Hercules, the constellation with which the god Marduk is most assuredly associated).

Similarly, for the "re-appearance" of the Great Square, the constellation Hercules will be reaching its zenith-point (its highest crossing point, as it passes due south for viewers in the northern hemisphere). This fact lends itself to the events of the text of Enuma Elish: Marduk is elevated to the position of king of the gods upon his demonstration of an ability to make the "garment" appear again.

Following the defeat of Tiamat (who is a personification of chaos), Marduk proceeds to establish the measures of the heavenly cycles (order), in the Fifth Tablet of Enuma Elish. He establishes the zodiac to divide the year, and he commands the god of the moon to determine the months and the days within each month. As Timothy J. Stephany observes in his introduction to Enuma Elish, this establishment of order out of chaos by the decree of Marduk is mirrored in the Genesis account by the decree of the God of the Bible during the creation text.[265]

It is noteworthy that the moon god of ancient Mesopotamia (whose name in Sumerian is Nanna, and in Akkadian his name is

Sin) is shown in one cylinder-seal in seated posture with extended arm, evocative of the outline of the constellation Virgo:

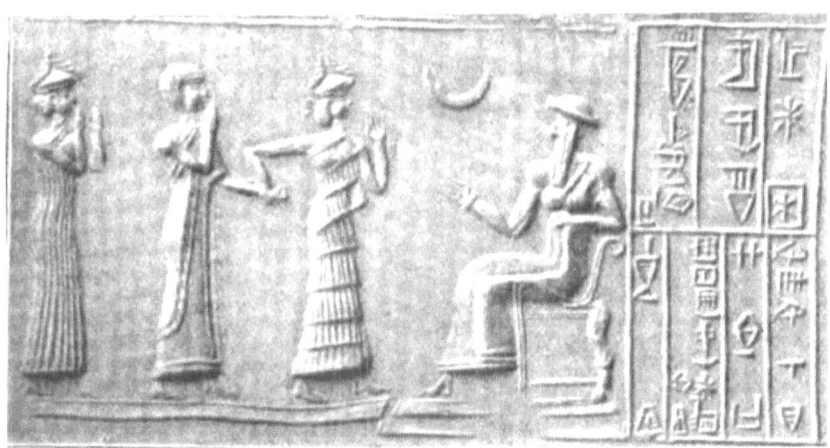

The cuneiform text on the seal itself indicates that the seal dates to the reign of Sumerian king Ur-Gur (or Ur-Nammu), who founded the famous Third Dynasty of Ur around 2112 BC. The god is seated on the right, and above his outstretched arm we see a crescent-moon shape. If the seated figure of the god in this ancient artwork is indeed related to the constellation Virgo (whose seated posture and outstretched arm create a very similar pattern in the heavens), then the crescent shape of the moon in this image would undoubtedly correspond to the arc of the Northern Crown.

There are similar examples of surviving artwork in which the sun-god Shamash is similarly depicted upon a throne with extended arm, and instead of the crescent moon of Sin, the radiating solar disc is depicted instead -- which almost certainly corresponds to the "whirling" form of the constellation Hercules, as we have now discussed many times. One example of such a depiction is presented below. These pieces of ancient artwork seem to indicate that, even though the sun god and moon god were

453

associated with the actual sun and moon in the heavens, aspects of these same gods were also visible in the constellations: the constellations whose outlines enable us to see the other gods of the Invisible Realm as well:

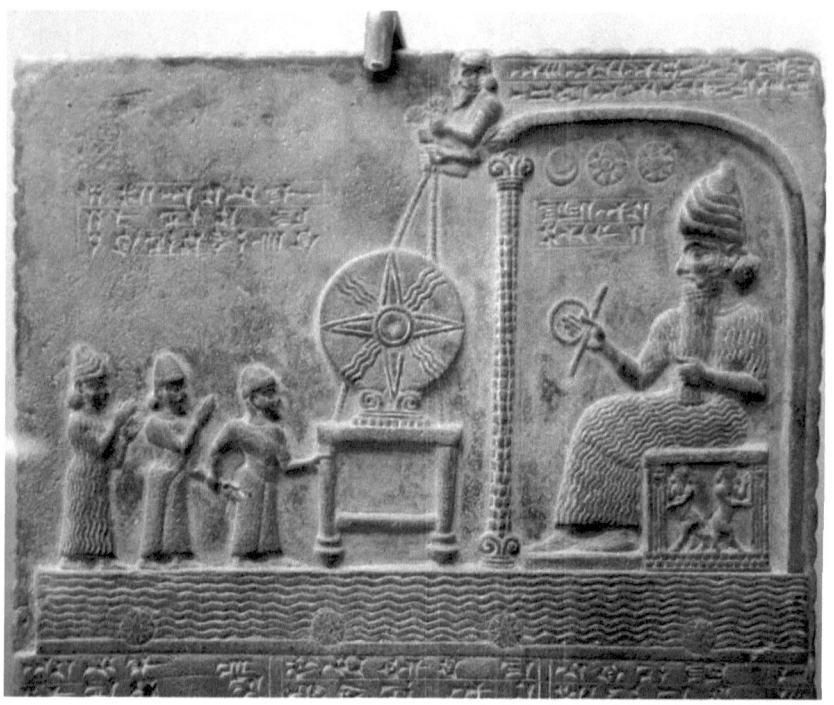

In the artwork above, the identification of the solar disc with the whirling form of the constellation Hercules is strengthened by the fact that it is depicted upon a table (suspended by a pair of triangular lines), which strongly suggests the outline of the central body of the constellation Ophiuchus, which consists of a tall rectangle (the table) surmounted by a triangle (the ropes).

Additionally, the identification of the seated god with the constellation Virgo is strengthened by the detail in the artwork of a small bearded figure holding a sprig of some type of vegetation. Because this small figure holding the leafy branch or branches is seen along a fairly direct line from the "outstretched arm" of the seated god, we can be reasonably confident that the sprig or branch in the artwork corresponds to the constellation Coma Berenices in the heavens, which means that the "outstretched arm" of the god on the throne corresponds to the outstretched arm of the constellation Virgo (whose outstretched arm points directly to the constellation Coma Berenices):

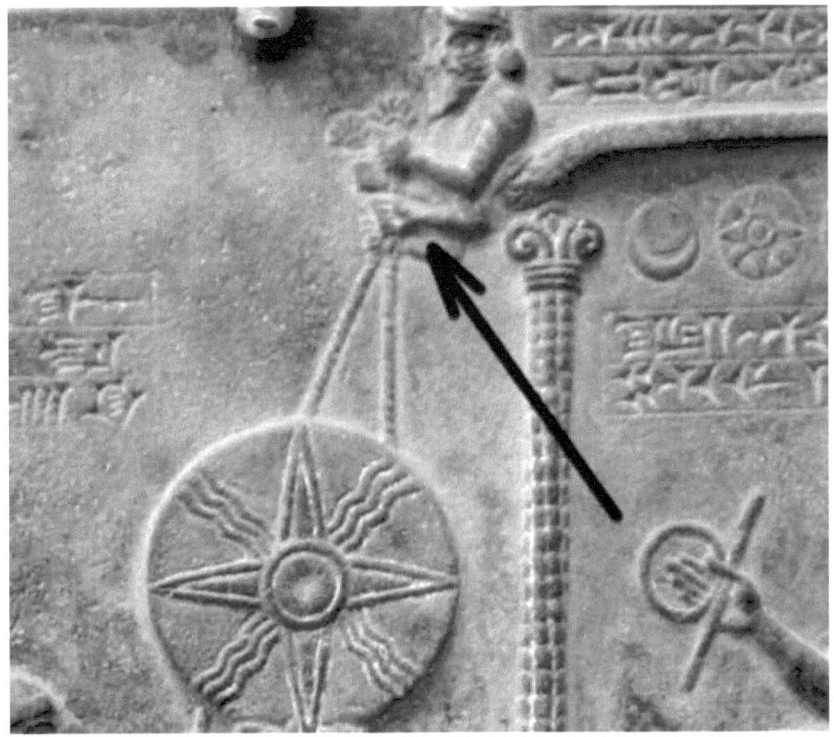

The conclusion of Enuma Elish is found in Tablet VII, and consists of the exaltation of Marduk by the other gods, after Marduk has defeated the forces of chaos and established the order of the heavens. They praise him with fifty titles of praise, and in conclusion the text of Enuma Elish declares:

123. By the name of "Fifty" did the great gods

124. Proclaim his fifty names, they made his path pre-eminent.

125. Let them be held in remembrance, and let the first man proclaim them;

126. Let the wise and the understanding consider them together![266]

The association of Marduk with the number fifty is noteworthy, because we can see echoes of this ancient association in other myth-systems, particularly in ancient Greece and Rome, where the figure of the hero Heracles (who is, obviously, associated like Marduk with the same constellation Hercules) has some association with the number fifty as well.

One manifestation of the connection between Heracles and the number fifty is found in the myth of the hero while still a youth just reaching adulthood, in which he learned of a king, named Thespius, who was seeking someone to slay a lion that was troubling the region. Heracles was happy to oblige, and while he was staying in the land of Thespiae in his quest to kill the lion, the king sent in his fifty daughters, one at a time, to sleep with the young hero.

The story is related in the *Bibliotheca* (or "Library") attributed to Apollodorus and probably written in the 2nd century AD, and in that version the author explains that the young hero was unaware that each night he was sleeping with a different maiden (Book 2, section 4). The same episode is also found in the *Bibliotheca historia* of Diodorus Siculus, which has been mentioned previously (see page 158), and which was probably written in the first century BC. In the account of Diodorus, each of the fifty daughters had a son by Heracles, who when they had grown to the threshold of manhood themselves went to Sardinia to found a colony, as had been directed by an oracle (see Book 4, section 29).

456

This story regarding the fifty sons of Heracles (and the fifty princesses with whom he slept, while slaying his first lion) seems to preserve some ancient association between the *constellation Hercules* and the *number fifty*, a connection which also surfaces in the fifty names given to the god Marduk.

Notable in the account of Apollodorus is the detail that, after slaying this first lion, young Heracles dresses himself in the skin of the animal, wearing its scalp over his head like a helmet. Most ancient artwork depicting Heracles shows the hero wearing the skin of a lion, with its scalp over his own head. The lion-head around the hero's head helps, along with the hero's full beard, to make the head of Heracles look quite square -- appropriate because one of the most distinctive aspects of the constellation Hercules is its square-shaped head. This "keystone" shape in the constellation is indeed its most recognizable feature in the night sky. Figures associated with the constellation Hercules will thus often have some aspect which makes their head appear square, whether a full beard (as with the figures of Zeus and of Heracles himself, as well as Thor in the Norse myths) or a kind of "fringe" or "ruff" (such as the fringe of serpents depicted on the heads of Gorgons in ancient artwork, almost resembling a square beard).

We will see a figure clad in the skin of a lion in the most famous ancient Mesopotamian myth as well, to which we will now turn.

The Gilgamesh Cycle and Atrahasis

Having now examined numerous pieces of evidence from the text of Enuma Elish (as well as related texts dealing with the Descent of Inanna and also with the identities of the Apkallu and the Anunnaki) which should establish beyond all reasonable doubt that the mythology of ancient Sumer and later descendant Mesopotamian civilizations employs the same system of celestial metaphor that we have seen in operation in other myths from around the globe, we can now proceed to examine a few of the celestial aspects of the myth-cycle which forms one of the earliest surviving epics in all of human literature: the Gilgamesh epic.

As Professor Andrew George of the University of London's School of Oriental and African Studies (SOAS) explains in the introduction to his 1999 translation of the various surviving texts containing the epic of Gilgamesh, a wide variety of ancient tablets from different periods and written in different languages have been discovered to contain portions of texts dealing with the exploits of Gilgamesh, but there are some significant variations in the narratives, and large gaps remain in all of the accounts, even in the most complete Gilgamesh narrative to survive. Professor George writes:

> Literary compositions that tell the story of Gilgamesh come down to us from several different periods and in several different languages. Some modern renderings disregard the enormous diversity of the material, so that the reader forms a mistaken impression of the epic's contents and state of preservation.[267]

The name of Gilgamesh appears in lists of deities in inscriptions going back as far as 2400 BC or even a couple of centuries earlier, and he is mentioned as a favorite god by Sumerian kings during the Third Dynasty of Ur (Ur III). We have fragments of five Sumerian texts containing portions of a Sumerian version of the Gilgamesh epic which were copied out, in the original Sumerian language, by later scribes in the Babylonian schools, where texts about the semi-divine hero were popular for practicing cuneiform and the art of textual inscription (around the year 1800 BC). In Sumerian, the central figure is called Bilgames rather than Gilgamesh, and the name of the mighty guardian of the Cedar Forest whose identity we will explore in more detail presently is named Huwawa, rather than Humbaba as he is called in the later Babylonian versions which have survived and which are more well-known than the Sumerian fragments. The original source of these Sumerian texts may have been the Ur III period, from around 2114 BC to 2004 BC.

The most well-known telling of the Gilgamesh epic comes from Babylonian versions, particularly one known as "He who saw the Deep," which is our most complete text of a version of the Gilgamesh epic (although even this one has several significant gaps in the text). It is often referred to as the Standard Version, and is believed to have been composed between 1100 BC and 1000 BC. Another much earlier Akkadian version, known as "Surpassing all other kings," dates back to 1700 BC but survives today only in fragments. Of the differences between the various versions and texts to have survived, Professor George writes:

> Like the Babylonian epic, the Sumerian poems of Gilgamesh are still in the process of reconstruction from hundreds of fragments of clay tablets stored in museums in many different countries. The more text that is recovered, the more one can observe the stark differences between the Sumerian poems and the Babylonian epic, and the more also one can

appreciate how skilfully the Old Babylonian poet of the latter worked into a seamless whole the traditional themes and stories that were his raw material. This is not to say that the poet of the Babylonian epic must have had the Sumerian poem before him, but he knew them, or something very similar, at least in outline.[268]

We will examine just a few of the celestial and esoteric aspects of the Gilgamesh cycle, based primarily on the Standard Version, and conclude with an examination of the figure of Uta-napishtim, who becomes the subject of an urgent quest undertaken by Gilgamesh towards the end of the epic. Uta-napishtim, who survived the Deluge, has previously been mentioned in this volume. He is related to similar persons named Ziusudra and Atrahasis in other texts from ancient Mesopotamia: we will conclude our examination of the Mesopotamian myths with a brief introduction to these ancient figures.

When the epic of Gilgamesh begins, the hero Gilgamesh is king in the city of Uruk (sometimes spelled Erech by modern authors), a great city north of Ur along the Euphrates River, in the southern region of Mesopotamia, in the heart of ancient Sumer. Gilgamesh, we are told, is two-thirds divine and one-third human: his mother is the goddess Ninsun, and his father the god Lugulbanda.

The opening of the Standard Version evokes the glory of ancient Uruk, the glory of its king who is described as without rival in kingly standing, taller and more powerful than all other men, his form drawn out by the Lady of the Gods and by the divine Nudimmud (also known as Enki or Ea). The opening of the poem also makes reference to the wisdom Gilgamesh eventually achieved during a life of wide and often weary traveling in search of secret and hidden knowledge, gaining "the sum of all wisdom," including wisdom from one who survived the great Deluge.[269]

However, at the outset of the poem, we see that Gilgamesh as king of Uruk caused great resentment among the people, by hassling the young men without cause, letting no son go free to his father (perhaps forcing them into his army, or into other involuntary servitude of some sort, or perhaps simply challenging them to combat -- the text is not specific, although it does say that when he takes up his weapons, no one is the equal of Gilgamesh), as well as letting no maiden go free to her bridegroom (demanding the right to have sex with all young brides first).

Because of this behavior, the fathers and mothers of the city appeal to the gods and goddesses, and their complaints are heard by the rulers of heaven.

The gods decide to fashion a companion for Gilgamesh, one mighty in strength, who can vie with Gilgamesh and occupy his overabundant energy, and they appeal to the goddess Aruru, who according to the Babylonian epic that we call the Standard Version was the great one who created mankind in the first place. The text tells us that Aruru washes her hands, takes some clay, and fashions a hero named Enkidu, whom she sets down in the wilderness, far from the habitation of others.

Of Enkidu, the text says:

> All his body is matted with hair,
> he bears long tresses like those of a woman:
> the hair of his head grows thickly as barley,
> he knows not a people, nor even a country.
>
> Coated in hair like the god of the animals,
> with the gazelles he grazes on grasses,

461

> *joining the throng* with the game at the water-hole,
> his heart *delighting* with the beasts in the water. (I. 105 - 112)²⁷⁰

This wild man who lives among the beasts of the fields is discovered by a young trapper, who comes upon Enkidu at the water-hole, surrounded by the herds of animals who also came to drink. The trapper goes back to his father and tells him what he has seen, that he has previously seen Enkidu's footprints at the watering-hole, and that the wild man has been pulling up the trapper's snares and freeing any beasts that have been caught.

The trapper's father gives his son a plan of action: do not rely on the strength of any man to solve the problem, but instead go into the city of Uruk and ask Shamhat the temple prostitute (her name means "something between 'good looking' and 'well endowed'" according to the glossary in the translation by Andrew George; in earlier texts her name is *Shamkutam*) to come with him to the wild: when she exposes her beauty to the wild man he will be unable to resist her, and after being with her, the animals will then shun him.²⁷¹ That outcome, presumably, would solve the problem of Enkidu releasing the game from the trapper's snares.

So the trapper goes to Uruk, and appeals to Gilgamesh the king. He explains to the king what is going on, describing Enkidu as being "as mighty as a rock from the sky" (the same formula used just a few stanzas earlier to describe Gilgamesh king of Uruk), and complaining that the wild man is filling in all the pits that are dug to catch the herds, pulling up all the snares, and generally releasing any game that has been captured.²⁷²

Speaking almost the same words used by the trapper's father, Gilgamesh advises leaving this situation to the beautiful Shamhat, and so at the king's command, the trapper and the prostitute head out into the wilderness, to wait by the water-hole.

When the herds of animals arrive at the water-hole, Enkidu among them, everything happens as predicted. In the translation of Andrew George, we read:

> Shamhat unfastened the cloth of her loins,
> she bared her sex and he took in her charms.
> She did not recoil, she took in his scent:
> she spread her clothing and he lay upon her.
>
> She did for the man the work of a woman,
> his passion caressed and embraced her.
> For six days and seven nights
> Enkidu was erect, as he coupled with Shamhat.
>
> When with her delights he was fully sated,
> he turned his gaze to his herd.
> The gazelles saw Enkidu, they started to run,
> the beasts of the field shied away from his presence.
>
> Enkidu had defiled his body so pure,
> his legs stood still, though his herd was in motion.
> Enkidu was weakened, could not run as before,
> but now he had *reason*, and wide understanding. (I. 188 - 202)[273]

Shamhat tells Enkidu that he is handsome, and just like a god. Why is he dwelling in the wild with the beasts, she asks him -- and she urges him to go to Uruk-the-Sheepfold, where the gods Anu and Ishtar are present in the temple, and where Gilgamesh the powerful king is perfect in strength, like a great wild bull.

Instinctively sensing that he should find a friend, Enkidu agrees to accompany Shamhat. He declares that he will challenge this Gilgamesh, whose strength is like a wild bull -- but Shamhat replies that Gilgamesh is beloved of the gods, and that moreover

Chapter Fifteen

Gilgamesh has already seen Enkidu in dreams: the two are going to become the closest of companions. Shamhat and Enkidu then make love again, and when they are ready to embark on the journey to Uruk, the text tells us that she strips off her clothes and gives part of her garment to Enkidu, and wears the other part herself.

This detail in the text of the Gilgamesh epic should ring a bell with readers who have read through this volume so far (or other volumes in this series, such as Volume Two about the mythology of ancient Greece). We have earlier noted a persistent pattern in which a female figure gives her garment to a male figure, often at the beginning of his journey (see the discussion in this volume beginning on page 220, focused on the sash given to Odysseus by the goddess Leucotheia at the beginning of his long journey home, and the parallels of this episode in the Odyssey with the depictions of Christ at his baptism at the beginning of his earthly ministry, as well as parallels to the sash given to Sir Gawaine in the story of *Gawaine and the Green Knight*).

I would argue that this detail in the story of Gilgamesh is no mere "throwaway line," but rather that it is a possible clue that the powerful figure of Enkidu may have an association with the constellation Ophiuchus, a figure in the sky who can be seen as "wearing a sash" (the two "serpent-halves" on either side of the constellation's central body being envisioned as the sash).

If so, then it is possible that the beautiful Shamhat corresponds to the heavenly form of the constellation Virgo, in close proximity to Ophiuchus and indeed lying on her back with legs spread apart in the direction of Ophiuchus. If this association between Virgo and Shamhat is correct, then it is possible that when she is described in the text as taking off her garments and lying down on them, the

464

long form of the constellation Hydra is envisioned as her garments on the ground beneath her. We will see other examples in which Hydra may play the role of clothing belonging to a female Virgo-figure, which has been stripped off.

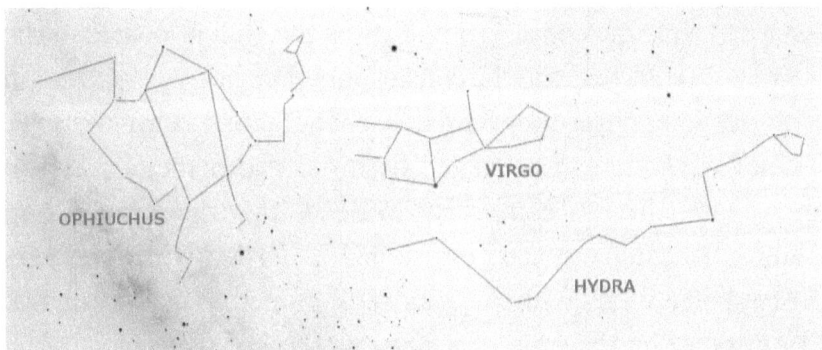

It should be noted, however, that (as we have just argued in the previous chapter), a garment which is laid out or spread out in myth will often be found to correspond to the Great Square of Pegasus. In that case, Shamhat would probably correspond to the constellation Andromeda, rather than Virgo, and Enkidu might then be associated with the constellation Perseus.

This interpretation does have some arguments in its favor. First, the head of the constellation Perseus actually projects into the band of the Milky Way in this part of the sky -- which would conform to the description of Enkidu coming to the watering-hole with the beasts of the field, and bringing his head down to the water to drink like an animal.

Additionally, the animals most frequently mentioned as accompanying Enkidu when he lives in the wild are gazelles, and it is possible that the Ram of Aries could play a gazelle. Aries has some faint stars which could be connected to give this constellation backwards-curving horns like a gazelle. Another animal mentioned in conjunction with Enkidu's rearing among the beasts of the wild is the wild ass. Gilgamesh later in the poem declares of Enkidu that Enkidu's mother was a gazelle, and his father was a wild ass, and that Enkidu was nursed on the milk of wild asses (Tablet VIII, lines 3 - 5).

As it happens, the constellation Taurus the Bull is located in the heavens directly beneath the constellation Perseus, a constellation with two long horns (appropriately enough, for a heavenly Bull). These *long horns* can alternately be envisioned as the *long ears* of an ass, and there is compelling evidence that the constellation Taurus the Bull was also envisioned as an ass with long ears (instead of as a bull with long horns) in numerous ancient myths. For instance, in the story of Samson in the Old Testament book of Judges, when Samson grasps the "jawbone of an ass," it is almost positive that Samson is Orion grasping the V-shaped Hyades, in the constellation Taurus (instead of being the jawbone of a bull, this V-shaped implement is called the jawbone of an ass in that story). Also, in the story of Balaam and the Ass in the book of Numbers, it can be shown beyond any doubt that the ass which Balaam rides is associated with the constellation Taurus (envisioned as an ass) and that Balaam himself is associated with the constellation Perseus.

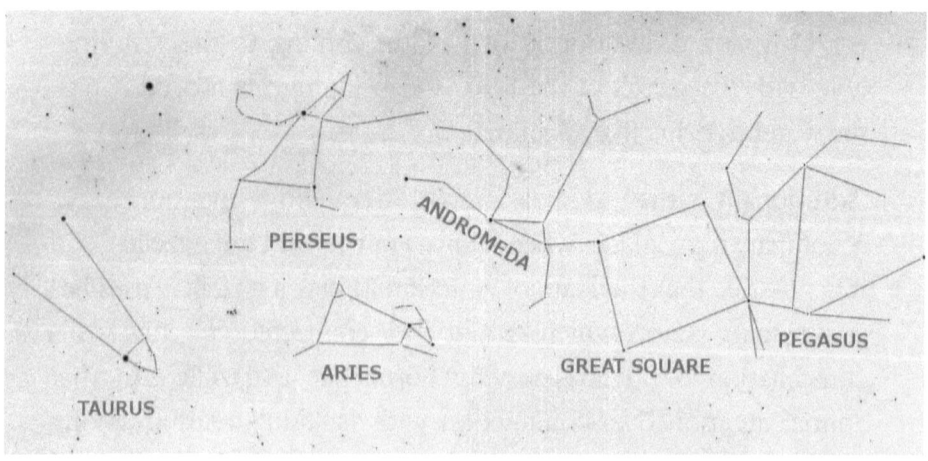

Due to the presence of both a "gazelle" (seen in the constellation Aries) and a "wild ass" (seen in the constellation Taurus) in close proximity to Perseus and Andromeda, I believe that this interpretation of the encounter between Enkidu and Shamhat is also quite plausible. The two regions of the sky are both a very good fit for the story of Enkidu and Shamhat, and I believe we should leave open the possibility that the ancient myths incorporated aspects of both connections.

Indeed, it is even possible that the first time Shamhat encounters Enkidu, when he comes to the watering hole among the beasts of the field (gazelles and perhaps also wild asses), he is associated with Perseus, a constellation which can be seen to be "dunking its head" in the band of the Milky Way (along with the long-horned or long-eared constellation Taurus):

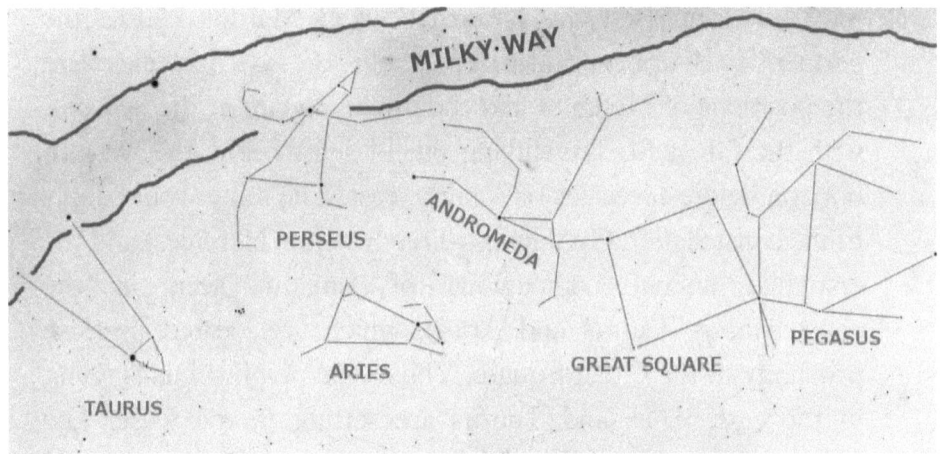

Perseus is in close proximity to both Aries and Taurus, as can be seen in the star-chart above. It is at this point, perhaps, that Shamhat first seduces Enkidu, and the two have intercourse for the first time. We see Shamhat represented in the form of Andromeda, her legs towards Perseus (elevated and parted) and her "garment" spread out behind her (in the form of the Great Square).

467

Chapter Fifteen

After their time together, however, Enkidu finds that the beasts of the field no longer associate with him: he has lost his innocence and purity, and now (perhaps) has descended to a different region of the Milky Way, to be associated with Ophiuchus. He continues to have sexual relations with Shamhat, now seen in the constellation Virgo, and she dresses him in part of her garment (the two serpent-halves of Ophiuchus, which fill the role of the *female garment given to other figures* associated with Ophiuchus in myth, such as Odysseus when his raft is destroyed by Poseidon and he is visited by the goddess Leucotheia, or Sir Gawaine in the story of the Green Knight, who is given a sash or girdle by the beautiful Lady Bertilak).

Now that he is associated with Ophiuchus, Enkidu finds that the animals who were once his companions all flee from him. We have just discussed the idea that when Marduk causes the garment to disappear and reappear, this episode may allegorize the positions of Hercules and the Great Square in the heavens, with the Great Square sinking out of sight below the western horizon before Hercules rises in the east. The same would apply to the constellation Ophiuchus (directly below Hercules) and the erstwhile animal companions of Enkidu (seen in the constellations Taurus and Aries), which are located in close proximity to the Great Square. Thus, when Ophiuchus is rising in the east, Aries and Taurus are setting in the west. The poignant depiction of Enkidu's loss of contact with the untamed realm of nature is depicted in the motions of the stars!

Note that the text informs us that Enkidu has both gained something and lost something as a result of his entry into a new world. He has lost his original purity and innocence -- his unconscious or uncontrived connection with nature -- while at the same time he has gained "reason" and "wide understanding." In psychological or even Freudian terms, it is as if the poem is depicting the *development* of our ego-mind, our reasoning mind, essential for functioning in a world with other men and women, and with that development the *simultaneous loss* of deep connection with our subconscious mind, our primal mind, our mind that is connected to the world of nature and which functions in harmony with the natural world and the cosmos. It is a loss or a disconnection which the ancient myths portray with many powerful metaphors, but perhaps none so ingenious as the portrayal of the change we see in Enkidu at this moment, when he can no longer keep up with the beasts of the field, and when the natural world no longer welcomes him but flees from him. Enkidu has learned the rules to a new game, but in doing so finds himself excluded from the old game. In this, his condition mirrors our own, showing us our own internal division and disconnection.

The reconnection to and reintegration with that part of ourselves which we have lost or forgotten will be the focus of many myths -- indeed, it is a central theme in all the myths we have encountered thus far, and in the myths which will be examined subsequently as we continue our tour through the Star Myths of the world.

As they journey to the city of Uruk, Enkidu and Shamhat come to a shepherd's camp, where the shepherds remark to one another that Enkidu is very much the same build as Gilgamesh, tall and proud as a battle-tower, and mighty as a rock from the sky. This comparison to a battlement or tower is a second clue that Enkidu might be associated with the constellation Ophiuchus (in addition to the earlier clue about wearing part of the garment of Shamhat). The constellation Ophiuchus resembles a great wall or tower, and will often be seen to play such a role in other Star Myths from other cultures as we progress through this multi-volume series.

The shepherds bring out bread and ale to set before Gilgamesh: Andrew George translates the text into English as "bread and ale," although other translators say "bread and wine," including Gerald J. Davis (2014), John Gardner and John Maier (1984), and Morris Jastrow and Albert Tobias Clay (1920).

Of course, if the meal given by the shepherds to Enkidu is *bread and wine*, then this scene appears to have some strong resonance with other famous bread and wine episodes in other ancient texts, including the encounter between Abram, later re-named Abraham, and Melchizedek in Genesis chapter 14, and of course the scene of the Last Supper in the gospel accounts of the New Testament.

In any case, the text of the Standard Version of the Gilgamesh epic informs us that Enkidu is initially hesitant to take the offering of food and drink from the shepherds, until Shamhat reassures him -- after which he eats the bread and downs seven goblets of the liquor! The drink has its effect on Enkidu -- the text tells us that his heart became merry and his face lit up, and he began to sing.[274]

The outline of Ophiuchus can be envisioned as holding a goblet: the "head-end" of the western serpent-half, which does indeed resemble a traditional wine-glass or goblet, and which appears as a goblet in many different myths around the globe. And, as we will see in *Star Myths of the World, Volume Three*, there are numerous reasons for seeing an association between Melchizedek (who brings forth bread and wine to give to Abram in Genesis 14: 18) and the figure of Ophiuchus in the heavens -- just as there are numerous reasons to see a connection between the figure of Ophiuchus and the figure of Jesus at the Last Supper in the gospel accounts.

470

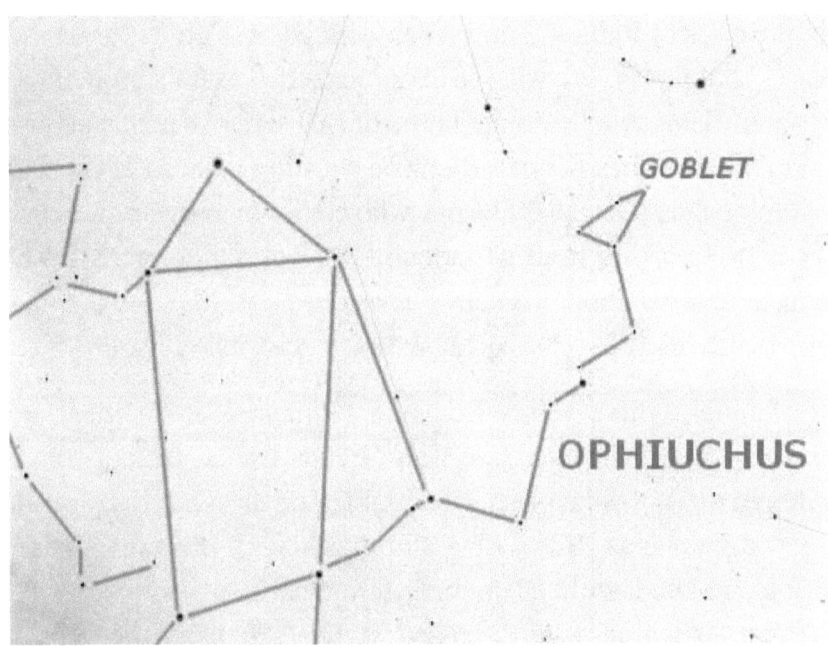

Thus, whatever the specific type of liquor brought forth by the shepherds to give to Enkidu in the Gilgamesh text, it is likely that we have here yet another indication of a possible connection between Enkidu and Ophiuchus.

Immediately following the verses which tell us how merry Enkidu became from drinking the seven goblets, the text informs us that:

> The barber groomed his body so hairy,
> anointed with oil he turned into a man.
> He put on a garment, became like a warrior,
> he took up his weapon to do battle with lions.[275]

The parallels to the story of Samson and Delilah in the book of Judges should be fairly obvious here -- and I am quite convinced that the same constellation plays the role of the "barber" who grooms the hairy body of Enkidu as that which plays the man Delilah calls upons to shear off the long uncut locks of the sleeping Samson in Judges 16: 19.

In the book of Judges, Samson is described as sleeping "upon the knees" of Delilah. We will see in our extended examination of the story of Samson in Volume Three of this series that this almost certainly describes Scorpio (Samson), resting its head at the feet of Ophiuchus (Delilah). The one who comes in to shear the *seven locks* of Samson's head is undoubtedly Sagittarius, the stars of which constellation (usually envisioned as a bow) could apparently also be seen as great shears or scissors!

Intriguingly, these verses from the Gilgamesh cycle (they are actually found in the so-called "Pennsylvania tablet," often referred to as "Gilgamesh P," a tablet of the Old Babylonian version known as "Surpassing all other kings") mention Enkidu being anointed with oil immediately after the mention of the barber. As will also be discussed in *Star Myths of the World, Volume Three*, the constellation Sagittarius is associated with pouring out oil and anointing with oil. Thus, these verses from the Old Babylonian version of Gilgamesh (the "Surpassing all other kings" version, dated back to around 1700 BC) provides important confirmation of the identification of the "barber" in both the Gilgamesh and Samson stories with the constellation Sagittarius.

Note the ease with which the ancient epic illustrates the transformation in Enkidu with regard to the world of nature: after sleeping with Shamhat, drinking with the shepherds, receiving a haircut and being anointed with oil, he now takes up his weapon to protect the flocks against lions. Once part of the natural world, he is now taking up his weapon against it.

Later on, the text tells us that a certain traveler was on his way to Uruk-the-Sheepfold to attend a wedding, perhaps of one of his friends or relatives. We don't know much about this young man on his way to the wedding whose route towards Uruk brings him past the camp of the shepherds (the text is fragmented at this point and there is a "lacuna" -- a "gap" or "hole" in the text due to damage to the surviving tablet; the word is related to the word "lagoon").

In any case, the text tells us that Enkidu and Shamhat were having their pleasure together when Enkidu lifted his eyes and noticed the man (perhaps the traveler was walking down the road to Uruk). He informs Shamhat that he wants to know where this man is going, so she calls out to the traveler, and goes up to speak to him, asking why he is hurrying so and where he is going.

The traveler informs them that he has been invited to a wedding, and further explains that as is customary in Uruk-the-Town-Square, Gilgamesh the king will go in to visit the bride and have intercourse with the wife-to-be, before the bridegroom himself. At this news, Enkidu's face grows furious, and he immediately sets off towards the city to confront the king. Shamhat follows.

When the pair reaches the town square of Uruk, a crowd gathers around them and immediately begin talking amongst themselves about Enkidu. Their words are related using a formula that has been related previously in the poem, such as when Enkidu and Shamhat arrive at the shepherd camp. The townspeople declare:

> "In build he is the image of Gilgamesh,
> but shorter in stature, and bigger of bone.
> For [sure it's the one who] was born in the uplands,
> animals' milk is what he was suckled on."[276]

Thus the translation of Professor George; a more literal 1920 translation of this passage from the "Surpassing all other kings" version preserved on the Pennsylvania Tablet, reads:

"Like the form of Gish he has suddenly become;
shorter in stature.
[In his structure high (?)], powerful,
. . . . overseeing (?)
In the land strong of power has he become.
Milk of cattle
He was accustomed to suck."[277]

The use of the shorter name "Gish" for "Gilgamesh" is indicative of the many forms the name of the semi-divine hero takes in different versions of the myth-cycle from different centuries and different parts of Mesopotamia. His name appears as *Gish*, and as *Gish-bil*, and as *Gish-bil-ga-mesh*, and as *Bilgamesh*, in addition to appearing as other variations.[278]

This description of Enkidu as being *like in form to Gilgamesh*, though *shorter in stature*, yet in structure *tall and powerful and overseeing*, may be clues to the celestial identity of Enkidu, probably referring again to Ophiuchus, a constellation which plays the role of a tall tower in some of the world's Star Myths, and indeed as a "far-seeing" tower in the Norse mythology, where (as discussed in Volume Four of this series) the constellation is associated with the Hlidskjálf of Odin: the High Seat or High Shelf, where Odin can ascend in order to see all things happening in the nine Norse worlds.

The first encounter between Gilgamesh and Enkidu is preserved in Tablet II of the Standard Version (with some lacunae), and in the Pennsylvania Tablet (Gilgamesh P). The wedding bed is all laid out, and the goddess of weddings has been invited to the consummation of the nuptials. But Enkidu blocks the door of the wedding-house with his foot, and does not allow Gilgamesh to enter. We can imagine the two staring at one another for a tense moment, before suddenly they lock in combat at the doorway of the wedding-house, in the Square of Uruk.

The text of Gilgamesh P tells us that they: "Seized (each other). Like oxen they fought" (P223 - 224).[279] At the wrestling of these two mighty combatants, the wall trembles and the threshold is demolished. Eventually, the verses inform us, Gilgamesh bends his knee to the ground, and his wrath is appeased (P227 - 229).

The setting in which this wrestling takes place is almost certainly the "doorway" formed by the constellation Ophiuchus itself, which plays the role of a gate, doorway, or other portal in many Star Myths. Additionally, the text itself tells us that the encounter takes place before the wedding-house or wedding pavilion for the bride and groom, which would also indicate Ophiuchus. The fact that Enkidu is *also* associated with Ophiuchus, as we've already been noticing, is not a problem for the ancient myths -- constellations often play more than one role in the same Star Myth without any apparent difficulty -- and the fact that the text tells us that Enkidu blocks the entrance to the wedding-house with his foot is a nice touch, if indeed (as I strongly suspect) both the *wedding-house* and *Enkidu* are both associated with the constellation Ophiuchus.

The identity of Gilgamesh, then, must almost certainly be the constellation Hercules. For one thing, the ancient texts specifically indicate that Gilgamesh "bends the knee" to conclude the combat between the two bull-like opponents, and as we've repeatedly seen, one of the distinctive aspects of the Hercules constellation is the kneeling posture created by the outline of the constellation. In addition, other lines of the Gilgamesh epic often describe him standing atop the great high wall of his city of Uruk,[280] and this description would certainly be consistent with the constellation Hercules, atop the tall, battlement-like outline of Ophiuchus.

Further, we have numerous surviving examples of ancient artwork, particularly from ancient Greece, in which a figure who is undoubtedly associated with the constellation Hercules (namely, the hero Heracles, in his distinctive lion-skin garment with its lifeless head over the hero's own head) is wrestling with an Ophiuchus-figure (just as Gilgamesh wrestles with Enkidu, whom we have been suspecting to be an Ophiuchus-figure as well).

For example, in the artwork below, from a beautiful hydria from ancient Greece now located in the Museum of Fine Art in Boston, we see Heracles wrestling with the figure of Triton (or Nereus):

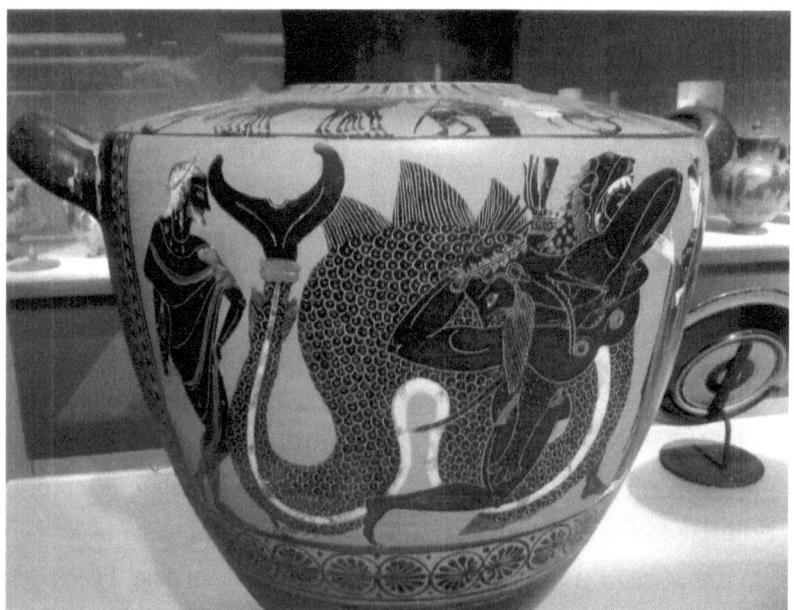

If we look closely, we can see that Heracles is depicted by the ancient artist in the characteristic deep-knee bend posture, indicative of the constellation Hercules. Triton, who has been put into a sort of head-lock or other wrestling embrace by Heracles, is depicted as a powerful "mer-man," with anthropomorphic upper torso (and crowned head) and serpentine lower body, which arches up sharply in the middle. I interpret this sharp "hump-shape" in the center of Triton's fishy, serpentine body as indicative of the outline of Ophiuchus. The flukes of the tail, on the left as we face the image, are in the correct position to correspond to Aquila (which is on the east or left of Ophiuchus as we face south from an observation point in the northern hemisphere). The crown on the head of Triton may indicate the Northern Crown, which is located on the west or right side of the central body of Ophiuchus.

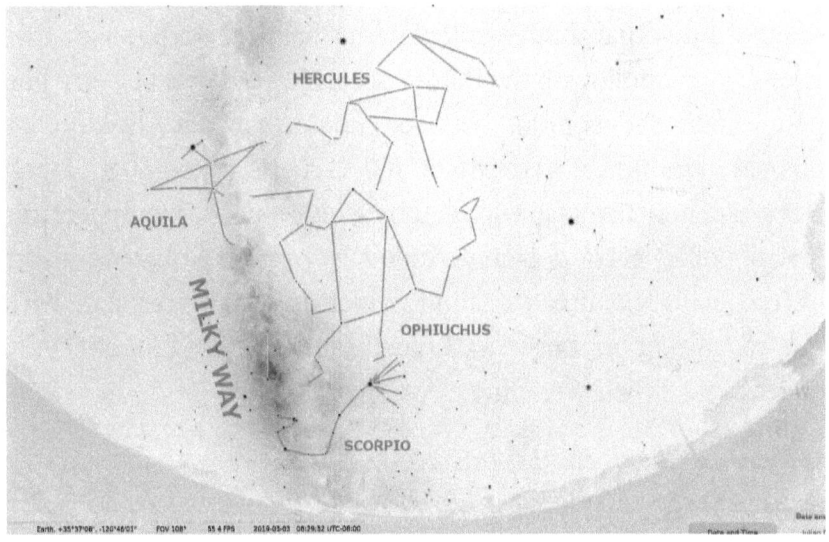

Based on the above textual clues, I believe we can with confidence conclude that the great wrestling-match between Gilgamesh and Enkidu before the doorway to the bride-house is seen in the heavens, and that the most likely constellations with which the two combatants are associated would be the constellations Hercules (Gilgamesh) and Ophiuchus (Enkidu).

However, there is one other possibile celestial explanation from a different part of the sky, one which I believe to be less likely (due to the abundance of textual clues and celestial correspondences noted above), but which is nevertheless worthy of mention. This possibility is suggested by the similarity on some levels between this first encounter between Enkidu and Gilgamesh, and the famous wrestling-scene at the ford of Jabbok described in the book of Genesis, chapter 32, between Jacob and the being described in verse 24 as "a man" and who is usually understood to be the Angel of the LORD, or in fact the LORD.

In that scene, the stranger perceives that he cannot prevail over Jacob (just as Gilgamesh cannot prevail over Enkidu), and therefore touches the hollow of Jacob's thigh, after which Jacob "halted" upon that thigh (walked with a halt due to the sinew that shrank in the hollow of the thigh), according to verses 25 - 32. The parallels to the combat between Gilgamesh and Enkidu go further, because as a result of the Genesis 32 combat, Jacob receives a new name as well as a blessing (indeed, Jacob declares he will not let his opponent go unless he is given a blessing, a sort of "reconciliation after wrestling" which appears to resonate with the reconciliation between Gilgamesh and Enkidu after the conclusion of their wrestling as well).

In *Star Myths of the World, Volume Three* (where the celestial aspects of the encounter at Jabbok or Peniel, between Jacob and the Angel, is discussed), we will see that all the clues in the Genesis 32 text point towards an identification of Jacob with the constellation Perseus (a constellation which appears to have one "twisted foot" or "shortened leg," and thus often plays a role in which an associated Perseus-figure is lame in the feet), and an identification of the Angel with the constellation Andromeda, which can be envisioned as reaching out to touch the constellation Perseus in the region of the hip closest to Andromeda.[281] Because the figures of Perseus and Andromeda can with certainty be seen to portray wrestling figures in that passage (and because the encounter between Jacob-Israel and the Angel of the LORD at the ford of Jabbok appears to have some strong parallels with the initial encounter between Enkidu and Gilgamesh), we should at least examine this region of the sky as a candidate for the wrestling match in the Gilgamesh epic.

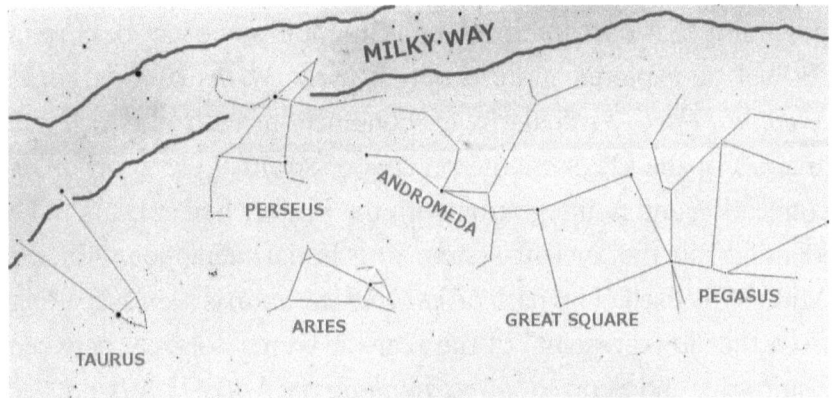

As it turns out, Andromeda and Perseus are found in close proximity in the heavens to the Great Square of Pegasus, and the text of the ancient tablets specify many times that this initial encounter between Gilgamesh and Enkidu takes place in the great Town *Square* of Uruk, sometimes called Uruk-the-Sheepfold.

This connection to a heavenly Square is enough on its own to suggest the possibility that the wrestling between Enkidu and Giglamesh may have a connection to the "wrestling figures" of Perseus and Andromeda. Adding to the evidence in support of this hypothesis is the fact that the constellation Aries the Ram is also found in the sky in close proximity to both Perseus and Andromeda, as well as to the Great Square (as seen in the star-chart on the preceding page), which suggests at the very least that the great square of Uruk-the-*Sheep*fold found in the text of the Gilgamesh tablets was seen in the sky in the Great Square of

Pegasus. Given that connection, and the frequent mention of Uruk-the-Sheepfold in the lines surrounding the combat between Gilgamesh and Enkidu, we should at least consider the possibility that the constellations Perseus and Andromeda portray the two battling heroes at this part of the story.

And, once again, I suggest that we should also be open to the possibility that *both* interpretations might in some way be correct. As will be explored more deeply in *Star Myths of the World, Volume Two*, particularly in conjunction with the celestial analysis of the Odyssey, the process of spiritual elevation or re-connection and re-integration with the Higher Self appears to be identified in the ancient system of celestial metaphor with the Milky Way itself. The *path of spiritual elevation* is seen ascending from the "lowest point" of the year (at winter solstice, between Sagittarius and Scorpio) *upwards along the Milky Way band*.

Perhaps, then, the wrestling between Gilgamesh and Enkidu was esoterically understood to *commence* at the "threshold of the bride-house" (i.e., the constellation Ophiuchus), which is a spiritual "low point" in the great heavenly cycles (near winter solstice), but to *conclude* at a "higher point" far above, along the path of the same Milky Way band, where Perseus and Andromeda wrestle near the "Sheepfold" Square of Uruk. This place of wrestling, as we see in the Genesis 32 text, is also a place of *blessing* and of *reconciliation* -- and after the combat between Gilgamesh and Enkidu, the two are no longer enemies but lifelong friends; indeed they become much closer than that. Gilgamesh and Enkidu, like Xbalanque and Hunahpu or Castor and Pollux, or many other pairs in ancient myth, become another example of "Hero Twins," representative of the reconciliation and re-integration of our divided condition: they actually represent one person, not two.

When understood in this light, we can begin to appreciate the incredible illustrative power of the characters of Gilgamesh and Enkidu as they apply to the human experience of each and every man and woman going through this life. The figures and metaphors are masterfully drawn, shedding light on aspects of our experience in ways very beneficial for us to understand.

Our "animal" senses -- our subconscious mind and sympathetic nervous system -- actually possess incredible sensitivity and awareness of a body of data which our conscious mind often fails to perceive at all. Sometimes, in fact, our conscious mind will deliberately ignore or keep itself from seeing information which our subconscious has already absorbed and perceived (such as when we absorb information which is threatening to the psychological structures which hold up the "sense of who we are" constructed by the conscious mind; our conscious mind will sometimes completely tune out data which might threaten its artificially-constructed "identity").

Our subconscious mind, in fact, is incredibly powerful and incredibly aware -- often far more aware than our conscious mind. But if we can *still* or *silence* the self-interested filtering system of the conscious mind and tap into what the subconscious already knows, we are capable of almost superhuman levels of insight. This explains why we will sometimes receive in dreams solutions to problems our conscious mind was unable to resolve (because, when we are asleep, our conscious mind shuts down, although our subconscious does not).

Pioneering German chemist August Kekule (1829 - 1896) recounted an incident in which, while wrestling with the question of the chemical structure of the hydrocarbon benzene, he dozed off and dreamed of a serpent grasping its own tail in its mouth, which his conscious mind upon awakening realized was the solution to his problem (the carbon atoms of a benzene molecule being arranged in a hexagonal ring, each with one hydrogen atom attached). Whether this anecdote told by Kekule was merely a story he liked to tell or whether it actually took place, the reason that it resonates so widely with so many (both in Kekule's day and in subsequent generations) is the fact that such "messages in dreams" are part of the human experience and familiar to most men and women at some point or another in their own lives.

I myself have on more than one occasion gone to sleep at night pondering some aspect of a myth and its possible celestial connections, and woken up in the morning with new insights far beyond anything I had arrived at the previous evening. These new insights often provided the "solution" to the problem with which I had been wrestling. Indeed, some of the insights you have been reading in this chapter came about in this very manner.

Where did those insights come from? They certainly were not the product of my conscious mind, as my conscious mind had been asleep, during which time I was, technically speaking, "unconscious." Indeed, unlike Kekule in his account, upon awakening I would not remember any specific dreams having to do with the solution to the question that I had been pondering the night before -- it was as if the solution was already present upon waking up in the morning. The subconscious, which continues to operate while we sleep (unencumbered by the rules and constructs and filters developed by the conscious mind over a lifetime of interacting with the structures of society and the norms of interpersonal relationships and identity-construction), must have provided the insight.

Indeed, the subconscious sometimes appears to exhibit perceptive power which cannot be explained by the laws of physics, and which borders on the superhuman or supernatural. Examples abound -- but one which has been documented too many times to be dismissed as mere coincidence are the premonitions about family members or loved ones, often far away and often received in the middle of the night, which are later confirmed as having been accurate, even if no explanation can be given by which the information could have been perceived through the ordinary five senses of sight, hearing, touch, taste, or scent.

In his haunting memoir entitled *Crazy for the Storm* (2009), Norman Ollestad recounts the terrible plane crash that took place on February 19, 1979, when a single-engine Cessna 172 carrying his father Norman Ollestad, Sr., his father's girlfriend Sandra Cressman, pilot Rob Arnold, and 11-year-old Norman Ollestad, crashed into the side of Mount Ontario in southern California, killing everyone but young Norman. The book recounts his harrowing journey down the extremely steep, snow-and-ice covered rock faces, chutes, and gulleys of the mountain, alone, through several situations where one false move or loss of resolve could have led to a very different outcome.

Without spoiling the book, which is well worth owning and reading in its entirety, Norman's memoir make very clear that he would not have survived without the traits his father had imparted to him as he was growing up, *but also* that he would not have survived had it not been for the actions of two other people whose actions on that tragic day in 1979 were critical to young Norman's being found at all, after he had made his way all the way down the mountain to a road. Both people acted on something that could be called sudden intuition or an

483

unexplained "hunch," and one of them felt that she had *heard* the crash itself (and says she had actually been awakened by it), even though when she told the sheriff's deputy about that, he explained to her that it was not possible based on her location at the time of the crash and the distance to the crash site itself.[282]

And there are countless other documented cases that can be put in this same category, suggesting that our subconscious can not only perceive critical information which our conscious mind fails to observe (or even deliberately filters out), but can also tap information which cannot be explained by the physical senses at all, as if our subconscious can sometimes link to information available to others, or to nature (or the universe) itself. And yet, in the process of becoming "entangled" in the structures of our identity within society, we lose touch with, discount, ignore, or otherwise reject this incredible aspect of ourselves.

Returning now to the epic of Gilgamesh, we might see in Enkidu's "loss of innocence" and disconnection from his original "state of nature" a picture of our own disconnection, not only from an amazing and powerful part of ourselves, but also from nature and the universe (to which our subconscious seems, in some way, to be connected). After Enkidu has intercourse with Shamhat, he loses his deep and uncontrived connection to the wild -- but, at the same time (the verses tell us), he gains new understanding. Our conscious mind and all its judgings and assessings and considerings is necessary for our operation in society, with other men and women, and it has its own merits: merits related to a different kind of knowledge and reasoning. But, through brilliant illustration, the epic of Gilgamesh conveys the profundity of what we lose at the same time that we gain this other mind, this other self.

And yet, the path forward, as illustrated by the events of the ancient text, does not lie through an attempt to somehow recapture the innocence Enkidu knew before his union with Shamhat, an attempt to recapture his wild state and his companionship with the animals of the field. Such an attempt would undoubtedly be futile anyway: the text makes clear that after intercourse with Shamhat, he is changed forever. He cannot go back.

Instead, Enkidu must embark upon a new path -- one which leads him to the encounter with Gilgamesh: Gilgamesh, who is the son of divine parents, and is himself "two-thirds" divine. In many ways, Gilgamesh represents the Higher Self, or the divine nature. Thus, the fact that the myth has Enkidu seeking out Gilgamesh rather than trying to somehow return to his state of nature (which was also a state of ignorance, although pure and innocent), indicates the direction we ourselves need to turn. We find ourselves in very much the same condition as Enkidu, following his separation from the wild and his loss of his earlier innocent state. Like him, we cannot go back to where we were -- but we can go forward. Like Enkidu, we should realize that we "need a friend." The friend with whom we should be seeking to connect is, in fact, our own Higher Self.

Gilgamesh probably represents the Higher Self in this ancient epic -- but as we see Gilgamesh at the opening of the epic, he too is lacking: in this case, lacking in compassion for and understanding of other men and women, an arrogant tyrant who oppresses and despoils his own subjects.

Perhaps these flaws in Gilgamesh's character at the outset of the epic cycle serve to illustrate for our understanding the condition of the soul before its incarnation, when it has not yet descended to "wrestle with" the lower realm of matter, and thus to convey to us some of the purpose for our coming down here in the first place, to learn lessons which are not available to a being of purely spiritual nature. Both parts of our nature have transformations to undergo: the god Eros needs the mortal Psyche as much as she needs him, and Gilgamesh will be transformed by Enkidu just as much as Enkidu by Gilgamesh.

The wrestling of Gilgamesh and Enkidu conveys to our understanding a reality which pertains to each and every one of us, cast down into the natural and physical world, cut off in many ways from our own nature (even our own subconscious mind), and yet in need of integration with our fuller self, our true self, our divine self, our Higher Self. This theme appears to be present in virtually all of the myth-systems found in the various cultures of the world.

Many times, the concept is illustrated through the use of *twins*, and in most cases of twinning there are significant differences between the two, because the two twins illustrate for us different aspects of our nature which must become reconnected and re-integrated: think of Eros and Psyche, or Jesus and Doubting Thomas, or Krishna and Arjuna (whom we will meet later in this volume), or Jacob and Esau, or Polydeuces and Castor, or Hunahpu and Xbalanque, among many others. In each case, I would argue that the twinned pair do not represent two different individuals at all, but rather the aspects of our own nature, which have become estranged as a consequence of our path down into this life we are each experiencing. The ancient myths point our way towards reconciliation.

Early in his brilliant masterpiece *Lost Light*, Alvin Boyd Kuhn makes a declaration which illuminates all that we've been discussing above. He says:

> Deity for man is at home, not afield in distant skies. The kingdom of heaven and the hope of glory are within. They lurk within the unfathomed depths of consciousness. Divinity lies buried under the heavier motions of the sensual nature and the incessant scurrying of the superficial mind.[283]

This truth is acted out for us in myth after myth, from culture after culture, under thousands of different costumes, in countless variations and permutations. The figures of Gilgamesh and Enkidu, however, stand out among this vast panoply of characters from world myth: drawn so perfectly, impressing upon our awareness the reality of our present condition, the poignancy of what we have lost and the urgency of the transformations we will undergo, and also the incredible treasure to which we already have access (although our conscious mind often remains blissfully ignorant, or even actively hostile, to the availability of everything that we really need).

We must rely on versions other than the Standard Version to learn about the conclusion of the combat between Gilgamesh and Enkidu, because there is a lacuna in Tablet II of the Standard Version at the fight episode. At the end of the fight, the text of Gilgamesh P ends. Thus, translator Andrew George at this point consults the Yale Tablet, which also contains part of the text from the "Surpassing all other kings" version of Gilgamesh (dated to the period around 1700 BC), but which is in worse condition than the Pennsylvania Tablet. There, in the Yale Tablet we learn that following the battle, Gilgamesh and Enkidu "kissed each other and formed a friendship."[284]

Modern scholars often interpret the bond between Gilgamesh and Enkidu (whose arrival has been foreshadowed to Gilgamesh in a dream as being a companion who will be "like a wife" to him, one he will love and embrace, and who will often save Gilgamesh's own life: Tablet I, 255 - 297)[285] as being in some way homosexual or homoerotic. However, I would argue that this interpretation fails to understand the *esoteric* aspect of these "twinning" oicotypes in ancient myth, which have to do not with two different terrestrial individuals but rather with the two natures present in each and every individual. These two natures, although estranged from one another, are supposed to be brought into harmony with one another. The relationship between them, the ancient myths and scriptures tell us (and show us) is even closer than that of a brother (indeed, this relationship with the divine twin or Higher Self is what I believe the Bible describes when it tells us "There is a friend *that* sticketh closer than a brother," in Proverbs 18: 24).

I would argue that all these metaphors, of twins or of combatants who later become fast friends, or of the intimate relationship between a husband and a wife in the myth of Eros and Psyche, are used by the ancient Star Myths of the world to convey to our deeper understanding (indeed, to our subconscious mind, because story and image can be a way to bypass the incessant filtering and judging of the conscious mind) an esoteric truth. We can see from overwhelming evidence that we are not talking about two literal or historical or terrestrial figures: Gilgamesh and Enkidu are undeniably drawn from celestial metaphor. Thus, their celestial and metaphorical nature should demonstrate beyond any doubt that the message we are to take from their relationship is an esoteric message, not a literalistic message.

As an aside, but very much related, we will see in Volume Two of this series that another famous relationship from ancient myth which is consistently interpreted by conventional academia as homosexual or homoerotic, the relationship between Achilles and Patroclus in the Iliad of ancient Greece, is also almost certainly intended to convey an esoteric rather than a literal message, and relates once again to the relationship between the ordinary mortal consciousness and the Higher Self.

Let us now skip ahead in the epic (over sections which are for the most part damaged and full of lacunae anyway) to the famous expedition of Gilgamesh and Enkidu to the great Forest of Cedar, to confront the powerful guardian of the forest, Humbaba (or Huwawa).

As the two prepare for their expedition to the Cedar Forest, the danger of the journey and in particular the power of Humbaba is related many times over, by the elders of the city, and most often by Enkidu himself, who knows of Humbaba from his own days in the wild. The formula describing the terrifying guardian of the forest is that "his roar is a whirlwind, flame (in) his jaws, and his very breath Death!" (Tablet III, Column 4, lines 2 - 3).[286] A section of Tablet II is translated by Andrew George as saying of Humbaba that his voice is the Deluge, his speech is fire, and his breath is death (Tablet II, 278 - 279).[287] All of these descriptions may contain clues to the celestial identity of Humbaba (Huwawa).

Craftsmen forge weapons for the expedition: in particular, a powerful axe (or axes) and a mighty sword. Then, the hero-twins go to the goddess Ninsun (the mother of Gilgamesh) to obtain a blessing for their endeavor, and she in turn ascends the parapet of the palace and burns incense and implores the sun god, Shamash (whose name is *Utu* in the Sumerian version), for assistance and protection for Gilgamesh in the upcoming fight against Humbaba. She also tells Enkidu that he is now like an adopted son to her, and she gives him her glorious necklace as an amulet and a pledge, and in her blessing to him wishes that the days may be long and the nights short while they travel together to the forest.

Gilgamesh and Enkidu also go to the seven elders of Uruk, who give them various pieces of advice, including the admonition to Gilgamesh that he should "wash his feet in the river of Humbaba," and the admonition to make sure that Gilgamesh keeps cool fresh water in his water-skin, in order to be able to pour out an offering of water for the sun-god Shamash daily (this advice is found in the version contained in the tablet known today as the Yale Tablet, or "Gilgamesh Y," lines 266 - 267). The two receive a farewell and blessing from the seven elders of Uruk.

Then they set off.

The journey to the Forest of Cedar is replete with celestial significance. At the entrance to the forest, they encounter a gate, which Enkidu addresses as though it were alive, with words of praise, before either he or Gilgamesh (the lines immediately prior are damaged) rips it out of its hinges and casts it aside. They enter the forest, marveling at the height of the trees and the beauty of the other foliage.

Along this journey, they cross seven successive hills or mountain ranges within the forest, each time stopping to rest and to receive a vision regarding the upcoming encounter with Humbaba, a vision which comes to Gilgamesh and which to him seems ominous but which Enkidu interprets as propitious.

These visions are given to Gilgamesh in dreams, and the text tells us that sleep comes over Gilgamesh in this way: first, he climbs a mountain, then pours out an offering of meal from a sack of meal or flour that he carries. Next, as he is squatting down on his haunches, sleep suddenly flows down over him and he is overcome with slumber. Then he wakes up just as suddenly, asking each time of Enkidu if his friend has called out to him or if some spirit has touched him, and indicating that he has an uncanny feeling, as if his flesh is all a-quiver.

The dreams each have fairly clear references to celestial characters, including a Thunderbird, a wild Bull, fire falling down from heaven, a great mountain, and a man enveloped in brilliance beneath the mountain, who gives Gilgamesh water to drink, and sets his feet back on the earth. Enkidu assures Gilgamesh that there is nothing to fear from the dreams and that they will surely slay Humbaba.

And, just as Enkidu encourages Gilgamesh, Gilgamesh does the same for Enkidu, when Enkidu confesses that in his apprehension his hands seem to have no strength. The two proceed towards the fateful encounter.

When they arrive at the center of the forest, Gilgamesh takes his axe and begins to chop down cedars. At this, the guardian appointed by Enlil, the great Humbaba, hears the commotion from a long ways off, and begins to storm through the woods towards the intruders, roaring out that they should not be violating the forest.

We are told in some badly mutilated lines that Humbaba is possessed of seven "glories" or "auras" (some translate them as "terrors"), which he eventually sends forth against the two heroes,

491

but to no avail. Gilgamesh takes out his tremendous axe and chops down seven mighty cedars in succession.

Humbaba comes forth out of his strong house of cedar. He sends forth the first of his auras. Enkidu continues to encourage Gilgamesh, who calls on Shamash for aid. The sun-god sends eight winds against the fearsome forest guardian: a north wind, a storm wind, an icy wind, a scorching wind, a whirlwind, a lightning wind, a flood wind, and a heart-stopping wind.

Then, Humbaba pleads for his life, and for mercy from Gilgamesh and Enkidu. But Enkidu urges Gilgamesh to slay the forest guardian. Tablet V tells us that at the urging of his friend, Gilgamesh draws forth the knife he carries at his side, and smites Humbaba in the neck. Another Old Babylonian tablet called the Ishchali Tablet informs us that as Humbaba falls, the ravines run with his blood (lines 22 - 25).[288]

In the same Ishchali Tablet, the heroes discuss how to deal with the "auras" of Humbaba, and Enkidu argues that if they focus on slaying Humbaba, the auras will be like chicks after their mother has been caught, saying:

> 'My friend, catch a bird and where go its chicks?
> Let us look for the auras later,
> as the chicks run here and there in the thicket!' (14 - 17)[289]

What is fascinating to me about this description of the auras of Humbaba is the specific comparison of them to "chicks," and in particular motherless chicks (even going so far as to describe them as "running here and there in the thicket"). This description resonates very strongly with other Star Myths from other cultures, specifically the omen at Aulis described by Agamemnon in the second book of the Iliad of ancient Greece, in which the king describes a great serpent which emerges from its hiding place beneath the sacrificial altar, and ascends a tree, pursuing a mother-sparrow and her brood of chicks, and devouring them all one by one! The celestial foundations of this portentious incident are discussed in *Star Myths of the World, Volume Two*, in which the serpent emerging from beneath the altar is identified as the constellation Scorpio, which devours the mother bird and her brood of chicks, who almost certainly correspond to the multiple heads of the same constellation (with the mother-bird possibly being associated with the star Antares in Scorpio).[290]

Equally intriguing is the fact that Jesus uses nearly the exact same metaphor in Matthew 23: 37 when beholding Jerusalem from afar, prior to the triumphal entry. In that verse he declares:

> O Jerusalem, Jerusalem, *thou* that killest the prophets, and stonest them which are sent unto thee, how often would I have gathered thy children together, even as a hen gathereth her chickens under *her* wings, and ye would not!

These metaphors, for the auras of Humbaba in the Gilgamesh epic, the omen at Aulis in the Iliad of ancient Greece, and the exclamation of Jesus prior to his entry into Jerusalem, are astonishingly similar, and I would argue that their similarity is no coincidence: they can all be shown to be based upon the same celestial metaphor involving Scorpio and perhaps Ophiuchus above it, which was evidently compared to a mother bird with all her chicks in the ancient system of metaphor found in the world's myths -- a metaphor which is not exactly "intuitively obvious" such that we would expect it to crop up independently in different cultures (just as the comparison of the Northern Crown to an arching infant is similarly obscure and yet similarly appears in the myths of multiple cultures around the globe).

This utterance attributed to the figure of Jesus in Matthew 23 is discussed in *Star Myths of the World, Volume Three,* where it is argued to be referring to the heads of Scorpio as the chicks -- and note that the same volume provides abundant evidence that Jesus himself is frequently associated with the constellation Ophiuchus, most notably during the scene of the Crucifixion itself.[291] Thus, this declaration of a desire to gather the children of the Holy City together, even as a hen gathers her chicks under her wings, may indicate a similar *identification of Jesus with Ophiuchus* here (gathering the "chicks" of Scorpio under the two "wings" of the constellation's outline) -- and indicating a possible association between Humbaba and Ophiuchus as well.

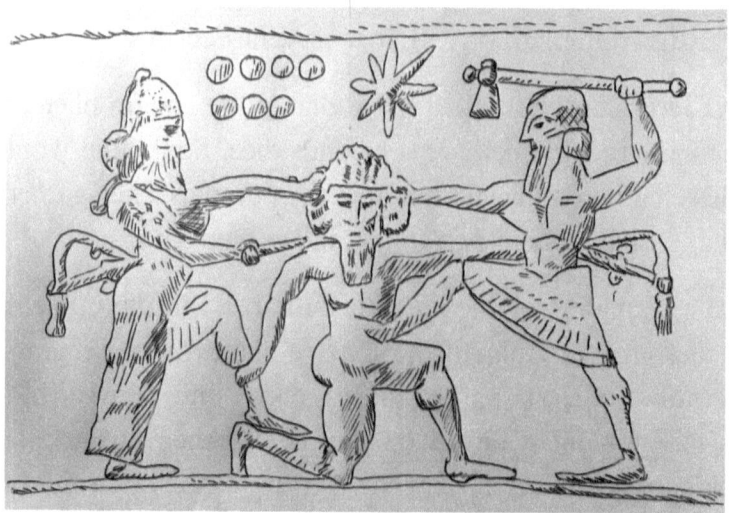

Ancient depictions of the slaying of Humbaba reinforce the interpretation of an association between Humbaba and the constellation Ophiuchus, such as the scene shown above from a Mesopotamian cylinder-seal. In the image, we see Humbaba flanked by the two heroes Gilgamesh and Enkidu, with the figure on the left (as we face it) holding a knife to the neck of Humbaba and thus likely representing Gilgamesh (since the text tells us that Gilgamesh smites Humbaba in the neck with his dagger), and the figure on the right wielding an upraised axe and standing in a posture which we have come to see as associated with the constellation Hercules. This figure on the right must thus be Enkidu, associated here with Hercules instead of with Ophiuchus as we have seen him in previous scenes (and note that in some of the ancient versions of the battle, it is Enkidu who chops off the head of Humbaba after Gilgamesh slays the guardian of the forest).

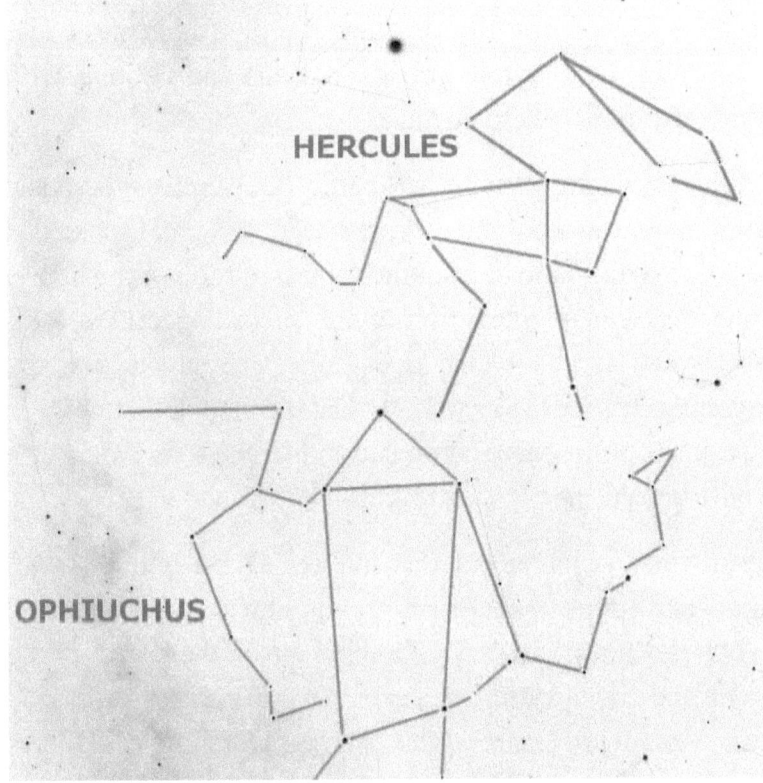

Note the eight-pointed star or solar disc above Humbaba, and offset slightly – we have by now seen this image depicted above figures associated with the constellation Ophiuchus frequently (see for example the images on pages 293, 294, 296, and 297, among others). This arrangement provides strong confirmation that Humbaba was associated with the constellation Ophiuchus, at least as suggested by depictions in some ancient artwork.

Note that Gilgamesh is similarly depicted in a body-outline reminiscent of the constellation Hercules, especially in the arrangement of his legs, but that instead of raising one arm overhead he is stabbing Humbaba in the neck. Recall that the same constellation Hercules also has a downward-reaching arm, pointing towards one side of the triangular "head" of the constellation Ophiuchus: this downward arm of Hercules could be envisioned as holding a short dagger or dirk and stabbing with it towards the "neck" of Ophiuchus:

However, since the downward hand of Hercules is really pointing more towards the "serpent-head" of the Ophiuchus constellation than to the head of the central portion of the figure, this interpretation of the action in the preceding cylinder-seal artwork is less certain. What does appear certain is that the ancient artist has envisioned both Enkidu and Gilgamesh as having aspects of the same constellation Hercules, as if the hero-twins have become nearly identical.

It is also worth pointing out that in *Star Myths of the World, Volume Two,* extensive analysis is presented which demonstrates that *wounds* dealt out to various combatants in the battles of the Iliad will nearly always correspond to *features on specific constellations,* with figures who are associated with Boötes receiving wounds to the head or face (consistent with the fact that this constellation has a "pipe" emanating from its face, which could instead be envisioned as a sword or arrow or spear penetrating the face from an assailant), and figures who are associated with Aquarius receiving woulds to the gut or bowels, (or through the lower back and going right on through to come out from the gut), because the outline of Aquarius features a straight "forward leg" which could be envisioned as a spear going into the gut or coming out of the gut.[292]

That same discussion noted that figures associated with the constellation Ophiuchus will usually be described as being wounded in the neck, collar, or upper chest area (sometimes just above the nipple), and the reason for this can be perceived by looking at the star-chart below, and noting that the left side of the constellation (holding the "tail-end" of the serpent) has a line which connects to the "neck" region, and which could thus be envisioned as a wound to the neck or throat:

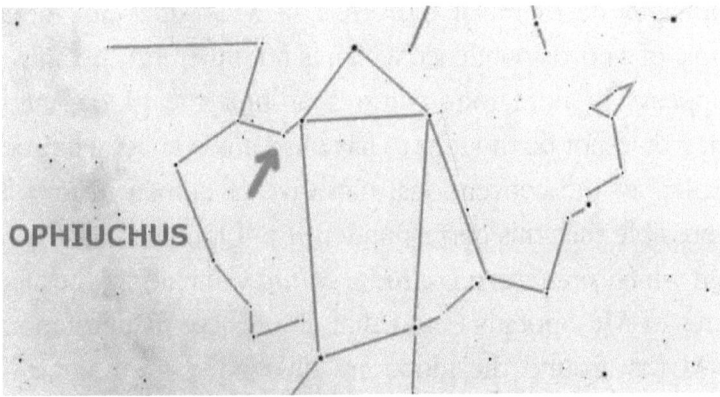

The star-chart above includes an arrow pointed towards the "arm" of Ophiuchus which could instead be envisioned as a weapon going into the neck or upper-torso region of the figure.

Thus, the fact that the ancient tablets specifically say that Humbaba is stabbed *in the neck* by Gilgamesh should be seen as yet another piece of evidence supporting a connection between Humbaba and Ophiuchus.

Yet more confirmation is provided by the formula, repeated many times in reference to Humbaba, that his roar is like the whirlwind (or the Deluge), his jaws are like fire, and his breath is Death itself.

Recall that we have already alleged that the two serpent-halves flanking the central body of Ophiuchus could be envisioned as terrible engulfing jaws. We previously noted this connection in the discussion of the fire-myth of the Pacific Northwest (involving Stag, who must dance through the snapping jaws of the door to the dwelling of the Old Man), as well as in the discussion of the jaws of Tiamat in her battle with Marduk in Enuma Elish (see pages 122 - 123 and 413 - 414).

We will see in Volume Four of this series that the same association of engulfing jaws around Ophiuchus can be found in the Norse myths, as well as in the famous artwork on the sarcophagus lid of Pakal the Great in Mesoamerica -- another example of a correspondence which is not inherently obvious and yet appears in numerous cultures around the globe, cultures which would not be thought to have had any contact whatsoever, according to the conventional narrative of human history. It is very possible that this correspondence to Ophiuchus is part of a system which *predates all of these cultures* (including the ancient cultures of Mesopotamia) and that all of these manifestations in Star Myths around the globe are descended from some now-forgotten predecessor culture whose system has been preserved in the world's far-flung ancient traditions.

The chopping down of the cedars which brings Humbaba running to try to stop Gilgamesh and Enkidu, as well as the chopping down of the great cedar in the center of the forest, appears to have a celestial foundation in the fact that the "whirling" form of the constellation Hercules was at times envisioned in ancient myth as a great tree, often a great tree upon a hill or mountain (because Ophiuchus would be envisioned as a hill or mountain with the "tree" of Hercules growing upon it).

Below is another ancient Mesopotamian cylinder-seal showing a great cedar-tree upon a hill or mountain:

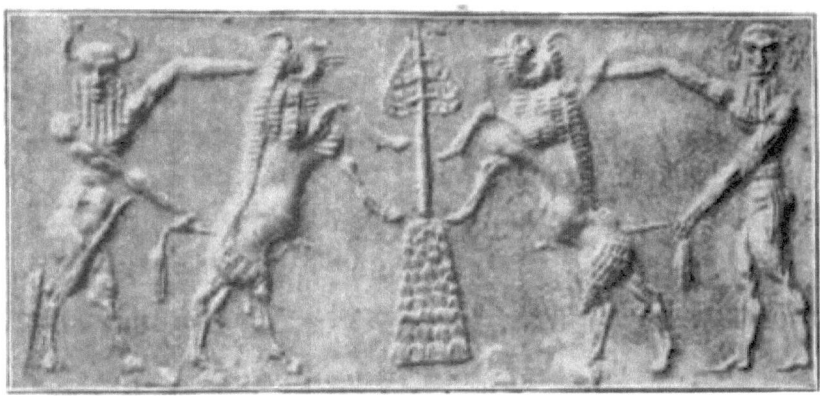

We can be certain that the two bulls flanking the tree and hill indicate Ophiuchus by looking at another cylinder-seal:

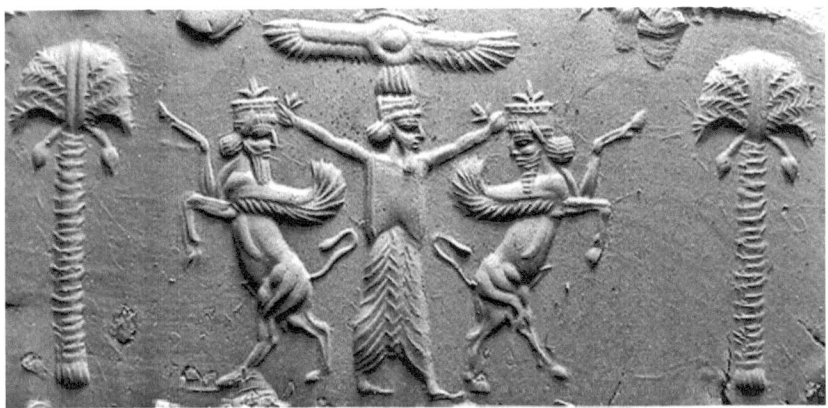

In the second image above, an anthropomorphic figure in the center is holding the forelocks of two rampant bull-figures (this pattern is indicative of what is called the "Master of Animals" icon). Above his head we see the familiar winged solar disc symbol, indicating beyond any doubt that this central anthropomorphic figure is associated with the central body of Ophiuchus (below the "whirling" outline of the constellation Hercules, which appears as the winged solar disc) and based on that identification we can see that the two flanking bull-figures whose hair he is holding are associated with the two "serpent-halves" flanking the central body of the same constellation (Ophiuchus).

Thus, in the cylinder-seal above on the preceding page, where we see a hill surmounted by a tree and flanked by two rampant bulls, we can thus be fairly certain once again that the central feature (in this case, a mound or hill) is associated with Ophiuchus, and that the tree above it (like the solar-disc in the lower seal depicted) is associated with the "whirling" outline of the constellation Hercules.

Note that a central tree under a solar disc is also a very common figure found in ancient Mesopotamian cylinder-seals which have survived to the present. Often the central tree (described by scholars as "the sacred tree") will be flanked by two symmetrical or nearly symmetrical figures, sometimes animals and often human. I would argue that all of these have an association with Ophiuchus (and its two "nearly symmetrical" serpent-halves) beneath Hercules. This fact indicates that *Ophiuchus itself* will at times be envisioned as a tree, and indeed we have already seen that the branching serpent-halves of Ophiuchus at times were envisioned as vines or branches in ancient myth (we will see this again in later volumes). Thus, the slaying of Humbaba and the chopping down of the central cedar are closely connected.

The description of the speech of Humbaba as being like a Deluge or like fire probably refers to the proximity of Ophiuchus to the bright part of the Milky Way galaxy, which is frequently envisioned in myth as a column as fire but also as a river of water, and at times as a gushing torrent of water. Indeed, as will be examined in much more detail in *Star Myths of the Bible*, this section of the Milky Way is associated with the water which pours down when the windows of heaven are opened and the fountains of the great deep are released, to initiate the Genesis Flood.[293]

Likewise, the description of Humbaba as having the roar of a whirlwind (literally, "his roar *is* a whirlwind," as translated by Professor George) almost certainly describes the whirling form of Hercules which is positioned in the sky above the open "jaws" of Ophiuchus, as if emanating from the gaping mouth of the forest guardian (such that the "roar" coming out of the jaws actually *is* the whirlwind-form of Hercules):

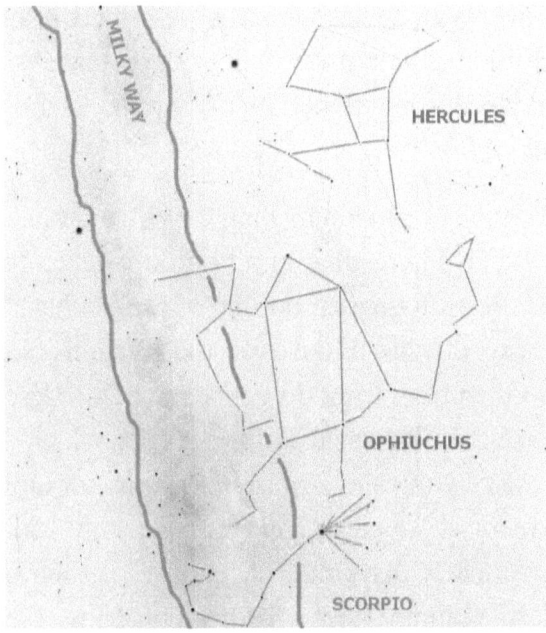

When Gilgamesh and Enkidu are traveling into the Cedar Forest on their way to Mount Lebanon, where the tallest cedar in the forest is located, the poem relates the same pattern of activity after each of the successive segments of the journey. In each case, the verses (using almost identical language) describe Gilgamesh and Enkidu facing the sun and digging a well, and then pouring fresh water in (as an offering to the sun god). Next, Gilgamesh climbs

501

to the top of the mountain (the travel involves crossing seven successive mountains) and pours out an offering of flour. Then, he calls out to the mountain to bring him a good dream, one which will reveal a good sign. Then Enkidu is described as making a "House of the Dream God" with a doorway in it, and Gilgamesh is described as "lying down like a net" at the doorway.

All of these actions can be seen to correspond to the same set of constellations we have been examining: when Gilgamesh climbs the mountain, he is Hercules atop the "hill-like" shape of Ophiuchus. The act of pouring out the flour undoubtedly refers to the Milky Way again, which is described in more than one sacred tradition as a pathway of flour or cornmeal spilled out (this correspondence is mentioned by de Santillana and von Dechend in *Hamlet's Mill*).[294]

The description of Enkidu making for Gilgamesh a "House of the Dream God" is interesting, and no doubt refers to the pavilion-shaped or doorway-shaped outline of Ophiuchus. At the foot of the doorway of this House of the Dream God, the poem describes Gilgamesh lying down like a net -- a description suited to describe either the constellation Scorpio, which does indeed lie down at the very threshold of the "doorway" of Ophiuchus in the night sky, or Hercules again (above the "doorway"). The constellation likely plays the "net" above the bed of Hephaestos discussed in Volume Two (which Hephaestus uses to catch his wife Aphrodite in an adulterous embrace with the god Ares).[295]

As mentioned earlier, each of the dreams described by Gilgamesh on each successive night can rather easily be connected to a feature of the heavens. There is even a dream about a man who gives Gilgamesh water to drink from his waterskin, which almost certainly corresponds to the constellation Aquarius.[296] In each case, the dream causes Gilgamesh to become uneasy, but Enkidu interprets the dream as propitious, and relating to the help they are certain to get from the god Shamash in their quest to defeat Humbaba (or, for some dreams, as help they will get from the god Lugulbanda, the father of Gilgamesh; Enkidu says that the man who in one dream gives Gilgamesh water from a wineskin to drink is the god Lugulbanda, which is a good indication of an association between Lugulbanda and Aquarius).

When the duo finally do encounter Humbaba (or Huwawa), the sun-god Shamash sends winds against the forest guardian,[297] thus indicating that Shamash himself is probably associated with the constellation Hercules when envisioned in "whirlwind" form. Such identification would be consistent with the evidence connecting solar discs and winged-sun symbology to the whirling Hercules. These patterns in the encounter with Humbaba parallel metaphors found in myths of other cultures as well.

Similarly, when the ancient texts describe the ravines running with his blood (as cited earlier, from the Ishchali Tablet), these rivers of blood draining down through the ravines probably correspond to the river-delta-shaped constellation of Scorpio immediately below Ophiuchus. We will see in Volume Two that on more than one occasion, a cave or pleasant grotto which is associated with Ophiuchus will be described as having fresh streams burbling down from the mouth of the cave, and these streams are associated with Scorpio. Such a scene is described when we meet the goddess Calypso in the Odyssey.[298]

Thus, we find in the text itself abundant indications that the slaying of Humbaba (Huwawa) envisions the same important section of the night sky containing the "vertically stacked" constellations of Scorpio, Ophiuchus and Hercules, with Scorpio corresponding to the "auras" and later the rivers of blood, Ophiuchus corresponding to Humbaba and also Enkidu, and Hercules playing the roles of Gilgamesh, the god Shamash, and the divine wind sent by Shamash. In some artwork, Enkidu is clearly envisioned as being associated with the constellation Hercules as well, sometimes wielding a large axe (and in some textual versions, Enkidu is the one to sever Humbaba's head after Humbaba is slain, an action which would correspond more naturally to a figure associated with Hercules, who stands above Ophiuchus with a menacing upraised weapon).[299]

Indeed, the battle with Huwawa very much corresponds to the exquisitely-detailed combat scene carved into the agate at Pylos discovered in 2017 and dubbed the Pylos Combat Agate, which was mentioned previously on pages 192 - 193, 210, and 265. The warrior associated with Hercules is slaying a figure associated with Ophiuchus; below this second figure, another warrior already lies dead upon the ground:

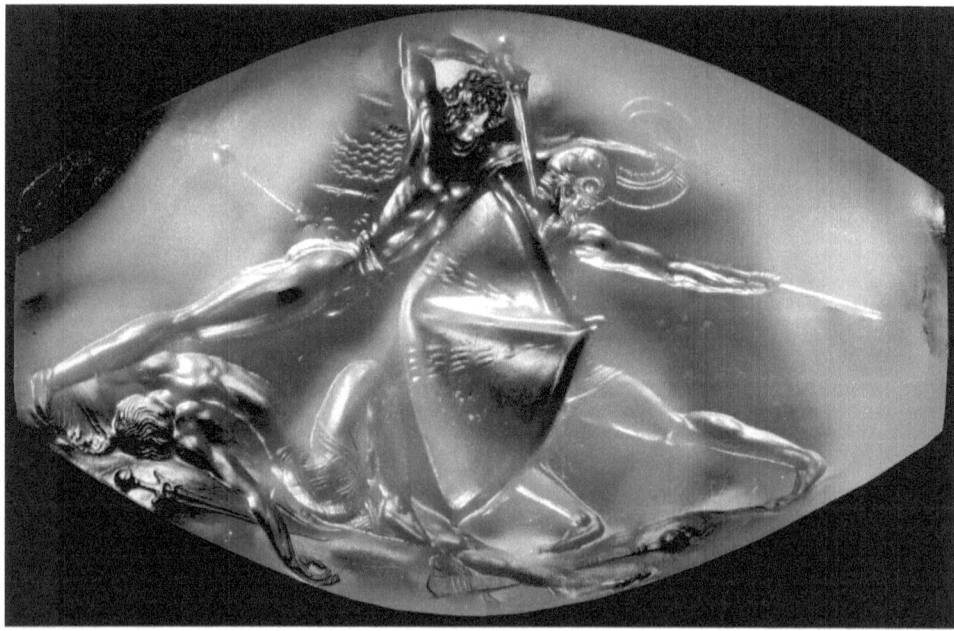

It is amazing to note that, long before this stunning agate (thought to be of possible Minoan origin, and to have been buried in a tomb which was sealed around 1500 BC), ancient Mesopotamian artwork diplays the same pattern, depicting Humbaba's slaying depicted Humbaba in the position of Ophiuchus being slain by Hercules-figures (in the case of Gilgamesh and Enkidu, both depicted as Hercules-figures).

Even more amazing is the fact that ancient Mesopotamian artwork has also survived depicting Humbaba's slaying but depicting him in the position of Scorpio rather than of Ophiuchus (I have argued that the figure on the ground in the Pylos Agate also shows clear connections to distinctive aspects of Scorpio, as well as of Sagittarius). These depictions of Humbaba in a position more evocative of Scorpio were also well known long before the Pylos Combat Agate came to light in 2017.

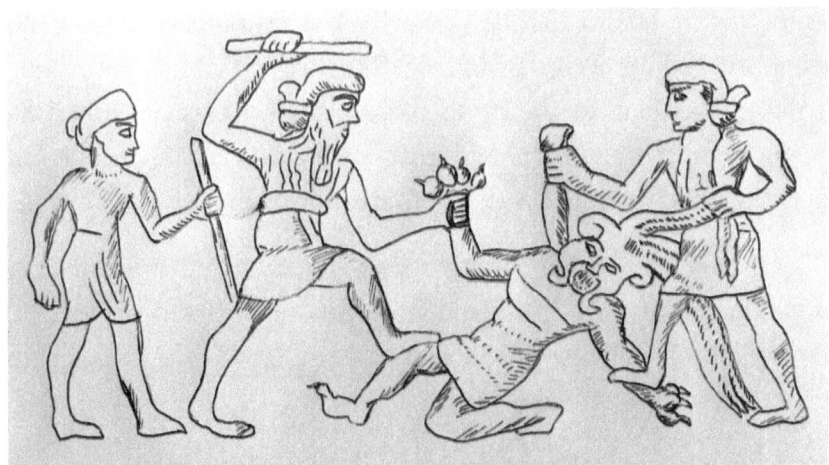

The scene above is a drawing of an ancient plaque from southern Mesopotamia dated to the early second millenium BC. Note the angle of Humbaba's body in the ancient artwork, consistent with the angle of Scorpio in the sky (relative to Ophiuchus, for example). We will see other examples of unmistakable Scorpio-figures depicted at this same angle in other ancient artwork from other cultures in later volumes in this series. Note too the long locks of hair atop the head of the unfortunate Humbaba: these long locks of hair almost certainly correspond to the "delta-shaped" top region of the constellation Scorpio (the part of Scorpio often envisioned as "multiple heads").

One intriguing correspondence which is suggested by the clear connection between Humbaba and Scorpio is the fact that the demigod Maui of the Pacific, as we have already seen, was sometimes described as having eight heads (and thus Maui has connections to Scorpio, in addition to other heavenly figures).

The reason this Scorpio connection between Maui and Humbaba is so interesting is that, when Humbaba is pleading with Gilgamesh and Enkidu to spare his life (in some versions of the battle with Humbaba) he specifically says that he did not know his mother or father – that he was an outcast, until Enlil established him as guardian of the forest.[300] This pattern is strikingly similar to the myth of Maui, who was described as being prematurely born and cast away, or even as being "an abortion" (as his older brothers often describe him).

Clearly, we are dealing with patterns which manifest again and again in the Star Myths of the world, patterns based on specific constellations which the ancient system imbued with specific characteristics and meaning.

But, what could be the esoteric meaning of this terrible scene of the slaying of Humbaba within the expedition to the Forest of Cedar described in the ancient tablets?

We have already in this volume discussed at some length some of the evidence indicating that the constellations themselves were imbued with additional esoteric significance based on their connection with larger celestial cycles, including the annual cycle of our earth's orbit around the sun (which creates the four great turning points of the solstices and equinoxes, each of which represented different aspects of the soul's own progress) but also the much longer cycle of the ages-long turning of the heavens we call precession (or the "precession of the equinoxes").

We have seen very strong evidence that the myth-cycle involving the slaying of Osiris in ancient Egypt, and the search for Osiris by the goddess Isis (with his eventual restoration, involving the actions of Horus the son of Isis and Osiris) is related to the great cycle of precession (for example, as Jane B. Sellers points out, Plutarch relates that Osiris is slain by his brother Set and Set's seventy-two henchmen).

Myths associated with precession often carry themes related to disconnection and loss -- the motion of precession itself, of course, "displaces" the very gears of the heavens themselves, causing constellations to be "held back" and eventually to lose their place and be replaced by others (just as the usurper Set displaces Osiris and takes his throne). Precession myths thus often involve dispossession, or a loss of connection to a previous condition of innocence (or even the end of a Golden Age).

We have already discussed at some length the significance of the "loss of innocence" dramatized in the life of Enkidu, who loses his connection with nature and with his primordial condition as part of his entanglements with society and society's ways, beginning with his seduction by Shamhat. In a sense, Enkidu experiences the "loss of a Golden Age," and as we discussed it is a loss which every one of us experiences at the hands of society as we are inexorably entwined in its interpersonal relations and norms and traditions and judgments, and as we build up the constructed mind and the constructed self, which cause us (like Enkidu) to lose contact with our primordial state, alienating us from our own subconscious and from certain aspects of ourself which were part of our natural inheritance.

It would be desirable to regain connection with this part of our being, but the myths indicate that the way to become reintegrated and whole is not to go backwards but to go forwards (and upwards). This disconnection or loss of innocence cannot be remedied by vainly trying to return to a primitive state once the "schism" has occurred. The schism must be *transcended* and a new integration must be effected, according to what I see the myths as depicting for our understanding. This is portrayed in the Osiris cycle, in which Isis searches for the coffin containing Osiris and retrieves it, and in which the son of Isis and Osiris -- Horus -- battles with Set and eventually restores his father.

In the Osiris myth, the slain Osiris in his casket was turned into a tree (which became the pillar holding up the palace of Byblos). This pillar has to be taken down, and we have seen that the giving of this pillar (containing the body of Osiris) has strong parallels to the taking down of the body of Christ from the Cross (the Cross also being referred to as "the Tree" in some Bible verses, such as Acts 5: 30 and 1 Peter 2: 24) and giving it to the Virgin Mary (see page 355). And in the expedition to the Forest of Cedars, we see the chopping down of a great tree as well.

All of these myths (and many more around the world) have to do with a great disconnection and displacement, and they use precessional imagery to evoke that theme. Indeed, the chopping down of a tree (or related symbology, such as the cracking of Yggdrasil in the Norse mythology, or the discussion of the displacement of the bedpost of Odysseus during the climactic scenes near the end of the Odyssey) is one of the clearest indications that a myth is evoking the great heaven-dislocating motion of precession. The slippage of the gears of heaven was also envisioned as a dislocation of the central pole around which the heavens themselves turn (and indeed, the motion of precession will cause the heavenly points of the very north and south celestial poles themselves to shift, as if the great central pole of heaven *has* been chopped down or damaged).[301]

Thus, I believe that the expedition to the Forest of Cedars and the chopping down of the tallest tree in the forest summons up the mighty theme of precession, and all of its esoteric meaning (having to do with our own dislocation and disconnection -- and our need to remedy that disconnection in order to once again become whole). For the great cycle of precession does not only evoke dislocation and disconnection, but also the ushering in of a new age, and new heaven and earth, and thus carries within it the theme of reconciliation, transcendence, and restoration.

There are many clues in the text itself that this famous expedition to the Cedar Forest is celestial and precessional in nature.

As they enter the Forest of Cedars, the heroes rip down a door at the entry to the forest, on their way to chopping down the highest cedar. The destruction of one door (and the later creation of a new door) also has precessional implications, as the authors of *Hamlet's Mill* explain (we saw one example of this when examining the Native American myth in which Deer jumps through the snapping door to retrieve fire).[302] In the discussion on pages 121 and 122 of this volume, we saw that this snapping doorway in the myth from the Pacific Northwest, like the snapping rocks of the Symplegades in the Greek myth of Jason and the Argonauts, was interpreted by the authors of *Hamlet's Mill* as representing one of the two equinox points, which are like "doors" or "gates" through which the sun must pass as it crosses the celestial equator twice each year (once on the way "down" to the lower half of the year, when nights are longer than days, and once again on the way back "up" to the summer half of the year, when hours of daylight are longer than hours of darkness).

Thus, a myth such as the expedition to the Cedar Forest, in which the heroes *rip down* one door and later establish a *new door* can be very directly interpreted as referring to the motion of precession, which "rips down" an old door and establishes a new one, by causing the sun's crossing point (at the equinoxes) to *move into a new zodiac constellation* for the succeeding precessional age.

One of the most heart-wrenching aspects of the Cedar Forest expedition is the fact that Humbaba appears to be profoundly wronged by Gilgamesh and Enkidu, who come off as bloodthirsty criminals. Humbaba (or Huwawa) pleads for his life, especially in the copies which have survived of the older Sumerian version of the myth, and offers the rationale that he is after all the rightfully appointed guardian of the Forest of Cedars. Gilgamesh seems amenable to this argument in most versions of the encounter, but Enkidu will have none of it and demands that Gilgamesh kill Humbaba immediately. Humbaba asks for mercy, but Gilgamesh and Enkidu (and by extension Shamash, who helps incapacitate Humbaba and who seems to be the deity whom Enkidu implicates as the one who most especially wants Humbaba destroyed) slay him instead.

What's more, they constantly refer to the fact that they *know* they are breaking the commands of Enlil in the killing of his rightful guardian. There appears to be nothing very praiseworthy in the act at all – and in fact much that could be condemned as terribly unrighteous.

The solution to the problem comes when we understand that this myth, like the myth of Set and Osiris, involves the depiction of precessional cycles – the end of an age, which we have already seen can be connected to the chopping down of a central tree. In this case, it seems that Humbaba is the rightfully-appointed guardian of the old Age – but the willful sun-god Shamash is determined to move into a new Age (and the shifting of the Ages is indeed a function of the sun's motion in rising from the background of one set of stars into another on the important equinox morning). Appropriately enough, these ancient texts tell us that it was the *sun-god* who overturned the order laid down by Enlil.

After slaying Humbaba, the heroes collect cedar from the sacred forest, including the tallest cedar in the forest, and use it to create a magnificent new door, one which will delight the gods (at the end of Tablet V). This represents the establishment of a new equinox, and of a new precessional age. I am convinced that the themes of these "precessional" world myths have to do with restoration as much as they have to do with separation -- and that they thus have to do with the deepest aspects of this incarnate life with which we must wrestle.

Without an understanding of the celestial aspects of the expedition to the Cedar Forest, and the esoteric significance with which the great heavenly cycles were imbued in the ancient system that informs virtually all of the world's known myth-traditions, we would have a difficult time making sense of the events of this violent expedition.

511

There are many other aspects of the Gilgamesh epic which could be profitably examined for their celestial content, including the slaying of the Great Bull of Heaven and the throwing of its haunch towards the face of Ishtar / Inanna (an episode which I believe can be fairly easily seen to be precessional in nature as well), but we will now move to conclude this introductory examination of the Star Myths of ancient Mesopotamia -- but only after first journeying with Gilgamesh to meet the important figure of Uta-napishtim who survived the great Deluge, and whose wisdom Gilgamesh seeks towards the end of the epic, as recorded on the surviving ancient tablets.

The episode of the slaying of the Bull of Heaven takes place in Tablet VI of the Standard Version of the Gilgamesh epic. The beginning of Tablet VII has not been preserved on any of the tablets of that text which have been discovered in the modern era thus far. However, as Professor Andrew George explains in his translation of the Gilgamesh texts, we do have a summary from "a fragmentary prose paraphrase, written in Hittite," and based upon an older version of Gilgamesh.[303] In that fragment, Enkidu has a dream in which he sees an assembly of the gods. He hears Anu, the father of Enlil and Enki among others, declare that because Gilgamesh and Enkidu have slain the Bull of Heaven, and have slain Humbaba who guarded the Forest of Cedar, one of those two heroes. Then Enlil decrees that of the two, Enkidu shall die and Gilgamesh shall not. Shamash the sun-god pleads for Enkidu, but to no avail.[304]

Enkidu lies down before Gilgamesh, tears flowing down like streams, and bewails this fate and the separation from Gilgamesh, whom he addresses as "O my brother, dear to me."[305] It is at about this point that the surviving text of Tablet VII of the Standard Version of the epic resumes. Enkidu begins a stream of curses.

He begins by cursing the great door of cedar he made for the temple. Next Enkidu curses the hunter who discovered him in the forest, in his natural state, and then goes on to curse Shamhat with a truly terrible string of curses, and concludes with his reason for cursing her: "Because [you made] me [weak, who was undefiled!] Yes, in the wild [you weakened] me, who was undefiled!" (VII, 130 - 131).[306]

At this point in the text, the god Shamash intervenes and in a voice from the sky, asks Enkidu why Enkidu should curse Shamhat, who fed him bread and liquor fit for a king, clothed him, and made him the companion of Gilgamesh himself. Shamash declares that Gilgamesh himself will supervise the funeral of Enkidu, and the people of Uruk will wail, and the very rulers of the underworld will all kiss Enkidu's feet. Shamash concludes by saying that after Enkidu is gone, Gilgamesh will wander the wilderness clad in a lion-skin, his hair matted, mourning for his friend and his brother.[307]

The words of the sun-god calm Enkidu's heart, and Enkidu then proceeds to bless Shamhat with a long list of blessings, saying "[My] mouth [that] cursed you shall bless [you] as well!"[308]

This theme of blessing versus cursing is very important across the ancient myths of the world. We see many verses in the text of the Old and New Testaments of the Bible dealing with the theme of blessing versus cursing, including in the story of Jacob and Esau, and the story of Balaam and the Ass, and many, many others. In the New Testament epistle of James chapter 3 we find a verse which is somewhat reminiscent of this passage in the Gilgamesh text, declaring "Out of the same mouth proceedeth blessing and cursing. My berthren, these things ought not so to be."

I have thought about this subject of blessing and cursing as it relates to the world's ancient myths at some length, and believe that we can see how closely it relates to the action of our being "cast down" into this material world (seemingly material, but actually simultaneously material and spiritual), in which we are "cut off" and disconnected from our previous state and divided even from our subconscious mind and our Higher Self.

If you think about most of the curse-words that you know or hear on a regular basis, you will readily agree that these words all have to do with *reducing* someone to their physical nature alone, denying that they are anything more than their physical characteristics, decreasing or diminishing them: objectifying them (reducing them to the status of an object).

But the world's myths and sacred traditions, as we have already seen, have as a central message the *elevation* of our spirit, the reconnection with that part of ourselves with whom we have temporarily become estranged, the re-integration with our Higher Self, the "discovery of fire" (meaning that divine spark present in each and every human soul), the recognition of our own spiritual nature and our unbreakable inner connection with the Infinite, and the fostering of such discovery and recognition in others as much as it is possible for us to encourage it. This, in a nutshell, describes the concept of *blessing*, and the ancient Star Myths encourage blessing rather than cursing -- both towards ourselves and towards others.

Note that the lines which describe Enkidu lying down and weeping, with tears that are described as flowing "like streams," may once again be describing Scorpio (whose river-delta-shaped upper region furnished the streams of blood in the "death of Humbaba" scene), particularly because Enkidu is then described as lifting his eyes up to the door, to curse it (the constellation Ophiuchus, above Scorpio) and also as cursing the beautiful Shamhat (whom we suspect to be associated with the constellation Virgo, in front of Scorpio).

We are not to curse our current incarnate condition -- and certainly not the ones who brought us into that condition -- but rather we are to seek to elevate our own spirit and that of others, as one of our most important goals during this incarnate life.

The remainder of Tablet VII describes dreams Enkidu relates regarding visits to the underworld, including one in which Enkidu describes being turned into a dove and taken down into the house of darkness (VII, 182ff),[309] from which none ever leave, in passages which are reminiscent of Maui's descent into the underworld in the form of a pigeon, as well as of episodes in Popol Vuh describing the Hero Twins in Xibalba.

Somewhere at the end of Tablet VII, in lines which have yet to be recovered on any surviving tablet, Enkidu dies, because Tablet VIII describes the funeral of Enkidu and the commemoration by Gilgamesh of his companion and brother. The pattern here is very similar to other myths having to do with the twinned nature of our own soul, according to my analysis. These include, for example, the mourning of Achilles for Patroclus (in the Iliad of ancient Greece) and the mourning of Jesus for Lazarus in the gospel accounts, both of which are addressed in later volumes of this series.

Gilgamesh, we learn (particularly in surviving older versions of the epic) refuses for days to surrender the body of Enkidu for burial, until he sees a maggot drop from the nose of his friend (see for instance the Sippar Tablets, dated to the eighteenth or seventeenth centuries BC, which describe this scene in section 2, verses 8 and 9).[310] This recognition of mortality has a profound effect on Gilgamesh. He realizes he too will one day be like the corpse of his friend, and thus begin his wanderings in the wilderness, dressed in a lion-skin, searching ultimately for the one who lives afar off and who was given immortality after surviving the great Deluge: Uta-napishti.

We will not here detail all the episodes of the wanderings of Gilgamesh in the wilderness, or all the details of the Mesopotamian Flood accounts. Suffice it to say that these can also be argued to be celestial in their foundations, although some of the encounters (such as the Scorpion-men) are more easily interpreted than others. The third volume of this series, *Star Myths of the Bible*, explores the celestial foundations of the Genesis Flood in detail, as well as the identity of Noah (who, along with his family, survives the Deluge in the Genesis account).

The Mesopotamian Flood-accounts are recorded in the Gilgamesh cycle (in Tablet XI of the Standard Version), as well as in other texts, including an Akkadian epic called Atrahasis, recorded on three tablets. Atrahasis (whose name means "Surpassing Wise" and is thought to be an epithet of Uta-napishti) and Uta-napishti are different names of the same flood-surviving figure, who is also called Ziusudra in Sumerian.[311]

The name *Ziusudra*, according to the glossary of Professor George's translation, means: "Life of Distant Days."[312] Professor Stephanie Dalley of Oxford notes that: "Sumerian Ziusudra is an approximate translation of Akkadian Ut-napishtim together with his epithet, in which the element *sudra* corresponds to Atrahasis' epithet *rūqu*, 'the far-distant.'"[313] *Uta-napishti* signifies: "I Found Life."[314]

The one who goes through the great Flood is one whose life is so full of days that it is a life of "distant days" -- indeed, as we will see, the gods actually declare to him and his wife that because they have gone through the Flood, they shall become like the gods. Thus, some logic (albeit one not yet immediately obvious) appears to inform this quest taken up by Gilgamesh after the death of Enkidu, in which he seeks to find his way to the distant dwelling-place of Uta-napishti. Let us undertake our own quest into the Mesopotamian source-myths in order to see if we can, through an examination of the esoteric celestial system, determine what that logic might be.

The story of the Deluge is told most fully in the three tablets of Atrahasis. This text is undoubtedly the source of the literalistic interpretation of Sitchin and his followers alleging that the Annunaki created humanity in order to perform physical labor for them, because in Atrahasis (unlike Enuma Elish, in which mankind is created in order to establish the worship of the gods and build shrines to them) humanity is indeed created in order to relieve the burden of the toiling Igigi -- although the idea that men toil in order to give gold needed by the Annunaki to run the atmosphere production on their alien planet is nowhere to be found. Indeed, the labor performed by the gods is specifically described as the construction of the great system of canals which enabled the watering of the fertile but arid lands between the two rivers, making possible the amazing civilizations of ancient Mesopotamia (the great canals were originally designed and built *by the gods*).

In Atrahasis, as has been mentioned previously during the discussion of the creation of humanity, the gods who grow tired of laboring (for 3,600 straight years, night and day) go to Ellil or Enlil, and demand relief from their toil. Enlil, listening to their complaint, decrees that mankind shall be created in order to do the work, and calls upon Anu to determine one god who will be slain so that his own life-blood and spirit can be mingled with clay in order to create mankind.

The texts tell us that the wise god Ilawela was chosen by the other gods to be the one who is to be slain, and whose spirit will be combined with the clay. The goddess Mami the midwife is directed to fashion men and women, and she does so, using fourteen pieces of clay to make seven males and seven females, combining the clay with the divine life-force provided by Ilawela, and informing them that they should never forget that although they are clay they also contain the divine and eternal spirit of the gods.

Thus is humanity created, and procreation between men and women begins shortly thereafter. However, after a space of six hundred years, or "not even six hundred years" as the text informs us, mankind had grown so plentiful upon the land that the din and clamor raised by the activities of the mortals began to greatly annoy the gods, and Enlil in particular.

Note here the parallels to the Genesis Flood account. The parallels between the Mesopotamian Deluge and the Genesis Flood, and indeed the world-wide flood oicotype, which is one of the most widespread myth-patterns of all, have been noted since the re-discovery and translation of the eleventh tablet of the Gilgamesh epic by the brilliant early Assyriologist George Smith (1840 - 1876) of the British Museum, who in November of 1872 noticed a passage on a tablet describing a Noah-figure landing his ark upon a mountain and sending out birds, including a raven and a dove, in order to find out whether it was safe to disembark.

In his book *Rise & Progress of Assyriology,* Wallis Budge writes that upon recognizing this Akkadian version of the Flood account on the tablet from the library of Asshurbanipal, Smith was so astonished "that he jumped up and rushed about the room in a great state of excitement, and, to the astonishment of those present, began to undress himself!"[315] The magnitude of the discovery was indeed enormous, and the shock to the paradigm prevalent in 1872 mirrored the shock Smith himself displayed. The tablet containing this Deluge description was many centuries older than the accepted dates for the composition of Genesis and the Pentateuch, but the parallels between them were undeniable.

So similar are many details in the Mesopotamian accounts and the Genesis description of the Flood that many scholars naturally assume that the Genesis account is descended from the Sumerian and Akkadian accounts (which are much earlier than Genesis, the surviving versions of Atrahasis being dated to about 1630 BC, and most estimates of the origin of the Gilgamesh cycle being even earlier than that).[316] Professor Dalley suggests in her 1989 book *Myths from Mesopotamia: Creation, the Flood, Gilgamesh, and Others* that most of the widespread flood myths from the ancient world descend from Atrahasis:

> Atrahasis the wise man, who built an ark and saved mankind from destruction, is a figure of immense prestige and antiquity to whom various literary and religious traditions were attached. He was known by a variety of names and epithets which were translated into different languages, sometimes with reinterpreted meanings, sometimes abbreviated, and in this way his fame spread over huge distances through a span of some five thousand years. In Mesopotamian literature he was the survivor of the Flood,

together with his wife, and was granted a form of immortality by the great gods. The story of the Flood was one of the most popular tales of ancient times, and is found in several ancient languages, reworked to suit different areas and cultures so that different settings and details are found in each version.[317]

While I of course agree with Professor Dalley that the oicotype of the great Flood is among the most widespread on the planet, I disagree that the other versions necessarily represent reworkings, retellings, or adaptations of a Mesopotamian original, and suggest that it is equally likely (if not vastly more likely) that all of the widespread variations around the globe are surviving remnants of a far older original, of which the Mesopotamian versions are but one later manifestation.

Indeed, similar Flood myths have been preserved among the Indigenous traditions of cultures in North, Central and South America, and it goes without saying that very few academics in the field of Assyriology or any other academic discipline today would admit the possibility that these too are variations or descendants of a Mesopotamian original.

There is a Flood account in the Popol Vuh of the Maya in which the gods send a Deluge to destroy their first attempts at creating human beings, men of clay with whom the gods are dissatisfied because of their inability to speak and therefore their inability to worship (echoing the stated purpose for the creation of mortal men and women found in Enuma Elish, where they are created to worship the gods).

In the Atrahasis account, as in the Genesis account, the gods (and in particular Ellil or Enlil) decide to destroy men and women because they have somehow overstepped their boundaries. In the Genesis account, this violation apparently involves the sexual relations between the "sons of God" and the "daughters of men" described in Genesis chapter 6, as well as the observation that: "the wickedness of man *was* great in the earth, and *that* every imagination of the thoughts of his heart *was* only evil continually" (Genesis 6: 4). In the Atrahasis account, we receive the added explanation that the clamor raised by the multitudes of men and women disturbed the tranquility of heaven and prevented Enlil from getting any sleep.

Thus to reduce their numbers, the gods first unleash disease upon humanity. As the disease takes its toll upon men and women, Atrahasis raises his voice to the gods to ask how long such misery and death shall be visited upon humanity, and the god Enki (or Ea) takes pity and instructs Atrahasis to call the elders together, institute a boycott of all further worship and offerings to the gods, but instead to offer a loaf of baked bread and a flour offering to the specific god who is sending the disease (in this case, Namtara) so that he will be ashamed to continue with that project. The people follow this advice, and the disease is stopped.

The text tells us that another period of time (six hundred years, or not even six hundred), and the clamor and racket again cause Enlil to become upset. A very similar pattern is then described, this time with a different god being instructed to withhold rain. The lack of rain leads to drought, and eventually to famine -- and seeing the misery it inflicts upon the people, Atrahasis again raises his voice to the gods, and is answered by Enki (or Ea), who provides a similar set of instructions, which being followed lead to the restoration of the rain and of the fruitfulness of the land to provide food for humanity.

After several more iterations of this same pattern, Enlil finally becomes enraged at Enki (Ea) for continuing to help humanity against the destructive plagues visited by the gods, complains again at the clamor created by men and women upon the earth, and commands Enki to send a great Flood upon them to wipe them out once and for all. Enki replies that he has no intention of doing such a thing and that violence of that sort is more characteristic of Enlil. This exchange takes place near the end of Tablet II of Atrahasis, at the conclusion of which Enlil determines to send a tremendous Deluge lasting six days and seven nights, and the council of the other gods assent to his plan.

Tablet III commences with Atrahasis being troubled by dreams foreshadowing the coming Flood. He calls out to his god, Enki (or Ea) to ask what the meaning could be. The god answers his servant, and tells Atrahasis to listen carefully. The ancient texts explain that Enki (or Ea) tells Atrahasis (or Ziusudra in the Sumerian version) to stand beside a wall in order to hear the words of the god. Here is a fragment describing the scene, as translated by Albert Tobias Clay in 1922:

> For . . . . . . the gods . . . . . .
> Zi-û-suddu standing at its side heard . . .
> At the wall on my left side stand . . . . . .
> At the wall I will speak a word to thee.
> My holy one, give attention!
> By our hand (?) a flood will be sent;
> To destroy the seed of mankind . . . .
> Is the decision, the word of the assembly [of the gods]
> The commands of Anu (and) En[lil . . .]
> Its (their) kingdom, its (their) reign . . .[318]

This encounter is translated and put into more understandable context by Timothy J. Stephany in his translation of Atrahasis (contained in the same volume as his translation of Enuma Elish):

> Enki raised his voice to be heard, speaking to his servant,
> "You say, 'It should be made known to me while dreaming'
> So pay heed to the substance that I will pass along to you.
> Wall, hear every utterance! Reed hut, attend to every word!
> Take apart your house and with the timbers construct a boat
> Put aside your property for the sake of saving living things
> The boat you construct must be sized with proper proportion
> The length of it and the width of it should be equivalent
> Put a roof upon it, like that which covers the deep Apsu,
> Cover it all so that even the sun might not peek inside!
> Construct within it both upper decks and lower decks
> The ropes must be made durable enough to endure strain,
> The bitumen must be made strong, to lend it sturdiness
> For I will make the rains fall upon you where you stand,
> Descending like a wealth of fowl, like a treasure of fish."[319]

These verses provide a wealth of detail from which the celestial foundations of the mighty Deluge and the survival of Atrahasis or Ziusudra or Uta-napishtim and his family can be teased out. Again, a more extensive discussion of the Flood account and all its various components, focusing on the version found in Genesis, is provided in the third volume of this series.

We have already seen evidence that the god Enki (or Ea) may be associated with the constellation Ophiuchus (see earlier discussion on pages 400 - 405). I believe that both the "wall" and the "reed hut" described in the verses above relate to the constellation Ophiuchus, which is described in just such a manner in other Star Myths from other cultures around the world, and especially in numerous Biblical texts (where Ophiuchus plays the role of the "booth" which shelters Jonah, for example, and the basket of "rushes" or reeds in which baby Moses floats). A notable verse is found in 2 Samuel 22: 30 and repeated again in Psalm 18:29, in which David declares in a song: "by my God I have leaped over a wall." Extensive analysis in *Star Myths of the World, Volume Three* (*Star Myths of the Bible*) establishes beyond any doubt that the figure of David is overwhelmingly associated with the constellation Hercules: if so, what is the identity of the "wall" over which the constellation Hercules can be said to be "leaping"? Clearly, these verses have their celestial foundation in the relative positions of the constellations Hercules and Ophiuchus, and indicate that Ophiuchus was anciently envisioned as a wall in some Star Myth manifestations.

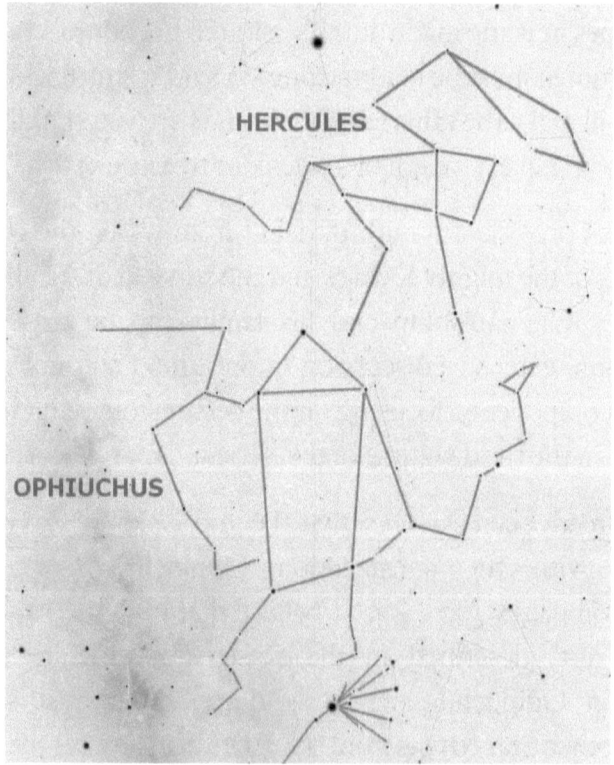

In the Atrahasis text, I would argue that it is also possible that Enki or Ea may be envisioned as correpsonding with Hercules, at least when he is whispering through "a chink in the wall" (a celestial connection which also finds its way into Shakespeare's *Midsummer Night's Dream,* of course). Note how Hercules appears to be bending down towards the western serpent-half of Ophiuchus (on the right of the image as we face it). In the ancient fragment translated by Albert Clay, above, we see that the text has Enki telling Ziusudra "at the wall on my left side stand."

Note that in the heavens, if we envision the constellation Hercules as having the front of its body towards us, then the upraised arm of the constellation (the arm holding the mighty sword or club or axe or thunderbolt-weapon) would be the right arm of the figure, while the downward-reaching arm would be the left arm of the same figure. Thus, if the god tells Ziusudra or Atrahasis to stand "at the wall" on his "left side," then this might indicate that Atrahasis is associated with Ophiuchus (anciently envisioned as a wall or a hut as well) while Enki is in this case associated with the constellation Hercules, telling Atrahasis where to stand as he gives him instructions on how to survive the Flood which will be sent by Enlil and the other gods.

Note also that the text of Atrahasis reveals that the god tells Atrahasis to tear down his own *house* in order to build the ark in which he will survive the Deluge. This detail may indicate that the boxy outline of Ophiuchus itself will *also play the ark* (after it plays the role of the house of Atrahasis, which is torn down). The text has Enki telling Atrahasis to "Put a roof upon it" like that which covers the deep Apsu, and Ophiuchus certainly has a roof shape at the top of the central body.

There is one objection which could be leveled at an identification of Ophiuchus with the ark which Atrahasis is instructed to build: the god tells Atrahasis to make its dimensions equal, such that its length and width are the same. The outline of Ophiuchus is definitely not square, but the Great Square of Pegasus certainly is, which means that we *could* interpret the command to tear down the house and build a square vessel as meaning that Ophiuchus serves as the "house" of Atrahasis, which is then torn down to make the "ark" of the Great Square. This interpretation is possible, although the Great Square does not have so satisfactory a roof as does Ophiuchus, and a roof is also mentioned in the text. However, since the roof is said to be "like that which covers the deep Apsu," it is possible to argue that the Milky Way itself, which arches above the Great Square, could be envisioned as this "watery roof."

I myself remain more partial to the identification of the ark of Atrahasis with Ophiuchus, especially because the instructions of Enki also specify that Atrahasis must coat the ark strongly with bitumen (this parallels the command of the LORD to Noah in Genesis 6: 14, that he must "pitch it within and without with pitch," with *pitch* being an English word derived from the same ancient root as that at the root of *bitumen*).

Many other (smaller) "arks" in world myth are described as being coated or "slimed" with bitumen or similar materials and set into the water amongst the reeds or rushes, usually containing an infant: for example, in Exodus 2: 3 the infant Moses is famously placed in an "ark of blurushes" which his mother has "daubed with slime and with pitch" and set adrift at the "river's brink" -- all descriptions which fit the constellation Ophiuchus at the edge of the Milky Way ("the river's brink") above the multiple heads of the constellation Scorpio (which play the river rushes or reeds --

see again the star-chart shown on page 524, where part of Scorpio is just visible below the "ark" of Ophiuchus).

Similarly, the ancient Akkadian king Sargon the Great (thought to have reigned in the period around and containing 2300 BC) inspired numerous later accounts of his birth and life, one of which (found on Assyrian tablets dated to about the 7th century BC) describe Sargon being conceived by a high priestess, who gave birth to him in secret, and placed him in a basket made of rushes, covered with a lid and sealed with bitumen, which she then set adrift in the river Euphrates. The similarities of this story with the Exodus account of baby Moses, as well as with other "baby cast adrift" myth-patterns from other cultures around the globe, have been remarked upon since the opening years of the twentieth century (tablets containing the story of baby Sargon were discovered in the 1800s). I believe these stories are all based upon the same constellations in the night sky, and their proximity to the great "river of stars," the Milky Way.

Thus, the presence of bitumen in the instructions of Enki to Atrahasis regarding the construction of the ark in which he will survive the Flood (and the presence of similar instructions given to Noah in the Genesis account) strongly implicates Ophiuchus as the celestial counterpart of the vessel being described. A final confirmatory clue is the detail of the ark as needing to have upper decks and lower decks, as well as strong *ropes*, to endure strain: the central body of the constellation Ophiuchus can be seen to have two sections to it (an "upper and lower deck," corresponding to the spaces within the tall rectangle and the triangular section under the roof), and of course it can also be envisioned as being flanked by two sturdy ropes (the serpent-halves).

The Deluge itself is foretold by Enki in a very interesting fashion: the god's description (as translated by Stephany) is that the rains will come down "like a wealth of fowl, like a treasure of fish." This description confirms the interpretation I have offered elsewhere (such as in Volume Three) for the floodwaters: they correspond to the Milky Way itself, pouring down from heaven upon the earth. The Milky Way band (particularly the brightest, widest section which stretches up from the region of Ara the Altar, between Scorpio and Sagittarius, and onward beside Ophiuchus and up past Hercules) contains of course the constellations of the two great birds Cygnus and Aquila ("like a wealth of fowl") and the delightful little constellation Delphinus, which appears as a salmon in both the Norse myths and in some sacred stories from Indigenous nations of North America (thus, this portion of the Milky Way also contains a "treasure of fish").

Returning now to the wanderings of Gilgamesh in search of Uta-napishti (who is also Ziusudra and Atrahasis), we will now "fast-forward" ahead to the meeting between Gilgamesh and the ancient survivor of the Deluge.

After the death of Enkidu, Gilgamesh wanders the wilderness in great sorrow, dressed in a lion's skin, his hair matted with grief, and eventually comes to the very edge of the world, where he first encounters the dreaded Scorpion-men at the base of a double-mountain called Mashu, whose top reaches to heaven and whose roots reach to the underworld. There dwell the Scorpion-men, whose great radiance is fearful, and whose glance (the text tells us) is death.

We can readily perceive that the Scorpion-men must relate to the constellation Scorpio, and most likely the constellation Scorpio in conjunction with Sagittarius (a more anthropomorphic figure, hence "Scorpion-men"). Between Sagittarius and Scorpio we find the "fearful radiance" of the brightest portion of the Milky Way. Above Scorpio we find the looming shape of the constellation Ophiuchus, which we will find playing the role of the *gates of the underworld* in many myth-traditions, and which also must play the role of the great twin-mountain Mashu, since the Scorpion-men are described as guarding the base of this mountain (and Ophiuchus is directly above Scorpio in the sky).

The Scorpion-men see Gilgamesh and one calls out to his mate that the flesh of this far-traveler is godlike, and that he is two-thirds divine and one-third mortal. They ask what business he has at the end of so far a road. Gilgamesh replies that he is seeking his great forefather Uta-napishtim, who found life eternal. Gilgamesh's hope is that Uta-napishtim will share that secret with him. The Scorpion-men tell him that no mortal has ever come this far, and that the road ahead lies through the great mountain. Only the great god Shamash, the sun, travels such a dark road. Gilgamesh, however, expresses his desire to go forward, and so the Scorpion-men wish him well.

Gilgamesh thus travels through the deep tunnel through the mountain, along the path that the sun would take each night, through the twelve hours of darkness: this concept is very similar to the passage through the *twelve hours of the night* depicted in some tombs of ancient Egypt, most notably in the *Book of the Amduat* and the *Book of Gates*, New Kingdom funerary texts describing the twelve-hour journey of the sun through the underworld (or the Duat). These texts themselves descend from an earlier funerary text called the *Book of the Two Ways* -- a title which is interesting since the mountain through which Gilgamesh must pass (in twelve "double-hours") is a Twin Mountain, and it is associated with Ophiuchus, and Ophiuchus

529

has two serpent-halves on either side of its central "mountain" body (the two serpent-halves possibly inspiring the description of "Two Ways," meaning "Two Roads" or "Two Highways or Pathways").

The journey of Gilgamesh through the mountain and the underworld path of the sun takes twelve double-hours, each hour described as bringing intense darkness, until the twelfth double-hour, when Gilgamesh emerges from the mountain ahead of the sun and beholds two trees full of fruit, a carnelian tree and a lapis lazuli tree (carnelian and lapis lazuli being semi-precious stones). These two trees are likely also based on celestial metaphor and associated with the two serpent-halves of Ophiuchus, which can be shown to play two trees (or two branching trunks of a single tree) in other Star Myths of the world, including the great branching olive-tree within whose shelter Odysseus spends the night after washing up on the shore of Phaeacia in the Odyssey (explored in Volume Two of this series).

Note also that, as far as modern parallels, the journey of Aragorn and his companions in the final book of the *Lord of the Rings* (*The Return of the King*) through the Paths of the Dead (under the mountain) can definitely be seen as evoking this ancient pattern which we see in the path taken by Gilgamesh the king in search of the dwelling-place of Uta-napishti the Distant.

After emerging from the great tunnel beneath the Twin Mountain, the same tunnel through which the sun must toil every night (likely described as "twinned" because it includes the *western horizon* and the *eastern horizon*, connected by the "lower way" beneath the earth), Gilgamesh is seen by the keeper of a tavern at the end of the world, Siduri (or Shiduri). She dwells at the edge of the vast empty sea across which no mortal has ever crossed, but only Shamash the sun (as she later informs Gilgamesh).

The authors of *Hamlet's Mill* spend some time musing on the significance of Siduri, and noting that scholars have since the discovery of the Gilgamesh tablets been trying to place the location of her tavern, perhaps somewhere along the edge of the Mediterranean. "Yet the hero's itinerary suggests a celestial landscape instead, and the scorpion-men should be sought around Scorpius," they argue[320] -- and it is certain that they are correct in this case, and that the "edge of the sea" where Siduri dwells is not to be found on our terrestrial geography but rather in the heavens.

The edge of the sea where Siduri tends her bar is almost certainly to be identified with the edge of the Milky Way band, which plays the role of the breakers washing up on the shore in many Star Myths (some of which we've already seen, such as the story of baby Maui cast into the sea-foam by his parents).

We don't have extensive description of Siduri herself with which to make a definitive identification. The text tells us that she keeps a tavern at the edge of the great sea (the tavern itself could be associated with the outline of Ophiuchus, which we have already seen to have been envisioned as a shelter). Note that Ophiuchus also can be envisioned as holding up a goblet (the "serpent-head" on the western side of the constellation). Thus, Siduri could perhaps be associated with Ophiuchus.

The text also declares that Siduri is "swathed in hoods and [veiled with] veils" (Tablet X, lines 1 - 4).[321] The text also tells us that Siduri has potstands (presumably full of liquor) and vats full of gold.[322] These descriptions suggest a possible association with the constellation Virgo, who is situated in the heavens adjacent to the great "cup" of Crater (a constellation between Virgo and Hydra). Also, the outline of Virgo suggests a woman wearing a veil or a hood:

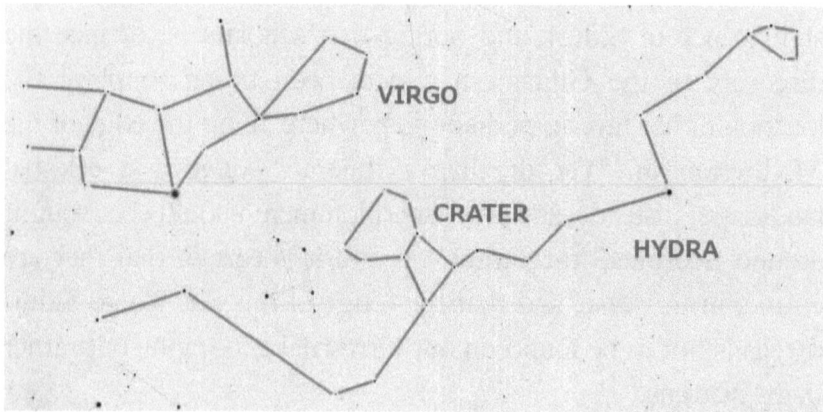

Without many textual clues to go on, it is difficult to make a positive identification of the celestial association of Siduri. I believe she is likely connected with either Sagittarius or Ophiuchus (both of which constellations could be seen as being on the "shore of the sea," if the shore is the band of the Milky Way, as I believe is most likely for the identification of the sea's edge in this portion of the epic), or else with Virgo as just discussed.

A connection with Virgo has some evidence in its favor, including the description of a "veil" or "hood" as well as the reference to vats, but the disadvantage of the Virgo identification is that the constellation cannot really be said to be on the "edge of the sea" (assuming the sea is the Milky Way). Virgo *is* located on the edge of the plunge down into the lower half of the year (during the precessional Age of Aries), which could be interpreted as being on the "edge of the sea" (with the "sea" being a metaphor for the lower half of the zodiac wheel, a metaphor for our life in this incarnate condition in the "lower realm"). Thus, an association with Virgo cannot be ruled out (and, if Siduri is Virgo, then

Ophiuchus could still be her tavern: Ophiuchus is located on the edge of the Milky Way and thus the "edge of the sea" as well).

The authors of *Hamlet's Mill* note that the figure of Siduri has many parallels in other myths around the globe, including the figure of "Mother Scorpion" found in myths of Central America, who receives the souls of those who are in between lives.[323]

Without doubt the figure of Siduri can be seen to have parallels with the jotun maiden Gunnlöd in Norse myth, whose celestial identity is discussed in Volume Four of this series. In that story, Odin seduces Gunnlöd in order to gain access to the vats of mead she guards (it is the Mead of Poetry, or the Song Mead). This clearly suggests a parallel to Siduri who keeps a tarvern at the edge of the world and has vats of some sort of liquor.

Gunnlöd herself lives in a cave beneath a formidable mountain (the Hnitbjörg) in Norse myth -- a sufficiently isolated location and one that may parallel the lonely tavern of Siduri at the edge of the world. The most direct parallel between the two stories, however, is certainly the fact that in order to reach Gunnlöd, Odin must transform himself into a serpent and slither through a long, dark tunnel which has been bored into the mountain using a tusk known as Rati (or Rati's Tusk), just as in the Gilgamesh epic, the wandering king comes to the tavern of Siduri after he has braved the dark tunnel which bores its way underneath the mountain of Mashu.

Thus, it would seem that Siduri and Gunnlöd have strong points of resonance: if so, this fact might also argue for an identification of Siduri with the constellation Virgo, since in Volume Four we see evidence that Gunnlöd may be associated with Virgo as well -- but we should keep the possibility open that Siduri could alternately be associated with either Sagittarius or Ophiuchus instead.

At the tavern of Siduri, Gilgamesh learns that the vast wasteland of ocean which lies between this world and the dwelling-place of Uta-napishti the Distant has never been crossed by a mortal. Only the sun-god Shamash has ever crossed that watery desert (although he crosses it every day, as he makes his way through the sky over the wide world). What's more, Siduri informs Gilgamesh that the sea contains a section midway across which are known as the Waters of Death -- any mortal who touches these waters will perish. However, she also tells Gilgamesh that there is a boatman named Ur-shanabi, who is the boatman of Uta-napishti: if anyone can get Gilgamesh across the sea, it will be Ur-shanabi, and his companions, known as the Stone Ones. Siduri suggests that Gilgamesh go to Ur-shanabi and let him see the wandering king's face.

The text then tells us that Gilgamesh loses no time in going in search of Ur-shanabi, and that when he sees the Stone Ones who crew the boat of Ur-shanabi, Gilgamesh takes up his axe and dagger and falls upon them in a violent assault, smashing up the Stone Ones and throwing them into the sea.

When Ur-shanabi arrives on the scene, and asks the king who he is and what he seeks, he explains to Gilgamesh that he has just destroyed the very Stone Ones who could have helped him in his quest. The Stone Ones are not harmed by the Waters of Death, but Gilgamesh has just smashed them to pieces and thrown them into the sea. Nevertheless, Ur-shanabi says that if Gilgamesh will go into the forest with his axe and cut down a number of long punting poles (three hundred in fact), then perhaps they can still cross the sea. The punting poles cannot be re-used, apparently, because if the mortals come in contact with the Waters of Death, they will perish. Thus, they need to leave the poles as they punt their way across the vast expanse to the distant land of Uta-napishtim.

I would guess that the Stone Ones smashed to pieces by Gilgamesh correspond again to Ophiuchus, envisioned this time as standing in the boat of Scorpio (a common way of seeing Ophiuchus in ancient myth). Gilgamesh is described as setting upon them with axe and dagger: these are the two weapons which we have already seen the Mesopotamian myths envision Hercules as wielding (the axe in his upraised arm and the dirk or dagger in his downward-reaching arm). The constellation Hercules can be envisioned as attacking Ophiuchus (just below Hercules) with these weapons.

When the boatman Ur-shanabi receives the poles cut by Gilgamesh, they set off across the sea. Most likely, Ur-shanabi at this point corresponds to Ophiuchus (since the Stone Ones are no more), standing in the boat, and carrying Gilgamesh with him (the constellation Hercules above Ophiuchus above Scorpio).

Where are they heading? They are almost certainly setting a course across the vast and relatively empty part of the sky just east of the bright region of the Milky Way (which is home to all of the important constellations on which most of the preceding mythical episodes are based). The empty region to the east of Sagittarius is referred to by H. A. Rey as the "wet region" of the sky, and it is relatively devoid of bright stars (other than Fomalhaut in the Southern Fish [Piscis Austrinus]).[324] H. A. Rey also refers to this part of the sky as "a very dull region."[325] This region represents the vast waste of ocean over which Ur-shanabi and Gilgamesh must travel in order to reach the dwelling-place of Uta-napishti the Distant.

In the middle of that "wet region" of the sky (as H. A. Rey calls it, probably due to the fact that its constellations are all water related, including Capricorn the "Sea-goat," Piscis Austrinus the Southern Fish, Cetus the Whale and Pisces the Fishes, as well as the fact that the region itself is vast and empty, like a wide ocean) we find the constellation Aquarius, the Water-bearer. This constellation almost certainly represents Uta-napishti the Distant in his faraway dwelling-place after the end of the Flood (he may have been associated with Ophiuchus prior to and during the Flood, as we've discussed above: yet another example of a connection in ancient myth between Aquarius-figures and Ophiuchus-figures).

Star Myths of the World, Volume Three provides abundant evidence to associate Noah with the constellation Aquarius, at least after the Flood when Noah settles down to plant the first vineyard (Great Square of Pegasus), then becomes drunk and passes out and is found by his sons Shem, Ham and Japheth. I would argue that Uta-napishti, whose story closely parallels that of Noah, is likewise associated with Aquarius after the Flood.

When Gilgamesh arrives at the distant home of Uta-napishti, borne there by Ur-shanabi, the ancient survivor of the Deluge greets him and asks the same series of questions that has been asked every time he has met people along the way (the same sequence, for example, was repeated when he met Siduri, and again when he met Ur-shanabi). Uta-napishti asks Gilgamesh why his cheeks are so hollow, his face so sunken, his mood so wretched, his visage so wasted, his heart so full of sorrow, his features so burned by exposure to frost and sun, and why he wanders the wild dressed in the skin of a lion (Tablet X. lines 212 and following).[326]

Gilgamesh replies with the same formulaic response which he has provided in answer each time to others as well: why shouldn't his cheeks be hollow, why shouldn't his face be sunken? He then goes on to recount the death of his beloved brother-in-arms Enkidu, and how he refused to surrender the body until he saw a maggot drop from Enkidu's nostril. Then, Gilgamesh explains, the fear of death came over him and he said to himself that he too would one day be in the same condition. It was at that point, he explains, that Gilgamesh became determined to seek out Uta-napishti the Distant, "of whom men tell" (X, 250).[327]

Now, having finally succeeded in his quest to reach the dwelling-place of his own great ancestor, Gilgamesh marvels: "I look at you, Uta-napishti, your form is no different, you are just like me, you are not any different, you are just like me" (XI, 1 - 4).[328] How is it, Gilgamesh asks, that Uta-napishti found the life eternal?

"Let me disclose, O Gilgamesh, a matter most secret," Uta-napishti begins (XI, 8 - 9).[329]

Uta-napisthi then relates the story of the Deluge in all its terrible detail -- and the level of detail in the Mesopotamian account paints (if possible) a yet more terrifying picture of the cataclysm than even the Genesis account of the Flood. The reader deserves to absorb the full text, found in the moving translation by Andrew George, to feel the impact of the ancient words, preserved across so vast a gulf of time down to the present day.

First Uta-napishti relates the decision of the council of the gods to send down the Deluge. Then, he relates the advice of Ea (or Enki), given to Uta-napishti through the wall as described earlier.

Uta-napishti relates that he understood the instructions of the god, and began the construction of the vessel that would bear him through the Flood. Then, Uta-napishti explains, he took aboard the boat his relatives, and all beasts both domestic and wild, along with representatives of every skill and craft known to civilization, and sealed the hatch.

The onset of the Deluge is described by Uta-napishti in awe-inspiring images: a black cloud arises on the horizon, and advancing within it with a bellowing roar was Adad the Storm God, with two gods going before him to bear his throne over mountain and plain (i.e. *Hercules atop Ophiuchus*). Uta-napishti recalls that:

> "The god Errakal was uprooting the mooring-poles,
> Ninurta, passing by, made the weirs overflow.
> The Anunnaki gods carried torches of fire,
> scorching the country with brilliant flashes.
>
> The stillness of the Storm God passed over the sky,
> and all that was bright then turned into darkness." XI, 102 - 107.[329]

Gale-force winds blow over the country for a day, flattening everything -- and when the Deluge itself arrives it comes with such force that no man or woman could recognize another, nor even make them out as the waters engulfed them. The gods themselves take fright at the awful cataclysm, and then begin to weep over the result.

Belet-Ili, the Mother Goddess who along with Ea made mankind, reproaches herself for allowing her children to be destroyed.

The downpour, along with the relentless wind, continues for six days and seven nights, and the ocean covers the face of the earth. But then, the storm subsides and all grows calm. Uta-napishti opens a vent, and feels the sun upon his cheeks. He too begins to weep.

The vessel runs aground upon the top of a mountain. Uta-napishti describes how he released birds, in a passage very similar to the Genesis account (and whose celestial foundations are explored in Volume Three of this series): first a dove, then a swallow, and finally a raven. The first two, finding no place to land, return to the boat, but the raven finds food and does not return.

At this, Uta-napishti says he brought out an offering, and made a sacrifice to the four winds, placing incense upon the mountain-top, and arranging flasks, with reed and cedar and myrtle beneath.

This description appears to reinforce our earlier analysis, that the ark of Uta-napishtim is associated with Ophiuchus (which also plays the role of a hill or mountain in many myths, including those of ancient Mesopotamia). When the text specifically describes Uta-napishti's sacrifice as being made "on the peak of the mountain" and as being offered "to the four winds," these verses perfectly describe Ophiuchus beneath the "whirling" outline of the constellation Hercules (the "four winds"):

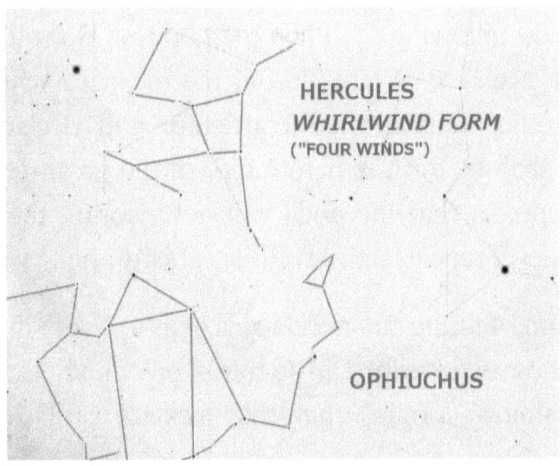

From the above image, we can also make out a likely celestial foundation for the "flasks" which Uta-napishti also arranges as part of his offering (the "serpent-head" of Ophiuchus, on the right of the central body of the constellation as we face the star-chart above).

Note that once again we have a clear parallel to the Genesis account, in which Noah is described building an altar to the LORD, and offering burnt offerings from the clean animals he brought on the ark (Genesis 8: 20). In the Biblical text, we read:

> And the LORD smelled a sweet savour; and the LORD said in his hearth, I will not again curse the ground any more for man's sake; for the imagination of man's heart is evil from his youth; neither will I again smite every living thing, as I have done. While the earth remaineth, seedtime and harvest, and cold and heat, and summer and winter, and day and night shall not cease. Genesis 8: 21 - 22.

The parallels between this passage and the account in Gilgamesh Tablet XI are quite astonishing, for there we read that the gods "did smell the savour" of the offering of Uta-napishti upon the mountain and gather around like flies as the man made sacrifice (XI, 161 and following).[330] Then the goddess Belet-ili arrives, and takes her necklace of lapis lazuli, the necklace which Anu had made for her during their courtship, and declares that this necklace shall be for a remembrance of the great desctruction of this Deluge, so that the gods will never forget them (and, it is implied, never repeat such a terrible catastrophe).

This action of lifting the necklace is akin to the fixing of the bow in the heavens described in Genesis 9: 13 - 16. It is very likely (indeed almost certain) that the necklace of Belet-Ili can be identified in the heavens in the form of the Northern Crown, Corona Borealis.

Then Enlil arrives on the scene, and seeing the boat of Uta-napishti he becomes enraged and exclaims that none were supposed to survive the Deluge. The god Nunurta immediately implicates Ea (or Enki). Then Ea responds to Enlil, turning the blame back upon him as the leader of the council of the gods, and asking how he could have ever decided to bring on such a catastrophe? Ea also explains that he himself never divulged any secrets to mortals, but only gave Atrahasis (as he here refers to Uta-napishti) a vision.[331] At the end of his accusation of Enlil, Ea tells Enlil to decide what to do with the man.

Uta-napishti describes to Gilgamesh what happens next:

> "Enlil came up inside the boat,
> he took hold of my hand and brought me on board.
> He brought aboard my wife and made her kneel at my side,
> he touched our foreheads, standing between us to bless us:
>
> 'In the past Uta-napishti was a mortal man,
> but now he and his wife shall become like us gods!
> Uta-napishti shall dwell far away, where the rivers flow forth!'
>
> So far away they took me, and settled me where the rivers flow forth. XI, 199 - 206.[332]

Thus were Uta-napishti and his wife made like the gods.

However, Uta-napishti then asks Gilgamesh who will convene for *him* the assembly of the gods? He challenges Gilgamesh to go without sleep for six days and seven nights -- a task Gilgamesh immediately fails.

Then, Uta-napishti commands that Gilgamesh's should be bathed, and his matted hair should be washed, and his animal pelts should be replaced with fine spotless garments. When it is time for Gilgamesh to depart, Uta-napishti again tells the king, "Let me disclose, O Gilgamesh, a matter most secret . . ."[333]

Uta-napishti describes a plant which grows deep beneath the water, the power of which can return Gilgamesh to the vigor of his youth. Gilgamesh wastes no time, but has Ur-shanabi row to the designated spot, where, affixing great stones to his feet, Gilgamesh sinks down beneath the waves and retrieves the plant.

With joy, Gilgamesh exclaims that he will take this plant home with him and test it out on an ancient citizen of Uruk, and then he will consume it himself to be once again as he was in his youth.

However, on the journey back across the leagues towards the great city, he finds a pleasant pool in which he bathes, and as he does so, a snake catches the scent of the "Plant of Heartbeat" and steals away with it. As it slithers away, the snake sheds its skin and disappears.

Gilgamesh sits down and weeps.

Thus ends the futile quest for immortality. The poem ends with Gilgamesh directing Ur-shanabi to climb the wall of Uruk and describe the city to him.

The fact that all of these episodes can be seen to be based upon celestial metaphor underscores the fact that the epic is esoteric in nature, revealing to our understanding deep truths through myth in much the same way that Mr. Miyagi's tasks instruct Daniel-san in the *Karate Kid*.

The plucking of the "Plant of Heartbeat" that will restore Gilgamesh to the vigor of youth has strong parallels to the plucking of the plant with black root and milky flower which the god Hermes plucks for Odysseus to protect the hero from the enchantment of the goddess Circe in the Odyssey. I believe it is likely that both are referring to the same celestial feature, related to the "water-streams" pouring down from the water-vessel of Aquarius (as discussed in more detail in *Star Myths of the World, Volume Two*).

Abundant evidence supports a connection between Noah and the constellation Aquarius and thus I believe it likely that Uta-napishti is associated with Noah as well. For one thing, Uta-napishti is sent to dwell "far away," and as we have already noted, Aquarius is located in the midst of the vast and relatively empty "wet region" of the night sky, far from the constellations near the Milky Way which play the characters in the majority of myths we have examined. For another thing, Uta-napishti is told by Enlil that he will dwell "where the rivers flow forth"[334] -- and as we will also see in Volume Two of this series, the V-shaped constellation Pisces was sometimes envisioned as the source of rivers (see the discussion on the voyage of Odysseus to the underworld, and the flowing together of the rivers Pyriphlegethon and Cocytus, in *Star Myths of the World, Volume Two*).[335] Thus Aquarius, adjacent to Pisces in the sky, is a figure who dwells "where the rivers flow forth."

As demonstrated in Volume Two, there is evidence which supports a connection between Aquarius and the god Hermes as well -- and thus, I believe that both the instruction about plucking the plant in the Gilgamesh epic (given by Uta-napishti, who is associated with Aquarius) and the instruction about plucking the plant called *molu* or *moly* in the Odyssey (given by Hermes, who

543

is also associated with Aquarius), can be shown to be based on the same region of the night sky.

When Gilgamesh stops to bathe in the pool, this scene is undoubtedly found in the heavens at the widest part of the Milky Way galaxy, at the Galactic Center -- a region which becomes a bathing pool or bathing spot in numerous ancient myths. The serpent stealing away with the precious plant in its mouth, of course, is Scorpio, located at that pool and heading away from it. The snake later sheds its skin as it slithers away, perhaps a sign of the effectiveness of the plant it has stolen (its youth is renewed, just as Uta-napishti promised). The shed skin may relate to the constellation Hydra, ahead of Scorpio in the sky and thus arranged in the heavens as though showing the progress of the snake as it slithers away from the pool where Gilgamesh is bathing:

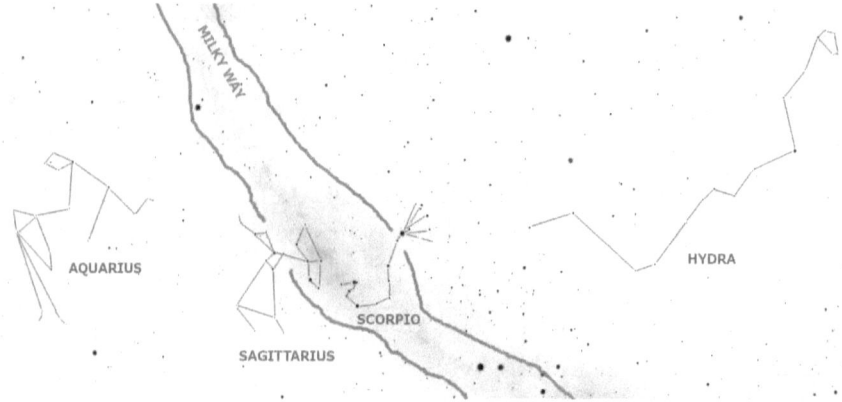

The star-chart above shows Aquarius on the left as we face the page. While not immediately intuitively obvious, I believe the long streams of water issuing from the water-vessel of the constellation were sometimes anciently envisioned as the stems of a mysterious and potent supernatural plant (the plant of the gods).

The water-pitcher itself might have been envisioned as the flower of this special plant.

Proceeding to the right (west) across the chart (from east in the left to west in the right as we face the chart), we come to the widening in the Milky Way where Gilgamesh stops to bathe. The constellation Sagittarius almost invariably plays the role of the bathing figure in myths involving this portion of the sky (this is one of the most common patterns in myth that I have encountered thus far).

As Gilgamesh bathes, we see Scorpio sneak up and steal away with the supernatural plant. Continuing towards the right of the chart (the west) we see the constellation Hydra, representing the serpent slithering away, and perhaps representing the skin that the snake sheds and leaves behind.

Gilgamesh sits down and weeps. Note that Odysseus in the Odyssey is also notable for weeping at certain points in the narrative. We will see in the discussion of the Odyssey in Volume Two of this series that Odysseus, like Gilgamesh, is most associated with the constellation Hercules -- and that the outline of Hercules can be envisioned as a weeping figure in the sky.

Thus, the events at the conclusion of the Gilgamesh cycle can clearly be seen to be based on celestial metaphor, as with all the other ancient myths we have examined -- and their meaning can thus be argued to be esoteric, not literal. But, what could these haunting episodes be trying to convey to our understanding?

I believe that these texts are intended to deliver a rather complex and profound message, through inspired myth -- a meaning which would be difficult to simply explain in a dry and didactic fashion, but which is tremendously helpful to our understanding here in this incarnate life.

It has to do with the toil of life in a body which we experience as men and women who are (as the myth of the creation of mankind from clay mixed with the life-blood of the god Ilawela demostrates) simultaneously mortal and divine. The fact that the gods create men and women to do the work on earth illustrates that the gods (who dwell in the realm of pure potentiality, rather than in the realm of matter) do not now experience the toils of this physical, incarnate existence into which we enter when we come down into the human form.

And it is down here in the human existence of this life that *we perform the work of the gods!*

Thus, we see that the first half of Atrahasis, which describes the revolt of the Igigi gods who no longer wish to perform physical labor, and describes the creation of mortal men and women to do the work instead, is in fact connected to the second half of Atrahasis, in which Atrahasis goes *through the Flood* and is made like the gods.

And how is it that Atrahasis / Uta-napishtim and his wife achieve "the life eternal"?

The ancient verses are very clear: they are made like the gods because by *going through the Flood!*

Now, this knowledge may not seem very helpful to you and me today, since you may be saying to yourself, "Well, that's all very nice for Uta-napishti and his wife -- but I didn't go through that Flood, so it doesn't do me much good to know that they achieved the life eternal by going through a Flood."

But that is exactly the point where we must remember that, based upon a super-abundance of evidence in the texts themselves, this Flood of which we read so often in the Star Myths of the world is *not a literal Flood*!

Of course, there may well have been one or more literal flood-cataclysms in earth's ancient past -- I do not deny that possibility and am in fact on record as arguing that the evidence in the geological record for a cataclysmic flood in earth's distant past is overwhelming.

But the Flood accounts that we find in the ancient myths are overwhelmingly *celestial* in nature -- and thus they are describing something esoteric, something metaphorical, and not something literal. We don't become "like the gods" by going through an ancient literal flood -- that would be impossible for us to accomplish today, since it happened ages ago. These ancient myths are intended to teach us about an entirely different Flood: one that each of us goes through and in fact a Flood through which each of us is actually going, right now!

It is the very same "Flood" that Odysseus can also be shown to endure, in the Odyssey of Greece, in which the hero is tossed about on the vast ocean by the wrath of Poseidon, going through a series of "spin cycles" as he traverses the watery obstacle-course between his starting point and his ultimate goal.

I would suggest that the Flood through which Uta-napishti must pass, and through which Odysseus must pass, is an esoteric reference to *this incarnate life* through which each of us must also pass -- through which each of us is in fact traveling right now.[336]

Further, the proper goal we are pursuing in this "ocean-crossing" experience in the human life is not some kind of eternal life in the body: the experience of Gilgamesh and his failure to achieve even mastery over sleep (let alone over death) is ample illustration of that fact.

Instead, there must be some lessons that we can only learn here in the turbulent sea which we traverse during our life in mortal form. We can see some rather dramatic changes in the character of Gilgamesh from the start of the epic to its conclusion, one of the most obvious being his complete lack of empathy for others at the start of the poem contrasted with his development of a much more empathetic nature as the poem goes on.

In the end, the sloughing off of the skin of the serpent as it slides away may be a symbol of the possibility that we ourselves will experience multiple incarnations, as we come down from the realm of the gods to toil our way through the life in a mortal body. While we are here, I believe that some of the important principles the Gilgamesh epic urges upon us include blessing rather than cursing, loving others as we love ourselves, and reconnecting with that part of ourselves from which we become estranged as an inevitable consequence of *first* the descent into the physical body and *second* the entanglements of human relationships and the complex demands of operating in a wider society.

How do we begin to reconnect with that part of us from whom we have become estranged? The answers are there in the myths, given to humanity in ancient times so remote they predate all the civilizations known to conventional academia (even predating the mysterious culture of Sumer, apparently). And, in addition to the myths, we have been given a variety of disciplines which also appear to have their roots in very ancient times, disciplines involving the *quieting* of the constructed, superficial mind, in order to become more aware of the wisdom of the neglected subconscious mind, which appears in some way to be connected to the wider universe and even to the realm of the gods.

These disciplines include practices such as Yoga, meditation, chanting, singing, drumming, Tantra, and many others.

I believe that once we begin to understand the esoteric language which the ancient myths can be shown to be speaking, the myths of ancient Mesopotamia will be seen to contain profound truths of great practical benefit, illustrating concepts that will help us hear the voice of our Higher Self and become reconnected with our "divine twin," as we make our way through the Deluge of this life in which we find ourselves.

Star Myths of Ancient India

Although it has been said many times already in this volume, and will be said many times again throughout this series, that our examination of the myths of any culture must necessarily be somewhat cursory, and that an entire multi-volume series examining celestial metaphor and esoteric meaning could be written exploring the myths of any single culture, this sentiment is perhaps more true of the myths of ancient India than of almost any other body of myth on our planet, so voluminous and variegated are the deities and episodes which fill the ancient scriptures and stories belonging to the heritage of the cultures of this region of the world.

The corpus of Sanskrit scripture of ancient India is believed to begin with the Vedas, of which the Rig Veda is acknowledged to be the oldest. The Rig Veda alone consists of 1,028 hymns, each averaging 10 verses long, traditionally totalling 10,800 *Panktis* (metrical counts of forty syllables) which thus are said to contain 432,000 syllables (both 108 and 432 being precessional numbers which appear again and again in ancient myth, as noted by the authors of *Hamlet's Mill*).[337]

Together with the other three Vedas (the Sama Veda, the Yajur Veda, and the Atharva Veda), these texts contain over 20,000 verses. The Rig Veda is thought to date to as early as 1200 BC, although some scholars assign an even earlier date.[338] In addition to the Vedas, the ancient texts of India also include the Upanishads (traditionally 108 in number),[339] as well as the great ancient Sanskrit epics of Mahabharata and Ramayana. Professor Wendy Doniger of the University of Chicago, a leading scholar of ancient Sanskrit textual traditions and of the mythologies of

550

ancient India, notes that "the *Mahabharata*, the great Epic of India" is "a compendium of over 100,000 verses (ten times as long as the *Iliad* and *Odyssey* combined)."[340] It should be noted that the number of verses in the canonical scriptures of the standard Bible (some of these verses being much shorter than the verses of the Iliad, the Odyssey, or the Sanskrit texts) is 31,102 of which 23,145 verses are in the Old Testament and 7,957 verses are in the New Testament.

Yet another corpus of ancient texts are the Brahmanas, lengthy Sanskrit commentaries upon the Vedic material, and thought to have been composed beginning around 900 BC.[341]

In addition to all these voluminous ancient Sanskrit texts, Professor Doniger explains that, "By far the most extensive sources of Hindu mythology, however, are the eighteen 'great' Purānas and the numerous 'minor' Purānas, veritable encylcopedias of Indian thought."[342] Of the vastness of the Puranas in comparison to the other ancient Sanskrit literature, Cornelia Dimmitt and J. A. B. van Buitenen write in the preface to their 1977 selection of the Puranas:

> While tradition ascribes to the *Mahābhārata* a *lakh* of couplets, or one hundred thousand, to the Purānas it assigns a *crore*, or ten million.[343]

Truly, then, we are faced with a wealth of ancient Sanskrit source material on the identity and exploits of the gods and supernatural beings within the cosmology of ancient India, perhaps surpassing in volume all other mythical literature. It will of course be impossible to even scratch the surface of such an extensive corpus -- volumes upon volumes could be filled with exploration of the Mahabharata alone, without even touching the Vedas or Puranas or other surviving ancient Sanskrit spiritual texts.

For the purposes of this volume, however, and for the purposes of establishing the thesis of this volume and wider series, it is not necessary to provide an exhaustive examination of any single body of ancient myth (from any single culture), but rather to provide enough evidence to establish beyond reasonable doubt that the myths within any given culture's corpus of myth ancient system can indeed be shown to stand upon the same foundation of celestial metaphor whose outline we have detected underneath the myths of so many other sacred traditions around our planet.

That the myths of ancient India support such a conclusion can be demonstrated beyond any doubt. We will begin by examining some of the most well-known individual gods and goddesses who are addressed in the Rig Veda (or in some cases introduced in other ancient texts), before discussing some of the central characters and most well-known episodes described in the massive epic of the Mahabharata.

The gods and goddesses found in the ancient Vedas continue to be worshiped today, in a stream which is more or less unbroken stretching back millennia, although there have of course been transformations and permutations through the centuries as "Vedic ritual tradition" evolved or developed into "the devotional system of Hinduism."[344] A discussion of this evolution is outside the scope of this volume: we will draw on textual evidence from the earliest Vedas to the more recent Puranas as we focus upon the indications that the myths of ancient India are built upon the same system of celestial metaphor found around the world, despite their distinctive atmosphere and flavor.

We will begin with an examination of the three gods who form a trinity known as the Trimurtri: the gods Brahma, Vishnu and Shiva.

The celestial identity of the god Vishnu is discussed in *Star Myths of the World, Volume Four: Norse Mythology*, in conjunction with the prophetic description of Ragnarok. In that fourth volume in this series, a quotation from French philologist and mythographer Georges Dumézil (1898 - 1986) is cited, from an article published in 1965, in which Dumézil argues for a possible "identity and common function" of the god Vishnu of ancient India and the god Vidar of Norse mythology (or Vidarr, as Dumézil's article spells the name).[345]

Dumézil makes this argument based on the fact that both Vishnu and Vidar intervene at a moment of cosmic crisis, in order to restore the world -- and that both do so by means of "steps" (Vidar by using his great shoe to split apart the jaws of Fenris Wolf, and Vishnu when, in his avatar as Vamana, he takes three steps to measure the entire world, his third step ending upon the head of king Mahabali). We will return to the story of Vamana presently, when discussing the concept of avatars. For now, it is enough to mention that *Star Myths of the World, Volume Four* presents some arguments for identifying Lord Vishnu with the constellation Ophiuchus (although some of his avatars may not).

Some of the supporting evidence given in Volume Four for an association between Vishnu and Ophiuchus include:

➢ The fact that Vishnu often stands atop a many-headed serpent (as Ophiuchus stands atop Scorpio)
➢ The fact that Vishnu is often depicted holding a conch shell and / or small lotus flower (the western serpent-head)
➢ The fact that Vishnu is sometimes accompanied by the eagle Garuda, King of Birds (and Aquila is adjacent to Ophiuchus in the heavens).

Chapter Sixteen

Below is an image of the god Vishnu, carved out of the sandstone in the famous Badami caves, in northern Karnataka, dating back to about the sixth century AD. The god is depicted seated upon the cosmic serpent Shesha (also known as Vasuki), whose multiple cobra-heads arch over the seated form of Vishnu like a canopy:

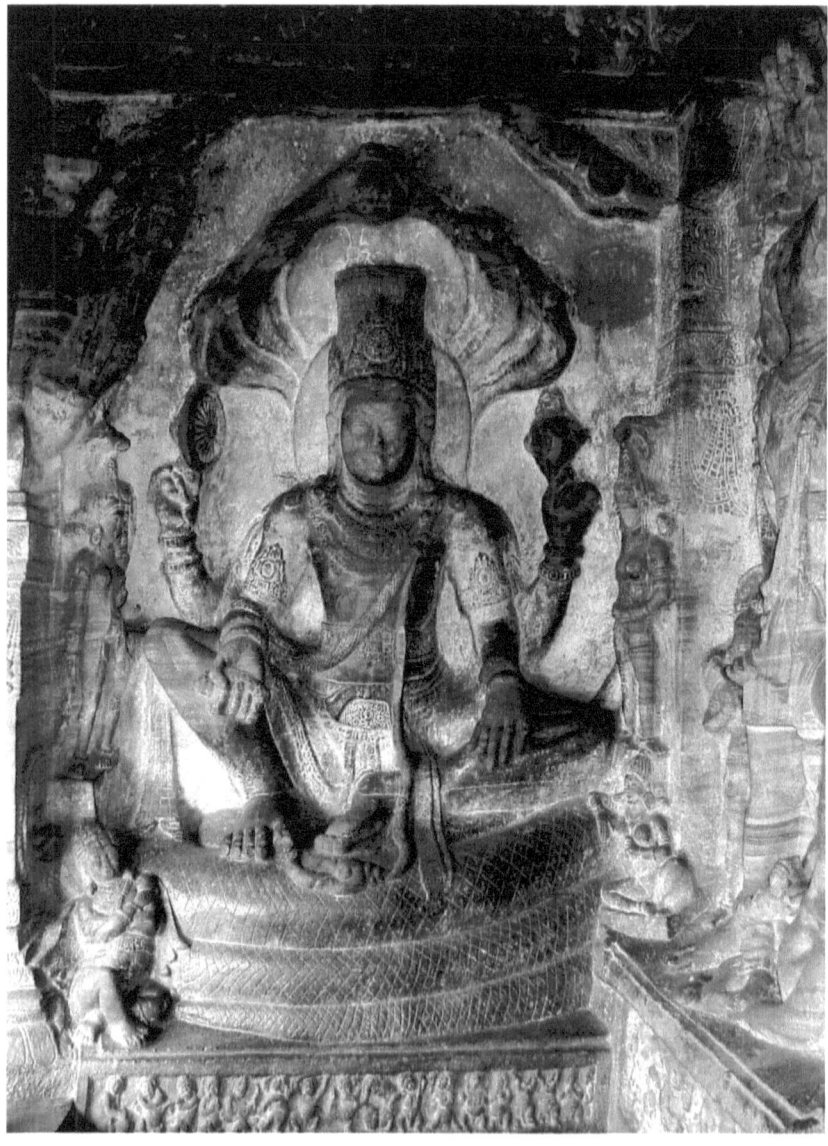

Below is the region of the sky containing Ophiuchus, showing the position of that constellation directly above the form of Scorpio:

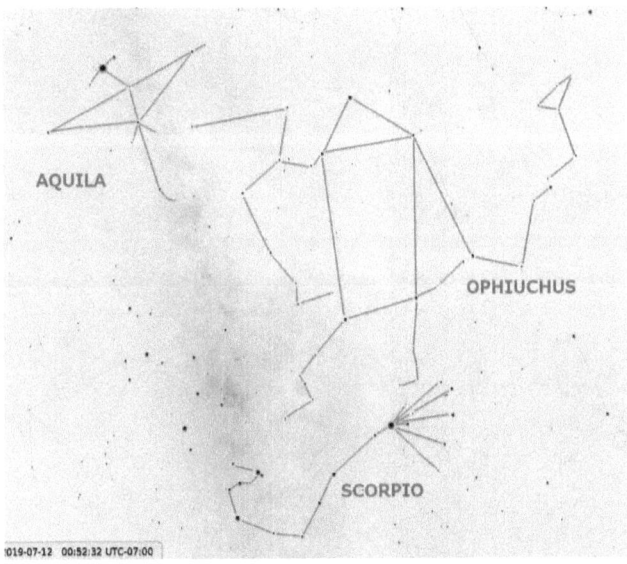

The form of Scorpio in the heavens is actually much larger and more impressive when seen in person than is implied by the star-chart when seen on paper -- truly an impressive and dazzling constellation, and appropriate for depicting the many-headed Nagaraja Shesha, king of all serpents, upon whom Vishnu sometimes sits or reclines in divine repose. Shesha is also referred to by the name *Ananta*, signifying "endless." This indicates that Shesha may be not just Scorpio and its multiple heads, but also whose body *continues* into the Milky Way and is thus identified with the Milky Way as well (as an extension of the sinuous form of Scorpio). The Milky Way forms a great *endless* ring in the sky, associated with a great serpent in many myth-systems.

In the carving from the Badami temple caves, we can just make out the form of the great King of Birds, Garuda the Eagle, located on the left side as we face the image of the god (on the god's right side), about adjacent to the upper of his two arms on that side

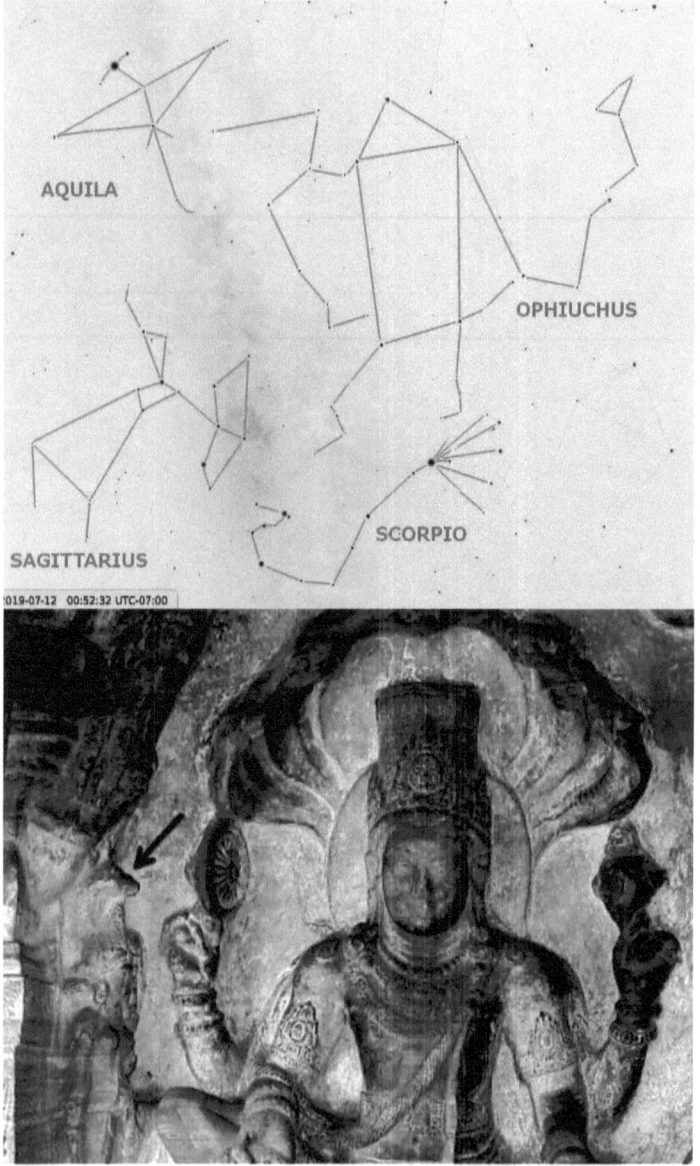

In the image at left, I have added an arrow pointing to what is likely the head of the great eagle, Garuda. Note that the artist has envisioned this eagle as being located in the correct position to

correspond to the constellation Aquila in the sky -- Aquila being located adjacent to the "upper hand" of Ophiuchus on the left side of the constellation as we face the star-chart above.

Indeed, the artist responsible for the image of Vishnu from the Badami caves has depicted Garuda the great eagle just above an image of a goddess, likely Vishnu's consort the goddess Lakshmi (difficult to see in this image, but she is standing facing towards the god just beneath the eagle indicated by the arrow here). Note that this location beneath the eagle would likely indicate that this goddess-wife of Vishnu is associated with the constellation Sagittarius in the heavens, located immediately below Aquila as shown in the star-chart above -- a constellation often associated with important goddesses in ancient myth around the world.

Below is a more recent painting from the nineteenth century depicting Vishnu and Lakshmi and Shesha:

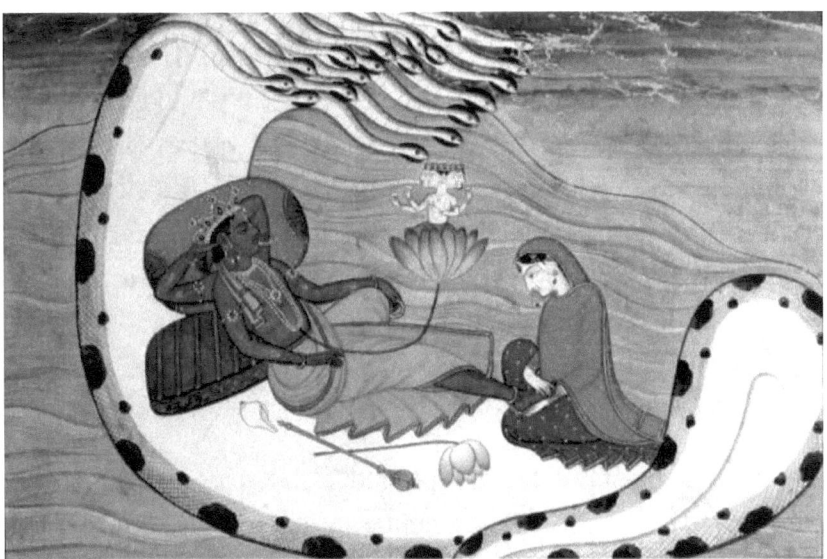

In this position of repose upon the great serpent, Vishnu is sometimes described as dreaming the universe into existence (in other words, this universe we inhabit is created by the dream of Vishnu accompanied by Lakshmi, upon the endless serpent of Ananta Shesha).

The discussion in Volume Four points out that the god Vishnu is the second person in the Trimurtri (or trinity of deities) consisting of Brahma, Vishnu, and Shiva. In this trinity, Brahma is described as the Creator, Vishnu as the Preserver, and Shiva as the Destroyer. From these descriptions, we can see that Vishnu must be the second person of the Trimurtri – and it is very significant, in that Christ is unequivocally the Second Person of the Christian Trinity, and (like Vishnu) is very often associated with the constellation Ophiuchus, as we will examine in more depth in *Star Myths of the World, Volume Three.*

Before turning our attention to Brahma the Creator, let us note another important feature of the god Vishnu, which is included in the nineteenth-century artwork depicted on the preceding page: a lotus which emerges from his navel in the form of a long stalk surmounted by a lotus-flower. We have already had occasion to note that the western "serpent-half" of the constellation Ophiuchus, which is surmounted by a small "circlet" or triangular wedge, is often envisioned in ancient myths as a lotus. See for example the discussion of artwork from ancient Assyria on page 294 of this volume, as well as discussion of the Eye of Horus which, after being torn out, becomes a lotus-flower (on page 366 of this volume).

Looking at the star-chart of Ophiuchus shown at right, it is very easy to understand why the ancient Sanskrit texts describe a lotus growing from the navel of the god Vishnu, if Vishnu is associated with the constellation Ophiuchus (the lotus-plant growing from his navel on the right):

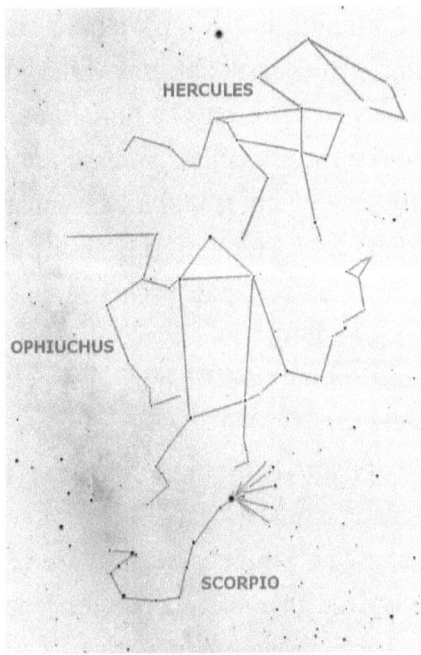

A text from the Puranas describes this lotus arising from the navel of Vishnu (also called Narayana), and describes the lord Brahma situated atop this lotus – which is a strong indication that Brahma the Creator is associated with the constellation Hercules, seen above the lotus of Ophiuchus in the heavens (as shown above). Here is a selection of the Sansrkit text, as translated by Cornelia Dimmitt and Johannes van Buitenen (all insertions in square brackets supply explanations found in the footnotes of the translation by Dimmitt and van Buitenen):

At the end of the last Eon [*kalpa*] when the three worlds were in darkness there was nothing but a solitary sea, no gods and so forth, no seers. In that undisturbed desolation slept the god Nārāyana, supreme person, lying on the bed that was the serpent Śesa. The all-knowing one who is contemplated by wise men had 1,000 heads, 1,000 eyes, 1,000 feet and 1,000 arms. Wearing a yellow robe, he was large-eyed, of vast dominion like a dark cloud, the soul of Yoga whose dwelling is the heart of *yogins*. Once during his sleep there arose in play from his navel a pure lotus, wondrous and divine, core of the three worlds. Spreading out 100 leagues, bright as the morning sun, it had a heavenly fragrance, with auspicious calyx and stamen. The lord Hiranyagarbha [Brahma] approached that place where the Archer [Vishnu] had been lying for a long time. The universal soul [Brahma], having made the eternal one [Vishnu] arise with his hand and infatuated by the other's illusion, spoke these sweet words: "Tell me, who are you, lying hidden here in darkness in this dreadful, desolate, solitary sea?" Hearing his words and smiling, the one whose banner bears Garuda [that is to say, Vishnu, who is "the one whose banner bears Garuda the eagle"] spoke to lord Brahman with a voice deep as the rumbling of a cloud: "Bhoh! Bhoh! Know me to be the god Nārāyana, origin and dissolution of the worlds, great lord of Yoga, the supreme person. See inside me the entire world, the continents with their mountains, the oceans and the seven seas, and also yourself, the grandfather of the worlds."

When he had said this, the universal soul, Hari [Vishnu], although he recognized the great *yogin*, asked Purusa, the creator [Brahma], "Who are you?" Beginning to laugh, the lord Brahmā, keeper of the Vedas, with lotus eyes, replied in these polished words, "I am creator and ordainer, the self-existent great-grandfather; in me is everything established; I am Brahmā who faces in all directions."[346]

After these introductions, Vishnu uses Yoga and enters into Brahma, emerging from his mouth. After emerging from the mouth of Brahma, Vishnu tells Brahma that the god should enter into Vishnu's belly, to see all the worlds therein. Brahma does so, roaming around inside Vishnu and seeing no limit to the worlds enclosed there. The text tells us that, all other doors out being shut by Vishnu, Brahma emerges from the navel of Vishnu:

> All doors being shut by the great-souled Janārdana, Brahmā found passage through the navel. Then the one born from a golden egg, the four-faced Brahmā who had entered therein by the power of Yoga, displayed himself on the lotus. Lord Brahmā, self-existent, the Grandfather, womb of creation, lustrous as the inside of a flower, shone there radiantly, resting on the lotus.[347]

From this description of Brahma resting upon the lotus, and from the earlier analysis showing that the lotus emanating from the navel of Vishnu must be the "serpent-head" on the west side of the constellation Ophiuchus, we can be quite confident that the god Brahma the Creator can be associated with the constellation Hercules (just as God the Father in the Christian Trinity can be seen to be associated with the constellation Hercules in the scriptures of the Bible, as shown in Volume Three of this series).

The line in the above-cited text which describes Lord Brahma as "the one born from a golden egg" may thus indicate that the *same celestial feature* envisioned as the lotus-flower atop the lotus stalk (that is, the "serpent-head" on the western serpent-half of Ophiuchus) also plays the role of the "golden egg" from which the god Brahma is described as being born. Note that this part of the constellation Ophiuchus has been seen to be depicted in the shape of an egg in many surviving pieces of ancient artwork from Mesopotamia, discussed earlier in this volume.

The god Brahma is often called by other names in ancient Sanskrit texts, including the Vedas and the Mahabharata, where the god is frequently referred to as Prajapati, meaning "lord of creatures."[348] He is also frequently referred to in these older texts as Grandfather.[349]

There are numerous ancient texts which imply or else state directly that Prajapati "poured out his seed" as part of an act (or acts) of creation at the beginning of the world, which is very reminiscent of the ancient Egyptian myths involving Atum -- a god whom we also saw (like Brahma or Prajapati) to be associated with the constellation Hercules (see pages 257 and 258 of this volume, for example).[350] This correspondence between the creation myths of ancient Egypt and of ancient India constitutes further confirmation that Brahma is associated with the constellation Hercules in the heavens.

Brahma is frequently described (and depicted) as having four faces and four arms (see for example the image shown on page 557). I believe that the four-fold nature of the god Brahma may originate from the fact that the constellation Hercules has a "four-fold" aspect when envisioned in "whirling" form, as we have seen previously:

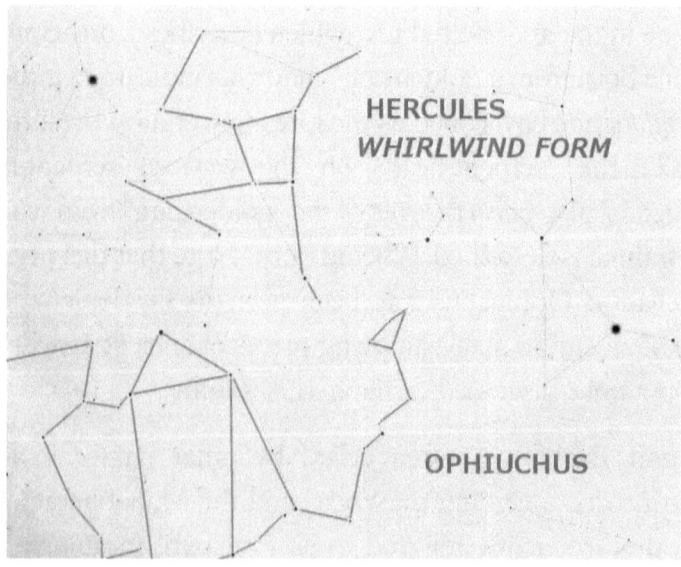

There are other clues which support the association of Brahma with the constellation Hercules. For one thing, he is described as the giver of the Vedas. The same "serpent-head" feature of Ophiuchus that is envisioned as a lotus and as an egg is also envisioned in other myths and sacred stories as a text (this is why, for example, Thoth who is associated with the constellation Hercules is the scribe of the gods in ancient Egypt: he is reaching towards the "tablet" in the heavens which is associated with the same serpent-head feature of the constellation Ophiuchus).

We will later see in our examination of the scriptures of the Old Testament that when the LORD inscribes the tablets of the Ten Commandments with the very finger of his hand, this action is associated with the constellation Hercules reaching down to the "tablet" held aloft by Ophiuchus.

Thus, the fact that Brahma of the four aspects is described as being the giver of the four Vedas corresponds to other Star Myths in which a deity associated with the constellation Hercules is the giver of sacred texts.

Thus, depictions of the god Brahma often show him holding a text in one hand, signifying his role as the giver of the Vedic texts (and indicating his connection to the constellation Hercules). In another hand, Brahma often holds a string of beads (a rosary), and this iconography almost certainly derives from the proximity of the constellation Hercules to the constellation Corona Borealis in the heavens (Corona Borealis is the Northern Crown). We have already seen many examples from other Star Myths around the globe in which a figure associated with the constellation Hercules is envisioned as reaching out to grasp the Northern Crown, because the lower downward-reaching arm of Hercules can be envisioned as being connected to the closest side of the arc of the Northern Crown (see for instance the discussion on pages 209 through 212 of this volume).

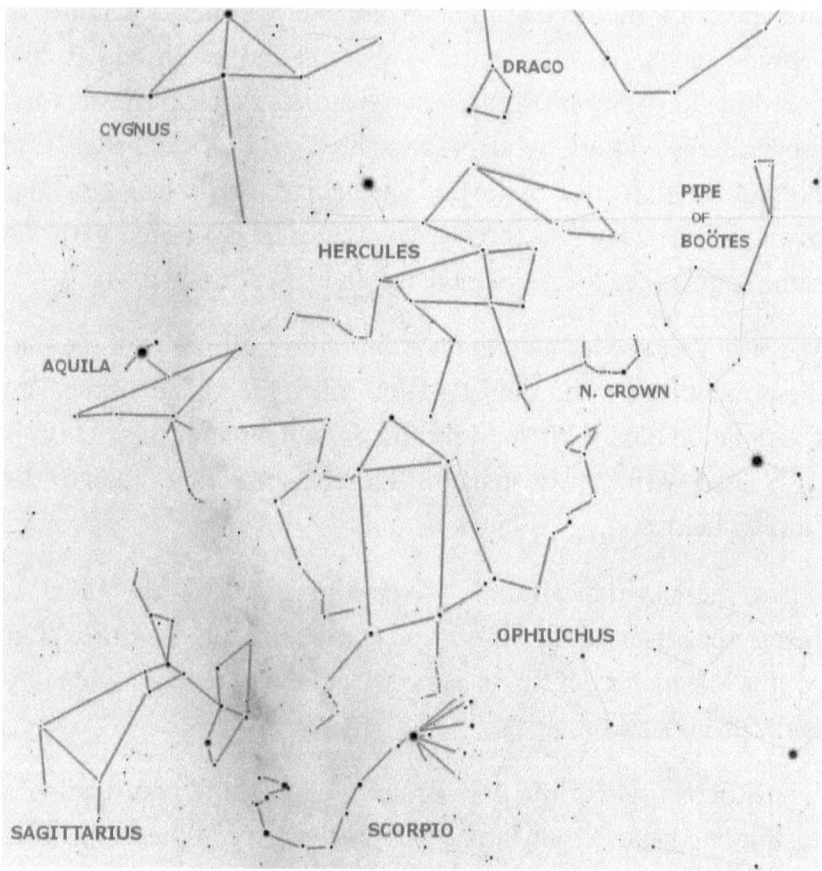

The other hands of Brahma will often be depicted as holding certain types of ladles or dippers, and these are probably indicative of the constellations of the Little Dipper (Ursa Minor) and perhaps of Draco (which are above the constellation Hercules in the sky) or even with the "pipe" of the constellation Boötes, which is also nearby (see the star-chart above).

Another important piece of evidence is the *vahana* or "vehicle" of the god. As we will see in our examination of other myths of ancient India, the gods and goddesses are often depicted riding upon a specific mount associated primarily with them, and known as their vahana. In the case of Brahma, the specific animal with which the god is associated as his vahana or vehicle is the long-necked *hamsa* or *hansa,* a Sanskrit word indicating a goose or swan. Clearly, this association with Brahma has to do with the fact that the constellation Cygnus the Swan (a constellation with a distinctively long neck) is seen flying in the heavens in close proximity to the constellation Hercules. In similar fashion, the vahana of the god Vishnu is Garuda the great eagle, and the constellation Aquila the Eagle is in close proximity to the constellation Ophiuchus (with which constellation the god Vishnu has been seen to be associated).

Below is a depiction of the god Brahma seated upon his vahana, a long-necked hamsa or hansa. In his hands he is holding a text, a string of beads or rosary, and other implements possibly associated with the ladle or dipper he often carries:

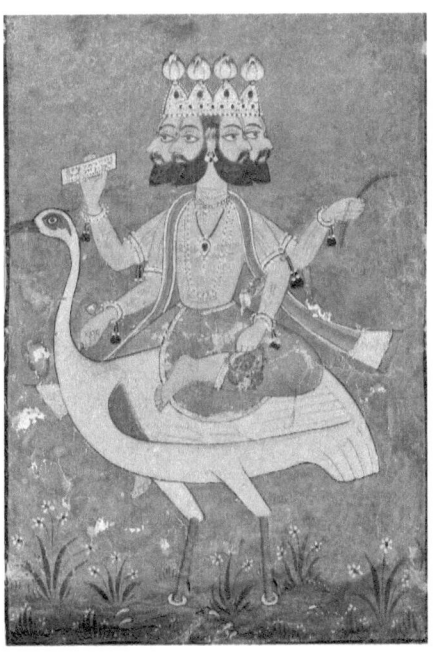

Having now identified the celestial associations of Brahma and Vishnu, this brings us to a discussion of the god Shiva, the third person of the Trimurtri and another very important god in the texts of ancient India. In the selected Puranas translated by Dimmitt and van Buitenen, the Lord Shiva and some of his characteristics and attributes are described as follows:

> Śiva means "auspicious," as does Śankara, which is the name most frequently employed in the Purānas. But a predecessor of this deity, who has terrifying attributes, is found in the *Rg Veda* under the name of Rudra, the "howler," also a popular Purānic appellation. The name is accounted for in the Purānas in a curious way:

>> Rudra, made from Brahmā's dying breath, leaped out of his mouth shining like a thousand suns, blazing like the Fire at the end of the Age. It was the god of gods, Rudra himself, howling most horribly. "Stop your roaring!" said Brahma to the bellowing god. "Because of your howling you will be known in the world as Rudra, the Howler!" (*Kūrma* I. 10. 23, 24)

> In the traditional Hindu trinity of gods in which Brahmā is called the creator, and Visnu the preserver, Śiva is known as the destroyer of the universe at the end of time, emphasizing his ferocious aspect as the deliverer of universal death. But just as Visnu plays all three divine roles for his devotees, Śiva is also regarded by his loyal followers as creator and protector.[351]

The same authors note that although Shiva is associated with destruction and with bringing about the end the universe at the close of each age, such a process is also a creative act.[352] Indeed, in a cyclical cosmology, the end of any one cycle marks the simultaneous beginning of another.

Perhaps because of this paradoxical connection between end and beginning, destruction and creation, Shiva is a god of stark contrasts, as noted by many scholars of Indian and Hindu myth. He is simultaneously celibate ascetic and devoted husband. He is typically portrayed and described as having the long matted locks or braids of an ascetic, part of which are piled atop his head in a triangular topknot. He is also typically depicted with serpents draped over his body, around his neck, and around his waist. Sometimes, he is depicted as being seated upon a tiger skin or leopard skin.

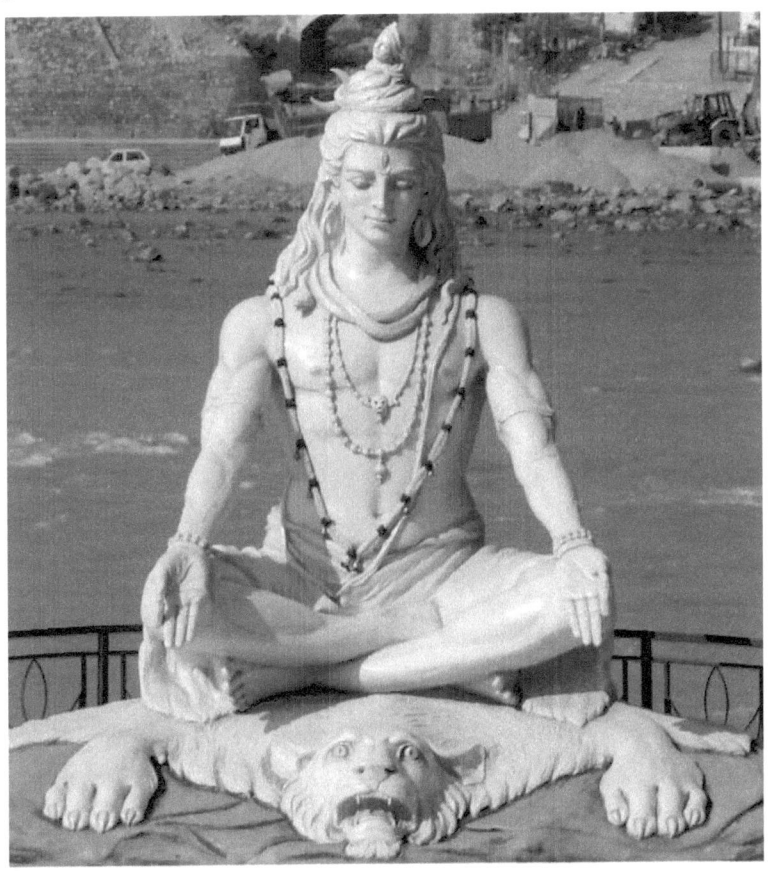

In the preceding image of a statue of Shiva in modern India (along the Ganges River in Uttarakhand in northern India, near Rishikesh) you can make out if you look closely the serpent wrapped around the shoulders of the god (the head of the serpent on our left as we face the image), as well as the crescent-shaped moon symbol in the piled-up hair atop Shiva's head (also on the left as we face the image).

Pre-modern depictions of the Lord Shiva also show the god with piled-up topknot and flanked by serpents, such as this statue from Aihole, dated to the period of AD 450 to AD 750):

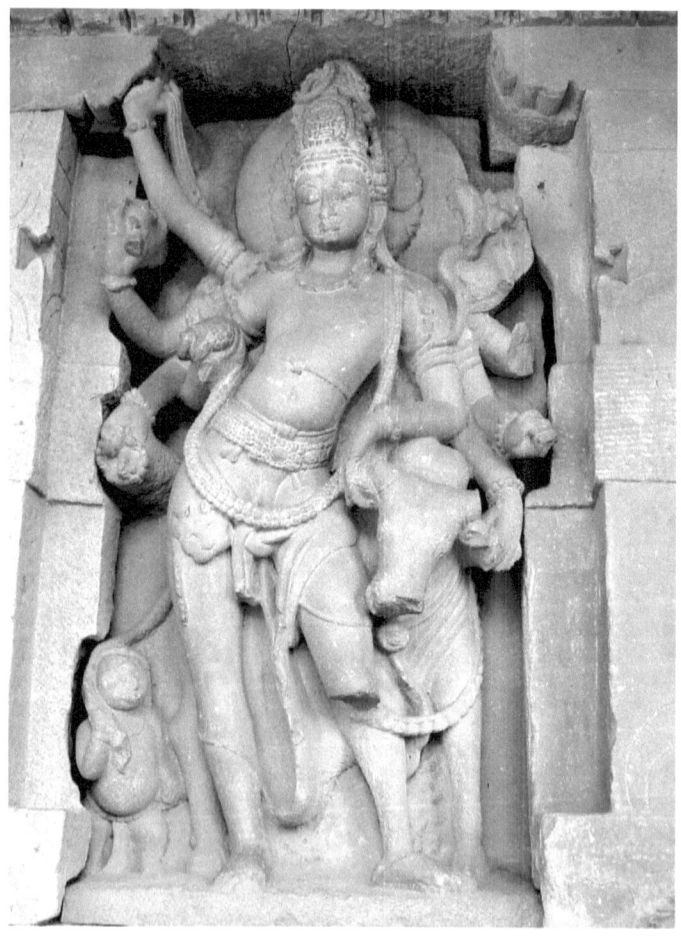

In this statue, you can see if you look closely that the god is wearing a tiger or leopard skin around his waist (the head of the animal is visible on his right upper leg, which is on the left as you view the image). The crescent-moon icon in his topknot is barely visible and partly broken-off at the top of his piled-up hair, and some long locks of hair cascade down to his shoulders on either side of the god's face. A cobra snake rears up over the shoulder of the god on the right side of the body as we face the image.

In their collection of Puranas, Cornellia Dimmitt and J. A. B. van Buitenen describe the most common details found in representations of the god:

> The iconographic accoutrements of Śiva are many. Some of the stories of their origins are to be found in the Purānas; some are not. Most commonly he dresses as a mendicant *yogin*, his body smeared with ashes, wearing a tiger-skin and adorned with a snake, the crescent moon in his hair and the Ganges river flowing from his matted top-knot. To defeat his enemies he carries a trident and a skull-topped club, sometimes also his bow Pināka or Ājagava. And as a dancing beggar he holds aloft a beggar's drum, or a human skull. He dwells on Mt. Kailāsa, famous as the place where his faithful followers hope to go after death.[353]

We have already identified Brahma the Creator with the constellation Hercules, and argued that Vishnu the Preserver is associated with the constellation Ophiuchus; with which celestial figure then will we find the god Shiva the Destroyer to be most closely connected?

Although the answer is surprising, virtually all of the evidence appears to point to a connection between Shiva and Ophiuchus as well, although this conclusion is somewhat unexpected due to the fact that we have just found evidence for a connection between Vishnu, the second god of the Trimurtri, and the same constellation Ophiuchus.

Nevertheless, the evidence for such a connection for Lord Shiva as well is quite compelling. The first clue is the fact that Shiva is frequently adorned with serpents, which is a clear indication of a possible connection with the constellation Ophiuchus, flanked as it is with the two great "serpent-halves." The triangular topknot may relate to the triangular outline at the top of the constellation, just as the crescent-moon symbol at the top of Shiva's hair likely points to the delicate crescent of Corona Borealis, above and just to the west of Ophiuchus in the heavens.

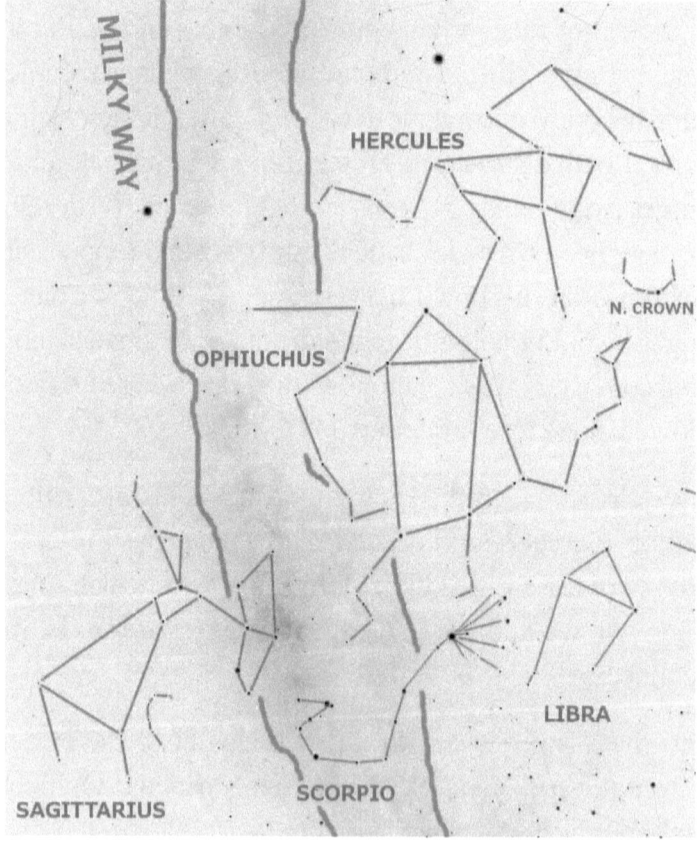

The long, unshorn locks of the god Shiva are said to tumble down and form the sacred river Ganga, the Ganges -- and I would attribute this aspect of Shiva to the close proximity of Ophiuchus to the widest and brightest part of the Milky Way, that heavenly *river of stars* which is associated in ancient myth around the world with specific sacred rivers on earth.

An additional clue connecting the god Shiva to the figure of Ophiuchus in the heavens is the text cited earlier (on page 566) which describes Shiva as originating by "leaping out of Brahma's mouth" (hence his Vedic appellation, "the Howler"). Deities or mythical figures associated with Ophiuchus often "descend from" deities or mythical figures associated with Hercules, and a description of Shiva literally springing from the head of Brahma brings to mind another very well-known deity associated with the constellation Ophiuchus who is described as springing from the head of a god associated with the constellation Hercules: the goddess Athena (associated with Ophiuchus, as discussed in *Star Myths of the World, Volume Two*) who springs from the head of her father Zeus (associated beyond any doubt with the constellation Hercules, as discussed in the same volume).

The association of the goddess Athena with the constellation Ophiuchus is helpful in this context, because we note that Athena in Greek myth is known for wearing the famous *Aegis*, a garment depicted as being fringed with serpents in ancient artwork (and upon which the serpent-fringed head of Medusa was sometimes said to have been fashioned after the hero Perseus slew Medusa).

The Aegis associated with Athena (as well as with her father Zeus) is a helpful clue in our examination of the celestial aspects of the god Shiva in the ancient texts of India because it may also help to explain the descriptions of the god as wearing a tiger's skin. I suspect that the dangling tail and paws of the tiger-skin and leopard-skin garments often worn by figures who are associated with Ophiuchus may have something to do with the long-tailed figure of Scorpio, just beneath Ophiuchus.

Other gods associated with Ophiuchus, such as Dionysus in the myths of ancient Greece, are frequently depicted as wearing a leopard-skin. Here is a detail of an ancient depiction of the god Dionysus from a piece of pottery in which a leopard-skin can easily be identified as being fastened around the neck and draped over the shoulders of the god:

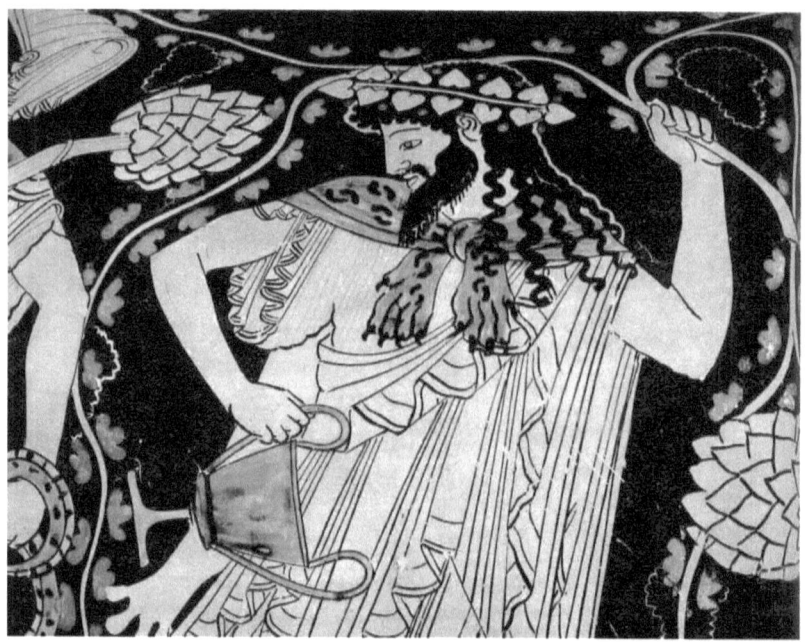

The god Dionysus has other characteristics which indicate a strong parallel with aspects of the god Shiva, most notable of them perhaps being the long unshorn locks of both deities. *Unshorn hair* is a distinctive characteristic of Dionysus. The wild and uncontrolled (and often destructive) dancing of the followers of Dionysus constitutes another parallel between the characteristics of Shiva and Dionysus.

Shiva is also associated with a specific mountain, Mt. Kailasa. Dionysus, too, is associated with a specific mountain: Mount Nysos, or Nysa (the god's name, in fact, signifies "Zeus of Nysos," or "the god (dios) of Nysos"). These many parallels between the two gods undoubtedly stem from the fact that both Shiva and Dionysus are associated with the same constellation, the constellation Ophiuchus -- and their association with a particular mountain is explained by the fact that the constellation Ophiuchus is often envisioned in Star Myths from many cultures as a mountain (usually a pleasant, wooded mountain).

Another aspect of the iconography of Lord Shiva mentioned in the quotation above from Dimmitt and van Buitenen is his carrying of a club topped with a human skull. This detail is almost certainly descriptive of the western "serpent-half" of the constellation Ophiuchus, the "serpent-head" on the right side of the central body as we face the star-chart shown on page 570 above. This part of the constellation could well be envisioned as a short club or stick topped by a skull.

In one of the episodes described in the Puranas, the god Shiva, referred to there as "the slayer of Trimura," is said to take on the form of "a young man carrying an *āsādha* staff, girdled with *munja* grass, wearing a sacred thread, carrying an umbrella, and wearing a deer-skin."[354] This description of the god in disguise is nevertheless revealing of an association with Ophiuchus, for in addition to wearing an animal skin and carrying a staff, Shiva in this instance carries an umbrella -- and we shall see that the constellation Ophiuchus is also frequently envisioned as having a kind of "canopy" or "umbrella" top (the large triangular top of the central body of the constellation).

Another Purana describes the dance of Shiva in the sky, at which sight the brahmins and yogins who witness this awe-inspiring sight utter a hymn which declares:

> "We behold you dancing, source of the world, lodged in our own hearts! By you does this wheel of Brahmā turn. You, sole guardian of the world, are filled with Māyā. We take refuge in you! We adore you! You are the soul of Yoga, the master of consciousness who dances the divine dance!"[355]

This text seems to imply that "this wheel of Brahmā" (the whirling form of the constellation Hercules) is envisioned as being turned by Lord Shiva (associated with Ophiuchus, just beneath Hercules in the heavens).

Another interpretation of the same passage above could also be that Lord Shiva, when envisioned as dancing in the sky, is then associated with the "whirling version" of the constellation Hercules, and in his dancing is envisioned as turning the wheel of Brahma (Brahma being the god more commonly associated with the constellation Hercules, rather than Shiva).

This interpretation (that Shiva temporarily assumes the form of the whirling version of Hercules, when Shiva is dancing in the sky) is strengthened by the fact that this aspect of the god Shiva (dancing) does not appear to be the god's normal manifestation. In the same Purana from which the above hymn to Shiva was quoted, we read that after this hymn was sung to him, the god Shiva "returned to his normal state," implying that his glorious and awe-inspiring *dancing form* is a special condition or form that Shiva assumes only under certain circumstances.

This interpretation of Shiva sometimes temporarily assuming an identification with the "whirling form" of the constellation

Hercules, during Shiva's dancing, is further supported by the famous sculptures of Shiva dancing, in the form of Nataraja (which means "Lord of the Dance"), surrounded by a ring of flame and with his hair streaming in all directions:

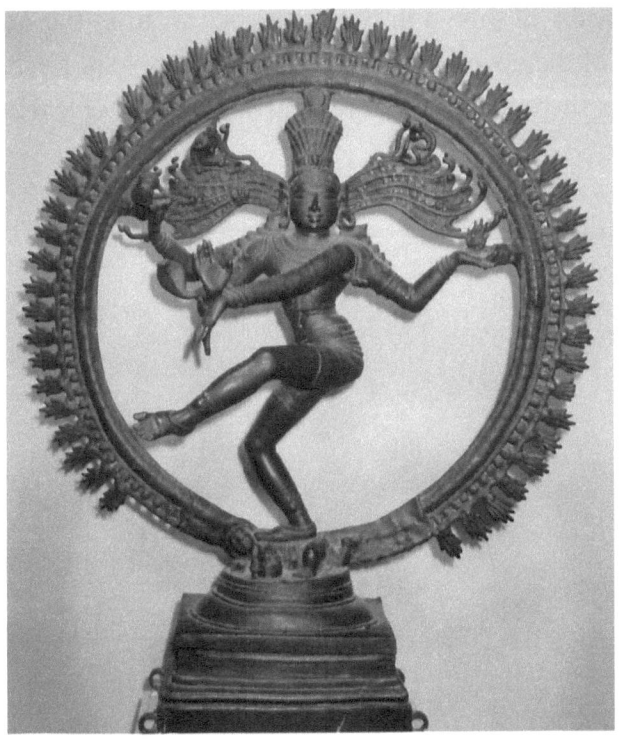

The reader can readily perceive that this famous depiction of Lord Shiva in ecstatic dance has parallels to the flaming solar disc iconography we have studied in previous chapters (such as those discussing the Star Myths of ancient Egypt and ancient Babylon) and which we identified with the whirling form of the constellation Hercules. In addition, the distinctive raised-leg posture of the god in these Nataraja depictions is evocative of the "standard outline" of the same constellation Hercules, as suggested by H. A. Rey in his books.

Another very well-known aspect of the god Shiva is his association with the symbol of the *linga* or *lingam*, the phallic symbol which is often carved out of stone and placed in temples and which to this day is anointed in worship at certain ceremonies and festivals, as shown in the image below, from the Ministry of Culture of the government of India, at a temple in Delhi where a lingam is surrounded and anointed with fruit, bel leaves, flowers and milk:

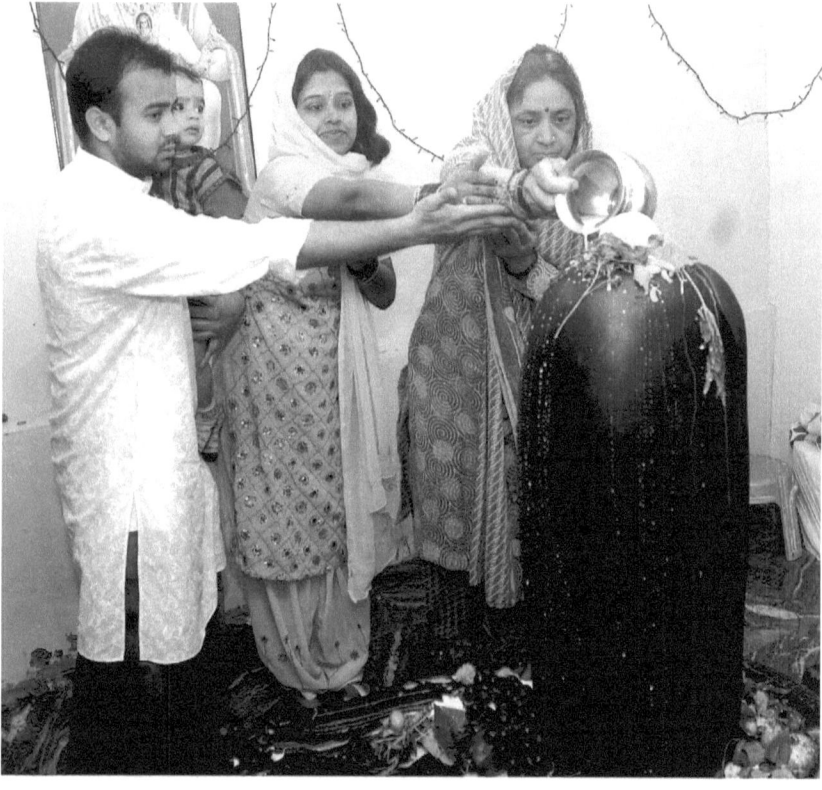

The word *lingam* itself comes from the Sanskrit word for the male sexual organ. Why is the god Shiva associated with the lingam? Cornelia Dimmitt and J. A. B. van Buitenen note that the symbol of the lingam which is always erect but which never ejaculates is another aspect of the contradictory nature of the god Shiva himself:

as the eternally erect linga refuses to expend its semen in physical release, it becomes the always potent generator of spiritual bliss [. . .] Thus, in Śiva, the denial or death of one virtue permits the generation of another. All opposites are really complements, each requiring the other's sacrifice for its own existence and growth. In death lies new life, and in denial, renewal. This is what is abundantly asserted through the complex personality of the great god Śiva.[356]

I would argue that the worship of this god who is so evidently associated with the characteristics of Ophiuchus in the form of the lingam may itself have a celestial foundation. As can be noted in the shape of the lingam sculptures found in the temples and surviving examples, the upper part of the representation is often slightly wider than the base, and may be seen as representative of the shape of the central portion of the constellation Ophiuchus itself, which is slightly narrower at the base than at the top, and which is surmounted by a triangle shape which could suggest a similarity to the male sexual member surmounted by the glans:

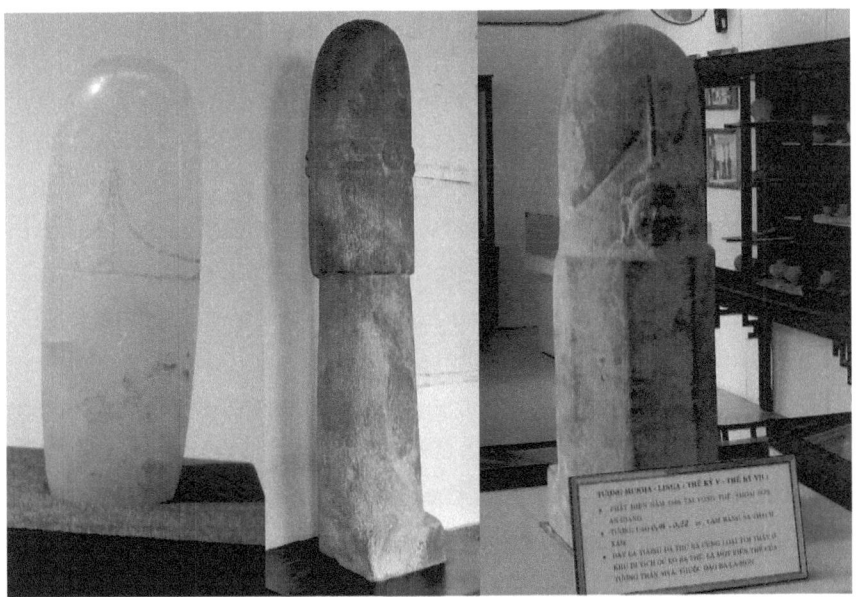

Compare the shape of the lingam statues shown on the preceding pages with the shape of the central column of the constellation Ophiuchus in the night sky:

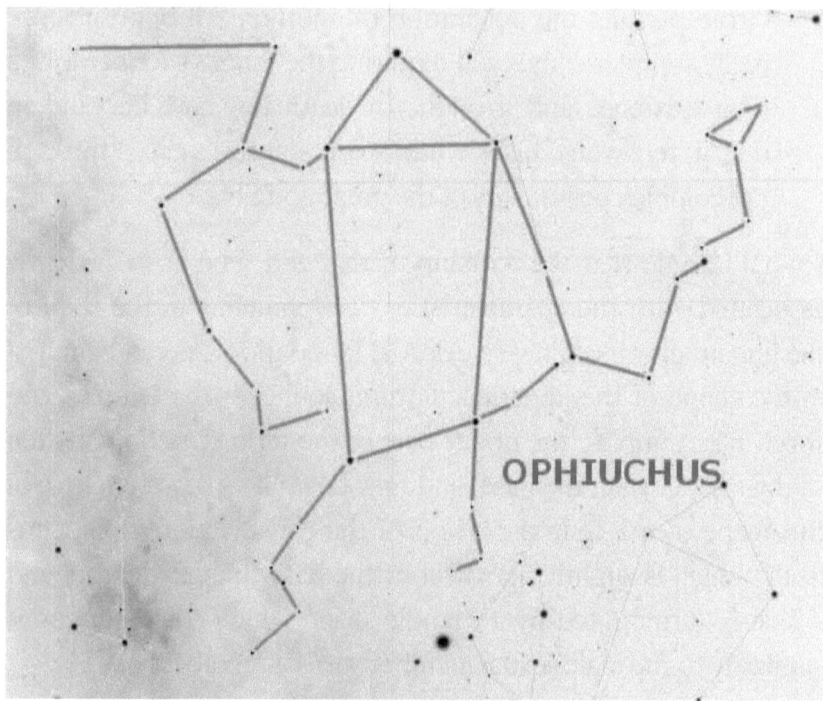

The central body of the constellation is slightly wider at the top than at the base, and is surmounted by a triangular section roughly proportionate to the glans atop a male phallus, which is very reminiscent of the lingam sculptures shown on the preceding pages. Note that the lingam sculptures themselves as found in existing temples and in museum pieces are often quite a bit wider and stouter than would be suggested by the male anatomy: they are actually shaped somewhat like a rounded vase or even an "overturned mortar" (see previously discussed myths in which Ophiuchus-figures are associated with overturned mortars, such as on pages 65 and 71). In other words, most lingam sculptures are suggestive more of the shape of the constellation Ophiuchus in the sky than of the shape of the actual human male anatomy.

It should be here pointed out that the lingam sculpture, while closely associated with the religion of India and the worship of the Lord Shiva in particular, is not exlusive to that culture and the worship of that god: ancient sources attest to representations of the phallus of Osiris in temples in ancient Egypt, for example (Plutarch mentions a representation of the phallus of Osiris being venerated in Egypt in section 18 of his discussion of the mythology of Isis and Osiris). And of course, we have already examined abundant evidence establishing a connection between the god Osiris of ancient Egypt and the celestial figure of Ophiuchus in the heavens: more evidence of a *worldwide* system.

Lest the reader should doubt this connection between the ancient shape of the lingam sculptures and the constellation Ophiuchus in the heavens, we can find Sanskrit texts which explicitly compare the lingam of Shiva with the shape of the sacred *mountain* of Shiva, a very strong indication that the lingam shape derives from the heavenly constellation, as there is abundant evidence from myths around the world in which Ophiuchus is associated with a mountain or plays the role of a mountain.

For example, in one of the Puranas translated by Cornelia Dimmitt and J. A. B. van Buitenen, dealing with the exploits of one of Vishnu's avatars (Varaha the Boar), the shape of the lingam is explicitly declared to be like the shape of the mountain of Lord Shiva! This comparison is indeed telling, and constitutes (in my opinion) conclusive evidence that both the lingam and the mountain are derived from the same celestial original: the constellation Ophiuchus. The text itself says:

> The ocean of Doomsday was roiled up by the heavy panting of this boar, who was adorned with gems, ornaments and glittering jewelry, shining like lofty piles of clouds filled with

lightning. Having assumed this vast, infinite, boar-like shape, the lord entered the netherworld in order to raise up the earth. There this mountainous boar blazed forth as radiantly as if he had gone to the foot of Maheśa's mountain, which is shaped like the *linga.*[357]

The title *Mahesha* signifies "Great Lord" and is one of the names of the Lord Shiva.[358] Thus we have in this Purana an explicit declaration that the shape of the lingam and the shape of the mountain of Shiva are identical -- which I would argue to be very strong confirmation that both are based upon the constellation Ophiuchus.

Indeed, there are many descriptions of Mount Meru, the central mountain of Vedic cosmology which upholds the heavens and separates them from the earth, in which the top is described as being wider than the base of the mountain. This, no doubt, is because Mount Meru can also be seen to be associated with the figure of Ophiuchus in the night sky.

Describing the vision of the earth found in the ancient Sanskrit texts, Dimmitt and van Buitenen write:

> Jambūdvīpa is the central continent, surrounded concentrically by six other circular lands separated by seven seas of different liquids. Holy Mt. Meru rises in the center of Jambūdvīpa, shaped "like the calyx of the lotus flower which is this earth" (*Kūrma* I.43.9), and wider at the top than at its base.[359]

Mount Meru is actually said to be the dwelling place of Brahma, Vishnu, and Shiva, and this association is appropriate if Vishnu and Shiva are both identified with the mountain-shaped constellation Ophiuchus and if Brahma is associated with the constellation Hercules directly above Ophiuchus.

Additionally, just as Mount Kailasa is associated with Lord Shiva, another central mountain, Mount Mandara, is associated with Lord Vishnu (who, as we have already established, is similarly identified with Ophiuchus in the heavens). Mount Mandara is described in the Puranas describing the churning of the heavenly Ocean of Milk, a scene which Graham Hancock has convincingly demonstrated to be representative of the great celestial turning of precession (building on a discussion found in *Hamlet's Mill*).[360]

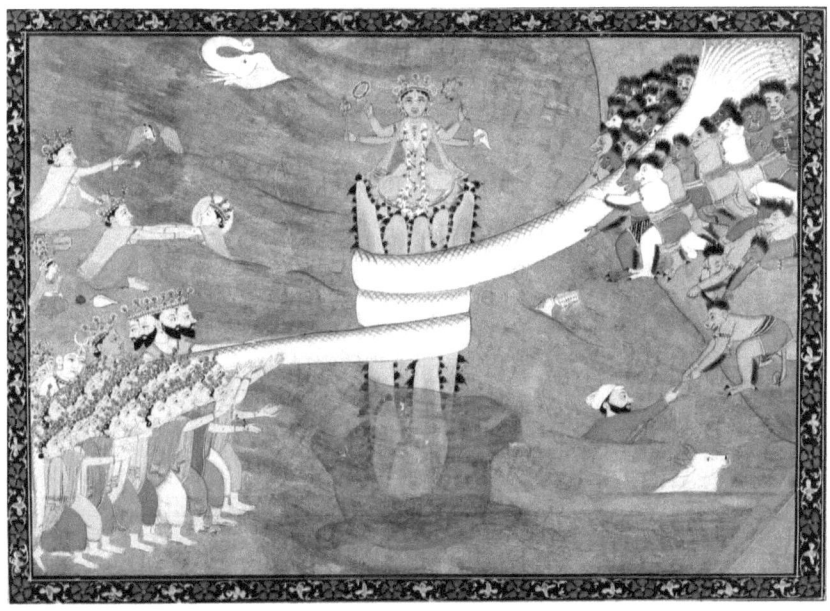

In the image above, Mount Mandara is depicted as the central "churning stick," which is being churned by the "tug-of-war" between the Daityas (malevolent spiritual beings) on one side and the gods and their supporters on the other. The great serpent Vasuki is acting as the twirling rope (note his multiple heads on the right side of the image as we face it). This episode took place when the gods needed *amrita* and Vishnu told them how to get it, by throwing herbs into the Ocean of Milk and then using the mountain as a churning stick to produce the nectar of the gods.[361]

581

In many, but not all, depictions of the scene of the churning of the Ocean of Milk, the top of the mountain will be slightly wider than the base, as in the scene on the preceding page (no doubt inspired by the fact that the heavenly mountain, Ophiuchus, grows slightly wider towards the top as we go upwards, prior to the triangular "capstone" at the apex of the constellation's central body).

The Puranas tell us that as the Ocean of Milk was being churned in order to produce the nectar, the vigorous motion caused the mountain to begin to sink, and thus Vishnu assumed his tortoise avatar, named Kurma, to support the base of the mountain:

> Because the unsupported mountain sank down into the water as they stirred up the sea, Visnu took the form of a tortoise and held Mt. Mandara on his back. From the milky ocean that was being churned in this way arose the poison Halāhala. Hara [that is, Shiva] took it into his throat, and because of this his throat turned blue.[362]

Most depictions of the churning of the Ocean of Milk will include Kurma at the base of Mount Mandara during the churning:

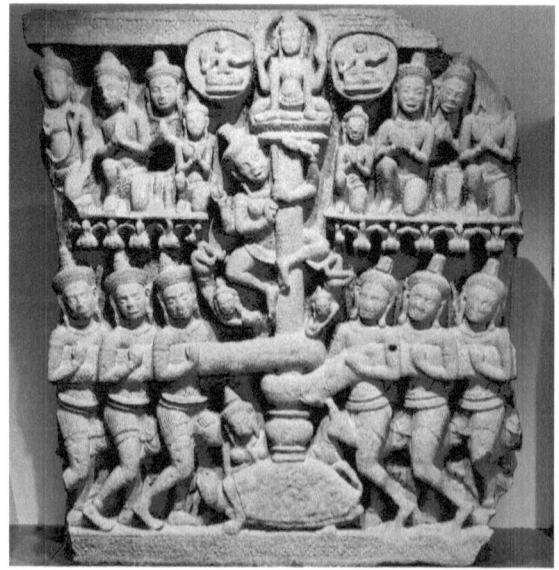

The tortoise avatar of the god Vishnu is almost certainly another way of envisioning the constellation Ophiuchus itself. The outline has a tall, humped central body with a "head" and a "tail" protruding from either end. Instead of being envisioned as an anthropomorphic figure holding a serpent, it could be envisioned as a central domed "shell" with a reptilian head and tail emerging from either side, plus two legs extending down below:

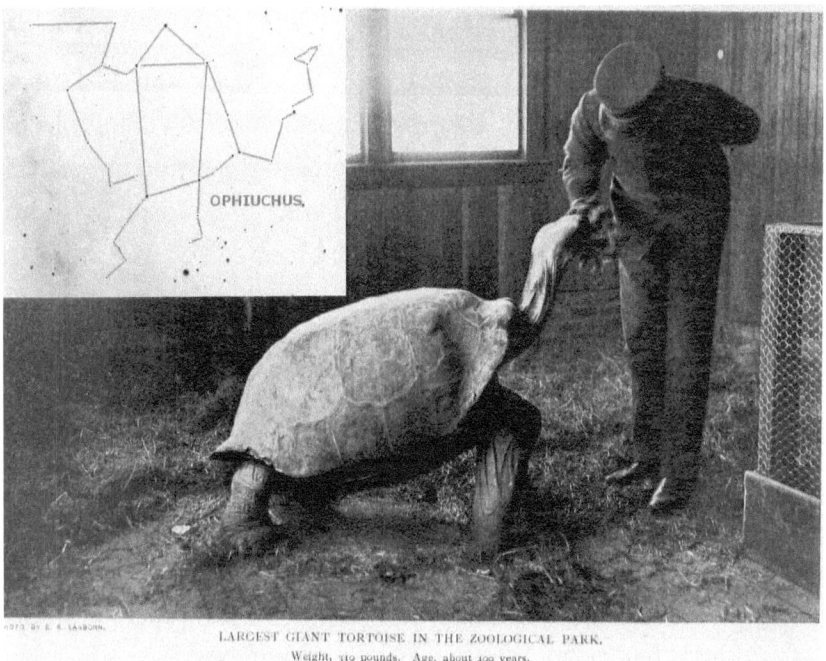

LARGEST GIANT TORTOISE IN THE ZOOLOGICAL PARK.
Weight, 310 pounds. Age, about 400 years.

Thus, the constellation Ophiuchus itself suggests the tortoise avatar of Vishnu, Kurma. The constellation also plays the role of Mount Mandara in the episode of the churning of the heavenly ocean -- and we can easily see from the star-chart above how the great serpent Vasuki could be envisioned as being wrapped around the central "mountain" in this particular myth. From the above analysis, it is clear that Mount Mandara is closely associated with the god Vishnu, just as Mount Kailasa is closely associated with the god Shiva -- and in both cases, the gods and their sacred mountains are almost certainly associated with Ophiuchus.

In addition to being envisioned as a great central mountain, the constellation Ophiuchus is also envisioned as a central pillar, and we find references in the ancient Sanskrit texts to an association between both Vishnu and Shiva with the characteristics of a pillar. Professor Wendy Doniger cites several examples in her book *Hindu Myths* of the use of the epithet *Sthanu* ("the Pillar") to refer to the god Shiva.[363] Similarly, in the Rig Veda, Vishnu is described as the one who "propped up the upper dwelling-place" to create space between earth and sky (recall the figure of the god Shu in ancient Egypt, who is likewise associated with Ophiuchus).[364]

As Professor Wendy Doniger notes in her translation of selections from the Rig Veda, when describing this act of propping up the heavens, the ancient text uses the important word *skambh* (a word much remarked-upon in the text of *Hamlet's Mill* by authors de Santillana and von Dechend).[365] Professor Doniger writes:

> The verb (*skambh*) is related to the noun for 'pillar,' the axis mundi that props heaven apart so that creation may take place. This pillar is also a measuring-stick for Visnu. Elsewhere this act is attributed to Varuna (5.85.5) [Varuna is an avatar of Vishnu], who measures out the earth with the sun as with a measure.[366]

Clearly, there is a super-abundance of evidence which supports an association between the god Shiva and the constellation Ophiuchus, and between the god Vishnu and the constellation Ophiuchus. Indeed, even more could be offered but at this point we have established the association and can move on to examine other aspects of the myths of ancient India. One additional item, however, should confirm the point being argued, and that is the fact that the ancient texts themselves recognize a deep connection between Vishnu and Shiva, to the point that the two actually blend together, in the form of the deity known as Hari-Hara. Cornelia Dimmitt and J. A. B. van Buitenen explain:

> Hari-Hara is half Visnu, half Śiva, asserting the identity of these two principal male deities of Hindu tradition. This image presents a monistic view of the origin of the universe by identifying both generative gods as a single divine being, and calling this combined entity by both their names at once: Hari is Visnu, and Hara is Śiva.[367]

Let us now move on to discuss celestial aspects of the goddess consort of Lord Shiva, but before doing so note in passing the important detail that Shiva himself takes on aspects of the goddess in an androgynous form known as Ardhanarinara (also Ardhanarishvara), meaning "half woman, half man."[368] This fact is notable on many levels, but for our purposes it is significant to note that Ophiuchus figures show up in myth as male characters and female characters, but often when male they have some adrogynous aspects to them, such as we see here in the case of the god Shiva, but also in the case of the god Dionysus (who shares many characteristics with Shiva, as we have already seen) as well as in the person of Jesus in the gospel texts (who is also associated closely with Ophiuchus in many episodes). Surely the reader has noticed that the depictions of Shiva presented earlier in this chapter (as well as many of the depictions of Dionysus from ancient Greece) share certain parallels with depictions of Jesus down through the centuries. I would argue that these are characteristics which were anciently associated with Ophiuchus, at least in some cases.

The consort of the god Shiva is the goddess Parvati, although similar to Shiva she has many aspects and in these different aspects the goddess has different names. Dimmitt and van Buitenen list some of them:

> As a loyal wife she is known as Pārvatī, the "mountain girl," daughter of the Himlālaya mountain, also as Umā, "mother," Gaurī, "white," and Satī, "virtuous."[369]

However, she also appears under the aspect of the great goddess Durga, "the inaccessible," as well as under the aspect of the violent goddess Kali.[370] I believe there is evidence to conclude that all these aspects of the goddess refer to the same constellation, the constellation Virgo in the sky, in close proximity to Ophiuchus. Indeed, figures associated with Virgo are sometimes envisioned in myth as giving birth to figures associated with Ophiuchus, although in the case of Parvati "the mountain born" it appears that Ophiuchus (often envisioned as a mountain) is the one who gives birth to Virgo (the goddess Parvati, described as the "daughter of the Himalaya mountain").

There is abundant evidence which indicates that the goddess Durga is associated with the constellation Virgo. One aspect of the goddess Durga which indicates an association with this constellation is the fact that she is frequently depicted as riding upon a lion, or as accompanied by a lion. The zodiac constellation Virgo in the heavens is found in very close proximity to the zodiac constellation Leo the Lion, and indeed follows directly behind Leo in the nightly procession of stars across the sky from east to west (in other words, Virgo is just east of Leo, and thus follows Leo as the heavens appear to turn due to the rotation of our planet towards the east, which causes the stars and constellations to appear to move towards the west, just as signposts and trees appear to move rearwards to a rider on a moving car or train).

Below is a star-chart showing the proximity of Virgo and Leo:

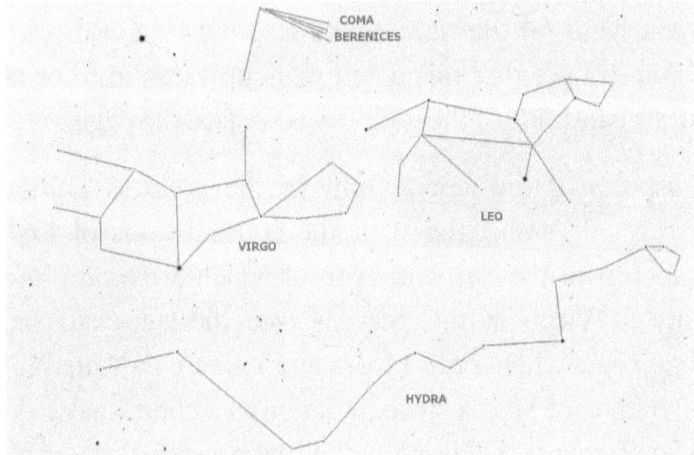

And below is an image of a set of modern-day icons for the worship of Durga during the annual festival of Durga Puja (also known as Durgotsava, Sharadotsav, Akalbodhan, Navaratri Puja, and other names):

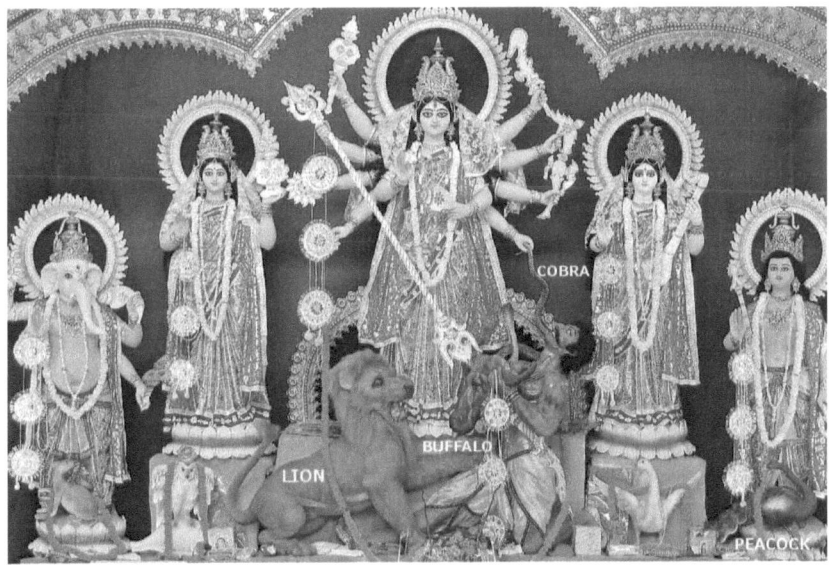

587

The goddess Durga is in the center and highest position, flanked by other deities. I have added labels to indicate the presence of a lion (self-evident, near the foot of the goddess and just to the left of her as we face the image), as well as a cobra (descending from her lowest hand on the right as we face the image: if you look closely you can see that this cobra rears upwards in front of the lower right-hand side of the goddess as we face the page).

These aspects of the iconography of the goddess Durga are almost certainly associated with the constellations of Leo the Lion and Hydra the Serpent, both of which are found in close proximity to Virgo in the heavens (see the star-chart on the preceding page, where both Hydra and Leo are indicated). Note that the outline of Hydra strongly suggests a cobra-snake, due to the circlet of stars at the "head-end" of the constellation.

Another figure commonly displayed in conjunction with the goddess Durga is a peacock. A peacock can be found in the preceding image of a Durga display on the preceding page, in the very lower-right corner of the picture as we face it. I have labeled the peacock in the lower-right corner (otherwise it might be difficult to spot in the image).

Based on my experience of looking at several hundred myths (at least) and several hundred depictions of sacred scenes from a variety of cultures, I am convinced that the symbol of a peacock is usually connected to the constellation of Coma Berenices (rather than the southern-hemisphere constellation known as Pavo the Peacock, which was mentioned earlier in conjunction with the Australian myth of Mirragan and Gurangatch). Coma Berenices, of course, is located in close proximity to Virgo as well. This constellation has a long spray of stars which appear to have been envisioned as the glorious tail of a peacock. In other artwork,

Coma Berenices will be envisioned as a sort of "whisk" or "feather-duster" implement with a cluster of feathers attached to a short handle (very reminiscent of the form of the constellation Coma Berenices itself).

Perhaps the most important attribute of the goddess Durga, also indicated in the Durga iconography shown above, is her fame as the slayer of the powerful Asura known as Mahish or Mahisa (or MahishAsura). Although it is a little difficult to see in the above iconography, I have labeled the severed head of a water buffalo in the modern display (it is located at the base of the long trident-like weapon held by the goddess, and is facing towards the left as if looking into the face of the lion at Durga's feet).

The story of the birth of the powerful buffalo-demon Mahish or Mahisa (whose name means "buffalo") is described in the Skanda Purana.[371] He grows so powerful that none of the gods can withstand him, and so they bring their energies together and the goddess is created (in other versions Durga is already pre-existent and the other gods give her aspects of their own weapons with which to oppose MahishAsura). The final defeat of the buffalo demon is described in the Markandeya Purana: in the end, Durga's power is far beyond his, and she cuts off his buffalo head with his own great sword (reminiscent of the beheading of Goliath by David with the giant's own sword as well).[372]

Star Myths of the World, Volume Three discusses the celestial foundations behind the episode of the slaying of Goliath by David (recounted in the scriptures in 1 Samuel chapter 17). The slaying of MahishAsura by Durga is likely based on different constellations from those which give us the story of David and Goliath. For one thing, the ancient Sanskrit texts describe Durga riding upon her ferocious lion when she goes forth to do battle with the great buffalo demon.[373]

Below is a stone relief carving from the Mahishamardini cave temple (or *mandapa*) in the Mahabalipuram temple complex of southern India, showing Durga riding her lion towards MahishAsura, who is depicted as a powerfully-built anthropomorphic male figure with a bull buffalo head. This scene is thought to have been carved during the 7th or 8th centuries AD.

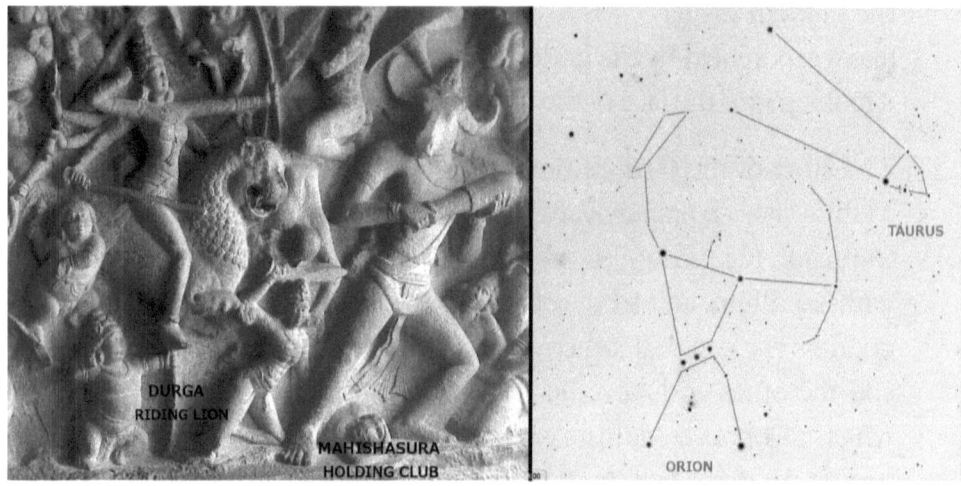

DURGA
RIDING LION

MAHISHASURA
HOLDING CLUB

TAURUS

ORION

Juxtaposed with the artwork from the Mahishamardini mandapa I have included the stars of the constellations Orion and Taurus, to show how closely the outline of the buffalo-demon in the cave temple carving can be seen to match the constellations in the heavens.

Everything in the posture of the buffalo-headed Asura in the temple art matches the outline of the constellation Orion, including the bend of Mahisha's left knee (the leg on the right as we face the image) – note the same bend in the leg on the right side of Orion as we face the constellation in the sky (the left knee of the constellation, if the outlined figure is envisioned facing towards us). Note also the prominent belt around the waist of MahishAsura in the sculpted temple wall, which of course corresponds to the famous three-star belt of the constellation Orion. Additionally, the sculpted figure has a long sash dangling from the belt, between the legs but more towards the Asura's straight leg (on the left as we face the sculpture). This long sash feature corresponds to a similar feature on the constellation itself, formed by the stars which are hang down as if from the belt of Orion, between the legs but closer to the straight leg on the left as we face the chart above. Note also that in the sculpture, Mahish is armed with a stout club, which also matches the bat-shaped weapon held aloft by the constellation Orion in the heavens.

In the scultpure of MahishAsura, the buffalo demon's head has not yet been severed by the goddess Durga -- but in the surviving texts it is very clear that this is exactly how the Asura meets his end. Turning to the star-chart of Orion and Taurus, we can see the likely celestial foundation for this myth. The bull-head outline of the stars of Taurus are visible in the heavens just above and to the right (to the west) of the constellation Orion. The figure of Orion itself can be envisioned as lacking a head. Thus, the stars themselves suggest that the bull-shaped head of Taurus has just been severed from the anthropomorphic man-shaped body of Orion, which appears to lack a head. It appears that the buffalo head has just been cut off, and is flying through the air above the headless outline of the body.

Note too that the outline of the goddess Durga, riding upon the lion in the sculpture, has close correspondence to the outline of the constellation Virgo in the heavens, including the angle of the hip and the distinctive outstretched arm (in this case, imagined as holding a bow in the extended arm of the goddess). Note that the

591

sculptor of the temple artwork has also depicted the hair of the goddess as being piled-up into a tall conical shape atop her head. This detail too can be seen as corresponding to the outline of the constellation Virgo, which has a rather elongated head.

But what could be the connection between Virgo and Orion in the night sky? The two constellations are rather far apart from one another. Indeed, if we look at a planetarium app or other depiction of the turning celestial background, we will see that the stars of Orion and Taurus are sinking down into the western horizon when the stars of Virgo are rising up from the eastern horizon -- and this fact, I'm convinced, gives rise to the myths in which the goddess Durga (associated with Virgo) slays the buffalo Asura Mahisha (associated with Orion and Taurus):

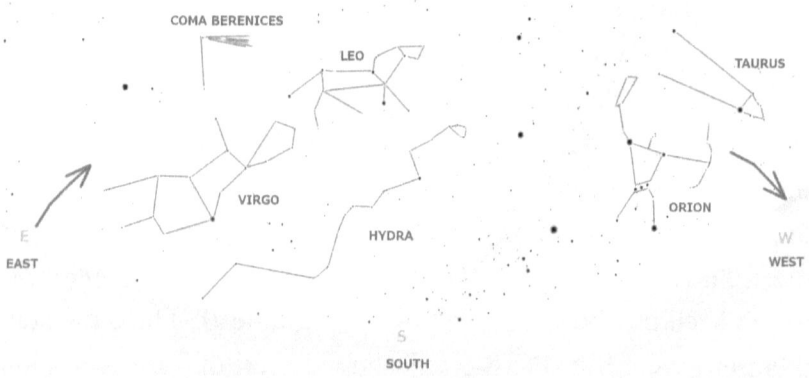

In the above star-chart, I have added arrows to give the reader the sense of the apparent motion of the sky, which rotates from east to west throughout the course of an individual night (due to the turning of our planet on its axis) as well as throughout the course of the year (due to the progress of our planet on its orbital journey around our central star, the sun). The turning of our planet on its axis causes heavenly bodies in the sky (including the sun and moon but also the stars and planets) to rise in the east and set in the west -- and this motion is indicated by the upward-arcing arrow rising out of the eastern horizon in the star-chart, and by the downward-arcing arrow descending into the western horizon on the other side of the chart.

From the chart above, we can see that as Virgo and the surrounding constellations (representative of the goddess Durga and her allies) are rising upwards from the eastern horizon towards the summit of the sky, the constellations Orion and Taurus are sinking down towards the western horizon, as if in defeat.

There are numerous ancient myths in which this type of "dual-horizon action" can be witnessed in operation. I was first introduced to this concept by the brilliant analysis on display in the lectures or "sermons" of the previously-introduced Reverend Robert Taylor of England (1784 - 1844), who points out this celestial action at work in the story of Adam and Eve and the Serpent being cast out of the Garden of Eden (sinking down into the west) at the same time that the constellation representing the cherubim with the flaming sword is rising up out of the eastern horizon (at the "east of Eden" as we are told in Genesis 3: 24).[374]

In similar fashion, Robert Taylor demonstrates that the story of the Magi (who came *from the east* and who then see the star of the holy child *in the east*, as told in the text of Matthew chapter 2) can be seen to be representative of the rising and setting of constellations which, as it turns out, are the same constellations which we are here discovering to form the basis for the ancient Sanskrit accounts relating the beheading of MahishAsura by the goddess Durga.[375]

Based on the above analysis and the clues left to us from the myths and ancient artwork (and existing iconography of the goddess Durga in annual festivals which continue in India to this very day), we can be fairly confident in our identification of the goddess with the constellation Virgo, and also our identification of the buffalo-demon Mahisa or Mahish with the constellation Orion (and his severed head, represented by the outline of Taurus).

Certain Sanskrit texts (and ancient tradition) appear to indicate that, despite their very different aspects, the goddess Parvati and the goddess Durga are one goddess. Cornelia Dimmitt and Johannes van Buitenen discuss this idea:

> Sometimes this fierce goddess is called the spouse of Śiva. Matching his two-sided personality, she is said to have two aspects also. As Pārvatī she is benign, and as Durgā she is destructive. That these are aspects of a single goddess, however, is sometimes clearly stated:
>
>> As good fortune, the goddess bestows wealth on men's homes in times of prosperity. In times of disaster she appears as misfortune for their annihilation (*Mārk.* 89. 36).[376]

The contrasting natures of the god Shiva, which the authors of the above passage see as paralleling the contrasting aspects of Parvati and Durga, are most often noted in his ascetic and celibate nature as a rigorous *yogin*, which is contrasted with his simultaneous portrayal as a loving husband and family man. The tension between these two aspects of Shiva is depicted in the ancient myths as creating a tension in Shiva's marriage to Parvati.

Dimmitt and van Buitenen describe Parvati's dilemma: "desiring children, she engages in a variety of subterfuges to seduce her reluctant, meditating husband."[377] They explain that:

> Offspring, in fact, are born to Pārvatī, but by odd means indeed. Ganeśa arises from the dirt washed off her body in

the bath. And Kārttikeya is restored to Śiva after being born in a reed thicket from his father's spilt seed, and raised by six of the seer's seven wives. Śiva is most clearly a reluctant spouse and parent, his marriage bringing to a focus again and again the tension inherent in his double nature, both erotic and ascetic.[378]

The description of the childhood of Karttikeya, "born in a reed thicket" and raised by six mothers has obvious parallels with the myth-pattern found around the world of infants who are cast-off in the reeds of a river (such as Moses in the Old Testament, or Sargon of Akkad in the traditions of ancient Mesopotamia), who are often described as being placed into a basket or an "ark" of reeds or rushes. We have seen that these myth-patterns correspond to the constellations of Scorpio and Ophiuchus, and the description of Karttikeya being raised by six of Shiva's seven wives certainly appears to point to the multi-headed constellation of Scorpio in this Star Myth as well. The association of Scorpio with reeds or rushes and with "cast-off babies" in myths literally around the globe is very noteworthy, and points to some common ancestor for this oicotype, in some predecessor culture which predates even the ancient cultures of India and of Mesopotamia.

Let us now pause to briefly examine the traditions surrounding the god Ganesha mentioned in the quotation above, who is another of the children of Parvati and Shiva. There are different accounts of the birth of Ganesha. In addition to the version in which Parvati creates this son from the dirt washed off in her bath, the Brhaddharma Purana describes a confrontation between Parvati and Shiva in which Parvati asks for a son and Shiva gives her a cloth doll, intending it as a sort of joke, but the cloth doll becomes a real child, Ganesha.[379]

In any case, the various myths are united in the fact that Ganesha eventually loses his head. In one version, Parvati stations Ganesha outside her bath, to prevent her from being disturbed, and when Ganesha tries to prevent Shiva from entering (not knowing the identity of his "father"), Shiva cuts off Ganesha's head using his trident.[380] In other versions, Shiva cuts off Ganesha's head with his hand, or with the flame from his third eye.[381]

Parvati is of course distraught by this turn of events, but Shiva promises to find a new head for their son, and replaces the severed head with an elephant head. In one version of the story, Shiva sends his servant Nandin (who is sometimes his attendant, sometimes his door-keeper, and sometimes a great bull) to cut off the head of anyone found sleeping with head facing to the north.[382] Nandin comes across the lord of elephants sleeping with his head facing to the north (considered inauspicious: the Sanskrit texts tell us that we should sleep with the head towards either the south or the east).[383] He cuts off the elephant's head and brings it to Lord Shiva, who fastens it to the body of Ganesha (and also causes the lord of elephants to be reincarnated, lest any reader was worried on that count).

The elephant-headed god Ganesha (also called Ganapati, especially in the south of India, among many other names and titles) remains one of the most beloved and widely worshipped deities in India today, as well as in many surrounding countries and cultures. He is known as the Remover of Obstacles (or "obviator of obstacles"), and the god of auspicious beginnings.

Ganesha is depicted in various postures and activities, but his distinctive elephant head makes the god very easy to identify. He is also frequently depicted being accompanied by his vahana (or "vehicle"), a mouse or shrew named Mushaka. In the images below, for example, we can see Ganesha seated above his mouse vahana:

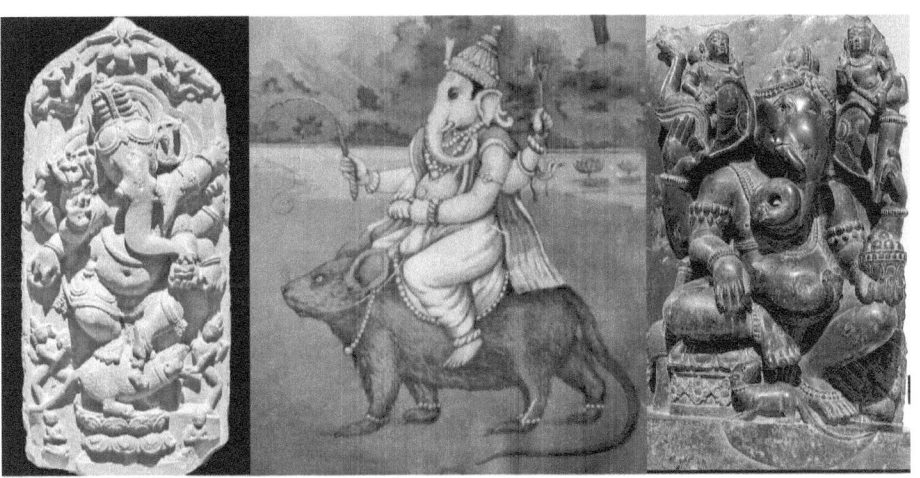

Is it possible that there might be fouund a celestial foundation to these myths? Perhaps it would be better to ask if it is possible that they might be found to *not* have a celestial foundation!

Knowing what you know by now of the constellations, can you think of a constellation which might be envisioned as having an elephant's head fastened atop a human body?

Thinking of the details of the common elements of the Ganesha myth just related, can you think of what surrounding constellations might be close to Ganesha in the heavens? Remember that we have already established, with a compelling abundance of evidence, that the god Shiva is most closely associated with the constellation Ophiuchus, and that Ganesha's mother Parvati is almost certainly associated with the constellation Virgo. Remember as well that in the myth, Ganesha "comes between" Shiva and Parvati (indeed, in a well-known version of the Ganesha myth, this fact is responsible for Shiva's act of cutting off Ganesha's head, not knowing that the boy is his son).

Below is a star-chart showing a now-familiar region of the heavens, containing numerous mythologically important constellations. If you haven't already identified a constellation which suggests a human body topped by an elephant's head, can you see such a constellation in the chart below (and, what's more, can you find that constellation to be situated *between* the constellations representing Shiva and Parvati)?

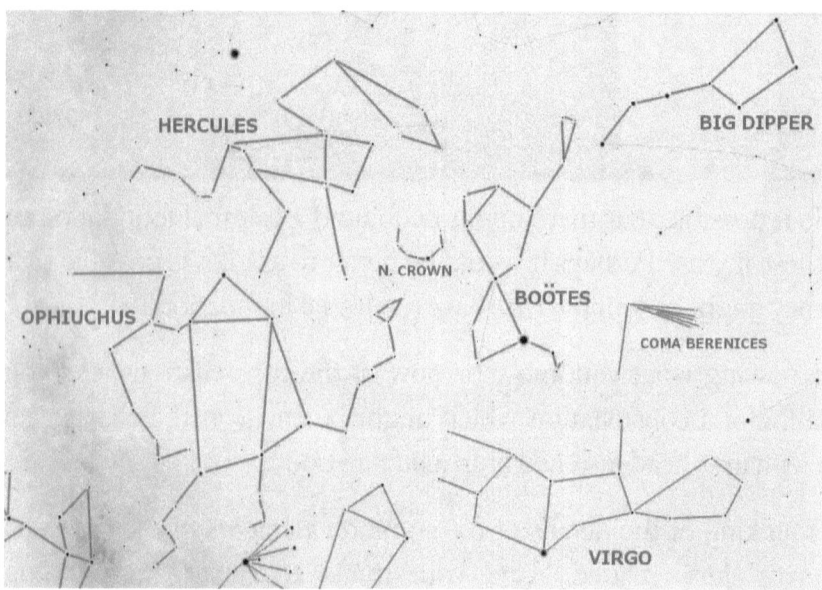

If, based on the details mentioned above, you suspect that the constellation Boötes the Herdsman might resemble a seated person with an elephant's head, then I am in agreement with you on the likely identification of the celestial figure of the Lord Ganesha. The distinctive feature of the constellation that resembles a long "pipe" protruding from the face would, of course, form the upward-curling trunk of the elephant head. And, as suggested by the Sanskrit texts themselves, the constellation

Boötes is located in close proximity to both Virgo (associated with Parvati) and Ophiuchus (associated with Shiva), and is indeed located "between them."

While the menacing form of Hercules can be seen rising up behind Boötes, as if preparing to sever the head of Boötes, we have seen very abundant evidence which indicates that Shiva is associated most closely with Ophiuchus, and it is Shiva who by almost all accounts beheads Ganesha before giving him an elephant head. In some accounts Shiva uses his trident, and in others he uses his hand: in either case, I believe the "serpent's head" feature of Ophiuchus, which extends closest to the back of the neck of Boötes, is envisioned as the agent of the beheading. The small triangle of stars that forms the "head" of the serpent held by Ophiuchus actually has three stars across the top, which may suggest the trident weapon which is often described as Shiva's preferred weapon:

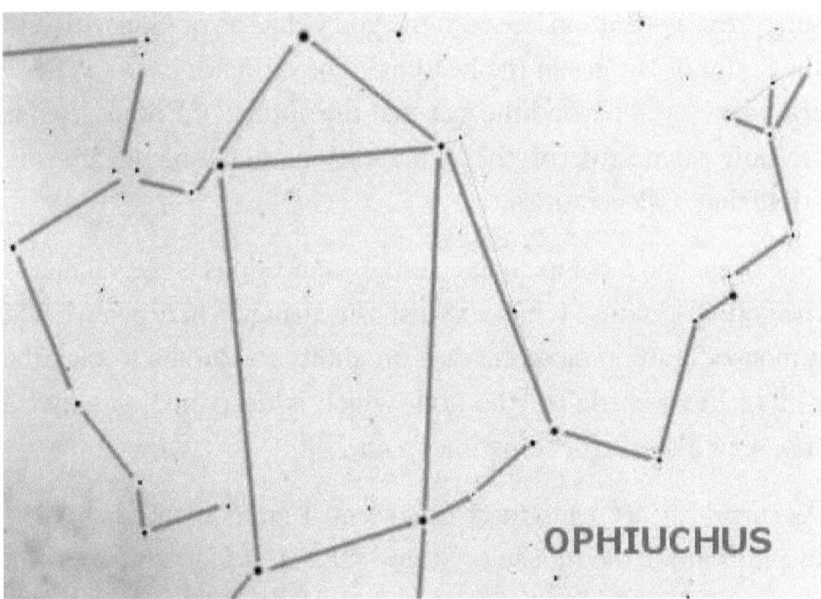

OPHIUCHUS

Of course, the same feature of Ophiuchus could be envisioned as the hand which the god uses in some accounts to cause his son's original head to fall to the ground. Indeed, the same "serpent-head" feature of Ophiuchus could also play the role of the "third eye" of Shiva which is used in some versions of the story to burn off Ganesha's head. We have already argued that the triangular or indeed "eye-shaped" circlet at the top of the western serpent-half of Ophiuchus might play the role of the Eye of Horus (such as when it is ripped out by the adversary Set). It is possible that this feature of Ophiuchus was (at least in some of the myths) envisioned as the "third eye" of Shiva! (It is also possible to argue that the "third eye" of Shiva is in the center of his forehead, where we usually envision someone's third eye: this interpretation could be suggested by the looking at the three stars which form the triangular top section of the central body of Ophiuchus, these three stars being mythologized as two eyes at the triangle's lower corners, with a third in between *and above* the other two).

What additional evidence can we find which supports this suggested association between the god Ganesha or Ganapati and the figure of Boötes in the heavens? The evidence in fact is fairly abundant, even beyond the fact that the outline of Boötes itself is strongly suggestive of the depictions of Ganesha in artwork stretching back centuries.

One of the most compelling celestial connections is the vahana of the god, his "mouse vehicle," Mushakavahana. Where can we find a mouse figure in close enough proximity to Boötes to play the role of the "vehicle" of the god, which is described as either a *mouse* or a *shrew* (or sometimes a *rat*)?

As surprising as it might at first seem, I am convinced that the inspiration for the mouse or shrew vahana of Ganesha is in fact the constellation Virgo, directly below Boötes! We have already seen more than one Star Myth in which the elongated head of the constellation Virgo is describeed as being similar to that of a rodent (see for example the story of the moon man and the *bandicoot woman,* from the Aboriginal people of Australia, or the figure of the goddess Xmucane in the Popol Vuh of the Maya, who is associated with the long-nosed *coatimundi:* both of these figures were argued to be associated with Virgo).

There are even some texts in which Ganesha is described as riding a lion or a peacock rather than a mouse, and both of these figures are also close enough to Boötes to serve as a mount for a god associated with Boötes. As we have already noted, I am convinced that the constellation of Coma Berenices is associated with the figure of a peacock in some ancient Star Myths -- and as you can see from the star-chart shown on page 598, Coma Berenices is found in very close proximity to the constellation Boötes in the sky. Also, we have already seen that Leo is very close to Virgo (indeed, just ahead of Virgo in the sky), and thus the alternate traditions in which Ganesha rides a lion or a peacock can be seen as additional evidence supporting an association between Ganesha and Boötes. However, Ganesha is most closely associated with a mouse, and this is because (I would argue) Virgo is directly below Boötes, and Virgo's head is pointing in the same direction that Boötes is facing, thus making it very easy to envision her as carrying the god Ganesha as she goes across the heavens.

There are other clues which support the identification of Ganesha with the heavenly figure of Boötes. For example, Ganesha is often depicted holding a rosary, and the Brhaddharma Purana tells us that the god Brahma gave Ganesha "a rosary of beads" after the elephant's head was placed on Ganesha's shoulders.[384] This rosary given by Brahma (Brahma being associated with the figure of the constellation Hercules in

601

the sky, as already established) is no doubt seen in the heavens in the form of the brilliant Northern Crown, which the constellation Hercules can be envisioned as grasping with the constellation's "lower hand" or "downward-reaching arm" -- and thus Brahma (Hercules) can be envisioned as holding out this celestial string of beads towards Ganesha (Boötes).

Similarly, Ganesha is frequently described as having broken one tusk, and frequently depicted with one tusk broken off. Indeed, one of the names of Ganesha is Ekadantaka, meaning "One-tusk," for this very reason.[385] The location of the broken-off tusk in the heavens is probably, once again, the Northern Crown, the curve of which constellation could very easily be envisioned as a broken-off elephant's tusk.

Another clue found in the descriptions of Ganesha is the passage in the Puranas which declares of the god with his new head that "his face was as bright as the moon."[386] We have already noted that in the same myth from the Aboriginal people of Australia in which we find the bandicoot woman, her companion is a "moon man," who is almost certainly associated with the constellation Boötes. Thus, I believe that texts such as the one which says of Ganesha that his face is like the moon could reflect an ancient tradition in which the head of the constellation Boötes was associated with the moon or seen to resemble the moon.

Additionally, I believe that it is also possible that when Nandi is sent by Shiva to cut off the head of anyone found lying with his head facing the north, Nandi the servant of Shiva is associated with the constellation Hercules, and that when he finds the lord of elephants facing to the north the myth is describing Hercules sneaking up behind the form of Boötes, whose face can be seen in the preceding star-chart (page 598) to be turned towards the Big

Dipper and thus generally *towards the north* (the north star, Polaris, being indiated by the front two stars of the Dipper's bowl, for which reason these two stars are called the "pointers").

From the foregoing analysis, it should be evident that the story of Ganesha is most certainly celestial in nature, as indeed we have found the other myths of ancient India and indeed of the world to be thus far. Before concluding this portion of the examination of the Star Myths of India, we will briefly discuss the figure of Indra, a central god of the Vedas although not included in the Trimurti of Brahma, Vishnu and Shiva, before looking at a few of the avatars of Vishnu. We will then close this chapter before transitioning to a discussion of some aspects of the Mahabharata in the following chapter.

The figure of Indra is central to the Rig Veda, the oldest of the great Sanskrit texts, but as Professor Wendy Doniger explains in her book on *Hindu Myths*, "none of the Rg Vedic hymns actually sets out to narrate a myth; rather, various myths are alluded to, often in enigmatic terms. To 'read' a Vedic myth about Indra, therefore, it is necessary to have recourse to later Indian commentaries, interpretations, and reworking of the Vedic myths, and then to re-examine the Vedic hymns themselves in the light of this knowledge."[387] This is noteworthy and parallels the situation with the Pyramid Texts (the oldest extant texts of ancient Egypt) and gods such as Osiris: the myths must thus be older still![388]

Knowing that Indra is a rain god, a warrior god, a king of the gods (known as Mahendra, or "Great Indra"),[389] and the deity in the pantheon of Vedic gods and goddesses who wields the thunderbolt weapon (known as the Vajra), we can by now surmise that Indra corresponds to the same constellation with which other thunderbolt-wielding gods, who are also usually rain gods and storm gods, and who are also often the most powerful gods in other pantheons, can be shown to be identified: the constellation Hercules.

Zeus of ancient Greece, and Jove of the ancient Latins, can both be shown to be associated with this same constellation -- and both are the leading gods of their respective pantheons, and the wielders of the thunderbolt weapon. We have seen the same correspondence with the constellation Hercules in the thunderbolt-wielding god Huracan of the Maya, whose very name gives us the name of the largest and most powerful of storms, and we will see this correspondence again in *Star Myths of the World, Volume Three* when we examine clear indications of association between the figure of Yahweh or Jehovah (whose name appears to be linguistically related to the name of *Jove*) and the same constellation Hercules in the heavens.

In the Rig Veda, Indra is described as being a slayer of a great dragon, a splitter of mountains, and a releaser of waters[390] -- all accomplishments associated with other gods who can be positively identified with the constellation Hercules (including Zeus who slays Typhon, Thor who battles with the Midgard Serpent, Marduk who defeats Tiamat, and the LORD Jah who subdues the Leviathan as described in Isaiah 27 and Psalm 74).

The passages which tell us that Indra splits open a mountain and releases the waters[391] are additional indications that Indra is indeed associated with the constellation Hercules, which is positioned above the mountain-shaped constellation Ophiuchus and can be envisioned as striking downwards towards Ophiuchus. The "waters" which are released thereby almost certainly correspond to the great river of the Milky Way itself, which flows directly past Ophiuchus and indeed can be envisioned as flowing out of Ophiuchus, since one foot of the constellation extends into the band of the Milky Way. Note that the action of striking a mountain to release water, attributed by the Rig Veda to the god Indra, closely parallels the passages in the Biblical books of Exodus and Numbers in which Moses is described as "smiting the rock" in order to cause water to come out of it, for the people to drink (see Exodus 17: 6 and Numbers 20: 10 - 11).

Heracles battling the nine-headed hydra is another example which falls into the same oicotype of myths involving a figure associated with the constellation Hercules fighting a dragon-like monster. The hydra in the case of the Heracles myth is almost certainly associated with the constellation Scorpio, which is often envisioned as having multiple heads arising from a serpentine body, and which is located directly below the constellation Ophiuchus (which is directly below the constellation Hercules), rather than with the *constellation* that bears the name Hydra, whose outline does not appear to have multiple heads.

In the case of Indra, the texts of the Rig Veda tell us that Indra battles the great dragon Vrtra, "the first-born of dragons."[392] Here is a passage from the translation of Wendy Doniger of a hymn to Indra found in the Rig Veda:

> I will tell the heroic deeds of Indra, those which the Wielder of the Thunderbolt first accomplished. He slew the dragon and released the waters; he split open the bellies of the mountain. He slew the dragon who lay upon the mountain; Tvastr fashioned the roaring thunderbolt for him. [. . .] Indra killed Vrtra, the greater enemy, the shoulderless one, with his great and deadly thunderbolt. Like the branches of a tree felled by an axe, the dragon lies prostrate upon the ground.

[. . .] Over him, as he lay like a broken reed, the swelling waters flowed for man.[393]

The textual evidence makes it very clear that the opponent of Indra in the above passage, the dragon Vrtra, can be identified with the constellation Scorpio (as can other dragon-like or serpent-like monsters battled by gods and heros associated with Hercules in other myth-traditions from around the world).

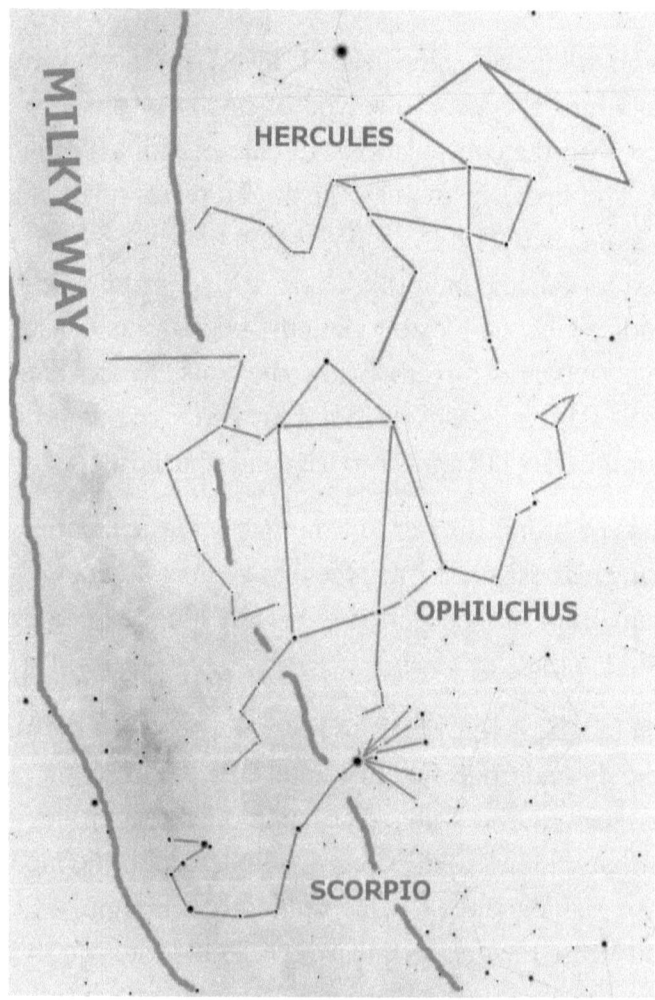

The text tells us that Vrtra lay prostrate on the ground, "like the branches of a tree felled by an axe," or "like a broken reed." Not

only is this an apt description of the constellation Scorpio, but we have already noted that myths in which an infant is cast upon the waters in an ark (such as the baby Moses, or the baby Sargon) are often described as being floated amongst the reeds (or bulrushes), as well as the fact that the ark or basket in which these infants are placed is usually described as being made out of reeds. Additionally, note many Biblical references to a broken or "bruised" reed, such as 2 Kings 18: 21, Isaiah 36: 6, and Isaiah 42: 3.

Additionally, we see that the text specifically tells us that as Vrtra lies there prostrate, like a broken reed, the waters flowed over his body. If, as suggested, the flowing-down column of the Milky Way in the heavens represents the waters that Indra releases from the mountain, then we can see from the preceding star-chart that these "waters" of the Milky Way do indeed flow over the prostrate body of the fallen dragon of Scorpio.

Intriguingly, the same passage cited above also declares that Indra prior to his battle with Vrtra "chose the Soma and drank the extract from the three bowls."[394] Soma is a drink of the gods in the Vedic tradition, described by Professor Doniger as "the ambrosial offering to the gods, by which they sustain their immortality; also a name of the moon, in which the ambrosia is stored; and sometimes incarnate as a god."[395] Indra is frequently described as drinking Soma, and Soma is closely associated with him and his powers.[396]

The fact that Indra is described as consuming Soma from "three bowls" has strong resonance with the Norse myth of Odin recovering the Mead of Poetry (the Song Mead), which was stored in three buckets or vats and guarded by a maiden inside a great mountain: this Norse myth is discussed at length in Volume Four of this series. However, in the Norse myths, as we will see,

Odin (who is most closely associated with the Song Mead) is *not* associated with the constellation Hercules.

Interstingly, in one of the hymns of the Rig Veda which is addressed to Soma personified, the powers of Soma are explicitly described as a "whirlwind." The hymn declares:

> This restless Soma -- you try to grab him but he breaks away and overpowers everything. He is a sage and a seer inspired by poetry.
> He covers the naked and heals all who are sick. The blind man sees; the lame man steps forth.
> [. . .]
> Be kind and merciful to us, Soma; be good to our heart, without confusing our powers in your whirlwind. (8.79)[397]

From this description of the power of Soma as a whirlwind, and from the connection between Soma and Indra, it is very likely that Soma is somehow associated with the "whirlwind" version of the constellation Hercules.

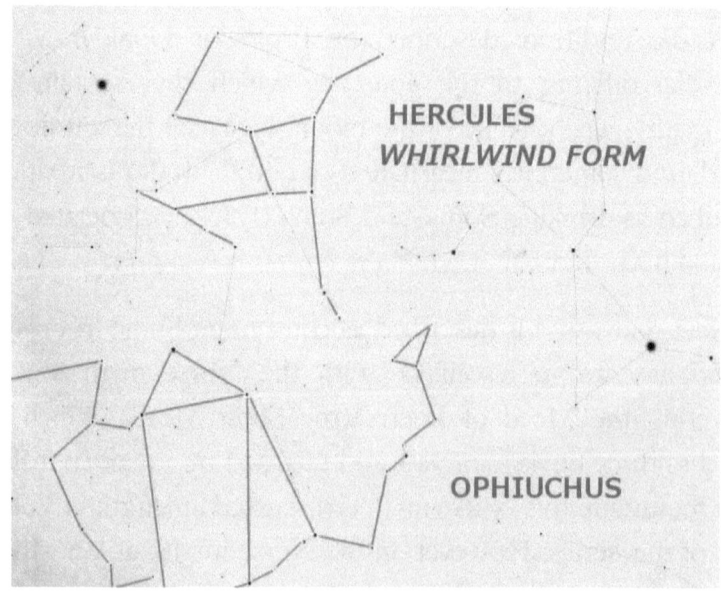

Positioned as this whirlwind is, above the "goblet" shape held in the hand of Ophiuchus (the western "serpent-head" feature of the Ophiuchus outline), it is possible that Soma is somehow associated with this goblet feature of Ophiuchus (which the constellation Hercules appears to be reaching down to grasp, as seen in the star-chart on page 606). The whirlwind form of Hercules above this goblet suggests the power which is contained within this ambrosial drink, while at the same time associating Soma with the god Indra, who is associated with the thunderstorm and with the constellation Hercules.

Below is a modern image of Indra from the 1850s. Note the position of the legs, with rear heel raised, characteristic of figures associated with the constellation Hercules, as well as the sword held overhead in very much the same position as the mighty weapon in the upraised arm of the constellation itself:

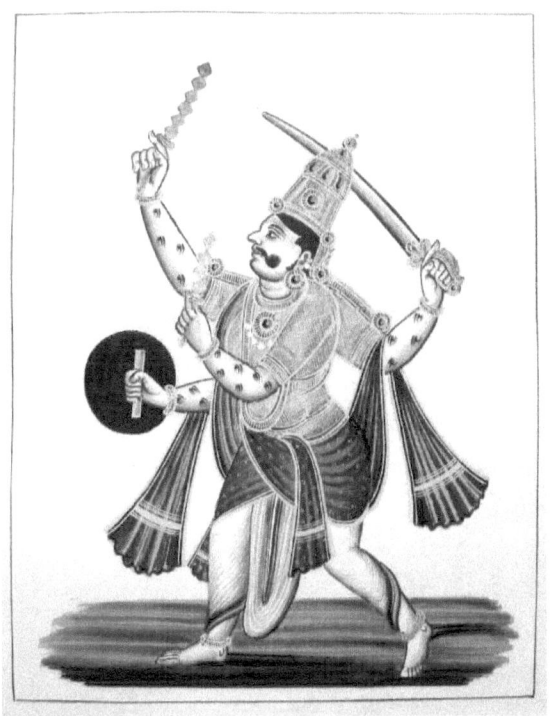

Two of the arms of the god are shown holding a symbol which is intended to represent the thunderbolt. Additionally, the lowest arm of the god is holding a disc-shaped shield, possibly associated with the Northern Crown which the constellation Hercules is often envisioned as grasping with its downward-reaching arm:

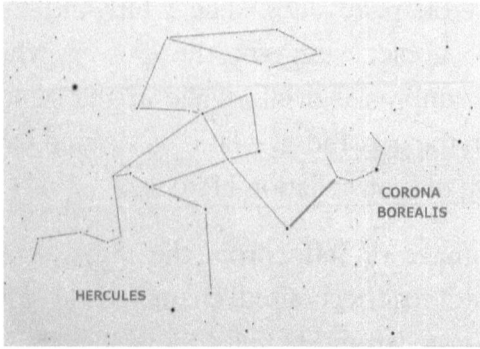

Below we present one more image of Indra, this one much older, from the Chennakesava Temple in southern India, which was completed and consecrated in the year we call AD 1258.

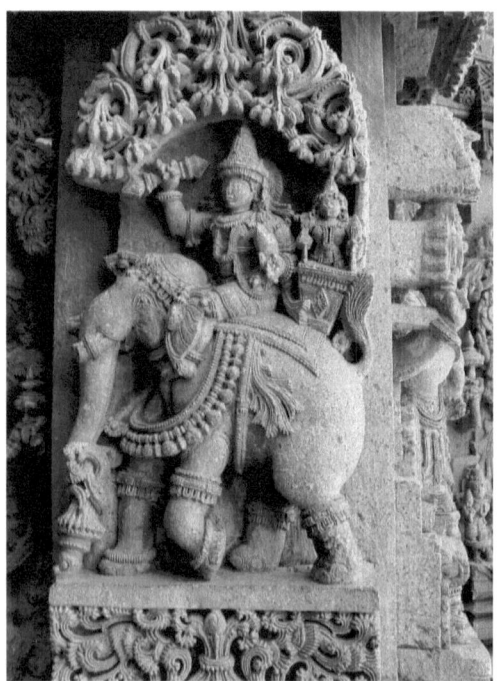

This carving shows Indra with arm upraised and holding the Vajra (the thunderbolt weapon) – clearly supportive of an identification with the constellation Hercules. However, it also depicts Indra upon his elephant vahana, the Lord of Elephants, Airavata. What constellation could represent this great elephant?

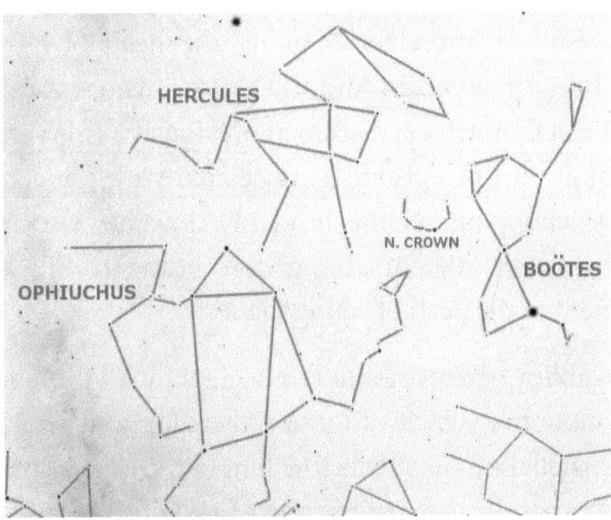

We have just finished looking at the identity of the god Ganesha or Ganapati, and concluded that an abundance of evidence points to an identification with the constellation Boötes in the heavens. Thus, having established a correspondence between Boötes and elephants, we could conclude that perhaps the vehicle or vahana of Indra, the Lord of Elephants Airavata, is associated with Boötes (a constellation quite near to the constellation Hercules).

But Ganesha is a deity with the body of a man and only the *head* of an elephant. Is it possible that the great Lord of Elephants himself is associated with a different constellation? Perhaps one directly below Hercules, and thus even more appropriate to serve as the "vehicle" upon which Indra rides?

I believe this possibility is in fact very likely: Airavata may be seen in the heavens in the outline of the now-familiar constellation

Ophiuchus, its long and serpentine western serpent-half being envisioned as the "trunk" of the great beast (in much the same way that we argued that Ophiuchus could be envisioned as the great tortoise avatar of Vishnu, Kurma).

Indeed, in one Purana account of the severing of an elephant head by Shiva's attendant Nandin, the head of the elephant Nandin brings belongs to Airavata himself, who was resting with his head facing north (as discussed previously). It is very possible that Nandin in this episode is associated with the constellation Hercules, chopping off the head of Airavata (associated with Ophiuchus) in order to bring the head to Shiva for the replacement of the head of young Ganesha.[398]

This possibility, that Airavata is associated with Ophiuchus (and that the mount or vehicle of Indra is then, logically enough, found in the constellation directly below him in the sky) is strengthened by the fact that the name of the great Lord of Elephants, Airavata, itself signifies in Sanskrit "born of the milky ocean" (Airavata being envisioned as a white elephant). Ophiuchus, as we have already discussed several times, is located immediately next to the Milky Way itself (the "milky ocean") and indeed has one foot in the Galaxy band.

This identification of Airavata with Ophiuchus strengthens the already strong evidence which argues that Indra is associated with the constellation Hercules. And it adds to an already enormous pile of evidence which demonstrates that the myths of ancient India, in common with the myths of so many other cultures around the globe, are infused at nearly every point with celestial metaphor.

Let us begin to transition to an examination of a few of the figures and episodes in the ancient Sanskrit epic Mahabharata by discussing some of the avatars of Vishnu and their celestial correspondences.

The concept of an avatar (also called an *avatara*) in the sense of an incarnation of a deity is almost exclusively related to the god Vishnu, who takes on various forms at various critical moments in mythical history, in order to restore balance to the universe. Cornelia Dimmitt and J. A. B. van Buitenen explain:

> As preserver and protector of the universe, the most important feature of lord Visnu lies in his *avatāras*, or "descents." Often called "incarnations," these *avatāras* are descents of a portion of the lord into animal or human form in order to redress the balance of good and evil in the world by supporting the forces of good. [. . .] Today it is common to list ten famous *avatāras* as the foundation of an evolutionary Vaisnavite theology, but in the Purānas this meaning of the *avatāras* is by no means so clear as it has become in recent times. [. . .] Each *avatāra*, however, does perform some heroic act on behalf of the welfare of mankind, and it is this unity of purpose that ties them all together as the work of Visnu.[399]

They further note that: "Śiva and the Goddess also show similar expansionist tendencies, but it is only Visnu who descends in *avatāras*."[400]

The number of avatars of Vishnu is seemingly endless. However, some Puranas name ten avatars, some list twelve. One Sanskrit text explicitly links the appearance of Vishnu's avatars with the end of each great Age, which could imply twelve avatars.[401] We will not examine all twelve (or even ten) of them here, but only enough to demonstrate that these avatars can be positively identified with specific constellations in the heavens, sometimes with the same constellation Ophiuchus with which Vishnu is primarily associated, and sometimes with other nearby constellations.

We have already examined the Kurma avatar of Vishnu, in which Vishnu is seen in the form of a great tortoise. As with his other avatars, Vishnu takes this form in order to restore order and balance to the cosmos; in the case of his Kurma avatar, it is because the gods are being defeated consistently by the Daityas, and they go to Vishnu seeking help. Vishnu instructs them in the making of heavenly nectar by churning the Ocean of Milk, and instructs them to enlist the aid of the Asuras to help in the process.

They set up Mount Mandara as a churning stick, and the great serpent Vasuki acts as a twirling rope tied about the mountain, but the churning action causes the mountain to sink down into the mud, and thus (the Puranas tell us) "Vishnu took the form of a tortoise and held Mt. Mandara on his back."[402]

This volume has already presented some evidence for seeing the Kurma avatar as another way of envisioning the constellation Ophiuchus, the same constellation with which the god is usually identified (see discussion on pages 582 - 583 of this volume).

In the case of Vishnu's fish avatar, Matsya (a name which literally signifies "fish" in Sanskrit),[403] the god takes on this form in order to preserve life and knowledge through the Great Flood. Vishnu descends as Matsya to warn one holy man, named Manu, of the coming dissolution of everything by water, and to instruct him to take all the seeds of life on earth, and all the Vedas and Puranas and all the sciences, into a great boat. Then, Vishnu's fish avatar Matsya will guide the boat through the Flood. Note the *nu* sound in Manu's name: this resonates with the names of *Noah*, *Uta-napishti*, *Oannes*, and even *John* the Baptist, all of whom can be seen to have strong ties to the constellation Ophiuchus (or to Aquarius, which as we've noted has a connection to Ophiuchus).

Vishnu's Matsya avatar is depicted as a combination between a fish and a man, with the torso and upper body of an anthropomorphic man emanating from a fish's mouth:

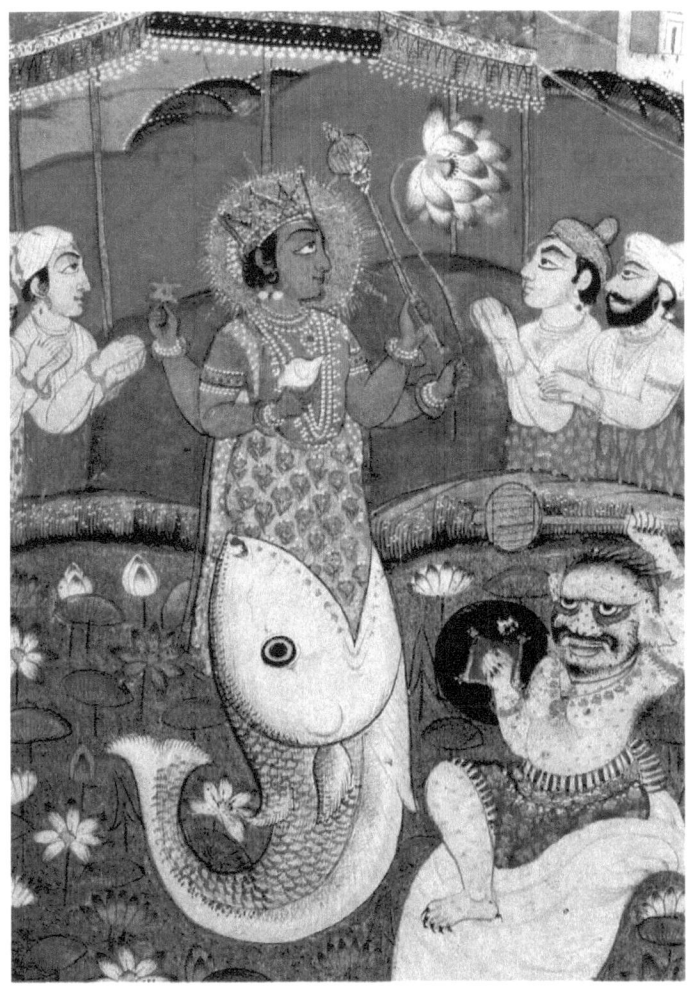

In the above depiction, note that the Matsya avatar includes the iconography normally associated with Vishnu, including his conch-shell (held in the hand in front of his chest in this painting), the lotus flower, and the crown upon his head. These items strengthen the argument that Matsya, like Vishnu himself, is connected with the constellation Ophiuchus.

Note that we have already examined the figure of a god, Triton, who wrestles with Heracles in the myths of ancient Greece, whose appearance (as a "mer-man" with torso and upper body of a powerful male human figure, and long fish-body below the waist, ending in an upturned tail with flukes) is remarkably similar to the depictions of the Matsya avatar of Vishnu (see pages 476 and 477 of this volume).

In that examination of Triton wrestling with Heracles, we offered evidence that Triton can be identified with Ophiuchus (his upturned tail and flukes likely being associated with the outspread wings of Aquila, nearby -- perhaps connected by the curving form of Scorpio beneath Ophiuchus):

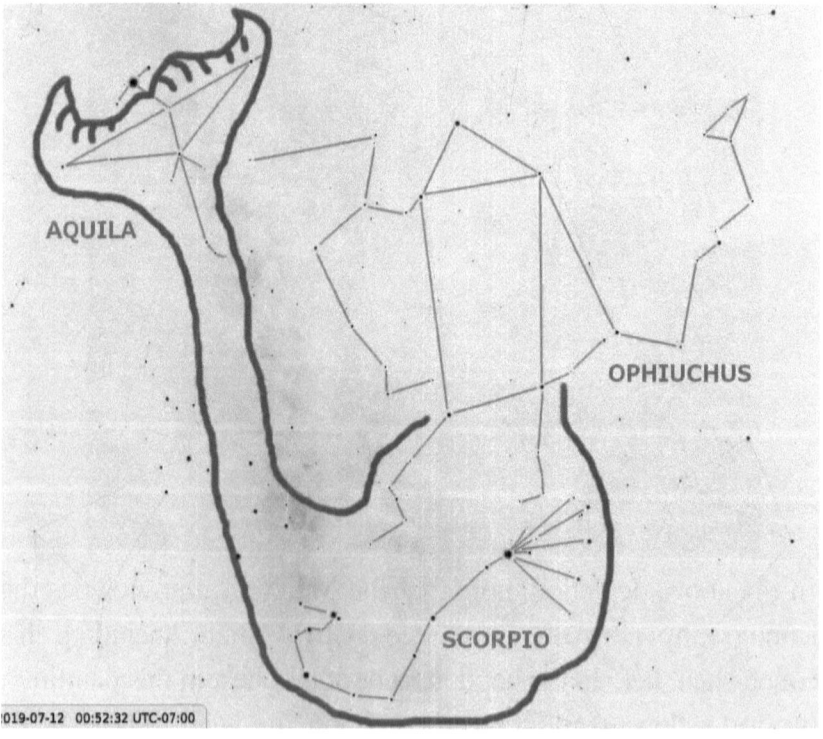

In the star-chart above, I have added thick additional lines to illustrate the fish-body with upturned tail and flukes. Below is another depiction of the Matsya avatar, from a modern statue:

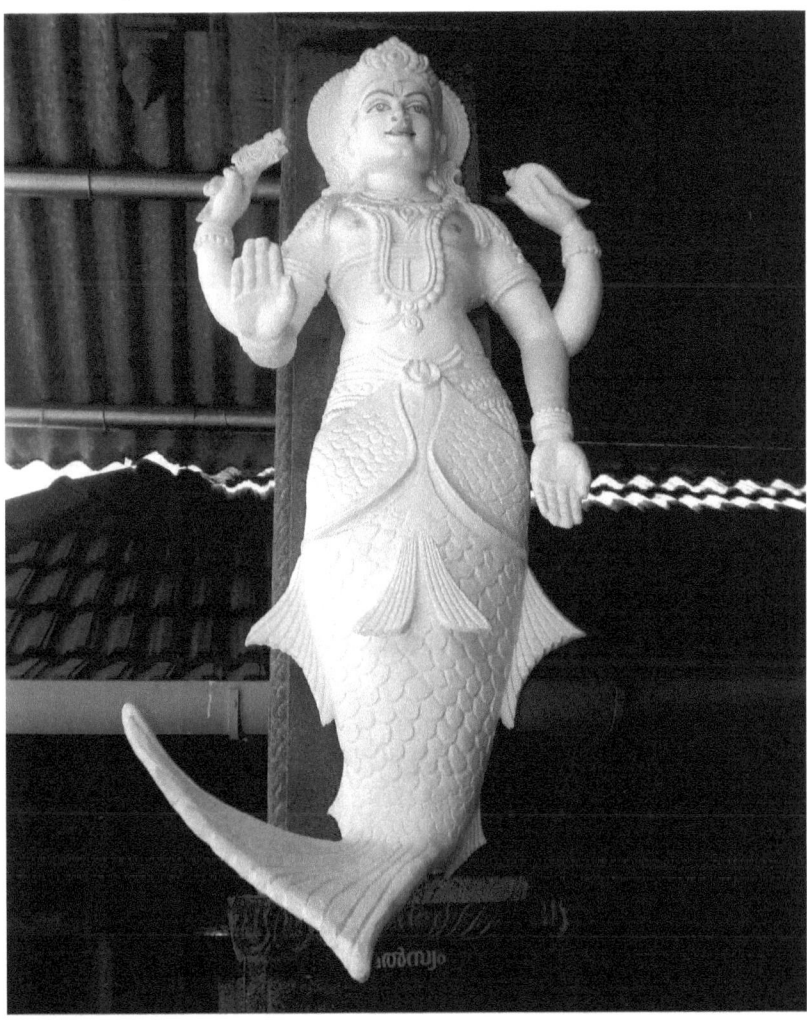

Another important avatar of Vishnu is Vamana, often referred to as Vishnu's dwarf avatar. The celestial associations of this avatar are touched upon in Volume Four of this series, with discussion of an observation put forward by Georges Dumézil regarding strong parallels between the figures of Vamana in Indian myth and Vidar or Viðarr in Norse myth (see page 553 of this volume).

Once again, this avatar of Vishnu is associated with the restoration of balance and order to the cosmos. In the case of the appearance of Vamana, the avatar appears in order to restore balance at the end of a sort of Golden Age ruled over by a mighty but benevolent Asura named Bali (or Mahabali, which means "Great Bali"). The Puranas tell us:

> When the end of an Age rolls around and time has lost its strength, then lord Visnu abandons his divine form to be born among men. When the gods and demons go to war, then Hari is born.
>
> Long ago when the Daitya Hiranyakaśipu ruled the triple world, and later when the three worlds were governed by Bali, there was real friendship between the gods and demons, who equally abided by the orders of these two rulers. But then the world became disordered, overrun with demons, and grievous and ferocious death-dealing war began between the demons and the gods who sought Bali's destruction.[404]

Note that battles between gods and an opposing category of supernatural beings often mark the end of an Age in the Star Myths of the world: the battle between the Titans and the Olympian gods which brings about an end to a now-nearly-forgotten Golden Age in the myths of ancient Greece, or the battle between the Norse gods and the forces of chaos which will take place at Ragnarok at the end of the Age, as foretold in the prophecy of the Volva in the Elder Edda.

As we have already discussed and as we will see again in future volumes of this series, the Age-ending battles or cataclysms are always the result of heavenly beings who "overstep their boundaries," such as the Genesis Flood described in the Bible, which (the text implies) results from the overstepping of boundaries by the "sons of God" who came in unto the daughters of men, described in Genesis 6: 4, immediately prior to the versees in which the LORD repents that he had made mankind on the earth and resolves to destroy the world with a Deluge.

As we saw in the passages on the Deluge of the myths of Mesopotamia, the shift in the precessional Ages is itself caused by the delaying of the background of stars, causing constellations to "overstep their bounds" and appear in a place where they are not "expected" to be (over the course of thousands of years). Thus, the description in ancient myth, of Ages being brought to an end when the gods and demons stop obeying the rules that are laid out for them, and instead begin to cross into one another's domains and struggle with one another, makes perfect sense as a way of esoterically allegorizing the heavenly cycle of precession.

The reader will note that the description just quoted, from the Puranas, where we see the ending of a Golden Age in which Mahabali presided over the three worlds and the gods and demons all abided by the rules, clearly describes just such a precessional shift: it is at these times that Vishnu is born as one of his avatars in order to preserve life, fulfilling his role as the Preserver within the Trimurtri.

Concerned over the situation described above, in which a ferocious war has begun between the demons and the gods who seek Bali's destruction, Vishnu announces to the virtuous Asita, mother of gods, that he will be born into the world through her, and in due time is born as the dwarf Vamana. Once grown to adulthood, Vamana disguises himself as a mendicant and attends a great sacrifice festival which Mahabali is holding as a means of consolidating and demonstrating his great earthly power.

Vanama requests a boon from the king, which was customary at such formal rituals. Bali asks Vamana what boon the dwarf would have the king give him, and Vamana requests as much land as the dwarf can cover in three paces.

The benevolent king replies, "What good are only three steps, best of striders? You should ask for a hundred or a hundred thousand steps!"[405] But Vamana replies, "I am content with only this much, lord of the Daityas. Give your wealth to other supplicants as you see fit."[406]

At this point, Vamana (who is of course an avatar of the god Vishnu) grows to enormous size and begins to take his three universe-encompassing strides.

With the first step, Vamana covers the entire earth. With the second step, he strides across the heavens. For the third step, the king offers his own head, and Vamana steps on it, sending Mahabali to the underworld.

Thus, the battle between the gods and the Asuras comes to an end, but so too does the prosperity of the Golden Age. However, Mahabali is permitted to return once each year, at the festival of Onam (still observed to this day), during which the abundance of that mythical time is again celebrated, with feasting, ritual dances, decorations of flowers, the wearing of costumes representing gods and demons, the wearing of new clothes, and other similarly symbolic activities.

As we will see on many occasions over the course of this multi-volume series, the constellation Hercules appears to have been envisioned as a dwarf in many of the Star Myths of the world. For example, the lion-headed god Bes of ancient Egypt can be confidently identified with the constellation Hercules, as mentioned earlier on pages 234 - 235 of this volume, and as discussed in more detail in later volumes as well. The dwarf Brokk who fashions the hammer of Thor in Norse myth can also be identified with Hercules, as mentioned on page 101 of this volume and as discussed in more detail in Volume Four of this series. And, in the myths of ancient India, it is very evident that the dwarf avatar of Vishnu, Vamana, is likewise associated with the constellation Hercules.

Below is a depiction of Vamana taking his third step and landing upon the head of Mahabali:

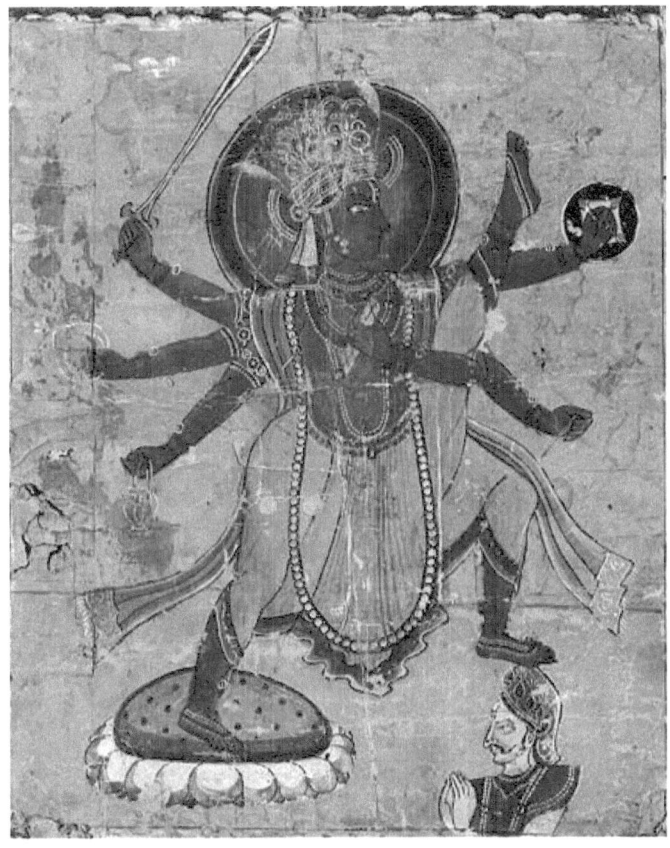

It should be self-evident to the reader at this point in the book that this iconography evokes the constellation Hercules in the sky.

Note in the preceding illustration that Vamana is brandishing a long club or sword in the arm that is upraised behind his own head, in very much the same way that the outline of Hercules brandishes a great club or sword in the heavens. Another arm, in front of Vamana's face, holds a small disc (perhaps a shield or buckler), likely indicative of the Northern Crown in front of the downward-reaching arm of the constellation Hercules. Most notable of all, of course, is the placement of Vamana's feet, which are evocative of the long stride the constellation Hercules appears to be taking -- and the fact that Hercules appears to be "stepping on the head" of the constellation Ophiuchus with his lead foot:

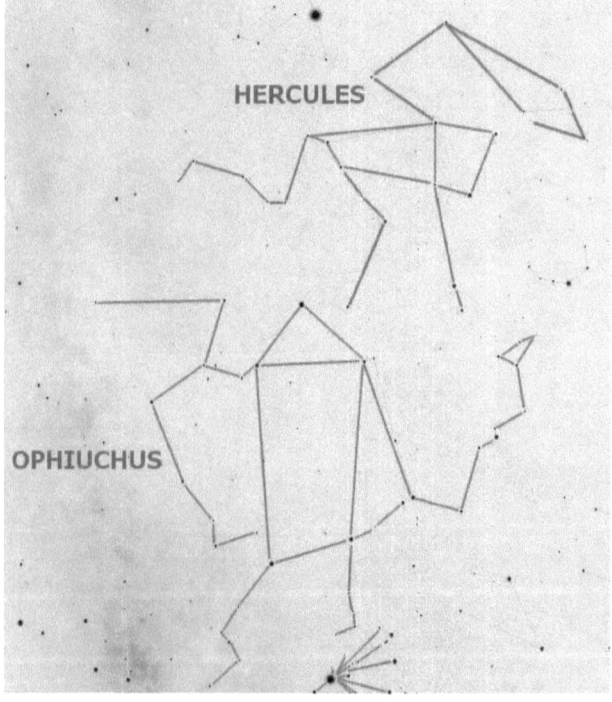

The above star-chart makes abundantly clear that Vamana is associated with Hercules, and king Mahabali is associated with the form of Ophiuchus. Note that if in our minds we rotate the constellation Hercules 90° counterclockwise and imagine the rear leg of Hercules being "planted" squarely on the floor, his forward leg would be stepping very high indeed! This is just how Vamana is portrayed in artwork:

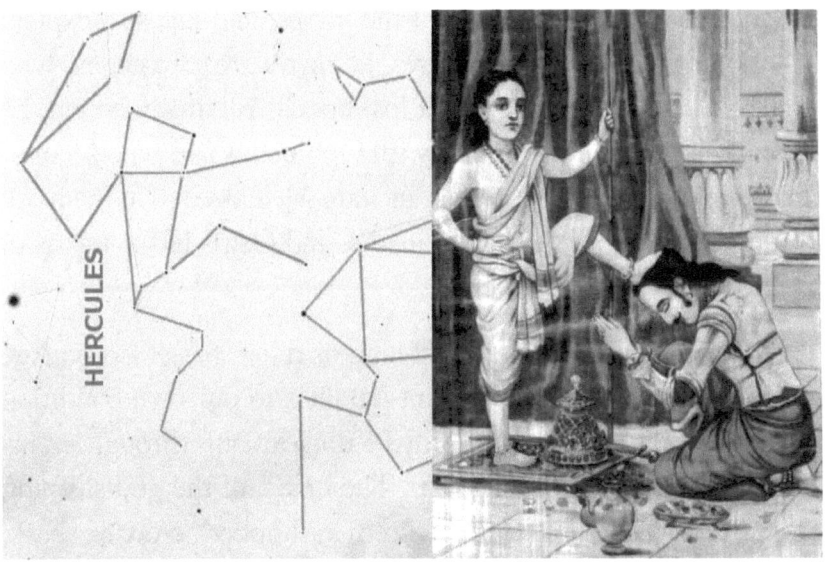

Clearly, in his avatar as Vamana, Vishnu is associated with the nearby constellation of Hercules.

Note that the banishing of a benevolent figure, often a ruler who presides over a lost Golden Age, to the netherworld for a period of time (but with a promised return) is an extraordinarily important and widespread myth-pattern or oicotype. The authors of *Hamlet's Mill* spend a great deal of time tracing out this myth-pattern around the globe, pointing out that we find it in the story of the Titan Kronos (banished to the underwater cave of Ogygia by Zeus), and in the myth of Saturn, and of Jamshyd, and of Osiris, and of Prometheus, and of King Arthur, and of many others.[407]

Based on the above analysis of the myth of Vamana and Bali, we can see that in at least one important example of this oicotype, the benevolent king who is banished can clearly be associated with

623

the constellation Ophiuchus (upon whose head the "great stride" of the constellation Hercules appears to land). This connection is very helpful in our analysis of the "vocabulary" and "grammar" of the ancient celestial language of the myths, and helps to explain why so many Ophiuchus-figures in myth are characters who evoke a sense of nostalgia for a lost epoch. Figures who can be shown to be closely associated with Ophiuchus and who seem to fit into this "nostalgic" category include Melchizedek in the book of Genesis, Odin in the Norse myths, and Osiris in the myths of ancient Egypt, among others.

The banishing of the benevolent king or ruler of the Golden Age to the underworld has important parallels to our own condition in this incarnate life, as Alvin Boyd Kuhn explains throughout his masterful 1940 book *Lost Light*. The image of the god sleeping beneath the waves is a figure of our own slumbering divine spark, buried within our incarnate body, which is composed primarily of the lower elements of earth and water (the mortal "clay").[408]

Thus this myth, and the annual festival associated with it, reminds us of the reality of this "sleeping divinity" -- and of the multitude of blessings which are available to us when we reconnect with that part of ourselves that has been lost during the process of entanglement with the rules and norms and strictures necessary for interaction in human society (recall the discussion of the myth of Enkidu from the texts of ancient Mesopotamia). We have, in actual fact, access to unlimited abundance through our unbreakable internal connection to an infinite realm, although most of the time we live and act as though we do not.

Other important incarnations of Vishnu include the godlike hero Rama, born to relieve the world of the depredations of the demon-king Ravana, and Parashurama, whose name literally means "Axe-Rama," an incarnation of Vishnu who subdues the warrior caste of *ksatriyas* when they overstep their bounds and disregard the sanctity of the *brahmins*. The adventures of Rama are recounted in the ancient epic Ramayana; in one episode of that epic, Rama must bend a bow which was once held by the god Shiva himself, and which no other king or warrior was able to bend, but which Rama bends with ease.

This episode, in which Rama wins as a wife the beautiful princess Sita, has clear parallels with an episode in the other ancient Sanskrit epic, the Mahabharata, in which Arjuna must perform a bow-trial which involves sending an arrow through a spinning disc to hit the eye of a fish-shaped target, in order to be considered by the beautiful princess Draupadi as a suitable candidate for marriage.

Both of these bow-trials have obvious parallels to the famous bow-trial recounted in the climactic scenes of the Odyssey of ancient Greece, an episode which can be shown to be founded upon celestial metaphor and which is explicated in detail in *Star Myths of the World, Volume Two*. Thus, we will not deal with them in this volume.

However, the avatar of Parashurama can be clearly seen to be another avatar of Vishnu which, like Vamana, is associated with the constellation Hercules in the heavens. We have already seen that the great weapon raised over the head of this constellation, and often envisioned in other myths as a great club, sword, mace, hammer, or even thunderbolt-weapon, can also be envisioned as a mighty battle-axe. Indeed, we spent some time earlier in this volume demonstrating that the figure of the thunder-god Shango or Xango of the Yoruba nation of Africa, who wields a powerful axe, is associated with the constellation Hercules, whose upraised weapon could be and obviously was envisioned as an axe in some of the Star Myths from cultures around the world.

Below is a depiction of Parashurama wielding his axe in battle, in which the distinctive characteristics of the constellation Hercules are clearly evident:

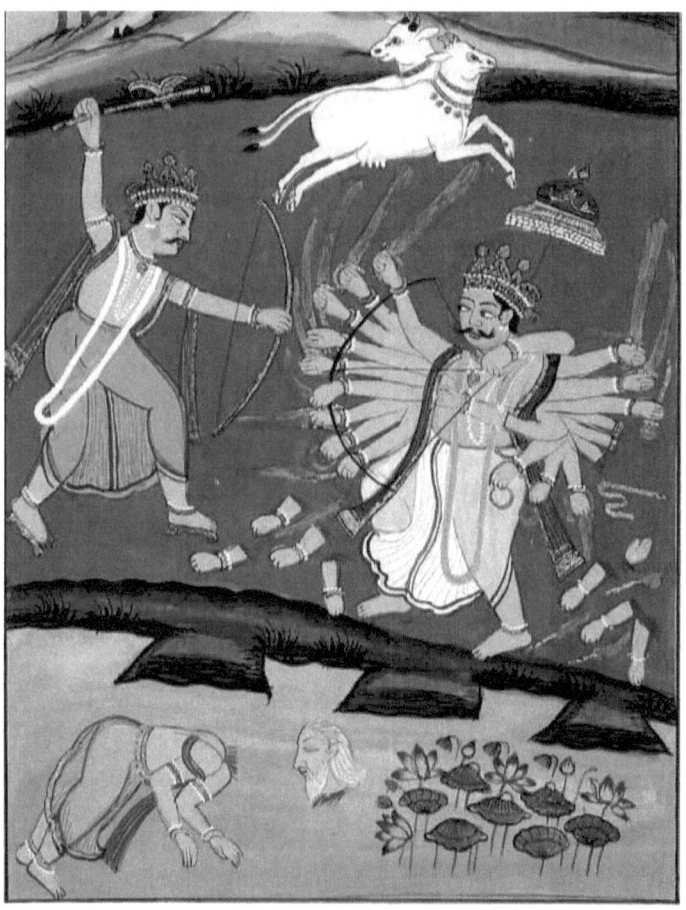

Parashurama, on the left, is depicted in the posture of the outline of the constellation Hercules, with his rear arm held aloft, brandishing an axe, and his lower arm extended forward of his face, and grasping a bow (most likely associated with the arc of the Northern Crown, towards which the lower arm of the constellation Hercules can be seen to be reaching). The rear leg of Parashurama has the heel up off the ground, which is almost invariably the case with artistic depictions of figures associated with the constellation Hercules.

Note that the ksatriya opponent of Parashurama in this depiction has a sort of "umbrella" or "canopy" above his head: this iconography in figures from the myths of India indicates an association with the constellation Ophiuchus, which has a large triangular top above the central rectangular body, the top being envisioned as a canopy or umbrella in many myths found in the ancient texts.

Another avatar of Vishnu described in the ancient texts but as a prophecy, the god not yet having incarnated in this form, is the great winged horse called Kalki, who will appear at the end of the current Yuga (the Kali Yuga). The celestial identity of Kalki is not difficult to decipher: we have a familiar constellation representing a winged horse, the great Pegasus, whose wing forms the Great Square of Pegasus, located between the wide "V" of the zodiac constellation Pisces.

It is appropriate that Kalki is the avatar whom the ancient texts describe as the one to incarnate at the end of the present age, because the constellation we call Pegasus, with whom Kalki is almost certainly to be identified, is situated at the constellation Pisces which does indeed mark the "current precessional Age," the one which only now is giving way to the next precessional Age (the Age of Aquarius, which follows the Age of Pisces).

Having at this point established, I hope, beyond any doubt the proposition that the avatars of Vishnu are based upon specific constellations, we will conclude this discussion and this chapter by briefly introducing one of the most important avatars of Vishnu: the god Krishna.

In the first edition of this volume, I argued that the god Krishna is associated with the constellation Boötes, based on a variety of clues.

First, as we will see in the upcoming chapter discussing the Mahabharata, Krishna acts as the divine charioteer of the warrior Arjuna -- and charioteers in the ancient myths are frequenly associated with the constellation Boötes.

Second, the god Krishna is frequently depicted playing a flute – indeed it is one of the god's most distinctive characteristics, and is featured in a large percentage of the surviving statues depicting Krishna. Obviously, the constellation Boötes has a long "pipe"-like feature as part of its outline, emanating from the head of the constellation near what would be the "mouth" region of the face, and thus Boötes becomes a good candidate for the god Krishna in myth.

Third, the constellation Boötes is traditionally known as the Herdsman, and often plays the role of a herdsman in various world myths. Because many myths describe the love of the cowherd women for Lord Krishna, including a myth which describes Krishna drawing the cowherd women out of their homes at night beneath the light of the moon and leading them in a circular dance known as the Rasa or Rasalila, this suggests a connection between Krishna and the constellation Boötes, which is a constellation associated with herds, and which is close to the Big Dipper and thus to the north celestial pole, making a sort of "circular dance" around the central northern point of the heavens (as does the Dipper itself).

For all these reasons, it seems likely that Krishna might be associated with Boötes, and I remain convinced that at times (especially when playing the role of divine charioteer, as he does for Arjuna in the Mahabharata) Krishna is indeed associated with this constellation. *However*, since the publication of the first edition of this first volume in the series, I have become convinced that the Lord Krishna is more closely associated with the constellation Ophiuchus, as is the Lord Vishnu of whom Krishna is an avatar.

One reason to suspect a possible association with Ophiuchus for Krishna is the fact that Krishna is almost invariably depicted as holding his flute out to one side as he plays it, not straight out from his mouth the way the "pipe" emerges from the mouth of Boötes in the outline of that constellation. This manner of holding the flute suggests that the "tail-end" of the serpent held by Ophiuchus, the eastern half which is located on the left side of the body as we face the star-chart below, plays the role of the flute of Krishna:

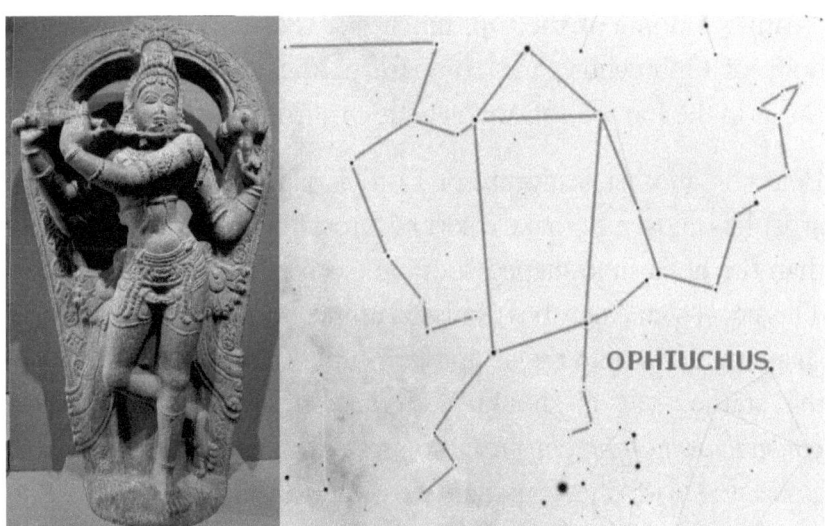

In the image above, which juxtaposes a star-chart of Ophiuchus with a 15th-century sculpture of the god, we can see how the left-half of the serpent of Ophiuchus, as outlined by H. A. Rey, could be envisioned as resembling a flute held sideways.

Indeed, in that sculpture, the artist has depicted two arms of Krishna holding the flute, extending to the left as we face the sculpture, but has added a third arm extending to the other side of Krishna's body (to the right as we face the image) which almost perfectly mirrors the other half of the serpent of Ophiuchus, on the right side of the central body as we face the star-chart shown above. This "third arm" depicted in the sculpture is holding some kind of weapon or other object which is strongly suggestive of a connection to the "serpent-head" on the right side of the body of Ophiuchus as we face the star-chart.

Note too in the above sculpture of Lord Krishna that the artist has supplied a kind of dome-topped "outline" to the figure of the god, and that this outline is suggestive of the shape of the constellation itself: narrower at the base than at the top, and consisting of two straight lines going upwards on the sides, then creating a dome at the top, much like the shape of the central body of Ophiuchus (and compare to the arch above the god Sokar in the Papyrus of Ani on page 272, from around 1270 BC!).

Below is another sculpture of Lord Krishna, and this time the artist has chosen to make a sort of "cross" behind the god, rather than the horseshoe-shaped "outline" seen in the previous image. This cross-shape may be dismissed as mere artistic choice, using a shape that will help the sculptor to support the multiple arms of the statue, but it should be noted that the *shape of the constellation Ophiuchus itself* suggests the shape now commonly associated with the Christian cross, and in fact I argue in *Star Myths of the World, Volume Three* (*Star Myths of the Bible*) that the Cross of Calvary is indeed based on the constellation Ophiuchus in the heavens. Thus, the sculpture seen on the opposite page, with its cruciform support, may be a clue that Krishna is associated with the same constellation Ophiuchus:

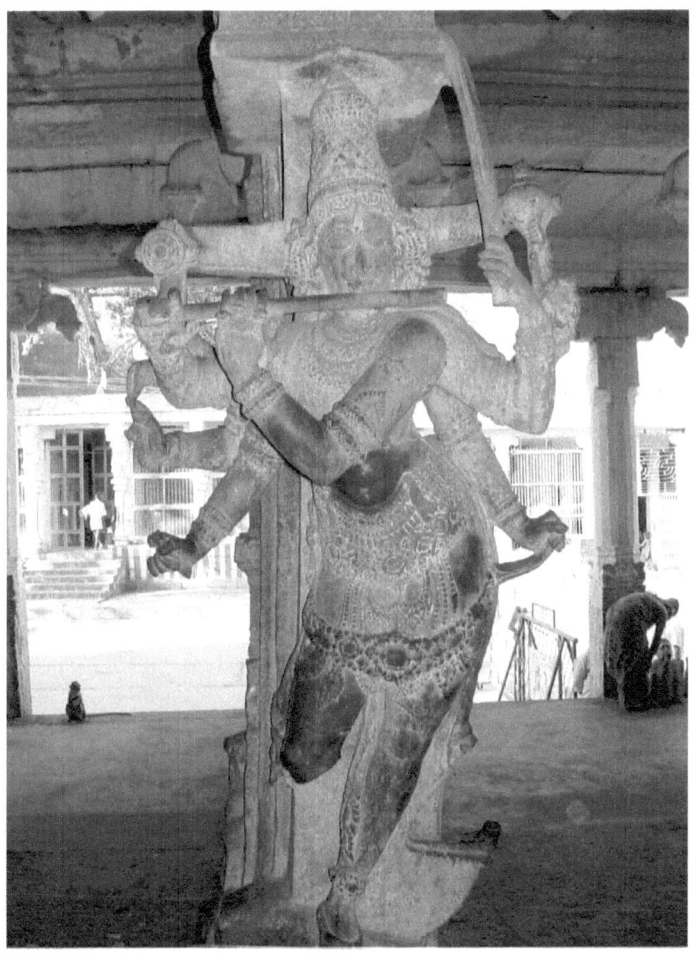

Note once again the flute, extending out to the left as we face the statue (which would be to the right for Krishna as he holds the flute).

Another reason to suspect that Krishna is associated with the constellation Ophiuchus is the fact that Krishna is also described in the ancient texts as having a conch-shell, which he sounds at important moments (such as at the start of the cataclysmic battle of Kurukshetra, in the Mahabharata). The conch-shell, as we have already mentioned, is part of the iconography of the god

Vishnu as well, which makes sense since Krishna is an avatar of Vishnu. And, as I have already argued, the conch-shell can very likely be identified with the "circlet" on the top of the western serpent-half of the constellation Ophiuchus (the "serpent-head" side of the constellation's outline). Thus, given his propensity for sounding the conch-shell trumpet, I believe that Krishna is most certainly associated with Ophiuchus as well.

Below is one more statue depicting the Lord Krishna, this one more modern than the previous two:

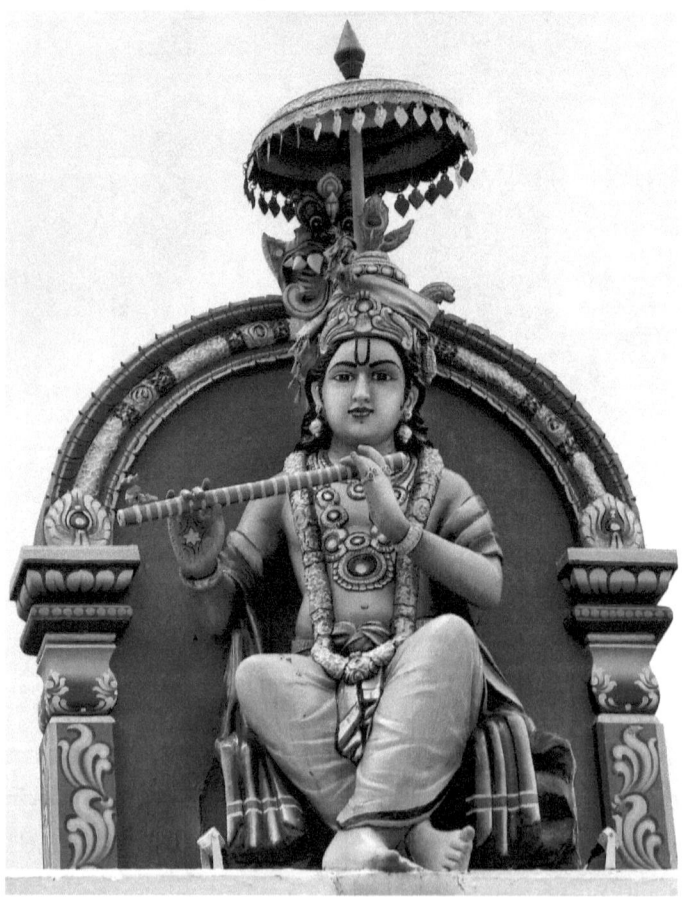

In the above statue, note that the god is protected above by a "parasol" or "umbrella" or "canopy." As noted earlier in our discussion of the avatar Parashurama, such a canopy or umbrella can be confidently associated with the outline of the constellation Ophiuchus. Note also that in the statue above, Krishna is depicted as seated in between *two pillars*: such positioning is strongly connected with the constellation Ophiuchus, which can be envisioned as having "two pillars" (one on either side of the central body). Indeed, King Solomon in the Old Testament scriptures is described as building a Temple in which two mighty pillars frame a central gate: I believe that both Solomon and his Temple gate with its two pillars can be identified with the constellation Ophiuchus (there is, of course, more discussion of the celestial identity of Solomon in Volume Three of this series).

We will have more to say about the god Krishna, who plays a central role in the ancient epic of the Mahabharata, in the upcoming chapter. It should be quite evident by now, however, that this important god is seen in the heavens in the outlines of specific constellations -- and that the same can be said for other figures and events described in the sacred texts of ancient India.

We will conclude this present discussion of the Star Myths of India at this point, and in subsequent chapters will discuss the celestial aspects of the Mahabharata and of the Bhagavad Gita (the Gita is contained in the Mahabharata), as well as of the figure of the Buddha (who is sometimes considered an avatar of Vishnu as well).

The Mahabharata

The great ancient epic of Mahabharata is described in its opening section as relating "the most eminent narrative that exists."[409]

It is said to have been recited by the ancient Rishi Vyasa, who asked the god Brahma for help in preserving the inspired utterances. Brahma nominated Ganesha for the task of writing down the verses as Vyasa recited them, and thus began the preservation of this immense inspired poem.[410]

The text itself relates that Ganesha agreed to record the verses, under the condition that Vyasa must continue reciting them, such that Ganesha's pen must never stop moving. Vyasa agreed, but only on the condition that whenever Ganesha might hear something which he did not comprehend, he would cease writing.[411] In this way, whenever Vyasa needed to slow down the transcribing of Ganesha, he would utter some difficult and "close-knit" *slokas* (or poetic lines), thus buying himself some time while Ganesha paused to consider their meaning.[412]

The introduction goes on to praise the poem of Vyasa by declaring of the Mahabharata that:

> The wisdom of this work, like unto an instrument of applying collyrium, hath opened the eyes of the inquisitive world blinded by the darkness of ignorance. As the sun dispelleth the darkness, so doth the Bharata by its discourses on religion, profit, pleasure and final release, dispel the ignorance of men.[413]

The Mahabharata is a massive epic. As already noted, it is by any way of counting the verses many times longer than both the Iliad and Odyssey of ancient Greece, combined. There is simply no way to do justice to the entire sweep of this ancient poem in the scope of this volume, and so this volume will endeavor to examine some of the most representative characters and incidents while commending further study of the full epic to all readers -- but the selections we will examine should leave little doubt that this revered ancient poem, which itself contains the Bhagavad Gita, one of the most beloved and oft-consulted scriptures on earth, is *celestial* in nature, its verses describing the adventures of characters who themselves can be seen to correspond to specific constellations in the heavens, operating within the same ancient system whose ruins seem to lie across every inhabited continent and island of our globe.

Before beginning an examination of some of the characters and events in this epic, it is appropriate to note how the entire massive poem begins. As with both the Iliad and the Odyssey of ancient Greece, the Mahabharata begins with an invocation of the divine. The first word of the epic is the sacred sound, "OM." Then, the poet declares: "Having bowed down to Narayana and Nara, the most exalted male being, and also to the goddess Saraswati, must the word Jaya be uttered."[414] *Narayana* is another name for the god Vishnu, "especially during the period of dissolution after a Yuga or Kalpa."[415] Narada or Nara is a sage who acts as a "frequent intermediary between gods and men."[416]

Perhaps the most appropriate place to begin our exploration of this majestic ancient text is with the terrible vow of Devavrata, which eventually leads to the tension over the rightful successor to the kingdom which forms the conflict in the plot of the Mahabharata. This vow comes about as follows: the ancient texts describe the kingdom whose capitol was the city of Hastinapura, ruled over in the distant past by king Shantanu. Shantanu was descended from the line of an ancestor known by the title of

Bharata, after whom the entire region of India, called *Bharatavarsa* (the "classical designation for the Indian subcontinent") was anciently named.[417] Bharata was the grandfather of Hasti, who founded the great city of Hastinapura. Four generations after Hasti, a son named Kuru became king of Hastinapura, and his name is important because the dynasty of Hastinapura were afterwards known as the *Kurus.* Six generations after Kuru, Shantanu became king of Hastinapura.[418]

One day while taking his customary walk along the banks of the great sacred river Ganga (the Ganges), the king was awe-struck at the sight of a gorgeous woman emerging from the water. Overcome with emotion, he immediately asked her hand in marriage, but she said that in order for her to accept, Shantanu would have to agree to her conditions:

> "thou must not interfere with me in anything I do, be it agreeable or disagreeable. Nor shalt thou ever address me unkindly. As long as thou shalt behave kindly I promise to live with thee. But I shall certainly leave thee the moment thou interferest with me or speakest to me an unkind word."[419]

The text informs us that the king readily agreed to these terms, and the two were married. The two were very happy together, and the king, "adhering to his promise, refrained from asking her anything."[420] Over the years, eight children "who in beauty were like the very celestials themselves" were born to the king and his consort, but as each was born, their mother would take the infant to the broad river Ganges and throw the child into the waters, saying "This is for thy good" as the child sank beneath the waters to rise no more.[421]

The king, looking on, was horrified and outraged, but remembering his promise, spoke not a word to his wife but looked on helplessly, until the eighth child. As the mother prepared to throw this one too into the great river, Shantanu could stand it no longer. He shouted, "Kill it not! Who art thou and whose? Why dost thou kill thine own children? Murderess of thy sons, the load of thy sin is great!"[422]

His wife stopped, and turned to speak to the king. She informed him that now, having saved the child, the time of her stay with Shantanu was at its end. For the first time she revealed her true identity, explaining to him that she was the goddess of the holy river itself, and telling him: "I am Ganga, the daughter of Jahnu. I am ever worshipped by the great sages; I have lived with thee so long for accomplishing the purpose of the celestials."[423]

She explained that once, the great Rishi Vasishtha (also known as the Rishi Apava) who was one of the Seven Sages and known for his great patience, was visited by eight Vasus (the Vasus being "a group of Vedic gods")[424] and that during their stay, while admiring Nandini, the cow of plenty possessed by Vasishtha (along with her calf), one of the Vasus, named Dyu, remarked to his wife that the milk of this cow could preserve for ten thousand years the youth of any mortal who consumed that milk. The wife of the Vasu implored her husband Dyu to steal the cow for her, so that her mortal friend on earth, a young maiden of great beauty, could live a long life free of disease or decripitude. Moved by his wife's request, and desiring to please her, Dyu (assisted by his brothers) stole the cow and her calf.[425]

Later, after the Vasus had departed, the great Rishi went looking for his cow and calf, and being unable to find them, the text tells us, "he saw by his ascetic vision that they had been stolen by the

Vasus."[426] The Rishi Apava then uttered a curse, saying that because the eight Vasus had stolen his milk cow, they would thus have to be born on earth as mortals. After this, he went back to his ascetic meditation. In the ancient texts, a Rishi designates an enlightened holy sage who has mastered all the mantras -- and the curse of a Rishi always come to pass.

Learning of the curse, the Vasus went back and apologized to Rishi Apava, hoping to pacify his anger. Apava replied that he would be merciful and free each of them from the curse of being born among mortals within one year of the time of their birth -- all except for Dyu, the instigator of the theft of the cow and her calf. Apava declared that Dyu would have to live on earth as a mortal man for a long life, but that, "Dyu, though dwelling on Earth, shall not beget children. He shall, however, be virtuous and conversant with the scriptures. He shall be an obedient son to his father, but he shall have to abstain from the pleasure of female companionship."[427]

The goddess Ganga then told Shantanu how the Vasus came to her, and begged her to throw each of them into the river as soon as they were born. So, she had done as they desired, in order to free them from their earthly life -- sparing only the eighth and final son, the incarnation of Dyu himself, whose lot was to live on earth for a long time, as specified in the curse of the great Rishi.

Having told Shantanu this account, Ganga told him that she would raise the child herself, sending him back to Shantanu when he was old enough. This boy, who was called Gangeya and more commonly Devavrata, as he grew up was taken by his mother to learn all the martial arts and use of weapons from Parashurama himself (an avatar of Vishnu discussed in the previous chapter), so that by the time he returned to Hastinapura he was a master of warfare of all kinds, as well as being conversant in all the branches of the Vedas. As a young man, Ganga brought him back to the king, and from that time on Devavrata lived in Hastinapura, and was immediately greatly respected due to his excellent disposition and unmatchable prowess at arms and fighting.

Shantanu was overjoyed to see what an accomplished son Devavrata proved himself to be, but he was very concerned about the succession of the kingdom, since he had only one son and what's more this son was very warlike and likely to participate in many battles. Shantanu was also concerned for his own fate after death, dependent as it was upon the prayers and remembrances of his descendants. If something should happen to his only son, he feared for both his kingdom and his own soul.

One day, while walking along the banks of the Ganges as was his custom, Shantanu encountered a young woman of tremendous beauty, and once again as he had long ago, he asked her for her hand in marriage. The maiden, named Satyavati, the daughter of the chief of fishermen, referred Shantanu to her father -- and when Shantanu spoke with him, he said his conditions were that her sons and not Shantanu's son by a previous wife should be in line for the throne, rather than Devavrata. Shantanu was not prepared to accept these terms, and though he was filled with desire for Satyavati, he rode sorrowfully back home to his palace.

However, Devavrata sensing something was troubling his father, inquired as to the cause, and upon learning the answer went to meet with the chief of fishermen. There, he declared that he would gladly renounce his claim to the throne so that Satyavati could marry Shantanu. But Satyavati's father was still not satisfied, pointing out that even if Devavrata decided not to rule, Devavrata's sons would have a claim to the throne and that this could supersede the claim of any children of Satyavati should she marry Shantanu.

Hearing this objection, Devavrata (moved, the text tells us, by desire to benefit his father), uttered a great and terrible vow: "I adopt the vow of *Brahmacharya* (study and meditation in celibacy). If I die sonless, I shall yet attain to regions of perennial bliss in heaven!"[428]

At these words, the Mahabharata tells us, the celestials began to rain down flowers from heaven upon the head of Devavrata, to show their approval of his selfless action, and to proclaim throughout the worlds that this one is "*Bhishma,*" a word which means "terrible" or "terrible vow." Thus, Devavrata is most commonly known by the name *Bhishma*, and he is a central figure in the Mahabharata.

The story about the drowning of the seven infants by the goddess Ganga and the saving of the eighth has some echoes with similar patterns elsewhere in world myth, such as the many myths involving the *casting away of a baby into the river* (a pattern we have already encountered in this volume, and will encounter again, more than once, before we're through -- and which is also of course very famous from the story of baby Moses in the Hebrew scriptures). It also has some resonance with the many examples of the "failed baptism" which often involves a pattern in which a female figure is stopped by a husband (such as in the story of the baptism of Achilles, in which the goddess mother of Achilles is dipping the boy in a fire or in the River Styx in order to make him invulnerable, and in some versions of the story the mortal father of the child intervenes to stop her, fearing for the child).

It is quite likely that there is a celestial foundation to this story of Ganga throwing seven children into the sacred river Ganges, while sparing the eighth. As with other variations on the infant cast into the river which center around Scorpio and Ophiuchus, there is likely a connection between the seven infants thrown in the water and the "many heads" of Scorpio, a constellation which is positioned such that it is "lying in" the brightest and widest part of the Milky Way galaxy (a "river of stars" which undoubtedly plays the role of the heavenly Ganges in the ancient myths of India).

If the Milky Way plays the role of the heavenly Ganges itself, it is quite possible that the goddess Ganga is associated with Sagittarius, immediately adjacent to the Milky Way and appearing as a beautiful woman stepping out of the river. The heads of Scorpio would then play her eight children, all of whom except one are drowned in the wide river. We've also seen that the constellation Virgo, lying on her back with her legs elevated, can be definitively shown in some Star Myths to have been envisioned as "giving birth" to figures associated with the constellation Scorpio (as we have already discussed, for example, in the Maui myths of the cultures of the Pacific). Thus, it is also possible that the goddess Ganga (at least when giving birth to the eight children) is associated with the constellation Virgo.

We've seen the constellation Scorpio envisioned as having seven, eight or nine heads in many Star Myths. In the story of Heracles fighting the Lernaean hydra, it has nine heads. In the myth of Maui, when baby Maui is thrown into the sea-foam, some versions of the story relate that the baby had eight heads. And, in the book of Revelation, the great red dragon who is described in Revelation chapter 12 and verse 3, standing "before the woman which was ready to be delivered, for to devour her child as soon as it was born" is of course Scorpio again, this time envisioned as having seven heads (the same number as the incarnate Vasus whom Ganga drowns).

Below is a star-chart showing the constellations Virgo and Scorpio, showing why certain ancient Star Myths envision Virgo as *giving birth* to a figure associated with Scorpio (or, in the case of Revelation 12, envisioning Scorpio as a seven-headed dragon standing before the woman who is in labor, waiting to devour her child as soon as she gives birth):

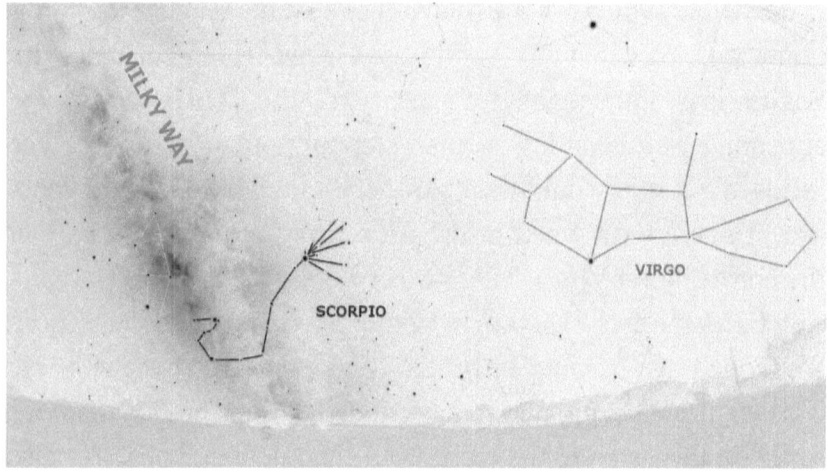

It is also possible to detect some parallel between this story and the story of the eight sons of Jesse in 1 Samuel 16, of whom seven pass before Samuel and are told that the LORD has not chosen any of the first seven. It is only when the eighth son, David, is brought before Samuel that the LORD declares, "Arise, anoint him: for this *is* he" (1 Samuel 16: 12).

In any case, there is no doubt in my mind that celestial metaphor is involved in this story and in most of the other episodes of the massive epic. We will soon see abundant evidence attesting to this fact. The figure of Bhishma is important for the entire plot of the epic, because his terrible vow of celibacy leads directly to the uncertainty and tension regarding the succession of kingship over

Hastinapura -- uncertainty which forms the main conflict in the poem, and leads ultimately to the battle of Kurukshetra.

Shantanu's second wife, Satyavati, bears him two sons. Note that this pattern of "two mothers" has been encountered before in world myth, and its likely esoteric meaning was discussed at some length in the chapter on the myths of ancient Egypt (see pages 358 through 360 of this volume, for example).

I believe it is very likely that Satyavati also corresponds to the constellation Sagittarius. The text tells us that she is the daughter of the chief of fishermen -- and we have already seen that the constellation Aquarius is associated with a fisherman figure in certain Star Myths (for example, in the story of Mirragan and Gurangatch of Australia). Sagittarius is located in close proximity to Aquarius in the night sky and may thus play a figure who is the daughter of an Aquarius-figure, as I believe Sagittarius does here in the story of Satyavati.

Another clue in the text suggesting that Satyavati may be associated with Sagittarius is the fact that, prior to meeting Shantanu, she was performing the duty of ferrying travelers across the river Yamuna, at the command of her father, for religious merit.[429] We have already seen that the constellation Scorpio could be envisioned as a boat, lying in the "river" of the Milky Way band, and thus it is very likely that Satyavati corresponds to Sagittarius, which can be seen "standing on the banks of the river (of the Milky Way) beside her boat (Scorpio)."

If indeed Ganga corresponds to Virgo (at least when giving birth to children) and Satyavati corresponds to Sagittarius (as I believe is also likely based on the text) then this pattern is very much consistent with other "two mother" oicotypes throughout world myth, in which the first mother usually corresponds to Virgo (the constellation situated at the point of the year's "downward plunge" into the lower half, symbolic of incarnation) and in which the second mother corresponds to Sagittarius (situated at the winter solstice, the "great turning point" of the year, symbolic of the end of the soul's downward motion and symbolic instead of the turn "back upwards" towards integration with spiritual things: the point of the "second birth"). The "two mothers" pattern is evident throughout the various stories and episodes contained in the Mahabharata.

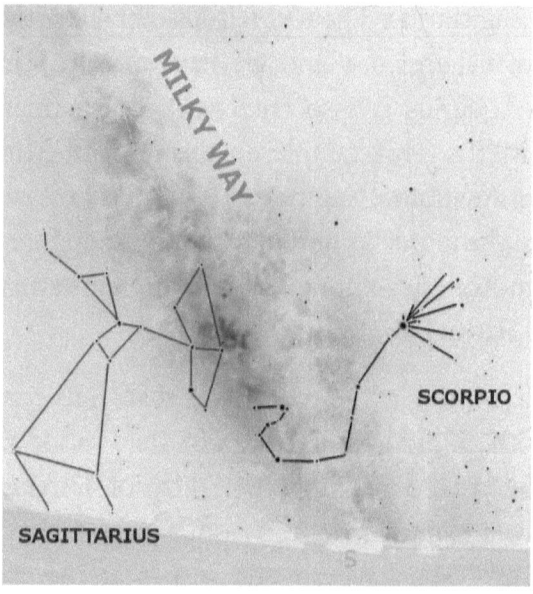

Shantanu eventually succumbs to the inexorable advance of Time, leaving Satyavati, and Bhishma, and Satyavati's two sons. After the death of Shantanu, Bhishma (who has renounced the throne) anoints the elder of the two sons of Shantanu as king -- but although this son, Chitrangada, is very accomplished as a fighter, he dies in battle against a celestial being before producing an heir. Bhishma then anoints the younger of the two sons of Satyavati, named Vichitravirya, as king, and being desirous to see Vichitravirya produce an heir, Bhishma looks for a bride for the boy (who had not yet reached manhood when his older brother Chitrangada was killed).

Hearing that the king of Kali was putting on a *swayamvara* for his three beautiful daughters, Bhishma took a single chariot and went to the capitol city of Kali. A *swayamvara* (or *svayamvara*) is an ancient tradition, described in the Vedas, by which a bride may select her own husband from among the suitors who attend -- and she may do so according to whatever criteria she herself determines. Acting by force, Bhishma abducted all three of the daughters of the king from their swayamvara, challenging all present to try and stop him (none could do so, Bhishma being a warrior of such surpassing ability).

While the eldest of these three abducted daughters, whose name was Amba, refused to marry the young king Vichitravirya, the other two sisters, named Ambika and Ambalika, married the king and spent seven happy years with him -- until Vichitravirya was afflicted with a terrible disease and succumbed, "setting like the evening sun."[430]

Now the succession of the Kuru throne was indeed in jeopardy. Satyavati begs Bhishma to produce an heir with Ambika or Ambalika (a tradition known as *niyogi*, specified in the anceint scriptures of India, allows a brother to produce an heir by the wife of a man who dies without an heir -- similar to the stipulation in the Biblical scriptures: see Deuteronomy 25: 5).

Satyavati releases Bhishma from the terrible vow he swore so many years before -- but Bhishma is adamant and refuses to break his vow. Since Bhishma will not renounce his vow of celibacy and produce an heir with either Ambika or Ambalika, Satyavati thinks of another option -- her first son, born to her during the years she was ferrying travellers across the river, prior to meeting Shantanu.

Chapter Seventeen

There was once a Rishi named Parasara who had traveled across the river, and by him Satyavati had borne a son, named Vyasa (or, more honorifically, Vyasadeva). This son had himself grown up to become a Rishi, and lived an ascetic life of meditation and severe austerity, in the Himalayas (he is also, according to the ancient texts, the composer of the Mahabharata itself).

So, Satyavati summoned Vyasadeva, and explained to the sage, her son, their predicament. He agreed to her plan and, under the custom of niyogi, went in to the chambers of Ambika. The next morning, Vyasa emerged from the quarters of Ambika, and informed Bhishma and Satyavati that Ambika would certainly bear a son -- but that, because Ambika herself had kept her eyes closed all night (Vyasa being horrifying to her sensibilities, on account of his physical condition following a life of hardship and asceticism), the child would be born blind.

Because this condition would prevent that child from ever ascending the throne as king, Satyavati and Bhishma urged Vyasadeva to try again some months later, this time with Ambalika. This time, having been instructed ahead of time, Ambalika was sure to keep her eyes open, but at the sight of Vyasa she turned pale. Thus, when the Rishi emerged the next morning, he informed Satyavati and Bhishma that the child Ambalika would bear would be pale.

Finally, after the birth of the first two sons mentioned below, Bhishma and Satyavati asked Vyasadeva to go in once more to Ambalika -- but this time Ambalika convinced one of her maidservants to dress up as Ambalika, so that Ambalika would not have to spend a second night with the sage (who was, of course, not fooled but spent the night with her anyway). From this union, a third son was conceived, but because the child was

646

born of Ambalika's maidservant, he would not be eligible for the throne.

In due time were born three sons, as predicted by Vyasa. The first, born of Ambika, was named Dhritarastra, and he was indeed born blind. The second, born of Ambalika, was named Pandu, and he was indeed remarkably pale (hence his name, which in Sanskrit indicates "pale"). The third, born of the maidservant, was named Vidura, and although not eligible for the throne, he became a great counselor renowned for his wisdom and rectitude.

Due to the vast scope of the Mahabharata and the need to explore some of the myths of a few more ancient cultures before the end of this volume, we will not here be able to explicate all aspects of each character or episode, or even the entire plot. We will press ahead to the identity of the sons of Pandu, who become the main protagonists of the great epic. However, it is enough to note in passing that with Amba and Ambalika we once again see an indication of the "two mothers" pattern at work in this ancient text of India.

Pandu will also manifest this pattern, having two wives, named Kunti and Madri. Kunti was given the name Pritha at her birth, but was more widely known as Kunti due to being raised by a king named Kuntibhoja, who was childless. Madri was a princess of the Madra kingdom.

Pandu became king of Hastinapura, his older brother being blind and thus considered incapable of ruling and of defending the kingdom in battle. Pandu was both wise and good, and was also an outstanding warrior, having been trained by none other than Bhishma. However, due to an incident in which he shoots a Rishi named Kindama who, while in the form of a stag was having sexual intercourse with a doe (who was in fact the Rishi's wife in the form of a deer as well), Pandu retires to the forest with his wives to live a simple life of penance, and Dhritarastra ascends the throne, supposedly as a kind of regent until coming of age of the sons of Pandu, but giving up the throne to them instead of to one of his own sons later proves to be too difficult for him. Dhritarastra displays constant internal tension between doing what he knows is right and acting in the interest of his own sons, who are openly arrogant and wicked.

Having retired to the forest to live among the brahmins and ascetics, Pandu begins to worry that he has no sons, and without sons there will be none to recite prayers and rituals for himself and his ancestors after he leaves this life. However, the dying Rishi Kindama, whom Pandu shot while the Rishi took the form of a deer, had cursed Pandu that because he had killed another being which was in the act of intercourse, Pandu himself would die the moment he embraced either of his wives out of sexual desire. Thus, Pandu saw no other way for his wives to bear offspring than to give themselves to another in his place.

When he presented this request to Kunti and Madri, however, they recoiled at the idea. Kunti then revealed that, long ago, her father's house had been visited by a great mystic named Rishi Durvasa. Grateful for the kind hospitality young Kunti had shown him. Durvasa had imparted to her a powerful mantra, which would allow her to invoke any god she chose, who would consummate sexual union with her and provide her with a son. Faced with the request of Pandu, Kunti proposed that she use the mantra now.

Pandu readily agreed to this idea, feeling that sons born of celestials would of course be the best possible heirs for the kingdom. And so, Kunti called upon the god of justice and duty,

Dharma, using the mantra taught to her by the Rishi Durvasa, long ago. Immediately, the god appeared, and when he asked Kunti what she desired and was told she wanted a son by him, the god immediately obliged.

In due time, a boy-child was born to Kunti from this union, and at the moment of his birth, a mysterious voice from the skies proclaimed: "This child shall be the best of men, the foremost of those that are virtuous. Endued with great prowess and truthful in speech, he shall certainly be the ruler of the earth. And this first child of Pandu shall be known by the name of Yudhishthira. Possessed of prowess and honesty of disposition, he sall be a famous king, known throughout the three worlds."[431]

Having obtained a son by such supernatural means, Pandu (we are told) wasted no time but asked Kunti to use her mantra again, this time to have a child who would be endowed with great strength. So, Kunti used her mantra to call upon the very god of the wind, Vayu, and when the god appeared she asked him for a son of great strength, capable of humbling the pride of every body.[432] Thus was conceived the great warrior Bhima; when he was born, an incorporeal voice annouced: "This child shall be the foremost of all endued with strength."[433]

The text further tells us that when Bhima was born, "he fell from his mother's lap upon the mountain breast," and "the violence of the fall broke into fragments the stone upon which he fell without his infant body being injured in the least."[434]

Pandu, still not satisfied with these two marvelous sons, next took counsel with the Rishis, and following their advice "commanded Kunti to observe an auspicious vow for one full year, while he himself commenced [. . .] to stand upon one leg from morning to evening, and practise other severe meditations with mind rapt in meditation, for glorifying the lord of the celestials."[435] After this year of devotion, Pandu was approached by Indra himself, who promised that Pandu would have another son, whose fame would reach throughout the three worlds, and who would promote the welfare of all.

Overjoyed, Pandu asked Kunti to use the mantra again, and this time she called upon Lord Indra to give her a son, and the ruler of heaven complied with her request. Of this union was born the child who would grow up to be the great warrior Arjuna.

Pandu suggested Kunti use the mantra yet again, but she declined -- but Pandu's other wife Madri requested that she be given use of the mantra, and when Kunti assented, Madri used the mantra to summon the twin gods known as the Ashvins. By them Madri had twin sons, of surpassing personal beauty, who were named Nakula and Sahadeva.

These five sons became known as the Pandavas because they were seen as the sons of Pandu, even though they were actually the sons of celestial gods by Pandu's wives Kunti and Madri (the "two mothers" pattern arising yet again in the Mahabharata). They would grow up into virtuous young men, and, through the training of their martial arts masters, into powerful warriors as well -- in fact, world-renowned warriors, virtually without equal.

At the same time these sons of Pandu were being born, each one year apart from the other for a total of five years (as we are told in the Mahabharata, in an echo of the five gods and goddesses of ancient Egypt including Isis and Osiris, who are born in each of five intercalary days), Pandu's older brother Dhritarastra and his wife Gandhari also conceived. Gandhari was a famously virtuous queen -- upon learning that the man she was pledged to marry was blind from birth, she fixed a sash about her own eyes, in order to share his condition, permanently choosing to give up her own sight to better empathize with Dhritarastra's situation. She had been promised by the sage Vyasa that she would bear a hundred sons -- and in one of the more bizarre episodes in world myth (which again is likely to be based upon a pattern in the stars), she gives birth to a "ball of flesh" after an unnaturally long period of gestation, and she is told by Vyasa to wait until it divides itself into 101 pieces, and put each piece in its own separate pot of ghee, place a lid over each, and only open the pots after two years.[436]

From these pots of ghee grow what might be called the first recorded "test-tube babies" (or in this case, "pot of ghee babies") -- the sons of Dhritarastra and Gandhari, 100 in number, plus one daughter. These sons would collectively become known as the Kauravas, which technically means "descendant of Kuru" (a title which would also apply to the Pandavas but which more particularly came to designate the descendants of Dhritarastra specifically, in contrast to the Pandavas).

The names of the 100 sons and the daughter are given in the Mahabharata (I. 117), but the most important of them are Duryodhana, the firstborn, and Dushashana, his favorite brother and right-hand man. Even as they are growing up, the sons of Dhritarastra (led by Duryodhana, the primary instigator of plots in the epic) developed a jealousy and hatred for their talented and popular cousins, the Pandavas.

Pandu and his wives rejoice at having such talented and virtuous sons. One fine spring day in the forest, however, while out among the beauty of nature with Madri, Pandu is overcome by desire for his wife and begins to embrace her. As they begin to make love, the curse placed upon Pandu by the Rishi long ago takes effect and Pandu dies. Madri chooses to join Pandu on the funeral pyre, declaring that she wants to satisfy his desire in the next life since she could not do so in this one, and Kunti and the five boys move back to the capitol.

To teach the five Pandavas the martial skills necessary to leaders and defenders of Hastinapur, Bhishma finds as their guru the great Drona, also called Dronacharya. Like Bhishma, Drona during his own youth was also trained by none other than Parashurama himself.

Drona teaches the boys to be masters at all kinds of fighting, and with all types of weapons, but also finds the weapon for which each one is most well-suited and encourages them to make that weapon their signature and special expertise. Yudhishthira becomes a master of the spear, as well as of battle from a chariot. The powerful Bhima becomes a master of the great mace. Arjuna becomes a master of the bow (but eventually becomes so skilled at all weapons that he surpasses all of them in every form of fighting). And the twins Nakula and Sahadeva become masters of the sword.

From these associations with specific weapons, as well as from the identities of the celestial gods summoned by the mantra to cause these five sons to be born to Kunti and Madri, we can begin to arrive at some conclusions regarding the celestial identity of the five famous Pandavas.

Yudhishthira is born of Kunti by the god Dharma, or righteousness and justice. Abundant evidence supports the conclusion that both Dharma and Yudhishthira can be identified with the constellation Ophiuchus in the heavens.

Examining first the god Dharma, he is the god of justice and righteousness and duty. In some of the Puranas he is explicitly associated with Yama, the god of death -- a god who can be seen to be associated with the constellation Ophiuchus (for example, Yama carries a dreaded noose with which he snares his victims: this noose can be identified with the "head" on the western half of the serpent held by Ophiuchus, which could easily be envisioned as a long, winding rope with a noose at the end). It should be noted that the god of the underworld in Greek mythology can also be identified with the same constellation Ophiuchus, as discussed in Volume Two of this series.

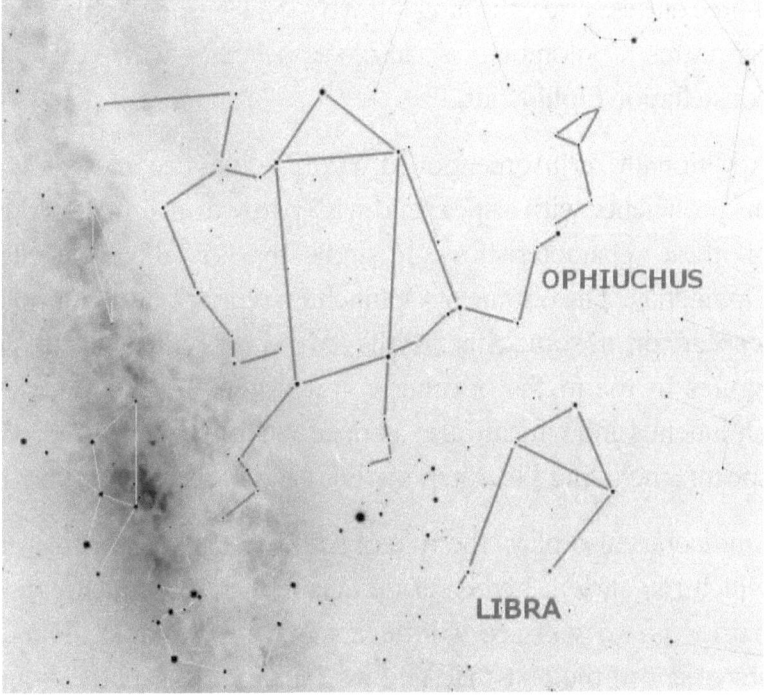

Additionally, as we can see in the above star-chart, the constellation Libra is located in very close proximity to Ophiuchus. The constellation Libra is envisioned as the Scales or Balances -- very appropriate to the god of justice and righteousness.

As befits his heritage as the descendant of the god of justice and righteousness, Yudhishthira is characterized by the qualities of wisdom, righteousness, patience, and placidity in situations that might cause others to panic. As the oldest of the five brothers, it is Yudhishthira who is anticipated to inherit the throne that was once occupied by their father Pandu, and everyone agrees that as the wisest and most devoted to righteousness and learning, Yudhishthira would be the best and most beneficient ruler. It should be noted that, as we will see beyond any doubt in Volume Three of this series, the king known for his wisdom in the Biblical scriptures, Solomon, is also associated with this same constellation Ophiuchus.

Additionally, as just mentioned, Yudhishthira becomes known for his proficiency with a spear and with battle from a war-cart. Both of these characteristics are indicative of the constellation Ophiuchus. The outline of Ophiuchus suggests a warrior holding a spear (or, in some Star Myths, *two* spears). We will see other figures in the myths of other cultures who are associated with Ophiuchus and who are also associated with a great spear (or two spears), including Hector in the Iliad and Odin in Norse myth.

Ophiuchus also plays the role of the "war-cars" or "war-carts" in which the ancient heroes of the Mahabharata frequently ride to battle, as we will see a little later in this volume. Thus, the statement in the text that Yudhishthira excels at battle from the war-car is consistent with his identification with the constellation Ophiuchus.

In the first edition of this first volume of Star Myths, I argued that Yudhishthira must be associated with the constellation Boötes, which is in fact a constellation often appearing as a charioteer in myth. Indeed, the constellation Boötes sits in front of the constellation Ophiuchus in the heavens, and thus could appear to be the driver or charioteer of the war-car represented by Ophiuchus. However, for the reasons laid out above, I am now convinced that Yudhishthira is associated with the constellation Ophiuchus rather than with Boötes.

There is one other important aspect of the figure of Yudhishthira which adds further evidence for his association with Ophiuchus. Yudhishthira has one great weakness -- a weakness which is almost the downfall of all the Pandavas, and which leads to a catastrophe that sets the course of the conflict between the Kauravas and the Pandavas towards all-out battle. This weakness is Yudhishthira's love of gambling, and particular gambling at dice. For reasons which will be examined when we reach the scene of the catastrophic dice game in the Mahabharata, there appears to have been an ancient association in the myths between table games and the constellation Ophiuchus.

The second of the Pandava brothers is the mighty Bhima, whose strength is so great that he sometimes uproots trees and swings them around at his foes. Bhima is an unquestionably Herculean figure (in strength, in temperament, and in prowess in battle), and the reader should have no difficulty in seeing that he is associated with the constellation Hercules.

As related earlier, Bhima is the son of Kunti by the wind god, Vayu. We have by now seen so much evidence in world myth that the "whirling form" of the constellation Hercules is associated with winds and hurricanes and whirlwinds and storms that the fact of Bhima's relation to the god of wind can be seen as powerful confirmatory evidence of Bhima's identification with the constellation Hercules.

Additionally, when Bhima was born the text of Mahabharata relates a rather unusual statement, declaring that: "While he fell from the lap of his mother upon the mountain breast, the violence of the fall broke into fragments the stone upon which he fell without his infant body being injured in the least."[437] A few lines later, the text adds this: "the infant, of body hard as the thunderbolt, falling down upon the mountain breast, broke into a hudred fragments, the rocky mass upon which he fell."[438]

This seems like a rather strange episode to appear in the epic. What is his mother doing dropping Bhima upon a mountain? Obviously, I would argue that this incident is celestial in its origin, and arises from the fact that the constellation Hercules is positioned directly above the constellation Ophiuchus -- and that, as we have already observed several times in this volume, Ophiuchus was often envisioned as a mountain in ancient myth (see for example the discussion of Ophiuchus as an ant-hill, mound, or mountain in Australian Aboriginal myth on page 42 of this volume, and in the Maya mythology preserved in the Popol Vuh on page 171, and in the story of Zeus crushing Typhon with Mount Aetna on page 369 of this volume, and in the Gilgamesh epic of ancient Mesopotamia as seen on pages 498 and 528 of this volume, among many others).

The fact that the text explicitly describes baby Bhima as having a body "hard as the thunderbolt" is yet additional confirmation of the association between Bhima and the constellation Hercules, the celestial figure who wields the thunderbolt weapon in the mythology of culture after culture around the world.

Additional confirmation of this identification of Bhima with Hercules, if any is needed, comes from the fact that Bhima invariably uses a great mace in battle (that is, when he is not uprooting a tree and using it as a tremendous club). The mace and the club are weapons associated with Hercules-figures (the mace used by characters in the epics of ancient India are envisioned as batons topped with an enormous metal ball, in outline not at all unlike the great hammer of Thor, or the great axe of Shango).

Depictions of Bhima confirm the identification with the constellation Hercules, preserving the now-familiar outline of that constellation. Here is a relatively modern version:

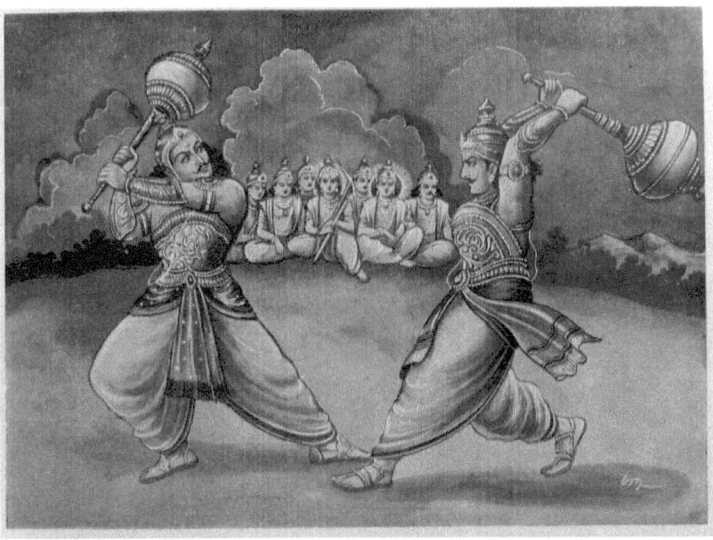

In the above fight, Bhima is battling with Duryodhana, the oldest of the one hundred sons of Dhritarastra and the principal plotter in their schemes to destroy the Pandavas. Both Duryodhana and Bhima use the mace as their primary weapon, which leads me to believe that Duryodhana is likely associated with the constellation Hercules as well (even though his strength is more ordinary compared to Bhima's superhuman physical power). Note the shape of the maces, as well as the conventions we've seen so many times in depictions of Hercules figures (rear leg of Bhima, on the right in this image, extended far behind, with heel raised).

Here is another depiction of Bhima in the same "outline of constellation Hercules" posture, this time from a gateway (known as the "Bhima Gateway") in a Vijayanagara-era ruin in Karnataka in India, next to a temple known as the Ganagitti Temple which has a date on it indicating it was built in the year we call AD 1385:

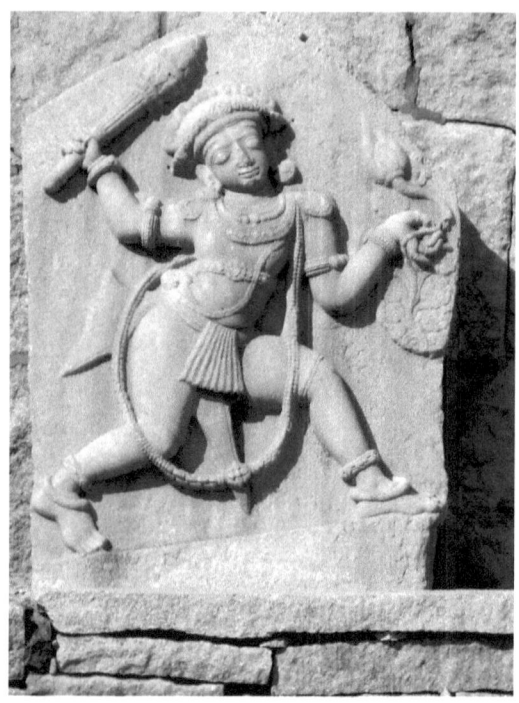

On this sculpture, the parallels to the outline of the constellation Hercules are undeniable and nearly perfect. It is interesting to note that Bhima here is depicted with a lotus in his forward hand (the one corresponding to the "downward-reaching" hand of the constellation Hercules). The downward-reaching hand of the constellation Hercules reaches towards the "serpent-head" on the western half of the serpent held by Ophiuchus, which we have already argued could play the role of a lotus-flower: this sculpture from the 1300s provides additional confirmation.

It is also notable that in other episodes in the Mahabharata, Bhima is described as slaying elephants, and in one particular episode he actually lifts up an entire elephant and hurls it at the chariot driven by one of his enemies, the warrior Karna (whose interesting birth-story we will examine a bit later). Bhima's act of hurling an elephant, in addition to demonstrating his enormous strength, also confirms his association with the constellation Hercules, as well as the association of Boötes with the figure of an elephant (as we argued in the discussion of the god Ganesha or Ganapati). Below is an illustration of Bhima hurling an elephant at Karna (Karna is driving a war-car or war-cart, pulled by horses):

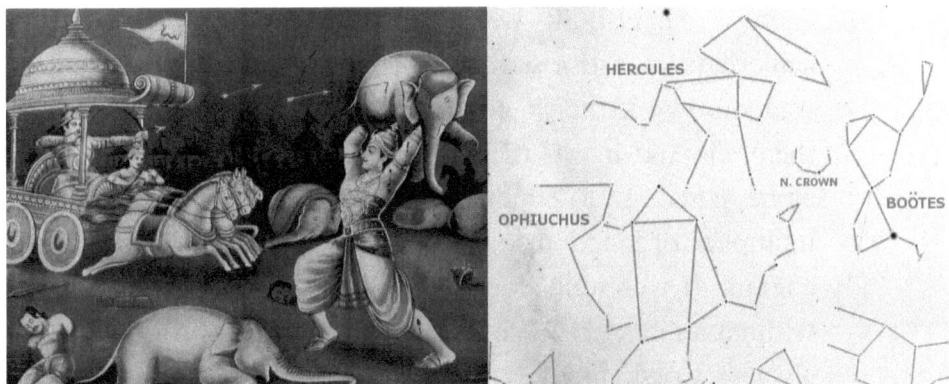

In the star-chart to the right of the drawing of the scene, you can see that Boötes is in front of Hercules and could be envisioned as the elephant thrown by Bhima, already hurtling through the air. From the above illustration you can also see why Boötes is often envisioned as a charioteer driving the "war-cart" of Ophiuchus, which follows behind Boötes. Note the charioteer at the front of the war-car in the illustration above: you can see him just in front of Karna in the cart (Karna is standing up and shooting arrows towards Bhima).

The third of the sons of Kunti is the mighty warrior Arjuna. Although Bhima is by far the strongest of the Pandavas, Arjuna is the most formidable warrior, mastering all the weapons to a degree surpassing all his brothers, and later in the epic even being transported to the celestial realm to be taught the use of celestial weapons beyond those available to ordinary mortals. Arjuna, however, is most closely associated with the bow, and most depictions of Arjuna show him holding one. Indeed, during the course of the epic he is given a heavenly bow by the fire-god Agni (who obtained it from the ocean-god, Varuna).

This bow, named Gandiva, is described in the text as:

> that wonderful jewel of a bow that was endued with great energy. That bow was the enhancer of fame and achievements, and it was incapable of being injured by any weapon. It was the chief of all weapons, and the grinder of them all. And it was the smiter of hostile armies and was alone equal to a hundred thousand bows. It was the multiplier of kingdoms, and was variegated with excellent colours. It was well-adorned, and beautiful to behold, and without a mark of weakness or injury anywhere. And it was always worshipped both by the celestials and the *Gandharvas.*[439]

(The Gandharvas are a category of celestials who are the heavenly musicians).[440]

Based on his strong association with archery and the bow, as well as on other clues in the text itself and the events described therein, I am convinced that Arjuna can be seen to be associated with the vitally important constellation of Sagittarius.

It is quite interesting to note in the passage of Mahabharata just cited, describing the bow Gandiva, that this celestial bow is said to be "variegated" in multiple colors. This description calls to mind the "coat of many colors" described in the book of Genesis in the Bible, and belonging to Joseph (see Genesis 37: 3). What makes this connection so intriguing is the fact that my independent analysis of the story and figure of Joseph in Genesis, published years before I noticed this description of Gandiva in the Mahabharata, confirms beyond a doubt that Joseph is associated with the *same constellation Sagittarius!* Joseph and his coat (as well as his other adventures) are discussed in *Star Myths of the World, Volume Three* (*Star Myths of the Bible*).

Arjuna receives the Gandiva bow, along with two inexhaustible quivers of arrows, at the hand of the fire-god, Agni, in order to help Agni consume a huge and wild forest, the Kandhava forest. This association of the bow with the fire-god and the burning of the forest may possibly be due to the fact that Sagittarius stands beside the widest and brightest portion of the Milky Way column, which was undoubtedly envisioned as a great blazing fire in many ancient Star Myths from around the globe.

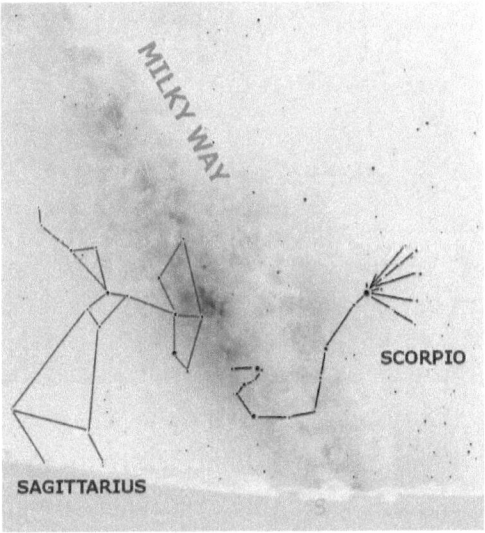

It is also notable that, near the end of the great epic, when the battles are all over and the Pandavas are departing for the Himalayas, Agni asks Arjuna to return the great celestial Gandiva bow to the gods.[441] The text in fact tells us that when they reached the shores of the sea (on their way to the mountains), "the Pandavas there beheld the deity of fire standing before them like a hill."[442] Agni tells Arjuna and the others that he obtained Gandiva from the ocean god Varuna, and now it must be given back to Varuna. Complying with the god's command, Arjuna throws the bow and its inexhaustible quivers into the sea.

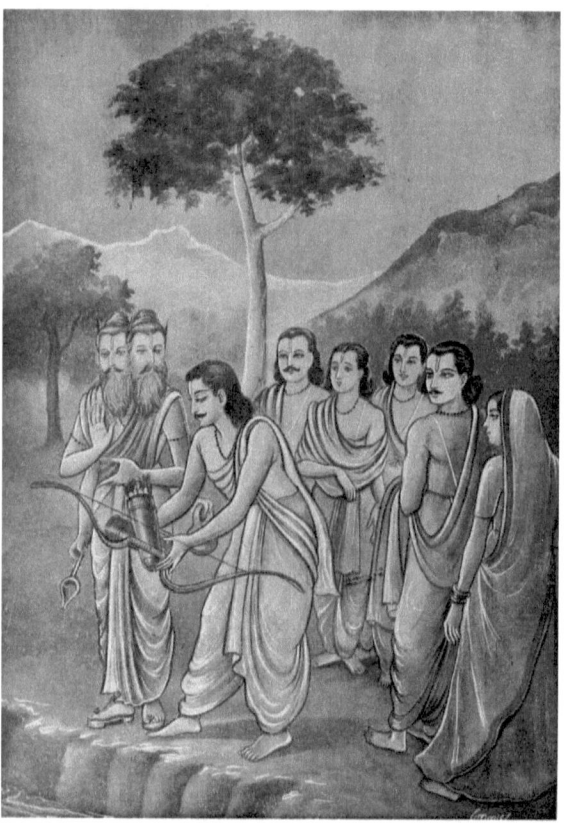

If you have any doubt that this episode in which Arjuna casts his invincible bow into the sea in order to return it to Varuna is based on the heavenly pattern seen in the constellation Sagittarius, who appears to be extending his (or her) bow into the "waters" of the Milky Way, turn back to the preceding page and observe again the position of Sagittarius relative to the widest part of the Milky

Way. In the star-chart below, the general outline of the Milky Way itself has been given outlines for ease of identification:

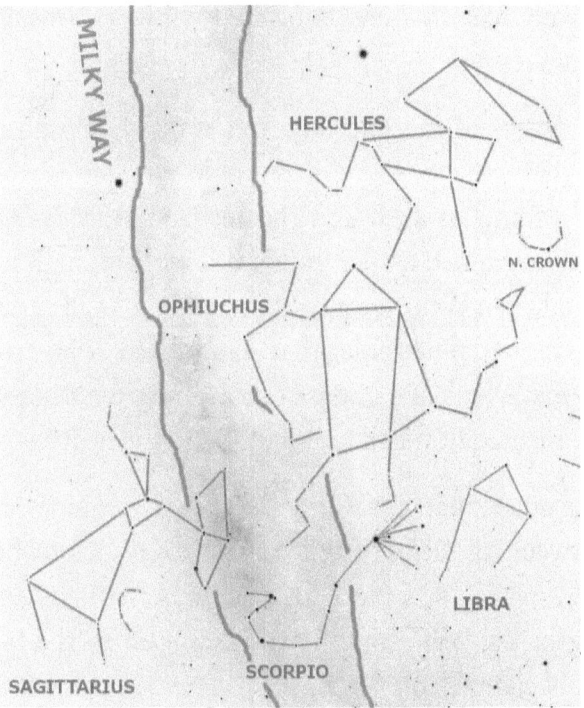

Indeed, the text cited just above from Mahabharata Book 17 and Section 1 tells us that the fire-god stood before Arjuna "like a hill," a description which indicates that Agni is identified with Ophiuchus, who does indeed stand before Sagittarius and who, as we've seen, is described as a hill or mountain in myths around the globe. Agni is also called "the deity of seven flames," no doubt referring to the multi-headed form of Scorpio just below Ophiuchus, envisioned as the seven flames Agni uses when he decides to consume something with fire.[443]

The fact that Arjuna receives his bow from Agni the god of fire, and returns the bow to the waters of the sea (for the god Varuna) is strong evidence that his bow is identified with the celestial bow which Sagittarius extends towards (and into) the Milky Way.

The other two Pandavas born after Arjuna are the two twins born to Madri, whose names are Nakula and Sahadeva. I believe it is fairly likely that they are associated with the constellation of the Twins of Gemini.

As for the origin of the one hundred sons of Dhritarastra and Gandhari, there seems to be a possible parallel between their birth from a lump of flesh and the birth of Rabbit Boy in the Lakota myth examined earlier in this volume, although it is only a possible parallel and one about which I am not at all certain. If so, then it is perhaps possible that Gandhari, who voluntarily chooses to make herself sightless out of unity with her husband, could be connected to the figure of Orion in the heavens.

We have argued that the Orion Nebula, Messier object 42, located between the legs of the constellation Orion (below the famous belt, in the "scabbard" or dagger sometimes envisioned dangling from the belt) could have been seen as the blood clot which later became Rabbit Boy (see page 130 of this volume). It is one of the brightest nebulae in the sky, and easily visible to the naked eye (on a clear night, away from light pollution).

Note that this explanation has in its favor the fact that the stars in the region of the "head" of Orion are extremely small and dim, giving rise to connotations of blindness or sightlessness in some mythical figures associated with this constellation. Orion himself, in some versions of his myth, is said to have been blinded by the father of a princess (a princess who was raped by Orion).

However, it is also possible to argue that the object to which Gandhari gives birth which later separates into the one hundred pieces that grow into the hundred sons might instead be associated with the multi-headed constellation Scorpio, to which the constellation Virgo can be envisioned as giving birth. If so, then it is possible that the constellations Libra and Ophiuchus which are adjacent to Scorpio might play a role of "jars of ghee, with lids on them," into which Gandhari is instructed to place the one hundred pieces which eventually grow into her sons, the Kauravas.

In this particular story, I don't believe there is enough textual evidence to be completely certain of the celestial referent.

Another important character in the Mahabharata who deserves at least brief mention is the figure of Karna. Karna in fact is the first son of Kunti, from prior to the time she met Pandu. When she was first given the marvelous mantra which she would later use to become the mother of Yudhishthira, Bhima and Arjuna, Kunti wanted to test out the mantra, to see if it really worked. So, one morning while she was all alone, she chanted the mantra while watching a beautiful sunrise -- and the sun god Surya himself appeared, ready to make love to her in order to give her a son.

Kunti explained that she was still just a maiden and had only been testing the mantra out of curiosity -- she was not yet ready to have a child. But the deity explained to her that since she had chanted the mantra, forces had now been set in motion that could not be undone: she would have to bear a child, but the god promised that even so she would, miraculously, not lose her virgin status.

The child born of this union was Karna, but Kunti kept the fact of his birth a secret. The baby was born, we are told, with "a natural coat of mail" and with "face brightened by ear-rings."[+++] After the baby was born, Kunti took him down to the river and set him adrift in a basket sealed with bee's wax -- a worldwide pattern which is by now very familiar (and we will examine yet another example of this oicotype before this volume is completed).

Karna can almost certainly be identified with the constellation Ophiuchus. For one thing, I am convinced that Ophiuchus (above the multi-headed constellation of Scorpio), or at times Scorpio itself (as with the case of eight-headed baby Maui), is the celestial original of all of these babies set adrift among the reeds or bulrushes, in baskets daubed with wax or bitumen or slime. For another, the fact that Karna's father is the sun-god again indicates the constellation Hercules, in whirling form, located immediately above Ophiuchus (we have seen abundant evidence for this identification, and numerous examples of Ophiuchus-figures being *descended from* Hercules-figures).

Another clue that Karna is associated with Ophiuchus is in the description of his "natural coat of mail." The constellation Ophiuchus is often envisioned as wearing a long mail coat, reaching down past its waist (due to the short legs of the constellation, which emerge beneath the long rectangular portion of the central body, as if Ophiuchus is a figure wearing a long coat of mail or a mighty breastplate). The goddess Athena, who is undoubtedly associated with the constellation Ophiuchus (and is descended from a Hercules-figure), is famous for her possession of the great breast-plate known as the Aegis, in the myths of ancient Greece. From this association of Ophiuchus with a coat of mail or a mighty breastplate, I believe it is fairly obvious that Karna can be identified with this same constellation as well.

As for the description of Karna wearing ear-rings, this detail is not one that I have encountered very often in other myths. Perhaps it is best to say that the description of Karna as having ear-rings, coupled with the near certainty that Karna is associated with Ophiuchus, is evidence in and of itself that Ophiuchus was envisioned in some ancient traditions as having ear-rings. The next question is why this constellation might be envisioned with such accessories. My best guess would be the fact that the "head" of Ophiuchus, a large and fairly distinctive triangle in the heavens, consists of three stars: one central star above two lower stars which make up the "base corners" of the triangle. It is at least possible that these two "lower corner" stars of the "head" of Ophiuchus play the role of ear-rings in this story.

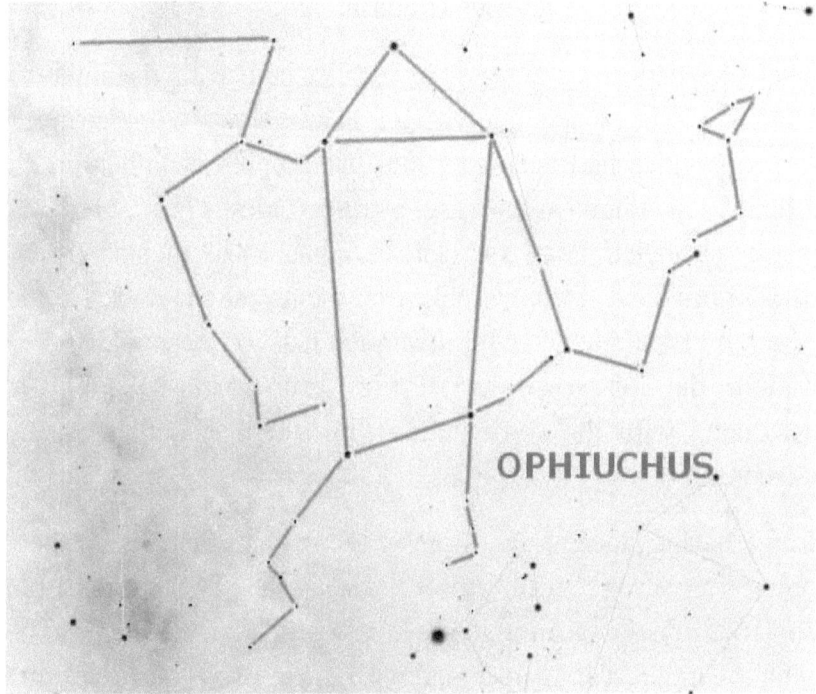

As the Pandavas and Kauravas grow up, the tension and animosity between them increases. At one point, jealous of the power of Bhima and his superiority in wrestling and other feats of strength, Duryodhana (whom the text describes as having "nectar on his tongue and a razor in his heart") tries to actually poison Bhima and then cast him into a body of water to drown.[445]

However, as the unconscious Bhima sinks down into the depths, the Nagas (divine serpents who live in deep underwater kingdoms) begin to bite him, and their venom acts to counter the effects of the poison. Bhima revives, begins fighting the nagas (giving them a good thrashing), and is eventually taken to their leader, Vasuki, who recognizes Bhima and wishes to help him. Vasuki and the other Nagas give Bhima a divine drink called *rasa*, contained in nectar-vessels known as *rasakunda*. Bhima quaffs down eight full vessels of rasa, each vessel endowing him with exponentially greater levels of strength.

There appears to be a possible parallel here with the myth of Heracles, who when he was an infant slew two enormous serpents which had been sent into his sleeping chambers in an attempt to kill him (in this case, by the goddess Hera). Heracles instead strangled the two serpents, holding one in each fist by the throat until dead. This myth likely envisions baby Heracles in the position of Ophiuchus, with a "serpent-half" on either side (even though the full-grown hero is, of course, most commonly associated with the constellation Hercules itself, in his many adventures).

Later, having failed in this attempt, Duryodhana and his brothers devise an even more treacherous plan. They order the construction of a vacation house in a distant land, causing it to be built of highly flammable material. Their plan is to trick the Pandavas into taking a relaxing vacation to this flammable house, and then set it alight as their cousins are sleeping.

However, the wise counselor Vidura, the youngest of the three brothers Dhritarastra's generation (Dhritarastra, Pandu and Vidura having been born of Ambika and Ambalika and a maidservant by Vyasadeva), discerned this treacherous plot, and met the Pandavas and their mother Kunti at the edge of the city as they were departing for their vacation in the special house. Speaking in a cryptic tongue which he and the learned

Yudhishthira understood, he told Yudhishthira that when a forest fire consumes a forest, those animals who are able to get to holes in the ground can survive the conflagration. Yudhishthira indicated that he understood the message of Vidura.

When the Pandavas reached the flammable vacation house, Yudhishthira, acting upon the cryptic message of Vidura, instructed his brothers to secretly construct an underground escape tunnel. They resolved to never all be asleep in the house at the same time, but instead one of the five brothers would always remain awake and on guard at any given time. Thus, when the house was eventually set ablaze by the agents of the Kauravas, in hopes of burning the Pandavas and their mother to death, everyone was already in the tunnel, and they escaped with their lives, following the tunnel deep into the woods where they could disappear from view for a time, letting the Kauravas and everyone else believe that the Pandavas and their mother had perished.

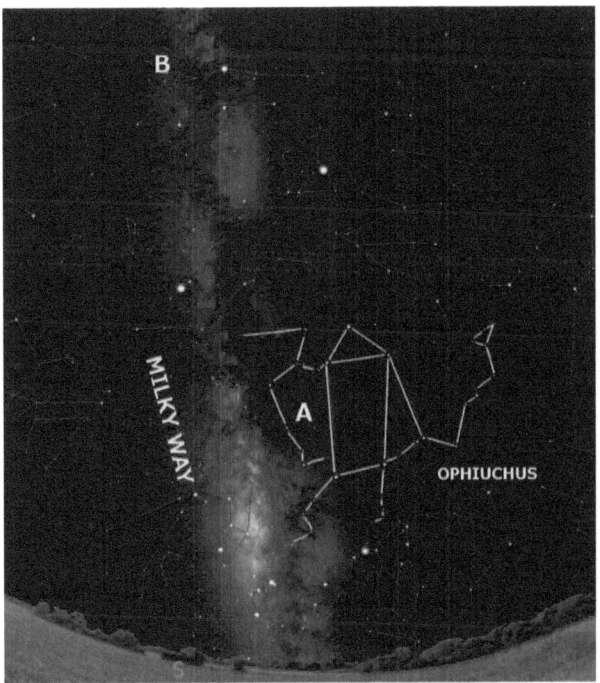

I am quite certain that this terrible incident in the epic also stems from a celestial original. Have a look at the star-chart on the preceding page, and see if you can discern for yourself the identity of the "flammable house" that the Kauravas prepared for the Pandavas and their mother, and if you can detect the "tunnel" which Yudhishthira (acting on the advice of Vidura) constructed for their getaway!

The house, of course, is seen in the heavens in the form of the constellation Ophiuchus, which plays the role of a house, a palace, a hut, a tent or "booth," a pavilion, and other similar structures and shelters in many, many Star Myths around the world.

Ophiuchus is situated just at the edge of the great band of the Milky Way in the night sky, and indeed is adjacent to the brightest portion of the Milky Way (the region believed to be the Galactic Center or Galactic Core, as it is most often called today). There is a great Dark Rift visible running across the Milky Way in a somewhat meandering, diagonal manner, originating just above the Galactic Core (we previously saw some Maya artwork which appears to have indicated this Dark Rift, on pages 185 through 187).

This Dark Rift is often viewed in the Star Myths as a sort of "passageway" or "bridge" or "crossing route" through the Milky Way (the Milky Way often being envisioned as a body of water, such as a great river or a sea, and also often being envisioned as a fire or a column of smoke). You can see the "pathway" formed by the Dark Rift in the black-and-white image on the preceding page, where I have marked the beginning of this passageway with the letter "A" on the Ophiuchus side of the Milky Way band (the western side), and with the letter "B" high above on the eastern side of the Milky Way. This passageway plays the role of the tunnel in the Mahabharata account, by which the five brothers and their mother make their escape from the blazing house.

Below is the same star-chart, this time in the more familiar color-inverted format, and with the general outlines of the Milky Way and the Dark Rift added in, to help indicate the pathway through the galaxy:

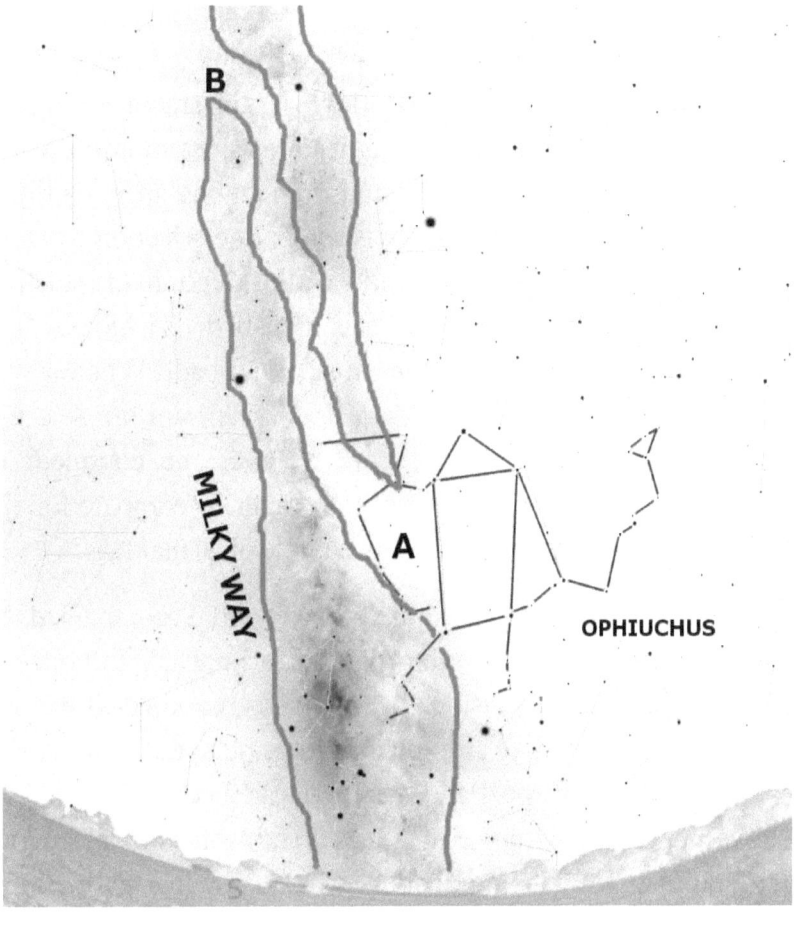

This Rift plays a major role in one of the most familiar episodes in the Bible, and is discussed in that capacity in detail in Volume Three of this series. Here in the Mahabharata, it is almost certainly the escape route in the incident of the burning house.

After experiencing full force the treachery of Duryodhana and his allies, the Pandavas and their mother determine to remain in hiding for a time, living deep in the forest among the ascetics and brahmins who also make their homes in secluded spots. The five brothers grow long hair and beards and dress in ascetic garments and sandals as if belonging to the brahmin caste instead of that of the ksatriyas.

We now arrive at one of the most memorable episodes in the entire epic of the Mahabharata: the swayamvara of Draupadi. Recall that a swayamvara (or svayamvara) is a ceremony in which an eligible bride selects her husband from among an assembly of suitors, setting any criteria she wishes for the selection process. King Drupada of the powerful and wealthy kingdom of Panchala in northern India had an accomplished, virtuous, and unbelievably gorgeous daughter named Draupadi. When it was announced that she was holding a swayamvara to select a husband, kings and warriors from all over the continent of Bharata flocked to Panchala's capitol, eager to compete for the attention of this most attractive and eligible of all maidens.

The Kuru princes, led by Duryodhana and accompanied by Karna, were among those who traveled to Panchala in hopes of winning Draupadi's decision. Karna, whose mother Kunti had set him afloat in the river after birth, had come to the capitol prior to the departure of the Pandavas, and had been befriended by Duryodhana, who witnessed Karna's great proficiency in warrior arts, and also Karna's humiliation at not knowing his heritage. Duryodhana instinctively realized that Karna could be turned into a powerful ally and a formidable opponent of the Pandavas, with the proper treatment and manipulation -- and Duryodhana was nothing if not masterful at manipulation.

At the swayamvara in the royal palace of Panchala, the king Drupada announced the criteria for Draupadi's selection of a husband. A cunning challenge had been devised in which a target in the shape of a fish had been suspended high above a reflecting pool. A slowly-spinning disc with a single hole in it had been placed just below the fish-target. The contestants at the swayamvara would be required to shoot an arrow at the fish, timing their shot so that the arrow would pass through the hole in the spinning disc. What's more, the winning shot must strike the fish-target directly in the eye.

But that was not even the most difficult part of the challenge: the contestants would not be allowed to look directly at the target while preparing to take their shot. They would instead have to look downwards into the reflecting pool while shooting upwards at the fish suspended above the spinning disc. Additionally, each participant would receive only a single try: failure on the first attempt would result in disqualification for consideration as an eligible husband.

There was yet one more stipulation: this shot would have to be made with a bow and arrows supplied by Drupada -- and he had instructed the crafting of a special bow for this occasion, extremely stiff and therefore nearly impossible for any ordinary man to string, let alone to draw and release a well-aimed shot. Indeed, the text informs us that Drupada had in his heart conceived the idea of making the bow so stiff that only Arjuna could string it and shoot it -- thus secretly hoping to have his incomparable daughter marry that incomparable prince.[446]

The text informs us that the machinery of this near-impossible target was set up in a grand arena, into which the crowds thronged, to watch the event, roaring like the sea. The arena was shielded with a great canopy, with beautiful mountains in the background. After introducing his daughter, whose beauty surpassed even the expectations of those assembled, the king announced the names and lineages of the gathered contestants.

One by one, the assembled kings and princes and mighty warriors came forward to attempt this unheard-of challenge of skill. Most could not even string the bow. Those few who could were unable to successfully pull back the bowstring, but were tossed to the ground by the stiffness of the bow itself.

Then up stepped Karna, and proceeded to lift up the great bow, stringing it with ease. As he began to draw it back to aim his shot, the princess cried out that she would by no means consent to marry a *Suta* (a son of two parents belonging to different castes). Embarassed again because of his origins, Karna throws down the bow with a laugh and walks away.[447]

When all the other assembled kings and princes had tried unsuccessfully to accomplish the seemingly impossible task, a young man stood up from among the crowd of brahmins assembled at the arena. It was in fact Arjuna in disguise: he and his Pandava brothers, dressed as brahmins, had come to the swayamvara as well. Arjuna addressed the king in a loud voice, and asked if he might be permitted to attempt the challenge.

At this, the crowd erupted in cheers and loud debate, particularly among the gathered brahmins, many of whom were overjoyed at the idea of one of their number competing for the hand of Draupadi, while others argued that it was not proper. Everyone commented on the obvious strength and build of the young brahmin standing beside the bow. When the debate died down, however, Arjuna spent a moment walking around the bow, praying to the god Ishana (a name of Shiva) the giver of boons, and remembering Lord Krishna as well.[448]

Then, in a flash, Arjuna picked up the bow and strung it with ease. Staring into the reflecting pool, he unleashed not one but five arrows so rapidly that all passed through the hole in the disc as it spun, piercing the eye of the fish and causing it to fall to the ground.

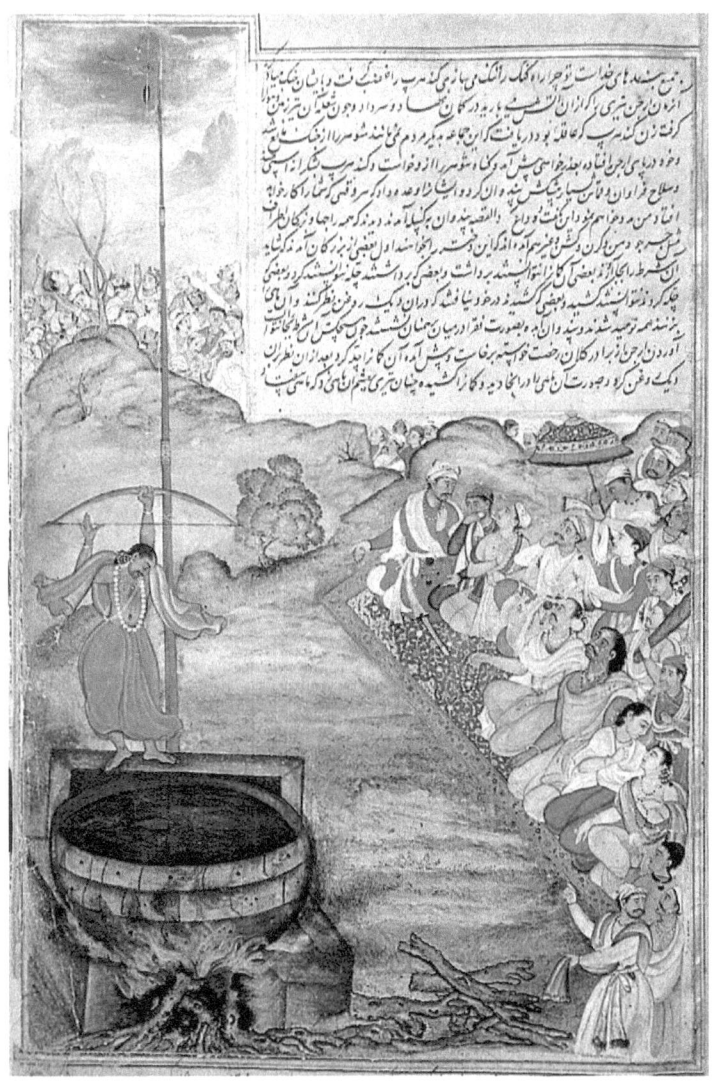

The illustration on the preceding page, from sixteenth century Persia, shows one imagining of the challenge of the swayamvara. Arjuna has his bow pointed in one direction as he looks in the other direction, down into the reflecting pool. An arrow pierces the eye of the fish, high above. The assembled crowds look on in amazement.

It may be difficult to make out the eye of the fish in the preceding image: here is a close-up of the upper-left corner of the painting to show the fish with an arrow piercing it from below.

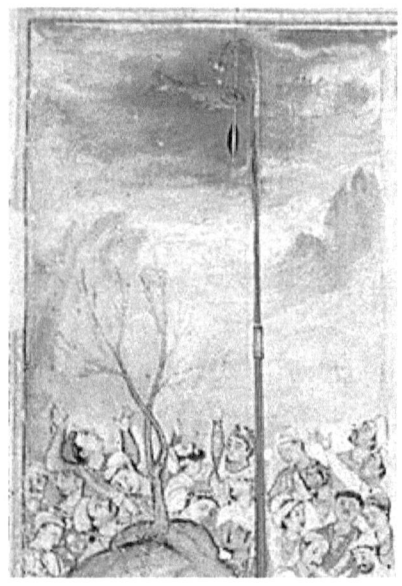

Note the many artistic elements in the painting which are evocative of a specific, and familiar, celestial region of the sky. For example, we see a hill with a tree on the top (the top part of the hill being visible in the close-up frame on this page). We also see a long "pathway" feature, widest at the point where Arjuna is perched over the reflecting pool, and tapering upwards as it winds towards a cleft in the hills to disappear over the horizon. This feature suggests the Milky Way itself, and suggests the region of the sky where the artist believed (correctly, in my opinion) that this swayamvara challenge takes place.

I would argue that in this challenge (perhaps differently from the bow-challenge in the Odyssey, which is discussed in detail in Volume Two of this series), the bowman is identified with the constellation Sagittarius, standing beside the widest part of the Milky Way (the Galactic Center) -- this widening feature in the galaxy frequently appearing in myth as a pool or bath.

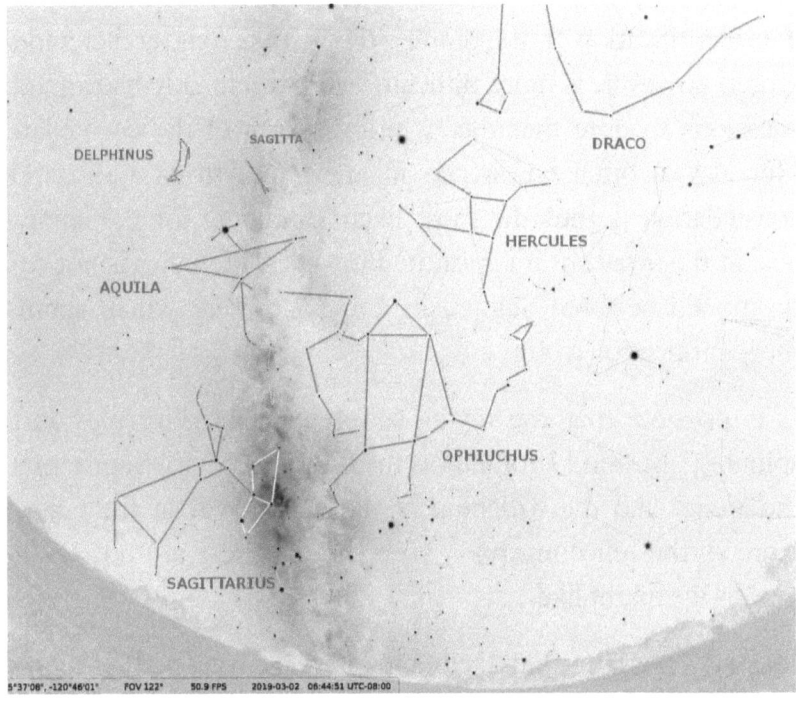

A distinctive feature of Sagittarius (besides of course the great bow) is the constellation's appearance of looking in one direction while walking in the opposite direction (a kind of "looking back" aspect which features in many Star Myths around the globe, including the story of Lot's wife in the book of Genesis, but also the worldwide pattern of the "failed retrieval from the dead" in which the rescuer *must not* look back).[449]

In this episode, I believe the story incorporates the "looking back" aspect of Sagittarius by having the contestants look down into a reflecting pool while shooting in the opposite direction.

The fish-shaped target in the swayamvara contest is likely identified with the beautiful little constellation Delphinus the Dolphin, located almost directly above the head of Sagittarius (associated with Arjuna) in the night sky, as seen in the star-chart on the preceding page.

The identification of the spinning disc between the archer and the target, however, is more difficult. We have already had multiple occasions to note that the "whirling" form of the constellation Hercules is often envisioned in ancient myth as a disc. This constellation is thus the most likely candidate for the spinning disc in the swayamvara episode. However, Hercules is not really positioned between Sagittarius and Delphinus, which confuses the identification a bit.

It is possible that the myths simply envision Hercules as the spinning disc and Delphinus as the fish-target, with Sagittarius as the archer and the widening of the Milky Way at the Galactic Core as the reflecting pool, even though these are not all "in a line" as we might like.

It is also possible that Delphinus is not envisioned as the fish-target but rather some star or constellation above Hercules (who plays the spinning disc), such as the head of the constellation Draco the Dragon.

Another possibility is that Hercules in this case does not actually play the role of the spinning disc. Perhaps the constellation Aquila the Eagle acts as the interfering disc instead. While not exactly disc-shaped, Aquila does contain a very bright star (Altair) which could function as the *hole in the disc* through which the arrow must pass in the attempt to hit the fish-shaped target (and note the wayward arrow above Aquila, in the form of the constellation Sagitta, whose very name means "the arrow").

I believe all of the above scenarios are good candidates for the celestial foundation of the swayamvara episode in the Mahabharata. I'm not certain which one is correct, but I think it should be quite apparent to the honest student of the ancient text that the scene is celestial in nature, and that it almost certainly describes this mythologically-important region of the heavens. Indeed, the text itself goes out of its way to describe pavilions, canopies, and mountains (all of them associated with Ophiuchus), as if directing us to this part of the night sky.

Thus Draupadi becomes the bride of not just Arjuna but all of the Pandavas. The epic itself explains the logic behind this arrangement, while including plenty of debate over the unusual nature of one woman being married to five men (the arrangment of one man married to multiple *wives* is treated as normal in these myths). Note the important fact that this pattern of *one woman with five husbands* is explicitly brought up in the gospels of the New Testament, in which Jesus encounters a Samaritan woman at the well (the episode is related in John chapter 4). What celestial feature might play the role of the well, and which constellation do you suppose plays the role of the woman in this particular passage of scripture?

Let's move ahead in the plot of the great epic to the terrible dice game entered into by Yudhishthira, the outcome of which is disastrous for the Pandavas and which eventually leads to the great Kurukshetra war which occupies much of the central books of the Mahabharata.

After winning Draupadi in marriage, the Pandavas and their mother Kunti eventually return to Hastinapura, where Bhishma and Vidura and the other honest counselors to Dhritarastra eventually convince the king to award the Pandavas half of the kingdom (Dhritarastra concedes to this advice, but gives the Pandavas an unpopulated wasteland for their half – which they cause to become prosperous, abundant, and beautifully developed with the help of the gods, including Indra).

Duryhodhana, the eldest of the Kuru brothers, cannot abide the sight of the Pandava realm becoming more and more prosperous and wealthy, and with his wicked uncle Shakuni (the brother of Dhritarastra's wife Gandhari) he hatches a plan to humiliate the Pandavas and seize everything they own, playing upon Yudhishthira's weakness for gambling and Shakuni's skill at dice (and ability to manipulate the dice through deceitful and underhanded methods).

Shakuni and Duryodhana approach Dhritarastra to convince the blind king to permit them to challenge Yudhishthira to a "friendly" game of dice, even while disclosing their intention (in the words of Shakuni) to "snatch this prosperity of Yudhishthira" for Dhritarastra and his sons.[450] Dhritarastra, as usual, puts up some resistance because he knows such a plan is evil, but then accedes. The king commands the immediate construction of:

> an assembly house of the most beautiful description, to be called the crystal-arched palace with a thousand columns, decked with gold and lapis lazuli, furnished with a hundred gates, and full two miles in length and in breadth the same.[451]

We noted earlier that Yudhishthira is associated with the constellation Ophiuchus, and that there is reason to suspect an ancient association between this constellation and gambling games played upon a table, such as dice. The description above of the assembly hall where the game will be played, with its arches and columns, suggests a possible connection to Ophiuchus -- but there is even stronger evidence to connect dicing with this constellation.

Below is an image of red-figure artwork on a hydria vase, dated to about 490 BC, showing Achilles and Ajax gambling at dice during some "down time" between the battles of the Trojan War:

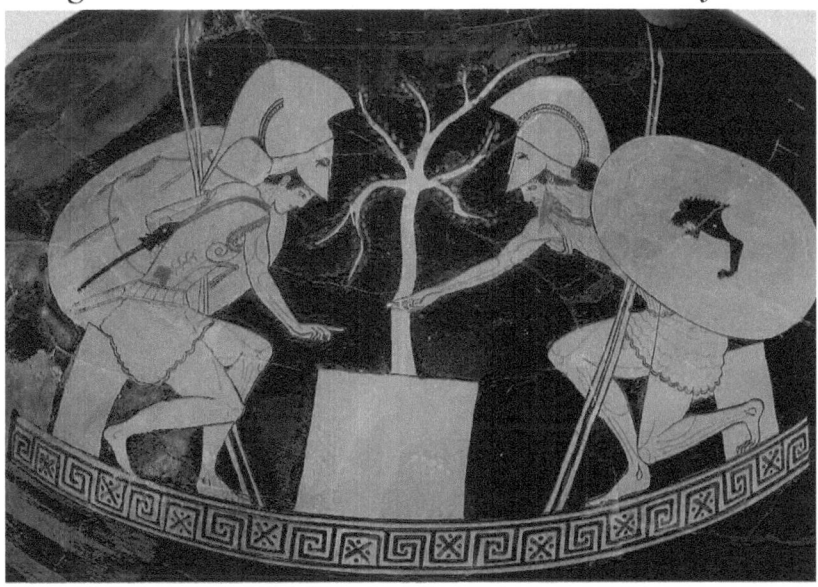

We see a scene of symmetry about a square table. In the background is a distinctive looking tree, rising up directly over the table upon which the game is taking place. I will argue that this scene, very popular in pottery from ancient Greece, provides strong evidence that these table-games were associated with Ophiuchus. In particular, the tree in this image is strongly reminiscent of the "whirling form" of the constellation Hercules, directly above the constellation Ophiuchus.

Here is another depiction of a similar scene. This time there is no tree present, but the fact that each warrior (as in the previous scene) holds two spears is indicative of the constellation Ophiuchus:

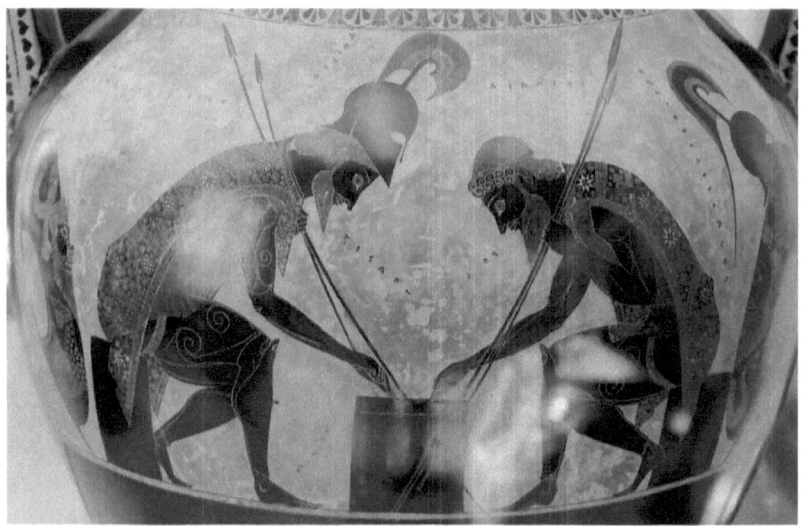

Note also that the artist of this ancient scene has opted to depict the helmet of the warrior on the right in the position we associate with the western serpent-half of Ophiuchus (the "serpent-head").

Below is yet another version of the same pattern:

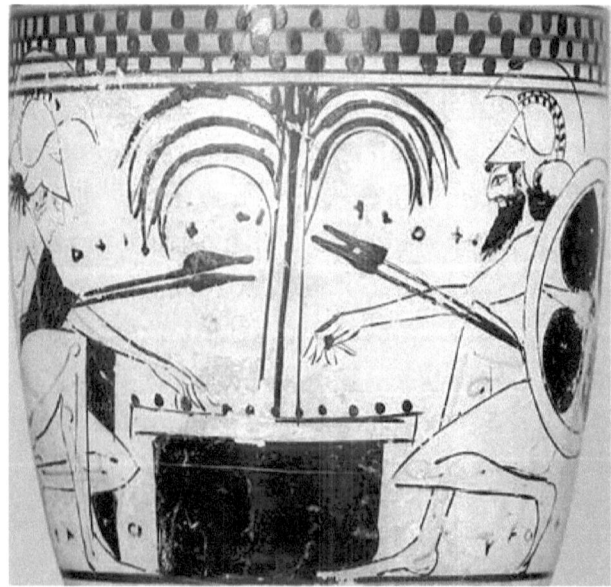

Again, we see a tree rising up over the dice-board, indicating that the table is associated with the central rectangle of Ophiuchus. In the above image the warriors again carry twin spears -- and they hold them in such a way as to suggest the triangular "top" or "head" of the central column of Ophiuchus.

Below is another example of the same pattern, this time with a new addition to the artwork, an addition which seals the argument for a connection between this gambling scene and Ophiuchus: the goddess Athena, who is undoubtedly connected to this constellation as discussed in the next volume in this series.

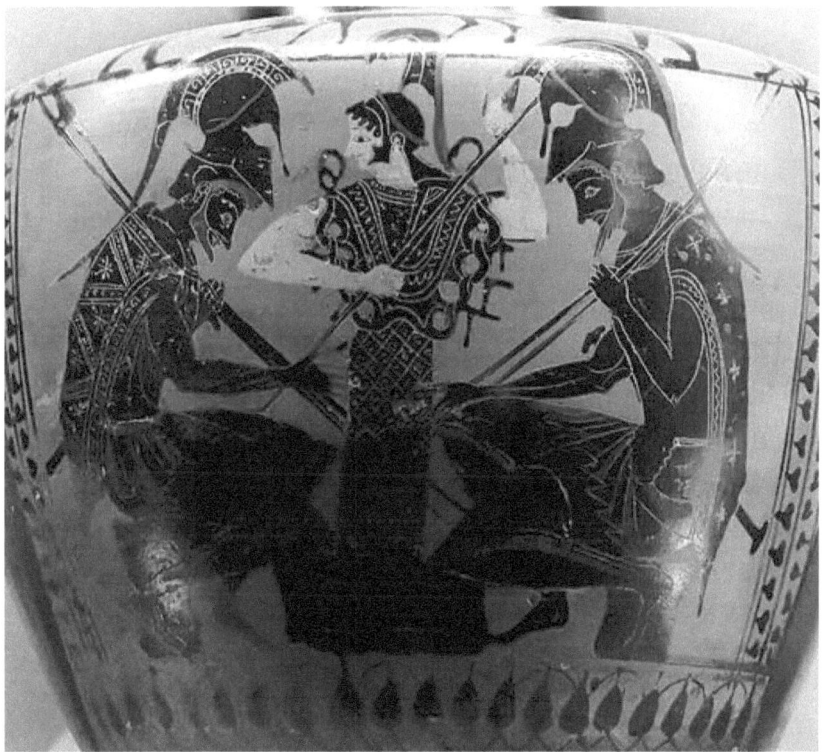

The reason it is worth taking the time to definitively establish this connection between gaming and Ophiuchus becomes clear when we realize that these ancient table-games were undoubtedly seen as representing the celestial cycles, particularly the inexorable and predetermined turning of the gears of precession, as the authors of *Hamlet's Mill* establish beyond any doubt during their chapter discussing Ragnarok and the end of the precessional Ages (the chapter itself is entitled "Twilight of the Gods").

There, beginning by citing a description of the aftermath of Ragnarok, and the mention in the Edda of the rediscovery after the cataclysm of the old golden gaming tables upon which the Æsir used to play, Hertha von Dechend and Giorgio de Santillana write:

> The rediscovery of the pieces of the game lying around in the grass, already told in the Völuspa, becomes clearer if one thinks of the Rigveda, where the gods themselves are said to go around like ayas, that is, casts of dice. It becomes more understandable still when one considers that the name of the Indian world-ages (Yuga) has been taken from the idiom of dicing. But both data could be dismissed as unrevealing were it forgotten that in several kinds of "proto-chess" -- to use an expression of J. Needham -- board games and dicing were combined: the number of eyes thrown by the dice determined the figure which was to be moved. That this very rule was also valid for *tafl*, the board game mentioned in the Völuspa, has been shown by A. G. van Hamel. Thus the dice forced the hands of the chess player -- a game called "planetary battles" by the Indians, and in 16th-century Europe still termed "Celestial War, or Astrologer's Game," whereas the Chinese chessboard shows the Milky Way dividing the two camps.[452]

We have already seen evidence that Ophiuchus plays a central role in ancient myths having to do with the turning of precessional Ages. This connection of Ophiuchus to the gaming-tables upon which the great cycles of the heavens are played out and dramatized, then, is a very significant and noteworthy development.

If these games dramatized the inescapable displacement of one set of "ruling constellations" by another set, due to the motion of precession, then the terrible dice game in the Mahabharata becomes much more understandable. When he gives in to the request of Duryodhana and Shakuni to set up the dice game with the Pandavas, Dhritarastra implies that he cannot stop what is about to happen, saying: "Even the great calamity, destructive of the lives of the Kshatriyas, cometh as destined by fate."[453] The text then goes on to comment:

> Having said this, the weak-minded Dhritarashtra regarded fate as supreme and unavoidable. And the king deprived of reason by Fate, and obedient to the counsels of his son, commanded his men in a loud voice [to build the assembly hall for the great dice game].[454]

The outcome of the dice game is indeed calamitous. Yudhishthira sits across from Shakuni, whom Duryodhana has appointed to play the game for him, Shakuni throwing the dice while Duryodhana supplies the stakes to be given to Yudhishthira if Shakuni's throw loses.

But Shakuni's throw never loses. Yudhishtira loses the first round, upon which he has bet a precious necklace from around his neck (perhaps indicative of the Northern Crown). From there, things go from bad to worse. Yudhishthira bets more and more wealth, and loses on every round. Each time, he increases the stakes he is gambling, in hopes of trying to win back what he has already lost in the previous throw of the dice.

As the terrible match goes on, Yudhishthira loses all of his possessions -- and eventually even gambles away his kingdom itself. Duryodhana and Shakuni are overjoyed. The assembled crowd is aghast. But no one makes a move to stop Yudhishthira, since he is after all a king, and since it is for Dhritarastra to decide if he wants to stop the proceedings. Eventually, however, Dhritarastra's brother Vidura can take no more, and implores Dhritarastra to stop the gambling before the one-sided outcome leads to the possibility of war.

Dhritarastra declines to intervene. Desperate to win back what he has lost, Yudhishtira now begins to gamble his brothers -- and continues to lose. First Nakula and Sahadeva are staked, and become the possessions of Duryodhana and Shakuni. Next come Bhima and Arjuna, and they too are lost. Finally, Yudhishthira gambles himself -- and upon losing becomes a slave.

And yet even at this point the awful game does not end, for Shakuni says to Yudhisthhira that it is sinful to bet oneself when one still has something else to bet -- and suggests Yudhishthira bet the beautiful Draupadi as a stake on the next throw of the dice, in order to try to win back his own freedom. Yudhishthira does so -- to the horror of the assembled onlookers.

As expected, Shakuni throws the dice and wins again.

The Kauravas are elated. They send an attendant to bring Draupadi to the assembly hall, telling the messenger that she no longer belongs in the royal quarters but must immediately get started scrubbing and cleaning, having become their slave, but she sends him back, asking to know whether Yudhishthira had already lost his own freedom before staking her in the game (a question which implies that if he had already become a slave, he himself would have no right at that point to stake Draupadi).

At this answer, Duryodhana becomes enraged and sends the second-oldest brother of the one hundred Kauravas, the cruel Dushashana, to drag her into the assembly hall by force.

When Dushashana confronts Draupadi in the chambers where she has been staying with her attendants, she pleads that she is in the monthly time of her cycle, and only wearing a single garment wrapped about her is in no condition to be taken to the assembly hall.[455] But Dushashana treats her with contempt, calling her a slave, and drags Draupadi by her long hair all the way down to the assembly hall.

Once there, the enraged Dushashana attempts to tear Draupadi's single garment off of her body -- but at this point Draupadi begins to pray to Lord Krishna, the avatar of Vishnu, calling upon him to "rescue me who am sinking in the Kaurava Ocean."[456]

The text of the Mahabharata relates what happens next, as Dushashana is trying to humiliate Draupadi and tear off her garment, and Draupadi with her hands over her eyes is calling out to Krishna for assistance:

> Hearing the words of Draupadi, Krishna was deeply moved. And leaving his seat, the benevolent one from compassion, arrived there on foot. And while Yajaseni [Draupadi] was crying aloud to Krishna, also called Vishnu and Hari and Nara, for protection, the illustrious Dharma, remaining unseen, covered her with excellent clothes of many hues. And, O monarch, as the attire of Draupadi was being draged, after one was taken off, another of the same kind appeared covering her. And thus did it continue till many clothes were seen. And, O exalted one, owing to the protection of Dharma, hundreds upon hundreds of robes of many hues came off Draupadi's person. And there arose then a deep

uproar of many, many voices. And the kings present in that assembly beholding that most extraordinary of all sights in the world, began to applaud Draupadi and censure the son of Dhritarashtra.[457]

The Pandavas have been sitting through this entire shameful spectacle humiliated, their upper robes remove as befitting their new status as slaves, but at the sight of Dushashana attempting to humiliate Draupadi by tearing off her garment, Bhima finally can stand no more, and bellows out a terrible oath in the midst of the assembly, declaring:

> "Hear these words of mine, ye Kshatriyas of the world. Words such as these were never before uttered by other men, nor will anybody in the future ever utter them. Ye lords of earth, if having spoken these words I do not accomplish them hereafter, let me not obtain the region of my deceased ancestors. Tearing open in battle, by sheer force, the breast of this wretch [Dushashana], this wicked-minded scoundrel of the Bharata race, if I do not drink his life-blood, let me not obtain the region of my ancestors."[458]

We could go on for thousands of pages relating the episodes in this marvelous ancient epic, but having reached one of the most famous scenes in the entire poem, let us now pause to examine some of the celestial correspondences before moving on to the great battle that this disastrous dice game presages.

Dushahashana dragging Draupadi to the assembly hall and then pulling at her clothing to try to disrobe her suggests the possibility that this second-oldest of the Kauravas is associated with the constellation Ophiuchus. We have already noted that the oldest brother, Duryodhana, is probaby associated with the constellation Hercules, based upon his skill at wrestling and proclivity for using the mace as his chosen weapon in combat. The two "serpent-halves" on either side of the central body of Ophiuchus are in some myths envisioned as a great sash, or winding-sheet, or other wrapping garment, and thus it is likely that Dushashana pulling on the covering of Draupadi is associated with this constellation. When he drags her by the hair, it is likely that Draupadi is associated with Scorpio, just beneath.

If so, then we can surmise that Draupadi herself is likely associated with either the constellation Virgo or the constellation Sagittarius, both of which often play the role of a beautiful female figure in the myths, and both of which are close enough to Ophiuchus to be envisioned as being disrobed as the Ophiuchus-figure pulls on their garment.

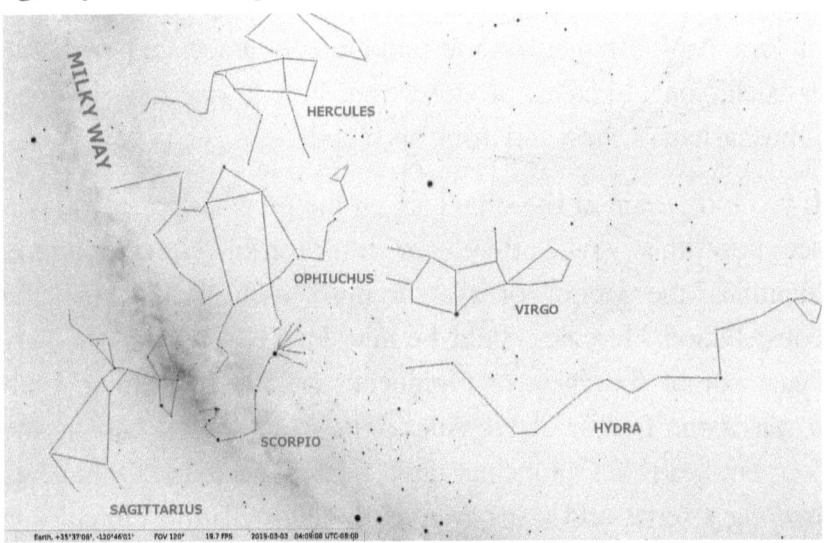

It is possible that Draupadi's never-ending sari, provided for her by Krishna to avoid her humliation at the hands of Dushashana, is seen in the heavens in the form of the constellation Hydra, winding its way towards Virgo and then perhaps envisioned as connecting with Scorpio and then the entire Milky Way, in an endless band. If so, then Draupadi is probably Virgo in this scene.

However, it is also possible that Draupadi is associated with Sagittarius, especially since the text itself specifically states that Lord Krishna provides her with "clothes of many hues," which is a characteristic of Sagittarius already remarked upon, in specific connection to the "coat of many colors" given to Joseph in the book of Genesis (Joseph also being associated with Sagittarius).

If so, then I think it likely that once again the entire Milky Way band becomes the endless source of covering garment supplied by the invisible Lord Krishna to Draupadi, even as Dushashana (associated with Ophiuchus) attempts to pull off all her clothing.

We can be very confident that Dushashana is indeed envisioned in the heavens in the constellation Ophiuchus based on Bhima's angry vow, uttered upon watching Dushashana's cruel treatment of Draupadi. Bhima, who is undoubtedly associated with the constellation Hercules, promises that he will one day rip open Dhushashana's chest and drink his blood.

If you look again at the star-chart on the previous page, you will see how this vow, uttered by a powerful Hercules-figure, identifies the victim of the promise with Ophiuchus: the constellation Hercules could be envisioned as pulling the very heart out of the chest of Ophiuchus below, and lifting it up towards the mouth of Hercules. The heart in this case is the "serpent-head" of Ophiuchus again, still connected to Ophiuchus by long arteries and veins even as the constellation Hercules is envisioned as reaching down and tearing it from the chest of the constellation below. Later in the epic, on the battlefield of Kurukshetra, Bhima will indeed fulfill this awful vow after killing Dushashana.

Thus, I believe that the famous scene of the attempted humiliation of Draupadi in front of all the assembled onlookers can be traced to constellations and celestial features in the night sky. It is noteworthy that this mythologically-important region, to which we keep returning again and again, is associated with the lowest point on the annual cycle of the earth's journey around the sun -- the point of winter solstice, where the plunge down into the lower realm reaches its very nadir, before turning back upwards towards spring equinox and eventual summer solstice.

I am convinced that the "code" or language employed by these myths involves the use of markers along the celestial cycles, such Sagittarius to evoke winter solstice, in order to convey messages associated with the *turning points* in those great cycles -- messages having to do with our own spiritual condition, and our soul's plunge into the material realm. The esoteric message associated with the great turning point of winter solstice, evoked by the constellation Sagittarius in particular, often has to do with our reconnection with the infinite realm, to which we always have access even at the very depths of our plunge in to matter.

The episode in which the Kauravas attempt to humiliate Draupadi illustrates this message most forcefully. Draupadi is pulled by her hair, made to feel the weakness of her physical condition, embarrassed by the fact of it being the time of month of her menstrual cycle, and dragged into an assembly hall in which all the symbols of social hierarchy, status, and rules of behavior are most evident and in force. There, a powerful and malevolent enemy attempts to strip her of her one garment of clothing -- an attempt to reduce her to the bare facts of her physical condition in a human body, to deny her spiritual nature and "rub her face" in her incarnate condition (so to speak).

But it is at this very point of maximum humiliation that Draupadi reaches out to the spiritual realm for succor. She calls upon Lord

Krishna, and -- because we actually have an unbreakable connection at all times to the Infinite World, the realm of the gods -- Krishna responds to her call even as Dushashana is still trying to disrobe her, and even as Draupadi is still calling upon the god for help.

It is one of the most powerful moments in the entire epic, and this memorable scene has become the subject of numerous artistic depictions over the centuries.

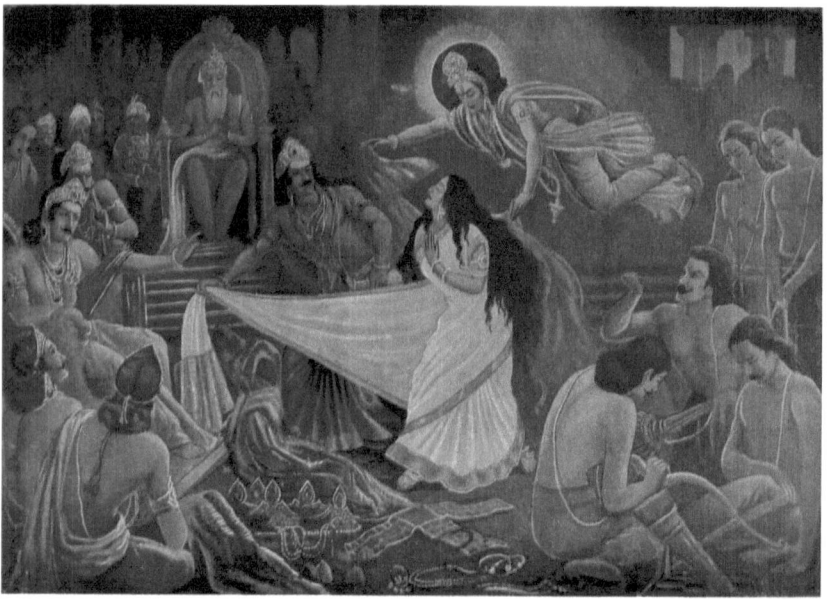

Refusing to be humiliated, Draupadi calls upon the Kuru elders to stand up for what is right. Then she addresses Dhritarastra directly and says he should be ashamed of himself for allowing such an unrighteous spectacle. With a heavy heart, Dhritarastra admits she is right, and offers Draupadi three boons. She asks for the restoration of her husbands' freedom and kingdom, and Dhritarastra grants her requests, to the chagrin of Duryodhana and Shakuni and the allies of the Kauravas.

However, as the Pandavas prepare to ride out of the city back to their own kingdom, Dhuryodhana persuades Dhritarastra to summon Yudhishthira to one more roll of the dice. Incredibly, Yudhishthira acquiesces to the request of the king his uncle, and this time the stakes for the game are decided to be: exile for the losers. Unsurprisingly, Shakuni's roll of the dice wins again.

The Pandavas end up being exiled for twelve years, followed by a thirteenth in which they are required to live incognito in some city without being discovered. The epic describes many adventures during these years, which would be profitable to examine, but at this point we have, in my assessment, provided substantial evidence which argues that the characters and episodes of the Mahabharata, in common with other ancient myths, scriptures and sacred stories the world over, are speaking the very same celestial language we have detected in our examination of other myths, and the same language we will encounter in future volumes of this series.

We will conclude our examination of the Mahabharata with a brief discussion of the great battle of Kurukshetra, including the conversation between Arjuna and Lord Krishna on the eve of battle, which becomes known as the Bhagavad Gita ("the Song of the Lord"), one of the most beloved and oft-consulted of all ancient scriptures worldwide.

The years of exile bring new maturity and experience to the Pandavas and their wife Draupadi. Much of the time is spent studying the ancient scriptures, along with side adventures including a sojourn by Arjuna among the heavenly realms, where he obtains celestial weapons and the knowledge required to wield them.

However, although the Pandavas acquire greater virtue during these long years, the Kauravas do not change their ways in the slightest, becoming all the more hostile and advancing their schemes to deny the Pandavas their right to even a *portion* of the kingdom (when, as sons of Pandu, the five brothers could arguably have a claim upon the *entire kingdom*, superior to the claim of Dhritarastra, let alone the claim of his sons). Unwilling to abide by the ancient precepts, even when advised by Bhishma and Vidura and a visit from Lord Krishna himself, the Kauravas make plans for a great war with the Pandavas, and the epic proceeds towards the battlefield of Kurukshetra.

There are very good reasons for understanding this mighty conflict as representative of the very same struggle between light and darkness that takes place every year as we orbit the sun: the progression through the equinoxes and solstices, and the interplay between days which are dominated by longer hours of darkness and those dominated by longer hours of daylight.

As we've seen, the heavenly cycles (including the annual cycle as well as other cycles both shorter and longer, all the way up through the cycle of precession) are imbued by the ancient system with esoteric and spiritual significance, such that they become representative of our own soul's progress down into this incarnate life, through its trials and challenges and obstacles, and of its rediscovery of and re-connection with our spiritual nature, our deeper nature, our Higher Self.

One indicator in the poem which argues that Kurukshetra functions in exactly this way is the fact that, on the very eve of the battle, Lord Krishna advises Arjuna to call upon the goddess Durga. Throughout the poem and the escalating tension between the Kauravas and the Pandavas, and the escalating acts of hostility initiated by Duryodhana and his brothers, Krishna has maintained a neutral posture of love and benevolent advice offered to both sets of cousins. In the epic, he himself is a cousin of the Kuru line, the ruler of a kingdom whose capitol is Dvaraka (or Dwaraka), even though he is simultaneously the Supreme Lord, identified with Vishnu and with Dharma (as we've already seen in citations from the text itself, such as in the episode of Draupadi's miraculous endless garment).

As open battle between the Pandavas and Kauravas becomes inevitable, both Arjuna and Duryodhana travel to Dvaraka to seek out Krishna and request that Krishna fight on their side of the upcoming battle. Krishna replies that he will help both of them, giving his services as a noncombatant to one side, and giving a vast army of his powerful Narayanas to the other. Krishna tells Arjuna that he can pick first, since Krishna saw Arjuna first as he was riding up, and Arjuna unhesitatingly chooses to have Krishna join his side, even as a noncombatant. Duryodhana smiles in his heart at this choice, valuing the vast army of Krishna's warriors more highly than he values having Krishna himself on his side as a noncombatant.

Thus Krishna joins the Pandava side, and will act as Arjuna's charioteer in the upcoming battle. On the eve of battle, as mentioned above, Krishna advises Arjuna to invoke the goddess Durga. The lines of battle are already drawn up, and the forces of each side are already arranged in preparation for the conflict to come. Krishna and Arjuna survey the scene from their war-car.

At the advice of Krishna, Arjuna alights on the ground and folds his hands, and utters a hymn to Durga, addressing her with terms that confirm some of the celestial associations of the goddess we have already examined, saying (in part):

"I bow to thee, O leader of *Yogins*, O thou that art identical with *Brahman*, O thou that dwellest in the forst of Mandara, O thou that art freed from decrepitude and decay, O Kali, [. . .] O wife of the universal destroyer, I bow to thee. O thou that rescuest from dangers, O thou that art endued with every auspicious attribute, O thou that art sprung from the *Kata* race, O thou that deservest the most regardful worship, O fierce one, O giver of victory, O victory's self, O thou that bearest a banner of peacock plumes [. . .], O thou that art always fond of buffalo's blood [. . .] O great goddess, let victory always attend me through thy grace on the field of battle. In inaccessible regions, where there is fear, in places of difficulty, in the abodes of thy worshippers and in the nether regions (*Patala*), thou always dwellest. Thou always defeatest the *Danavas*. Thou art the unconsciousness, the sleep, the illusion, the modesty, the beauty of (all creatures). Thou art the twilight, thou art the day, thou art Savitri, and thou art the mother. Thou art contentment, thou art growth, thou art light. It is thou that supportest the Sun and the Moon and that makes them shine. Thou art the prosperity of those that are prosperous. The *Siddhas* and the *Charanas* behold thee in contemplation."[459]

Some of these words of worship from Arjuna recorded in the Mahabharata confirm our previous identification of the goddess Durga, slayer of the buffalo-headed MashishAsura, with the constellation Virgo in the heavens, including the declaration that she "bearest a banner of peacock plumes": we have earlier argued that the constellation Coma Berenices is associated in the myths of ancient India and some other cultures with the long feathers of a peacock.

Seeing Arjuna's devotion, the goddess herself appears in the firmament, and declares to him:

> "Within a short time thou shalt conquer thy foes, O Pandava. O invincible one, thou hast Narayana (again) for aiding thee. Thou art incapable of being defeated by foes, even by the wielder of the thunderbolt himself."[460]

The appearance of Durga on the eve of the great battle, as well as her words of encouragement to Arjuna, strengthen the argument that the struggle at Kurukshetra is indeed representative of our plunge down into this incarnate life. As we have noted previously, in the great annual cycle, the constellation Virgo is stationed at the verge of the autumnal equinox: at the verge, that is, of the downward plunge into the lower half of the year.

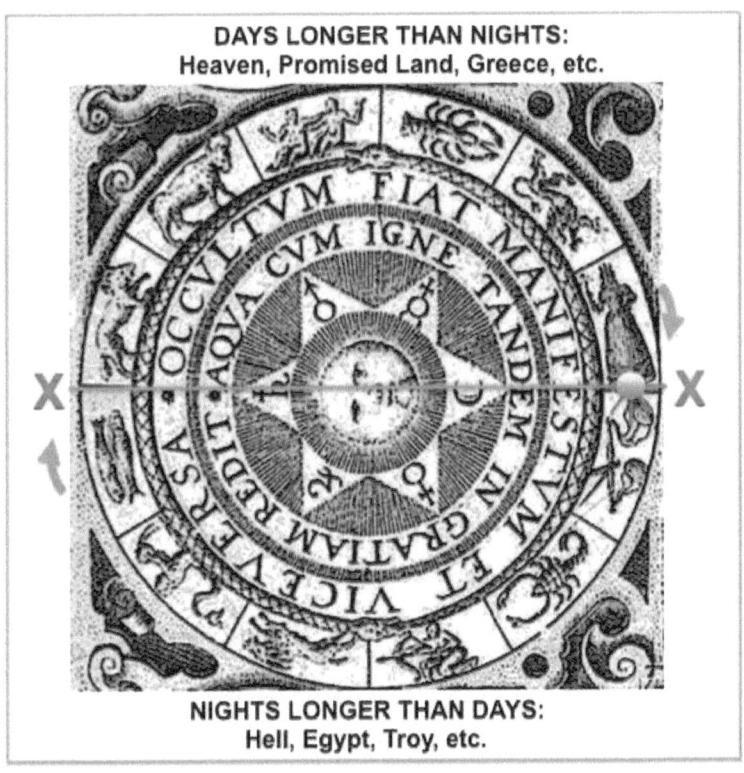

DAYS LONGER THAN NIGHTS:
Heaven, Promised Land, Greece, etc.

NIGHTS LONGER THAN DAYS:
Hell, Egypt, Troy, etc.

I am thus convinced that the words of the goddess to Arjuna are intended to be seen as words addressed to each one of us who comes down into this incarnate realm -- words of encouragement for the soul's struggle through material existence and interaction with the realm represented by the lower half of the wheel (the same struggle represented by the "ocean crossing" discussed earlier in conjunction with the myth of Uta-napishti in the myths of ancient Mesopotamia).

Indeed, more than one ancient Sanskrit text, including the Mahabharata but also the Katha Upanishad (or Kathopanishad), compares the body through which we go through this incarnate life to a chariot or war-car, implying that Arjuna and Krishna in the lead-up to the battle of Kurukshetra are representative of our own condition in this life, steering our "chariot" but with access to the "divine charioteer," should we choose to avail ourselves of his help.

In an earlier chapter, the wise counselor Vidura gave this advice to his brother Dhritarastra:

> One's body, O king, is one's car; the soul within is the driver; and the senses are its steeds. Drawn by those excellent steeds, when well-trained, they that are wise, pleasantly performeth the journey of life, and awake in peace. The horses that are unbroken and incapable of being controlled, always lead an unskilful driver to destruction in the course of the journey; so one's senses, unsubdued, lead only to destruction.[461]

The next day, despite the presence of Lord Krishna to guide his chariot, and the encouragement of the goddess Durga who has told him that he is incapable of being defeated in the upcoming battle, the heroic Arjuna finds himself wracked by doubts, even as the two sides are preparing to roll towards one another for the initial clash. The conch-shells are blowing on both sides, along with horns, accompanied by the clash of cymbals and the beating of drums. Both Arjuna and Krishna stand up in their war-car and blow their conch-shells.

Then, Arjuna instructs Krishna to drive his car out to the space between the two armies -- and when he does so, Arjuna seeing the presence of so many of his relatives and friends and his martial arts instructors from the time of his youth on both sides, tells Krishna that he has lost all strength in his limbs, and his body trembles, his mouth is dry, his hair stands on end, and his skin burns. Arjuna feels he cannot proceed in such a war, which would bring him into open conflict with his own kinsmen and preceptors: he would prefer to throw away his weapons (including the great bow Gandiva) and sit down on the ground, even if it means his own death.

This is the beginning of the Bhagavad Gita, "the essence of religion, the knowledge of Brahma, and the system of Yoga."[462]

The Bhagavad Gita is a section of the Mahabharata consisting of Lord Krishna's instructions to Arjuna during Arjuna's period of doubt and despair prior to the commencement of hostilites in the great battle. The name *Bhagavad Gita* signifies "Song of the Lord" in Sanskrit, with *gita* signifying "song." The text in fact is often referred to simply as the *Gita* ("the Song").

The reluctance on the part of Arjuna to partipate in the battle (despite the evidence that he is by far the most qualified warrior present on either side, and virtually invincible) actually mirrors very closely the *reluctance or doubt* of many other mythical figures in the sacred traditions of other cultures, including the withdrawal of Achilles from the battlefield at the beginning of the

Iliad of ancient Greece, or the doubt exhibited by Thomas in the gospel account of John, as well as the doubt exhibited by Psyche in the story of Eros and Psyche (or Cupid and Psyche) as related by various ancient sources including by Apuleius (thought to have lived c. AD 125 - c. 170) in his *Metamorphoses* (better known as the *Golden Tale of the Ass*, or simply the *Golden Ass*).

And, just as the figure of Jesus in the gospel story encourages Thomas to trust in him, and the figure of Eros in the account related by Apuleius encourages Psyche over and over to trust in him (and then restores her when she fails to do so), so also the Lord Krishna in the Mahabharata encourages Arjuna to perform his duty upon the battlefield, in the section known as the Bhagavad Gita.

The nature of the instruction which Krishna imparts to Arjuna makes it very clear that this encouragement is for each one of us in this incarnate life: it is not advice given exclusively to an ancient nearly-invincible warrior named Arjuna, who is in fact the son of Indra, about to embark upon a literal battle. In fact, much of the advice seems to have little to do with situations one might encounter upon the battlefield.

Some of the declarations of Lord Krishna in the Gita include:

> He that abstains
> To help the rolling wheels of this great world,
> Glutting his idle sense, lives a lost life,
> Shameful and vain. (Chapter 3, verse 16)[463]

> Therefore, thy task prescribed
> With spirit unattached gladly perform,
> Since in the performance of plain duty man
> Mounts to his highest bliss. (Chapter 3, verse 19)[464]

To cease from works
Is well, and to do works in holiness
Is well; and both conduct to bliss supreme;
But of these twain the btter way is his
Who working piously refraineth not.
That is the true Renouncer, firm and fixed,
Who -- seeking nought, rejecting nought -- dwells proof
Against the "opposites." O valiant Prince!
In doing, such breaks lightly from all deed:
'Tis the new scholar talks as they were two,
This Sânkhya and this Yôga: wise men know
Who husbands one plucks golden fruit of both!
The region of high rest which Sânkhyans reach
Yogins attain. Who sees these twain as one
Sees with clear eyes! (Chapter 5, verses 2 - 5)[465]

In other words, Krishna tells Arjuna, the paths of action and inaction are actually the same. The goal is action without attachment:

Because the perfect Yôgin acts -- but acts
Unmoved by passions and unbound by deeds,
Setting result aside. (Chapter 6, verse 4)[466]

As Professor Victor H. Mair of the University of Pennsylvania explains in his valuable commentary accompanying his translation of the Tao Te Ching (or Dao De Jing, sometimes written "Dao de jing" or "Daodejing"), which we will examine in a subsequent chapter, this goal of *right action without attachment to the outcome* is central to the Gita -- and to the Tao. Speaking of the concept of *wu-wei* (literally "without exertion" or "non-exertion") in the Tao Te Ching, Professor Mair writes:

If Tao and *te* are the most significant static or nounal concepts in the *Tao Te Ching*, *wu-wei* is certainly the most important dynamic or verbal notion set forth in the classic. Of all the Old Master's ideas, it is also the most difficult to grasp. *Wu-wei* does not imply the absence of action. Rather, it indicates spontaneity and noninterference; that is, letting things follow their own natural course. For the ruler, this implies reliance on capable officials and the avoidance of an authoritarian posture. For the individual, it means accomplishing what is necessary without ulterior motive. Some commentators have explained *wu-wei* as connoting "nonpurposive" or "nonassertive" action.[467]

Thus, this "reluctance" or "doubting" we see displayed in Arjuna may have multiple layers of meaning for us. It may represent the soul's reluctance to incarnate in the body in the first place. More significantly for those of us who are already here in the body, it may have to do with our reluctance (enamored as we are with the material condition in which our soul is enmeshed, and the pleasures and demands concomitant with that condition) to make that "great turn" towards integration with our Higher Self, and our difficulty with shaking off the net of entanglements that keep us from availing ourselves of our own inner connection to the Infinite.

From the message of Lord Krishna to Arjuna, escaping from this dilemma clearly involves the question of action versus nonaction -- and the way through the dilemma involves reaching the place where action and inaction are united rather than opposed. Achieving such a state will, in and of itself, require escape from the doubts and entanglements which cause our action to be tainted by desire for approval or reward, or by fear of negative consequences even if our actions are right.

Elaborating further on the theme of nonassertive action as it relates to the Gita and the Tao Te Ching, Professor Mair writes:

> The chief lesson Krishna has to offer Arjuna is that altruistic or disinterested action (*niskāma karma*) leads to realization of Brahma. That is to say, one should act without regard or desire for the fruits (*phala*) of one's action. This idea is repeated over and over again in countless different formulations. These passages are of great importance for understanding the enigmatic concept of "nonaction" that is so prominent in the *Tao Te Ching*. "The person of superior integrity takes no action," says the Old Master, "nor has he a purpose for acting." We are told straightaway to "act through nonaction" and that "through nonaction, no action is left undone." In spite of the fact that this idea appears a dozen times and is obviously central to the Old Master's teachings, we can only vaguely surmise from the *Tao Te Ching* the specific implications of *wu-wei* (nonaction).
>
> However, when we read the *Bhagavad Gītā*, we discover an exceedingly elaborate analysis of the nature and purpose of nonaction. The ideal of action without attachment is conveyed in many guises throughout the *Bhagavad Gītā*, for example, *akrta* (nonaction), *akarma* (inaction), *naiskarmya* (freedom from action or actionlessness), *karmanām anārambhān* (noncommencement of action), and so forth. Krishna refers to himself as the "eternal nondoer" and states that the Yogin should think, "I do not do anything." He declares that he "sits indifferently unattached by these actions." Elsewhere he condemns sitting and remembering. All of this reminds us of the "sitting and forgetting"

advocated by the Taoists that later developed into a type of meditative practice.[468]

I believe that the Bhagavad Gita not only *tells* us about the path of action without attachment to the outcome, but also *shows* us the way by which this ideal is to be attained -- and it does so through the aforementioned metaphor of the chariot or war-car in which Arjuna will ride into the battle, with Krishna as his charioteer.

This beautiful and functional metaphor, in which the *divine twin* holds the reins which guide and control the horses (who represent our senses) can in fact be shown to be based upon a celestial pattern.

Below is one of many illustrations of Arjuna in the chariot with Krishna as his charioteer, to which I have added annotations:

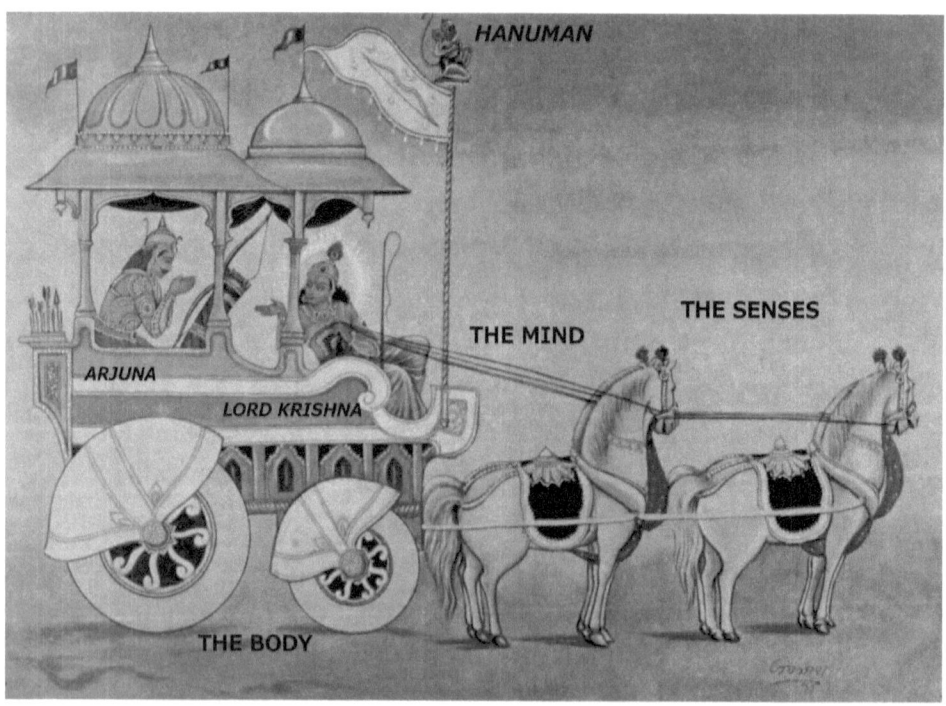

As we have already argued, the distinctive war-cars with canopies on top described in the ancient Sanskrit texts including the Mahabharata can be identified with the "canopy-topped" constellation of Ophiuchus in the heavens. We have also previously argued that Lord Krishna himself (who is an avatar of Vishnu) is also associated with Ophiuchus, and that this fact probably explains his frequent depiction in the act of playing the flute. However, when he takes on the role of charioteer, or driver of the war-car, it is very likely that Krishna is visible just ahead of the war-car of Ophiuchus, in the outline of the constellation Boötes, a constellation which can be shown to play a charioteer or a cart-driver in other mythologies, including in the Iliad of ancient Greece and in the Norse myths contained in the Eddas:

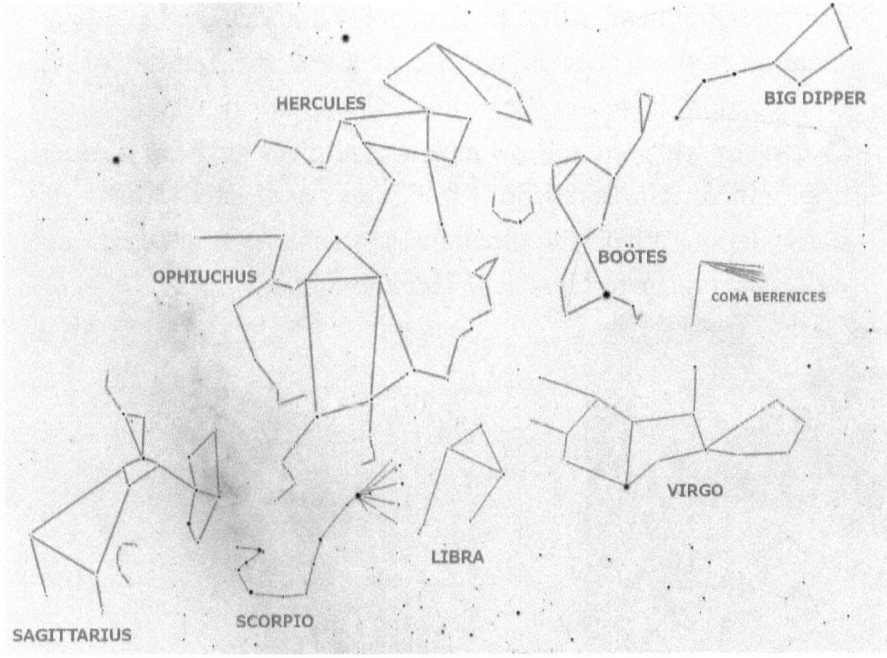

We can envision the celestial charioteer Boötes as connected to the Big Dipper, the bowl of which consists of a "team of four strong horses," by the long "reins" of the Dipper's handle.

Thus, the scene in the image on page 704 is mirrored in the sky: Ophiuchus is the war-car, Boötes represents Krishna the divine charioteer, and the stars at the front of the Dipper are the steeds. Above the war-car of Arjuna and Krishna flutters the banner bearing the image of the god Hanuman, a banner which Arjuna was given by the gods when he was given the chariot itself. This image of Hanuman atop the chariot confirms the identification of the war-car with the constellation Ophiuchus -- because we can positively identify the god Hanuman with the constellation Hercules, and Hercules is directly above Ophiuchus just as the Hanuman banner is directly above the chariot!

Reasons for identifying Hanuman with the constellation Hercules are many. First, Hanuman is often depicted in a deep-lunging posture that is characteristic of the outline of the constellation Hercules. In addition, Hanuman has a sort of "beard" or "ruff" around his face, which gives his head a square appearance, characteristic of figures associated with this constellation (other Hercules figures often have a full beard, such as Zeus, or the hero Heracles / Hercules himself).

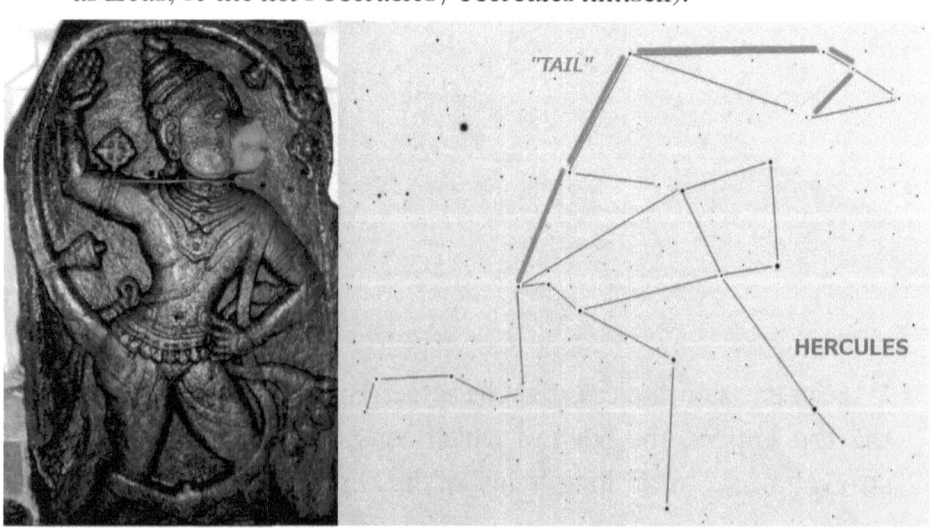

Hanuman of course has a long tail, and this can be envisioned in the outline of Hercules either by envisioning the long extended rear-leg of the outline as the tail of the god, or by envisioning slightly different lines connecting the stars usually seen as outlining the weapon curving over the constellation's back to create the outline of a tail arching over the back instead. One way of envisioning such an outline is shown in the image above.

Another strong piece of evidence linking Hanuman to the constellation Hercules is the fact that, like Bhima, Hanuman's favored weapon is a great mace. In the image below, we see Hanuman holding an enormous mace:

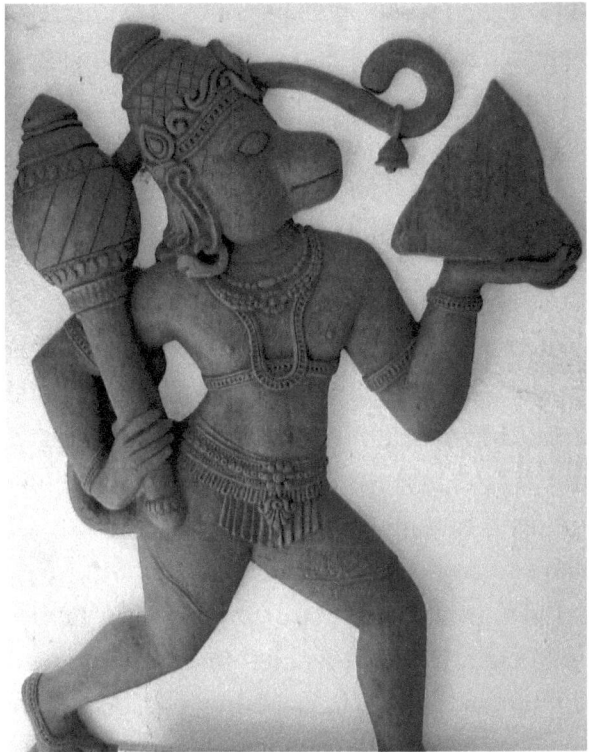

In the above image, Hanuman is also holding the top of a mountain, a popular aspect of his iconography stemming from an episode in the ancient Sanskrit epic Ramayana in which he must obtain herbs found in the Himalayas to heal Rama's brother. Not knowing which herb to select, Hanuman brings the entire mountaintop. This episode can be seen as confirming Hanuman's identification with the constellation Hercules: the "mountaintop" he pulls up is no doubt the triangular upper portion of the constellation Ophiuchus, directly below Hercules. Recall the discussion of the Benben stone of ancient Egypt, on pages 256 and 260 of this volume.

The identification of Hanuman with the constellation Hercules and of the top of Ophiuchus with a triangular mountain also sheds light on a tradition remarked upon by Graham Hancock in *Fingerprints of the Gods*. Speaking of the *Pyramid* of Uxmal, he notes on page 152 a Maya legend which asserts that "a dwarf with supernatural powers had raised the building in just one night." Note that we have seen that dwarves in myth are also associated with the constellation Hercules (see pages 620 - 623 of this volume); the pyramid, again, is the top triangle of Ophiuchus.

There is an episode in the Mahabharata in which mighty Bhima (also associated with the constellation Hercules and also favoring the great mace as his chosen weapon) encounters Hanuman lying beneath a banana tree, and (not recognizing him as the god Hanuman) tells the god to move out of his way. Hanuman tells Bhima to move Hanuman's tail and go past -- but Bhima finds that, for all his tremendous strength, he cannot move the monkey-god's tail. Then, perceiving that he must be in the presence of a supernatural being, Bhima asks Hanuman who he is – and is told that he is Hanuman, who is in fact Bhima's older brother, both of them being sons of the wind-god, Vayu.[469]

This encounter dispels all doubts, if any remained at this point, that Hanuman is associated with the constellation Hercules.

That identification, in turn, confirms that the scene of Arjuna and Krishna in the great war-car before the start of the Kurukshetra war (beneath the banner of Hanuman) can be identified with the constellations described above (ranging from Ophiuchus to the Big Dipper, and perhaps even to Sagittarius, with which constellation Arjuna is undoubtedly associated).

Because we can see beyond any doubt that this chariot bearing Arjuna and Lord Krishna is celestial in nature, we can be confident that its meaning is esoteric and spiritual, rather than literal and terrestrial, and can thus avoid wasting our time and energy trying to determine if indeed Kurukshetra was an actual literal battle in which historical figures corresponding to Arjuna and his brothers, or Krishna from Dwaraka, fought over physical and earthly terrain. Instead, we should (I would argue) realize that if the war-car being described can be found in the heavens, it is trying to illustrate for our understanding some truth regarding invisible matters, and the truth that it is attempting to illustrate will likely have to do with the subject matter of the Gita itself: the concept of *right action without attachment*, of *acting as though not acting at all*, connected (as Professor Victor Mair has demonstrated) to the concept of *wu-wei* in the Dao De Jing.

How do we achieve this "action through nonaction"? Looking to the image of the chariot of Arjuna, itself based upon a celestial pattern, we can *see* the answer: we achieve it by giving the reins to the divine twin, represented in the Sanskrit epic by Krishna himself, acting as charioteer.

Based on the metaphor of the chariot which Vidura explained to Dhritarastra (and particularly the version of the metaphor found in the Kathopanishad, in verses or mantras 3 through 6 of the third section of part one), there is a clear distinction between the *mind itself* (identified with the *reins* in the Kathopanishad, which help control the horses, who themselves represent the senses and emotions) and the one who *holds the reins* and who thus is actually "behind" or "above" the mind itself.

In the Bhagavad Gita, we are given a picture of the god Krishna himself holding the reins and steering the chariot. At the same time, we are given an image of Arjuna wracked by doubt, uncertain of how to act, torn by competing loyalties and social bonds (bonds and norms which begin to be layered onto our conscious mind from our earliest days as an infant).

Krishna directs Arjuna towards *action without attachment*: without fear of negative consequences, without hope of reward or positive outcome -- perceiving what is right and acting as if the mind itself is not even acting. The way to achieve such a state is to place the reins in the hands of our Higher Self, which means transcending the net of attachments that have been cast over our being since our earliest days, and which continues to be stitched and strengthened and expanded as we go through our lives. That tangle of attachments will increasingly *bog us down and confuse our action* unless we make a regular practice of connecting with the deeper part of ourselves which is in touch with the Infinite (that is, unbounded, unentangled, un-netted).

Like Psyche in the myth of Eros and Psyche, we need to trust in Eros (although we, like her, are always prone to doubting); like Arjuna, we need to place the reins in the hands of the divine charioteer.

We could continue for thousands of additional pages exploring the celestial metaphor unfolded for us in the Mahabharata, and the profound messages these stories are trying to illustrate for our understanding and benefit. However, having at this point (I hope) established beyond any doubt or objection that the myths of India found in the ancient Sanskrit texts employ the same mysterious system we have found operating all around the world (and perhaps originating in the long-lost "yuga called Krita when the one eternal religion was extant," which Hanuman describes to Bhima during their encounter in the Mahabharata), we will close this chapter for now, and proceed to the final stations on this volume's tour.

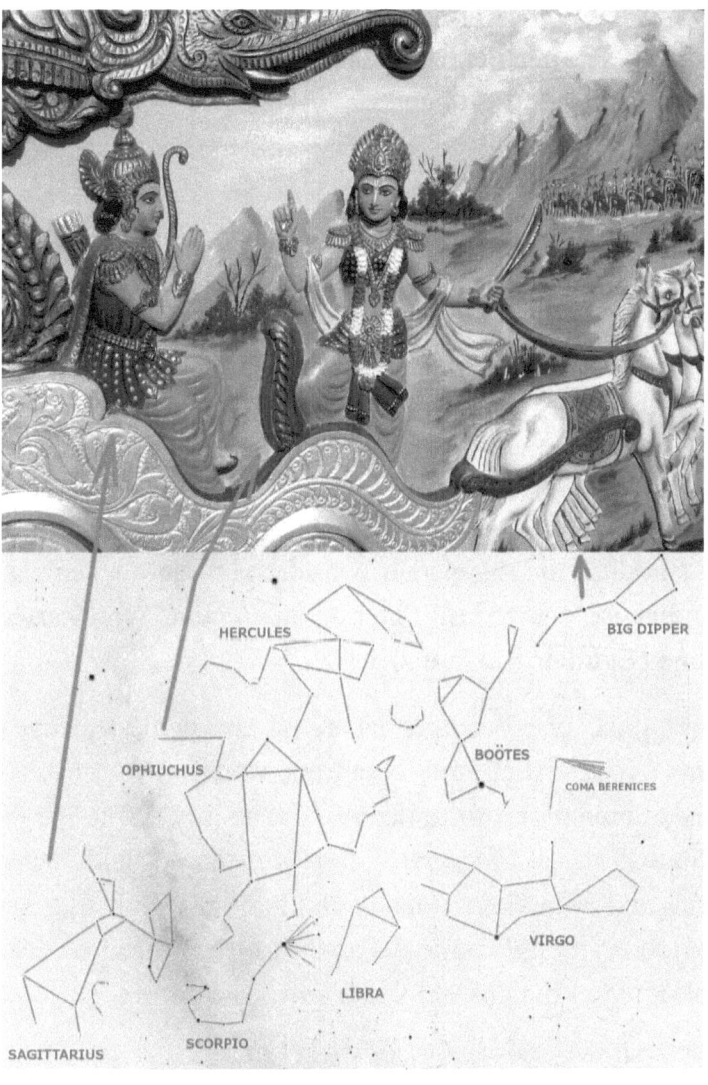

The Life of the Buddha

In addition to producing the Vedas and Puranas and ancient Sanskrit epics such as the Mahabharata, which seem to multiply divinity after divinity and celestial being after celestial being, ancient India was also the home of the original Buddhist tradition, which in comparison appears to be almost a complete counter-impulse to the endless multiplication of divinities.

Instead of focusing on pantheons of gods and goddesses, the ancient Buddhist texts focus on the life and teachings of the Buddha, who according to tradition and the account in some of the earliest texts (such as the texts of the Pali Canon, usually arranged into three *pitaka* or "baskets" of texts and hence sometimes referred to as the *Tripitaka* or the *Tipitaka*) was born a prince and renounced his life of luxury to seek Awakening.

Many conventional scholars treat the life of the individual who would become *the Buddha* (a name meaning *the Awakened* or *the Enlightened*) as historical or at least semi-historical in nature: if some aspects are considered embellishments, the basic outline of the Buddha's life is generally considered to have taken place in human history, enacted by a literal human being who started his life named Siddhartha Gautama.

And yet once one becomes aware of the endlessly repeating patterns of celestial allegory operating around the world, even a cursory examination of the details of the story of the life of the Buddha will reveal *the same system of metaphor* underlying the episodes and events of the life of Siddhartha -- and suggest that *virtually every detail* in the accounts can be traced to celestial metaphor rather than to literal and terrestrial history.

The basic outlines of the life of the Buddha are fairly well-known and well-established. Since the Pali Canon is probably the oldest known collection of original texts in which the life and teachings of the Buddha have been preserved, we will base the description in this chapter on passages from those "baskets" (the word *Pali* refers to a specific vernacular of Sanskrit from the northern part of India close to the Himalayas; it is the sacred language of Theravada Buddhism).

These teachings were probably committed to writing during the period of the first century BC to first century AD, after being passed down from generation to generation in oral format for centuries. Traditionally, the Buddha is usually believed to have walked the earth during the second half of the fifth century BC.

The texts tell us that the young prince Siddhartha was born to the royal parents Sudhodhana (his father) and Maya (his mother). Siddhartha's father was from the Sakyan clan - associated with the sun.

Like the Pandavas and many other related figures in ancient myth, the young Siddhartha exhibits the familiar "two mothers" arrangement: it is said that his mother Maya dies soon after Siddhartha was born (seven days after, in most accounts), and he is raised by his "second mother" or his mother's sister, Pajapati.

Siddhartha's mother Maya is said to have conceived the child after being visited in a dream by a great white elephant. Upon waking the next morning, she discovered that she was pregnant. Note that this story thus describes an "immaculate conception," in that (like the story of the birth of the Christ in the gospel accounts, among many others related in the Star Myths of the world), no sexual intercourse is necessary for Maya to be found to be with child.

Indeed, the mother of the Buddha-to-be is described in many ancient texts and commentaries as being of impeccable character, giving generous alms and performing the proper holy-day vows, as well as being free from any previous sexual relations or any lustful thoughts, as well as having abstained from taking any life, abstaining from theft, from evil conduct, from lying, and from taking any wine or strong drink.[470]

Below is a sculpted bas-relief showing Maya dreaming of the white elephant, which in the ancient texts is specifically described as entering her side. This sculpture is thought to date to the period of AD 100 through AD 300:

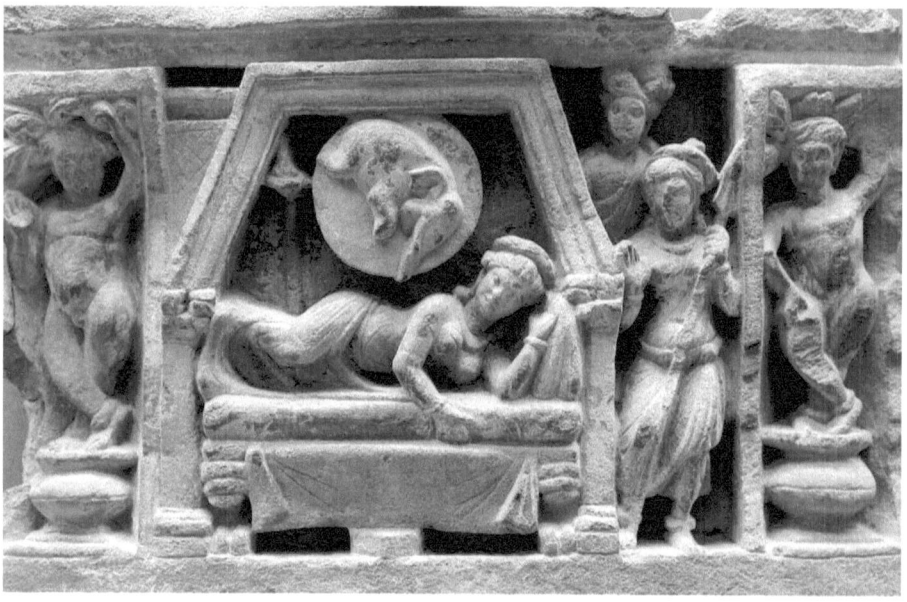

Not only does Maya see the elephant go into her side during the dream, but according to some traditions the child would be born from her side as well. Does this tradition indicate that Queen Maya was delivered using some type of caesarian section? Or is it (as I believe to be more likely) a celestial detail?

Below we see two examples of an oft-depicted scene showing the child of Maya being born from her side:

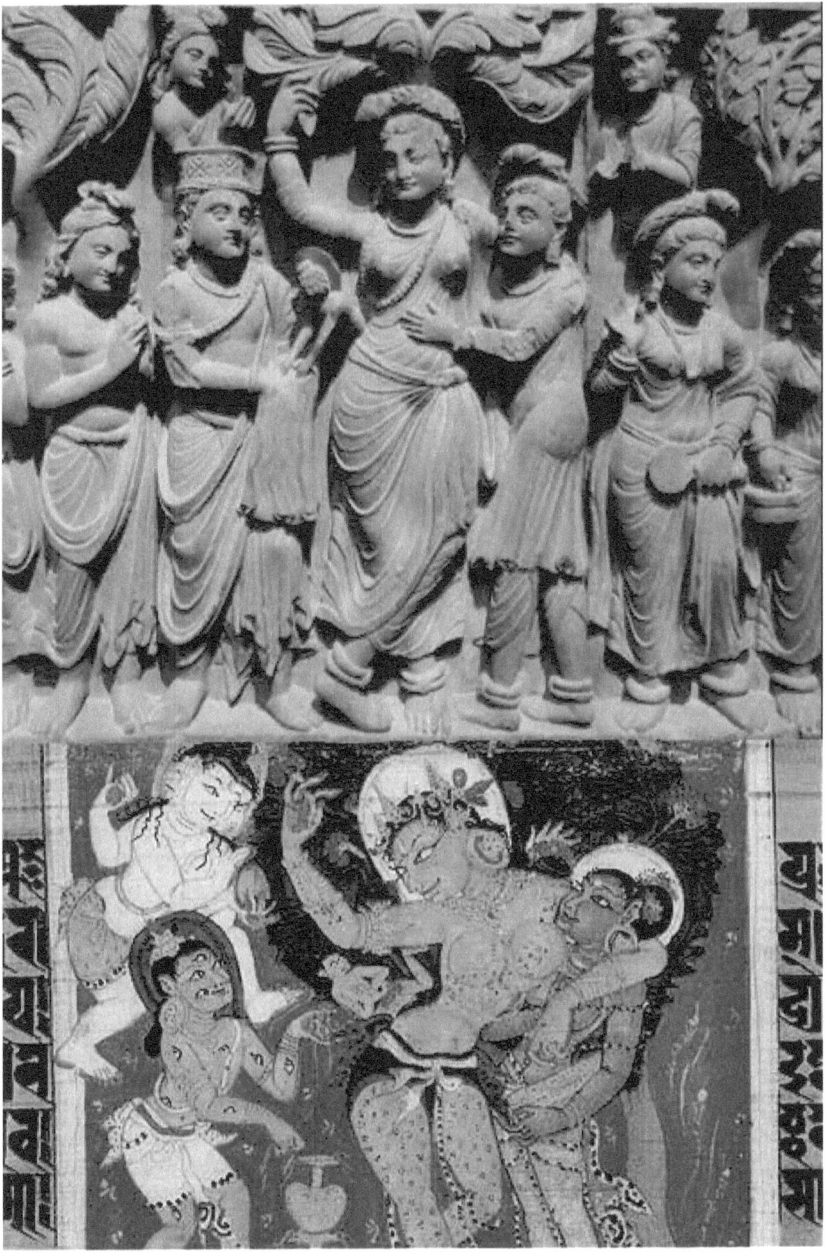

Despite the fact that the two portrayals of the infant being born out of the side of Maya come from two different cultures separated from one another by centuries, the position of the child and the body posture of Maya herself are almost identical. The top image is of a sculpted bas-relief from the period of the Kushan Empire, dating perhaps to the late 100s or early 200s AD. The bottom image comes from the period of the Pala Empire, which was not founded until AD 750 and in a region farther to the south than the Kushan Empire centuries before. Nevertheless, the artwork in both cases depicts Maya with the same angle of the body, the same bend at the hip, the same crossed legs, the same upraised arm on the same side as the bend of the hip, and both depict the baby emerging from the same point.

Upon the birth of the one who would become the Buddha (called at this point the *Bodhisatta*, which means "the Buddha-to-be" in Pali, akin to *Bodhisattva* in other forms of Sanskrit), the great seer Asita was in the midst of his meditation when he sees the Thirty Devas ("a class of gods, antagonists to the Asuras, or demons"[47]), all dressed in pure white, celebrating ecstatically, holding up banners and cheering.

In response to his questions regarding the cause of their celebration, Asita is told:

> "The Bodhisatta, the foremost jewel, unequaled,
> Has been born for welfare and ease in the human world,
> In a town in the Sakyan countryside, Lumbini.
> That's why we're all so wildly elated.
> He, the highest of all beings,
> The utmost person,
> A bull among men, foremost of all people,
> Will set turning the Wheel,

In the grove named after the seers,
Like a strong, roaring lion,
The conqueror of beasts."[472]

Asita seeks out the prince, and going to the palace of
Sudhodhana and Maya, is welcomed into their presence (being a
famous sage) and shown the special child. Upon entering the
presence of the Buddha-to-be, Asita experiences ecstatic rapture,
and sees a vision:

The devas held in the sky
a many-spoked sunshade
of a thousand circles.
Gold-handled whisks
waved up & down,
but those holding the whisks and the sunshade
couldn't be seen.[473]

Asita is allowed to hold the child, and declares: "this one is
unsurpassed, the highest of the biped race."[474]

Suddenly, Asita begins to weep, and the concerned parents ask if
the seer foreses any danger to their child the prince. He explains
that he foresees no harm to the prince – it is for himself that Asita
is weeping, because he knows his own death is imminent. Asita
declares:

"This prince will touch
the ultimate self-awakening.
He, seeing the utmost purity,
will set rolling the Wheel of Dhamma
through sympathy for the welfare of many.
His holy life will spread far and wide.
But as for me,
my life here has no long remainder;

my death will take place before then.

I won't get to hear

the Dhamma of this one with the peerless role.

That's why I'm stricken, afflicted and pained."[475]

The parallels between these traditions regarding the birth of the Buddha (written down well before the New Testament period, and supposedly describing events from the fifth century BC) and the descriptions of the birth of the Christ described in the gospels are striking. Not only do we have the description of a virgin birth to a woman described as blameless in her conduct, but we also have celestial rejoicing (among the devas in the Buddha account, and among the angels in the gospel texts), as well as the visit of an aged prophet in both stories -- aged prophets who make startlingly similar proclamations in each case.

In the gospel according to Luke, the following episode is recounted in chapter 2:

> 25 And behold, there was a man in Jerusalem, whose name *was* Simeon; and the same man *was* just and devout, waiting for the consolation of Israel; and the Holy Ghost was upon him.
>
> 26 And it was revealed unto him by the Holy Ghost, that he should not see death, before he had seen the Lord's Christ.
>
> 27 And he came by the spirit into the temple: and when the parents brought in the child Jesus, to do for him after the custom of the law,
>
> 28 Then took he him up in his arms, and blessed God, and said,
>
> 29 Lord, now lettest thou thy servant depart in peace, according to thy word:
>
> 30 For mine eyes have seen thy salvation,
>
> 31 Which thou hast prepared before the face of all people;

₃₂ A light to lighten the Gentiles, and the glory of thy people Israel.

₃₃ And Joseph and his mother marvelled at those things which were spoken of him.

₃₄ And Simeon blessed them, and said unto Mary his mother, Behold, this *child* is set for the fall and rising again of many in Israel; and for a sign which shall be spoken against;

₃₅ (Yea, a sword shall pierce through thy own soul also,) that the thoughts of many hearts may be revealed.

Note the numerous similarities:

> ➢ both Simeon and Asita receive knowledge of the special child's birth through contact with the divine realm
> ➢ both Simeon and Asita are advanced in age, and waiting for the birth of the special child: having held the baby in their arms, they declare that they will now depart this world
> ➢ both Simeon and Asita prophesy about the future of the child, using very similar terms (terms which are, in fact, celestial in nature)

Clearly, the accounts of the birth of the Buddha and of the birth of the Christ are very different in many superficial details, and yet underneath they appear to be following an almost identical pattern! What can account for these obvious parallels between them? Are the gospel accounts copies or altered versions of the earlier Buddha traditions?

Not necessarily (although it is of course a possible explanation); more likely, I believe, is that both traditions preserve aspects of some far older system, and that their similarities stem from their origin as celestial metaphor, and the passed-down memories of some ancient original, founded upon figures in this part of the sky.

We examine the overwhelming evidence that the characters and events in the Bible, virtually from first to last, are based on this ancient system in Volume Three of this series. Let's examine the evidence that the traditions surrounding the Buddha's birth are likewise based on celestial metaphor, before examining the "prophecy of Asita" for its celestial content.

The episode in which Maya envisions an elephant descending into her side likely describes the constellation Virgo in the night sky, with Boötes above:

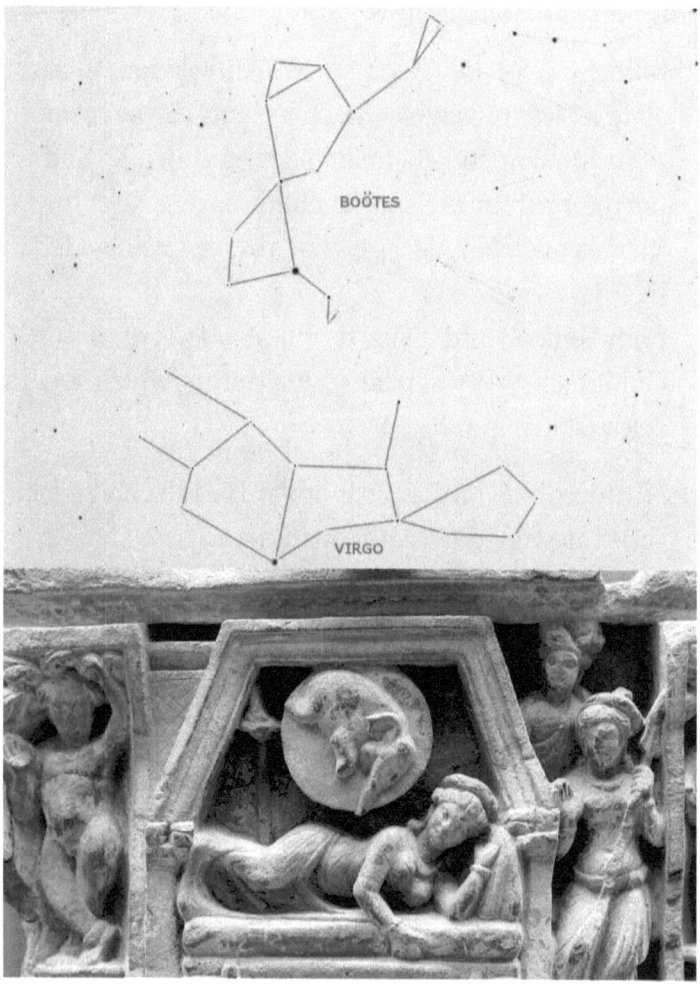

The depictions of Maya giving birth from her side are more difficult. We could conclude that since the elephant goes into her side in the dream, the baby coming out of her side is simply Boötes again, this time envisioned as coming out of the side of Virgo -- but the depictions of Maya in the oft-depicted scene of her giving birth to the Buddha-to-be out of her side do not appear to me to represent a posture suggestive of Virgo. On the other hand, the imagery is highly suggestive of the outline of Sagittarius:

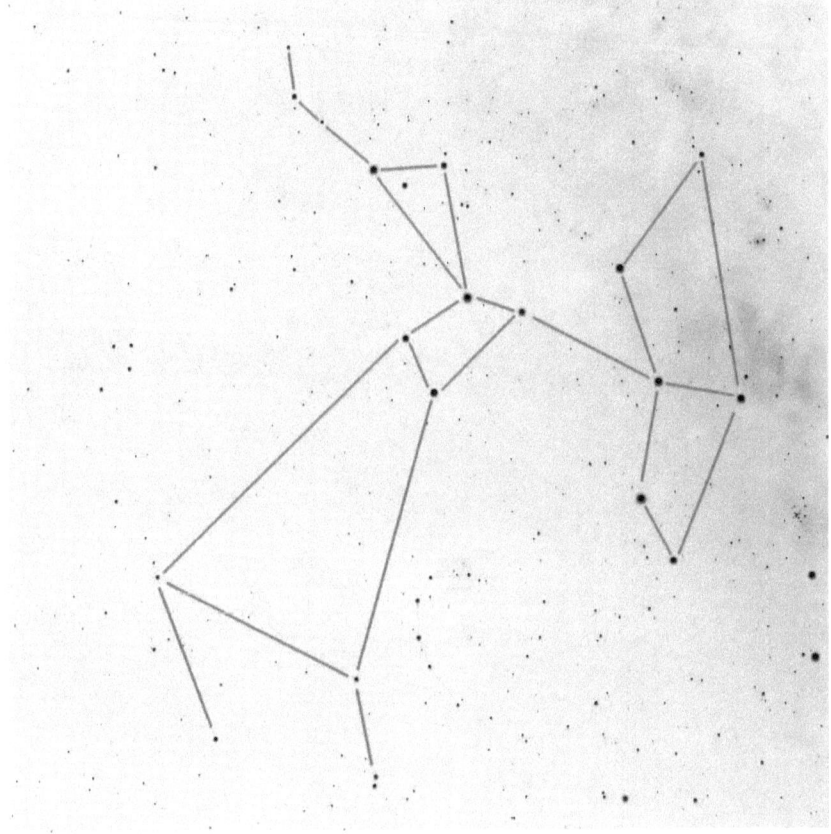

If you turn back to the images of this birth-scene on page 715, you will note similarities to the celestial outline above, including the bend in the hip, the inclination of the head, and perhaps most noticeable of all the upraised arm on the left of the images as we look at them on the page, corresponding to the curved "plume" atop the head of Sagittarius on the left (or eastern) side of the constellation as we look at the star-chart above.

I must admit that, although the depictions of the birth-scene (one from the Kushan Empire, and one from the Pala Empire) appear to depict Maya in a posture most reminiscent of the outline of Sagittarius, yet the identification with specific stars of the baby itself emerging from Maya's side is not at all certain to me yet.

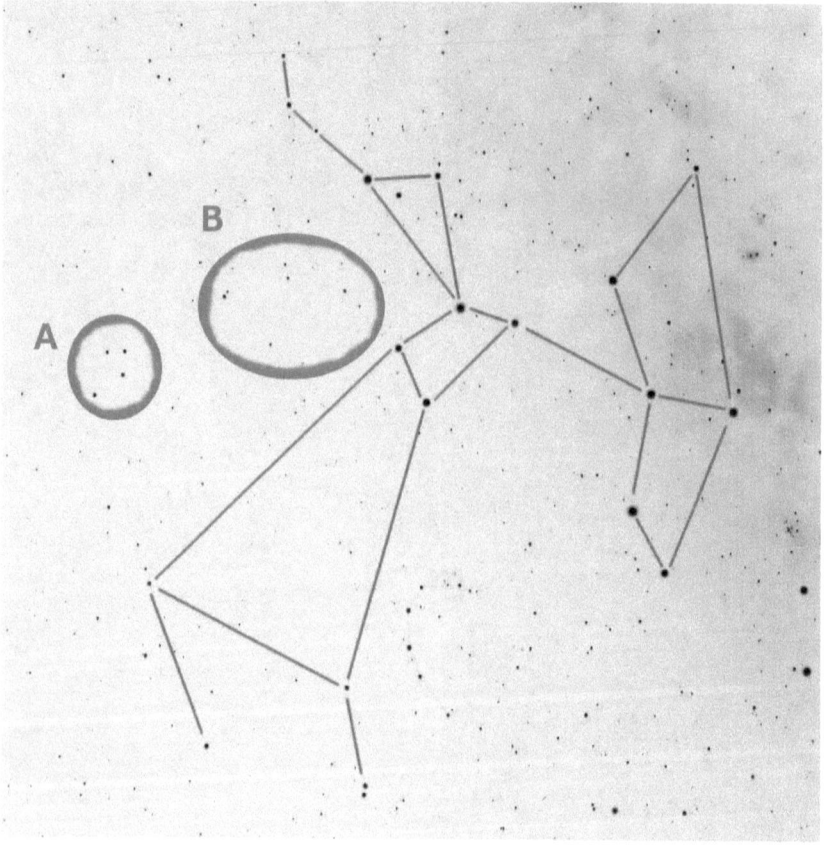

There is a group of stars in the circled area labeled "A" above. These stars make up the "tuft" at the end of the "tail" of Sagittarius when envisioned as a centaur (see discussion on page 421 of this volume). There is another group of stars in the region marked "B" above. Both of these groupings are possible candidates for the baby seen emerging from the side, but neither is completely satisfactory. The stars in the circle marked "A" are brighter and more easily seen, but the stars in the oval marked "B" are closer to the position in which the baby is depicted in the images shown on page 715.

The most I'd say at this point is that the artwork down through the centuries appears to envision Maya in the *posture of Sagittarius*, although I am uncertain which stars would then represent the baby emerging from her side in those depictions.

There is one other possible candidate for the constellation being depicted in the ancient artwork showing Maya giving birth from her side, and that is the constellation Perseus:

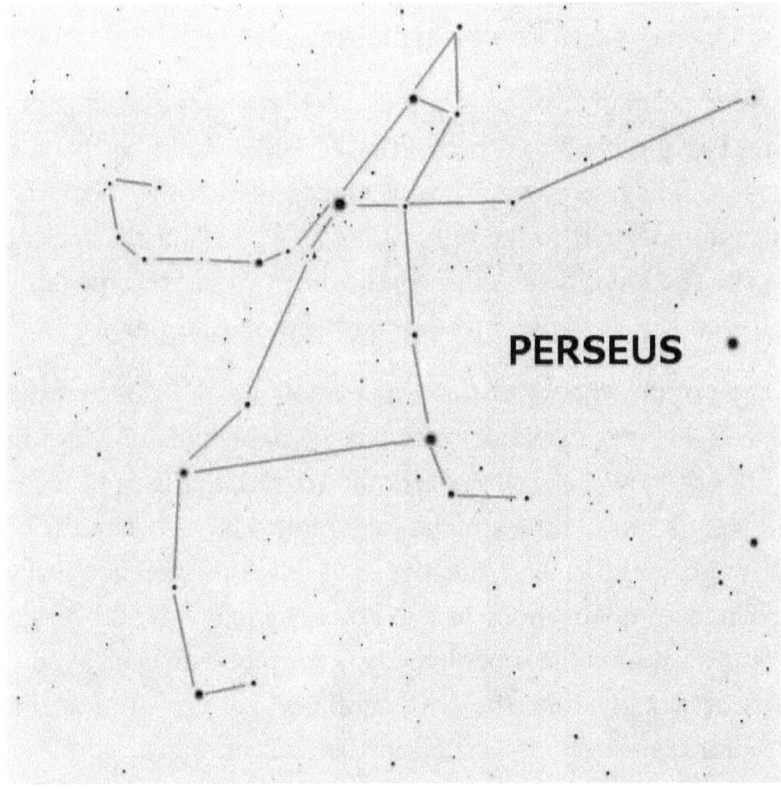

This suggestion does have some things going for it. For starters, the identity of the baby emerging from the side is very obvious (the "arm" on the left side of the constellation as we face Perseus in the star-chart is in perfect position to play the role of the infant depicted in the ancient artwork).

For another thing, figures associated with the constellation Perseus are very often represented in artwork as having their legs crossed, as does Maya in the artwork shown on page 715 (the reason for this cross-legged association of Perseus is the fact that the foot on the left of the constellation is "twisted," which is how it is described in some myths based on this constellation, but instead of being twisted it could simply be envisioned as the foot from the opposite-side leg, crossed over the other leg, in which case the foot of the crossed-over leg would point the way that the foot of Perseus is seen to point in the sky).

One other point in favor of a Perseus association for the depiction of Maya giving birth to a baby from her side would be the fact that it would explain why Maya is embracing another beautiful woman immediately to the right of her as we look at the ancient artwork. The identity of that second woman would then be fairly easy to deduce: she represents the constellation Andromeda.

A couple of drawbacks to this explanation are the fact that the outline of Perseus does not resemble the depictions of Maya in the artwork shown as well as the outline of Sagittarius appears to do. Also, it seems a little strange for Maya to be associated with both Virgo and Perseus: the two constellations are not really linked in many myths. For Maya to be associated with both Virgo and Sagittarius, on the other hand, would not be unusual at all -- indeed, it would evoke the "two mothers" pattern once again, since Virgo is usually associated in the ancient system with our "first birth" and Sagittarius with our "second birth." Thus, if Maya is in some way an embodiment of both figures, it would make the baby special indeed, evoking the "second birth" at the time of the baby's physical birth into this world, and thus perhaps foreshadowing his attainment of Awakening.

Moving on to the prophecy of Asita, we note first that when he was alerted to the birth of the Buddha-to-be by the rejoicing devas, the celestials informed him that one whom they call both a lion and a bull will "set turning the Wheel." Next, in a vision, Asita sees a "many-spoked sunshade with a thousand circles" as well as whisks which are waving up and down (although "those holding the whisks and the sunshade couldn't be seen").

This imagery is clearly celestial in nature. We've already argued that the constellation Coma Berenices (Berenice's Hair) is often described or depicted as a "whisk" in ancient myth and in ancient artwork. It is often included in descriptions and in artwork to point us towards the region of the sky in which Coma Berenices is located (in the region surrounded by Virgo, Boötes and Hercules. Below we see whisks in an image of Ganesha:

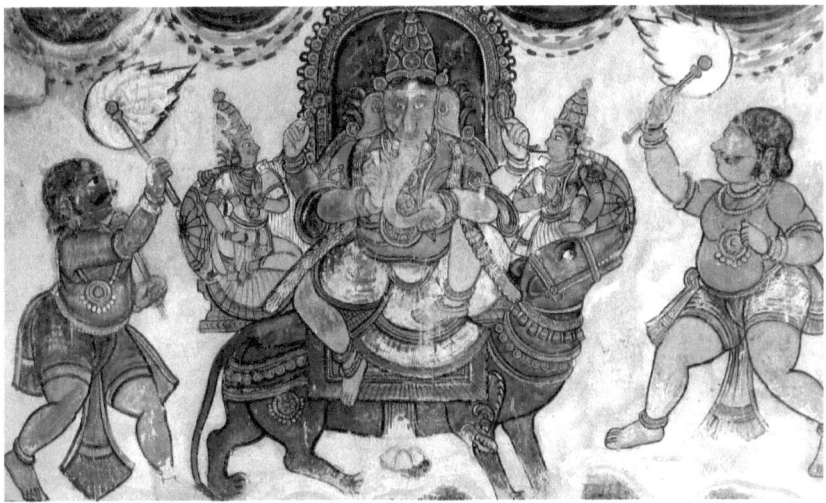

Those holding the whisk would typically *not* be seen, if the whisk is associated with Coma Berenices, since it seems to "float" above the constellation Virgo (although in some cases a connecting line is envisioned from the outstretched arm of Virgo to the "handle" of the constellation Coma). The fact that these whisks are described as having handles (in this case, "golden handles") makes the identification with Coma Berenices more certain.

The many-spoked sunshade may be a reference to the triangular top portion of the central body of Ophiuchus, a feature which (as we have seen) could be envisioned as a sort of parasol or sunshade. However, the fact that it is "many-spoked" suggests that the text here may be referring instead to the great wheel of the zodiac itself, which turns across the sky once per year, and which is likewise seen to turn through the great Ages of precession. The imagery of the zodiac band as a great many-spoked wheel is also found in the famous vision of Ezekiel which is discussed at length in *Star Myths of the World, Volume Three.*[476]

That this great many-spoked wheel of the zodiac, with each zodiac sign being a "pie-shaped section" of the wheel bounded by spokes, is what the texts are actually describing is evident from the many other references to the Wheel, or the Wheel of Dhamma (Dharma) which the Buddha-to-be is going to "set turning" or "set rolling."

This great Wheel is mentioned in each of the important passages about Asita's vision and prophecy: when he first hears the devas celebrating in heaven, when he has another vision in the presence of the child, and when he declares to the child's parents that this child will "touch the ultimate self-awakening" and "set rolling the Wheel of Dhamma through sympathy for the welfare of many."

Note too that the number of devas described in the text may be significant: they are explicitly described as the "Thirty Devas." There are thirty degrees in one zodiac house, if we divide the year into twelve stations using the zodiac (360 degrees for a full circle divided by twelve zodiac segments results in 30 degrees per zodiac segment). Thus the number 30 evokes the twelve-sectioned "wheel of the year" (its sections being the zodiac signs).

Very noteworthy it is that the prophecy uttered by the aged Simeon in the episode described in the gospel according to Luke also appears to be referencing the same majestic celestial machinery! Simeon declares: "this child is set for the fall and rising again of many in Israel; and for a sign which shall be spoken against" (Luke 2: 34). Such a declaration can be seen as a description of the turning of the same great Wheel, which will result in the "fall and rising again of many in Israel" (that is to say, the fall and rising again of many *zodiac houses in the sky* – the twelve tribes of Israel being explicitly linked to the zodiac constellations by passages in Genesis 49 and Deuteronomy 33, as examined in depth in Volume Three of this series).[477]

That the child in either case is declared to be one who will "set turning" this great Wheel (or, in the case of the Luke passage, "set [. . .] the fall and rising again of many in Israel") seems to indicate a connection to not just the annual motion of progress through the zodiac (which moves its way across the heavens in one year) but also the great Ages-long motion of precession, whose inexorable progress causes the "fall" and the "rising again" of the zodiac constellations which form the backdrop of stars for the sun at the critical stations of the year: the spring equinox, summer solstice, fall equinox, and winter solstice.

Because both the Buddha (as we'll see) and the Christ appear to be closely identified with the constellation Ophiuchus, the reference to precession here may well be yet another piece of evidence for the suspected connection between Ophiuchus and the motion of precession which we have mentioned earlier. Recall our discussion of evidence in myth which connects Ophiuchus to pivot in the celestial tug-of-war that churns the infinite Ocean of Milk. Recall also the connection between Ophiuchus and the "dice games" which ancient myth associates with the irresistible motion of precession. And note the many Ophiuchus-figures (such as Baldr and Osiris and Jesus and Kronos) whose death or banishment are connected to the end of an Age.

It is interesting that the prophecy of Simeon declares that this child will not only be set for the falling and rising again of many in Israel (in the zodiac band) but will also be "a sign that is spoken against" (Luke 2: 34). There is a tradition that the constellation Ophiuchus can be seen as the "thirteenth zodiac sign" because (as mentioned previously) the path of the ecliptic does cross through part of Ophiuchus (one of the legs of the constellation). Some argue that Ophiuchus was removed at some point (one argument being that Ophiuchus was removed from a more ancient and more matriarchal system, in which a great Goddess was worshipped, in order to reduce the zodiac to the more solar and thus, according to the argument, more patriarchal system: although I myself have not thus far seen enough evidence to support such an assertion, it nevertheless should be considered as one among many possibilities), thus making Ophiuchus a sort of "outcast" among the zodiac, an assoication which may be referenced by the phrase "a sign that is spoken against."

Along these lines of investigation, it is interesting to note that in the exile of the Pandavas following the disastrous dice game (discussed in the previous chapter and shown to be connected to the mighty turning of the wheels of precession), the five princes are required to live in the wilderness for twelve full years, *followed by an additional thirteenth year* in which they must live in a populated city but without being recognized! Could this thirteenth year be a cryptic reference to the "thirteenth sign" which is "no longer recognized"?

In any case, it should be at this point uncontroversial to assert that the descriptions of the birth of the Buddha exhibit abundant evidence which shows them to be based upon the same system of celestial metaphor which underlies the myths, scriptures and sacred traditions of so many other cultures around the globe. While those arguing that the Buddha was a literal historical figure might dismiss these "miraculous birth stories" as "later accretions" or "embellsihments" added to the fundamentally historical account, an examination of the rest of the story of the life of the Buddha indicates that the other familiar details of the life-story are likely based on celestial metaphor as well.

As he grows up, Siddhartha enjoys every luxury. He spends his time among three palaces: one for the cold season, one for the hot season, and one for the rainy season. The three palaces have beautiful ponds containing lotuses blooming: red-lotuses in the pond at one palace, white-lotuses in the pond at another palace, and blue-lotuses in the lotus-pond in the remaining palace. But as he grows to manhood, the prince begins to realize that the unconsidered intoxication with youth, health, and life -- and the unthinking revulsion at the marks of advanced age, at the signs of illness and disease, and at death itself -- are all contradictory, since all those who hold those intoxications and revulsions are themselves subject to the effects of age, of disease, and of death.

And so, at the age of twenty-nine, Siddhartha decides that he must renounce his life of ease and luxury and pursue a holy life as a wandering ascetic, without a house in which to lay his head, subsisting on the alms distributed by the people out of their charitable intentions, and carrying with him no possessions but a robe and a bowl.

He shaves off his beard and his hair, and (despite the weeping and grieving of his two parents) goes forth into the life of the wandering ascetic: he is still unawakened, but is now going forth to pursue a holy life and to search for ultimate awakening.

As he wanders, the Bodhisatta collects alms from the villages, but then retreats to secluded places, to meditate upon recollection of his past lives, upon the passing away and reappearance of beings, upon the equanimity that can be maintained in any circumstance whether pleasurable or painful, and upon the development of mindfulness, internal composure, assurance, knowledge, and sympathy.

Those who follow him to see where he would meditate would sometimes find him seated before a great cleft in a rock, or at the holy mountain in the foothills of the Himalayas, but most famously, of course, the Bodhisatta sits beneath the great tree by the river Nerañjara, the tree which is sometimes called "the Bodhi tree" or "the Bo tree" (in reference to the pursuit of *Bodhi*, or "awakening").

The tree is traditionally understood to have been a *ficus religiosa* or "sacred fig," also known as a *pipal* (in Hindi) or an *ashwanth* (in Sanskrit). Some texts describe it as a banyan tree, however (which is a completely different tree from a *ficus religiosa*). There are numerous trees at sacred sites in India which are popularly believed to be the very tree under which the Bodhisatta sat, or said to be descended from a cutting from that original sacred fig tree, just as there is a tree at the supposed site of the battle of Kurukshetra said to be the site of Lord Krishna's instruction to Arjuna (which became the text of the Bhagavad Gita). While I obviously believe the sites where these mythical events take place are to be found *in the heavens,* I also believe that these ancient myths are describing realities which pertain to each and every individual man or woman -- and thus, to the extent that men and women go to these sites, then these sites do indeed become "the place where the Buddha sits" or "the place where Krishna speaks to Arjuna," because those myths describe a reality which is undeniably present *within* individual men and women.

As the Bodhisatta sits beneath the tree, he is tempted and attacked by the demon Mara, and in some versions by the daughters of Mara as well, usually described as being three in number. Note that the pattern of three female figures under a tree is extremely widespread in ancient myth, and is seen for example in the Norns who sit beneath Yggdrasil in the Norse myths, and who are almost certainly related to the three Fates of Greek mythology as well.

Regarding all of the commotion around him as merely the arising and passing away of all things, the Bodhisatta remains motionless and unperturbed. He sits motionless for days and days on end -- according to most traditions, for seven times seven days without moving. In some texts, the Buddha later recounts the experience of abstaining from food until he became so emaciated that when he grasped his torso beneath the ribcage, his hand encircled his own spine.

At last, having demonstrated the discipline of tranquility and unattachment in the face of all possible distractions and aggravations, including the charge of a powerful demon mounted on a mighty elephant, and the seductions of the three irresistably beautiful daughters of Mara, and a host of other incitements, he attained Enlightenment. From henceforth, he would be the Buddha – the Awakened One.

I'm convinced that the message of this story has nothing to do with the question of whether any man or woman could sit motionless for forty-nine days in a row. The story is not, I'm convinced, about someone else who lived long ago, and who was given a destiny even before birth which set him apart from all other men and women who would ever live. Instead, I would argue that this story is illustrating for us the detachment necessary to overcome the assaults and temptations which Mara will impose upon *every* human life.

In other words, it is conveying a message which is nearly identical to that conveyed by Krishna to Arjuna in the Bhagavad Gita, discussed in the previous chapter. And, like the episode in which the Bhagavad Gita is given, we can see that this story is esoteric in nature because its details, as in all the other previous myths we have examined, are celestial. The details point us towards the great celestial cycles, and the "falling and rising again" of the heavenly figures, arising and disappearing in an endless wheel, the "rolling of the Wheel of Dharma."

As with the Bhagavad Gita itself, the celestial metaphor itself contains the key to unlocking the mystery of how such "right action without attachment" can be obtained. In the story of the Buddha, with its emphasis on the turning of the Wheel and the arising and departing of all beings, and all experiences, and all things, we glimpse the attitude or awareness which we must achieve in order to become immune to the attacks and entanglements of Mara and Mara's allies and offspring.

Let's go back through some of the details in the life of the Buddha in order to briefly explore some of the celestial metaphor with which his story is replete.

The early life of Siddhartha, spent among three palaces (one for each of three seasons) emphasizes to us once more the connection between this prince and the heavenly cycles, the rotating wheel whose motions he eventually learns to observe with detachment. The palaces with their pools and lotuses describe characteristics we recognize as belonging to the constellation Ophiuchus, which often plays the role of a palace or a tower or a tent or a pavilion or a house or a hut or other shelter, and which stands next to the widest and brightest part of the Milky Way band (a widening which plays the role of a pool in countless myths around the world, and almost certainly does so here: each palace being represented by Ophiuchus, and each pool with the widest and brightest part of the Milky Way, adjacent to Ophiuchus).

The lotus plant is another detail we've now seen to be often associated with Ophiuchus, and in particular the "serpent-head" on the western side of the constellation: this serpent-half is sometimes envisioned as running all the way down across the central body of the constellation to terminate in the wide part of the Milky Way,[478] and thus these lotus plants described in the story of the life of the Buddha could well be envisioned as *growing from* the lovely pools next to each palace in the story.

The description of the Bodhisatta or Bodhisattva sitting in meditation *upon a hill*, or in the *cleft of a great rock*, or (most famously) *beneath a fig tree* can all be shown to also be connected to the outline and characteristics of the constellation Ophiuchus.

The constellation Ophiuchus itself is often envisioned as a hill or a mountain in the world's Star Myths. Thus the accounts of Buddha meditating *at the top of a hill* may indicate an identification with this constellation. In addition, as we have discussed, the two "serpent halves" on either side of the central body of the constellation can be demonstrated to have been envisioned as great "jaws" yawning open as if to swallow up that central figure (see for example the discussions on pages 122 - 123, 134, and 413 of this volume; it may also explain the Symplegades).

Once we are familiar with this way of envisioning the constellation Ophiuchus, then we can understand the traditions which tell us that the followers of the Bodhisatta would sometimes find him meditating *within a great cleft* in a rock: the central body of the constellation represents the meditating Bodhisatta, and the serpent-halves on either side represent the walls of the rock-cleft:

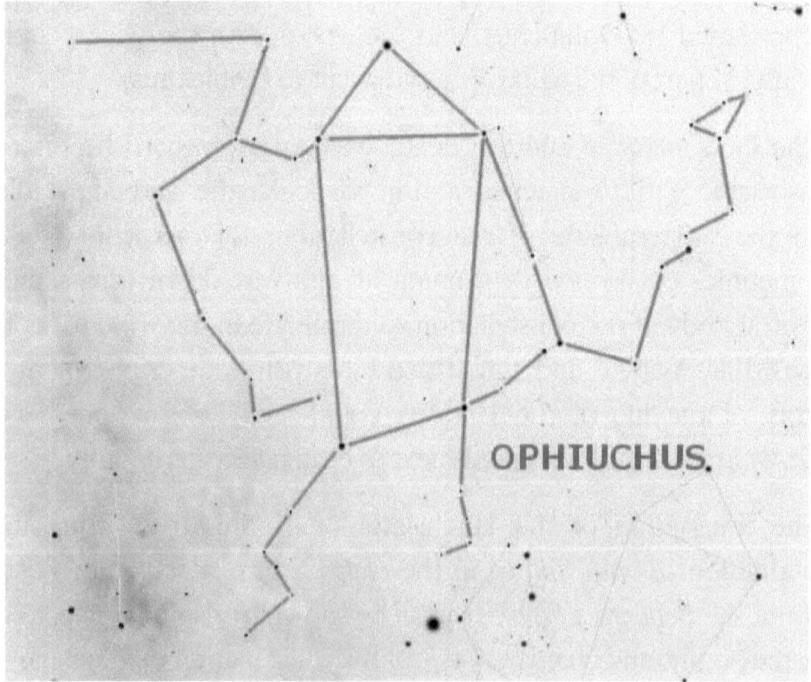

OPHIUCHUS.

Below we see a statue of a Buddha, positioned in between two pillars – two pillars being another common indicator that we are dealing with the constellation Ophiuchus (as mentioned previously, we will see that the figure of Solomon in the book of Kings in the Bible is associated with this same constellation):

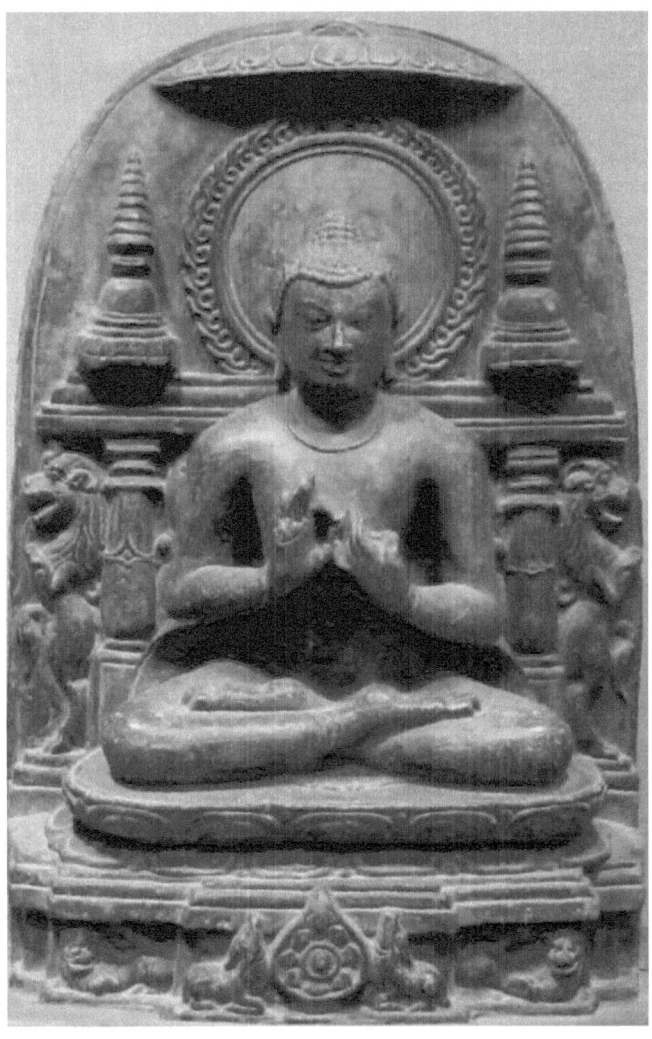

Note the canopy or parasol or sunshade (another clue pointing to Ophiuchus) at the top of this statue, which comes from the Pala Empire and is dated to the eleventh century AD.

735

By far the most well-known position for the Buddha (or the Bodhisatta) to meditate, of course, is *beneath the sacred fig tree.* Here too we can be quite confident that Ophiuchus is indicated, underneath the constellation Hercules envisioned in its "whirling" form. Hercules resembles a tree and is seen playing the role of a tree in numerous Star Myths from around the world:

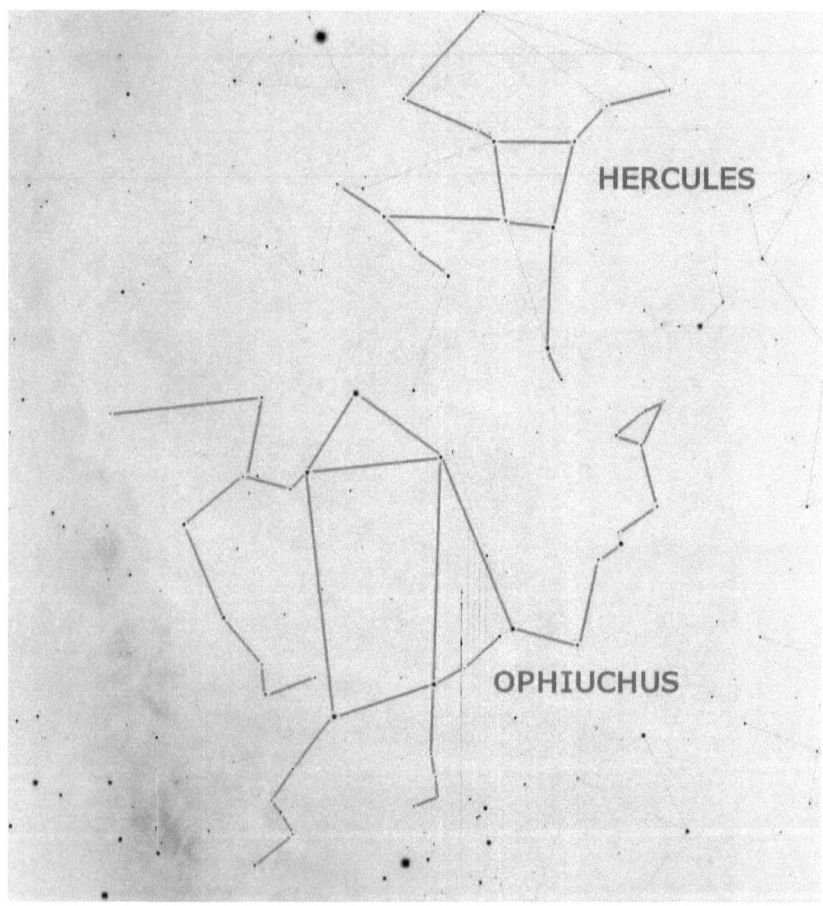

That this tree-like outline was often specifically envisioned as a *fig tree* is evident from numerous other examples in myth and scripture. For example, when Odysseus is sucked down into the vortex of Charybdis in Book 12 of the Odyssey, the long-suffering hero clings to a helpful fig tree atop an ocean rock after the monster spits him back up. That fig tree corresponds to the tree-shaped outline of Hercules atop the craggy outline of Ophiuchus.

Again, in the gospel account according to John, Jesus tells Nathanael that he saw him while Nathanael was "under the fig tree," before Philip had even summoned Nathanael to come see the teacher (John 1: 46 - 50). Later, in the story of the triumphal entry into Jerusalem, Jesus curses a fig tree such that it withers (this incident is discussed in *Star Myths of the World, Volume Three*, and related to the figure of Hercules above Ophiuchus in that instance as well). The cursing of the fig tree incident is described in Matthew 21 and also in Mark 11; in the Matthew account Jesus specifically compares his ability to cause it to wither with the ability to *tell mountains to be removed and cast into the sea*, thus bringing in a reference to Ophiuchus in conjunction with a discussion of a fig tree, and indicating beyond doubt that we are dealing with a celestial feature in these passages.[479]

Note too in the eleventh-century statue of the Buddha shown on page 735 the presence of a radiant disc, apparently ringed with little tongues of fire, behind the head of the seated Buddha. This is a common feature in depictions of the Buddha, and I would suggest that it likely represents the "whirling disc" form of the constellation Hercules, located just above the constellation Ophiuchus in the heavens.

The attack of Mara is also described in terms we can recognize as indicating celestial metaphor. When the demon mounts a tremendous elephant and charges at the meditating Bodhisattva, we can be fairly confident that (like Indra, who also rides an elephant, discussed in a previous chapter) Mara can be identified with the constellation Hercules above Ophiuchus.

The three seductive daughters of Mara are likely to be embodiments of the two undulating serpent-halves on either side of the central figure of Ophiuchus, as well as of the prostrate figure of Scorpio just below this same central part of the constellation (Siddhartha in meditation being identified with the central column of Ophiuchus, and the two serpent-halves plus Scorpio surround him, like the daughters of Mara who are trying to distract the meditating young man).

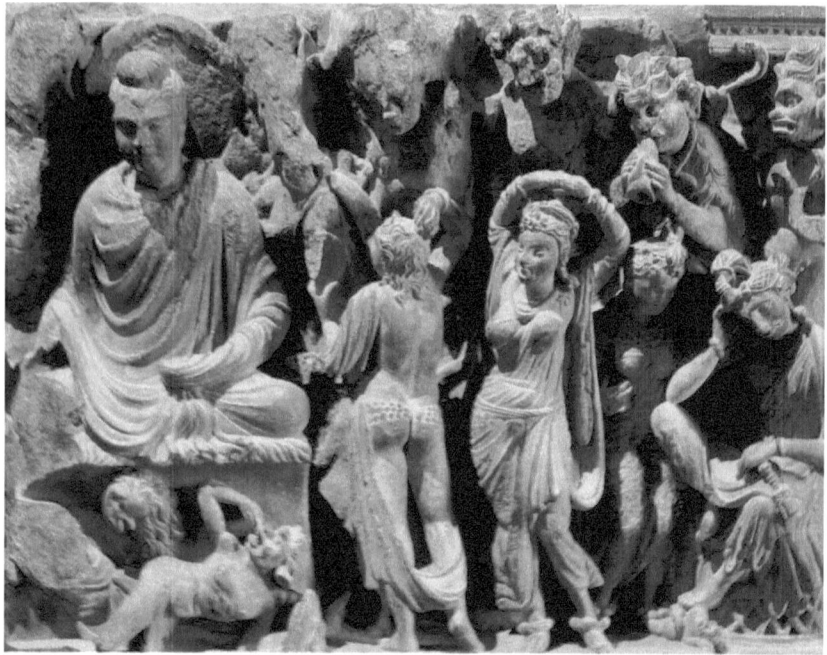

Above is one depiction of the daughters of Mara attempting to seduce Siddhartha as he meditates, from the Kushan Empire period.

Finally, just in case any additional evidence is at this point needed to conclude beyond any doubt that the figure of the Buddha is understood to be associated with the constellation Ophiuchus, here is a statue showing a seated Buddha beneath a tree, with a figure standing behind and above him holding a great club, wearing a full beard, and covered in powerful muscles -- all the characteristics of the hero Heracles or Hercules (as well as of the god Zeus or Jove):

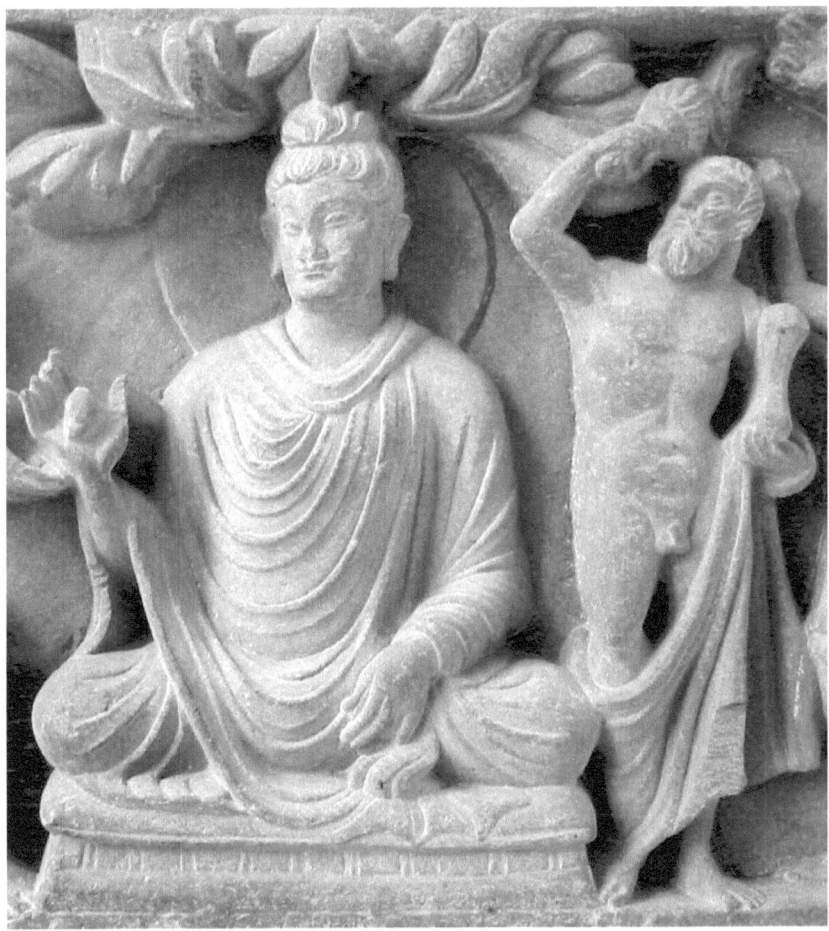

The statue is from the 2nd century AD, and the figure behind the Buddha can be identified as Vajrapani, whose name literally means "Vajra-in-hand." The Vajra is another name for the thunderbolt weapon in Sanskrit, usually wielded by the god Indra. Vajrapani is a protective being who guards the Buddha and who represents the Buddha's great strength (having achieved Enlightenment). Other beings who protect the Buddha are personifications of the Buddha's wisdom and his compassion.

Chapter Eighteen

That the figure of Vajrapani is associated beyond any doubt with the constellation Hercules should be abundantly clear. In the past, I thought this statue proved that the figure of the Buddha was associated with the placid-looking constellation of Boötes, since Hercules stands above and behind Boötes in the heavens.

However, as we have just seen, other evidence linking the figure of the Buddha to the constellation Ophiuchus is simply overwhelming, and I now realize that I was previously mistaken. This statue with Vajrapani actually helps confirm the identification of the Buddha with Ophiuchus. If you look closely at the 2nd-century sculpture, you will see that in the upraised palm of the figure of the Buddha there is an object resembling an egg! We have already seen abundant evidence, stretching all the way back to artwork from ancient Mesopotamia, which indicates that this upraised hand holding an egg-shaped object is a clear indication of the constellation Ophiuchus. See for example the images and discussion on pages 294 and 295 of this volume.

At this point, it should be very clear that the stories of the life of the Buddha, in common with sacred tradition the world over, are based on celestial metaphor (and, what's more, based on the same system we see in operation in so many other cultures located in so many other parts of the world). The passages in which the Buddha says he became so thin during his meditation ordeal that he could place his hands around his spine may indicate a borrowing of imagery from the constellation Scorpio, just beneath the constellation Ophiuchus.

This reference to what we might call "Scorpio imagery" during a grueling ordeal seems to have a parallel in the text of Psalm 22, in which the speaker is describing a grievous trial of some sort, in which he is "compassed" (surrounded on all sides) and beset by enemies who gape at him like bulls or like lions, causing him to declare: "I am poured out like water, and all my bones are out of joint: my heart is like wax; it is melted in the midst of my bowels" (Psalm 22: 12 - 14). During this trial, the speaker says, he remembers how in the past those who called on God would be delivered, but of such rescue the speaker despairs, saying famously, "But I *am* a worm, and no man; a reproach of men, and despised of the people" (Psalm 22: 6). Later, he declares "I may tell all my bones: they look and stare upon me" (Psalm 22: 17).

Does this imagery not recall the ordeal of the Bodhisattva, when he is beneath the tree and becomes so emaciated he can encircle his spine with his hands? It evokes Scorpio, saying "I am a worm and no man," (Scorpio being envisioned as a serpent and as a worm in addition to as a scorpion in ancient myth). This same Psalm is often referenced in relation to the Crucifixion event, due to the verse in Psalm 22 which declares "they pierced my hands and my feet" (Psalm 22: 16). And indeed, as we will see in a later volume, the Crucifixion scene -- beyond any doubt -- is centered upon this same constellation Ophiuchus.

What does it all mean?

We have seen that Ophiuchus in the ancient system forms the very center around which turn the Ages of precession. We have also seen that Ophiuchus was seen as being both "part of the zodiac" but also "separate from it." We see the Buddha achieve Awakening when he is able to view all around him with detachment, as the *arising and passing away again* of all beings and actions and struggles.

As philosopher Marshall McLuhan (1911 - 1980) famously said, "the medium is the message."

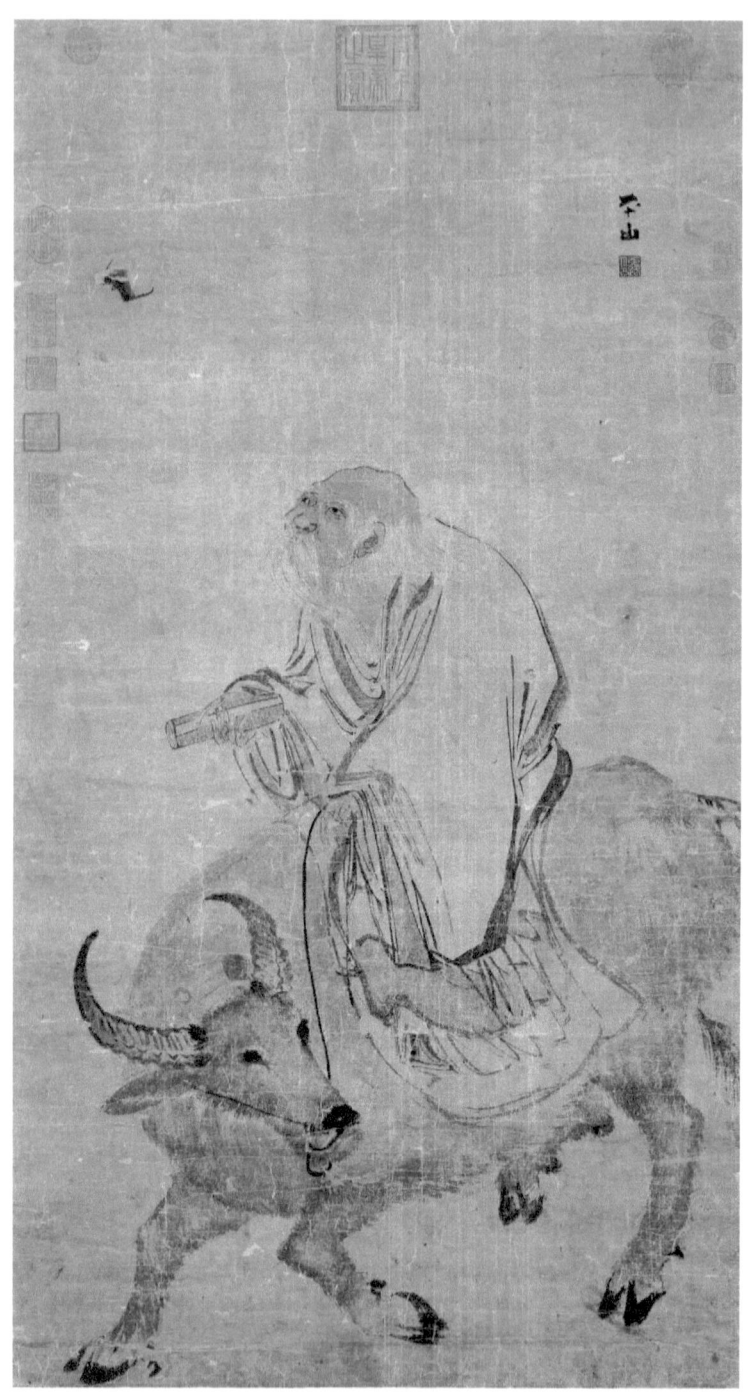

742

Star Myths of Ancient China: the Dao De Jing

We have now examined the story of the life of the Buddha and concluded that it is difficult to argue that any of it is based upon literal history at all, arguing instead that it is far more likely the story employs the great celestial cycles in order to point us towards profound truths, as do virtually all the other Star Myths of the world.

When it comes to the founding texts of Taoism (or Daoism), however, it seems that we have at last come to a spiritual tradition passed down to us from the ancient world which is based strictly upon philosophical and even practical principles, without any attendant celestial elaboration or extended allegory.

And yet, while that is certainly how things appear at first glance, I am convinced by the evidence that the traditions and teachings of Taoism can be shown to fit into the same world-wide phenomenon that we have been examining, and to hearken back to some of the same metaphors regarding the cycles of the heavens in order to convey the ancient message.

The foundational text known as the 道德經, which is usually rendered into our alphabet as *Tao Te Ching* or *Dao De Jing*, has now been found on texts dating back to 170 BC - 190 BC (for the Ma Wang Dui silk texts, discovered in 1973) and to before 300 BC (for the bamboo tablets of Guodian, discovered in 1993).

The name of the title has been interpreted as signifying "The Classic Book of Integrity and the Way" by noted scholar of Chinese language and culture Victor H. Mair, Professor of Chinese Language and Literature in the Department of Oriental Studies at the University of Pennsylvania since 1979 (the word 德

Te or *De* understood best as signifying "integrity" and the word 道 *Tao* or *Dao* signifying "way" or "road").[480] The word 經 (*Ching* or *Jing*) signifies "classic," as in a book or text which is recognized as a classic.

The origin of the Tao Te Ching is attributed to a figure known to us as 老子 *Lao Tzu* (or *Laozi*), and as with the individual named Siddhartha Gautama, scholars generally understand him to have been a literal figure located in actual historical space and time.

The encyclopedic history compiled by the Grand Historian Si Ma Qian 司馬遷 (135 BC - 86 BC), gives us one of the earliest (if not *the* earliest) surviving accounts of the Lao Tzu story.

It should be noted that the massive history of Si Ma Qian, which relates events stretching all the way back to the reign of the Yellow Emperor, contains numerous clues that many of its personages are actually metaphorical incarnations of celestial figures (including the Yellow Emperor himself, who has many aspects which connect him to Saturn and to Saturnian figures the world over, some of which are explored in *Hamlet's Mill*).

Si Ma Qian's text 太史公書 (*Records of the Grand Historian*, also simply called the 史記 *Records of the Scribe*) gives the Lao Tzu story in these words:

> Lao-Tze cultivated the Tao and its attributes, the chief aim of his studies being how to keep himself concealed and remain unknown. He continued to reside at the capitol of Chau, but after a long time, seeing the decay of the dynasty, he left it and went away to the barrier-gate, leading out of the kingdom on the northwest. Yin Hsi, the warden of the gate, said to him, "You are about to withdraw yourself out of sight. Let me insist on your first composing for me a book." On this,

Lao-Tze wrote a book in two parts, setting forth his views on the Tao and its attributes, in more than 5,000 characters. He then went away, and it is not known where he died. He was a superior man, who liked to keep himself unknown.[481]

While it is not mentioned in this version from Si Ma Qian, there is a tradition that Lao Tzu traveled on the back of a water buffalo, and it is upon the back of this animal that Lao Tzu is often depicted, riding towards the west and leaving the kingdom of China, as in the painting by Zhang Lu 張路 (1464 - 1538), shown on page 742.

Other later texts and traditions also elaborate upon the story a bit further, describing the warden of the gate (尹喜 Yin Hsi or Yinxi) as desiring to become the disciple of Lao Tzu, and as being accepted by the master (usually after various professed rejections by Lao Tzu, and tests of Yinxi's determination to follow the Tao). In many of those stories, Yinxi leaves his post at the western gate to follow the Old Master into the west as his disciple, and the two are never again seen in China (in some accounts, they traveled to India).

In one interesting variation, recorded in the seventh-century (AD) text entitled 三洞珠囊 (literally "Three Grottoes Pearl Purse"), or *Purse of Pearls from the Three Grottoes*, sometimes called the *Pearly Bag of the Three Caverns*, Lao Tzu accepts Yinxi but tells him to live alone practicing the Tao for three years. After three years, Yinxi is to send a black sheep to the market, which will be the agreed-upon sign to Lao Tzu that his disciple is ready to meet again.[482]

Although the story of Lao Tzu departing the kingdom on the back of a water buffalo seems to be rather short on details that could identify it as belonging to the category of Star Myth, I believe there are many reasons to conclude that this story, as with so many others which have come down to us from ancient times, is in fact based upon the celestial cycles.

The Tao Te Ching itself is filled with details which seem to relate to the turning of the great Wheel of the heavens, and to the endless "rising and falling" of the myriad things 萬物 (the very concept we discovered to be central to the message of the life of the Buddha and reflected in the celestial clues contained in the ancient Buddhist accounts and traditions).

Let's begin with the identity of the Old Master himself, Lao Tzu, whose name in Chinese characters is written 老子 which individually are the symbols for "Old Man" and "child."

The first word 老 is pronounced *lao* in Mandarin and *louh* (rhymes with "dough") in Cantonese, and is used as a term of respect to this day in common conversation, and placed in front of the person's family surname, as in English in previous centuries we might say "Old Man Brown" or "Old Man Miller," although in modern times this usage is now no longer seen in English (or at least is no longer considered to be polite).

The second word 子 is pronounced *jai* or *dzai* in Cantonese and *dze* or *dzuh* in Mandarin, and although it is said that in ancient times this word signified "Master," it is certain that it most commonly means a *son*, a *young child* or a *descendant* in general.

Why might a figure with such a name, "Old Man / Child," be described as riding on a buffalo and departing into the west? Does the fact that Lao Tzu's famous encounter takes place at the "barrier-gate" have any possible significance? And what are we to make of the fact that Si Ma Qian tells us that Lao Tzu liked to "keep himself concealed and remain unknown"?

In previous examinations of myths involving a water buffalo (particularly in the myth of the goddess Durga, who slays MahishAsura who has the head of a water buffalo, as well as in the story of Shango and the hartebeest described on page 80 of this volume) we argued for a connection with the zodiac constellation of Taurus the Bull in the night sky. I would suggest that the story of Lao Tzu departing from China towards the west, while riding on the back of a water buffalo, is connected with the same important zodiac constellation.

Si Ma Qian's account says that Lao Tzu departed through a "barrier gate" and it is at this "gate" that he was stopped and asked to write down his wisdom before departing from sight forever.

If the buffalo on which Lao Tzu rides away is related to Taurus, then it is also likely that this "barrier gate" represents more than just the boundary of the constellation itself, or even the western horizon into which Taurus (and all other zodiac constellations, in their turn) will eventually sink due to the nightly turning of the earth on its axis. As we have already discussed many times (such as in the Native American myth of the Old Man and his Daughter, or the great cedar door in the Gilgamesh epic), these "gates" and "doorways" and other narrow passages found in the ancient myths can often be tied to the "crossing points" of the equinoxes, where the line of the ecliptic crosses the celestial equator twice per year, and where the sun's journey crosses from the "upper half" where days are longer than nights to the "lower half" where nights are longer than days, and back again.

If so, then it is certainly a possibility that the departure of Lao Tzu has to do with the end of a specific precessional Age: the end of the Age of Taurus, which gave way to the Age of Aries.

The fact that in some legends Yinxi is said to send a "black sheep" to the marketplace as a signal for Lao Tzu to come forth and meet him would appear to be additional evidence which suggests that this story should be understood in celestial terms. Aries the Ram is the zodiac house which *follows* the zodiac house of Taurus in terms of precessional Ages, even though Aries *leads* Taurus across the night sky during the nightly rotation from east to west. In other words, in the shift of Ages from the Age of Taurus to the Age of Aries, the Ram of Aries is "sent forth" while Taurus is still "in hiding" below the horizon – as a signal for Lao Tzu to come out of hiding and meet with his disciple Yinxi.

If the tradition of Lao Tzu riding a buffalo associates him with the constellation Taurus, and with the end of the Age of Taurus and the arrival of the Age of Aries, then this opens up an entirely new perspective on the *name* of 老子 ("Old Man" / "child") as well, and on the traditions or legends, easy to dismiss as mere fabulous embellishments, that the Old Master was born with a full head of white hair, even as an infant.

There are even popular stories in which the mother of 老子 is said to have conceived when watching a falling star -- i.e., another example of an "immaculate conception" or virgin birth -- and that she then carried the baby within her womb for sixty-two long years, only delivering the child when she leaned against a plum tree. For this reason, 老子 was born already having a long grey or white beard and long earlobes: such traditions seem to contradict the conventional argument that the second character in Lao Tzu's name, 子, signifies "Master" and instead suggests that the character signifies "child," just as it still does to this day.

If Lao Tzu represents a point on the Great Wheel of the zodiac (and a precessional Age - the Age of Taurus), then the designation of his name in terms of both "old man" and "child" may well be intended to convey the very same concept that we are familiar with in the western traditions of "Father Time" and "Baby New Year" which were (and in some cases still are) often depicted in magazines and newspapers each year at the changing of the annual cycle.

The old "year," represented by an aged figure with a long beard and bent posture, gave way to a "new year," represented by a plump and happy little baby, often depicted as carrying the same accessories or props as the old man (such as a large sickle or scythe, and sometimes an hourglass as well). The symbolism dramatizes the fact that the point of New Year is simultaneously an *ending-point* and a *starting-point* on the circle. Below is one such illustration from New Year 1910 (I have added the Chinese characters for the name of 老子):

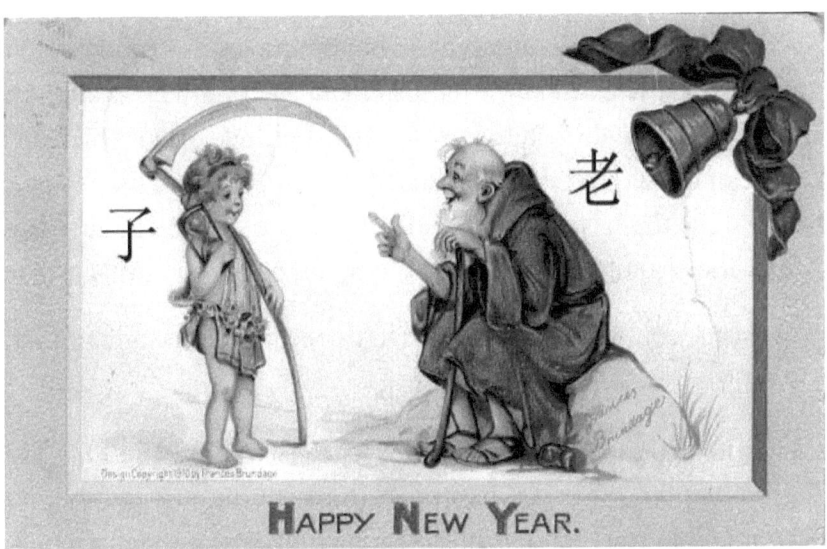

HAPPY NEW YEAR.

In other words, it is very possible that the combination of the symbol for an *old man* and the symbol for *a child* in the name of Lao Tzu is intended to convey the very same concept: he stands at the ending point of one Age and the beginning of another, just as Taurus or any other sign in the zodiac wheel can be seen as an "ending point" and a "beginning point" on the circle (which of course has no actual beginning and end).

Now recall that we have already had occasion to see this very same concept being dramatized in other Star Myths, such as the birth of the Buddha - in which the aged Asita comes to visit the parents of the child, to foretell the significance of the child's life, and makes clear that he (the old sage) will be leaving the stage before the child will ever accomplish all these things. Similarly, in the New Testament scriptures the aged Simeon comes to the parents of the baby to foretell the significance of the birth, and to declare that having seen the birth of the awaited one, Simeon can now depart in peace from this life.

Those familiar with the New Testament scriptures will also perhaps have remembered by now that Christ declares himself to be "the alpha and the omega," the beginning and the end, which proclamation is celestial in nature, made by one who is himself identified with a sign on the great circle - a circle upon which any point can be said to be *the end* and *the beginning* simultaneously. See also the discussion of the god Khepri (the young sun) and Ra-Atum (the old sun) from ancient Egypt, on page 290 of this text.

Now what could any of this have to do with the message of Dao De Jing?   Everything.

Listen to Professor Victor H. Mair's translation of the Dao De Jing's Chapter 48. It is Chapter 48 in the traditional numbering of chapters in the Dao De Jing, but is numbered as Chapter 11 in Professor Mair's 1990 translation based on the Ma Wang Dui silk texts (because in the Ma Wang Dui texts, the chapters are arranged differently from the arrangement which would come to be used in later centuries, and which is now more familiar to us):

The pursuit of learning results in daily increase,
Hearing the Way leads to daily decrease.
Decrease and again decrease,
    until you reach nonaction.
Through nonaction,
    no action is left undone.

Should one desire to gain all under heaven,
One should remain ever free of involvements.
For,
    Just as surely as one becomes involved,
    One is unfit for gaining all under heaven.[483]

Does this teaching sound at all familiar? If you have read the two preceding chapters, discussing the Bhagavad Gita in the Mahabharata and discussing the story of life of the Buddha, then it should.

"The pursuit of learning results in daily increase" -- daily increase of entanglements, daily increase of attachments, daily increase of "*shoulds*" and "*coulds*" ("I should have . . ." or "I could . . ."), of casting one's mind forward into the future and backwards into the past: the daily increase in the netting that this chapter refers to as "involvements."

And yet the advice of Lord Krishna in the Bhagavad Gita (as Victor Mair points out in his outstanding and very helpful Afterword to that 1990 translation) is "the ideal of action without attachment."[484]

And how can we achieve such an ideal?

Perhaps it has something to do with the understanding that the beginning point and the ending point are the same.

Perhaps it has something to do with observing the turning of the great Wheel, while at the same time remaining unattached to it.

Perhaps it has something to do with the curious status of the constellation Ophiuchus, the so-called "thirteenth zodiac sign" -- part of the wheel but not part of the zodiac. There is another tradition that Lao Tzu had twelve previous incarnations, and that the Lao Tzu who wrote down the Dao De Jing before he rode off into the west was the thirteenth.

One could even make the argument that the descriptions of Lao Tzu as having *long ears* (or long ear-lobes) might have something to do with an association with the constellation Ophiuchus, with its two serpent-halves somehow envisioned as enormous ears, although I would only suggest that as an outside possibility.

In any event, the text of the Dao De Jing itself contains the theme of the arising and passing away again of all things (or of the "myriad" or "ten thousand things" 萬物), the unfolding of all things from the Dao and their eventual re-folding back into the Dao.

Discussing this concept in his Afterword, Professor Mair says: "The Tao, ineffable and without attribute, is identified with nonbeing, yet it is the source of all creation, which is characterized as being."[485]

The interplay of these two, "is" and "is not," and the arising of "is" out of "is not" and back again, runs through the text.[486]

Professor Mair discusses the arising of the myriad things out of the undifferentiated, undefined, undefinable Tao. Explaining the phrase 萬物 "myriad things" (which Professor Mair says is pronounced "*wawn-woo*"), he writes:

Literally "ten thousand objects," this expression refers to all things in the universe that have existence or being, in contrast to their origin -- the Tao -- which is without existence. The figure "ten thousand" signifies the vast variety of creatures and things in the world. It stands in opposition to the unity of the Tao from which they spring. The Old Chinese pronunciation of *wan-wu* was roughly *myanh-var.* This expression is clearly related to English "many varieties." The connection between *myanh* and "many" is obvious without having to cite earlier Indo-European antecedents. Still more striking is the affinity between Chinese *var* and the Indo-European root *var* of "variety," since both originally referred to the multi-colored fur of animals (compare English "vair" and "miniver"). The earliest character used to write *wu* actually depicts a speckled bovine.[487]

This insight into the etymology of the words is fascinating -- as is the connection between Old Chinese and words which survive in modern English. Another example of (older) words in English with the same *var* root would be "variegated," which we have already encountered in discussing important mythical concepts, such as Joseph's many-colored coat and its parallels in the Mahabharata, including Arjuna's miraculous many-hued bow Govinda, and Draupadi's miraculous many-hued sari supplied to her by the invisible Lord Krishna so that Dushashana could not strip her naked in front of the assembly after the disastrous dice game.

Notably, all of the figures with which this "multi-colored" description is used (Joseph's coat in Genesis, and Arjuna and Draupadi in Mahabharata) appear to be associated with the same constellation in the heavens: Sagittarius.

As we've already discussed at length, Sagittarius and Scorpio flank the widest and brightest section of the Milky Way -- the Galactic Core, where stars in our galaxy are now thought to be born. It is also the region which contains the Dark Rift, seen by the ancient Maya as the galactic *birth canal*. Additionally, the region of Sagittarius in the heavens marked the zodiac sign through which the sun traveled just prior to the "great turning point of the year" during the Age of Aries: the point of winter solstice, the point of "second birth." All of these celestial connections appear to have resonance with the arising of the "myriad things" in the Dao De Jing -- and the insight provided by Professor Mair that the word 物 in Old Chinese has etymological connections to the root *var*, which shows up in our words "variety" and "variegated," which may have celestial connections in the ancient system with the constellation Sagittarius.

Even more astonishing, unless my Chinese character analysis is mistaken, is the fact that the other word in this word-pair 萬物 (the first word in the pair, 萬, representing "myriad" or "ten thousand") is also the original symbol for the word "scorpion"! This introduces the almost incredible possibility that the important phrase 萬物 in Dao De Jing points us towards Scorpio (萬) and Sagittarius – and thus towards the Galactic Center between the two, which (according to modern astronomers, may be the origin of all the stars in our galaxy).

One other very noteworthy point in Professor Mair's comments on the phrase 萬物 should be mentioned in passing, and that is the assertion that the earliest form of the character used to write the word *wu* (the second word in the phrase "myriad things") "actually depicts a speckled bovine." Although he does not pursue it in his Afterword to his translation of Dao De Jing, this observation by Victor Mair may well open a window upon a very confusing and poorly understood passage of scripture in the book of Genesis, in which Jacob's uncle Laban agrees to Jacob's suggestion that Jacob's compensation for his labor shall be "all the speckled and spotted cattle, and all the brown cattle among the sheep, and the spotted and speckled among the goats" (Genesis 30: 32). Jacob takes rods of green poplar, of hazel, and of chesnut, and "pilled white strakes in them," and sets them before the flocks in their watering troughs, so that they should conceive "cattle ringstraked, speckled, and spotted," which (unlikely as it seems) duly occurs (Genesis 30: 37 - 39).

Does this passage somehow connect to Sagittarius and its connection with "variegation"? I do not have enough evidence at this time to say for certain -- although it seems to be a strong possibility. More importantly, however, we can at this time say with a fair degree of confidence that the great turning of the cycles of the heavens were connected in this ancient system with the endless arising and passing away of the "myriad things" -- with their arising out of the undefined Infinite, and their endless return back to that same boundless Tao (as Professor Mair puts it, "the endless return of those myriad creatures to the cosmic principle from which they arose").[488]

Indeed, this great spoked wheel (which we also saw mentioned prominently in the story of the birth of the Buddha, and which we will see again in the famous vision of Ezekiel, discussed in Volume Three), is described in the Dao De Jing, in a well-known passage in Chapter 11 (under the conventional numeration).

There, we read (in the translation of Victor Mair, in the chapter numbered 55 in his arrangement of the Ma Wang Dui text):

Thirty spokes converge on a single hub,
but it is in the space where there is nothing
that the usefulness of the cart lies.[489]

Professor Mair also notes the importance of this passage, and points out its powerful resonance with an ancient Sanskrit text (the Mundaka Upanishad) which uses a very similar metaphor for the internal energy channels in the human body which all "come together like spokes in the hub of a wheel."[490] It is at this hub, the text of the Upanishad tells us, where the Infinite principle and the individual soul come together and "move about, becoming manifold."[491]

As Professor Mair points out, these texts clearly have to do with an ancient and esoteric system of Yogic meditation and energy circulation, which by the second century BC "had received explicit and elaborate codification in written form."[492] But it is also apparent, I believe, that the ancient understanding of what was going on, involving the harmonizing of the individual self with the Infinite, through practices including meditation and Yoga and the circulation of prana or chi, was expressed using celestial metaphor and the mighty cycles of the infinite realm above our heads. Certainly metaphors such as the wheel of thirty spokes evoke other celestial metaphor we have visited earlier in this volume, and which we will see again -- and so apparently do many other aspects of the Dao De Jing and the traditions surrounding its creation.

There are of course many more myths and traditions from the vast culture of ancient China which could themselves form the basis of an entire volume (or, more appropriately, a multi-volume series) which explored them in search of evidence of celestial metaphor. Some of these I have touched upon in previously published blog posts and videos over the years, including:

- ➤ the story of the cowherd and the weaver girl and the famous magpie bridge (which is explicitly celestial in its content, and which is very notable for many reasons, among them being the fact that "weaving at the loom" is an important mythical component found several times in the Odyssey and other Greek myths, and in the Norse myths, and in the Bible including in the Star Myth of Samson),
- ➤ or the story of the Jade Emperor and his loss of the Bird of Heaven, and the subsequent threat to the survival of humanity on earth (averted by the Emperor's daughter) celebrated each year at the Lantern Festival which marks the end of the Chinese Lunar New Year celebration,
- ➤ or the story of Da Mo (Bodhidharma) and Shen Guang (discussed in the subsequent chapter),

And many, many others -- far too many to include in this volume. Our purpose has been to demonstrate that the same world-wide system includes the traditions of ancient China: the ancient system is truly global in its scope. As well, this chapter was intended to open some new perspectives on the teaching of the Dao De Jing, by relating its content and message to the celestial cycles which it invokes, and which it uses to help us to grasp what it is trying to convey to our understanding.

Indeed, I am convinced that the ancient myths are all preserving and conveying a very similar message, regarding right action without attachment -- a message which we can better grasp and embody as we meditate upon the vast and endless cycles by which all things are consantly unfolding out of, and folding back into, the infinite and ineffable Tao.

757

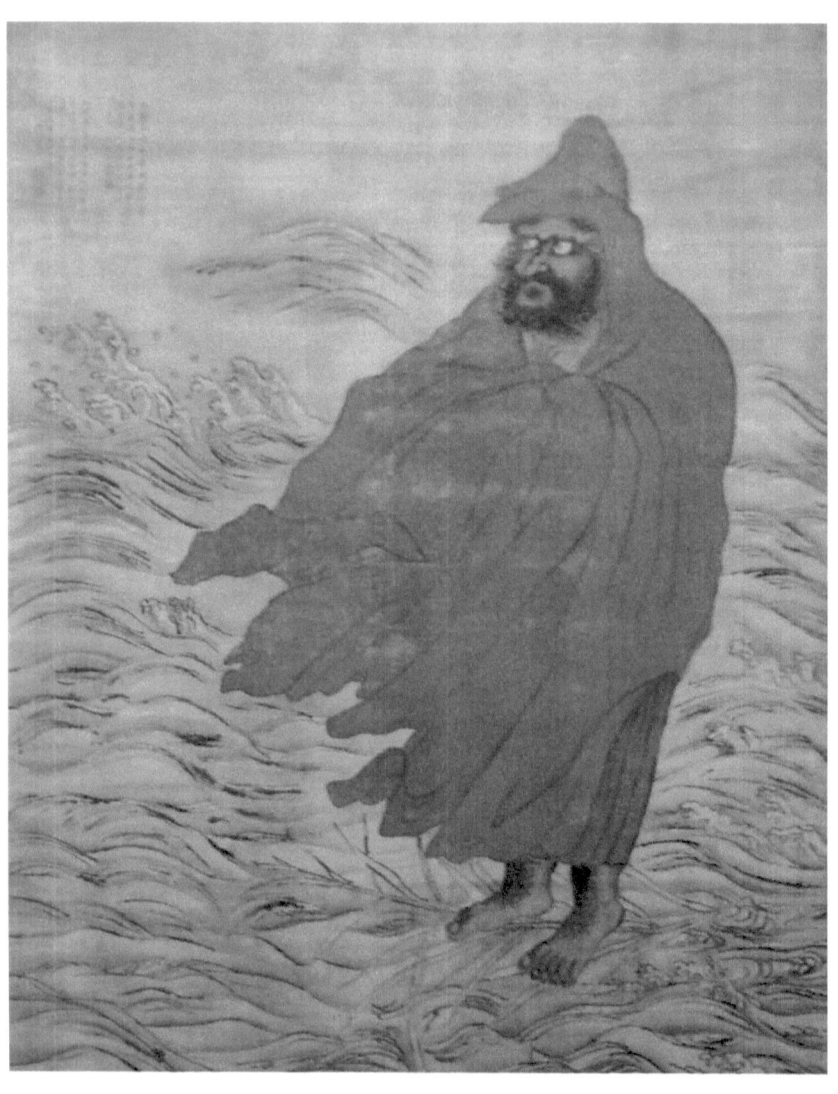

758

Da Mo or Bodhidharma

The figure of Da Mo is credited with the propagation of a new understanding of Buddhism which would transform not only China but many cultures in the surrounding region, including those of Vietnam, Korea, and eventually Japan, and which would come to be known as *Ch'an* or *Chan* Buddhism -- called in Korea *Sŏn* and in Japan *Zen* Buddhism.

The word *Ch'an* is considered to be a Chinese adaptation of the Sanskrit word *Dhyana*, meaning "mind training" -- with a particular emphasis on meditation. Philosopher Hu Shih (1891 - 1962), however, once declared that "Chinese Zennism arose not out of Indian yoga or Dhyana but as a revolt against it,"[493] although this argument could certainly be debated, as the actual origins of Ch'an or Zen are shrouded in legend, and thus very difficult to examine objectively.

Once again, as with the figures of Lao Tzu and the Buddha himself, in Da Mo we find a figure who is often considered to have been historical, but whose life story in the accounts show unmistakeable signs of the very same ancient pattern of celestial metaphor we have encountered again and again in sacred traditions around the world.

Tracing the early history of Ch'an Buddhism in China lies outside of the scope of this volume, although it is a fascinating area of investigation. We will here concern ourselves with the most well-known aspects of the legend of Da Mo, for the purpose of examining their incorporation of the ancient worldwide system which we have been tracing all the way around the globe, and the points of resonance with the esoteric message we have glimpsed within the other celestial myths explored in previous chapters.

Chapter Twenty

Discussing the earliest accounts of the arrival of Bodhidharma, who would come to be called Da Mo (達磨) in China and later Daruma in Japan, Andy Ferguson writes in *Tracking Bodhidharma: A Journey to the Heart of Chinese Culture* that:

> The most widely believed account of Bodhidharma's life claims that he arrived in China in the year 527 in Guangzhou. He then immediately traveled to Nanjing at the invitation of Emperor Wu of the Liang dynasty. Emperor Wu believed deeply in Buddhism, elevating it to the status of a state religion. He invited Buddhist teachers from all over Asia to visit his palace and teach the religion's philosophy, and tradition says that Bodhidharma was likewise invited to perform this service. The central story that Zen has preserved about Bodidarma is that when he met Emperor Wu in Nanjing at the latters invitation in 527 CE, the two did not have the same views about proper Buddhist theory and practice. Emperor Wu expected Bodhidharma to praise him for the material and public support he had provided to Buddhism, but instead Bodhidharma rejected the emperor's religious activities. This was, of course, a big affront to the "Bodhisattva Emperor." Thereafter, says this traditional account, Bodhidharma crossed the Yang-tse River (folklore says he did so on a single stalk of bamboo) and proceeded north to live at Shaolin Temple in North Central China. He allegedly lived in a cave on a mountain behind Shaolin Temple for nine years before dying in the year 536.[494]

This traditional outline, Andy Ferguson writes, "is first seen in texts from about four hundred years after Bodhidharma lived," and "is almost certainly not an accurate account of Bodhidharma's life."[495] Ferguson writes:

Da Mo or Bodhidharma

Serious scholars believe that a book called the *Continued Biographies of Eminent Monks* (which I'll hereafter call the *Continued Biographies*), a book written around the year 650, a time much closer to when Bodhidharma lived, provides a far more reliable account of his life. The author, the monk Daoxuan, probably knew Zen monks who were Bodhidharma's second generation of disciples.[496]

I would suggest, however, that it is very possible that the figure we know of as Da Mo (or Bodhidharma, or Daruma) was entirely legendary (or at least that the story which has come down to us about his life is based more on celestial metaphor than on any terrestrial history), and that accounts written closer to the year he allegedly came to China are not necessarily any more accurate than later accounts.

Professor Jeffrey L. Broughton, Professor Emeritus of Religious Studies at California State University, Long Beach and a specialist in Buddhist Studies and early Ch'an texts, explains that the very earliest biography of Bodhidharma was compiled by "T'an-lin, an erudite Sanskritist active in the first half of the sixth century in North China" but one whose "scholarly credentials eventually led to his demotion within the Ch'an genealogy."[497] Of the record left by T'an-lin, Professor Broughton writes:

> The *Biography* is exceedingly simple. T'an-lin gives us but four points: the Dharma Master was the third son of a great South Indian king; he "crossed distant mountains and seas" to propagate Buddhism in North China; some ridiculed him; he acquired two younger Chinese disciples who served him for several years.[498]

Of the record of Bodhidharma's life found in the *Continued Biographies of Eminent Monks* by the monk Daoxuan (whose name is also rendered *Tao-hsüan* in a different system of transcribing Chinese into Latin alphabetical characters), "the first redaction of which was completed in 645,"[499] Professor Broughton writes that:

> The *Continued Biographies of Eminent Monks* contains not only a Bodhidharma entry, but an entry on the Dharma Master's disciple Hui-k'o. In addition, in his general comments at the end of his section on meditation practioners, Tao-hsüan ventures a critique of Bodhidharma's style of meditation. The Bodhidharma entry is nothing more than a very slightly reworked version of T'an-lin's *Biography* and *Two Entrances*. The only real addition is the mention of the age of 150, which Tao-hsüan clearly picked up from the *Record of the Buddhist Monasteries of Lo-yang*. Tao-hsüan provides T'an-lin's third son of an Indian king with a Brahmin or priestly lineage and has the disciples Hui-k'o and Tao-yü serving for four or five years rather than T'an-lin's several years.[500]

Professor Broughton notes another addition from Daoxuan or Tao-hsüan, and that is a "specific itinerary" for Da Mo's travels: "a sea voyage to South China and a subsequent trek across the Yangtze River to the North."[501] Ostensibly taking the histories of Da Mo's travels as literal and historical, Professor Broughton notes that based on this itinerary and the statement in *Continued Biographies of Eminent Monks* which says that Da Mo arrived on China's southern coast within the boundaries controled by the Sung Dynasty, "we might deduce that he must have arrived by 479, the year in which the Sung fell."[502]

Again, however, I would argue that it is quite possible that the stories of Bodhidharma or Da Mo are describing an entirely celestial figure, whose "travel itinerary" moves through the starry realms above our heads. Exhibit A in such an argument would be the fact that we have already seen numerous examples in which a mighty river, one which is central to a culture (such as the Ganga or Ganges in India) will be associated with the great "river of stars" which stretches through the heavenly landscape: the Milky Way. The fact that Da Mo is said to have crossed the great Yangtze River of China (the longest river in all of Asia, and the third-longest in the world) on a stalk of bamboo indicates that the river he crosses in the ancient accounts is no ordinary terrestrial river (nor even an *extraordinary* terrestrial river)!

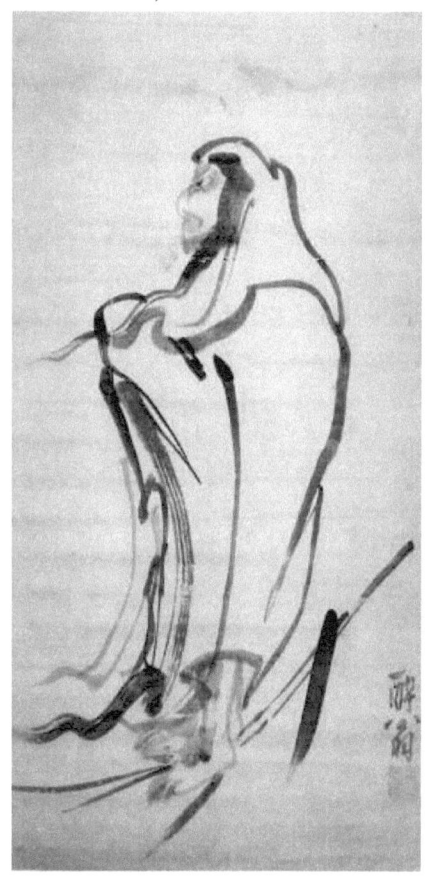

The crossing of the great river upon a bamboo reed is in fact one of the most well-known and oft-depicted episodes in the Da Mo legend. At right we see one example, by Gim Myeong-guk of Korea (c. 1600 - c. 1665), showing Da Mo standing on a broken branch. Another example can be found at the start of this chapter, showing Daruma crossing the water while his robes and hood are whipped by the winds. If you look closely beneath his feet, you can make out the bamboo reed upon which he is standing. Somehow, this reed enables him to practically "walk on water."

Obviously, no amount of meditation that I know of will enable anyone, even a Zen master or the son of a king, to stand upon a broken bamboo branch and cross a river -- but as we have already seen in the discussion of the myths of ancient India, the constellation Scorpio is sometimes described as a "broken branch" or a "broken reed" (see the discussion of Indra's battle with the dragon Vrtra on pages 606 - 607 of this volume). Scorpio does resemble a reed (which is why the "baby cast adrift" oicotype often mentions reeds or rushes, such as the story of Moses among the bulrushes), and many verses in the Old Testament scriptures make reference to a "broken" or a "bruised reed."

If Scorpio plays the broken bamboo reed upon which Da Mo crosses the mighty Yangtze, then what constellation plays the role of Da Mo himself? Obviously, that would the one "standing upon" the broken reed of Scorpio: Ophiuchus, who appears to be standing upright upon the form of the constellation Scorpio, and "riding" this reed across the heavenly river of the Milky Way:

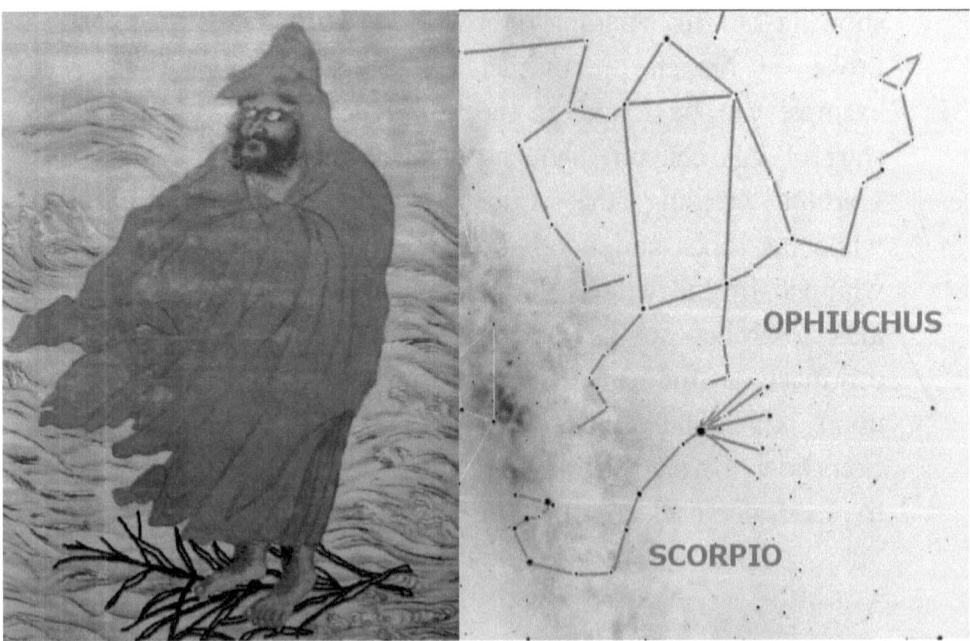

In the image on the preceding page, I have (in order to enable greater ease of visibility) darkened the outline of the artwork's original broken bamboo reed beneath the feet of the figure of Daruma, upon which the sage is standing as he crosses the great river. Juxtaposed with the star-chart of the constellations Ophiuchus and Scorpio, it is easy to see just how much the story (and the traditional depictions of this episode in art) resembles the heavenly original.

Note too that the tradition, mentioned in even the earliest accounts we have of the legend of Bodhidharma, that the traveling master is the *son of a great king*, is also consistent with a celestial identification of Da Mo with the constellation Ophiuchus. As we have discussed regarding numerous mythical figures thus far, characters associated with one constellation will often be described in myth as being *descended from* characters associated with the constellation *directly above* them.

In the case of Da Mo, who appears to be associated with the constellation Ophiuchus based on the legend of his crossing of the river on a reed, we can look upwards in the night sky and perceive the "great king" from whom Bodhidharma is said to be descended: the powerful form of the constellation Hercules.

Numerous other Star Myths can be referenced in order to support this assertion (many of them already examined earlier in this same volume), including the descent of Shu (associated with Ophiuchus) from Atum (associated with Hercules) in ancient Egypt, or the descent of Shiva (associated with Ophiuchus) from the head of Brahman (associated with Hercules) in ancient India, or the descent of Athena (associated with Ophiuchus) from the head of Zeus (associated with Hercules). Thus, I would argue that the description of Bodhidharma as the son of a king could be seen as an indication that the sage is associated with Ophiuchus, and as additional confirmatory evidence backing up the identification with Ophiuchus which we find in the story of Da Mo's crossing of the Yangtze River on a single stalk of bamboo.

Note too that the crossing of the river in the "travel itinerary" given in the early accounts takes Da Mo from South China into North China. Recall the argument of Virginia Lee Davis and Jane B. Sellers (introduced on pages 361 - 362 of this present volume) that the constellations on the side of the Milky Way containing the north celestial pole were considered to be in the "northern kingdom" in the system of ancient myth. Ophiuchus and Scorpio, as can be seen on the full-sky star-chart found on page 388 of this volume, appear to be just emerging into the "northern half" side of the Milky Way band. In other words, the reputed path of Da Mo's travels appears to conform *to the layout of the constellations* in the sky. Da Mo, corresponding to Ophiuchus, can be seen to have crossed the "great river" (the Milky Way) upon the "broken reed" (Scorpio) and in doing so to have moved *from the South into the North* of the heavenly landscape.

All of the analysis thus far suggests that the storyline, even as it is presented in the very earliest accounts, is based upon a heavenly pattern, and not upon literal, terrestrial, historical events.

The continuing adventures of Da Mo after crossing the river into the north of China would appear to further support his identification with the figure of Ophiuchus, and to further support the conclusion that the life of Da Mo as it has been told down through the centuries is actually based upon celestial metaphor.

The next important detail of the Bodhidharma story we will examine is the sage's reputation for tremendous periods of motionless meditation. Tradition relates that Da Mo made his way north to Mount Sung, and the famous monastery of Shaolin located there. There, it is said,

> he took to sitting-in-meditation before a wall, keeping silence throughout the day. This mystified all who saw him, and they called him "the wall-gazing Brahman."

> With regard to the term "wall-gazing" (*pi-kuan* in Chinese), many have taken it in the literal sense. But some have given it a spiritual interpretation by saying that the word "wall" has the connotation of shutting out external dust or distractions. Following this line, Suzuki observes that "the underlying meaning of 'wall-contempation' must be found in the subjective condition of a Zen master, which is highly concentrated and rigidly exclusive of all ideas and sensuous images."[503]

Whether or not this "wall-gazing" is taken "in the literal sense" by practitioners of meditation who follow Bodhidharma's example, there are a number of reasons why we, as Star Myth investigators, should not take the *stories themselves* too literally.

We have already seen evidence suggesting an identification between Da Mo and the constellation Ophiuchus, and the descriptions of his "wall-gazing" meditation only strengthen that association. First, we have by now seen numerous examples of ancient myths in which Ophiuchus plays the role of a hill or mound or mountain: the fact that Da Mo seeks out Mount Sung in order to begin his famous meditation suggests the possibility that the accounts and traditions are giving us hints of his celestial identity (Ophiuchus) with this detail.

Second, we have also seen evidence that Ophiuchus can play the role of a hall or temple or pavilion in myth, and thus it is quite likely that the accounts which tell us that Da Mo made his way to the Shaolin Temple in order to begin his long meditation may be yet another clue that we are dealing with an Ophiuchus-figure in these stories.

Third, we have even seen evidence which identifies the constellation Ophiuchus with a wall! Turn back in this volume, for example, to the story of Atrahasis in the myths of ancient Mesopotamia, in which the god Enki (or Ea) whispers to Atrahasis through the wall instructions which will enable Atrahasis to build a boat and survive the coming Deluge (see discussion on pages 523 - 525 of this volume). In that discussion, we also pointed to an identification of Ophiuchus with the wall over which David tells us he leaps, mentioned in Psalm 18: 29 and also in 2 Samuel 22: 30. Thus, whatever the meaning of "wall-gazing" as a form of meditation, the mention of a wall (along with the mention of a hill and of a temple) is a clue that we are here dealing with an Ophiuchus-figure, in the person of Bodhidharma or Da Mo.

We have already had occasion to observe, in myths from other cultures, that figures who sit for extended periods of meditation are almost invariably associated with the constellation Ophiuchus. We saw evidence, for example, that the Lord Shiva is associated with Ophiuchus. Later, we saw evidence to associate the figure of the Buddha with the same constellation.

There is also an account contained within the Mahabharata of ancient India, an account not among those we examined in our discussion of Mahabharata in previous chapters, concerning a sage named Rishi Chyavana who meditated so long and so deeply that he was eventually covered over by a termite mound or ant-hill! This episode is found in Book 3, section 122 of the Mahabharata, and is recounted to the Pandavas by another Rishi named Lomasa, during their time of exile from Hastinapura. Speaking to Yudhishthira, Rishi Lomasa explains:

> 'A son was born to the great saint Bhrigu, Chyavana by name. And he, of an exceedingly resplendent form, began to practise austerities by the side of yonder lake. And, O Pandu's son! O protector of men! he of mighty energy assumed the posture called *Vira*, quiet and still like an inanimate post, and for a long period, remained at the same spot of ground. And he was turned into an anthill covered with creepers. And after the lapse of a long period, swarms of ants enveloped him. And covered all over with ants, the sagacious saint looked exactly like a heap of earth. And he went on practising austerities, enveloped on all sides with that ant-hill.'[504]

This story adds still further confirmatory evidence for seeing an association between the constellation Ophiuchus and the various figures in myth described as meditating for unbelievably long periods of time. Note that we have already seen evidence for a connection between Ophiuchus and a termite-mound described in myth (in the very first chapter of this volume, in the discussion of a myth from the Indigenous Aboriginal people of Australia, on pages 42 - 43).

That Chyavana, who meditates until he is covered-over with an ant-hill, is also associated with Ophiuchus can be inferred from additional clues included in the text of Mahabharata cited above, such as the fact that his place of meditation is *by the side of a lake*, and the fact that he is described as being as "quiet and still as an inanimate post" (a *post* being another common manifestation of Ophiuchus in myth, such as the myths in which Ophiuchus plays the role of the central post that becomes the churning-stick of heaven, during the episode of the Churning of the Ocean of Milk).

Thus, the story of Chyavana who meditates until he is buried beneath an ant-hill simultaneously confirms the connection between Ophiuchus and mounds of all sorts, as well as the connection between Ophiuchus and deeply-meditating figures in ancient myth -- and strengthens our argument that Da Mo in his wall-gazing meditation can be seen to be yet another manifestation of this same vital constellation.

The severity of Da Mo's meditation is similarly super-human. In an introduction to his translation of the *Zen Teaching of Bodhidharma*, Red Pine (Bill Porter) writes:

> To keep from falling asleep while meditating, he cut off his eyelids, and where they fell, tea bushes grew. Since then, tea has become the beverage of not only monks but everyone in the Orient. Faithful to this tradition, artists invariably depict Bodhidharma with bulging, lidless eyes.[505]

Note that the tradition of tea bushes (or tea trees) growing from the severed eyelids of Da Mo is obviously legend -- and one which may well have a celestial origin that adds still further evidence for an identification with Ophiuchus. We have already seen an absolutely overwhelming number of myths in which the whirling form of Hercule is envisioned as a tree or a bush (and we will see more examples in subsequent volumes in this series). Often, this tree is envisioned as growing out of the "serpent-head" feature on the western side of the constellation Ophiuchus -- a feature which we have already seen to play the role of an eye in numerous myths!

See for example the discussion on pages 266 and 366 of this volume.

Instead of playing the role of an *eye* that has been torn out, however, as in the story of the "Contendings of Seth and Horus" from ancient Egypt, this "serpent-head" could instead play the role of an *eyelid* that has been cut off and is now being held in the "hand" of Ophiuchus on the constellation's western side:

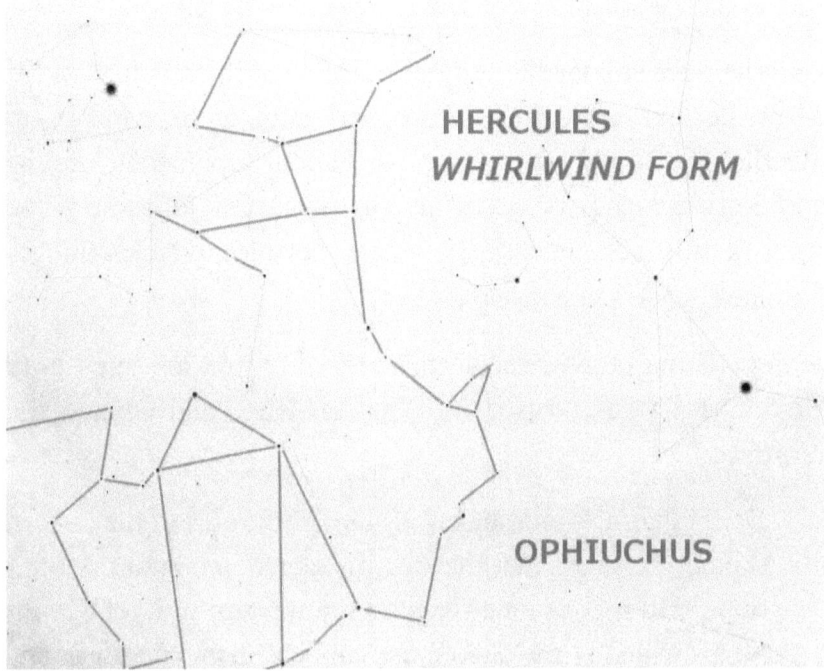

In the above diagram, I have added a "connecting line" which could be envisioned (and very evidently *was envisioned* by the keepers of the ancient worldwide system) joining the "whirling form" of the constellation Hercules to the "serpent-head" feature on the west side of Ophiuchus (the right side as we face the star-chart on this page). This line, when envisioned, enables us to see the "tree-like" outline of Hercules growing up out of the "serpent-head" on the west side of Ophiuchus. If the serpent-head feature is indeed the celestial "eyelid" of Da Mo, which the sage has cut off in order to meditate without interruption, then this identification explains the rather strange tradition which informs us that the first tea-bushes or tea-trees grew up from the severed eyelids of Bodhidharma!

Once again, we see evidence which points very strongly towards an identification of Da Mo (Bodhidharma) with the constellation Ophiuchus -- and for a celestial interpretation of the events traditionally associated with the Zen ancestor's life.

And there are still further examples related in the accounts of Da Mo's life and adventures which add even more evidence to identify the sage with the constellation Ophiuchus, if any additional evidence is needed at this point. One of these is the story of Shen Guang (神光), whose devotion enables him to become Da Mo's first disciple.

Jeffrey Broughton relates this legend, picking up after Bodhidharma has crossed the Yangtze River and entered the North:

> Bodhidharma's journey brings him to the area of the eastern capital Lo-yang and the nearby sacred mountain Mount Sung. He spends nine years on the western peak of Mount Sung, which is the site of the famous Shao-lin Monastery. (This western peak is known as "Few Caves" or "Small Caves"). A fortyish Chinese monk by the name of Shen-kuang, who is well versed in classical Chinese literature, soon encounters the Indian. Whenever Shen-kuang asks a question of the master, he receives only silence. In order to show his sincerity in seeking the teaching of Buddhism, Shen-kuang stands in the deep nocturnal snow. Bodhidharma's response to this gesture is to ask the Chinese monk why he is standing in the snow and to inform him that

he is pursuing Dharma in a petty frame of mind. Shen-kuang thereupon takes a dagger, cuts off his left arm, and politely lays it before the patriarch. The Indian master accepts this demonstration of sincerity and renames his Chinese disciple Hui-k'o, a name meaning something like "his wisdom will do."[506]

In some versions of this myth, Shen Guang (or Shen-kuang) stands guard over the motionless meditating Da Mo, day and night, in all kinds of weather, hoping to attract the master's attention. Failing to do so, Shen Guang finally cuts off his own arm in order to prove his devotion and his burning desire to become the master's disciple.

It seems very likely that we have here another example of the pattern we earlier saw displayed in the story of Buddha and Vajrapani, discussed on pages 738 - 740 of this present volume. In that discussion, we saw artwork which depicts Vajrapani as a Heracles-like (or Hercules-like) figure, brandishing the Vajra or thunderbolt weapon overhead, and standing behind and above the form of the seated Buddha, who is meditating while cross-legged on the ground (see the image of the sculpture from the second century AD on page 739).

That this imagery and this ancient tradition involving Vajrapani and the Buddha are based upon the constellations Hercules and Ophiuchus is beyond any doubt. As we saw, the seated Buddha has one hand elevated, and in it he holds a small egg-shaped object: an artistic element which indicates the constellation Ophiuchus and which is found in artwork from ancient Mesopotamia as well (with parallels to artwork from ancient Egypt and to that of other cultures such as ancient Greece).

Based on our understanding of the celestial correspondences in the Vajrapani - Buddha scene, as well as the celestial correspondences in other Hercules - Ophiuchus depictions from other settings, we can with a fair degree of confidence determine that this story involving Shen Guang standing over the meditating Da Mo is based on the very same constellations in the night sky, with Shen Guang corresponding to the constellation Hercules and Da Mo once again corresponding to Ophiuchus (we have already seen abundant evidence connecting Da Mo with Ophiuchus).

The reader can find numerous examples of artwork depicting Shen Guang (later given the name Hui-k'o) standing behind the meditating form of Da Mo (or Bodhidharma, or Daruma) simply by searching the web. The image below, however, shows beyond any doubt the correspondences to the constellations in the sky:

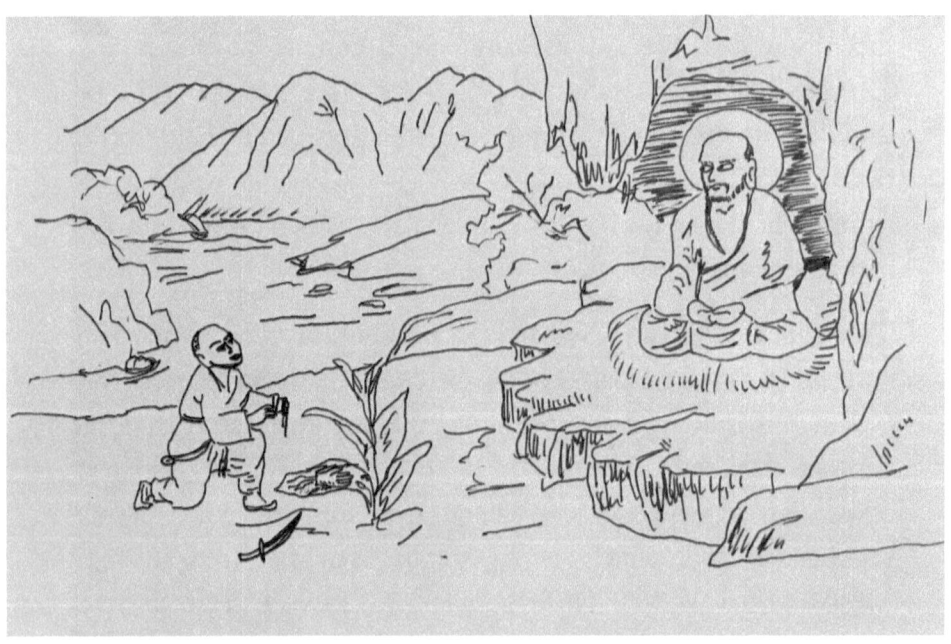

The drawing above is my rendition of a mural in the Bohyunson Temple in Goseong, near the southern tip of the Korean

Peninsula, based upon a photograph of the mural found on the website of Dale Quarrington, *Dale's Temple Adventures.*[507]

As should be immediately obvious, Shen Guang (who later receives the name Hui-k'o) is depicted in the characteristic posture associated with the constellation Hercules, and which ancient artwork around the globe frequently employs when depicting a figure associated with this constellation.

In the artwork, Shen Guang has cut off his own hand in order to demonstrate his resolve to Da Mo. He has placed the severed hand upon a large leaf belonging to a plant nearby. The long, curved knife or short sword Shen Guang must have used can be seen lying on the ground nearby.

Note that in the heavens, the constellation Hercules reaches down with one hand towards the "serpent-head" feature on the west side of the constellation Ophiuchus, while at the same time brandishing his mighty weapon (which could be envisioned as a great sword) threateningly over his own head, in this case apparently envisioned as preparing to strike off his own hand:

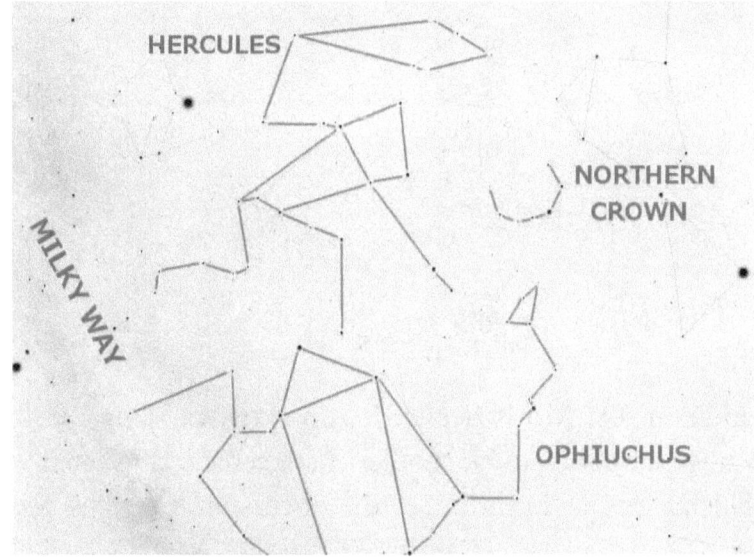

In addition to the remarkable similarity between the depiction of Shen Guang (Hui-k'o) in the temple mural and the outline of the constellation Hercules in the night sky (and to other depictions of Hercules-related figures from ancient artwork around the globe), there are a number of other noteworthy details in this mural from the Bohyunson Temple.

First, observe that Da Mo is depicted as though seated cross-legged and meditating in an arched cave-mouth. We have already had occasion to note that other Ophiuchus-figures are often depicted underneath an arch, or under a dome-like canopy or parasol (see for instance the depictions of Vishnu shown on pages 554 and 557 of this volume, or the depictions of Krishna shown on pages 629 and 632 of this volume, or the depiction of the Buddha shown on page 735, or even the depiction of Sokar on page 272).

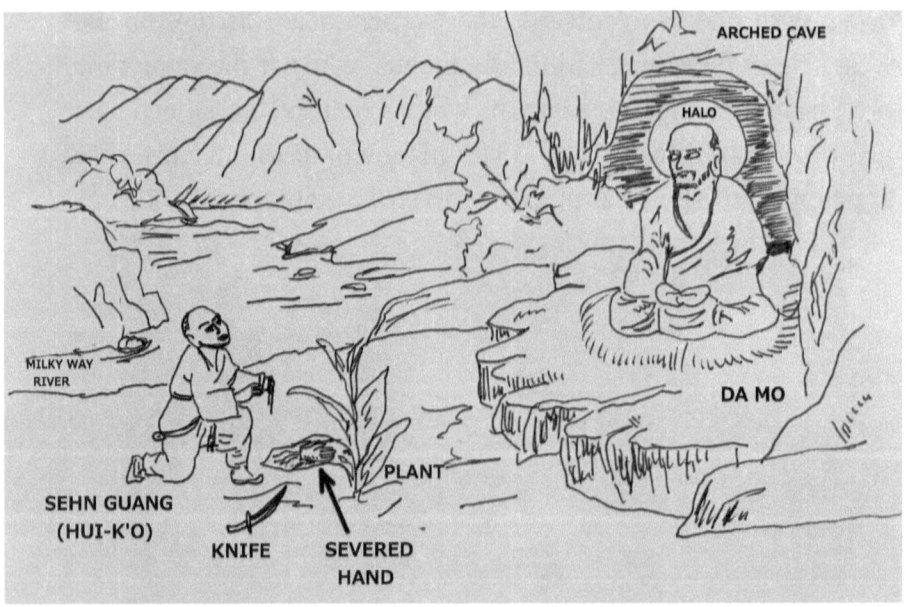

In addition, Da Mo is depicted with extremely long earlobes, which we have seen to be another characteristic associated with Ophiuchus-figures in myth (see the discussion regarding Karna from the Mahabharata on page 665 - 667 of this volume, as well as the mention of the long ear-lobes of Lao Tzu, discussed on page 752).

Da Mo's staring, bulging eyes have already been mentioned in conjunction with the legend of his having cut off his own eyelids: this mural certainly follows the convention of depicting the sage with such staring eyeballs. The master is also depicted with a halo behind his head, possibly indicative of the whirling form of Hercules positioned above Ophiuchus.

The artist has included a river which winds its way down from the upper part of the painting and on past the extended rear leg of Shen Guang (on the left side of the image as we face it on the page), just as the Milky Way galaxy itself winds its way down past the extended rear leg of the constellation Hercules in the heavens.

Shen Guang's severed hand rests upon a large leaf of the plant directly in front of him. I am convinced that the "severed arm motif" found in this and other Star Myths from around the globe are based upon the constellation Coma Berenices, envisioned as a severed arm (a severed arm still spurting blood, no less). We have already seen a severed arm in another myth, from the Popol Vuh of the Maya, when Seven Macaw tears Hunapuh's arm off (see pages 184 and 194 of this volume). We saw another example in the incident of the severed hand of Horus (see page 366).

Additionally, there is another famous arm torn off in a myth, from another culture separated by yet another ocean from the lands that are home to the Da Mo tradition: the arm of the monster Grendel, torn off by the hero Beowulf in the Anglo-Saxon poem *Beowulf.* Like the arm torn off in the Popol Vuh, this severed arm in the *Beowulf* poem is promptly hung up in a high place. I would suggest that these "severed arm myths" found in cultures separated from one another by great distances and wide oceans represent yet further powerful evidence for the existence of the ancient worldwide system which underlies the ancient myths of cultures found on every inhabited continent and island, the outlines of which we have been tracing throughout this volume, and whose origins appear to stem from an age long before the rise of any culture or civilization known to conventional history.

Very much akin to the tradition of Ch'an Buddhism itself, the spread of which is attributed to this legendary figure, the Star Myths of the world are about *showing us* rather than telling us. They employ esoteric metaphor to convey their truths to our deeper understanding, truths which our "rational" or "superficial mind" would probably reject (in much the same way that Mr. Miyagi teaches Daniel-san karate using the method of "wax-on, wax-off," bypassing Daniel-san's critical and doubt-filled ego-mind).

This approach is employed because the myths are designed to help us to overcome and transcend the "doubting twin" of our socially-constructed ego-mind, which constantly balances and decides between the rules and norms and strictures and precepts which it has created for itself as well as receiving from society beginning immediately upon birth, and to rediscover that deeper (and indeed infinite) wellspring to which we always have access, but which lies beneath (and is thus *obscured, overlooked* and *forgotten by*) the "scurrying of the superficial mind."[508]

For this reason, the ancient myths do not address their message to the superficial mind -- they bypass the superficial mind altogether, using powerful esoteric stories, cutting directly through to what R. A. Schwaller de Lubicz called "intelligence-of-the-heart" in his 1960 text *Esoterism & Symbol.*[509]

This "intelligence-of-the-heart," Schwaller explains, is "inaccessible to cerebral intelligence."[510] Explaining further, he writes:

> Esoterism can be neither written nor spoken, and hence cannot be betrayed. One must be prepared to grasp it, to see it, to hear it. This preparation is not a knowing but a being-able [...]. [511]

But if this deeper understanding, this esoteric grasping, can be "neither written nor spoken," as Schwaller here asserts, then what is the purpose of the ancient myths and scriptures? What is the purpose of esoteric writings and stories in general?

Their purpose, Schwaller asserts, is not to explain or to teach, but rather to *evoke* -- a word which means to "call forth." Schwaller writes:

> Thus esoteric teaching is strictly *evocation*, and can be nothing other than that. Initiation does not reside in any text whatsoever, but in the cultivation of intelligence-of-the-heart. Then there is no longer anything occult or secret, because the intention of the enlightened, the prophets, and the "messengers from above" is never to conceal -- quite the contrary.[512]

I am convinced that the myths themselves are designed to *evoke* -- to call forth understanding when we are "prepared to grasp it." It is when we are ready that the realization will come to us: when we hear the story of Enkidu and Gilgamesh, for example, and suddenly exclaim, "Ah!" because we have unexpectedly *grasped it* (we could have the same experience while reading a story from the Popol Vuh, or contemplating the stories of the life of Da Mo).

This is exactly how Zen is evoked in the disciple by the master, in the tradition of the "transmission of the lamp." It is not that the master "explains" to the disciple: that does not work.

A notable example of this evocation and realization is provided to us in the Da Mo story, here explained by Wu Jinxiong (John Ching Hsiung Wu, 1899 - 1986) in his 1960 text *Golden Age of Zen*. In this episode, Hui-k'o has come to Da Mo and explained that he has not yet found peace within:

> Hui-k'o said to him, "My mind has not found peace[,] I beg you, master, to pacify it for me." He [Da Mo] said, "Bring forth your mind to me and I will pacify it for you." After a long silence, Hui-k'o told his master that he had searched for the mind but could not find it. Thereupon the master said, "Behold, I have already pacified the mind for you!"

This marked the beginning of the transmission of the lamp, and Bodhidharma became the First Patriarch of the Chinese School of Zen. The method he employed is a typical instance of the via negativa, so characteristic of the whole tradition of Zen. Bodhidharma did not deny, any more than the later masters, the existence of the mind. But the "mind" which Hui-k'o was trying so desperately to find and to pacify was not the true mind, but merely a faint reflection of it. The true mind is always peaceful; there can be no restlessness about it. Besides, the true mind is the subject that thinks. As soon as we begin to think about it or try to do something about it, it is no longer the subject, but an object, which cannot be the true mind. By saying that he had already pacified it, the master was pointing at the true mind, which, being always in peace, really has no need of pacification. By asking the disciple to bring forth the mind, he made him discover for himself that the falsely objectified mind was but an illusion.

This prepared him for the discovery of the true mind through a direct intuitive perception called into action by the unexpected words of the master.[513]

Thus, at least, the explication by Wu Jinxiong: this represents his own atttempt to articulate a realization which Hui-k'o supposedly achieved in the story, but which is not explained in the story and hence is actually a realization which *the story evoked within Wu Jinxiong* (Hui-k'o himself perhaps never even having been an actual historical personage, but rather a figure in a story designed and intended to evoke realization within the one who hears the story).

This is very much how the ancient myths of the world operate: no one else can tell you what they mean, but that is not because they are intended to *conceal* -- as Schwaller de Lubicz says, "quite the contrary."

They are designed to evoke, to call forth, to spark the realization within the one who is prepared to grasp it, in much the same way that Mr. Miyagi's teaching was designed to elicit an "Ah ha!" within Daniel-san, but not because Mr. Miyagi *explained* anything to Daniel-san in words, addressing his "cerebral intelligence." Such an approach would have been fruitless, and Daniel-san would never have been able to grasp what Mr. Miyagi's esoteric approach enabled Daniel-san to grasp.

Perhaps now the reader can understand why the ancient authors gave us stories about a Zen master named Bodhidharma or Da Mo, stories which can be shown to be based upon celestial metaphor and not upon literal and terrestrial history. Perhaps now we understand why the historicity of these stories "does not really matter" -- as Alvin Boyd Kuhn puts it, they are "*a thousand times more precious as myths than as alleged history.*"[514]

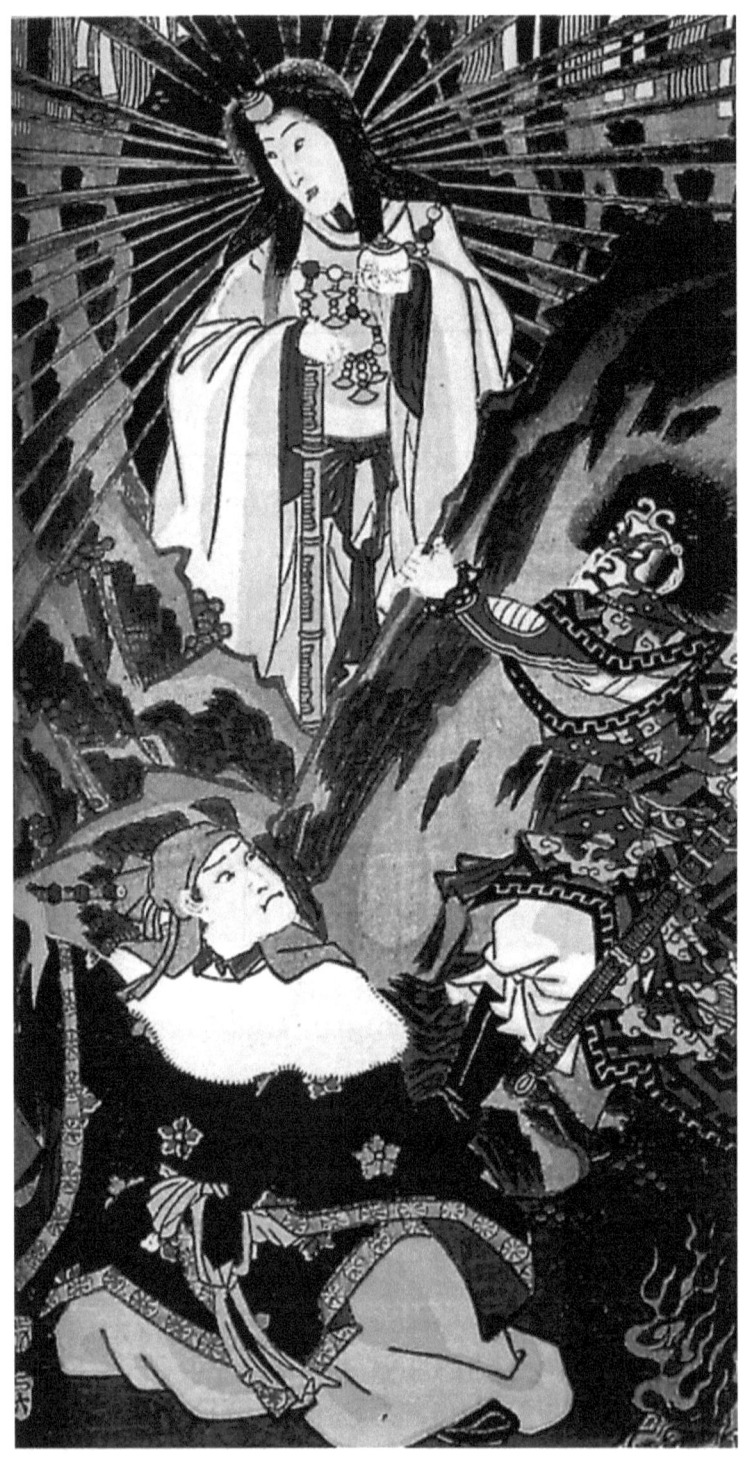

782

Star Myths of Ancient Japan: the Kojiki

At this point in our tour of the ancient myths, we have circled the globe. We have examined myths from Australia, and proceeded to explore myths from nearly every inhabited continent, as well as from the islands which stretch across the vast expanse of the Pacific Ocean. We now conclude with an examination of a few of the myths of ancient Japan (a land which in the people's own language is called 日本 *Nihon*, "Sun's Origin").

In his 1960 book *Shinto: the Kami Way*, eminent Shinto scholar Dr. Sokyo Ono (1904 - 1990), a professor at Kokugakuin University of Tokyo and a lecturer in the Association of Shinto Shrines -- described by Hideo Kishimoto (1903 - 1964) as "one who has devoted his entire professional life to the study of this faith" -- writes:

> Shinto, the indigenous faith of the Japanese people, is relatively unknown among the religions of the world. Many people are familiar with the torii, the typical gateway to Shinto shrines, and some have a vague impression of the unique ornamentation which adorns many shrine roofs. Yet to all but a few, the shrines to which the torii leads and the Shinto faith which it symbolies are very much an enigma.[515]

A preface to the same work, by co-author William Parsons Woodard (1896 - 1973), founder of the International Institute for the Study of Religions, declares:

> [. . .] except for the student who has the interest, ability, and almost inexhaustible resources in time for his investigation, Shinto remains practically a closed book.

> Actually there are very few people, Japanese or foreign, who understand Shinto thoroughly and are able to explain it in

detail. These scholars, including the author of this booklet, are the first to admit that there are many things which cannot be clearly explained because in some areas there is still no certain knowledge.[516]

And yet, although it displays its own distinctive character, stemming from the ancient indigenous culture of the islands of Japan (or Nihon), and although it is in the words of Professor Sokyo Ono in the same book "as indigenous as the people that brought the Japanese nation into existence and ushered in its new civilization,"[517] yet there are within the most ancient surviving records describing the lives and genealogies of the *kami* of this indigenous tradition unmistakeable indications of connection to the same ancient system we have found in all the other ancient sacred traditions we have examined on our trip around the globe.

The word *Shinto* 神道 signifies "spirit path" or "spirit way" and in Japanese these two characters are pronounced *kami no michi* and mean "the Kami Way," the word *kami* being a Japanese word worthy of closer examination. In his 1972 book entitled *The Allied Occupation of Japan 1945 - 1952 and Japanese Religions*, the same William P. Woodard discusses the kami within the tradition of Shinto:

> *Shinto* is the cluster of the beliefs and customs of the Japanese people centering in the kami, a term which designates spiritual entities, forces or qualities that are believed to exist everywhere, in man and in nature. Usually without gender and often without anything akin to personality, the kami are believed to infuse the universe, and life for the devout Shintoist is lived in harmony with and in gratitude to them. In its traditional usage in Shinto the word kami (singular or plural) may be translated deity(ies),

spirit(s), god(s), or divine (e.g., *kamikaze*: divine wind), but it should never be translated God. In the interest of clarity it is better to leave it untranslated.[518]

Of the practice of integrating one's life with the reality of the spirit world and the kami, Professor Ono in his book *Shinto: the Kami Way* writes:

> In its personal aspects "Shinto" implies faith in the kami, usages practiced in accordance with the mind of the kami, and spiritual life attained through the worship of and in communion with the kami. To those who worship kami, "Shinto" is a collective noun denoting all faiths. It is an all-inclusive term embracing the various faiths which are comprehended in the kami-idea.[519]

The oldest surviving text describing the origin of the kami was completed in the year commonly called AD 712. This text is known as the 古事記 *Ko Ji Ki* (or, more commonly, Kojiki), which literally means "Old Matters Record" or, as it is usually rendered, "A Record of Ancient Matters." That it preserves knowledge which had been passed down for centuries prior to the composition of the text we have today is evident from the fact that in its original preface, the author expresses concern that certain accounts are being altered or emended and that thus there is a danger of knowledge being lost or forgotten.

As Professor Ono goes on to explain regarding the Kojiki:

> Shinto itself does not possess sacred scriptures, such as are found in many other religions, -- a fact which is a significant indication of the character of the Shinto faith itself. Nevertheless, there are certain ancient records that are regarded as authoritative and provide its historical as well as its spiritual basis.

The earliest of these were compiled by Imperial order and contain the mythology and early history of the Japanese people. The *Kojiki* ("Record of Ancient Matters") is the oldest extant Japanese historical record. Its date is 712 of the Christian era. It provides an account of events down to the year 628. Though written in Chinese ideographs the style is ancient, pure Japanese and through it we can know something of the style of the earlier oral transmission from generation to generation. Consequently it is especially valued.[520]

For our brief examination of just a few of the sacred traditions regarding the kami of Nihon, we will rely primarily on the myths contained in the Kojiki.

I will be the first to admit that the account provided by the Kojiki does not lend itself to easy examination for Star Myth content. Often little or no details are provided about many of the kami who are mentioned, beyond their names. When activities and episodes *are* related, the details are sometimes so sparse that confident identification with specific constellations is difficult or impossible.

Nevertheless, within this record of ancient matters we are occasionally provided with a glimpse -- and at times even a clear vista -- which confirms beyond doubt that the ancient understanding of the kami expresses itself using the same language that we have found the world's other Star Myths to be speaking: such episodes provide all the evidence we need to state with confidence that the ancient indigenous tradition of Nihon belongs to the same world-wide system which we have found to be operating in all the other cultures we have examined thus far.

One of these episodes, the story of Amaterasu and her retreat to the cave, is extremely well-known and indeed foundational to the history of Japan, in that the emperors and empresses were thought to be descendants of Amaterasu. Let's now turn to the ancient text in order to identify some clear connections in this story as related in the Kojiki to specific (and now-familiar) constellations, as well as connections regarding a few other important kami described in the Kojiki.

The opening descriptions of the first kami at the start of the Kojiki are quite terse, but even here we catch occasional glimpses which seem to resonate with myths we have examined already in this volume. Here is the poem's beginning, from the 1882 translation by Basil Hall Chamberlain (1850 - 1935), who was a professor of Japanese at Tokyo Imperial University, a translation which has some drawbacks but is yet valuable for being very literal to the text and honest in its explanation of difficult spots:

> The names of the Deities [kami] that were born in the Plain of High Heaven [Takama-no-hara] when the Heaven and Earth began were the Deity Master-of-the-August-Centre-of-Heaven, next the High-August-Producing-Wondrous-Deity, next the Divine-Producing-Wondrous-Deity. These three Deities [kami] were all Deities born alone, and hid their persons. The names of the Deities [kami] that were born next from a thing that sprouted up like unto a reed-shoot when the earth, young and like unto a floating oil, drifted about medusa-like, were the Pleasant-Reed-Shoot-Prince-Elder Deity, next the Heavenly-Eternally-Standing-Deity. These two Deities [kami] were likewise born alone, and hid their persons.[521]

The more recent 2014 translation by Professor Gustav Heldt of the University of Virginia renders the names of these original kami in a less unwieldy fashion as follows (in the same order as given above): "Master Mighty Center of Heaven," "the spirit Lofty Growth," "the spirit Sacred Growth," "Fine Budding Reed Lad," and "Ever-Standing Heaven."[522]

Additionally, the 2014 translation by Professor Heldt describes the young land as "floating like tallow on water" (as opposed to being "like unto a floating oil," in the 1882 translation by Chamberlain), and as "drifting like a jellyfish" rather than "drifted about medusa-like" (although note that "medusa" is actually a term for jellyfish, and is undoubtedly what Chamberlain is indicating when he says "medusa").[523]

Note that, despite the paucity of detail supplied in the original text, we can still surmise (if we had to guess) which constellations might correspond to deities who are described as "Mighty Center of Heaven" (or "August Center of Heaven"), or as "Heavenly Eternally Standing Deity." If I had to guess, although there is by no means enough textual detail provided for a confident analysis, I would propose that a *Center-of-Heaven* kami would probably correspond to the constellation Hercules in whirling form, and that an *Eternally-Standing* kami who holds up the heavens would correspond to the constellation Ophiuchus, in much the same way that we saw the Egyptian god Shu holding up the heavens in the discussion on pages 261 - 262 of this volume.

Similarly, the description of the earth drifting about like a jellyfish or a medusa, and something sprouting up "like unto a reed-shoot" evokes earlier discussions of babies cast adrift amongst the reeds or bulrushes, often in baskets which are also made of reeds. We have seen that these "baskets of reeds" (or, in the case of the basket in which baby Moses is cast adrift, baskets specifically described as an "ark") are often associated with the constellation Ophiuchus above Scorpio, with Scorpio presumably looking like a bunch of reeds. Indeed, a "thing which sprouted up like unto a reed-shoot" is probably a reference to the constellation Scorpio, which (when envisioned in its "multiple-heads" form) resembles a sprouting ear of wheat or barley.

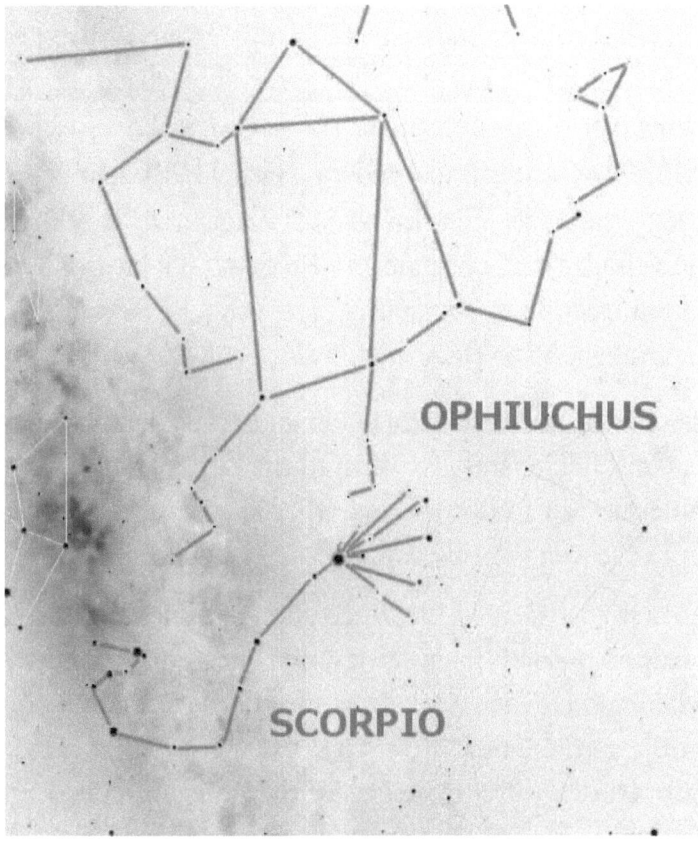

Recall as well that, in addition to the infant Moses and the baby Sargon and the infant Karna who were set adrift *in baskets* in a river, we must also add to this myth-pattern the baby Maui, who was cast into the sea-foam by his parents (apparently *sans* basket). Do you remember that when his parents abandoned Maui at the shore, he was wrapped up by *jellyfish* for protection?

If we had to guess what constellation or region of the night sky is being referenced in these opening verses of the Kojiki which mention a "sprouting reed" and a "floating jellyfish," I would unhesitatingly point to the region of the constellation Scorpio, based on what we know from our examinations thus far.

The text of the Kojiki then goes on to introduce two more individual kami, followed by a group of five pairs of kami (these five pairs all brothers and sisters). In this group of five pairs of brother-and-sister kami, the last pair introduced is a very important pair of spirits named 伊邪那岐 *Izanagi* and his sister 伊邪那美命 *Izanami,* translated by Basil Hall Chamberlain as "the Deity the Male-Who-Invites" (Izanagi) and "the Deity the Female-Who-Invites" (Izanami).[524] Professor Heldt in his recent translation calls them the spirits "He Who Beckoned" and his sister spirit "She Who Beckoned."[525]

The assembled heavenly kami command Izanagi and Izanami to "make, consolidate, and give birth to this drifting land." In order to enable the pair to do this, the other kami give to Izanagi and Izanami a "heavenly jeweled spear."[526]

> So the two Deities, standing upon the Floating Bridge of Heaven, pushed down the jeweled spear and stirred with it, whereupon, when they had stirred the brine till it went curdle-curdle, and drew [the spear] up, the brine that dripped down from the end of the spear was piled up and became an island. This is the Island of Onogoro.[527]

We can already detect important clues regarding the identity of Izanagi and Izanami in this passage regarding the creation of the islands and the firming up of lands which previously only drifted. First, as we have already argued and as we will see supported by abundant evidence in Volume Two of the series, the use of the specific weapon of a *spear* or halberd-like weapon is very often a characteristic of the constellation Ophiuchus. Second, the description of the two kami "standing upon the Floating Bridge of Heaven" may be an additional indication of the constellation Ophiuchus, which can clearly be seen to have one foot in (or upon) the Milky Way band: standing, as it were, upon the Floating Bridge of Heaven (if that bridge corresponds to the Milky Way, as I believe to be quite likely). Note that the guardian Heimdal who stands upon the Rainbow Bridge of Asgard is argued in Volume Four to correspond to the constellation Ophiuchus as well:

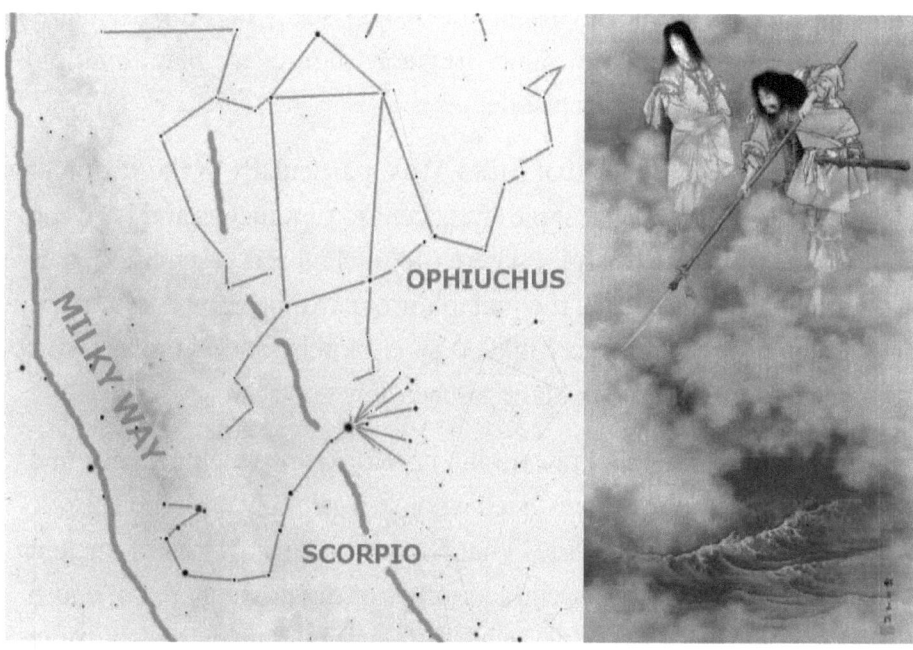

In the above star-chart, the outline of the Milky Way band has been added for ease of identification. Can you see why Izanagi and Izanami are described as "standing on the bridge" and how they might be envisioned as "stirring the brine" with their spear in order to make it go "curdle curdle"?

The rendering by Basil Hall Chamberlain of the curdling process as "curdle curdle" is explained in one of his footnotes; he says:

> It is not easy to find in English a word which will aptly render the original Japanese onomatopoeia *koworokoworo*. The meaning may also be "till it made a curdling sound."[528]

The Milky Way almost certainly plays the role of the brine which is curdled, in addition to being the floating bridge of heaven. It is not unusual for a heavenly feature to play two roles in a single myth (just as some movies feature the same actor playing multiple roles, sometimes of characters who look very different from one another), and the myths in the Kojiki seem to be particularly prone to using the same heavenly figure to play multiple characters in a single episode.

If one looks at the actual Milky Way, particularly in the region of its brightest and widest part (adjacent to Ophiuchus and between Sagittarius and Scorpio, where Ophiuchus can be envisioned as stirring with a spear), the metaphor of curdling can be seen to be aptly appropriate: the Milky Way is blotchy and clumpy in this region, and marked by dark patches here and there.

Note too that this episode in the Kojiki in which Izanagi and Izanami churn the briny deep resonates strongly with the episode examined in the previous chapter on the Star Myths of ancient India, in which the assembled forces of the heavenly realm churn the great Ocean of Milk, using Mount Mandara as the churning stick and the serpent Vasuki as the twirling rope (see for instance page 581 of this volume). We noted when discussing that episode that the metaphor almost certainly involves the constellation Ophiuchus in that case as well.

After they have made the Island of Onogoro, the text tells us they descended to it, and there "found a mighty pillar of heaven and a spacious hall."⁵²⁹ Once again, if it need even be repeated, these are characteristics of Ophiuchus, a constellation which often plays a great door, a palace, a tower, or similar structure in myth. Izanagi and Izanami, noticing their different physical features (explicitly calling attention to the difference between their reproductive organs and proposing to join them together) resolve to walk around the great pillar of heaven they have found (Izanagi from the right and Izanami from the left), and then join together in bed to consummate their desire.

As they are walking around the pillar, Izanami speaks first and says of Izanagi, "What a charming and desireable young man!" and Izanagi says of Izanami, "What a charming and desireable maiden!" However, Izanagi then expresses his concern that it was not proper for the woman to have spoken first.

Because of this impropriety, the text informs us, the child born of their first union is born limbless and unable to stand. This child is named 蛭子 Hiruko, literally "Leech-child." With characteristic economy of description, the Kojiki tells us: "This child they placed in a boat of reeds, and let it float away."⁵³⁰

Thus, here in the ancient mythology of Nihon we find yet another example of a world-wide oicotype, the baby cast adrift in a vessel made of reeds. Surely the advocates of the conventional theory do not propose that all of these stories, with such remarkable parallels (including the explicit mention of *reeds* or *rushes* in virtually all of them, save only the Maui version, which instead has jellyfish) simply arose independently of one another in all these different cultures, located in all these different parts of the globe!

And yet the hypothesis that they must all have had some sort of contact with one another or that the myth-pattern might have migrated over the centuries from one culture to another seems equally untenable. Are we to believe that the story of Sargon of ancient Mesopotamia somehow influenced the myths of the cultures of the islands of the Pacific? How would proponents of the conventional theory of myth and the conventional timeline of human history explain the transfer of such a myth pattern from the ancient land of Assyria to the islands that stretch from Hawaii to New Zealand, while also somehow making its way into the scriptures of the Bible, the Mahabarata of ancient India, and the mythology of the indigenous inhabitants of ancient Japan?

Of course, there is also the famous solution proposed in 1916 by Carl Gustav Jung (1875 - 1961), involving "archetypes" preserved within the "collective unconscious" in which archetypal symbols preserved somehow beyond the limitations of individual consciousness form a kind of ocean out of which images and patterns can arise across great distances or across great gulfs of time.

While agreeing that there do appear to be strong reasons to believe that the individual unconscious does at times appear to "know" or "sense" things beyond what that individual could have perceived using the five physical senses (see for instance the discussion on pages 483 - 484 of this volume), it is quite evident from Jung's writings that he was unaware of the celestial pattern upon which the world's myths (with their recurring myth-patterns or oicotypes) can be shown to be based. Without ruling out the possibility of a "collective unconscious," I would nevertheless suggest that it is not the best explanation for the evidence that we find in the myths of the world (although given the recurrence of patterns such as the child set adrift in a vessel made of reeds, we certainly need to search for *some* explanation, thus necessitating the proposal of some sort of hypothesis to try to account for this phenomenon, one of which is that proposed by Jung).

The evidence for a *celestial* explanation for all these patterns and parallels around the world is abundant and compelling, and explains what we find in the myths of the world very well -- but we are still left with the question of how this system can possibly be found underlying myths of the indigenous inhabitants of Nihon and of the ancient Mesopotamians and so on around the globe.

The evidence that the ancient system was already fully developed in the earliest surviving texts of ancient India and ancient Egypt and ancient Mesopotamia suggests that it belongs to some even more ancient (though now unknown) culture -- and we could perhaps argue that it then spread via the "collective unconscious" from that extremely ancient (and now forgotten) source to all the cultures and peoples of the earth who have arisen in the subsequent centuries.

I am not convinced that we need to resort to a collective unconscious to explain its diffusion around the globe. It is equally likely, in my opinion, that this ancient system was known worldwide during that time of extreme antiquity, and that after some great world-wide catastrophe, the survivors preserved some memory of it which formed the seeds for the ancient traditions that were then passed down in the cultures that arose (millennia later) following that ancient disaster. However, I do not rule out a "collective unconscious" as part of the explanation. We simply do not know at this time.

Whatever the actual explanation, we have here in the laconic description of the fate of the Leech-child Hiruko the same

795

common elements of the myth-pattern or oicotype that we have perceived in the ancient myths of India, and of Mesopotamia, and which we will examine in the story of Moses in Volume Three of this series, and to some degree in the story of baby Maui, thrown into the sea by his parents. And, I would argue that Hiruko, like baby Maui, can be identified with the constellation Scorpio. The resemblance of the constellation Scorpio to a leech, or a maggot, or a worm, is fairly self-evident.

Scorpio, of course, is situated in the heavens directly underneath the figure of Ophiuchus -- and I am fairly confident that Izunagi and Izunami are both together associated with this constellation. Note that we have already seen that the god Shiva (who is also associated with Ophiuchus) has a manifestation, Ardhanarinara, in which he is "half male and half female," or simultaneously male and female.

The text from the Kojiki describes Izanagi and Izanami walking around a central pillar -- this suggests that they are (at least during this circumambulation of the pillar) associated with the two "serpent-halves" of Ophiuchus, the central body of the constellation being the pillar. Note that one serpent-half can quite obviously be seen as suggestive of the male phallus, and the other serpent-half can just as easily be seen as having a space which would suggest the female yoni (guess which is which):

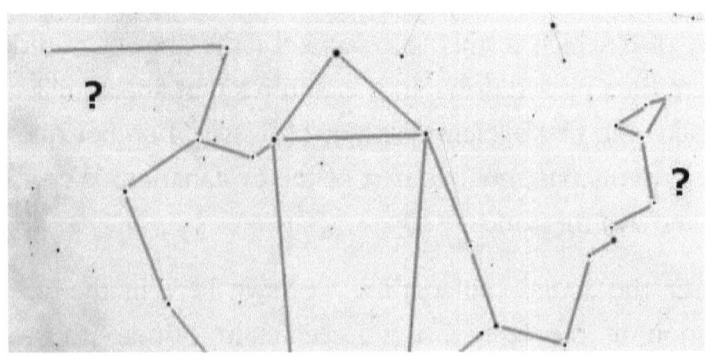

In his 1968 translation of the Kojiki, linguist and scholar Donald L. Philippi (1930 - 1993) cites 本居宣長 Motoori Norinaga (1730 - 1801), one of the most prominent scholars of the Kojiki and Shinto, regarding the motion of circling the central pillar by Izanagi and Izanami, quoting Motoori directly in the passage below:

> It seems to have been an ancient ceremony to precede conjugal intercourse by walking around a pillar. Here, the performance of this ceremony at the beginning of the conjugal intercourse must be of the deepest significance [. . .] But since there is no explanation [of the ceremony], its meaning cannot be fathomed by ordinary mortals. If one were to venture a conjecture, however, first of all, the man is above in sexual intercourse, like heaven or the roof which spreads over the house; the woman is below, like the supporting earth, or the floor of the house. The pillar stands between them, strengthening and connecting top and bottom, and thus no doubt the idea is to strengthen and connect the couple. *Kojiki-den*, I, 193.[531]

Donald Philippi then adds that "Hirata Atsutane (1776 - 1843) and Suzuki Shigetane (1812 - 63), also *kokugakusha* of the late Edo period, agreed that the pillar is a phallus (Matsumura, II, 207)."[532]

These interpretations may well be correct on one level -- but based upon the identification we are now building to the constellation Ophiuchus, it is evident that the central pillar can as well be seen to parallel the celestial identity of the lingam of Lord Shiva, likewise a pillar representative of the phallus and likewise a pillar associated with the central body of the same constellation Ophiuchus (as discussed on pages 576 - 580 of this volume).

There are also many commentaries down through the centuries which have pointed out a likely linguistic connection between the names *Izanagi* and *Izanami* and the name of the god *Ishana* (one of the names of the Lord Shiva, to whom Arjuna prayed during the bow-trial at the swayamvara of Draupadi, as we saw on page 675).

There are many more children born to Izanagi and Izanami, but we will fast forward a little now and find out that the final child of the pair is named Fire-Shining-Elder, and in giving birth to him his mother is burned to the point that she dies.

She descends to the underworld, and Izanagi goes down to find her, in a pattern very similar to the Orpheus story and other "retrieval from the land of the dead" myths found around the world. Izanami informs Izanagi that it is too late: she has already eaten of the food from the furnace or stove belonging to the god of the underworld (this is a pattern found in other "underworld retrieval" myths, a pattern examined in detail in my 2017 book *Astrotheology for Life*).

Izanami tells him not to look at her, and goes into the palace of the underworld to consult with the deities of death about the possibility of returning to the land of the living. Izanagi waits and waits, but she stays in the palace for so long that he finally lights a match which he has made from an end-tooth broken off from the comb he uses to hold his hair in a bun. Note that this pattern (including the comb) has strong echoes with the story of Deer Hunter and White Corn Maiden which we examined earlier in this volume (and may indicate an identification with Sagittarius).

The light from the match made from the tooth of the comb reveals the figure of his erstwhile lover, now rotting and swarming with maggots (this incident probably envisions

Izanami, in her skeletal and rotting state, with the constellation Scorpio). Horrified, Izanagi flees, and Izanami sends denizens of the underworld to pursue him (but he distracts them) and finally pursues him herself as he flees to the upper realm. Izanagi finally stops her by throwing down a great rock to block up the gate of the land of death (the rock standing in the middle of the "Even Pass of Hades," in the translation of Basil Hall Chamberlain).[533] So, standing opposite one another with the rock in between, they bid one another farewell, and Izanami stays below to become the queen of the underworld (an end result with obvious echoes to the fate of Persephone in Greek myth).

Note that this great rock in the midst of a pass is no doubt another reference to Ophiuchus (the "pass" being formed by the two serpent-halves, envisioned as the sides of a mountain pass, with the "rock" in between being the central body of the constellation). It is significant to note that Ophiuchus plays the role of the *gate of the underworld* in a great many world myths, including in the Norse myths and in the myths of ancient Greece (discussed in Volumes Four and Two of this series, respectively).

Upon returning from the land of the dead, Izanagi washes off the pollution of the land of the dead, and in doing so are born more kami. Among these are the goddess 天照 *Amaterasu* (born from his left eye, her name is translated as Heaven-Shining-Great-August-Deity by Chamberlain: the characters of her name literally mean "Heaven's Shine" or "Heaven's Splendor" or "Heaven's Illuminator") and the god 須佐之男命 *Susano'o* (born from Izanagi's nose, this kami's name is translated His Brave-Swift-Impetuous-Male-Augustness by Chamberlain: the characters of his name literally signify "Commander Beard -- Male" or something to that effect, according to my own loose translation of the ideograms).

Which constellations could be associated with these two important kami, born from the eyes of Izanagi? We will have to look for clues in the text itself, but recalling that we have already argued that Izanagi is most closely associated with Ophiuchus, and recalling that the Eye of Horus was earlier argued to be envisioned in the "serpent-head" feature of Ophiuchus (the head-end at the westernmost point of the constellation), it is possible that this brother-and-sister pair are associated with a constellation close to (and seen as arising from) this "eye" on the western serpent-half of that constellation.

Next Izanagi bestows a beautiful jewel-string, a delightfully jingling necklace, upon Amaterasu, and tells her to rule the "Plain-of-High-Heaven."[534] And Izanagi directs Susano'o to rule the "Sea-Plain."

But Brave-Swift-Impetuous-Male has other plans. First, we are told that he "cried and wept till his eight-grasp beard reached to the pit of his stomach," which causes disaster upon the earth and, the text tells us, "portents of woe" which arise in "the myriad things."[535] Izanagi is surprised and asks Susano'o why he is behaving this way instead of ruling the land with which he was entrusted. Susano'o replies that he would prefer to go live with his deceased mother -- whereupon Izanagi angrily "expelled him with a divine expulsion."[536]

Next, Susano'o ascends to heaven, shaking the mountains -- and Amaterasu (who has tied the string of jewels in her hair) becomes alarmed at the noise Susano'o is making, and takes up a bow and a quiver of arrows, "and stood valiantly like unto a mighty man," asking Susano'o why he is ascending up there. Susano'o assures Amaterasu he means her no harm, and then invites her to swear oaths to one another and produce children together. To this she agrees, and they produce more kami descendents. In between the listing of their offspring, the text tells us that Susano'o frequently begs Amaterasu to give him the jewels twisted in her hair.

From these accounts in the text, it is likely that Susano'o can be identified with the constellation Hercules, particularly given the fact that he ascends to heaven and causes the mountains to tremble. This identification is not completely certain at this point, but it does seem likely, particularly in that Susano'o is identified as a god of storms. The fact that he frequently begs for the string of jewels may also be a clue to an identification with Hercules, in that Hercules (as we've frequently remarked, and illustrated in star-charts such as the one on page 210) appears to be reaching out towards Corona Borealis, the Northern Crown (which could be envisioned as either a necklace or a tiara of jewels to be worn in the hair as a crown).

On the other hand, Izanagi tries to give Susano'o command over the "Sea-Plain," which likely corresponds to the "wet region" of the sky, in which the constellation Aquarius is situated. However, since Susano'o does not accept this domain but instead ascends to heaven and causes the mountains to shake, it seems most likely he is associated with Hercules rather than Aquarius. Additional support for this identification with Hercules is the fact that Susano'o is elsewhere described as wielding a great "ten-hand-breadth sword," which is certainly suggestive of the constellation Hercules in the heavens, brandishing a great sword-shaped weapon over his head and back.

Indeed, I suspect that both Amaterasu and Susano'o, who are generated from the eyes of Izanagi after he washes out the pollution of the underworld, may have some connection to the constellation Hercules, which is situated above Ophiuchus and which (particularly when envisioned in "whirling" form) rises up from the "eye" of the serpent-head on the western serpent-half of Ophiuchus. Note that by her name, "Heaven's Illuminator," Amaterasu seems to be a sun goddess (this is certainly how she is usually described), and we have seen much evidence that the whirling form of the constellation Hercules is envisioned in some myth systems as the great solar disc, radiating beams of light (particularly in the solar iconography of ancient Egypt). The fact that Izanagi gives Amaterasu a beautiful necklace may also indicate her identification with the constellation Hercules, a constellation immediately adjacent to Corona Borealis and closely connected with it in many myths.

In the above-cited passages from the text, when Amaterasu picks up a bow and stands "valiantly like unto a man," however, Amaterasu seems to be associated with characteristics of the constellation Sagittarius (which of course wields a great bow). In this passage, she is also described as winding the jeweled cord into her hair -- and Sagittarius is notable for the long "plume" which curves up above the head of the constellation. This plume in the outline of the constellation could very well be what is indicated by the frequent reference to Amaterasu winding the jewelled string into her hair (see star-chart on the page opposite).

The association with Sagittarius becomes important in the next episode involving Amaterasu and Susano'o, because Sagittarius will be shown to have a close connection with the act of weaving at the loom in many other Star Myths, particularly in the myths of ancient Greece (where we find Sagittarius-figures engaged in weaving *many* times in Volume Two of this series) but also in the Norse myths (as discussed in *Star Myths of the World, Volume Four*).

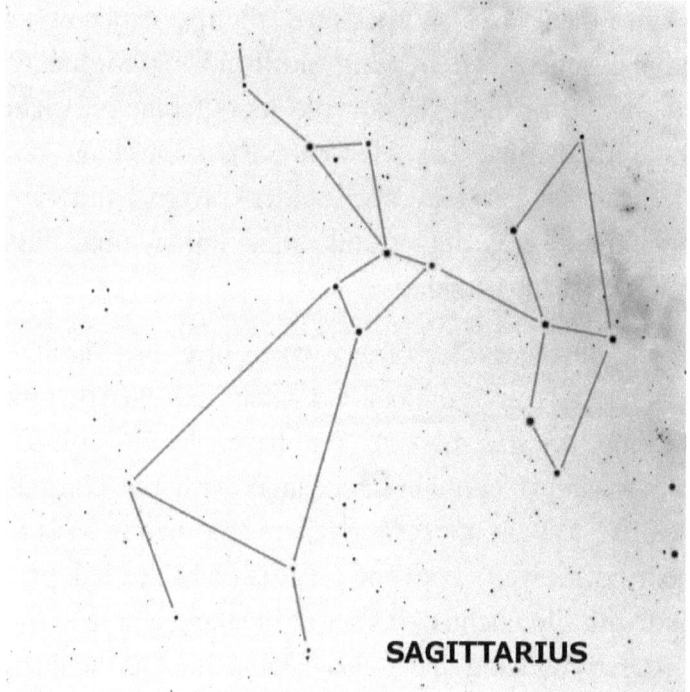

SAGITTARIUS

After the two have children, the Kojiki tells us Susano'o becomes impetuous, and goes on a rampage: "he broke down the divisions of the ricefields laid out by the Heaven-Shining-Great-August-Deity [Amaterasu], filled up the ditches, and moreover strewed excrements in the palace where she partook of the great food."[537]

Amaterasu tries to excuse his behavior, but this only makes Susano'o become even more violent. As Amaterasu was "overseeing the weaving of sacred robes inside the hallowed sanctum of the weaving hall,"[538] (in Gustav Heldt's translation of the text), Susano'o breaks a hole in the top of the weaving-hall, and through it let fall "a heavenly piebald horse which he had flayed with a backward flaying," (in Basil Hall Chamberlain's translation).[539]

At this shocking behavior, "the women weaving the heavenly garments were so much alarmed" that they jabbed their weaving shuttles into themselves and perished (the text explicitly tells us where they jammed their weaving shuttles).[540] So frightened and upset at this horrifying behavior and its outcome is Amaterasu that she retreats into her Heavenly Rock-Dwelling (Gustav Heldt translates it as "Heaven's Boulder Cavern") and slams the door behind her, securing it and going into hiding, plunging heaven and earth into darkness.[541]

What could all this rather bizarre chain of events signify? The actions described can be understood when we realize that the text is describing *celestial* figures. We have already argued that Susano'o is almost certainly associated with the constellation Hercules. While I am not certain what could be the basis for the excrement he strewed about the great feast hall (a hall probably identified with Ophiuchus), his act of breaking a hole in the roof of the sacred weaving hall (also Ophiuchus) is familiar: the "whirling" version of Hercules has been associated with a hole in a building before (in the African myth of Kintu and Nambi):

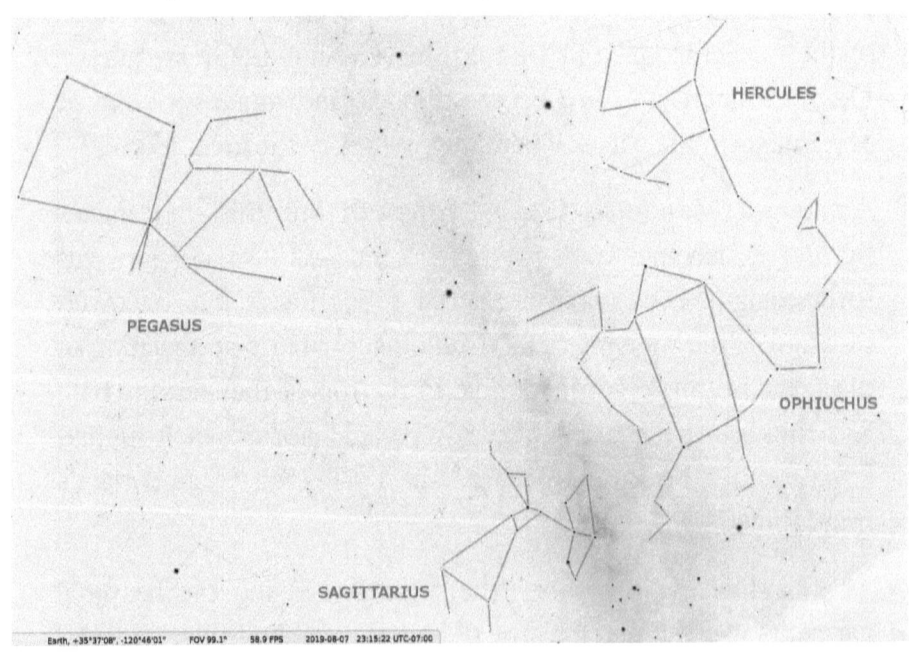

Note that there is also a story in the gospel about breaking a hole in a roof in order to lower a man down to Jesus for healing (in the gospel according to Mark, chapter 2).

The "piebald horse flayed backward" (that is to say, "beginning at the tail" as Basil Hall Chamberlain explains in a footnote)[542] can be confidently identified as the constellation Pegasus, with the *Great Square* representing the skin which is peeled off the body starting at the tail:

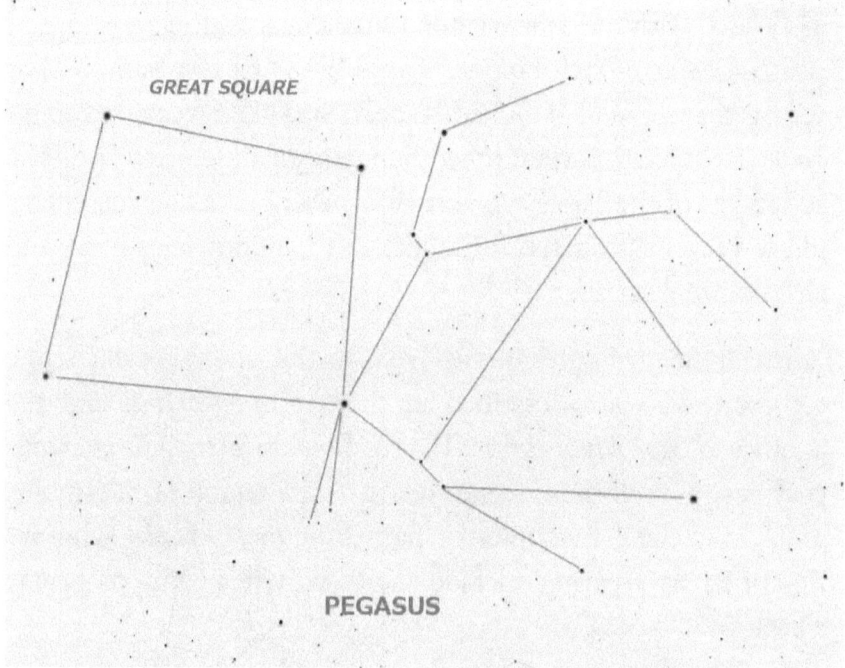

The casting down of this backward-flayed piebald horse through the hole in the roof by the impetuous Susano'o takes place while Amaterasu and her accompanying kami are weaving. The act of weaving is an important motif in many of the world's myths, and in the numerous myths I have examined, I have always concluded that it is closely associated with the constellations Sagittarius and Ophiuchus, with Ophiuchus possibly representing a loom (or, in this case, a "weaving hall") and the Milky Way itself possibly playing the tapestry or fabric which Sagittarius or Ophiuchus is weaving.

In the Norse myths recorded in the eddic texts, there is an entire poem in the Elder Edda describing the encounter of Odin with a giant whose name is Mighty Weaver: this encounter is explored in *Star Myths of the World, Volume Four* and found to be describing the constellations Sagittarius and Ophiuchus.

In the scriptures of the Bible, the giant Goliath is shown to be associated with the constellation Ophiuchus, as discussed in *Star Myths of the World, Volume Three*. The text of 1 Samuel 17: 7 tells us that the staff of Goliath's spear "*was* like a weaver's beam." Indeed, there are several other giants or gigantic warriors in the scriptures of the Bible who are also described as having spears like a weaver's beam (see 2 Samuel 21: 19, 1 Chronicles 11: 23, and also 1 Chronicles 20: 5).

There are many figures in the Greek myths (and especially in the Odyssey) who are described in the act of weaving, and the analysis in *Star Myths of the World, Volume Two* finds evidence that here as well these scenes relate to the region of Sagittarius and Ophiuchus. Examples of figures in the Odyssey who are described as weaving include Calypso, Circe, and of course Penelope.

Star Myths of the World, Volume Two also provides evidence showing that the outline of the bow of Sagittarius corresponds very closely to the shape of certain types of ancient hand-operated shuttles.[543]

In other words, the evidence that these events described in the Kojiki (which are otherwise quite inexplicable and somewhat disturbing) are based upon celestial figures is quite strong.

Sometimes, those who encounter my arguments that the world's ancient myths, from virtually every culture on the globe, can be shown to be based on the stars reply that such an argument makes sense: after all, most of the same stars can be seen from just about every place on earth. However, parallels such as the one just noted, in which the region containing Sagittarius and Ophiuchus is repeatedly associated with the act of weaving (in cultures which are far apart from one another, such as the cultures that produced the Hebrew scriptures of the Bible, the Elder Edda of Scandinavia and Iceland, the Odyssey of ancient Greece, and the Kojiki of ancient Japan) are simply not easily explained by the simple fact that "the stars can be seen around the globe."

First of all, we would not necessarily expect the same outlining-system to be independently adopted by cultures with no contact with one another (and no contact with some common predecessor culture). Secondly, even if different cultures *did* adopt the same (or roughly similar) constellations, we would not necessarily expect multiple cultures to independently envision those constellations as being associated with the act of weaving at a loom. It is simply not immediately obvious that such should be the case. When we find the same pattern emerging in cultures separated so widely around our planet, we realize that this evidence poses a severe challenge to the conventional paradigm of our shared human history.

At the final insulting action of Susano'o, the goddess Amaterasu has had enough. She enters her Heavenly Rock-Dwelling and closes the great door fast behind her. All of heaven is plunged into darkness, as well as the Central Land of Reed-Plains.

We are told by the text that the kami "assemble in a divine assembly in the bed of the Tranquil River of Heaven," and ask a kami whose name Basil Hall Chamberlain renders as "Thought-Includer" to think of a plan. The kami all help in the preparation of the plan. Here are some of their preparations (Heldt translates):

> They sought out One Eye, the smith of heaven.
> They bade the mighty one Stone Mold Crone make a mirror.
> They bade the mighty one Jewel Ancestor make long strnads strung with many curved pendants.
> They summoned the mighty one Little Roof of Heaven and the mighty one Solemn Soul and had them prepare a divination by removing the shoulder bone of a true stag from Mount Gleaming in heaven and gathering wood from the bird cherries on its slopes to burn it with.
> They uprooted by its roots a many-branched hallowed evergreen that flourished on Mount Gleaming in heaven.
> From its upper branches they hung long strands strung with many curved pendants.
> From its middle branches they hung a massive mirror.
> From its lower branches they hung prayer strips made of white mulberry paper and blue hemp.
> The mighty one Solemn Soul bore these things aloft in solemn offering.
> The mighty one Little Roof of Heaven intoned solemn hymns in prayer.
> The spirit Strong-Armed Man of Heaven stood in hiding by the cavern entrance.[544]

With the preparations all in order, the kami are ready to put their plan into action. The kami named *Ame-no-Uzume-no-mikoto* 天宇受売命 prepares to begin her dance. Basil Hall Chamberlain translates her name as "Her Augustness Heavenly-Alarming Female" and Gustav Heldt translates it as "Wreathed Woman of Heaven."[545]

The text tells us that Ame-no-Uzume binds up the leaves of the bamboo-grass from the mountain "in a posy for her hands," and lays a "soundingboard before the door of the Heavenly Rock-Dwelling" to dance upon.[546] Basil Hall Chamberlain in a footnote regarding this "soundingboard" says that the slightly later work *Nihon Shoki* or *Nihongi* records this object with a character that means "tub" or "trough" or "manger."[547] Then the text tells us that Uzume "stamped loudly on it and became possessed, showing her breasts and pushing the girdle of her skirt down past her privates."[548]

At this display, all the assembled kami begin to laugh. Their laughter shakes the Plain of High Heaven. The sound of the laughing of eight hundred myriad kami all together reaches Amaterasu inside her Boulder Cavern. She cracks open the door just a little bit and asks why Uzume would be singing and dancing, and all the assembled kami laughing, with the world plunged into darkness?

Uzume replies that they were laughing and dancing due to the arrival of a kami even more illustrious than Amaterasu herself! As Uzume is giving her answer, Little Roof of Heaven and Solemn Soul place the mirror before Amaterasu. Seeing her own reflection, Amaterasu begins to come out a bit further past the door to gaze at the reflection.

At this, Heavenly-Hand-Strength-Male-Deity (or "Strong-Armed Man of Heaven" as his name is rendered by Gustav Heldt) takes Amaterasu's hand and draws her out all the way from the cave. At the same time, "the mighty one Solemn Soul drew forth a sacred boundary rope whose straw ends hung down, stretched it out behind her mighty back, and spoke, saying: 'You shall not turn back past here!'"[549]

Of this boundary rope, which in the original is called *shiri-kume-naha*, Basil Hall Chamberlain says in a footnote:

> rope made of straw drawn up by the roots, which stick out from the end of the rope. Straw ropes thus manufactured are still used in certain ceremonies and are called shime-naha, a corrpution of the Archaic term.[550]

These ropes are still used today to create or demarcate a sacred space, and to prevent the movement of spirits.[551] Below is an image of a sacred torii gate with shimenawa:

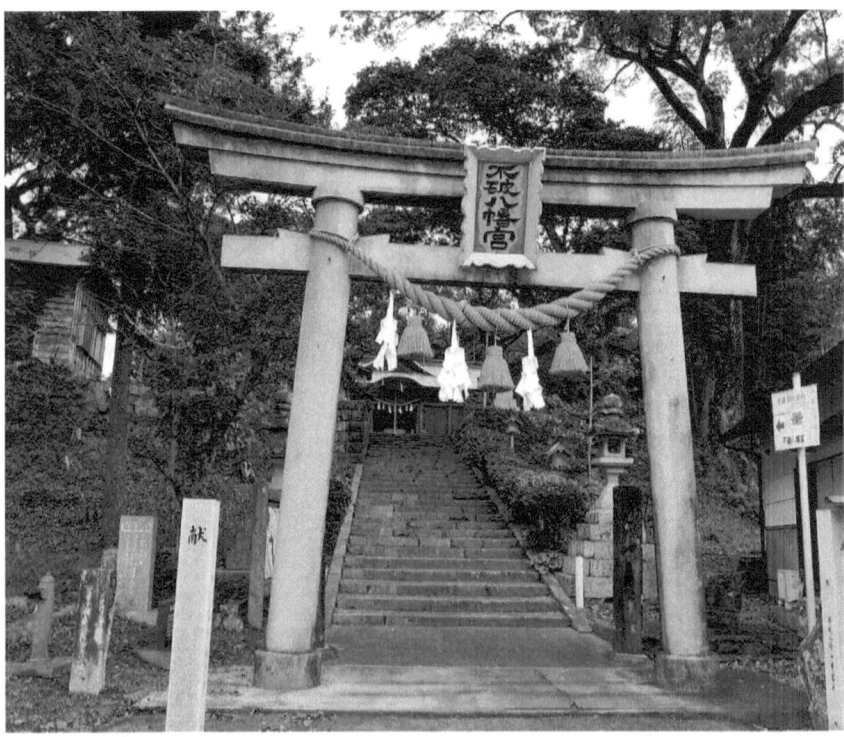

Such is the nature of the rope which was pulled over the opening to the Rock-Dwelling to prevent Amaterasu from retreating again into hiding.

Below is another shimenawa rope, joining the famous Meoto Iwa
or "Married Couple" rocks in the sea off the shore of Futami in
Mie Prefecture. These rocky islets are said to represent Izanagi
and Izanami; the rice straw rope which binds them weighs over a
ton and must be replaced several times a year due to the impact of
wind and water:

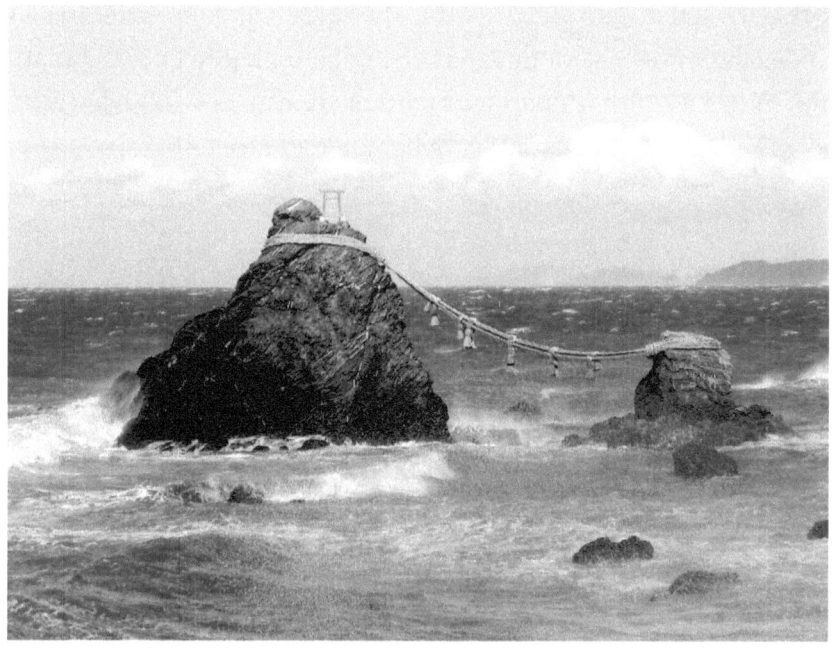

Note the presence of a torii on the larger of the two rocks. There
is clearly a connection between the torii gate (which marks a place
of crossing between the sacred and the mundane) and the
shimenawa rope (which similarly demarcates the boundaries of
sacred spaces).

What can we glean from this ancient myth which may point to the
presence of the ancient foundations -- foundations that, although
now fragmented, can yet be detected underneath myths from so
many cultures and climes around the globe, connecting even the
most superficially dissimilar?

To begin with, many of the kami mentioned in the preparations for the plot to bring back Amaterasu from her self-imposed exile can be tentatively identified with specific constellations. For example, we meet "One Eye, the smith of heaven" -- and note that in Volume Two of this series we will discover that the giant Cyclopes of Greek mythology (who are also mighty smiths) are beyond doubt associated with the constellation Aquarius, a constellation whose outline has a single eye, and who often plays the role of a smith (due to the fact that we can envision his water-vessel instead as a celestial set of hammer and tongs):

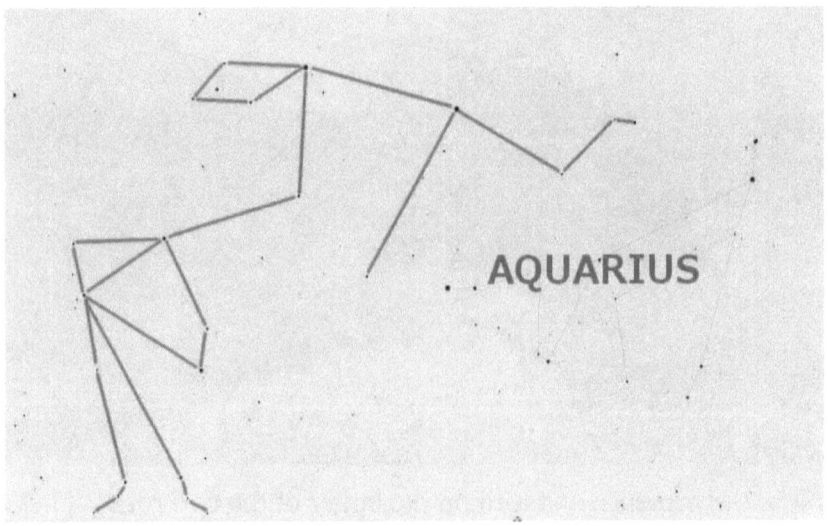

AQUARIUS

The introduction of a kami smith named One Eye, then, resonates strongly with smith-figures in other myths.

We also meet a kami named "Little Roof of Heaven" who, along with Solemn Soul, are responsible for many of the preparations for their plan to lure Amaterasu back out of her rocky cave. Given the fact that I am convinced that the rocky cavern into which Amaterasu retreats is the great "cleft in the rock" formed by Ophiuchus in the heavens (when the two serpent-halves are viewed as though the cliff-walls of a great split in a mountain, with a central figure in between these walls), I believe we will find Little Roof of Heaven in close proximity to Ophiuchus. I would suggest that the kami named Little Roof of Heaven likely corresponds to the constellation Libra, immediately adjacent to Ophiuchus, and like Ophiuchus shaped like a roof supported by two posts, except that Libra is smaller than Ophiuchus (and hence Libra is the "Little Roof of Heaven," while Ophiuchus has a larger roof):

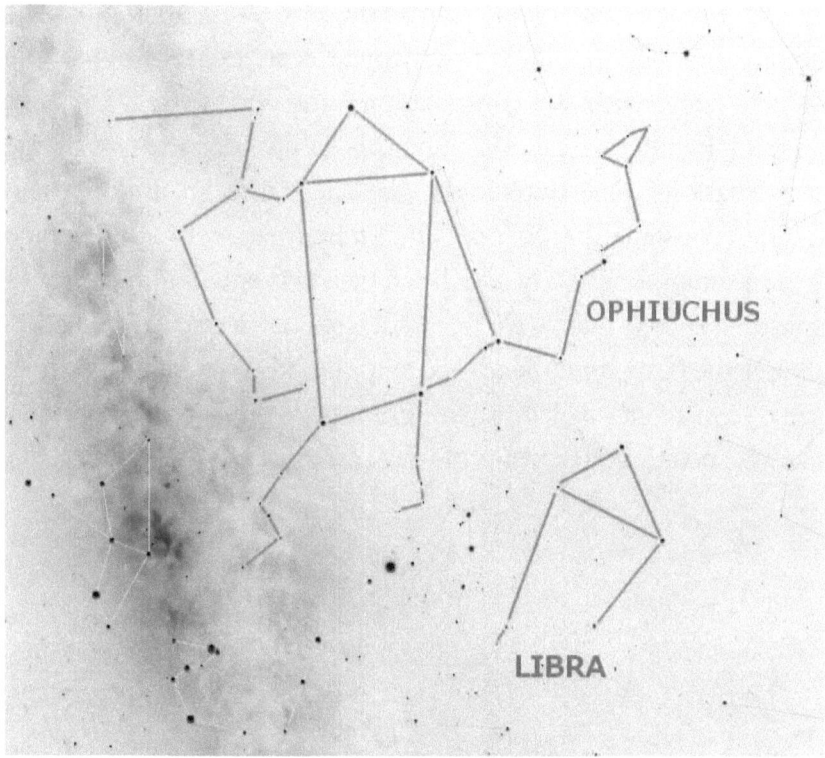

What about the identity of the string of jewels, eight feet long, which the kami hang on the upper branches of the hallowed evergreen that they brought from the top of Mount Gleaming in heaven? Well, the tree atop the mountain we have seen to be associated with the constellation Hercules above Ophiuchus, and thus it is likely that the necklace hung in the branches of this tree

813

corresponds to the constellation Corona Borealis, which (as we have mentioned many times) can be envisioned as connected to one arm (or branch) of the constellation Hercules.

And what of the identity of Ame-no-Uzume, whose sexually explicit dance causes the kami to shake the heavens with their laughter, and arouses the curiosity of Amaterasu to come and inquire as to what is going on?

I believe that certain clues, such as the posy of bamboo grass she holds in her hand, point strongly towards an identification of the kami Uzume with the constellation Virgo in the heavens. The posy of bamboo grass, of course, is easily identified with the constellation Coma Berenices in the celestial realm, a "posy" held by the constellation Virgo. The overturned tub upon which Uzume stamps as she begins her dance and enters into a state of spiritual trance may well be associated with the constellation Crater the Cup, underneath Virgo in the sky (or perhaps with the same constellation Libra we examined previously, which is likewise positioned beneath the feet of Virgo in the heavens):

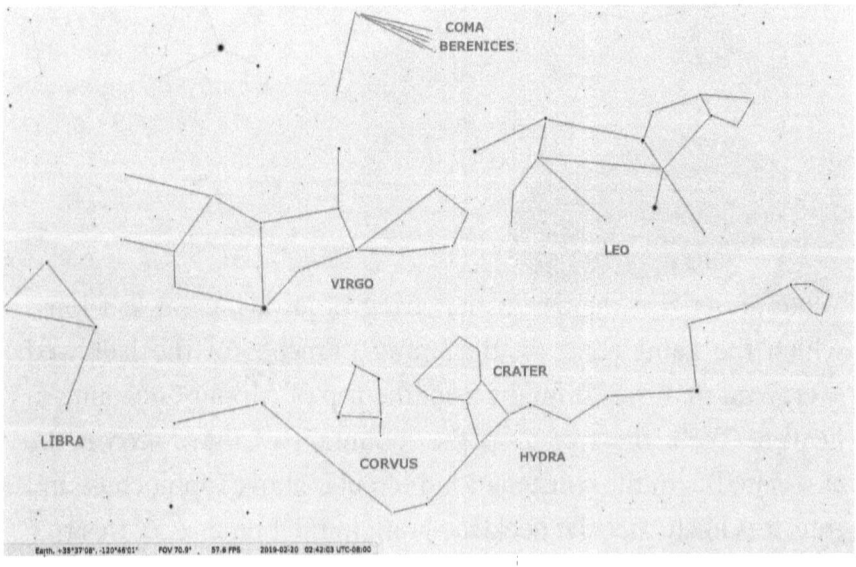

Note that in the above star-chart I have also drawn the lines which form the shape of the constellation Corvus the Crow, which stands close by to the constellation Virgo in the heavens and thus is closely associated with Virgo-figures in some myths. This constellation appears to have been envisioned as a rooster in some ancient myth -- and some depictions of the kami Uzume feature an accompanying rooster (also note her extended arm):

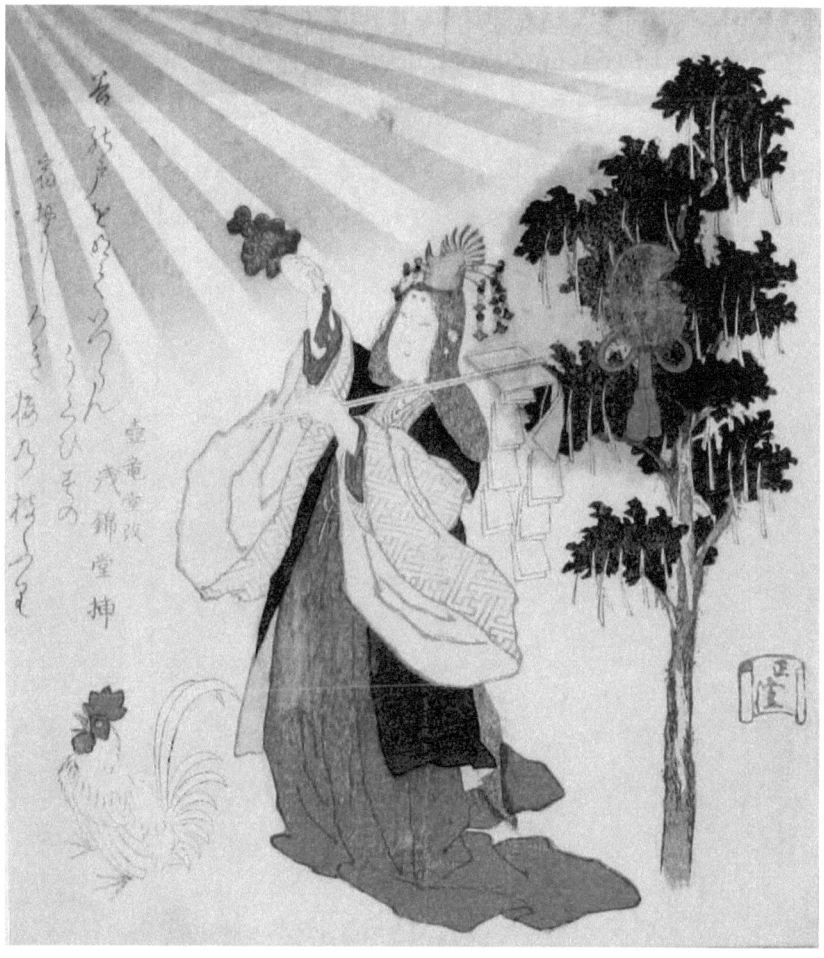

As Amaterasu peeks out of her rock-cavern and inquires about the cause of the commotion, Little Roof of Heaven and Solemn Soul hold up the mirror and place it before her.

What could be the celestial original for this mirror? In the past, I thought that it might be seen in a large circle of very faint stars located in front of the upper body and face of the constellation Virgo. However, as I have analyzed this myth further, and realized that in this story the sun-goddess Amaterasu has hidden herself within the cleft of the rock that can be identified with the constellation Ophiuchus, I realized that the mirror must be held up to the figure peeking out from within this rock-cleft, not the figure doing the dancing (Virgo being identified with Uzume in this episode).

It came to me that the mirror in this story is almost certainly seen in the form of the familiar serpent-head of Ophiuchus!

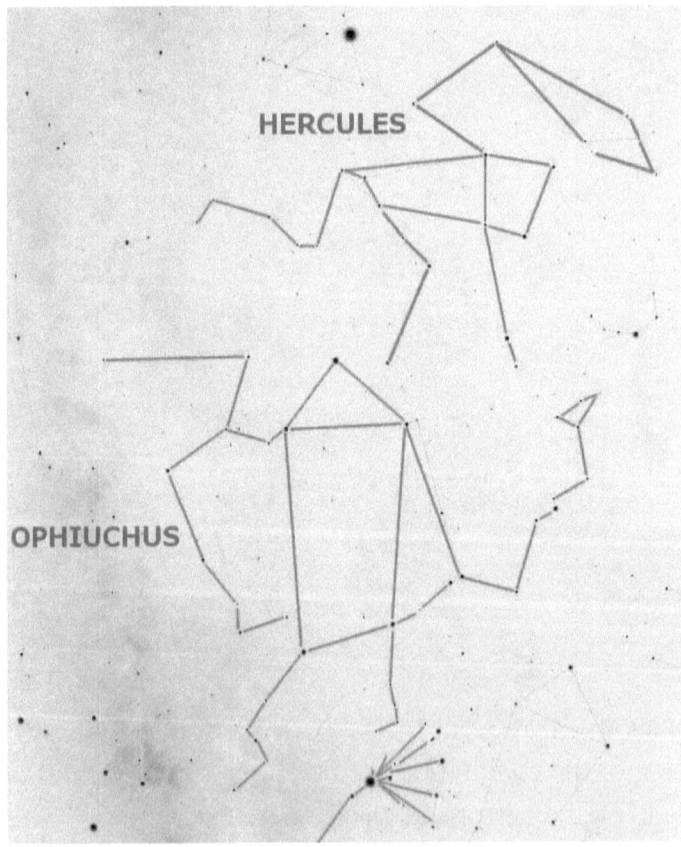

As she creeps forward to investigate the image in the mirror, Heavenly-Hand-Strength-Male-Deity (translated *Strong-Armed Man of Heaven* by Gustav Heldt) takes her hand and draws her out. Heavenly-Hand-Strength-Male-Deity can be identified with the constellation Hercules, who reaches down towards Ophiuchus as if to lead Amaterasu out by the hand when she comes to investigate the cause of the laughter of the assembled kami.

And what could be the identity of the great sacred boundary-rope which is drawn across the entrance to the boulder-cave, so that Amaterasu cannot go back? That rope can be identified with the two "serpent-halves" held by the constellation Ophiuchus, here envisioned as a great shimenawa which closes off the gate of the cave.

The torii gate itself, which has become an emblem representing Shinto and known the world over, may well be patterned upon the celestial form of Ophiuchus in heaven, which itself represents a gate in many myths (and whose central body consists of rising parallel "pillars" on either side, topped by an "upper space" enclosed by the top triangle, just as the torii has two vertical pillars topped by an additional "upper space" which, even though not triangular, can perhaps be seen as patterned after or somehow descended from the overall shape of Ophiuchus). The close association between the torii and the shimenawa may well stem from the fact that both the gate and the ropes are connected to the same centrally-important constellation in the night sky.

The authors of *Hamlet's Mill* address the significance of the bawdy dance of Uzume, in Appendix 36 of their text. They note that sexually explicit dance appears in numerous myths from around the globe, nearly always to placate an angry goddess or to bring back a sun deity:

> Amaterasu [. . .] was caused to come out again only by the lascivious dances of "the ugly sky-female," Uzume, dancing with the celestial jewel-tree upon her head, amidst 800,000 gods assembled in the Milky Way, and producing fire afterward. Egyptian Ra, who had retired from a world which he did not like anymore, was "persuaded" by the same kind of jokes by Isis to take up again his duties ("And then the great god laughed at her"). The motif emerges again in the Edda, where Loke and a he-goat make the angry Skadi laugh, preventing her, thus, from avenging the murder of her father, Thiassi. The story has also survived, although in dull disguise, in the Polynesian Marquesas Islands and, in excellent shape, with the Cherokee Indians; there the sex appeal is missing, admittedly, but the *agelastos* character is Mother Sun, desolate about the death of her only duaghter: a true Demeter [. . .].[552]

The term *agelastos* which is used in the above discussion from Hamlet's Mill refers to the name of a rock in Greek myth upon which the goddess Demeter sits after the abduction of Persephone, threatening to withdraw her life-giving grain forever if Persephone is not returned. The word *agelastos* (or *agelasta*) means "laughterless" or "without a smile" in Greek. Demeter must be made to smile, a pattern in numerous myths around the globe. She is finally made to laugh by the indecent dance of an old woman named Iambe (after whose name comes the adjective *iambic*, as in iambic verse or iambic pentameter: the dance itself was done in the iambic meter, according to some versions of the myth).

Once again, the world-wide scope of this particular (and very specific) myth-pattern defies explanation via the conventional paradigms taught in academia to this day.

Note too that the withdrawal of Amaterasu parallels not only the threatened withdrawal of Demeter but also the previously-mentioned withdrawal of Achilles from the Trojan War (to sulk in his tent), the previously-examined withdrawal of Arjuna at the start of the Battle of Kurukshetra (where he is located in a war-car which is likewise associated with Ophiuchus), as well as the delay by Jesus mentioned in the gospels when Lazarus was sick (mentioned in John II: 6).

These are truly astonishing parallels which we find between the ancient mythology of Nihon and myth-patterns which surface literally around the world. The explanation for these parallels, I am convinced, is found in the fact that the myths of the world retain a common foundation and speak a common language -- a language of celestial metaphor, built upon a foundation laid down in remote antiquity of such great age that the system was already many centuries old (at least) before the rise of the oldest civilizations known to conventional history.

There are certainly more myths from ancient Japan which could be explored for their celestial content, as can be said of the myths of all the cultures which we have visited (too briefly) in this volume. However, at this point we have I trust provided enough evidence to prove once again beyond the shadow of a doubt that the myths of Nihon, in common with the received ancient wisdom of *virtually every other culture* on this earth, employ a shared system of astronomical allegory.

While outside the scope of this volume, it is worth pointing out in passing that the sacred rituals of the Shinto tradition, enacted down through the centuries in a form that preserves their ancient outlines, have been argued by Jenichiro Oyabe (1867 - 1941) to have astonishing parallels to observances recorded in the Hebrew scriptures of the so-called Old Testament. He points out abundant examples to support his argument, including the carrying of an ark called the *mikoshi* into the water on a significant day of the year, the pattern of the shrines themselves which resembles the layout directed for the tabernacle in the Old Testament, the use of uncut or unhewn stones in the walls surrounding the Grand Shrine of Ise, and the keeping of sacred shrine relics within an inner sanctum hidden from view, with strong parallels to the Holy of Holies described in the Old Testament scriptures. He also makes numerous arguments for linguistic parallels between terms from the Hebrew scriptures and corresponding Japanese words.[553]

While Dr. Oyabe has (if correct in identifying at least *some* of his alleged parallels) performed a valuable service by using his knowledge of Shinto to analyze similarities between the rituals, locoi and objects described in the Old Testament and the ceremonies and shrines and accessories which have been and continue to be used in the indigenous Kami Way of Nihon, evidence which appears to point to *some* kind of connection (if not by actual contact between cultures then by close adherence to some now-unknown common source), this evidence and commonality by no means indicates that the persons and events described in the Hebrew scriptures describe literal and terrestrial history.

Indeed, as demonstrated in *Star Myths of the World, Volume Three* (*Star Myths of the Bible*), the characters and events found in the Old Testament, as well as the New Testament, can be shown to be celestial metaphor, from start to finish. Thus, it is

820

mistaken to conclude (as Jenichiro Oyabe apparently concluded) that Japan was influenced by -- or indeed settled by -- a so-called "lost tribe" of ancient Israel. These "tribes" or groupings described in the Old Testament can be shown to be *tribes or groupings of stars* (primarily stars which make up the zodiac ring of constellations).

Rather, as we have argued throughout, it is better to conclude that *both sets of myths are based on the stars* -- and a shared foundation of celestial metaphor. Having seen that the figures and events described in the Kojiki are based upon this esoteric system of allegory, it is reasonable to believe that they are designed to convey an esoteric message, and not an overt or literal message confined to describing events in terrestrial history (or even embellished terrestrial history).

Based upon some of the parallels noted above regarding figures who "doubt" or "withdraw" in other celestially-founded myths from around the world (in which category we can include Achilles and Arjuna and Doubting Thomas, for example), we can suggest that the *meaning* of story of the withdrawal of the sun-goddess Amaterasu has little or nothing to do with the actual annual cycle of the sun with regards to the decline of the sun's power during the winter, or even its "standstill" at the critical point of winter solstice. Yes, the story may use those aspects of the solar cycle as the metaphor *through which* it conveys its esoteric meaning, but the ultimate *meaning* of the myth is not the obvious fact that "the sun's path across the sky grows lower and lower during the winter months, culminating in a low-point at winter solstice."

Rather, I would propose that the esoteric message of this myth, as with so many of the others we have studied, has to do with the elusiveness of our own divine nature, and our own Higher Self, from whom our conscious mind has been severed or separated, in part by the entangling net of "connections" and "attachments" which we begin to weave as part of our integration into human society (and which is also woven for us by our families and the other institutions into which we are incorporated), and in part by the very fact of our traumatic plunge out of the realm of spirit and into the realm of matter and incarnation in the physical body itself.

The stories of Achilles withdrawing from the battlefield, or of Jesus going down into the tomb, or of Amaterasu shutting herself up within the great rock cavern indicate that the deeper subconscious, and the divine and indeed infinite realm with which that subconscious is mysteriously connected, is now hidden, and difficult to find: it has withdrawn to a deep and dark place. To reconnect with and become integrated again with our inner connection to the Infinite, we must search for the divine in a deep and dark place as well. That deep and dark place is within. To reconnect, then, requires meditation in darkness and in silence, the myths seem to imply.

They also imply that there must be some sort of mocking or ridicule or *sense of detachment* from the realities of the physical body, depicted in this story by the bawdy dance of Uzume, a dance which has its counterpart in other myths around the globe as noted by the authors of *Hamlet's Mill*. Perhaps Uzume can bare her breasts and pull at her nipples and tug her skirt down to her thighs in front of an assembly of laughing gods because she does not take these things so seriously that she is overly attached to them, or at least because she is showing us that we ourselves must have a sense of detachment regarding the incarnate realm.

This assertion should not be understood to imply that I believe the myths are at all advocating indecent exposure in public (or that I advocate it) -- quite to the contrary. Again, I do not believe they are teaching their lessons in a *literal* but rather in an esoteric fashion. I would suggest that what may be implied by this recurring pattern of the indecent dance that brings a smile to the goddess (helping her to redisover her own sense of humor, if you will) may instead have to do with the entire understanding of our incarnation in a human body in the first place: it may well be that the myths are teaching that our understanding of this condition in which we find ourselves should be that of amusement, because we find the entire arrangement somewhat funny.

It is like the Buddha observing the attacks of Mara and the blandishments of Mara's daughters with detachment, or Krishna telling Arjuna to act rightly but without attachment to the outcome: as if not acting at all. It seems safe to say that we can laugh at something when we have one step of remove from it, when we can step outside of our entanglement with (or identification with) a situation and see it as funny. Perhaps this is why the goddess must be made to laugh in so many myths: it is an enactment of the "one step of remove" that is being demonstrated in other myths we have examined -- the same kind of "detachment from entanglement" that is allegorized in the giving of the reins of the chariot to Lord Krishna in the battle of Kurukshetra.

Indeed, I would argue that the myths are imparting to us the same lesson, over and over, using different metaphors in hopes that *one* (at least) will enable us to grasp their profound message. If we do not get it from one story, perhaps we will see it when presented in a different way.

We earlier examined a metaphor of "invisible furniture," to represent the "invisible truths" that the myths want to reveal to us (truths about the Invisible Realm, with which we are actually connected, although we are usually unaware of this connection, which is why we often trip and stumble over the invisible furniture that is all around us).

If we were in a room that had a number of invisible chairs and a couple of invisible tables and other pieces of furniture, we would not be able to see these objects directly (because they are invisible). But if we were to drape over these invisible pieces of furniture a number of sheets or blankets (visible sheets and visible blankets), then we would be able to see the outlines of those invisible objects, by seeing the sheets and blankets draped over the furniture, and given shape by the invisible objects underneath.

The world's ancient Star Myths, I suggest, are like these sheets and blankets, draped over the invisible furniture below. They enable us to perceive invisible truths, which we would be unable to perceive on our own. The fabric and texture and designs upon these sheets vary greatly from one culture to the next, and from one myth-family to another. The texture and feel of the Norse myths are very different from the texture and feel of the myths of ancient India -- and yet I would argue that they are simply different blankets or coverings which have been draped over the same invisible truths underneath, in order to enable us to see and to grasp what would otherwise cause us to stumble.

Sometimes the covering fabric is thin and gauzy, and barely embellished with mythical designs at all (such as in the Dao De Jing, for instance, in which we do not find elaborate tales of gods and goddesses and monsters and heros and kings and queens, although we still find esoteric language and celestial metaphor being employed, as we have now seen). Other times, the blankets are thick and plush and elaborately embroidered with fantastical designs, memorable characters, and interconnecting plots. But they are all intended to enable us to see *beyond* the fabric itself (*beneath* the fabric itself), to the invisible substance that is underneath.

Thus, with this story of Amaterasu hiding within the cave, and the enthusiastic and divinely-inspired dance of Ame-no-Uzume, we will conclude this tour through the Star Myths of cultures which stretch across the entire globe and which yet are connected by a single coherent celestial system. We have explored some representative myths of the Indigenous Aboriginal people of Australia, of the cultures of Africa, of the nations and civilizations of the Americas, of the people living on the tropical islands which dot the vast expanse of the Pacific Ocean, of the cultures of ancient Egypt, ancient Mesopotamia, ancient India, ancient China, and ancient Japan.

These myths have filled hundreds of pages, and yet we have only barely scratched the surface of the material available in any single one of these cultures. And we have of necessity overlooked and neglected many other cultures altogether, whose myths and sacred stories likewise constitute a priceless treasure within the inheritance of the family of humanity worldwide, and which could (and perhaps someday will) fill many more volumes of analysis exploring their celestial content and esoteric widsom.

And, as mentioned many times within the course of our tour, there are three full additional volumes of similar exploration still to come, in subsequent volumes in this series, as well as other books I've written outside of this series but which also explore the ancient worldwide system of Star Myths.

I hope that your relationship with the world's ancient myths will be a blessing to you in your life, as it has been and continues to be for me.

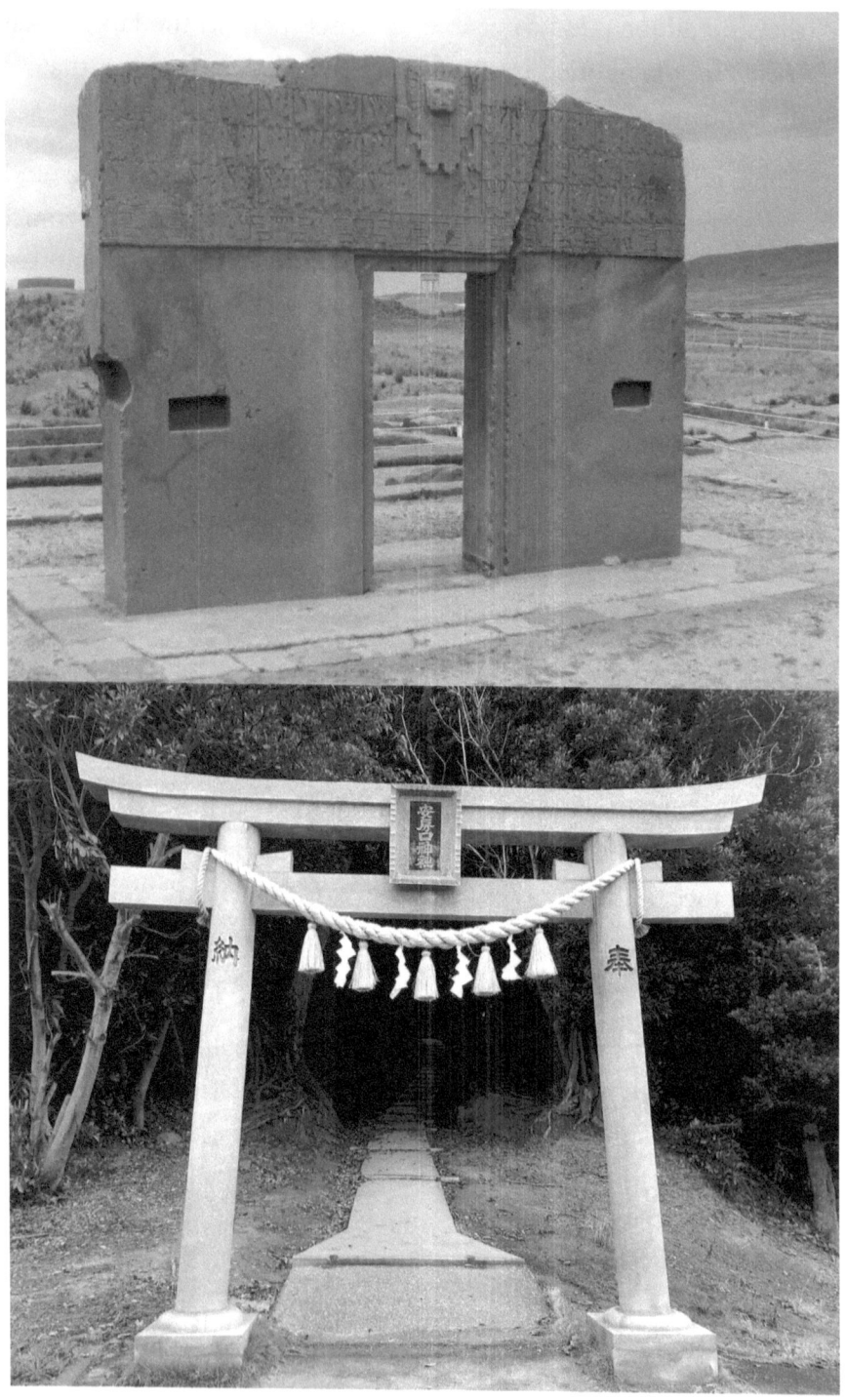

826

Concluding Thoughts

After several hundred pages including hundreds of star charts and examples from ancient artwork we have reached the end of this new edition of the first volume of the Star Myth series, but our journey is only just beginning.

We have seen compelling (and, I would argue, conclusive) evidence which argues that the world's ancient myths, scriptures and sacred stories, from virtually every culture on every inhabitable piece of land across our globe, share a common foundation -- a foundation of tremendous antiquity, and one which is patterned upon a very specific way of looking at the stars and their heavenly cycles, and which utilizes an esoteric "language" or "code" which assigns particular meaning to those cycles in order to dramatize and convey profound truths to us for our benefit and blessing.

The vast extent of this ancient system, whose fragmented ruins still peek (out as it were) from beneath the surface soil, and from between the jungle foliage or from beneath the surface of windswept desert sands or snowy northern landscapes, has necessitated the sheer length of this present volume, even though (as I have often felt compelled to explain), we have here only barely introduced the evidence available in the world's sacred traditions, and have only visited a small sampling of the world's cultures.

I could of course have divided this present volume into a number of shorter books, each examining for example the myths of a different continent, but in doing so I felt something might have been lost: the ability to present a very broad sweep of myths from literally around the globe, and to see again and again certain patterns and oicotypes emerging which argue very strongly that the world's ancient traditions all belong to a single amazing system, and in doing so to provide -- as much as it is possible to now do so for this long-forgotten language of celestial metaphor -- a kind of "Rosetta Stone" which enables us to begin to piece together the vocabulary and grammar and even some of the logic of this ancient inheritance of the human race.

We have seen, for example, the pattern of the "baby cast adrift upon the water," manifesting itself in the legends of ancient Mesopotamia surrounding Sargon of Akkad, and in the Sanskrit texts of ancient India concerning baby Karna (himself a product of a kind of "immaculate conception" by his mother Kunti and the god of the sun), and in the story of Hiruko the Leech-child preserved in the Kojiki of ancient Japan, and in the story of baby Maui who is cast into the sea-foam by his parents -- and of course in the story of baby Moses, placed into the Nile "in an ark of bulrushes" which is "daubed with slime and with pitch" in the book of Exodus.

The similarities in the characteristics of these stories, found in cultures which almost certainly did not have any contact or communication with one another, speaks to their descent from some common point of origin, as well as to their allegorization of a very specific part of the sky containing the constellations Scorpio and Ophiuchus, as well as the brightest part of the great Milky Way itself.

These patterns contain such specific detail across many cultures that they are extremely unlikely to have been generated independently of one another in multiple different cultures over and over again without any connection whatsoever. They involve a common way of seeing the outlines of constellations,

constellations which in many cases are difficult to trace out unless one actually knows the system of outlining which appears to have been shared by all these ancient cultures (and which can be seen manifesting itself in ancient artwork from around the world).

Other examples abound. We have seen the myth-pattern or oicotype of the "baby snatched up," which manifests itself in the story of Maui's rescue from the sea-shore by his powerful ancestor Tama-nui-ki-te-Rangi, and in the story of baby Achilles dipped into either a special fire or into the River Styx, with echoes to the story of the goddess Isis dipping an infant in the fire when she arrives in the kingdom of Byblos to search for the slain god Osiris, and we will see in a later volume in this series (when we take a deeper dive into the celestial foundation of the stories preserved in the Old and New Testaments of the Bible) that this same pattern underlies the famous episode known as the "Judgment of Solomon," in which the king orders a baby to be cut in half (the baby is not, in fact, actually cut in half in that story).

In all of these stories, we find compelling evidence that the stars of the constellation Hercules, reaching out to grasp the arc of stars known as Corona Borealis or the Northern Crown, provides the celestial original for the details of the mythological drama. It is *extremely* unlikely that cultures as widely separated as those in which we find these manifestations of the "baby snatched up" pattern settled upon this way of interpreting the stars independently: the constellation Hercules itself is not easy to trace out, and yet it was evidently envisioned in the very same way in cultures around the globe, and while the arc of the Northern Crown is in fact very easy to identify, it is extremely unusual to think of it as an infant, and one would not expect it to be imagined that way in one culture, let alone in many separate cultures.

Concluding Thoughts

And yet we need not conclude that the ancient Egyptians somehow interacted with the cultures found across the Pacific islands from Hawai'i to Aotearoa to Rapa Nui. The evidence points to an origin of this worldwide system in some predecessor culture which predates the earliest civilizations known to conventional history, some culture of such remote antiquity that it was perhaps as far removed in time from the founding dynasties of ancient Egypt as that ancient culture is distant in time from our own day.

We have in this volume, for example, seen evidence which suggests that the "satchel" pattern shown in ancient artwork from Mesopotamia -- a pattern which manifests itself in artwork elsewhere on our globe, as researchers such as Graham Hancock and Richard Cassaro and others have demonstrated -- may be a depiction of the constellation Libra, envisioned as an accessory carried by figures associated with the constellation Ophiuchus (a constellation of tremendous importance in the ancient worldwide system of myth, as we have seen in our journey through the myths in this book).

Indeed, I am not the first to point out that one of the remarkable pillars in the recently-uncovered (within just the past twenty years) ancient site known as Göbekli Tepe are inscribed with symbology that appears to be celestial in design, particularly on one of the many large T-shaped pillars uncovered in Enclosure D, a pillar that has been called "Pillar 43."

This pillar contains relief carvings depicting a scorpion next to a large vulture-like bird. The wings of the bird, as noted by Paul Burley in 2011 and discussed in Graham Hancock's *Magicians of the Gods* (2015) as well as in my own 2017 book *Astrotheology for Life*, are depicted with an angle strongly suggestive of the stars which make up the outline of the "bow" held by the constellation Sagittarius -- which in fact is the zodiac constellation adjacent to Scorpio in the heavens![554]

Very notable for our discussion of the "satchel" held by Ophiuchus-figures in ancient art, the same Pillar 43 also features three such satchels, above the scorpion and vulture:

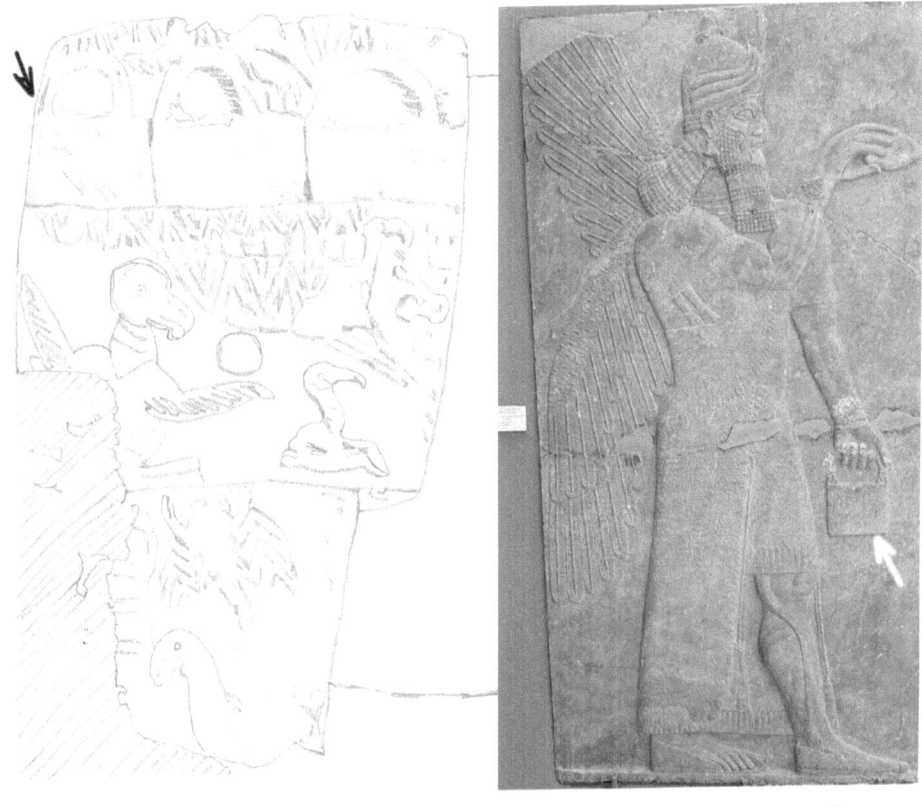

The image above shows at left a drawing I made of the artwork on Pillar 43, with an arrow indicating the leftmost of three "satchel" designs, juxtaposed with a relief from ancient Mesopotamia which we saw earlier (on page 442 -- and see also the image on page 439), of an anthropomorphic being holding an "egg" or "pinecone" in one hand (elevated) and holding a "satchel" or "purse" or "handbag" in the other hand (extended downwards).

Concluding Thoughts

The presence of this handbag-shape on artwork found on a pillar at Göbekli Tepe, a site of incredible antiquity (thought to have been deliberately buried not later than the year 8000 BC), suggests the possibility that the ancient worldwide system we are investigating in this volume has its origins in a time long before any culture or civilization known to the keepers of academic orthodoxy, an advanced culture whose very existence those orthodox academicians refuse to contemplate or consider, let alone admit. And yet the evidence pointing to the existence of such a culture is becoming more and more difficult to ignore.

The reader should also be made aware of the fact that figures holding the very same type of "satchel" or "handbag" artifact have been found in the Americas. The evidence is so plain that it simply cannot be denied (it can only be studiously ignored by those who wish to avoid facing the implications of these clues).

On the opposite page is an image showing the amazing artwork on a stele found at La Venta, in the heartland of the ancient Olmec civilization, about whom little is known. The Olmecs are sometimes referred to as the "mother culture" of Mesoamerica, dating back as early as 1800 BC. The famous "colossal heads" of the Olmecs (also found at La Venta) are thought to have been carved during the period between 850 BC and 700 BC.

The carved stele below is known as Monument 19 from La Venta. It depicts a crouching Olmec figure wearing what appears to be some kind of elaborate headgear, over whom rises a tremendous feathered serpent.

The crouching figure can be clearly seen to be holding a satchel or handbag in his extended arm, the outline of which bears an uncanny resemblance to the satchels depicted on other artwork from other parts of the globe, including the satchels shown on artwork from the civilizations of ancient Mesopotamia:

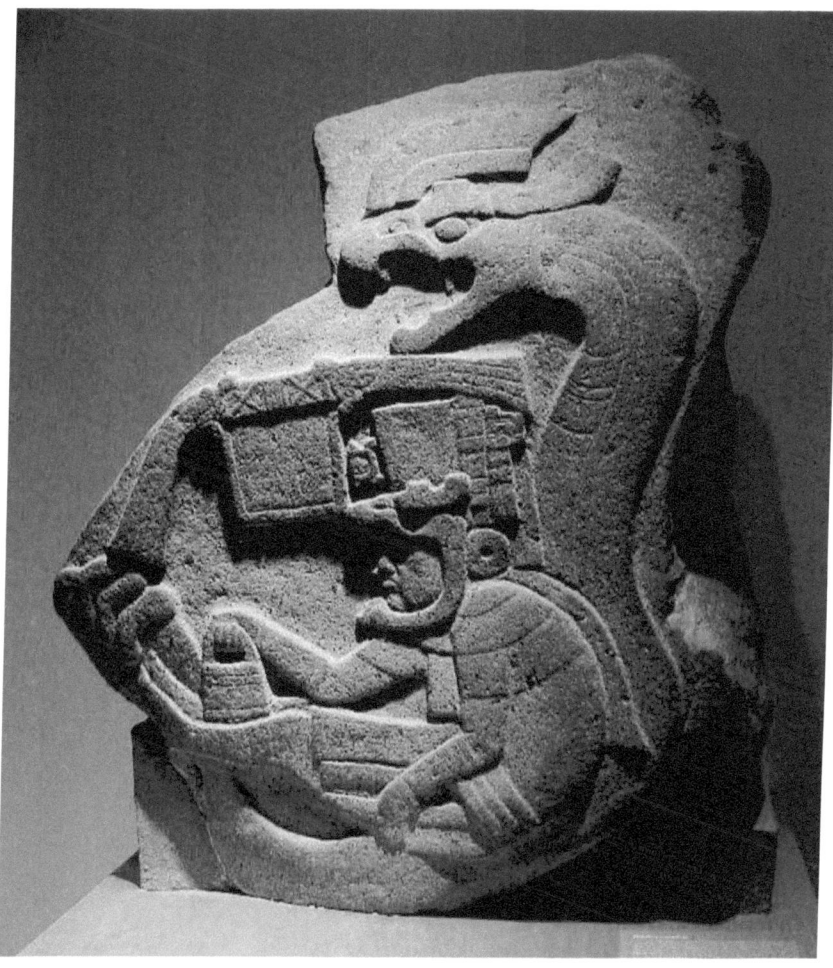

Once again, I would argue that this artwork follows celestial patterns, with the helmeted figure likely associated in some way with Ophiuchus, holding a satchel likely associated with the constellation Libra. Note the "arch" over the head of the crouching figure, which we have noted many times on other Ophiuchus-linked artwork around the globe (such as in the fifteenth-century Krishna sculpture shown on page 629).

Concluding Thoughts

The feathered serpent in this Olmec stele may represent the "western serpent-half" of Ophiuchus (the "serpent-head" side of the serpent of Ophiuchus). We saw evidence to support a connection between Ophiuchus and the deity called Plumed Serpent in the Popol Vuh of the Maya, discussed for instance on page 173 of this volume.

The connection between Ophiuchus and sacred portals, which we saw in the torii gates of Shinto, is found in the Americas as well, such as in the famous "Gate of the Sun" at Tiwanaku:

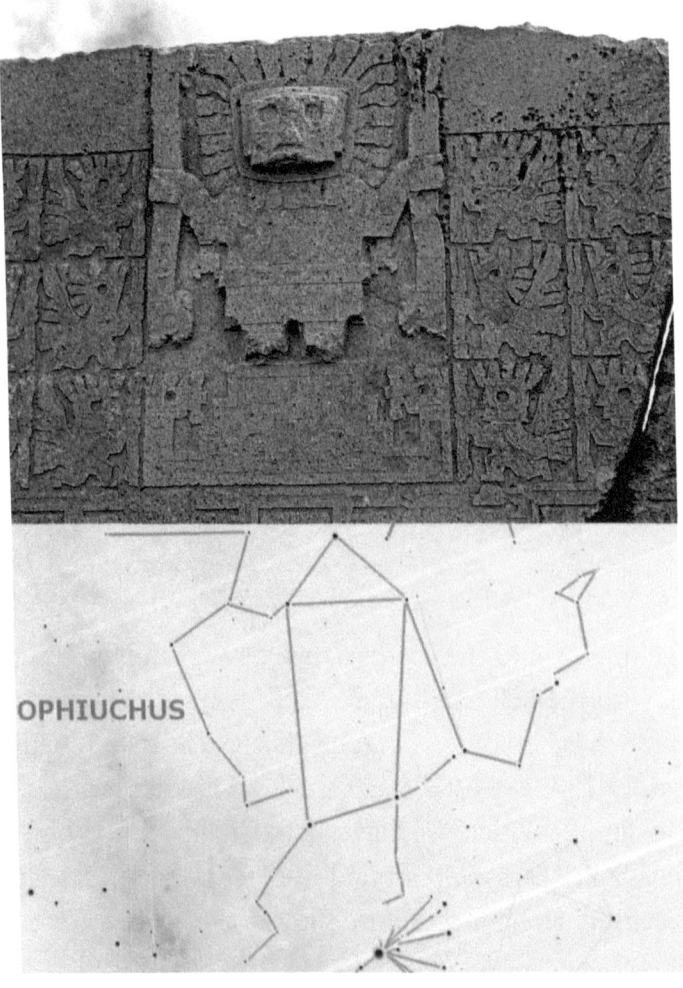

Lest any object that the similarity between the figure atop the *gate-shaped* monument and the constellation in the sky is mere coincidence, look more closely at the image above and you will see that the designers of this gate have included numerous smaller winged figures repeated in the square pattern on either side of the larger central icon. These winged figures display the distinctive "deep-knee bend" posture which we have seen to be characteristic of the constellation Ophiuchus and which is so clearly seen in depictions of the hero Heracles in the artwork of ancient Greece, for example:

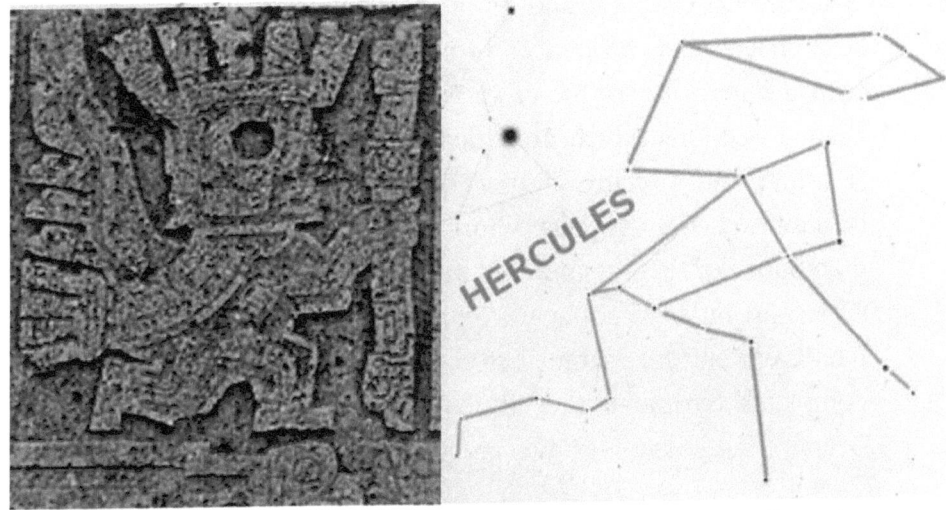

Note the characteristic raised heel on the rear leg, as well as the possession of what in other cultures would likely be identified as a thunderbolt-weapon (an implement almost exclusively associated with mythical figures who are associated with this constellation).

The existence of such figures atop the great "Gate of the Sun" at Tiwanaku displaying such characteristics, which we have seen again and again in other artwork from the complete other side of the planet, and which can be unequivocally linked to the outline of the constellation Hercules in the heavens, simply cannot be denied and points to the existence of a *worldwide system*.

835

Concluding Thoughts

The evidence pointing to the existence of some now-forgotten predecessor culture, traces of which can be found around the globe, is overwhelming -- and the point I am trying to establish in the disucssion above is that the evidence we find in mythology goes hand-in-hand with the abundant archaeological evidence found in monuments, artwork, and other types of physical artifacts the world over.

Other researchers of the worldwide evidence for a "lost civilization" have recognized the importance of mythology and mythological evidence and its interconnection with the physical or archaeological evidence: Graham Hancock's breakthrough book *Fingerprints of the Gods* (1995) contains two entire multi-chapter sections which are titled "The Mystery of the Myths" (Parts IV and V of an eight-part book). The first of these sections is subtitled, "A Species with Amnesia,"[555] which is an apt metaphor for expressing the implications of what the myths appear to indicate about our current condition with respect to whatever culture came before and which has now been completely written-out of the conventional paradigm and the overall consciousness of men and women around the world.

But the full and astonishing scope of the evidence contained in the myths which points to the undeniable existence of some extremely ancient and now-forgotten predecessor culture cannot be appreciated or apprehended until we begin to decipher the constellational "code" or language that the myths around the world all employ, and which is now beginning to come into view, as we complete the initial stage of our world-wide tour through the myths found in every longitudinal section of our planet.

As we noted in our discussion of the efforts to decipher the Mesopotamian cuneiform writing-system during the nineteenth century, the system itself contained unmistakable indications of the existence of some previously unknown civilization which had designed the cuneiform system, because the system itself was evidently not created with the Semitic Babylonian and Akkadian languages in mind. That previously-unknown civilization turned out to be the Sumerians, a mysterious and tremendously accomplished culture whose existence until that point in the 1800s had been completely forgotten.

And yet even after the evidence for the existence of the Sumerian civilization became clear (beginning with the discovery of an inscription mentioning the "king of Sumer and Akkad" which was publicized in 1869), a group of scholars led by one very prominent Assyriologist continued to deny the possibility of the existence of any non-Semitic culture in Mesopotamia, and to publish scholarly article after scholarly article arguing for the rejection of the idea of the existence of the Sumerians!

This scholarly resistence, which went on for three full decades within the academic community, beginning in the 1870s and continuing into the twentieth century, is no mere historical curiosity: it closely parallels the situation in which we find ourselves at this very moment, over a hundred years later!

One has to wonder if there is an agenda beyond mere academic obtuseness and venality behind this stubborn refusal to consider the evidence revealing the bankruptcy of the dominant paradigm.

If so, it may lie in the fact that the violent overthrow of the last remnants of the ancient system which was accomplished by the proponents of literalist Christianity at the end of the Roman empire established the oligopoly (the self-styled "aristocracy," meaning "rule by those who are intrinsically *better*," from the Greek word *aristos*: "best") that controled western Europe for the following fifteen centuries -- and which gave rise to the system of colonialist imperialism whose beneficiaries were more than willing to impoverish vast portions of the globe and billions of men and women in order to gain and retain control over the natural resources bestowed by the gods for the benefit of humanity.

Wherever and whenever this exploitative system has been challenged, literalistic interpretations of ancient myths and scriptures (usually literalistic interpretations of the scriptures of the Bible in Europe, but not exclusively) have been used as an important tool of reaction against any attempts to reform the oligopolistic structures of control.

Indeed, as George Orwell incisively perceived and dramatized, the control of the narrative of history constitutes a critical aspect of the control of thought, which turns out to be just as essential as the mechanisms of military, political, and economic control for subduing and exploiting other men and women. As Orwell wrote in his best-known work, *Nineteen Eighty-Four*:

> And if all others accepted the lie which the Party imposed -- if all records told the same tale -- then the lie passed into history and became truth. "Who controls the past," ran the Party slogan, "controls the future: who controls the present controls the past."[556]

But, as Martin Luther King, Jr. said in his speech delivered on March 25, 1965 at the climax of the march on Selma: "How long? Not long! Because no lie can live forever!"[557] Note that Dr. King explicitly recognized the deep connection between the structures of colonialism and the forces of racism, exploitation, and economic oppression, declaring in a 1962 address to the American Negro Leadership Conference on Africa that:

Colonialism and segregation are nearly synonymous; they are legitimate first cousins because their common end is economic exploitation, political domination, and the debasing of the human personality."[558]

It is my deep conviction that the ancient myths entrusted to humanity, when we listen to them in the language that they are actually speaking (which is a celestial language, a metaphorical language, and an esoteric language) offer real healing for the division each one of us experiences at our most individual and internal level (the division from our deeper subconscious self which takes place as a result of our incorporation into society and its norms and structures, as dramatized in the experience of Enkidu in the ancient Mesopotamian epic of Gilgamesh), and at the same time they offer real healing and real solutions for the deep divisions and problems we face on a societal level and indeed on a global level.

It should go without saying that I categorically reject the attempts by fascists and racists during the modern era to co-opt ancient mythologies such as the Norse myths or the myths of India (including the Mahabharata and the Bhagavad Gita) to support odious racist theories -- which is still going on to this day and represents a grave threat to human freedom, prosperity, equality, and democracy.

The analysis and evidence presented in this book should prove beyond any shadow of doubt that those myths, like all the other myths entrusted to the varied cultures of our shared planet, are not literal and historical in nature, but rather esoteric. They are not speaking of figures or groups from which actual men and women who are alive today are descended -- and thus they cannot properly be used to elevate one group above another, or as a basis for denigrating and exploiting any so-called "race" or ethnicity or family of mankind.

On the contrary, they teach the inherent, unbreakable, and undeniable connection to the divine -- to the Infinite -- within each and every man and woman who has ever lived. This divine spark is buried deep within and beneath the superficial exterior -- not just our *physical* exterior but even beneath the "superficial mind," in the words of Alvin Boyd Kuhn.[559]

The fact that the ancient myths are focused primarily upon this reality cannot at this point be denied. To try to use them, then, as a supposed basis for judging, exploiting, oppressing, dehumanizing, or doing violence to other men and women based upon their external bodily features, their physical heritage as part of one or another family of mankind, their skin's pigmentation, their sex, or any of the other ways which attempt to falesly deny the inherent dignity and divine spirit present in every other man, woman and child we will ever meet constitutes a gross violation, even a complete inversion, of the demonstrable message of the world's ancient wisdom preserved in the myths.

What is the path the myths show us? We have seen that it involves detachment, and (as Krishna tells Arjuna in the Bhagavad Gita) doing what is right without regard for the outcome. It involves blessing and not cursing -- but this too requires detachment from the tangle of society-based norms and structures which are imposed on us (and which we impose upon ourselves), and reconnecting with the source of blessing: that part of ourselves which is connected to the unbounded and infinite, and to which everyone else around us is in fact connected as well.

The more we begin to apprehend this connection to the unbounded realm, the more we open ourselves up to help from the gods, who are always ready to work through men and women, and who appear at the moment they are called, as we see demonstrated time and again in the various myths of the world.

The myths declare that you -- yes, you yourself -- have access to the infinite realm, the invisible realm, the absolutely boundless realm . . . the realm of the gods. Indeed, the myths not only declare this truth, they demonstrate it again and again. The gods work out their will through men and women.

The gods do not shoot the bow for Arjuna: they *give* him the bow (and other divine weapons), and they are with him when he uses it. When Arjuna shoots the arrow through the eye of the fish in the swayamvara of Draupadi, he whispers a prayer to Ishana (Shiva) and to Krishna, and they are with him as he draws back the arrow -- but they are acting through Arjuna, who is the one shooting the target.

We see the same pattern again and again in the other myths we have examined, including in the Gilgamesh cycle, or in the Popol Vuh. We will see it again in the Odyssey of ancient Greece, examined in the next volume of this series.

These stories are not about someone else. They are about you. They are about each one of us.

We are all involved in the great battle of Kurukshetra. As Arjuna learned, there is no avoiding this battle. The way forward, as Krishna tells him, is to do what is right, without attachment, without worrying about the outcome.

"Welcome back to the fight. This time I know our side will win."

End Notes

1. Kuhn, *Stable and the Manger*, 4.

2. Kuhn, *Lost Light*, 46.

3. *Ibid.*

4. Fagles, Odyssey, 165.

5. *Ibid*, 166.

6. *Lost Light*, 46.

7. *Ibid.*

8. Cassaro, "Lion's Gaze."

9. *Ibid.*

10. *Ibid.*

11. Reference to the "dust of centuries" is from de Santillana and von Dechend, *Hamlet's Mill*, 4 - 5.

12. Rey, *The Stars: A New Way to See Them*, 11.

13. Frazer, *Myths of the Origin of Fire*, 9.

14. *Ibid.*

15. *Ibid.*

16. *Ibid*, 15, and note that Frazer in his text cites an older source for this story, an 1899 book by Baldwin Spencer and F. J. Gillen.

17. *Ibid.*

18. *Hamlet's Mill*, 140, 321.

19. Thomas, *Some Myths and Legends of the Australian Aborigines*.

20. *Ibid.*

21. *Star Myths of the World, Volume Three*, 627.

22. See *Star Myths of the World, Volume Two*, 279 - 280.

23. *Star Myths of the World, Volume Three*, 600 - 601.

24. Parrinder, *African Mythology*, 16.

25. *Ibid*, 17.

26. *Ibid*, 18.

27. *Ibid*, 34 - 35.

28. *Hamlet's Mill*, 80.

29. *Ibid.*

30. *Ibid.*

31. Georges and Jones, *Folkloristics*, 150.

32. Bascom, *Sixteen Cowries*, 44.

33. *Ibid*, 45.

34. Beier, *Yoruba Myths*, 32 - 33.

35. *Sixteen Cowries*, 45.

36. It is also remotely possible that Oya could be associated with Ophiuchus, immediately above Scorpio, rather than Scorpio (Ophiuchus would then be imagined as giving birth to nine children, i. e. to Scorpio). However, Ophiuchus does not precede Hercules in the heavens as obviously as does Virgo. Additionally, the detail about Oya

having a second form as an antelope supports her identification with Virgo, a constellation closely associated with Centaurus in other Star Myths from around the world, as discussed on pages 82 through 84 of this volume.

37. *Sixteen Cowries*, 45.

38. *Yoruba Myths*, 33.

39. *Sixteen Cowries*, 46.

40. *African Mythology*, 41.

41. *Myths of the Origin of Fire*, 164.

42. *Ibid.*

43. *Ibid.*

44. *Ibid*, 165.

45. *Ibid*, 1.

46. *Ibid.*

47. *Hamlet's Mill*, 5.

48. *Ibid*, 190 - 191.

49. *Ibid*, 321 - 322.

50. *Ibid*, 318.

51. *Star Myths of the World, Volume Four*, 423 - 438.

52. Erdoes and Ortiz, *American Indian Myths and Legends*, 5.

53. *Ibid.*

54. *Ibid*, 6.

55. *Ibid.*

56. *Ibid.*

57. *Ibid.*

58. *Ibid.*

59. *Ibid*, 7.

60. *Ibid.*

61. *Ibid.*

62. *Ibid*, 8.

63. *Ibid.*

64. *Stable and the Manger*, 4.

65. *American Indian Myths and Legends*, 173.

66. *Ibid.*

67. *Ibid*, 173 - 174.

68. *Ibid*, 174.

69. *Ibid*, 175.

70. *Star Myths of the World, Volume Three*, 530 - 537.

71. Quotations are from the Giles translation of 1800, *Odyssey of Homer; construed literally, and word for word*, Volume 4, pages 157 - 158.

72. *Star Myths of the World, Volume Two*, 634 - 636.

73. Quotation is from the Buckley translation of 1896, *First Thirteen Books of the Odyssey of Homer, Literally Translated*, page 183.

74. *Star Myths of the World, Volume Two*, 540 - 542.

75. Christenson, *Popol Vuh*, preface.

76. Tedlock, *Popol Vuh*, 21.

77. Christenson, *Popol Vuh*, 26.

78. *Ibid*, 27.

79. *Ibid*, 23.

80. Diodorus Siculus, *Bibliotheca*, Book V and section 19; discussed in *Undying Stars*, 303 ff.

81. See for instance discussion in *Astrotheology for Life*, 244 - 261.

82. See for instance Mertz, *Mystic Symbol*, 93.

83. The name *Balam* appears in Christenson, Popol Vuh, page 191. In a footnote discussing the derivation of the name *Xbalanque*, Professor Christenson writes: "*B'alan* is undoubtedly an archaic spelling of *b'alam* (jaguar), m/n letter substitutions being fairly common in Quiché. [. . .] The Maya closely identified the jaguar with the sun, particularly in its journey through the underworld at night" (Christenson, *Popol Vuh*, page 81, note 164). Whether there is indeed some linguistic connection between *Ba'al / the Ba'alim* of the cultures of the eastern Mediterranean and the word *b'alam* ("jaguar" which is "closely identified with the sun"), these correspondences would appear to invite further investigation.

84. Christenson, *Popol Vuh*, 7 - 8.

85. *Ibid*, 60.

86. *Ibid*, page 59, note 56.

87. *Ibid*, page 60, note 62. Note that the authors of *Hamlet's Mill* also point out that the name of this Maya god means "one-leg" (see *Hamlet's Mill*, pages 126 - 127).

88. *Ibid*, page 52, note 19.

89. *Ibid*, pages 52 - 53, note 20.

90. *Ibid*, 59 - 60.

91. *Ibid*, 62.

92. *Star Myths of the World, Volume Two*, 448 - 450.

93. *Ibid*, 259.

94. *Ibid*.

95. Tedlock, *Popol Vuh*, 64.

96. Hancock, *Fingerprints of the Gods*, 47, 103.

97. *Ibid*, 102, and see his note 2 on page 517 for the sources of this quotation.

98. *Ibid*.

99. *Star Myths of the World, Volume Three*, 716 - 717.

100. Tedlock, *Popol Vuh*, 99.

101. Christenson, *Popol Vuh*, 80.

102. *Ibid*, 82.

103. *Ibid*.

104. *Ibid*, page 82, note 165.

105. *Ibid*, page 81, note 163.

106. Christenson, *Popol Vuh*, 88.

107. *Ibid*, page 82, note 166.

108. *Ibid*, page 83, note 170.

109. See for instance *Lost Light*, 146 - 175.

110. Heyerdahl, *American Indians in the Pacific*, 13.

111. Luomala, *Maui of a Thousand Tricks*, 4 - 10.

112. *Ibid*, 21.

113. *Ibid*, 13, 24.

114. Curnow, "Te Rangiheke, Wiremu Maihi," and also Simmons, "Sources of Sir George Grey's Nga Mahi a Nga Tupuna Maori."

115. *Maui of a Thousand Tricks*, 39.

116. *Ibid*, 32.

117. *The Stars: A New Way to See Them*, 36.

118. *Hamlet's Mill*, 4 - 5.

119. *Ibid*.

120. *Maui of a Thousand Tricks*, 41 - 42.

121. *Ibid*, 42.

122. *Ibid*, 43.

118. *Ibid*.

119. *Ibid*, 43, 58.

120. *Ibid*, 43.

121. Whatahoro, *Lore of the Whare-wānanga*, 12.

122. Simmons, "Sources of Sir George Grey's Nga Mahi a Nga Tupuna Maori," 172.

123. *Star Myths of the World, Volume Three*, 740 - 741, note 99.

124. *Maui of a Thousand Tricks*, 46.

125. *Ibid*, 68.

126. *Myths of the Origin of Fire*, 100 ff.

127. *Hamlet's Mill*, 319.

128. *Ibid*, 427.

129. *Ibid*, 320.

130. *Ibid*.

131. Kuhn, *Easter: the Birthday of the Gods*, 4 - 5.

132. Prichard, *An Analysis of the Egyptian Mythology*, 36.

133. *Ibid*, 157. For the passage referenced from Herodotus, see the edition of *Histories* listed below in the Bibliography, pages 146 - 147.

134. Pinch, *Egyptian Myth: A Very Short Introduction*, 9.

135. Müller, *Egyptian Mythology*, 3.

136. *Ibid*, 20.

137. *Ibid*, 4.

138. *Ibid*.

139. Brewer and Teeter, *Egypt and the Egyptians*, 140.

140. *Ibid*.

141. Pinch, *Handbook of Egyptian Mythology*, 111.

142. *Pyramid Texts*, trans. Mercer, page 206.

143. Willems, *Coffin of Heqata*, page 466, note d.

144. Pinch, *Handbook of Egyptian Mythology*, 111.

145. *Ibid*, 65.

146. *Ibid*.

147. *Ibid*.

148. Budge, *Gods of the Egyptians*, 104.

149. Pinch, *Handbook of Egyptian Mythology*, 112.

150. *Star Myths of the World, Volume Four*, 179.

151. Pinch, *Egyptian Myth: A Very Short Introduction*, 49.

152. Pinch, *Handbook of Egyptian Mythology*, 203.

153. *Ibid*, 38.

154. *Ibid*, 62 - 63.

155. Plutarch, *Of Isis and Osiris*, section 9.

156. *Ibid*.

157. Teeter, Emily. "The Life of Ritual." *Ancient Egypt*. Ed. David P. Silverman. Oxford: Oxford UP, 1997. 148 - 165. Quotation is from page 158.

158. Pinch, *Handbook of Egyptian Mythology*, 153.

159. *Egypt and the Egyptians*, 52.

160. *Hamlet's Mill*, 389.

161. "Life of Ritual," in *Ancient Egypt*, 155.

162. Budge, *Egyptian Hieroglyphic Dictionary*, Volume 2, page 886.

163. Müller, *Egyptian Mythology*, 33.

164. *Egyptian Hieroglyphic Dictionary*, Volume 2, page 886.

165. Prichard, *An Analysis of the Egyptian Mythology*, 128 - 129.

166. *Star Myths of the World, Volume Three*, 465-467.

167. *Undying Stars*, 280. Note that the argument by Ralph Ellis, referenced therein, that the name Jehovah may be a variant of Djeheuty, is found for example in his book *Tempest and Exodus*, pages 133 - 134. Intriguingly, although the arguments of Mr. Ellis consistently literalize the characters and events described in Biblical scripture (arguing for instance that characters such as Adam and Eve, Abraham, David, and others are all historical Egyptian kings and queens), while I provide evidence which argues that these characters and events are actually based upon constellations, his argument for a connection between the name Djeheuty and the name Jehovah may have merit, in that (as I demonstrate in *Star Myths of the World, Volume Three*), the figure of Jehovah God is associated with the constellation Hercules in the heavens (see for instance the discussion of the encounter with the LORD when Adam and Eve are hiding after eating from the fruit of the tree, or the discussion of the scene of Jacob's Ladder, for instance). Similarly, as detailed in this volume, the figure of the god Thoth (or Djeheuty) can be shown to be associated with the same constellation Hercules in the night sky.

168. Massey, *Paul the Gnostic Opponent of Peter*, 18.

847

169. Ritner, Robert K. "The Cult of the Dead." *Ancient Egypt*. Ed. David P. Silverman. Oxford: Oxford UP, 1997. 132 - 147. Quotation is from page 134.

170. Plutarch, *Moralia*, 13.

171. *Ibid.*

172. *Ibid*, 15.

173. *Ibid*, 16.

174. *Ibid*, 18.

175. *Ibid.*

176. Jones, "Towards a Chronology of Plutarch's Works," 61 - 74.

177. Pinch, *Handbook of Egyptian Mythology*, 128.

178. *Pyramid Texts*, trans. Mercer, page 153.

179. Neugebauer, *Exact Sciences in Antiquity*, 87.

180. *Ibid*, 85.

181. *Of Isis and Osiris*, section 15.

182. Budge, *Book of the Dead*, 172.

183. Budge, *Osiris and the Egyptian Resurrection*, 63.

184. *Hamlet's Mill*, 67.

185. *Ibid*, 67 - 68.

186. *Ibid*, 12 ff.

187. Sellers, *Death of Gods in Ancient Egypt*, 26 - 27.

188. *Ibid*, 193 - 196.

189. *Ibid*, 185 - 196.

190. See *Hamlet's Mill*, 162 and *Death of Gods in Ancient Egypt*, 191.

191. *Hamlet's Mill*, 252 and 258.

192. *Of Isis and Osiris*, section 15.

193. *Ibid*, section 16.

194. Pinch, *Handbook of Egyptian Mythology*, 128.

195. *Lost Light*, 416.

196. *Ibid*, 403.

197. *Ibid*, 415 - 416.

198. *Of Isis and Osiris*, section 14.

199. *Lost Light*, 7 - 8.

200. *Death of Gods in Ancient Egypt*, 90.

201. *Ibid*, 90 - 94.

202. *Ibid*, 94.

203. "Contendings of Horus and Seth," in *Literature of Ancient Egypt*, Simmons ed., pages 99 - 103. Page 99 (note that the ancient text tells us that after cutting off his tainted hands and throwing them in the water, Isis restores a new set of hands to Horus).

204. *Ibid.*

205. *Ibid*, 100.

206. *Death of Gods in Ancient Egypt*, 96.

207. *Ibid*, 97.

208. Massey, *Ancient Egypt, the Light of the World*, Volume 2, page 303.

209. *Lost Light*, 549 - 550.

210. Budge, *Book of the Dead*, Volume I, pages 180 - 183, 177.

211. *Lost Light*, 550.

212. *Ibid*, 551.

213. Crawford, *Sumer and the Sumerians*, 10.

214. Kramer, *Sumerians*, 5 ff.

215. *Ibid*, 19.

216. *Ibid*.

217. *Ibid*, 21. See also King, *Babylonian Religion and Mythology*, 2.

218. Kramer, *Sumerians*, 21 - 22.

219. *Ibid*, 21.

220. King, *Babylonian Religion and Mythology*, 6.

221. *Ibid*.

222. Heidel, *Babylonian Genesis*, 1 - 2.

223. Stephany, *Enuma Elish*, iii.

224. *Babylonian Genesis*, 10 - 11.

225. *Ibid*, 3.

226. King, *Seven Tablets of Creation*, Volume I, page 5.

227. *Ibid*, 13.

228. *Ibid*.

229. *Ibid*, 17.

230. *Ibid*.

231. *Hamlet's Mill*, 153.

232. *Ibid*, 152 - 153, italics in original.

233. *Ibid*.

234. *Ibid*, 244 - 246.

235. *Seven Tablets of Creation*, Volume I, page 35.

236. *Ibid*, 61.

237. *Ibid*.

238. *Ibid*, 63 - 65.

239. *Star Myths of the World, Volume Two*, 496 - 497.

240. *Seven Tablets of Creation*, Volume I, page 69.

241. *Ibid*, 71 - 73.

242. *Star Myths of the World, Volume Four*, 426 - 448.

243. Stephany, *Enuma Elish*, i - ii.

244. *Ibid*.

245. *Ibid*, ii.

246. *Hamlet's Mill*, 424.

247. Verbrugghe and Wickersham, *Berossos and Manetho*, 13.

248. *Ibid*, 16.

249. *Ibid*, 44.

250. *Ibid*, 17.

251. *Ibid*, 44.

252. See for instance *Star Myths of the World, Volume Three*, 599 - 601.

253. McIntosh, *Ancient Mesopotamia: New Perspectives*, 321.

254. Dalley, *Myths from Mesopotamia*, 3.

255. *Ibid*, 9.

256. Leick, *A Dictionary of Ancient Near Eastern Mythology*, 8.

257. *Hamlet's Mill*, 274.

258. *Ibid*, 285.

259. *Ibid*, 348.

260. *Seven Tablets of Creation*, Volume I, page 43.

261. *Ibid*, 87, note 7.

262. *Ibid*, 87 - 89.

263. *Ibid*, 89, note 1.

264. *Ibid*, 61.

265. Stephany, *Enuma Elish*, iii.

266. *Seven Tablets of Creation*, Volume I, pages 111 - 113.

267. George, *Epic of Gilgamesh*, xv.

268. *Ibid*, 141.

269. *Ibid*, page 1. (Tablet I, line 16).

270. *Ibid*, 5.

271. *Ibid*, 225.

272. *Ibid*, 6.

273. *Ibid*, 8.

274. *Ibid*, 14. (Pennsylvania Tablet, 100 - 105).

275. *Ibid* (Pennsylvania Tablet, 106 - 111).

276. *Ibid*, 15 (Pennsylvania Tablet, 179 - 185).

277. Jastrow and Clay, *An Old Babylonian Version of the Gilgamesh Epic*, 67.

278. *Ibid*, 29.

279. *Ibid*, 68.

280. See for example the Sumerian text of *Bilgames and Akka*, lines 89 ff.

281. *Star Myths of the World, Volume Three*, 385.

282. Ollestad, *Crazy for the Storm*, 263 - 264.

283. *Lost Light*, 46.

284. George, *Epic of Gilgamesh*, 17.

285. *Ibid*, 10 - 11.

286. Thompson, *Epic of Gilgamesh*, 20.

287. George, *Epic of Gilgamesh*, 21.

288. *Ibid*, 46.

289. *Ibid*, 45.

290. *Star Myths of the World, Volume Two*, 145 - 146, 433 - 437.

291. *Star Myths of the World, Volume Three*, 657 - 658, 690 - 696.

292. *Star Mtyhs of the World, Volume Two*, 384 - 387.

293. *Star Myths of the World, Volume Three*, 295 ff.

294. *Hamlet's Mill*, 249.

295. *Star Myths of the World, Volume Two*, 496 - 497.

296. George, *Epic of Gilgamesh*, 37.

297. See for example Tablet III line 90, and Tablet V lines 135 - 140.

298. *Star Myths of the World, Volume Two*, 448 - 450.

299. See for instance George, *Epic of Gilgamesh*, 160 (from the text of the version known as "Sumerian A").

300. See for instance George, *Epic of Gilgamesh*, 159, 165. Note that Huwawa in pleading to Gilgamesh (or, in this Sumerian text, Bilgames) declares that he never knew a mother or a father but was raised by the mountain (Sumerian Version A, lines 155 - 156): this again indicates a connection between Huwawa and Ophiuchus (which plays a mountain in many other myths), as well as perhaps an identification of Huwawa with Scorpio (the constellation that could be seen as "descended from" the "mountain" of Ophiuchus, since Scorpio is located directly *below* Ophiuchus).

301. See for instance *Hamlet's Mill*, 448 - 450.

302. *Hamlet's Mill*, 318.

303. George, *Epic of Gilgamesh*, 54.

304. *Ibid*, 55.

305. *Ibid.*

306. *Ibid*, 58.

307. *Ibid*, 58 - 59 (Tablet VII, lines 134 - 147).

308. *Ibid*, 59.

309. *Ibid*, 61.

310. *Ibid*, 122 - 124.

311. *Ibid*, 222.

312. *Ibid*, 225.

313. Dalley, *Myths from Mesopotamia*, 2.

314. George, *Epic of Gilgamesh*, 225.

315. Budge, *Rise & Progress of Assyriology*, 153.

316. Lambert and Millard, *Atra-hasis: The Babylonian story of the flood*, 32.

317. Dalley, *Myths from Mesopotamia*, 1.

318. Clay, *A Hebrew Deluge Story in Cuneiform*, 70.

319. Stephany, *Enuma Elish*, 96 - 97. Note once again that the quoted passage is found in the Atrahasis, which is also contained in Stephany's volume containing his translation of Enuma Elish.

320. *Hamlet's Mill*, 294.

321. George, *Epic of Gilgamesh*, 76.

322. *Ibid.*

851

323. *Hamlet's Mill*, 295.

324. *The Stars: A New Way to See Them*, 56 - 57.

325. *Ibid*, 56.

326. George, *Epic of Gilgamesh*, 83-84.

327. *Ibid*, 85.

328. *Ibid*, 88.

329. *Ibid*.

330. *Ibid*, 94.

331. *Ibid*, 94 - 95.

332. *Ibid*, 95.

333. *Ibid*, 98 (See Tablet XI, line 281).

334. *Ibid*, 95 (See Tablet XI, line 205).

335. *Star Myths of the World, Volume Two*, 560 - 561.

336. Notably, Stephanie Dalley says of the name of *Odysseus* on page 2 of her 1989 book *Myths from Mesopotamia*:

> It has been suggested that the name Ulysses, used by the Romans for Odysseus, Comes from the Hittite *ullu(ya)š*, as a translation of Atrahasis' epithet 'the far-distant,' and that the names Odysseus and Outis may be based on a pronunciation of the logogram for Ut-napishtim, which is UD.ZI.

Dalley attributes this observation to H. Schretter's 1974 text *Alter Orient und Hellas*, page 13, and adds: "There is no evidence, however, that UD.ZI was ever pronounced phonetically" (in note 3 on page 2).

337. Doniger, *Rig Veda*, 11. Precessional numbers are discussed in *Hamlet's Mill*, 7 and 162.

338. Doniger, *Hindu Myths*, 17.

339. Doniger, *Rig Veda*, footnote on page 12.

340. Doniger, *Hindu Myths*, 15.

341. *Ibid*, 17.

342. *Ibid*, 15.

343. Dimmitt and van Buitenen, *Classical Hindu Mythology*, xii.

344. *Ibid*, 8.

345. *Star Myths of the World, Volume Four*, 440 - 441.

346. Dimmitt and van Buitenen, *Classical Hindu Mythology*, 30 - 31.

347. *Ibid*, 31.

348. Doniger, *Hindu Myths*, 35 - 36, 350.

349. *Ibid*, 36 - 37.

350. *Ibid*, 30 ff.

351. Dimmitt and van Buitenen, *Classical Hindu Mythology*, 149.

352. *Ibid*, 148.

353. *Ibid*, 150.

354. *Ibid*, 159.

355. *Ibid*, 202 - 203.

852

356. *Ibid*, 154.

357. *Ibid*, 76.

358. *Ibid*, 355.

359. Dimmitt and van Buitenen, *Classical Hindu Mythology*, 27.

360. *Fingerprints of the Gods*, 260 - 261.

361. Dimmitt and van Buitenen, *Classical Hindu Mythology*, 96.

362. *Ibid*, 74.

363. Doniger, *Hindu Myths*, 37 - 39, 129, 134 - 137, 354.

364. Doniger, *Rig Veda*, 226.

365. *Hamlet's Mill*, 227, 232 - 233, 261, 306, 317, 321.

366. Doniger, *Rig Veda*, page 227 note 3.

367. Dimmitt and van Buitenen, *Classical Hindu Mythology*, 153.

368. *Ibid*, 153, 351.

369. *Ibid*, 150.

370. *Ibid*.

371. Doniger, *Hindu Myths*, 238 ff.

372. *Ibid*, 248 - 249.

373. *Ibid*, 247.

374. Taylor, *Astronomico-Theological Lectures*, 158.

375. Taylor, *Devil's Pulpit*, 43 - 44. The celestial foundations of the story of the visit of the Magi from Matthew chapter 2 is also discussed in *Star Myths of the World, Volume Three*, 583 - 595.

376. Dimmitt and van Buitenen, *Classical Hindu Mythology*, 225.

377. *Ibid*, 223.

378. *Ibid*, 151.

379. Doniger, *Hindu Myths*, 262 - 265.

380. Dimmitt and van Buitenen, *Classical Hindu Mythology*, 180 - 183.

381. Doniger, *Hindu Myths*, 265.

382. *Ibid*, 266.

383. See for example *Mahabharata*, Book 13 (Anusasana Parva), section 104, in which Bhishma tells Yudhishthira: "One should never sleep with head turned towards the north or the west."

384. Doniger, *Hindu Myths*, 268.

385. *Ibid*.

386. *Ibid*.

387. Doniger, *Rig Veda*, 56.

388. The Pyramid Texts are the oldest extant *extended* texts from ancient Egypt; some texts older than the Pyramid Texts survive but only short inscriptions, not extended narratives or mythical accounts.

389. Dimmitt and van Buitenen, *Classical Hindu Mythology*, 95.

390. Doniger, *Hindu Myths*, 75.

391. *Ibid*. Also Doniger *Rig Veda* 167 note 11, commenting on Rig Veda 1. 85.

392. Doniger, *Hindu Myths*, 75.

393. *Ibid*, 74 - 75.

394. *Ibid*, 75.

395. *Ibid*, 354.

396. Doniger, *Rig Veda*, 119.

397. *Ibid*, 121.

398. Doniger, *Hindu Myths*, 266 - 267.

399. Dimmitt and van Buitenen, *Classical Hindu Mythology*, 62.

400. *Ibid*, 63.

401. *Ibid*, 67.

402. *Ibid*, 74.

403. *Ibid*, 355.

404. *Ibid*, 67.

405. *Ibid*, 81.

406. *Ibid*.

407. *Hamlet's Mill*, 146 - 148. Note that to this list of figures banished to the underworld or to a cave for a time (with a promised return) we could also add the figure of Christ, of whom the Apostles' Creed declares: "He descended into hell: the third day he rose again from the dead." As we shall see in *Star Myths of the World, Volume Three*, Jesus is closely associated with the constellation Ophiuchus, just as in the story of Vamana and Mahabali, Mahabali is associated with Ophiuchus. Mahabali is sent to the underworld by Vamana, as are so many other Ophiuchus figures, including Baldr (along with those named on page 623 such as Osiris).

408. *Lost Light*, 159, 182, 564 - 567.

409. *Mahabharata*, trans. Ganguli, Book I, section 1.

410. *Ibid*, Book I, section 1.

411. *Ibid*.

412. *Ibid*.

413. *Ibid*.

414. *Ibid*.

415. Dimmitt and van Buitenen, *Classical Hindu Mythology*, 356.

416. *Ibid*, 355 -356.

417. *Ibid*, 352.

418. *Mahabharata*, trans. Ganguli, Book I, section 95.

419. *Ibid*, Book I, section 98.

420. *Ibid*, Book I, section 98.

421. *Ibid*.

422. *Ibid*.

423. *Ibid*, Book I, section 99.

424. Dimmitt and van Buitenen, *Classical Hindu Mythology*, 359.

425. *Mahabharata*, trans. Ganguli, Book I, section 99.

426. *Ibid*.

427. *Ibid.*

428. *Ibid.* Book I, section 100. Parenthetical in the original Ganguli translation.

429. *Ibid.*

430. *Ibid,* Book I, section 102.

431. *Ibid,* Book I, section 123.

432. *Ibid.*

433. *Ibid.*

434. *Ibid.*

435. *Ibid.*

436. *Ibid,* Book I, section 115.

437. *Ibid,* section 123.

438. *Ibid.*

439. *Ibid,* Book I, section 227.

440. Dimmitt and van Buitenen, *Classical Hindu Mythology,* 353.

441. *Mahabharata,* trans. Ganguli, Book 17, section 1.

442. *Ibid.*

443. The figure of Agni is discussed at some length in *Hamlet's Mill,* and the authors obviously consider Agni to be a figure of great importance. Their observations about Agni are worth visiting in light of the evidence presented in this present volume which suggests a connection between Agni and the constellation Ophiuchus, standing above Scorpio (see discussion on page 663). The authors of *Hamlet's Mill* argue that, "Agni, however, is a title, and the Rigveda stresses time and again that three Agnis already have gone away, 'consumed' by the 'sacrificial service'" (Appendix 38, pages 428 - 429). This observation is significant, in that we discuss in this volume the abundant evidence that figures associated with Ophiuchus (including Agni, but also Baldr of Norse myth, Jesus of the New Testament, Osiris of ancient Egypt, Kronos of ancient Greece, and many others) are closely identified with the turning of the great Ages of precession. Another notable detail provided by von Dechend and de Santillana in *Hamlet's Mill* is the observation that "one of the Agnis had 'seven mothers,' like Heimdal" (429). As I have already concluded based on separate study of the Norse myths, previous to taking up this more-detailed analysis of Agni for this second edition of Volume One, Heimdal is undoubtedly associated with the constellation Ophiuchus as well (see *Star Myths of the World, Volume Four,* pages 420 - 422). There, I argued that Heimdal's parentage by nine mothers undoubtedly stems from the fact that Ophiuchus is positioned directly above Scorpio, the multiple heads of Scorpio playing the role of the multiple mothers of Heimdal. Here as well, the detail that Agni has multiple mothers (in this case, seven) helps confirm our identification of this god with Ophiuchus. The authors of *Hamlet's Mill* also note of Heimdal that one of his epithets, *Vindler,* means (quoting Viktor Rydberg's *Teutonic Mythology,* 1907 and page 234) "to twist or turn, wind, to turn anything around rapidly. As the epithet 'the turner' is given to that god who brought friction-fire (bore-fire) to man, and who is himself the personification of this fire, then it must be synonymous with 'the borer.'" (*Hamlet's Mill,* 159). This discussion by de

Santillana and von Dechend (following Rydberg) of Heimdal (an Ophiuchus figure, as I have argued) with the motion of winding or boring resonates strongly with the discussion in this volume of the overwhelming evidence that Ophiuchus plays the "churning stick" in the great *Amritamanthana*, or "Churning of the Milky Ocean" (see discussion on page 581 of this volume, for example). The authors of Hamlet's Mill note that Tezcatlipoca (an important god of the Aztecs, whose name means "Smoking Mirror") is also described as drilling fire, "in the year 2-Reed, after the flood" (*Hamlet's Mill*, 322) -- which indicates a possible connection with Ophiuchus as well (although not necessarily an identification with Ophiuchus, since it also is possible that Hercules, just above Ophiuchus, can be seen as turning the drill). Finally, the authors of *Hamlet's Mill* also reference a myth related in the Bhagavata Purana in which th virtuous prince Dhruva "stood on one leg for more than a month, motionless," after which a heavenly voice announces: "The stars, and their figures, and also the planets shall turn around you" -- and Dhruva ascends to what the authors of Hamlet's Mill describe as "Pole star" but which is also described in the text they cite from the Bhagavata Purana as "the exalted seat of Vishnu" (*Hamlet's Mill*, 138). The descriptions here seem to indicate Ophiuchus once again, as the great central "churning stick" around which everything else revolves -- and which is certainly the "seat of Vishnu" as well, as we have discussed in this volume in the examination of the celestial correspondence between Vishnu and Ophiuchus. This action of Dhruva raises the possibility that Ophiuchus was sometimes envisioned as "standing on one leg" -- perhaps because one leg of the constellation is within the Milky Way band and hence more obscured than the other. Note that Pandu in the Mahabharata also stands upon one leg from morning to evening for a full year, prior to the conception by Kunti through the god Indra of the peerless Arjuna (see page 649 of this volume), which raises the possibility that Pandu as well can be identified with Ophiuchus. In any case, this discussion reveals that Agni is undoubtedly associated with Ophiuchus, and that Ophiuchus is a constellation of tremendous significance in the ancient worldwide system of celestial metaphor underlying the myths.

444. *Mahabharata*, trans. Ganguli, Book 1, section 58.

445. *Ibid*, Book 1, section 128.

446. *Ibid*, Book 1, section 187.

447. *Ibid*, Book 1, section 189.

448. *Ibid*, Book 1, section 190.

449. *Star Myths of the World, Volume Three*, 339 - 340 (the episode involving Lot's wife); *Astrotheology for Life*, 159 - 190 (discussion of the "failed retrieval from the dead").

450. *Mahabharata*, trans. Ganguli, Book 2, section 55.

451. *Ibid*.

452. *Hamlet's Mill*, 161 - 162.

453. *Mahabharata*, trans. Ganguli, Book 2, section 55.

454. *Ibid*.

455. The condition of Draupadi when she is dragged, being in the time of her monthly period, recalls the condition of the woman in the gospel account who has the

continuous flow of blood and who is healed by Jesus (see the gospel according to Matthew, chapter 9). I discuss this incident in the gospel accounts, and its celestial foundations, in *Star Myths of the World, Volume Three*, pages 628 - 633. The Draupadi episode undoubtedly involves the very same constellations (in both cases, the female figure being associated with either Virgo or Scorpio -- and probably with both constellations at different points of the story).

456. *Mahabharata*, trans. Ganguli, Book 2, section 67.

457. *Ibid.*

458. *Ibid.*

459. *Ibid*, Book 6, section 23.

460. *Ibid.*

461. *Ibid*, Book 5, section 34.

462. *Ibid*, Book 6, section 35.

463. Arnold, *The Song Celestial*, 40.

464. *Ibid.*

465. *Ibid*, 55 - 56.

466. *Ibid*, 62 - 63.

467. *Tao Te Ching*, trans. Mair, 138.

468. *Ibid*, 141 - 147.

469. *Mahabharata*, trans. Ganguli, Book 3, sections 145 - 148.

470. See for example the Majjhima Nikaya, Sutta 123, verses 6 - 7.

471. Dimmitt and van Buitenen, *Classical Hindu Mythology*, 353.

472. "Nalaka Sutta," trans. Bhikku.

473. *Ibid.*

474. *Ibid.*

475. *Ibid.*

476. *Star Myths of the World, Volume Three*, pages 170 - 202.

477. *Ibid*, 84 - 87, 388 - 411.

478. See for instance the discussion in *Star Myths of the World, Volume Four*, page 323.

479. See *Star Myths of the World, Volume Three*, 663 - 668. The description of a mountain being "removed and cast into the sea" becomes much easier to understand if the mountain is the constellation, which the turning of the heavens will cause to "be removed and cast down into the western horizon."

480. *Tao Te Ching*, trans. Mair, xiii - xiv.

481. Si Ma Qian, *Records of the Grand Historian*, section 63. The translation cited is from *Medieval China*, ed. Horne, pages 396 - 397.

482. See for example Livia Kohn's "The Lao-tzu Myth," published in *Lao-tzu and the Tao-te-ching* (Kohn and LaFargue, eds.), pages 41 - 62, page 56.

483. *Tao Te Ching*, trans. Mair, 16.

484. *Ibid*, 142.

485. *Ibid*, 138.

486. See Victor Mair's discussion of the words "BEING, NONBEING" in Part II of his Afterword to the translation of the Ma Wang Dui texts, *Ibid*, 138.

487. *Ibid*, 139.

488. *Ibid*.

489. *Ibid*, 70.

490. *Ibid*, 156.

491. *Ibid*.

492. *Ibid*, 156 - 157.

493. Wu, *Golden Age of Zen*, 28.

494. Ferguson, *Tracking Bodhidharma*, 12 - 13.

495. *Ibid*, 13.

496. *Ibid*.

497. Broughton, *Bodhidharma Anthology*, 53.

498. *Ibid*.

499. *Ibid*, 55.

500. *Ibid*, 55 - 56.

501. *Ibid*, 56.

502. *Ibid*.

503. *Golden Age of Zen*, 42.

504. *Mahabharata*, trans. Ganguli, Book 3, section 122.

505. *Zen Teaching of Bodhidharma*, Red Pine, ix.

506. *Bodhidharma Anthology*, 3.

507. See Quarrington, "Bodhidharma –달마 (5th to 6th Cent.)," *Dale's Temple Adventures*, July 22, 20014. koreantemples.com/?p=9074

508. The phrase "scurrying of the superficial mind" is taken from a quotation by Alvin Boyd Kuhn which was cited earlier, on page 487 and which is found in its original entirety on page 46 of Kuhn's *Lost Light* (see also note 281 above).

509. Schwaller de Lubicz, *Esoterism & Symbol*, 75.

510. *Ibid*, 3.

511. *Ibid*.

512. *Ibid*, 75.

513. *Golden Age of Zen*, 46 - 47.

514. *Lost Light*, 24 (emphasis in the original).

515. Ono, *Shinto*, 1.

516. *Ibid*, ix.

517. *Ibid*, 1.

518. Woodard, *Allied Occupation of Japan 1945 - 1952*, 10.

519. *Shinto*, 3.

520. *Ibid*, 9 - 10.

521. *Kojiki*, trans. Chamberlain, section I, page 15.

522. *Kojiki*, trans. Heldt, 7.

523. *Ibid*.

524. *Kojiki*, trans. Chamberlain, section II, page 17.

525. *Kojiki*, trans. Heldt, 8.

526. *Kojiki*, trans. Chamberlain, section III, page 19.

527. *Ibid*.

528. *Ibid*, note 4.

529. *Kojiki*, trans. Heldt, 9.

530. *Kojiki*, trans. Chamberlain, section IV, page 21.

531. *Kojiki*, trans. Philippi, 398.

532. *Ibid*.

533. *Kojiki*, trans. Chamberlain, section IX, page 41.

534. *Ibid*, Section XI, page 50.

535. *Ibid*, Section XII, page 51.

536. *Ibid*.

537. *Ibid*, Section XV, page 61.

538. *Kojiki*, trans. Heldt, 22.

539. *Kojiki*, trans. Chamberlain, Section XV, page 62.

540. *Ibid*. See also *Kojiki*, trans. Heldt, 23.

541. *Ibid*, Section XVI, page 63. See also *Kojiki*, trans. Heldt, 23.

542. *Ibid*, Section XV, page 62, note 10.

543. *Star Myths of the World, Volume Two*, 544 - 545.

544. *Kojiki*, trans. Heldt, 23 - 24.

545. *Kojiki*, trans. Chamberlain, section XVI, page 65; *Kojiki*, trans. Heldt, 24.

546. *Kojiki*, trans. Chamberlain, section XVI, page 64.

547. *Ibid*, page 64, note 31.

548. *Kojiki*, trans. Heldt, 24.

549. *Ibid*.

550. *Kojiki*, trans. Chamberlain, section XVI, page 65, note 34.

551. *Ibid*.

552. *Hamlet's Mill*, 425.

553. "Japanese Author Traces Nippon Origin to Hebrew Race." *Jewish Daily Bulletin*, 15 August 1929: 3 - 4.

554. See Burley, "Göbekli Tepe: Temples Communicating an Ancient Cosmic Geography," March 2013; see also Hancock, *Magicians of the Gods*, 308 - 325; and see also *Astrotheology for Life*, 250 - 253.

555. *Fingerprints of the Gods*, 185.

556. Orwell, *Nineteen Eighty-Four*, 32.

557. King, "Our God is Marching On!", 25 March 1965.

558. King, "Address to the American Negro Leadership Conference on Africa," November 1962.

559. *Lost Light*, 24.

Image Credits

listed by page number

8. Draupadi calls upon Krishna. Wikimedia commons.
https://commons.wikimedia.org/wiki/File:1940s_Indian_Hindu_Print_Draupadi_Vastraharan_2.jpg

36. Pig-footed Bandicoots, Australia. Wikimedia commons.
https://commons.wikimedia.org/wiki/File:PigFootedBandicoot.jpg

43. Cathedral Termite Mound, Australia. Wikimedia commons.
https://commons.wikimedia.org/wiki/File:Cathedral_Termite_Mound_-_brewbooks.jpg

59. Woman with Mortar & Pestle, Tanzania. Wikimedia commons.
https://commons.wikimedia.org/wiki/File:Bundesarchiv_Bild_105-DOA0285,_Deutsch-Ostafrika,_Einheimische_beim_Mehlstampfen.jpg

61. Ngoni girls, Malawi, c. 1910. Wikimedia commons.
https://commons.wikimedia.org/wiki/File:%22Young_Ngoni_girls,_Livingstonia%22,_Malawi,_ca.1910_(imp-cswc-GB-237-CSWC47-LS4-1-015).jpg

70. Xango (also spelled Shango). Wikimedia commons.
https://commons.wikimedia.org/wiki/File:Representação_de_Xangô_MN_01.jpg

164. Zeus, Huracan with Thunderbolts. Wikimedia commons.
Top: https://commons.wikimedia.org/wiki/File:Combat_de_Zeus_contre_Typhon.jpg
Bottom: https://commons.wikimedia.org/wiki/File:Dresden_codex,_page_2.jpg

167. Collared peccary (top), coati (bottom). Wikimedia commons.
Top: https://commons.wikimedia.org/wiki/File:Collared_Peccary_crossing_the_road.jpg
Bottom: https://commons.wikimedia.org/wiki/File:MexicanCoati2.jpg

175. Khafre sculpture, Sovereign Plumed Serpent. Wikimedia commons.
Left:
https://commons.wikimedia.org/wiki/File:Ägyptisches_Museum_Kairo_2016-03-29_Chephren_03.jpg
Right: https://commons.wikimedia.org/w/index.php?title=File:Förstemann_Dresden_Codex.pdf&page=3

185. Blowgunner, bird, scorpion, serpent. Author's rendition of original artwork from a Maya vase photographed by Justin Kerr and designated K1226.

209. Heracles grasping curved crest, three examples from ancient artwork. Wikimedia commons.
Left: https://commons.wikimedia.org/wiki/File:Heracles_Amazons_Met_61.11.16.jpg
Center: https://commons.wikimedia.org/wiki/File:Herakles_Amazons_MAR_Palermo_NI1897.jpg
Right: https://commons.wikimedia.org/wiki/File:Herakles_Kyknos_Louvre_F36.jpg

211. Heracles and Achelous. Wikimedia commons.
https://commons.wikimedia.org/wiki/File:Herakles_Achelous_Louvre_G365.jpg

218. New Zealand Wood Pigeon. Wikimedia commons.
https://commons.wikimedia.org/wiki/File:Keulemans,_John_Gerrard_1842-1912_-New_Zealand_pigeon._Carpophaga_Novae_Zealandiae._(one-half_natural_size)._-_J._G._Keulemans_delt._and_lith._(Plate_XXIV._1888)._(21014153784).jpg

860

235. Staring Image of Maui Carved atop Rafters.
Maning, *Old New Zealand*, page 338.

262. Shu separating Nut and Geb. Wikimedia commons.
https://commons.wikimedia.org/wiki/File:Geb,_Nut,_Shu.jpg

264. Nut and Geb showing serpent head. Budge, *Gods of the Egyptians*, Vol 2, p 104.

268. Zeus defeating Typhon. Wikimedia commons.
Same image information as image on page 164.

272. Sokar, from illustration in Papyrus of Ani. Wikimedia commons.
https://commons.wikimedia.org/wiki/File:BD_Sokar-Osiris.jpg

273. Khonsu with sidelock; two views. Wikimedia commons.
left: https://commons.wikimedia.org/wiki/File:Statue_Khonsu_Weigall.jpg
right: https://commons.wikimedia.org/wiki/File:Karnak_Khonsou_080519.jpg

276. Zeus with horns of Ammon. Wikimedia commons.
https://commons.wikimedia.org/wiki/File:Zeus_Ammon_(Antikensammlung_München).jpg

277. Statue of Khnum, from time of Psamtik I (664BC - 610BC). Wikimedia commons.
https://commons.wikimedia.org/wiki/File:Egyptian_-_Khnum_-_Walters_22342_-_Three_Quarter.jpg

278. Khnum at the potter's wheel; two views. Wikimedia commons.
left: https://commons.wikimedia.org/wiki/File:Chnum-ihy-isis.jpg
right: https://commons.wikimedia.org/wiki/File:DendaraMamisiKhnum-10.jpg

283. Amun-Ra from Deir el-Medina. Wikimedia commons.
https://commons.wikimedia.org/wiki/File:Amun-Ra_kamutef_2.jpg

290. Scarab pectoral of Tutankhamun. Wikimedia commons.
https://commons.wikimedia.org/wiki/File:Tutankhamun_scarab1.jpg

291. Winged scarab, ancient Egypt. Wikimedia commons.
https://commons.wikimedia.org/wiki/File:Egyptian_winged_scarab_beetle.jpg

293. Assyrian youth with Winged Sun above. Wikimedia commons.
https://commons.wikimedia.org/wiki/File:Panel_with_a_youth_grasping_a_tree;_winged_sun_disc_above_MET_vs59_107_5.jpg

294. Assyrian holding vine; Winged Sun above. Wikimedia commons.
https://commons.wikimedia.org/wiki/File:Furniture_plaque_carved_in_relief_with_a_male_figure_grasping_a_tree;_winged_sun_disc_above_MET_DP110643.jpg

296. Funerary stele showing winged solar disc. Wikimedia commons.
https://commons.wikimedia.org/wiki/File:Osiris,_Horus,_and_Isis._Funerary_stele_of_Tjrerei_for_Ra-Horakhty._From_Egypt._Roman_period,_1st_to_2nd_century_CE._State_Museum_of_Egyptian_Art,_Munich.jpg

297. Akhenaten and Nefertiti, upraised arms; Aten above. Wikimedia commons.
https://commons.wikimedia.org/wiki/File:C%2BB-Egypt-Fig12-AkhnatenWorshippingSun.PNG

303. Ivory seal, tomb of Den; smiting scene. Wikimedia commons.
https://commons.wikimedia.org/wiki/File:IvoryLabelOfDen-BritishMuseum-August19-08.jpg

306. Illustrations of Thoth. Wikimedia commons.
https://commons.wikimedia.org/wiki/File:Thoth_(in_illustrated_List_of_the_principal_Egyptian
Divinities)(1888)_-_TIMEA.jpg

309. Wall relief from Luxor showing Thoth. Wikimedia commons.
https://commons.wikimedia.org/wiki/File:Luxor_temple_15.jpg

322. Isis receiving the Djed pillar from Byblos. Wikimedia commons.
https://commons.wikimedia.org/wiki/File:Abydos_seti_16_det2.JPG

325. Rectangular star-clock from tomb of Seti I. Wikimedia commons.
https://commons.wikimedia.org/wiki/File:Seti1-Lepsius-III-137-b.jpg

329. Osiris upon a lion couch. From Budge, *Osiris and the Egyptian Resurrection*, Volume 2, page 25.

345. Thetis dips Achilles in the River Styx. Wikimedia commons.
https://commons.wikimedia.org/wiki/File:Nicolai_Abildgaard_-
_Thetis_Immersing_her_Infant_Son_Achilles_in_the_River_Styx_to_Make_him_Invulnerable_-
KMS3353-_Statens_Museum_for_Kunst.jpg

347. Ankh and Djed supporting solar disc. Wikimedia commons.
https://commons.wikimedia.org/wiki/File:BD_Ankh,_Djed,_and_Sun.jpg

354. Isis with child Horus. Wikimedia commons.
https://commons.wikimedia.org/wiki/File:Statuette_of_Isis_and_Horus_MET_DP241030.jpg

355. Isis and pillar (same as page 322); Pietá by Michelangelo. Wikimedia commons.
https://commons.wikimedia.org/wiki/File:Michelangelo%27s_Pieta_5450_cropncleaned_edit.jpg

357. Winged Isis from a panel at Abydos. Wikimedia commons.
https://commons.wikimedia.org/wiki/File:Ägyptischer_Maler_um_1360_v._Chr._001.jpg

388. Messier star chart, full sky. Wikimedia commons.
https://commons.wikimedia.org/wiki/File:MessierStarChart.svg

400. Seal of Adda showing Enki. Wikimedia commons.
https://commons.wikimedia.org/wiki/File:Ea_(Babilonian)_-_EnKi_(Sumerian).jpg

404. Seal showing Enki and Ziusudra. Wikimedia commons.
https://commons.wikimedia.org/wiki/File:GalzuEnjiWarnsNoahFloodSItchin2000p194_150ht_copy.jpg

405. Zeus defeating Typhon. Wikimedia commons.
Same image source as image on pages 164 and 268.

411. Figure often associated with Marduk. Wikimedia commons.
https://commons.wikimedia.org/wiki/File:Chaos_Monster_and_Sun_God.png

423. Lammasu from palace at Nimrud. Wikimedia commons.
https://commons.wikimedia.org/wiki/File:Lamassu_from_the_Throne_Room_(Room_B)_of_the_North-
West_Palace_at_Nimrud,_Iraq,_9th_century_BC,_now_in_the_British_Museum,_London.jpg

425. Apkallu and Bishop's Mitre. Wikimedia commons.
left:
https://commons.wikimedia.org/wiki/File:Plate_6_fish_god_(A_second_series_of_the_monuments_of_Nineveh)_1853_(cropped).jpg
right: https://commons.wikimedia.org/wiki/File:Henry_Chichele.jpg

439. Eagle-headed Apkallu. Wikimedia commons.
https://commons.wikimedia.org/wiki/File:Wall_relief_depicting_an_eagle-headed_and_winged_man,_Apkallu,_from_Nimrud..JPG

441. Archangel Michael with Scales. Wikimedia commons.
left: https://commons.wikimedia.org/wiki/File:San_Michele_Arcangelo_Bartolomeo_Vivarini_GAC.jpg
right:
https://commons.wikimedia.org/wiki/File:São_Miguel_Arcanjo,_oficina_de_Garcia_Fernandes_(atr.).jpg

442. Winged man with pinecone and satchel. Wikimedia commons.
https://commons.wikimedia.org/wiki/File:A_winged_human-headed_Apkallu_holding_a_bucket_and_a_pine_cone._From_Nimrud,_Iraq._883-859_BCE._Ancient_Orient_Museum,_Istanbul.jpg

453. Cylinder-seal showing worshipers and the god Sin.
From King, *Babylonian Religion and Mythology*, 15.

454. Relief showing worshipers and the god Shamash.
https://commons.wikimedia.org/wiki/File:Tablet_of_Shamash_relief.jpg

455. Same as image on page 454, cropped and with arrow added.

476. Hydria with Heracles wrestling Triton, Boston Museum of Fine Art.
Photograph taken by the author.

494. Drawing based on ancient scene of slaying of Humbaba on cylinder seal shown at
https://wiki.uiowa.edu/display/theatre/Humbaba+Dramaturgical+Information

499. Ancient cylinder-seals from Mesopotamia.
Top: from Leonard W. King, page 162.
Bottom: Wikimedia commons.
https://commons.wikimedia.org/wiki/File:Cylinder_Seal,_Achaemenid,_modern_impression_05.jpg

504. Pylos Combat Agate. Originally found on Wikimedia commons. Later at "Object lesson: the Pylos Combat Agate," *Current World Archaeology*, May 24, 2018. Original source: Department of Classics, University of Cincinnati.

505. Drawing based on another of many ancient scenes showing slaying of Humbaba, from a plaque (VA 7246) now housed in the Vorderasiatisches Museum in Berlin.

554. Vishnu and Shesha, Badami Caves. Wikimedia commons.
https://commons.wikimedia.org/wiki/File:Badami_Cave_3_si05-1613.jpg

557. Vishnu, Lakshmi, Shesha. Wikimedia commons.
https://commons.wikimedia.org/wiki/File:Vishnu_and_Lakshmi_on_Shesha_Naga,_ca_1870.jpg

567. Shiva statue, Uttarakhand. Wikimedia commons.
https://commons.wikimedia.org/wiki/File:Now_memory_Shiva_statue_near_Paramarth_Niketan.jpg

568. Shiva statue, Aihole. Wikimedia commons.
https://commons.wikimedia.org/wiki/File:Le_temple_de_Durga_(Aihole,_Inde)_(14379845811).jpg

572. Dionysus from ancient kleophrades. Wikimedia commons.
https://commons.wikimedia.org/wiki/File:Dionysus-kleophrades1.jpg
See also:
https://commons.wikimedia.org/wiki/File:Dionysos_thiasos_Staatliche_Antikensammlungen_2344.jpg

575. Shiva Nataraja sculpture. Wikimedia commons.
https://upload.wikimedia.org/wikipedia/commons/a/a2/Shiva_Nataraja_Delhi_National_Museu
m_n101-06.jpg

576. Maha Shivaratri celebration. Wikimedia commons.
https://commons.wikimedia.org/wiki/File:Lord_Shiva_devotees_offering_milk,_flowers,_fruits_a
nd_bel_leaves_on_a_Shivaling_for_seeking_divine_blessings,_in_a_city_temple_at_the_celebrati
on_of_Maha_Shivaratri,_in_New_Delhi_on_February_23,_2009_(1).jpg

577. Shiva Lingam, three examples. Wikimedia commons.
left: https://commons.wikimedia.org/wiki/File:Cattien_rock_crystal_linga.png
center: https://commons.wikimedia.org/wiki/File:Shiva_Linga_-_Kushan_Period_-_Maholi_-
_ACCN_15-652_-_Government_Museum_-_Mathura_2013-02-23_4948.JPG
right: https://commons.wikimedia.org/wiki/File:Lingga.jpg

581. Churning the Ocean of Milk. Wikimedia commons.
https://commons.wikimedia.org/wiki/File:Kurma,_the_tortoise_incarnation_of_Vishnu.jpg

582. Churning the Ocean of Milk. Wikimedia commons.
https://commons.wikimedia.org/wiki/File:Barattage_de_l%27ocean_de_lait.jpg

583. Tortoise circa 1901. Wikimedia commons.
https://commons.wikimedia.org/wiki/File:Annual_report_-
_New_York_Zoological_Society_(1901)_(17810443573).jpg

587. Durga celebration 2011. Wikimedia commons.
https://commons.wikimedia.org/wiki/File:Durga,_Burdwan,_2011.JPG

590. Durga and MahishAsura. Wikimedia commons.
https://commons.wikimedia.org/wiki/File:Durga_Slays_Mahisasura.jpg

597. Three images of Ganesha. Wikimedia commons.
left: http://commons.wikimedia.org/wiki/File:Ganesh_(musée_d%27art_asiatique_de_Berlin).jpg
center: https://commons.wikimedia.org/wiki/File:Ganesh_on_his_vahana,_a_mouse_or_rat.jpg
right: https://commons.wikimedia.org/wiki/File:Ganesha,_India,_1200s-
1300s_AD,_black_schist,_remnants_of_gesso_and_puja_pigment_-_Dallas_Museum_of_Art_-
_DSC05066.jpg

609. Painting of Indra, c. 1850. Wikimedia commons.
https://commons.wikimedia.org/wiki/File:Indra_with_thunder_olt.jpg

610. Indra on Airavata. Wikimedia commons.
https://commons.wikimedia.org/wiki/File:Somnathpur_si0823.jpg

615. Matsya avatar painting. Wikimedia commons.
https://commons.wikimedia.org/wiki/File:Matsya_painting.jpg

617. Matsya avatar sculpture. Wikimedia commons.
https://commons.wikimedia.org/wiki/File:Deshaavathaarami_malsyam.jpg

621. Painting of Vamana and Bali. Wikimedia commons.
https://en.wikipedia.org/wiki/File:Vamana1.jpg

626. Parashurama in battle. Wikimedia commons.
https://commons.wikimedia.org/wiki/File:Parashurama_killing_Kartavirya_Arjuna.jpg

629. Krishna sculpture, 15th century. Wikimedia commons.
https://commons.wikimedia.org/wiki/File:A_15th_Century_Hindu_Art,_Hindu_deity_Krishna,_Asian_Art_Museum_of_San_Francisco.jpg

630. Krishna sculpture, Madurai. Wikimedia commons.
https://commons.wikimedia.org/wiki/File:Madurai_si0727.jpg

632. Krishna sculpture, Singapore. Wikimedia commons.
https://commons.wikimedia.org/wiki/File:Sri_Mariamman_Temple_Singapore_2_amk.jpg

657. Bhima fights Duryodhana. Wikimedia commons.
https://commons.wikimedia.org/wiki/File:Duel_between_Duryodhana_and_Bhima.jpg

659. Bhima throws an elephant. Wikimedia commons.
https://commons.wikimedia.org/wiki/File:Bhima_throws_an_elephant_at_Karna%27s_chariot.jpg

662. Arjuna returns Gandiva to the sea. Wikimedia commons.
https://commons.wikimedia.org/wiki/File:Arjuna_throws_his_weapons_in_water_as_advised_by_Agni.jpg

675. Arjuna hits the mark. Wikimedia commons.
https://commons.wikimedia.org/wiki/File:Arjun_hits_the_target.jpg

681. Ajax and Achilles gaming. Wikimedia commons.
https://commons.wikimedia.org/wiki/File:Ajax_and_Achilles_gaming,_ca._490_BCE_Attributed_to_the_Berlin_Painter_Met_Museum_of_Art_Pub_Domain_DP260740.jpg

681. Ajax and Achilles gaming, two scenes. Wikimedia commons.
Top: https://commons.wikimedia.org/wiki/File:Akhilleus_Aias_MGEt_16757.jpg
Bottom: https://commons.wikimedia.org/wiki/File:Achilles_Ajax_dice_Louvre_MNB911.jpg

704. Arjuna and Krishna in the War-Car. Wikimedia commons.
https://commons.wikimedia.org/wiki/File:Bhagavatgeeta.jpg

706. Hanuman. Wikimedia commons.
https://commons.wikimedia.org/wiki/File:Hanuman_Bjgur.jpg

707. Hanuman. Wikimedia commons.
https://commons.wikimedia.org/wiki/File:Hanuman_in_Terra_Cotta.jpg

711. Bhagavad Gita. Wikimedia commons.
https://commons.wikimedia.org/wiki/Bhagavad_Gita#/media/File:Bhagavata_Gita_Bishnupur_Arnab_Dutta_2011.JPG

714. Maya's dream of the elephant. Wikimedia commons.
https://commons.wikimedia.org/wiki/File:Dream_Queen_Maya_BM_OA_1932.7-9.1.jpg

715. Maya gives birth to the Buddha-to-be. Wikimedia commons.
Top: https://commons.wikimedia.org/wiki/File:Four_Scenes_from_the_Life_of_the_Buddha_-_Birth_of_the_Buddha_-_Kushan_dynasty,_late_2nd_to_early_3rd_century_AD,_Gandhara,_schist_-_Freer_Gallery_of_Art_-_DSC05128.JPG
Bottom: https://commons.wikimedia.org/wiki/File:Astasahasrika_Prajnaparamita_Queen_Maya_Birth.jpeg

725. Ganesha, Thanjavur. Wikimedia commons.
https://commons.wikimedia.org/wiki/File:Tanjore_ganesh.jpg

735. Buddha statue, Pala Empire. Wikimedia commons.
https://commons.wikimedia.org/wiki/File:%27Buddha%27s_First_Sermon%27,_chlorite_statue_from_India,_Pala_dynasty,_11th_century,_Honolulu_Academy_of_Arts.JPG

738. Buddha and the daughters of Mara. Wikimedia commons.
https://commons.wikimedia.org/wiki/File:Versuchung_des_Buddha_Museum_Rietberg_RVI_25.jpg

739. Buddha and Vajrapani. Wikimedia commons.
https://commons.wikimedia.org/wiki/File:Buddha-Vajrapani-Herakles.JPG

742. Lao Tzu departs, by Zhang Lu. Wikimedia commons.
https://commons.wikimedia.org/wiki/File:Zhang_Lu-Laozi_Riding_an_Ox.jpg

749. Baby New Year, 1910. Wikimedia commons.
https://commons.wikimedia.org/wiki/File:PostcardHappyNewYearOldManKidScytheHourglass1910.jpg

758. Daruma painting, Sojiji Temple. Wikimedia commons
https://commons.wikimedia.org/wiki/File:Sojiji_Bodhidharma_painting.jpg

763. Bodhidharma on bamboo reed. Wikimedia commons.
https://commons.wikimedia.org/wiki/File:Kim_Myeongguk-Bodhidharma_crossing_a_river_with_a_broken_branch.jpg

758. Amaterasu emerging from the Rock. Wikimedia commons.
https://commons.wikimedia.org/wiki/File:Amaterasu_cave_crop.jpg

767. Izanagi and Izanami. Wikimedia commons.
https://commons.wikimedia.org/wiki/File:Kobayashi_Izanami_and_Izanagi.jpg

786. Torii at Fuba-hachimangu, Kochi. Wikimedia commons.
https://en.wikipedia.org/wiki/File:Fuba_Hachimangu_01.JPG

787. Meoto Iwa, Mie. Wikimedia commons.
https://commons.wikimedia.org/wiki/File:Meotoiwa.jpg

791. Ame-no-Uzumi and a Rooster. Wikimedia commons.
https://commons.wikimedia.org/wiki/File:The_Goddess_Uzume_with_Rooster_and_Mirror_(Harvard_Art_Museums).jpeg

826. Puerta del Sol, Tiwanaku and Awaguchi Shrine Torii. Wikimedia commons.
Top: https://commons.wikimedia.org/wiki/File:Puerta_del_Sol_en_Tiwanaku_(Bolivia).jpg
Bottom: https://commons.wikimedia.org/wiki/File:Awaguchi_Shrine_torii_1.jpg

833. La Venta Monument 19; Olmec. Wikimedia commons.
https://commons.wikimedia.org/wiki/File:La_Venta_Stele_19_(Delange).jpg

834 and 835. Detail from Gate of the Sun, Tiwanaku.
Wikimedia commons.
https://commons.wikimedia.org/wiki/File:Flickr_-_archer10_(Dennis)_-_Bolivia-68.jpg

Bibliography

Apuleius. *The Golden Ass.* Trans. Jack Lindsay. Bloomington: Indiana UP, 1960.

Arnold, Edwin. *The Song Celestial, or Bhagavad-Gita (From the Mahabharata.* London: Trübner, 1900.

Ataç, Mehmet-Ali. *Mythology of Kingship in Neo-Assyrian Art.* Cambridge: Cambridge UP, 2010.

Bascom, William. *Sixteen Cowries: Yoruba Divination from Africa to the New World.* Bloomington: Indiana UP, 1980. First Midland Book Edition 1993.

Beier, Ulli and Georgina . *Yoruba Myths.* Cambridge: Cambridge UP, 1980.

Brewer, Douglas J. and Emily Teeter. *Egypt and the Egyptians.* Second Ed. Cambridge: Cambridge UP, 2007.

Broughton, Jeffrey L. *Bodhidharma Anthology: The Earliest Records of Zen.* Berkeley: University of California Press, 1999.

Budge, Ernst Alfred Thompson Wallis, trans. *The Book of the Dead: An English Translation of the Theban Recension, English Translation in Three Volumes.* Vol VI in *Books on Egypt and Chaldaea,* Ten Vols. Budge and King. London: Kegan Paul, 1901.

Budge, Ernst Alfred Thompson Wallis. *Egyptian Hieroglyphic Dictionary, in two volumes.* Vol 2. London: John Murray, 1920.

Budge, Ernst Alfred Thompson Wallis. *Gods of the Egyptians: Or, Studies in Egyptian Mythology.* Two Vols. London: Metheun, 1904.

Budge, Ernst Alfred Thompson Wallis. *Osiris and the Egyptian Resurrection.* Two Vols. London: P. L. Warner, 1911.

Budge, Ernst Alfred Thompson Wallis. *Rise & Progress of Assyriology.* London: Richard Clay & Sons, 1925.

Burley, Paul. "Göbekli Tepe: Temples Communicating an Ancient Cosmic Geography." Originally written in June, 2011 and published in March, 2013 at www.grahamhancock.com/forums/BurleyP1.php.

Cassaro, Richard. "Lion's Gaze: An Ancient Occult Parable." Blog post on *Richard Cassaro: Discovery & Revival of Lost Ancient Wisdom,* December 29, 2015. www.richardcassaro.com/the-lions-gaze-an-occult-parable/

Clay, Albert T. *A Hebrew Deluge Story in Cuneiform, and other Epic Fragments in the Pierpont Morgan Library. Yale Oriental Series, Researches,* Volume 3. New Haven: Yale UP, 1922.

Crawford, Harriet. *Sumer and the Sumerians.* Cambridge: Cambridge UP, 1991. Second ed. 2004.

Curnow, Jenifer. "Te Rangikaheke, Wiremu Maihi." *Dictionary of New Zealand Biography*, first published 1990. *Te Ara: the Encyclopedia of New Zealand.* https://teara.govt.nz/en/biographies/1t66/te-rangikahek-wiremu-maihi

Dalley, Stephanie. *Myths from Mesopotamia: Creation, the Flood, Gilgamesh, and Others.* Rev Ed. Oxford: Oxford UP, 1989. Rev Ed. 2000.

Davis, Gerald J. *Gilgamesh: A New Translation.* NY: Insignia, 2014.

De Santillana, Giorgio and Hertha von Dechend. *Hamlet's Mill: An Essay on Myth and the Frame of Time.* Boston: Godine, 1969. First paperback ed. 1977.

Dimmitt, Cornelia and J. A. B. van Buitenen, eds. and trans. *Classical Hindu Mythology: A Reader in the Sanskrit Puranas.* Philadelphia: Temple UP, 1978.

Diodorus Siculus. *Library of History.* Trans. C. H. Oldfather. Online LacusCurtius version of the original Loeb Classical Library edition. Cambridge: Harvard UP, 1933 - 1967.

Doniger, Wendy, trans. *Hindu Myths: A Sourcebook translated from The Sanskrit.* London: Penguin, 1975.

Doniger, Wendy, trans. *Rig Veda: An Anthology.* London: Penguin, 1981.

Edmunds, Albert J. *Canonical Account of the Birth of Gotama the Buddha.* Open Court, Volume XII: 1819. https://www.sacred-texts.com/journals/oc/cabgb.htm

Ellis, Ralph. *Tempest and Exodus: The biblical Exodus was the Hyksos Exodus from Egypt.* Cheshire: Edfu Books, 2000.

Enuma Elish: The Babylonian Creation Epic. Trans. Timothy J. Stephany. Createspace, 2013. Second Ed. 2014.

Epic of Gilgamesh: A new translation from a collation of the cuneiform tablets in the British Museum rendered literally into English hexameters. Trans. R. Campbell Thompson. London: Luzac, 1928.

Epic of Gilgamesh: The Babylonian Epic Poem and Other Texts in Akkadian and Sumerian. Trans. Andrew George. London: Penguin, 1999.

Erdoes, Richard and Alonso Ortiz, eds. *American Indian Myths and Legends.* NY: Pantheon, 1984.

Frazer, James. *Myths of the Origin of Fire: An Essay.* London: Macmillan, 1930. Reissued in 1974 by Hacker Art Books, NY.

Gardner, John and John Maier. *Gilgamesh: Translated from the Sin-leqi-unninnī version.* NY: Vintage Books, 1984. First Vintage Books Ed, 1985.

Georges, Robert A. and Michael Owen Jones. *Folkloristics: An Introduction.* Bloomington: Indiana UP, 1995.

Hancock, Graham. *Fingerprints of the Gods.* NY: Crown, 1995.

Hancock, Graham. *Magicians of the Gods: The Forgotten Wisdom of Earth's Lost Civilization*. NY: Thomas Dunne, 2015.

Heidel, Alexander. *Babylonian Genesis: The Story of Creation*. Chicago: U Chicago P, 1942. Second Ed, 1951.

Herodotus. *The Histories*. Trans. Aubrey de Sélincourt. Harmondsworth: Penguin, 1954. Rev. Ed. 1972.

Heyerdahl, Thor. *American Indians in the Pacific: the Theory behind the Kon-Tiki Expedition*. London: Allen & Unwin, 1952.

Homer. *Iliad*. Trans. Robert Fagles. NY: Viking Penguin, 1990.

Homer. *Odyssey*. Trans. Theodore Alois Buckley. *First Thirteen Books of the Odyssey of Homer, Literally Translated with Explanatory Notes*. Philadelphia: David McKay, 1896.

Homer. *Odyssey*. Trans. Robert Fagles. NY: Viking Penguin, 1996.

Homer. *Odyssey*. Trans. the Rev. Dr. Giles. *Odyssey of Homer; Construed Literally, and Word for Word*. London: James Cornish, 1800. Four vols.

Horne, Charles F, ed. *Medieval China. Sacred Books and Early Literature of the East* [Series, 14 vols]. Volume 12. NY: Parke, Austin & Lipscombe, 1917.

Jastrow, Morris and Albert T. Clay. *An Old Babylonian Version of the Gilgamesh Epic, on the Basis of Recently Discovered Texts. Yale Oriental Series, Researches*. Volume IV, Part 3. New Haven: Yale UP, 1920.

"Japanese Author Traces Nippon Origin to Hebrew Race." *Jewish Daily Bulletin*. 15 August, 1929. 3 - 4.

Jones, C. P. "Towards a Chronology of Plutarch's Works." *Journal of Roman Studies*, Volume 56, Parts 1 and 2 (1966). 61 - 74.

King, L. W. *Babylonian Religion and Mythology. Books on Egypt and Chaldaea*, Volume IV. London: Kegan, 1903.

King, L. W. *Seven Tablets of Creation, or the Babylonian and Assyrian Legends Concerning the Creation of the World and of Mankind*. Two Vols. London: Luzac, 1902.

King, Martin Luther, Jr. "Address to the American Negro Leadership Conference on Africa." Harriman, NY. November, 1962.
https://thekingcenter.org/archive/mlks-address-american-negro-leadership-conference-africa [accessed January 2018; link no longer active]

King, Martin Luther, Jr. "Our God is Marching On!" Selma, Alabama. 25 March 1965.
https://kinginstitute.stanford.edu/our-god-marching

Ko-ji-ki, or "Records of Ancient Matters." Trans. Basil Hall Chamberlain. 1919.
www.sacred-texts.com/shi/kj/kj000.htm

870

Kojiki: an account of ancient matters. O no Yasumaro. Trans. Gustav Heldt. NY: Columbia UP, 2014.

Kojiki. Trans. Donald L. Philippi. Tokyo: U Tokyo P, 1968.

Kramer, Samuel Noah. *Sumerians: Their History, Culture, and Character.* Chicago: U Chicago P, 1963. Paperback ed, 1971.

Kuhn, Alvin Boyd. *Easter: the Birthday of the Gods.* Wheaton: Theosophical Society Press, 1966. Second ed. [Lecture originally delivered in 1936].

Kuhn, Alvin Boyd. *Lost Light: An Interpretation of Ancient Scriptures.* Elizabeth, New Jersey: Academy Press, 1940.

Kuhn, Alvin Boyd. *The Stable and the Manger.* Wheaton, Illinois: Theosophical Press, 1936.
https://archive.org/stream/TheStableAndTheManager/AlvinBoydKuhn-TheStableAndTheManager#page/no/mode/2up
  [note: the URL says "manager" instead of "manger" both times]

Lambert, W. G. and A. R. Millard. *Atra-hasis: The Babylonian story of the flood.* Oxford: Clarendon, 1969.

Lao Tzu. *Tao Te Ching: The Classic Book of Integrity and the Way.* Trans. Victor H. Mair. NY: Bantam, 1990.

Lao-tzu and the Tao-te-ching. Livia Kohn and Michael LaFargue, eds. Albany: SUNY Press, 1998.

Leick, Gwendolyn. *A Dictionary of Ancient Near Eastern Mythology.* London, Routledge: 1991.

Luomala, Katharine. *Maui of a Thousand Tricks: His Oceanic and European Biographers.* Honolulu: Bernice P. Bishop Museum, 1949.

Mahabharata of Krishna-Dwaipayana Vyasa. Trans. Kisari Mohan Ganguli, trans. Calcutta: Pratap Chandra Roy, 1896.
http://www.sacred-texts.com/hin/maha/index.htm

[Maning, Frederick Edward]. *Old New Zealand: A Tale of the Good Old Times and a History of the War in the North Against Chief Heke, in the Year 1845.* "By A Pakeha Maori." Christchurch: Whitcombe and Tombs, 1906.

Massey, Gerald. *Ancient Egypt, the Light of the World.* Two Vols. London: Unwin, 1907.

Massey, Gerald. "Paul the Gnostic Opponent of Peter, not an Apostle of Historic Christianity." n.d.
www.gerald-massey.org.uk/massey/dpr_02_paul_as_a_gnostic.htm

Mathisen, David Warner. *Astrotheology for Life: Unlocking the Esoteric Wisdom of Ancient Myth.* Paso Robles: Beowulf, 2017.

871

Mathisen, David Warner. *Star Myths of the World, and how to interpret them, Volume Two: Myths of Ancient Greece.* Paso Robles: Beowulf, 2016.

Mathisen, David Warner. *Star Myths of the World, and how to interpret them, Volume Three: Star Myths of the Bible.* Paso Robles: Beowulf, 2016.

Mathisen, David Warner. *Star Myths of the World, and how to interpret them, Volume Four: Norse Mythology.* Paso Robles: Beowulf, 2018.

Mathisen, David Warner. *Undying Stars: The truth that unites the world's ancient wisdom, and the conspiracy to keep it from you.* Paso Robles: Beowulf, 2014.

Mertz, Henriette. *Mystic Symbol: Mark of the Michigan Mound Builders.* Originally published in Gaithersburg, Maryland: Global Books, 1986. Republished Colfax, Wisconsin: Ancient American Magazine / Hayriver Press, 2004.

McIntosh, Jane R. *Ancient Mesopotamia: New Perspectives.* Santa Barbara: ABC-CLIO, 2005.

Müller, Max. *Egyptian Mythology.* In *Mythology of All Races, in Thirteen Volumes.* Louis Herbert Gray, ed. Volume 12. Boston: Marshall Jones, 1918.

"Nalaka Sutta: To Nalaka" (Sn 3.11), Trans. Thanissaro Bhikku. *Access to Insight* (BCBS Edition), 30 November 2013.
http://www.accesstoinsight.org/tipitaka/kn/snp/snp.3.11.than.html.

Nemet-Nejat, Karen Rhea. *Daily life in ancient Mesopotamia. Daily life through history* (Series). Westport: Greenwood, 1998.

Neugebauer, Otto E. *The Exact Sciences in Antiquity.* 2nd ed. New York: Dover, 1969.

"Object lesson: the Pylos Combat Agate." *Current World Archaeology.* Issue 89. May 24, 2018.

Ollestad, Norman. *Crazy for the Storm: A Memoir of Survival.* NY: Ecco, 2009.

Ono, Sokyo and William P. Woodard. *Shinto: the Kami Way.* Boston: Tuttle, 1962.

Orwell, George. *Nineteen Eighty-Four.* NY: Harcourt Brace Jovanovich, 1949. Signet reprint (paperback), 1981.

Parrinder, Geoffrey. *African Mythology.* London: Hamlyn, 1967.

Pinch, Geraldine. *Egyptian Myth: A Very Short Introduction.* Oxford: Oxford UP, 2004.

Pinch, Geraldine. *Handbook of Egyptian Mythology. Handbooks of World Mythology.* Santa Barbara: ABC-CLIO, 2002.

Plutarch. *Of Isis and Osiris,* in *Moralia.* Trans. Frank Cole Babbitt. 1936. Loeb Classical Library volume V, online version at
http://penelope.uchicago.edu/Thayer/E/Roman/Texts/Plutarch/Moralia/Isis_and_Osiris*/home.html

Popol Vuh: the Mayan Book of the Dawn of Life, rev. ed. Trans. Dennis Tedlock. NY: Touchstone, 1996.

Popol Vuh: Sacred Book of the Quiché Maya People. Trans. Allen J. Christenson. Electronic version of original 2003 publication. Mesoweb: www.mesoweb.com/publications/Christenson/PopolVuh.pdf

Prichard, James Cowles. *An Analysis of the Egyptian Mythology: To Which is Subjoined, A Critical Examination of the Remains of Egyptian Chronology.* London: John and Arthur Arch, 1819.

Pyramid Texts. Trans. Samuel A. B. Mercer. NY: Longmans, Green, 1952. online version www.sacred-texts.com/egyp/pyt/pyt28.htm Scanned online May 2004, John Bruno Hare, redactor.

Quarrington, Dale. "Bodhidharma --달마 (5th to 6th Cent.)" *Dale's Temple Adventures.* July 22, 2014. koreantemples.com/?p=9074

Russian Fairy Tales. Trans. Marie Ponsot. NY: Golden Press, 1960.

Schwaller de Lubicz, R. A. *Esoterism & Symbol.* Originally published in French under the title *Propos sur Esotérisme et Symbole* by La Colombe, Editions du Vieux Colombier, in 1960. Trans. André and Goldian vandenBroeck, 1985. Rochester, Vermont: Inner Traditions, 1985.

Sellers, Jane B. *Death of Gods in Ancient Egypt: A Study of the Threshold of Myth and the Frame of Time.* Lexington, Kentucky: Lulu Books, 1992.

Silverman, David P. ed. *Ancient Egypt.* Oxford: Oxford UP, 1997.

Simmons, David. "The Sources of Sir George Grey's Nga Mahi A Nga Tupuna." *Journal of the Polynesian Society,* Volume 75, No. 2, 1966. 177 - 188.

Simpson, William Kelly, ed. *Literature of Ancient Egypt: An Anthology of Stories, Instructions, Stelae, Autobiographies, and Poetry.* Third Ed. New Haven: Yale UP, 2003.

Taylor, Robert. *Astronomico-Theological Lectures.* NY: Calvin Blanchard, 1857.

Taylor, Robert. *Devil's Pulpit: or, Astro-Theological Sermons by the Reverend Robert Taylor.* NY: Calvin Blanchard, 1857.

Thomas, W. J. *Some Myths and Legends of the Australian Aborigines.* Melbourne: Whitcombe & Tombs, 1923. www.sacred-texts/com/aus/mla/mlaoo.htm

Verbrugghe, Gerald P. and John M. Wickersham. *Berossos and Manetho, Introduced and Translated; Native Traditions in Ancient Mesopotamia and Egypt.* Ann Arbor: U of Michigan P, 1996. First paperback ed. 2001.

Whatahoro, H. T. *Lore of the Whare-wānanga: Or Teachings of the Maori College on Religion, Cosmogony, and History.* Vol 1. Cambridge: Cambridge UP, 1913.

Willems, Harco. *Coffin of Heqata (Cairo JDE 36418): A Case Study of Egyptian Funerary Culture of the Early Middle Kingdom*. Leuven: Peeters, 1996.

Woodard, William P. *Allied Occupation of Japan 1945 - 1952 and Japanese Religions*. Leiden: Brill, 1972.

Wu, John C. H. *Golden Age of Zen: Zen masters of the Tang dyasty*. Bloomington: World Wisdom, 2003. Originally edition published Taipai: National War College, 1967.

Zen Teaching of Bodhidharma. Trans. Red Pine. NY: North Point, 1987.

Index

878

884

897

referenced in the phrase "authors of *Hamlet's Mill*" on 330, 340, 379, 399, 438, 448, 509 – 510, 531, 533, 550, 566, 594, 623, 817, 822, and 845 n.87)

Von Sydow, Carl Wilhelm (1878 - 1952) 68

Vrtra 605 – 607, 764

Vyasa, Vyasadeva 634, 646 – 647, 651, 668

Wag-feast 324

Wagons (See *Carts*)

Wagtails 226 – 227

Wall (Ophiuchus as) 134, 469, 475, 522 – 525, 537, 542, 734, 767 – 768, 770, 812 - 813

"Wall-gazing," "Wall-contemplation" 767 – 768, 770

War-car, war-cart (See *Carts*)

Warramungu 31 – 32, 37

Warra-pulla-pulla 31 – 33

Water buffalo (See *Buffalo*)

"Waters above" and "Waters below" 386 – 389, 391, 397, 431, 443

Waters of Death 534 – 535

Watusi 92

Waung 38 – 39, 41 – 44

Weaving, Weavers 134, 757, 802 – 807, 822

Weeping 320, 448, 514, 538 – 539, 542, 545, 717, 730

Wellington, New Zealand 200

West, John Anthony (1932 - 2018) 379

"Wet region" 535 – 536, 543, 801

Whalebone 232

Whambeyan limestone caves 48

Wheel of Brahma 574

Wheel of Dharma, Wheel of Dhamma 717, 726, 732

"Whirling form" of Hercules 97, 119, 133 – 134, 223, 267 – 268, 292 – 295, 297, 348, 368, 409, 453 – 454, 498 – 500, 503, 539, 562, 574 – 575, 608 – 609, 655, 666, 678, 681, 736 – 737, 770 – 771, 777, 788, 802, 804

Whirlpools 96 – 97, 105 – 106, 115 – 116, 118 – 119, 223

Whirlwinds 223, 408 – 409, 489, 492, 497, 501, 503, 608 – 609, 655

Whisks 589, 717, 725 – 726

White-Bone-Snake 123

White Corn Maiden 140 – 146, 148 – 153, 180, 798

White River Rosebud Reservation 125

White River Sioux 125, 133, 205

Wickersham, John M. 426 – 427

Willems, Harco 257

Wilson, Horace Hayman (1786 - 1860) 66

Wind 72, 142, 223 – 224, 408 – 409, 412, 415, 489, 492, 497, 501, 503 – 504, 538 – 539, 608 – 609, 649, 655, 708, 755, 785, 811

Wine 136, 176, 278, 324, 430, 470, 503, 714

Wine-glass (See *Goblet*)

Winged scarab (See *Scarabs*)

Winged Sun 267, 293 – 297, 348, 429, 499

Wingeecaribee River 48

Wiremu Maihi Te Rangikaheke (See *Te Rangikaheke, Wiremu Maihi*)

Wollondilly River 48 – 49

Woman at the well 679

Woodard, William Parsons (1896 - 1973) 783 – 784

Woodpeckers, Woodpecker 236 – 238, 240 – 243

World Tree (See *Yggdrasil*)

Worms 184, 207, 226, 741, 796

Wounds, celestial aspects 496 – 497

Wu, Emperor 760

Wu, Jinxiong (John Ching Hsiung Wu) (1899 - 1986) 780 – 781

Wu-wei 701 – 703, 709

Xango (See *Shango*)

Xbalanque 181, 183, 190, 194, 480, 486, 845 n.83

Xibalba 173 – 174, 181, 190, 195 – 196, 515

Xpiyacoc 162, 165 – 168, 184

Xmucane 162, 165 – 166, 168, 184, 601

Yahweh 160, 163, 224, 285, 301, 604

Yajur Veda 550

Yale Tablet 487, 490

Yale University 361

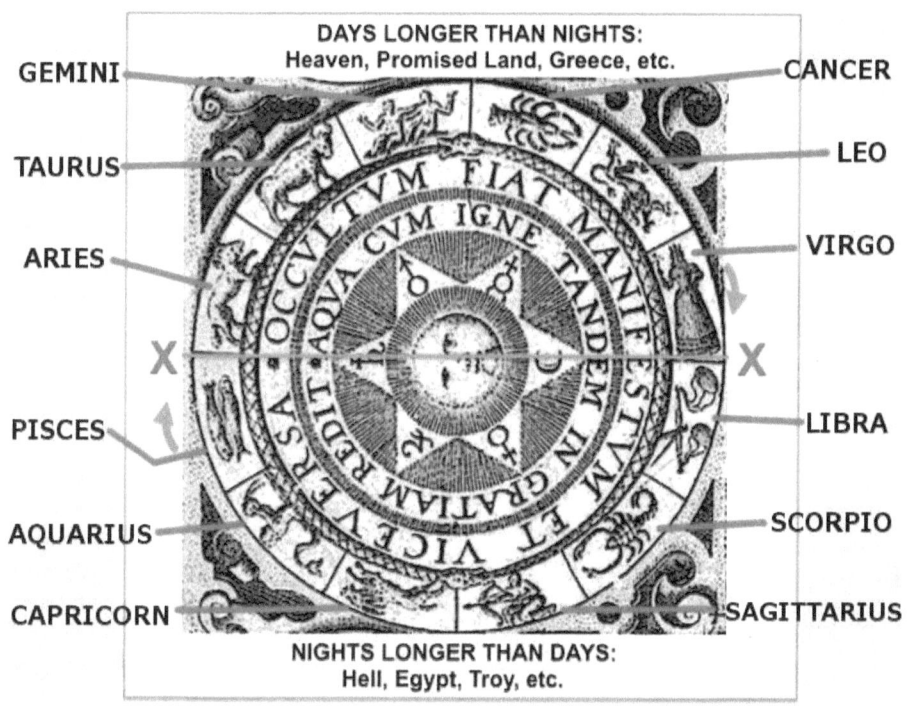

DAYS LONGER THAN NIGHTS:
Heaven, Promised Land, Greece, etc.

GEMINI

TAURUS

ARIES

PISCES

AQUARIUS

CAPRICORN

CANCER

LEO

VIRGO

LIBRA

SCORPIO

SAGITTARIUS

NIGHTS LONGER THAN DAYS:
Hell, Egypt, Troy, etc.

www.ingramcontent.com/pod-product-compliance
Lightning Source LLC
Chambersburg PA
CBHW030247290526

45785CB00001B/1